SARGONIC AND GUTIAN PERIODS

(2334–2113 BC)

THE ROYAL INSCRIPTIONS OF MESOPOTAMIA

Volumes Published

ASSYRIAN PERIODS

1 Assyrian Rulers of the Third and Second Millennia BC (TO 1115 BC)
A. KIRK GRAYSON

2 Assyrian Rulers of the Early First Millennium BC I (1114–859 BC)
A. KIRK GRAYSON

EARLY PERIODS

2 Sargonic and Gutian Periods (2334–2113 BC)
DOUGLAS FRAYNE

4 Old Babylonian Period (2003–1595 BC)
DOUGLAS FRAYNE

SUPPLEMENTS

1 Royal Inscriptions on Clay Cones from Ashur now in Istanbul
V. DONBAZ and A. KIRK GRAYSON

THE ROYAL INSCRIPTIONS OF MESOPOTAMIA

EARLY PERIODS / VOLUME 2

Sargonic and Gutian Periods

(2334 – 2113 BC)

DOUGLAS FRAYNE

UNIVERSITY OF TORONTO PRESS

Toronto Buffalo London

University of Toronto Press 1993
Toronto Buffalo London
Reprinted in paperback 2014

ISBN 978-0-8020-0593-9 (cloth)
ISBN 978-1-4426-2375-0 (paper)

Printed on acid-free paper

Canadian Cataloguing in Publication Data

Frayne, Douglas
Sargonic and Gutian periods (2334–2113 BC)

(The Royal inscriptions of Mesopotamia. Early periods ; v. 2)
Includes bibliographical references.
ISBN 978-0-8020-0593-9 (bound) ISBN 978-1-4426-2375-0 (pbk.)

1. Cuneiform inscriptions, Sumerian. 2. Cuneiform inscriptions, Akkadian.
3. Sumerian language – Texts. 4. Akkadian language – Texts.
5. Assyria – Kings and rulers. 6. Assyria – History – Sources.
I. Title. II. Series.

PJ3815.F73 1993 935′.01 C93-094893-9

The research and publication of this volume
have been supported by
the Social Sciences and Humanities Research Council of Canada
and the University of Toronto.

To

my parents

Contents

Preface

Many people have helped in the preparation of this volume and I would like to acknowledge gratefully their assistance here.

Foremost, I must thank Professor A.K. Grayson for the conception and bringing into being of the Royal Inscriptions of Mesopotamia Project and for his ongoing efforts to sustain the project. The continued financial support of the Social Sciences and Humanities Research Council of Canada has made the research and publication of this volume possible, and is deeply appreciated.

I would like to thank D.O. Edzard, Editor-in-Charge of Early Periods, for his time and care in reading the manuscript and for his invaluable advice on numerous scholarly matters. The assistance of R. Biggs, W.G. Lambert, and P. Steinkeller, who kindly served as readers for the volume, is also gratefully acknowledged. Special thanks must be extended to B. Foster of Yale University; his careful collations of texts from various European collections for RIM greatly assisted in the preparation of this volume. In particular, his study of a lengthy, previously unedited Narām-Sîn inscription in Jena, research made possible by funds provided by the SSHRCC, provides an important addition to the Narām-Sîn corpus. He also kindly made available to the author a photo of Ni 3200, a large Sammeltafel in Istanbul containing Old Babylonian copies of several Old Akkadian inscriptions; this enabled collation of the inscriptions and the chance to provide for the first time in the RIM scores a complete transliteration of these important texts. I also thank G. Frame, A.K. Grayson, and R.F.G Sweet, who carefully read the manuscript and offered numerous valuable suggestions which improved the volume.

Several scholars gave advice, collated texts, or provided new information for the volume; these include P.-A. Beaulieu, R. Biggs, J. Black, G. Frame, A. George, J. Marzahn, H. Neumann, J. Oelsner, D. Potts, Å. Sjöberg, P. Steinkeller, and R. Zettler. Again, I must thank the RIM headquarters staff: K. Glaser, Project Manager; H. Grau, Project Secretary, and R. Westerby, Assistant Systems Manager, for their tireless efforts to convert the computer files of the initial manuscript into a publishable form.

Toronto
May 1993

D.R.F.

Editorial Notes

With the exceptions noted below, the editorial principles followed in the preparation of this volume are the same as those employed in the three volumes already published in The Royal Inscriptions of Mesopotamia series (RIMA 1 [1987] and 2 [1991], and RIME 4 [1990]). These principles are set out in full in the RIM Project's Editorial Manual (2nd ed., Toronto, 1990) and will be familiar to users of the previous volumes. But for the benefit of readers who make their first acquaintance with the RIM series with this volume, the following should be said.

This volume belongs to the sub-series allotted to the Early Periods; it is therefore a RIME volume, specifically RIME 2. Its purpose is to provide reliable editions of all royal inscriptions, in a rather loose sense of that term, of the Sargonic and Gutian periods as defined in the Introduction. Each text is identified by a four-element designator, e.g., E2.3.4.5. In this example E2 identifies the sub-series and volume (Early, volume 2), the second element identifies the dynasty according to the sequence given in the list of Contents (pp. vii-viii), the third element gives the number of the ruler in that dynasty, and the fourth element indicates the text of the ruler in the order assigned by the editor

Texts which cannot be assigned to a particular ruler are designated 0 for the dynasty and 0 for the ruler, and are then given a text number in a sequence beginning 1001. They are found on pp. 308 ff. in the section entitled Unattributed.

Brief non-royal inscriptions have been included in the volume if they mention a king or a member of the royal family, e.g., inscriptions on objects dedicated to rulers. These follow the royal inscriptions of the relevant reign and are given a text number in a sequence beginning 2001.

In the case of texts with multiple exemplars, the text is given as a master text reconstructed from the combined evidence of the witnesses, which are always listed in a catalogue after a brief introduction to the text. Variants from the master text, without distinction of major and minor, are given in a critical apparatus at the foot of the page. They are listed according to the line numbering of the master text, in bold face; the number in normal typeface that follows the line number indicates the exemplar. Complete transliterations of all exemplars, except for bricks and seals (and, in a few cases, bowls), are given in the style of musical scores on the microfiches found in a pocket inside the back cover.

An exception to the rule that complete transliterations of all exemplars are given only in the microfiches occurs with text E2.13.6.3, the famous historical-literary account of Utu-ḫegal's expulsion of the Guti. The justification for this departure from normal practice is given on p. 283.

Attention is called to the abbreviations c, p, and n in the catalogues of exemplars. They indicate, respectively, whether an exemplar has been collated by autopsy, collated from a photograph, or not collated.

In the transliterations, the use of lower-case roman typeface for Sumerian and lower-case italic for Akkadian will be obvious to the reader. In the translations, italic is used to indicate uncertainty or a word left in the original language. Sign values are normally given according to Borger, Zeichenliste. But note as innovations of this volume the values śi$_4$ (SU$_4$, si$_4$; Borger śí), śi$_{11}$ (SIG, si$_{11}$; Borger śì), śe$_{11}$ (SIG, se$_{11}$; Borger śé), śu$_4$ (SU$_4$, su$_4$; Borger śú), śum (SUM, sum; Borger śúm), śum$_6$ (TAG, sum$_6$; Borger śum), áś (ÁŠ, ás; Borger aś), íś (IŠ, ís; Borger iś), and úś (UŠ, ús; Borger uś) for the transliteration of Old Akkadian. The rationale for these innovations is given in the Introduction.

The manuscript was prepared on an Apple Macintosh IIsi computer, using MicroSoft Word 5.0 and CuneiformOriental font, and the camera-ready copy submitted to the publisher was printed on a Linotronic 300 PostScript typesetter.

Toronto
May 1993

R. F. G. Sweet
Editor-in-Chief

Bibliographical Abbreviations

AASF	Annales Academia Scientiarum Fennicae, Series B. Helsinki, 1909–
AASOR	The Annual of the American Schools of Oriental Research. New Haven, 1919–
AfO	Archiv für Orientforschung, vols. 3– (vols. 1–2 = AfK). Berlin, Graz, and Horn, 1926–
AHw	W. von Soden, Akkadisches Handwörterbuch, 3 vols. Wiesbaden, 1965–81
AJ	The Antiquaries Journal, Being the Journal of the Society of Antiquaries of London. London, 1921–
AJSL	American Journal of Semitic Languages and Literatures. Chicago, 1884–1941
Algaze, Kurban Höyük 2	G. Algaze (ed.), Town and Country in Southeastern Anatolia, Volume 2 (=OIP 110). Chicago, 1990
Amiet, L'art d'Agadé	P. Amiet, L'art d'Agadé au Musée du Louvre. Paris, 1976
Amiet, MDP 43	P. Amiet, Glyptique susienne des origines à l'époque de Perses achéménides. Cachets, sceaux-cylindres et empreintes antiques découverts à Suse de 1913 à 1967, 2 vols. Paris, 1972
Andrae, AIT	W. Andrae, Die archaischen Ischtar-Tempel in Assur (=WVDOG 39). Leipzig, 1922
André-Leicknam, Naissance de l'écriture	B. André-Leicknam, Naissance de l'écriture cunéiformes et hiéroglyphes, 4e édition. Paris, 1982
ANEP[2]	J.B. Pritchard (ed.), The Ancient Near East in Pictures Relating to the Old Testament, 2nd edition. Princeton, 1969
ANET[3]	J.B. Pritchard (ed.), Ancient Near Eastern Texts Relating to the Old Testament, 3rd edition. Princeton, 1969
AnOr	Analecta Orientalia. Rome, 1931–
AO	Der Alte Orient. Leipzig, 1901–45
AOAT	Alter Orient und Altes Testament. Neukirchen-Vluyn, 1968–
AoF	Altorientalische Forschungen. Berlin, 1974–
AOS	American Oriental Studies. New Haven, 1935–
APA	Acta praehistorica et archaeologica. Berlin, 1970–
ArOr	Archív Orientální. Prague, 1930–
ARRIM	Annual Review of the Royal Inscriptions of Mesopotamia Project. Toronto, 1983–1991
AS	Assyriological Studies. Chicago, 1931–
ASJ	Acta Sumerologica. Hiroshima, 1979–
ATAT[2]	H. Gressmann (ed.), Altorientalische Texte zum Alten Testament, 2. Auflage. Berlin and Leipzig, 1926
BA	Beiträge der Assyriologie und semitischen Sprachwissenschaft, vols. 1–10. Leipzig, 1890–1927
Babyloniaca	Babyloniaca, études de philologie assyro-babylonienne. Paris, 1907–37
Bagh. For.	Baghdader Forschungen. Mainz am Rhein, 1979–
Bagh. Mitt.	Baghdader Mitteilungen. Berlin, 1960–
Ball, Light	C.J. Ball, Light from the East, or the Witness of the Monuments. London, 1899
Banks, Bismya	E.J. Banks, Bismya, or The Lost City of Adab. New York and London, 1912
Barnett and Wiseman, Fifty Masterpieces	R.D. Barnett and D.J. Wiseman, Fifty Masterpieces of Ancient Near Eastern Art in the Department of Western Asiatic Antiquities in the British Museum. London, 1969
Barton, PBS 9/1	G. Barton, Sumerian Business and Administrative Documents from the Earliest Times to the Dynasty of Agade (=PBS 9/1). Philadelphia, 1915
Barton, RISA	G.A. Barton, The Royal Inscriptions of Sumer and Akkad (=Library of Ancient Semitic Inscriptions 1). New Haven, 1929
Basmachi, Treasures	F. Basmachi, Treasures of the Iraq Museum. Baghdad, 1976
BASOR	Bulletin of the American Schools of Oriental Research. New Haven, 1919–
BE	Babylonian Expedition of the University of Pennsylvania, Series A: Cuneiform Texts, vols. 1–14. Philadelphia, 1893–1914
Beaulieu, Nabonidus	P.-A. Beaulieu, The Reign of Nabonidus King of Babylon 556–539 B.C. (=YNER 10). New Haven and London, 1989
BE Res	Babylonian Expedition of the University of Pennsylvania, Series D: Researches and Treatises, vols. 1, 3–5. Philadelphia, 1904–10
Bezold, Literatur	C. Bezold, Babylonisch-Assyriche Literatur. Leipzig, 1886

BibMes	Bibliotheca Mesopotamica. Malibu, 1975–
Biggs, Abū Ṣalābīkh	R.D. Biggs, Inscriptions from Tell Abū Ṣalābīkh (=OIP 99). Chicago and London, 1974
BIN	Babylonian Inscriptions in the Collection of J.B. Nies. New Haven, 1917–
BiOr	Bibliotheca Orientalis. Leiden, 1943
BJVF	Berliner Jahrbuch für Vor- und Frühgeschichte. Berlin, 1961–
BM Guide	British Museum. A Guide to the Babylonian and Assyrian Antiquities, 3rd edition. London, 1922
BMFB	Bulletin of the Museum of Fine Arts, Boston. Boston, 1903–
BMQ	British Museum Quarterly, vols. 1–37. London, 1926–73
BNYPL	Bulletin of the New York Public Library. New York, 1897–
Böhl, Leiden Coll.	F.M.T. Böhl, Medeelingen uit de Leidische Verzameling van spijkerschrift-Inscripties, 3 vols. Amsterdam, 1933–36
Boehmer, Glyptik	R.M. Boehmer, Die Entwicklung der Glyptik während der Akkad-Zeit. Berlin, 1965
Börker-Klähn, Bildstelen	J. Börker-Klähn, Altvorderasiatische Bildstelen und Vergleichbare Felsreliefs (=Bagh. For. 4). Mainz am Rhein, 1982
Boese, Weihplatten	J. Boese, Altmesopotamische Weihplatten, Eine sumerische Denkmalsgattung des 3. Jahrtausends v. Chr. Berlin and New York, 1971
Borger, EAK 1	R. Borger, Einleitung in die assyrischen Königsinschriften, Erster Teil: Das zweite Jahrtausend v. Chr. (=Handbuch der Orientalistik Ergänzungsband V/1/1). Leiden, 1961
Borger, Zeichenliste	R. Borger, Assyrisch-Babylonische Zeichenliste, 2. Auflage (=AOAT 33/33A). Neukirchen-Vluyn, 1981
Braun-Holzinger, Bronzen	E.A. Braun-Holzinger, Figürliche Bronzen aus Mesopotamia (=Prähistorische Bronzefunde I/4). Munich, 1984
Brinkman, PKB	J.A. Brinkman, A Political History of Post-Kassite Babylonia 1158–722 B.C. (=AnOr 43). Rome, 1968
BRM	Babylonian Records in the Library of J. Pierpont Morgan, 4 vols. New Haven, New York, 1912–23
BSMS	Bulletin of the (Canadian) Society for Mesopotamian Studies. Toronto, 1981–
Buchanan and Hallo, Early Near Eastern Seals	B. Buchanan and W.W. Hallo, Early Near Eastern Seals in the Yale Babylonian Collection. New Haven and London, 1981
van Buren, Fauna	E.D. van Buren, The Fauna of Ancient Mesopotamia as Represented in Art (=AnOr 18). Rome, 1939
CAD	The Assyrian Dictionary of the Oriental Institute of the University of Chicago. Chicago, 1956–
Cagni (ed.), Il bilinguismo	L. Cagni (ed.), Il bilinguismo a Ebla. Atti del convegno internazionale (Napoli 19–22 aprile 1982). Naples, 1984
CAH	I.E.S. Edwards, C.J. Gadd, N.G.L. Hammond, et al. (eds.), The Cambridge Ancient History, 2nd and 3rd editions. Cambridge, 1970–
Calmeyer, Datierbare Bronzen	P. Calmeyer. Datierbare Bronzen aus Luristan und Kirmanshah. Berlin, 1969
Cameron, Iran	G.G. Cameron, History of Early Iran. Chicago, 1936
CCT	Cuneiform Texts from Cappadocian Tablets in the British Museum
Christian, Altertumskunde	V. Christian, Altertumskunde des Zweistromslandes von der Vorzeit bis zum Ende der Achämenidenherrschaft I. Leipzig, 1940
Clay, YOS 1	A. Clay, Miscellaneous Inscriptions in the Yale Babylonian Collection. New Haven, 1915
de Clercq, Collection	H.F.X. de Clercq and J. Ménant, Collection de Clercq, catalogue méthodique et raisonné, antiquités assyriennes, cylindres orientaux, cachets, briques, bronzes, bas-reliefs etc., 2 vols. Paris, 1888/1903
Cohen, Enmerkar	S. Cohen, Enmerkar and the Lord of Aratta. Ph.D. dissertation, University of Pennsylvania, 1973
Collon, Cylinder Seals 2	D. Collon, Catalogue of the Western Asiatic Seals in the British Museum. Cylinder Seals II: Akkadian, Post Akkadian, Ur III Periods. London, 1982
Collon, First Impressions	D. Collon, First Impressions: Cylinder Seals in the Ancient Near East. London, 1987
Contenau, Glyptique Syro-Hittite	G. Contenau, La Glyptique Syro-Hittite. Paris, 1922
Contenau, Manuel	G. Contenau, Manuel d'archéologie orientale, 4 vols. Paris, 1927–47
Cooper, Curse	J.S. Cooper, The Curse of Agade. Baltimore, 1983
CRAIB	Comptes-rendus des séances de l'académie des inscriptions et belles-lettres. Paris, 1857–
Cros, Tello	G. Cros, Nouvelles fouilles de Tello, Mission française de Chaldée. Paris, 1910
CRRA	Compte Rendu de la Rencontre Assyriologique Internationale. [various locations], 1950–
CT	Cuneiform Texts from Babylonian Tablets in the British Museum. London, 1896–
Cullimore, Oriental Cylinders	Cullimore, Oriental Cylinders. Impressions of Ancient Oriental Cylinders, or Rolling Seals of the Babylonians, Assyrians, and Medo-Persians. London, 1842–43
DAFI	Cahiers de la Délégation archéologique française en Iran. Paris, 1971–
Damas. Mitt.	Damaszener Mitteilungen. Mainz am Rhein, 1983–

Deimel, Šumerische Grammatik^{2}	A. Deimel, Šumerische Grammatik mit Übungsstücken und zwei Anhängen, 2nd edition. Rome, 1939
Delaporte, Bibliothèque Nationale	L. Delaporte, Catalogue des cylindres orientaux et des cachets assyro-babyloniens, perses et syro-cappadociens de la Bibliothèque Nationale. Paris, 1910
Delaporte, Louvre 1	L. Delaporte, Musée du Louvre. Catalogue des cylindres, cachets et pierres gravées de style oriental, tome I: Fouilles et Missions. Paris, 1920
Delaporte, Louvre 2	L. Delaporte, Musée du Louvre. Catalogue des cylindres, cachets et pierres gravées de style oriental, tome II: Aquisitions. Paris, 1923
Delougaz, Private Houses	P. Delougaz, H. Hill, and S. Lloyd, Private Houses and Graves in the Diyala Region (=OIP 88). Chicago, 1967
Delougaz, Temple Oval	P. Delougaz and T. Jacobsen, The Temple Oval at Khafājah (=OIP 53). Chicago, 1940
Dunham, Foundations	S. Dunham, A Study of Ancient Mesopotamian Foundations. Ph.D. dissertation, Columbia University, 1980
Durand, Mohammed Diyab	J.-M. Durand, Recherches en Haute Mésopotamie: Tell Mohammed Diyab. Campagnes 1990–1991 (=Mémoires de N.A.B.U. 2). Paris, 1992
Dürr, Trésors	N. Dürr, et al., Trésors de l'Ancien Iran. Geneva, 1966
Ebeling, IAK	E. Ebeling, B. Meissner, and E.F. Weidner, Die Inschriften der altassyrischen Könige (=Altorientalische Bibliothek 1). Leipzig, 1926
Edzard, Rép. Géogr. 1	D.O. Edzard, G. Farber, and E. Sollberger, Die Orts- und Gewässernamen der präsargonischen und sargonischen Zeit. Wiesbaden, 1977
Edzard, Rép. Géogr. 2	D.O. Edzard and G. Farber, Die Orts- und Gewässer namen der Zeit der 3. Dynastie von Ur. Wiesbaden, 1974
Ehrich, Chronologies	R. Ehrich, Chronologies in Old World Archaeology. Chicago and London, 1965
Eichler, Tall al-Hamīdīya 2	S. Eichler, M. Wäfler, and D. Warburton, Tall al-Ḥamīdīya 2. Symposion, Recent Excavations in the Upper Khabur Region, Berne, December 9–11, 1986. Göttingen, 1990
Ellis, Foundation Deposits	R.S. Ellis, Foundation Deposits in Ancient Mesopotamia (=YNER 2). New Haven and London, 1968
Erlenmeyer Collection	Anonymous, Ancient Near Eastern Texts from the Erlenmeyer Collection. London, 1988
Fadhil, Arraphe	A. Fadhil, Studien zur Topographie und Prosopographie der Provinzstädte des Königsreichs Arrapḫe (=Bagh. For. 6). Mainz am Rhein, 1983
Falkenstein, Inschriften Gudeas	A. Falkenstein, Die Inschriften Gudeas von Lagaš I. Einleitung (=AnOr 30). Rome, 1966
FAOS	Freiburger altorientalische Studien. Wiesbaden and Stuttgart, 1975–
Fisher, Nippur 1	C. Fisher, Part I, Babylonian Expedition of the University of Pennsylvania, Excavations at Nippur, plans, details and photographs of the buildings, with numerous objects found in them during the excavations of 1889, 1890, 1893–1896, 1899–1900, with descriptive text. Philadelphia, 1905/6
Foster, Umma	B. Foster, Umma in the Sargonic Period (=Memoirs of the Connecticut Academy of Arts and Sciences vol. 20). Hamden, 1982
Frankfort, Art and Architecture	H. Frankfort, The Art and Architecture of the Ancient Orient. Harmondsworth, 1954
Frankfort, Cylinder Seals	H. Frankfort, Cylinder Seals: A Documentary Essay on the Art and Religion of the Ancient Near East. London, 1939
Frankfort, Stratified Cylinder Seals	H. Frankfort, Stratified Cylinder Seals from the Diyala Region (=OIP 72). Chicago, 1955
Franzaroli, Studies Ebla	P. Franzaroli (ed.), Studies on the Language of Ebla (=Quaderni di Semitistica 13). Florence, 1984
Frayne, Early Dynastic List	D.R. Frayne, The Early Dynastic List of Geographical Names. New Haven, 1992
FuB	Forschungen und Berichte. Berlin, 1957–
Fürtwängler, Gemmen	A. Fürtwängler, Die Antiken Gemmen. Berlin and Leipzig, 1900
Gadd, Early Dynasties	C.J. Gadd, The Early Dynasties of Sumer and Akkad. London, 1921
Gadd, Reading-book	C.J. Gadd, A Sumerian Reading-book. Oxford, 1924
Gadd, UET 1	C.J. Gadd, L. Legrain, and S. Smith, Royal Inscriptions. London, 1928
Gelb, Hurrians	I.J. Gelb, Hurrians and Subarians (=Studies in Ancient Oriental Civilization 22). Chicago, 1944
Gelb, Land Tenure	I.J. Gelb, P. Steinkeller and R.M. Whiting, Earliest Land Tenure Systems in the Near East: Ancient Kudurrus (=OIP 104). Chicago, 1991
Gelb, MAD 1	I.J. Gelb, Sargonic Texts from the Diyala Region. Chicago, 1952
Gelb, MAD 3	I.J. Gelb, Glossary of Old Akkadian. Chicago, 1957
Gelb, MAD 2^{2}	I.J. Gelb, Old Akkadian Writing and Grammar, 2nd edition. Chicago, 1961
Gelb, OAIC	I.J. Gelb, Old Akkadian Inscriptions in the Chicago Natural History Museum, Texts of Legal and Business Interest (=Fieldiana: Anthropology 44/2). Chicago, 1955
Gelb and Kienast, Königsinschriften	I.J. Gelb and B. Kienast, Die Altakkadischen Königsinschriften des dritten Jahrtausends v. Chr. (=FAOS 7). Stuttgart, 1990

de Genouillac, Kich	H. de Genouillac, Premières recherches archéologique à Kich (Fouilles françaises d'El-'Akhymer, mission d'Henri de Genouillac, 1911–12), 2 vols. Paris, 1924/25
Ghirshman, Kunstschätze	R. Ghirshman, Kunstschätze aus Iran von der prähistorischen bis zur Islamischen Zeit. Zürich, 1962
Ghirshman, Perse	R. Ghirshman, Perse: Proto-Iraniens, Médes, Achéménides. Paris, 1963
Ghirshman, Sept milles	R. Ghirshman, Sept milles ans d'art en Iran. Paris, 1961
Gibson and Biggs, Seals	M. Gibson and R.D. Biggs, Seals and Sealing in the Ancient Near East (=BibMes 6). Malibu, 1977
Grayson, Chronicles	A.K. Grayson, Assyrian and Babylonian Chronicles (=Texts from Cuneiform Sources 5). Locust Valley, 1975
Grayson, RIMA 1	A.K. Grayson, Assyrian Rulers of the Third and Second Millennia BC (To 1115 BC). Toronto, 1987
Grégoire, Lagash	J.-P. Grégoire, La province méridionale de l'état de Lagash. Luxemburg, 1962
Grégoire, MVN 10	J.-P. Grégoire, Inscriptions et archives administratives cunéiformes , 1e partie. Rome, 1981
Gressmann, ATAT^2	H. Gressmann, Altorientalische Texte zum Alten Testament, 2nd edition. Berlin and Leipzig, 1926
Gressmann, ATBAT	H. Gressmann, Altorientalische Texte und Bilder zum Alten Testament. Tübingen, 1909
Groneberg, Rép. Géogr. 3	B. Groneberg, Die Orts- und Gewässernamen der altbabylonischen Zeit. Wiesbaden, 1980
Haas , Hurriter	V. Haas (ed.), Hurriter und Hurritisch (=Konstanzer Altorientalische Symposien 2. Konstanz, 1988
Hallo, Royal Titles	W.W. Hallo, Early Mesopotamian Royal Titles, a Philologic and Historical Analysis (=AOS 43). New Haven, 1957
HBKWS	Handuch der Kunstwissenschaft
Heinrich, Fara	E. Heinrich, Fara, Ergebnisse der Ausgrabungen der Deutschen Orient-Gesellschaft in Fara und Abu Hatab 1902/03. Berlin, 1931
Hilprecht, BE 1	H.V. Hilprecht, Old Babylonian Inscriptions Chiefly from Nippur, 2 vols. Philadelphia, 1893/96
Hilprecht, Bêl–Tempel	H.V. Hilprecht, Die Ausgrabungen der Universität von Pennsylvania in Bêl-Tempel zu Nippur. Leipzig, 1903
Hilprecht, Deluge Story	H.V. Hilprecht, The Earliest Version of the Babylonian Deluge Story and the Temple Library of Nippur (=BE Res 5/1). Philadelphia, 1910
Hilprecht, Explorations	H.V. Hilprecht, Explorations in Bible Lands during the 19th Century. Philadelphia, 1903
Hilprecht, Recent Research	H.V. Hilprecht (ed.), Recent Research in Bible Lands, Its Progress and Results. Philadelphia, 1898
Hommel, Geschichte	F. Hommel, Geschichte Babyloniens und Assyriens. Berlin, (1885–) 1888
Hrouda, Isin 2	B. Hrouda (ed.), Isin-Išān Baḥrīyāt II. Die Ergebnisse der Ausgrabungen 1975–1978 (=Bayerische Akademie der Wissenschaften philosophisch-historische Klasse NF 87). Munich, 1981
Hrouda, Vorderasien 1	B. Hrouda, Vorderasien 1: Mesopotamien, Babylonien, Iran und Anatolien. Handbuch der Archäologie. Munich, 1971
HSS	Harvard Semitic Series. Cambridge Mass., 1912–
HUCA	Hebrew Union College Annual. Cincinnati, 1924–
ILN	The Illustrated London News. London, 1842–
IrAnt	Iranica Antiqua. Ghent, 1961–
Iraq Museum Guide	Anonymous, A Guide to the Iraq Museum Collections. Baghdad, 1942
ITT	Inventaire des tablettes de Tello conservées aux Musée Impérial Ottoman. 5 vols. Paris, 1910–21
JA	Journal asiatique. Paris, 1822–
Jacobsen, Copenhagen	T. Jacobsen, Cuneiform Texts in the National Museum, Copenhagen, Chiefly of Economical Contents. Leiden, 1939
Jacobsen, Cylinder Seals	H. Frankfort and T. Jacobsen, Stratified Cylinder Seals from the Diyala Region (=OIP 72). Chicago, 1955
Jacobsen, Gimilsin Temple	T. Jacobsen, The Gimilsin Temple and the Palace of the Rulers at Tell Asmar (=OIP 43). Chicago, 1940
Jacobsen, Jerwan	T. Jacobsen, Sennacherib's Aqueduct at Jerwan (=OIP 24). Chicago, 1935
Jacobsen, OIC 13	T. Jacobsen, H. Frankfort, and C. Preusser, Tell Asmar and Khafaje, the First Season's Work in Eshnunna 1930/31. Chicago, 1932
Jacobsen, SKL	T. Jacobsen, The Sumerian King List (=AS 11). Chicago, 1939
JANES	Journal of the Ancient Near Eastern Society of Columbia University. New York, 1968–
Janneau, Dynastie	Ch.-Guill. Janneau, Une dynastie chaldéenne: les rois d'Ur. Paris, 1911
JAOS	Journal of the American Oriental Society. New Haven, 1893–
JBAA	Journal of the British Archaeological Association. London, 1848–
JCS	Journal of Cuneiform Studies. New Haven and Cambridge, Mass., 1947–

Jean, Religion	C.-F. Jean, La religion sumérienne d'après les documents sumériennes antérieurs à la dynastie d'Isin (–2816). Paris, 1931
Jeremias, HAOG	A. Jeremias, Handbuch der altorientalischen Geisteskultur. Leipzig, 1929
JNES	Journal of Near Eastern Studies. Chicago, 1942–
Johns, ADD	C.H.W. Johns, Assyrian Deeds and Documents Recording the Transfer of Property Including the so-called private contracts, legal decisions and proclamations preserved in the Kouyunjik Collections of the British Museum Chiefly of the 7th Century B.C., 4 vols. Cambridge, 1898–1923
JRAS	Journal of the Royal Asiatic Society. London, 1834–
JSOR	Journal of the Society of Oriental Research, vols. 1–16. Chicago and Toronto, 1917–32
Kärki, KDDU	I. Kärki, Die Königsinschriften der dritten Dynastie von Ur (=Studia Orientalia 58). Helsinki, 1986
KB	Keilinschriftliche Bibliothek, Sammlung von assyrischen und babylonischen Texten in Umschrift und Übersetzung, vols. 1–6. Berlin, 1889–1915
Kessler, Nordmesopotamien	K. Kessler, Untersuchungen zur historischen Topographie Nordmesopotamiens nach keilschriftliche Quellen des 1. Jahrtausends v. Chr. (=Beihefte zum Tübinger Atlas des Vorderen Orients, Reihe B, Nr. 26). Wiesbaden, 1980
King, Antique Gems	C.W. King, Antique Gems, their origin, uses and value. London, 1860
King, Antique Gems and Rings	C.W. King, Antique Gems and Rings. London, 1872
King, Early History	L.W. King, A History of Sumer and Akkad: An Account of the Early Races of Babylonia from Prehistoric Times to the Foundation of the Babylonian Monarchy. London, 1910
Klengel and Marzahn, Sumer	E. Klengel-Brandt and J. Marzahn, Sumer (=VAM Kleine Schriften 5). Berlin, 1983
Komoróczy, Sumer	G. Komoróczy, 'Fénylö ölednek édes öröben ...' A Sumer irodalom kistükre. Budapest, 1970
Kramer Anniversary	B. Eichler (ed.), Kramer Anniversary Volume: Cuneiform Studies in Honor of Samuel Noah Kramer (=AOAT 25). Neukirchen-Vluyn, 1976
Kramer, ISET 2	S.N. Kramer, Istanbul Arkeoloji Müzelerinde Bulunan: Sumer Edebî Tablet ve Parçalari 2 (=TTKY 6/13a). Ankara, 1976
Kramer, Sumerians	S.N. Kramer, The Sumerians, Their History, Culture, and Character. Chicago and London, 1963
Kupper, Nomades	J.-R. Kupper, Les nomades en Mésopotamie au temps des rois de Mari. Paris, 1957
Kutscher, Brockmon Tablets	R. Kutscher, The Brockmon Tablets of the University of Haifa: Royal Inscriptions (=Shay Series of the Zinman Institute of Archaeology). Haifa, 1989
Lajard, Mithra	Introduction à l'étude du culte publique et des mystères de Mithra en Orient et en Occident. Paris, 1847
LAK	A. Deimel, Liste der archaischen Keilschriftzeichen von Fara (=WVDOG 40). Leipzig, 1922
Lambert, BWL	W.G. Lambert, Babylonian Wisdom Literature. Oxford, 1960
Larsen, City-State	M.T. Larsen, The Old Assyrian City-State and Its Colonies (=Mesopotamia 4). Copenhagen, 1976
Layard, Discoveries	A.H. Layard, Discoveries among the Ruins of Nineveh and Babylon, with Travels in Armenia, Kurdistan and the Desert. London, 1853
Legrain, Luristan Bronzes	L. Legrain, Luristan Bronzes in the University Museum. Philadelphia, 1934
Legrain, PBS 15	L. Legrain, Royal Inscriptions and Fragments from Nippur and Babylon. Philadelphia, 1926
Legrain, UE 3	L. Legrain, Archaic Seal-impressions. London and Philadelphia, 1936
Legrain, UE 10	L. Legrain, Seal Cylinders. London and Philadelphia, 1951
Lehmann-Haupt, Mat.	C.F. Lehmann-Haupt, Materialien zur älteren Geschichte Armeniens und Mesopotamiens. Berlin, 1907
Luckenbill, Adab	D.D. Luckenbill, Inscriptions from Adab (=OIP 14). Chicago, 1930
Luckenbill, ARAB	D.D. Luckenbill, Ancient Records of Assyria and Babylonia, 2 vols. Chicago, 1926–27
MAD	Materials for the Assyrian Dictionary. Chicago, 1952–
MAIB	Mémoires de l'institut national de France, académie des inscriptions et belles-lettres. Paris, 1899–
MAM	Mission Archéologique de Mari
MAOG	Mitteilungen der Altorientalischen Gesellschaft. Leipzig, 1925–43
MAOV	Mitteilungen des Akademisch-Orientalischen Vereins zu Berlin (I). Berlin, 1887
MARI	Mari, Annales de Recherches Interdisciplinaires. Paris, 1982–
Martin, Fara	H.P. Martin, Fara: A Reconstruction of the Ancient Mesopotamian City of Shuruppak. Birmingham, 1988
Maspéro, Histoire	G. Maspéro, Histoire ancienne des peuples de l'Orient classique, 3 vols. Paris, 1895–99
McCown, Nippur 1	D.E. McCown, R.C. Haines, and D. Hansen, Nippur I: Temple of Enlil, Scribal Quarter, and Soundings (=OIP 78). Chicago, 1967
MDOG	Mitteilungen der Deutschen Orient-Gesellschaft. Berlin, 1898–
MDP	Mémoires de la Délégation en Perse. Paris, 1900–

MEE	Materiali epigrafici di Ebla. Naples 1979–
Meek, HSS 10	T.J. Meek, Excavations at Nuzi 3: Old Akkadian, Sumerian, and Cappadocian Texts from Nuzi. Cambridge, Mass., 1935
Meissner, BuA	B. Meissner, Babylonien und Assyrien, 2 vols. Heidelberg, 1920/25
Meissner, IAK	E. Ebeling, B. Meissner, and E. Weidner, Die Inschriften der altassyrischen Könige (=Altorientalische Bibliothek 1). Leipzig, 1926
Mélanges Birot	J.-M. Durand and J.-R. Kupper (eds.), Miscellanea babyloniaca. Mélanges offerts à Maurice Birot. Paris, 1985
Ménant, Babylone	M.J. Ménant, Babylone et la Chaldée. Paris, 1875
Ménant, Glyptique	M.J. Ménant, Les pierres gravées de la Haute-Asie, recherches sur la glyptique orientale, 2 vols. Paris, 1883/86
Ménant, Manuel	M.J. Ménant, Manuel de la langue assyrienne. Paris, 1880
Merhav, Treasures	R. Merhav (ed.), Treasures of the Bible Lands: The Elie Borowski Collection. Tel Aviv, 1987
Mesopotamia	Meopotamia: Rivista di Archeoligia. Turin, 1966–
Meyer, Sumerier und Semiten	E. Meyer, Sumerier und Semiten in Babylonien. Berlin, 1906
de Meyer (ed.), Tell ed-Dēr 3	L. de Meyer (ed.), Tell ed-Dēr: Soundings at Abū Habbah (Sippar). Louvain, 1980
Micali, Monumenti	G. Micali, Monumenti inediti a illustrazione della storia degli antichi populi Italiani. Florence, 1844
Middleton, Engraved Gems	J.H. Middleton, The Engraved Gems of Classical Times with a Catalogue of Gems in the Fitzwilliam Museum. Cambridge, 1891
Middleton, Lewis Collection	J.H. Middleton, The Lewis Collection of Gems and Rings in the possession of Corpus Christi College, Cambridge. Cambridge, 1892
MJ	Museum Journal of the University Museum, University of Pennsylvania, vols. 1–24. Philadelphia, 1910–35
Moortgat Festschrift	K. Bittel, et al. (eds.), Vorderasiatische Archäologie. Studien und Aufsätze Anton Moortgat zum fünfundsechzigsten Geburtstag gewidmet von Kollegen, Freunden und Schülern. Berlin, 1964
Moortgat, Kunst	A. Moortgat, Die Kunst der alten Mesopotamien. Die klassische Kunst Vorderasiens. Cologne, 1967
Moortgat, VAR	A. Moortgat, Vorderasiatische Rollsiegel: Ein Beitrag zur Geschichte der Steinschneidekunst. Berlin, 1940
de Morgan, MSP 4/1	J. de Morgan, Mission scientifique en Perse 4/1. Paris, 1896
MP	Monuments et mémoires publiés par l'académie des inscriptions et belles-lettres. Paris
MSL	B. Landsberger, et al. (eds.), Materials for the Sumerian Lexicon. Rome, 1937–
Muscarella, Ladders	O.W. Muscarella (ed.), Ladders to Heaven: Art Treasures from Lands of the Bible. Toronto, 1981
MVAG	Mitteilungen der Vorderasiatisch-Aegyptischen Gesellschaft, vols. 1–44. Berlin and Leipzig, 1896–1939
MVN	Materiali per il vocabolario neosumerico. Rome, 1974–
NABU	Nouvelles assyriologiques bréves et utilitaires. Paris, 1987–
Nashef, Rép. Géogr. 4	K. Nashef, Die Orts- und Gewässernamen der altassyrischen Zeit. Wiesbaden, 1991
Nashef, Rép. Géogr. 5	K. Nashef, Die Orts- und Gewässernamen der mittelbabylonischen und mittelassyrischen Zeit. Wiesbaden, 1982
Nestmann, Excavations	C. Nestmann, Excavations at Bismya. Ph.D. dissertation, University of Chicago, 1949
OECT	Oxford Editions of Cuneiform Texts. Oxford, London, and Paris, 1923–
OIC	Oriental Institute Communications. Chicago, 1922–
OIP	Oriental Institute Publications. Chicago, 1924–
OLZ	Orientalistische Literaturzeitung. Berlin and Leipzig, 1898–
Open Court	The Open Court, a Monthly Magazine. Chicago, 1886–
Opificius, Geschnittene Steine	R. Mayer-Opificius, Geschittene Steine der Antike. Münzen und Medaillen A.G. Basel, 1968
Oppenheim, Letters	A.L. Oppenheim, Letters from Mesopotamia. Official, Business, and Private Letters on Clay Tablets from Two Millennia. Chicago, 1965
Oppert, EM 1	J. Oppert, Expédition scientifique en Mésopotamie ... Tome 1: Relation du voyage et résultats de l'expédition. Paris, 1863
OrAnt	Oriens Antiquus, Rivista del Centro per le Antichità e la Storia dell'Arte del Vicino Oriente. Rome, 1962–
von der Osten, Newell	H.H von der Osten, Ancient Oriental Seals in the Collection of Mr. Edward T. Newell (=OIP 22). Chicago, 1934
Owen, NATN	D. Owen, Neo-Sumerian Archival Texts Primarily from Nippur in the University Museum, the Oriental Institute and the Iraq Museum. Winona Lake, 1982
Parrot, Glyptique mésopotamienne	A. Parrot, Glyptique mésopotamienne: Fouilles de Lagash (Tello) et de Larsa (Senkereh) (1931–1933). Paris, 1954
Parrot, Tello	A. Parrot, Tello, vingt campagnes de fouilles (1877–1933). Paris, 1948

PBS	Publications of the Babylonian Section, University Museum, University of Pennsylvania, 15 vols. Philadelphia, 1911–26
Perrot and Chipiez, Chaldée et Assyrie	G. Perrot and C. Chipiez, Histoire de l'art dans l'antiquité, tome 2: Chaldée et Assyrie. Paris, 1884
Peters, Nippur	J.P. Peters, Nippur, or Explorations and Adventures on the Euphrates. The Narrative of the University of Pennsylvania Expedition to Babylonia in the Years 1888–1890, 2 vols. New York and London, 1897
Pettinato, MEE 2	G. Pettinato, Testi amministrativi della biblioteca L. 2769. Part 1 (=MEE 2). Naples, 1980
Pézard and Pottier, Catalogue	M. Pézard and E. Pottier, Musée du Louvre, Catalogue des antiquités de la Susiane (mission J. de Morgan), 2nd edition. Paris, 1926
Poebel, PBS 4/1	A. Poebel, Historical Texts. Philadelphia, 1914
Poebel, PBS 5	A. Poebel, Historical and Grammatical Texts. Philadelphia, 1914
Pohl, TMH 5	A. Pohl, Vorsargonische und sargonische Wirtschaftstexte (=TMH 5). Leipzig, 1935
Pope, Survey	A.U. Pope, A Survey of Persian Art from Prehistoric Times to the Present, vol. 1. New York and London, 1938
Porada, Corpus	E. Porada, Corpus of Ancient Near Eastern Seals in North American Collections, 1: The Collection of the Pierpont Morgan Library (=Bollingen Series 14). Washington, 1948
Preusser, Wohnhäuser	C. Preusser. Die Wohnhäuser in Assur (=WVDOG 64). Berlin, 1953
PSBA	Proceedings of the Society of Biblical Archaeology, vols. 1–40. London, 1878–1918
1 R	H.C. Rawlinson and E. Norris, The Cuneiform Inscriptions of Western Asia, vol. 1: A Selection from the Historical Inscriptions of Chaldaea, Assyria, and Babylonia. London, 1861
RA	Revue d'assyriologie et d'archéologie orientale. Paris, 1886–
Radau, EBH	H. Radau, Early Babylonian History down to the End of the Fourth Dynasty of Ur. New York and London, 1900
Rassam, Asshur	H. Rassam, Asshur and the Land of Nimrod. New York, 1897
REC	Thureau-Dangin, Recherches sur l'origine de l'écriture cunéiformes, 1re partie: Les formes archaiques et leurs équivalents modernes. Paris, 1898
Rép. Géogr.	W. Röllig (ed.), Beihefte zum Tübinger Atlas des vorderen Orients, Reihe B, Nr. 7: Répertoire Géographique des Textes Cunéiformes. Wiesbaden, 1974–
RHA	Revue hittite et asianique. Paris, 1930–
RHR	Revue de l'histoire des religions. Annales du Musée Guimet. Paris, 1880–
RIM	The Royal Inscriptions of Mesopotamia Project. Toronto
RIMA	The Royal Inscriptions of Mesopotamia, Assyrian Periods. Toronto, 1987–
RIME	The Royal Inscriptions of Mesopotamia, Early Periods. Toronto, 1990–
RIMS	The Royal Inscriptions of Mesopotamia, Supplements. Toronto, 1984–
RLA	Reallexikon der Assyriologie. Berlin, 1932–
RLV	Reallexikon der Vorgeschichte, vols. 1–15. Berlin, 1924-32
Rocznik Orientalistyczny	Polska akademia nauk komitet nauk orientalistycznych, Rocznik Orientalistyczny. Warsaw, 1914–
Roscher, Lexikon II/1	W.H. Roscher, Ausführliches Lexikon des griechenischen und römischen Mythologie II/1. Leipzig, 1890–94
RSO	Rivista degli studi orientali. Rome, 1907–
RT	Receuil de travaux relatifs à la philologie et à l'archéologie égyptiennes et assyriennes, vols. 1–40. Paris, 1870-1923
Rutten, Encyclopédie	M. Rutten, Encyclopédie photographique de l'art. 2 vols. Paris, 1935–36
Salonen, Türen	A. Salonen, Die Türen des alten Mesopotamien, eine lexikalische und kulturgeschichtliche Untersuchung (=AASF 124). Helsinki, 1961
de Sarzec, Découvertes	E. de Sarzec, Découvertes en Chaldée par Ernest de Sarzec, ouvrage accompagné de planches, publié par les soins de Léon Heuzey, avec le concours de Arthur Amiaud et François Thureau-Dangin pour la partie épigraphique, 2 vols. Paris, 1884/1912
SCCNH	Studies on the Civilization and Culture of Nuzi and the Hurrians.
Scheil, MDP 2	V. Scheil, Textes élamites-sémitiques, 1e série. Paris, 1900
Scheil, MDP 4	V. Scheil, Textes élamites-sémitiques, 2e série. Paris, 1902
Scheil, MDP 6	V. Scheil, Textes élamites-sémitiques, 3e série. Paris, 1905
Scheil, MDP 10	V. Scheil, Textes élamites-sémitiques, 4e série. Paris, 1908
Scheil, MDP 14	V. Scheil, Textes élamites-sémitiques, 5e série. Paris, 1913
Scheil, MDP 28	V. Scheil, Mélanges épigraphiques. Paris, 1939
Schroeder, KAH 2	O. Schroeder, Keilschrifttexte aus Assur historischen Inhalts, Zweites Heft (=WVDOG 37). Leipzig, 1922
SEb	Studi Eblaiti, vols. 1–7. Rome, 1979–84
Selz, Bankettszene	G. Selz, Die Bankettszene: Entwicklung eines 'überzeitlichen' Bildmotivs in Mesopotamien; von der frühdynastischen bis zur Akkad-Zeit (=FAOS 11). Wiesbaden, 1983
Seux, ERAS	M.-J. Seux, Épithètes royales akkadiennes et sumériennes. Paris, 1967

Shileiko, VN	V.K. Shileiko, Votivnie nadpisi šumerijskich pravitelej. Petrograd, 1915
Sjöberg, Temple Hymns	Å. W. Sjöberg and E. Bergmann, The Collection of the Sumerian Temple Hymns (=TCS 3). Locust Valley, 1969
SKL	T. Jacobsen, The Sumerian King List (=AS 11). Chicago, 1939
SMEA	Studi Micenei ed Egeo-Anatolici
Smick, Cuneiform Documents	E.B. Smick, Cuneiform Documents of the Third Millennium in the John F. Lewis Collection in the Public Library of Philadelphia. Ph.D. dissertation, Dropsie College, 1951
G. Smith, Chaldean Genesis	G. Smith, The Chaldean Account of the Genesis, Containing the Description of the Creation, the Fall of Man, the Deluge, the Tower of Babel, the Times of the Patriarchs, and Nimrod; Babylonian Fables, and Legends of the Gods, from the Cuneiform Inscriptions. London, 1875
von Soden, GAG	W. von Soden, Grundriss der akkadischen Grammatik (=AnOr 33). Rome, 1952
Sollberger, UET 8	E. Sollberger, Royal Inscriptions Part 2. London, 1965
Sollberger and Kupper, IRSA	E. Sollberger and J.R. Kupper, Inscriptions royales sumériennes et akkadiennes. Paris, 1971
Solyman, Götterwaffen	T. Solyman, Die Entstehung und Entwicklung der Götterwaffen im alten Mesopotamien und ihre Bedeutung. Beirut, 1968
Speleers, Catalogue	L. Speleers, Catalogue des intailles et empreintes orientales des Musées Royaux du Cinquantenaire. Brussels, 1917
Speleers, Catalogue Suppl.	L. Speleers. Catalogue des intailles et empreintes orientales des Musées Royaux du Cinquantenaire, Supplément. Brussels, 1943
Spycket, Statuaire	A. Spycket, La statuaire du Proche-Orient ancien (= Handbuch der Orientalistik 7/1/2/B 2). Leiden and Cologne, 1981
Spycket, Statues	A. Spycket, Les statues de culte dans les textes mésopotamiens des origines à la Ire dynastie de Babylone (=Cahiers de la Revue Biblique 9). Paris, 1968
Steible, ASBW 2	H. Steible, Die altsumerischen Bau- und Weihinschriften. Teil 2. Kommentar zu den Inschriften aus 'Lagaš', Inschriften ausserhalb von 'Lagaš' (=FAOS 5). Wiesbaden, 1982
Steible, NSBW 2	H. Steible, Die neusumerischen Bau und Weihinschriften. Teil 2. Kommentar zu den Gudea-Statuen; Inschriften der III. Dynastie von Ur; Inschriften der IV. und 'V' Dynastie von Uruk; Varia. Stuttgart, 1991
Steinkeller, Texts Baghdad	P. Steinkeller and J.N. Postgate, Third-Millennium Legal and Administrative Texts in the Iraq Museum, Baghdad. Winona Lake, 1992
Stephens, YOS 9	F.J. Stephens, Votive and Historical Texts from Babylonia and Assyria. New Haven, 1937
Steve, Tchoga Zanbil 3	M.J. Steve, Tchoga Zanbil (Dur-Untash), volume III. Textes élamites et accadiens de Tchoga Zanbil (=MDP 41). Paris, 1967
Stol, Studies	M. Stol, Studies in Old Babylonian History. Leiden, 1976
Stol, Trees	M. Stol, On Trees, Mountains, and Millstones in the Ancient Near East. Leiden, 1979
Strommenger and Hirmer, Mesopotamien	E. Strommenger and M. Hirmer, Fünf Jahrtausende Mesopotamien: die Kunst von den Anfängen um 5000 v. Chr. bis zu Alexander. Munich, 1962
Studies Diakonoff	Societies and Languages of the Ancient Near East. Studies in Honour of I.M. Diakonoff. Warminster, 1982
Studies Molin	I. Seybold (ed.), Meqor ḫajjim. Festschrift für Georg Molin zu seinem 75. Geburtstag. Graz, 1983
Studies Sjöberg	H. Behrens, et al. (eds.), Dumu-e_2-dub-ba-a: Studies in Honor of Åke W. Sjöberg (=Occasional Publications of the Samuel Noah Kramer Fund 11). Philadelphia, 1989
Studies Tadmor	M. Cogan and I. Ephᶜal (eds.), *Ah, Assyria* ... Studies in Assyrian History and Ancient Near Eastern Historiography Presented to Hayim Tadmor (=Scripta Hierosolymitana, Publications of the Hebrew University of Jerusalem, vol. 33). Jerusalem, 1991
Symbolae Böhl	M.A. Beek et al. (eds.), Symbolae Biblicae et Mesopotamicae Francisco Mario Theodoro de Liagre Böhl Dedicatae. Leiden, 1973
TCS	Texts from Cuneiform Sources. Locust Valley, New York, 1966–
TCL	Textes cunéiformes du Musée du Louvre, Département des Antiquités Orientales. Paris, 1910–
Thureau-Dangin, Chronologie	F. Thureau-Dangin, La chronologie des dynasties de Sumer et d'Accad. Paris, 1918
Thureau-Dangin, ISA	F. Thureau-Dangin, Les inscriptions de Sumer et d'Akkad, transcription et traduction. Paris, 1905
Thureau-Dangin, RTC	F. Thureau-Dangin, Recueil de tablettes chaldéennes. Paris, 1903
Thureau-Dangin, SAK	F. Thureau-Dangin, Die sumerischen und akkadischen Königsinscriften (=VAB 1). Leipzig, 1907
TMH	Texte und Materialien der Frau Professor Hilprecht Collection of Babylonian Antiquities in Eigentum der Universität Jena
TSBA	Transactions of the Society of Biblical Archaeology. London, 1872–93
TTKY	Türk Tarih Kurumu Yayınlarından. Ankara

TUAT	O. Kaiser (ed.), Texte aus der Umwelt des Alten Testaments. Gütersloh, 1982–
UE	Ur Excavations. Oxford, London, and Philadelphia, 1926–
UET	Ur Excavations, Texts. London, 1928–
UF	Ugarit-Forschungen, Internationales Jahrbuch für die Altertumskunde Syrien-Palästinas. Neukirchen-Vluyn, 1969–
UMB	The University Museum Bulletin. Philadelphia
Unger, AuBK	E. Unger, Assyrische und babylonische Kunst. Breslau, 1921
Unger, Naram-Sin	J.P. Naab and E. Unger, Pir Hüseyin'de Naram-Sin stelinin keşfi/ Die Entdeckung der Stele des Naram-Sin in Pir Hüseyin. İstanbul, 1934
Unger, Siegelbildforschung	E. Unger, Der Beginn der altmesopotamischen Siegelbildforschung: Eine Leistung der Österreichischen Orientalistik (=Sitzungsberichte der Österreichenische Akademie der Wissenschaften, philosophisch-historische Klasse 250/2). Vienna, 1966
Unger, SuAK	E. Unger, Sumerische und akkadische Kunst. Breslau, 1926
UVB	Vorläufiger Bericht über die von (dem Deutschen Archäologischen Institut und der Deutschen Orient-Gesellschaft aus Mitteln) der Deutschen Forschungsgemeinschaft unternommenen Ausgrabungen in Uruk-Warka. Berlin, 1930–
Uzunoğlu, IESEM	E. Uzunoğlu (ed.), İstanbul Eski Şark Eserleri Müsezi. Istanbul, 1974
VAB	Vorderasiatische Bibliothek. Leipzig, 1907–16
VAM	Vorderasiatisches Museum, Berlin
VAS	Vorderasiatische Schriftdenkmäler der Königlichen Museen zu Berlin. Leipzig and Berlin, 1907–
Vogelzang and Vanstiphout, Epic Literature	M.E. Vogelzang and H.L.J. Vanstiphout (eds.), Mesopotamian Epic Literature: Oral or Aural? Lewiston, N.Y., 1992
Walker, CBI	C.B.F. Walker, Cuneiform Brick Inscriptions in the British Museum, the Ashmolean Museum, Oxford, the City of Birmingham Museums and Art Gallery, the City of Bristol Museum and Art Gallery. London, 1981
Ward, Morgan	W.H. Ward, Cylinders and Other Ancient Oriental Seals in the Library of J. Pierpont Morgan. New Haven, 1920
Ward, Seals	W.H. Ward, The Seal Cylinders of Western Asia. Washington, 1910
Weidner, IAK	E. Ebeling, B. Meissner, and E. Weidner, Die Inschriften der altassyrischen Könige (=Altorientalische Bibliothek 1). Leipzig, 1926
Westenhoz, OSP 1	A. Westenholz, Old Sumerian and Old Akkadian Texts in Philadelphia Chiefly from Nippur. Part One. Literary and Lexical Texts and the Earliest Administrative Documents from Nippur (=BibMes 1). Malibu, 1975
Westenholz, OSP 2	A. Westenholz, Old Sumerian and Old Akkadian Texts in Philadelphia. Part Two: The 'Akkadian' Texts, the Enlilmeba Texts, and the Onion Archive (=Carsten Niebuhr Institute of Ancient Near Eastern Studies Publications 3). Copenhagen, 1987
Westenholz, Texts Jena	A. Westenholz, Early Cuneiform Texts in Jena. Pre-Sargonic and Sargonic Documents from Nippur and Fara in the Hilprecht-Sammlung vorderasiatischer Altertümer Institut für Altertumswissenschaften der Friedrich-Schiller-Universität, Jena. Copenhagen, 1975
Winckler, AOF	H. Winckler, Altorientalische Forschungen, 3 vols. Leipzig, 1893–1905
Winckler and Böhden, ABK	H. Winckler and E. Böhden, Altbabylonische Keilschrifttexte zum Gebrauch bei Vorlesungen. Leipzig, 1892
Wiseman and Forman, Seals	D.J. Wiseman and W. and B. Forman, Cylinder Seals of Western Asia. London, 1959
WO	Die Welt des Orients. Wuppertal, Stuttgart, and Göttingen, 1947–
Woolley, Sumerian Art	C.L. Woolley, The Development of Sumerian Art. New York, 1935
Woolley, UE 2	C.L. Woolley, The Royal Cemetery. London and Philadelphia, 1934
Woolley, UE 4	C.L. Woolley, The Early Periods. London and Philadelphia, 1955
Woolley, UE 5	C.L. Woolley, The Ziggurat and Its Surroundings. London and Philadelphia, 1939
Woolley, UE 6	C.L. Woolley, The Buildings of the Third Dynasty. London and Philadelphia, 1974
Woolley, UE 8	C.L. Woolley, The Kassite Period and the Period of the Assyrian Kings. London, 1965
Woolley and Mallowan, UE 7	L.W. Woolley and M. Mallowan, The Old Babylonian Period. London and Philadelphia, 1976
WVDOG	Wissenschaftliche Veröffentlichungen der Deutschen Orient-Gesellschaft. Leipzig and Berlin, 1901–
WZJ	Wissenschaftliche Zeitschrift der Friedrich Schiller Universität Jena. Jena, 1951–
WZKM	Wiener Zeitschrift für die Kunde des Morgenlandes. Vienna, 1887–
Yang, Sargonic Archive	Z. Yang, A Study of the Sargonic Archive from Adab. Ph.D. dissertation, University of Chicago, 1986
Yang, Sargonic Inscriptions	Z. Yang, Sargonic Inscriptions from Adab (=Institute for the History of Ancient Civilizations, Period Publications on Ancient Civilizations 1). Changchun, 1989
YNER	Yale Near Eastern Researches. New Haven and London, 1967–
YOS	Yale Oriental Series, Babylonian Texts. New Haven, 1915–
ZA	Zeitschrift für Assyriologie und verwandte Gebiete. Berlin, 1886–
Zadok, Elamite Onomasticon	R. Zadok, The Elamite Onomasticon. Naples, 1984

ZDMG	Zeitschrift der Deutschen Morgenländischen Gesellschaft. Leipzig and Wiesbaden, 1879–
Zervos, L'art	C. Zervos, L'art de la Mésopotamie de la fin du quatrième millénaire au XVe siècle avant notre ère. Paris, 1935

Other Abbreviations

c	collated
cm	centimetre(s)
col(s).	column(s)
dia.	diameter
DN	divine name
dupl.	duplicate
E	east
ED	Early Dynastic
ed(s).	editor(s)
ex(s).	exemplar(s)
fig(s).	figure(s)
frgm(s).	fragment(s)
GN	geographical name
MB	Middle Babylonian
n	not collated
N	north
NA	Neo-Assyrian
n(n).	note(s)
NB	Neo-Babylonian
no(s).	number(s)
NS	New Series
OAkk.	Old Akkadian
OB	Old Babylonian
obv.	obverse
OS	Old Series
p	collated from photo
p(p).	page(s)
pl(s).	plate(s)
PN	personal name
reg.	registration
rev.	reverse
RN	royal name
S	south
W	west
var(s).	variant(s)
vol(s).	volume(s)

+	Between object numbers indicates physical join
(+)	Indicates fragments from same object but no physical join

Object Signatures

When the same signature is used for more than one group, the first group in this list is meant unless otherwise indicated. For example, 'A' always means the Istanbul collection unless stated otherwise.

A	1) Aššur collection of the Arkeoloji Müzeleri, Istanbul
	2) Asiatic collection of the Oriental Institute, Chicago
ÄS	Collection of the Ägyptologische Staatssammlung, Munich
AH	Abu Habba collection of the British Museum, London
AO	Collection of Antiquités Orientales of the Musée du Louvre, Paris
As	Excavation numbers of the Chicago excavations at Tell Asmar, Iraq
Ash	Collection of the Ashmolean Museum, Oxford
Ass	Prefix of excavation numbers from the German excavations at Aššur
Ass ph	Prefix of excavation photos from the German excavations at Aššur
Bab	Excavation numbers of the German excavations at Babylon
Bab ph	Prefix of excavation photos from the German excavations at Babylon
BE	1) Signature of objects in the Babylon collection of the Vorderasiatische Museum, Berlin
	2) Prefix of excavation numbers from the German excavations at Babylon
BLMJ	Bible Lands Museum, Jerusalem
BM	British Museum, London
BT	William and Sylvia Brockmon Collection of Cuneiform Tablets at the University of Haifa
CBS	Babylonian Section of the University Museum, Philadelphia
EŞ	Eşki Şark Eserleri Müzesi of the Arkeoloji Müzeleri, Istanbul
FLP	John Frederick Lewis collection of the Free Library of Philadelphia
HS	Hilprecht collection of Babylonian Antiquities of Fr. Schiller University, Jena
IB	Excavation numbers of the Munich expedition to Isin-Išān Bahrīyāt
IM	Iraq Museum, Baghdad
Kh	Prefix of field numbers from the American excavations at Khafajah
L	1) Signature of objects in the collection of the University Museum, Philadelphia
	2) Lagash collection of the Arkeoloji Müzeleri, Istanbul
LB	Tablets in the Liagre Böhl collection
M	1) Signature of objects in the Mari collection of the Musée du Louvre, Paris
	2) Prefix of excavation numbers from the French excavations at Mari, Syria
MAH	Musée d'Art et d'Histoire, Geneva
MFAB	Museum of Fine Arts, Boston
MLC	J. Pierpont Morgan collection of the Yale University Library, New Haven
MM	1) Signature of objects in the collection of the Museo Monserrat, Barcelona
MMA	Metropolitan Museum of Art, New York
N	Nippur collection of the University Museum, Philadelphia
Ni	Nippur collection of the Arkeoloji Müzeleri, Istanbul
NBC	James B. Nies collection of the Yale University Library, New Haven
N-T	Excavation numbers of inscribed objects from the American excavations at Nippur
O	Objects in the Section du Proche Orient of the Musées Royaux du Cinquantenaire, Brussels
OI	Oriental Institute, Chicago
ROM	Royal Ontario Museum, Toronto
Sb	Susa collection of the Musée du Louvre, Paris
TA	Object numbers of the Chicago excavations at Tell Asmar, Iraq
Th	R.C. Thompson collection of the British Museum, London
U	Prefix of excavation numbers from the British-American excavations at Ur, Iraq
UM	University Museum, Philadelphia
VA	Vorderasiatische Museum, Berlin
VA Ass	Aššur collection of the Vorderasiatische Museum, Berlin
VA Bab	Babylon collection of the Vorderasiatische Museum, Berlin
VAT	Tablets in the collection of the Vorderasiatische Museum, Berlin
W	Excavation numbers of the German excavations at Uruk/Warka
YBC	Babylonian collection of the Yale University Library, New Haven

SARGONIC AND GUTIAN PERIODS

(2334–2113 BC)

INTRODUCTION

The time period covered by the inscriptions edited in this volume extends from the accession of Sargon of Akkad to the end of the Gutian period, the latter arbitrarily defined here as the beginning of the reign of Ur-Nammu of Ur. According to J.A. Brinkman's chronology (found in an appendix to A.L. Oppenheim, Ancient Mesopotamia, second edition), this corresponds to 2334–2113 B.C. These are, of course, not precise dates; the details of the chronology of this period remain to be sorted out. The following terminology is used in this volume. This phase of ancient Mesopotamian history is designated as the Sargonic and Gutian periods; the dialect of the Akkadian language in which most of the royal inscriptions of this period are recorded is called Old Akkadian. The term Akkadian refers to the archaeological levels which have yielded artifacts of this period. Original inscriptions of the Sargonic and Gutian periods are not particularly numerous; they are, however, supplemented by the evidence of several Old Babylonian tablet copies of Old Akkadian inscriptions. The latter are an invaluable source for the reconstruction of the history of this period. The Sargonic period marks the first time the Akkadian language was extensively used for royal inscriptions. The majority of inscriptions in this volume are recorded in that language; a minority are known in bilingual (Sumerian and Akkadian) versions, and a handful are in Sumerian alone. While the previous editors of the Old Akkadian inscriptions, H. Hirsch, and I. Gelb and B. Kienast, have carefully separated the original inscriptions from the Old Babylonian tablet copies in their editions, the author has decided, in the case of duplicates, to edit the two sources together. Since the details concerning the date of an exemplar, whether original monument or later copy, are clearly set out in the catalogue, there should be no undue confusion for the reader.

The relative lack of sources for Sargonic times compared with those of the Old Babylonian period means that the chronological arrangement provided in the author's RIME 4 is not feasible here; rather, the inscriptions are arranged thematically. This means that texts of a particular type — those describing military campaigns, building inscriptions, votive inscriptions, and the like — are grouped together.

Concerning the system of transliteration of texts, the values given in Borger, Zeichenliste are employed, with the one modification. I. Gelb (MAD 2 p. 35) has proposed a series of four different voiceless sibilants for the earliest stages of Old Akkadian as shown in the following chart. In the Old Akkadian column of the chart, S stands for voiceless sibilant.

Old Akkadian	Old Babylonian	Arabic	Hebrew	Old Akkadian Syllabary			
a) S_1	s	s	š	SA	SE_{11}	SI	SU
b) S_2	š	š	ś (sīn)	SA	SE_{11}	SI	SU
c) S_3	š	ṯ	š	ŠA	ŠE	ŠI	ŠU
d) S_4	š	—	—	SÁ	ŠÈ	—	SU_4

The author, following the practice of Gelb and Kienast in their editions, has opted for a clear differentiation between Old Akkadian S_1 and S_2; in this volume the latter is transliterated as ś. This differentiation can present problems for the modern editor, since in many cases the Old Akkadian syllabary is ambiguous on this question. The IŠ sign, for example, can represent either /iš/ or /iś/, and in many cases the correct value can be determined only by comparison with other forms of a particular substantive or verb. If the Akkadian lemmata fail to clarify the issue, the comparative evidence of other Semitic languages can be called upon. For instance, the infinitive *sa-ma-um* in Eblaite argues that the first phoneme of the verb 'to hear' in Old Akkadian is ś rather than š. Of interest is the fact that the evidence of the examples collected by Gelb in MAD 3 would not have been sufficient to determine its correct value. If comparative evidence was lacking so that the author was unable to determine the more precise nature of the original sibilant, here it was simply given a value VŠ.

Another problem arises in the transliteration of signs containing the Old Akkadian phoneme ś. Since the phoneme coalesced with š in post-Old Akkadian texts, and since the scholars who established the modern system for Akkadian transliteration based their values to a large degree on these later texts, they did not find it necessary to provide a complete roster of values for all possible combinations of syllables with ś. Generally, the value given to the ś signs was the same as that for the S series; for example, śa = sa, śi = si, śu = su, etc. However, this principle was not universally applied. For example, SU_4 was given the value śú, SI_{11} was read as śì, and ÁŠ was rendered as aś. One could argue that a simpler system would be one that consistently assigned the values of the s signs to the ś signs. In such a system SU_4 would be read $śu_4$, SI_{11} as $śi_{11}$, and ÁŠ with value áś, and so forth. This transliteration system would have the advantage of not significantly adding to the number of signs for the Old Akkadian syllabary, and by consistently deriving the ś values from the s values would provide a reading that should be immediately recognized by the scholar. In the hope that such a system will lessen the confusion concerning the transliteration of the ś series of signs, it has been adopted for the present volume.

Following the suggestion of Krebernik (ZA 81 [1991] p. 136) we have interpreted the graphemes PA_4.ŠEŠ 'anointed priest' and ŠA.DÚ 'mountain' to be pseudosumerograms rather than syllabic writings. The same applies for NI.$ŚI_{11}$ 'people'. We have read the É sign in Sumerian PNs as é, not as ʾà.

With respect to the numbering of texts, we note that the main series refers to the royal inscriptions of the king, the 1000 series to royal inscriptions whose attribution is uncertain, and the 2000 series to servant seals and votive inscriptions. If a seal or a votive inscription belongs to the king or a member of the royal family, it is edited in the main series.

Akkad

E2.1.1

There is a particular scarcity of sources concerning the foundation and early expansion of the Akkadian state. In order to understand better the process of its state formation we should first examine the political situation that existed in Babylonia at the end of the Early Dynastic period, that is, in the period immediately preceding the one treated in this volume. P. Steinkeller has recently written on this subject (in an article 'History of Mesopotamia [Third Millennium]' Anchor Bible Dictionary 4 [1991] pp. 725–26):

> To begin with the question of N[orthern] government, the most striking fact is that the N[orth] never seems to have developed a system of independent city states, even remotely comparable to that of the S[outh]. On the contrary, there are strong reasons to believe that during the Early Dynastic II and III periods (ca. 2750–2300) N[orthern] Babylonia formed, for most of the time, a single territorial state, whose gravity-point usually remained at Kish. The qualification 'usually' we just applied to the role of Kish is necessary, for we know that the political landscape of the N[orth] involved two other major powers, Mari and Akshak, which actively competed with Kish for the control of N[orthern] Babylonia. And, if we can trust the testimony of the 'Sumerian King List' (henceforth SKL), on at least two occasions, first Mari and then Akshak actually achieved ascendancy over Kish (Jacobsen 1939: 103–7).

Some idea of the extent of the Kišite state in what may have been its maximum extent in Early Dynastic times may be provided by the geographical list edited by G. Pettinato in Orientalia NS 47 (1978) pp. 63–73, if, as I have argued (in a monograph entitled The Early Dynastic List of Geographical Names, American Oriental Series vol. 74, p. 87), the toponyms enumerated in the list were cities controlled by Kiš, or those with which it had trade relations.

To the triad of competing northern powers — Kiš, Mari, and Akšak — there was added, in late Early Dynastic times, a fourth — Agade. To this day the location of the city remains unknown; a recent discussion (C. Wall-Romana, JNES 49 [1990] pp. 205–45) posits a location for the city somewhere in the area of the confluence of the Diyala and Tigris rivers. Now, the early Old Babylonian texts from Ešnunna edited by R. Whiting exhibit a number of features of the 'hymno-epic' dialect which, in turn, is thought to have inherited many of its grammatical features from the Old Akkadian language. It is not unlikely that the Old Akkadian language, as attested in the royal inscriptions of the Sargonic kings, displays features of the dialect of the capital regiòn. If this be true, it would support the hypothesis of a location for the city of Agade in the Diyala region, although it would not be proof of it. The early Akkadian state may have been a small breakaway league of cities on the eastern fringes of the Kišite kingdom which under Sargon's leadership contended, as Mari and Akšak had done earlier, for hegemony over the area that was later designated Babylonia. While no details of the struggle between Kiš and Agade are known, the final outcome — the defeat of Kiš and the incorporation of its realm into the domains of Agade — is certain; the events are alluded to in the literary composition 'Curse of Agade': 'After Enlil's frown / Had slain Kish by means of the Bull of Heaven ...' According to the Sumerian King List and other historical sources, the founder of the Akkadian state was Sargon, a man of apparently humble origins. For the various traditions concerning his birth the reader is referred to B. Lewis' monograph, The Sargon Legend.

Sargon

E2.1.1

According to the Sumerian King List, Sargon had a lengthy reign of 56 years (2334–2279). Unfortunately, the lack of any date list for the king makes it impossible at this time to provide a secure chronology for even the major events of his reign. We do not know, for example, whether Sargon year 1 is the year he acceded to the throne in Agade or whether he became king at Agade at some later time. While some scholars have maintained that Šarru-kīn was a throne name adopted by Sargon when he declared his independence from Ur-Zababa, the king of Kiš whom he had served as cupbearer, it is more likely to have been his birth name; a parallel would be provided by the Old Akkadian PN Šarru-dān. Sargon asserted his independence with the founding of his capital at Agade. Although the evidence of the Sumerian Sargon Legend (most recently edited on the basis of a new exemplar by Cooper and Heimpel in JAOS 103 [1983] pp. 67–82) suggests that the fall of Kiš was brought about as a result of the defeat of Ur-Zababa by Sargon, it is noteworthy that fully five Kišite royal names follow Ur-Zababa in the Sumerian King List. The last of these, Nannia, might possibly be connected with the Nanni who appears in the ancient proverb collections as the epitome of a hapless ruler (see Gurney and Kramer, OECT 5 pp. 38–39), although this is uncertain. Presumably as a consequence of his defeat of Kiš, Sargon adopted the title LUGAL KIŠ, which in the context of the Sargonic royal inscriptions should be translated 'king of the world'. Having consolidated his control over Babylonia, Sargon next moved against the south. In this campaign his rival was Lugal-zage-si of Uruk, a ruler who had established a small empire in southern Mesopotamia comprising the cities of Uruk, Ur, Eridu, Umma, Zabala, KI.AN, Larsa, and probably Adab and Keš. In all fifty city governors are said to have been under Lugal-zage-si's control (see E2.1.1.2 line 16). Apparently a major confrontation took place at or near Uruk, with the result that Sargon soundly defeated the king of Uruk, took him captive in a neck stock, and paraded the former 'king of the land' in triumph before the gate of the god Enlil in Nippur. Further campaigns against Eninmar and Lagaš completed Sargon's conquest of Sumer.

Other major events of the reign of Sargon included a campaign against the lands of Elam and Paraḫšum in the east, and an apparent razzia to the north-west against Mari, Iarmuti, and Ebla. An idea of the extent of the Sargonic state carved out by Sargon may be gained by a study of the list of cult centres appearing in the En-ḫedu-ana compilation of temple hymns, for, as C. Wilcke (ZA 62 [1972] pp. 47–48) has argued, it is likely that En-ḫedu-ana created this work in order to honour her father. Thus, from this literary source we would conclude that Sargon's empire stretched from Eridu in the south to Hiza on the middle Tigris in the north, and from Kazallu in the west to Dēr in the east.

I. Year Names and Events of the Reign

Since a secure chronology for the events of Sargon's reign has not yet been established, the following list of year names implies no chronological order.

(i) The Defeat of Uruk and the South

See inscriptions E2.1.1.1–7.

(ii) The Elamite Campaigns

(a) mu *śar-um*-GI-*né* URU×A.KI mu-ḫul-a 'The year Sargon destroyed Arawa'. HS 931: A. Pohl, TMH 5 no. 181 and A. Westenholz, Texts Jena no. 181.
(a′) mu URU×A.KI ḫul-a. 'The year Arawa was destroyed'. HS 836: A. Pohl, TMH 5 no. 86 and A. Westenholz, Texts Jena no. 86.
(b) m[u *śar-um*]-GI-*né* ⸢NIM⸣.KI mu-ḫul-a 'The year Sargon destroyed Elam'. HS 835: A. Pohl, TMH 5 no. 85 and A. Westenholz, Texts Jena no. 85.

Year name (a), known in two slightly different forms, records Sargon's defeat of the city of Arawa. This important settlement, thought to lie on the western fringes of Elam, was designated by the ancients as the 'bolt of Elam'. Its defeat probably marked the first stage of Sargon's conquests in the east. Further evidence of the Arawa campaign is found in the mention in E2.1.1.8, caption 3, of the booty from this city. The conquest of Elam itself, in this case a probable reference to the defeat of Susa and its region, is recorded in year name (b). As a consequence of his eastern wars Sargon adopted the title 'conqueror of Elam and Paraḫšum', which we find in E2.1.1.8–9. E2.1.1.10, incised on a victory stele found in excavations at Susa. The stele may have been carved to celebrate the defeat of the Elamites, although this is uncertain.

(iii) The Euphrates Campaign

(c) mu ma-rí.KI-a ḫul-a 'The year Mari was destroyed'. CBS 8424: A. Westenholz, OSP 1 no. 102; HS 830: A. Pohl, TMH 5 no. 80 and A. Westenholz, Texts Jena no. 80.

Although no king is named in year name (c), the references to Mari in E2.1.1.1 and to the conquest of the region of the Upper Euphrates in E2.1.1.11 make its attribution to Sargon likely. The French excavators of Mari have found clear evidence of destruction levels of the Pre-Sargonic Palace I, and according to M. Lebeau (MARI 4 p. 135) the reoccupation of the palace dates to the beginning or middle phase of the Sargonic period. Thus an assignment of the destruction of Mari to Sargon is supported by both textual and archaeological evidence.

(iv) The Simurrian Campaign

(d) mu *śar-um*-GI śi-mur-um.KI-šè ⸢ì⸣-gin-⸢na-a⸣ 'The year Sargon went (on a campaign) to Simurrum'. HS 901: A. Pohl, TMH 5 no. 151 and A. Westenholz, Texts Jena no. 151; N 474: A. Westenholz, OSP 1 no. 145.

The strategic city of Simurrum, located somewhere in the Jebel Ḥamrīn region not far from its junction with the al-ʿUẓaim river, was, according to the evidence of year name (d), the object of a campaign by Sargon; unfortunately, no royal inscription provides us with details of the campaign. Control of the city by the Sargonic kings was apparently not maintained, since the city was once again the target of an attack by Narām-Sîn (see the discussion to Narām-Sîn year names [hh]–[ii] below).

1

Although few contemporary inscriptions of Sargon remain, there is a sizeable number known from later Old Babylonian tablet copies: two large Sammeltafeln from Nippur, one in Philadelphia (CBS 13972), the other in Istanbul (Ni 3200), contain copies of several Sargon inscriptions. Throughout this volume, whenever these two Old Babylonian Sammeltafeln are sources for an inscription, they are designated as exemplars 1 and 2, respectively. The Philadelphia tablet consists of two main fragments. The first, designated in the bibliography as fragment 1, was published in copy by Poebel; the second, designated as fragment 2, was joined to fragment 1 and published nine years later by Legrain.

In the catalogue for this text and for other inscriptions recorded on Sammeltafeln, we have indicated the line numbers according to their position on the original Sammeltafeln (tablet lines) as well as their numbering in the reconstructed text (text lines). The column numbers of the Philadelphia tablet, following the convention of Gelb and Kienast, are numbered consecutively, so that rev. col. i appears in the chart as rev. xv. The columns of the Istanbul tablet, on the other hand, are numbered i–x on the reverse.

The originals of these copies may have been inscribed on triumphal steles that once stood in the courtyard of Enlil's Ekur temple in Nippur.

The first inscription, which is found in Sumerian and Akkadian versions, deals with the defeat of Uruk, Ur, E-Ninmar, and the area around Lagaš. It mentions the capture of Lugal-zage-si, king of Uruk.

CATALOGUE

Sumerian version

Ex.	Museum number	Tablet lines preserved	Text lines preserved	cpn
1	CBS 13972	obv. i 6–21, 26–29, 31–53	6–21, 26–29, 31–53	c
		obv. iii 2–11, 14–16, 18–41	63–72, 75–77, 79–102	
		obv. iii 42–43	Colophon	
2	Ni 3200	obv. i 22–32	24–37	p
		obv. iii 26–29	84–87	

Akkadian version

Ex.	Museum number	Tablet lines preserved	Text lines preserved	cpn
1	CBS 13972	obv. ii 8–19, 23–60	8–19, 23–60	c
		obv.iv 2–5, 10–41	68–71, 76–109	
		obv. iv 44–45	Colophon	
		obv. iii 44–47	Caption 1	
		obv. iv 46–48	Caption 1′	
		obv. iv 49–51	Caption 2′	
		obv. iv 52–54	Caption 3′	
2	Ni 3200	obv. ii 23–35	27–36	p

COMMENTARY

The line count and translation follow the Akkadian version. Where the Sumerian translation varies from the Akkadian, the divergence is recorded in the notes.

In line 5 and passim in this volume, we have translated the logogram ^{d}INANNA in Akkadian contexts 'the goddess Aštar'. For the reading Aštar instead of Eštar in (Pre)-Sargonic sources, see the comments of Krebernik in ZA 81 (1991) pp. 135–36. For the translation of lines 94–101, see D. Edzard in Studies Tadmor pp. 258–263. In this, and following Akkadian texts, the logogram SUḪUŠ is assumed to stand for *išdā*; hence the translation 'foundations'.

BIBLIOGRAPHY

1914 PBS 4/1 pp. 173–76 no. 34 A–B (ex. 1, frgm. 1, edition)
1914 Poebel, PBS 5 pl. XX no. 34 (ex. 1, frgm. 1, copy)
1923 Legrain, MJ 14 pp. 204 and 207–10 (ex. 1, frgm. 2, photo, copy, edition)
1926 Legrain, PBS 15 pp. 12–13 and pls. XV no. 41 (ex.1, frgm. 2, copy, edition); pl. III–V (ex. 1, frgms. 1–2, photo)
1929 Barton, RISA pp. 100–107 Sharrukin 1 (ex. 1, edition)
1961 Gelb, MAD 2² p. 193 Sargon Late Copies no. 1 Aa+b (ex. 1, study)
1963 Hirsch, AfO 20 pp. 2–3 and 34–37 Sargon b 1 (exs. 1–2, edition)
1969 Oppenheim in ANET³ p. 267 (ex. 1, translation)
1971 Sollberger and Kupper, IRSA IIA1a (exs. 1–2, translation
1990 Gelb and Kienast, Königsinschriften pp. 157–63 and pls. I–III, XI–XII Sargon C 1 (exs. 1–2, photo, edition); p. 140 (ex. 1, copy)
1991 Edzard, in Studies Tadmor pp. 158–63 (lines 86–101, study)

TEXT

Sumerian	Akkadian	
1) [*śar-um*-GI]	1) [*śar-ru*-GI]	1–11) [Sargon, king of Agade, bailiff of the goddess Aštar, king of the world, anointed priest of the god An], lord of the land, governor for the god Enlil,
2) [lugal]-	2) [LUGAL]	
3) [ag-ge-dè.KI]	3) [*a-kà-dè*.KI]	
4) [maškim]-	4) [MAŠKIM.GI$_4$]	
5) [^{d}inanna]	5) [^{d}INANNA]	
6) [lu]gal-K[IŠ]	6) [LUGAL KIŠ]	
7) [gúd]a-an-na	7) [PA$_4$.ŠEŠ AN]	
8) ⸢lugal⸣-	8) ⸢LUGAL⸣	
9) ⸢kalam-ma⸣	9) KALAM.MA.KI	
10) énsi-gal-	10) ÉNSI	
11) ^{d}en-líl	11) ^{d}*en-líl*	
12) uru unu.KI	12) URU.KI	12–22) conquered the city of Uruk and destroyed its walls. He was [victorious] over Uruk in battle, [conquered the city],
	13) UNU.KI	
13) e-ḫul	14) SAG.GIŠ.RA	
	15) *ù*	
14) ⸢bàd⸣-bi	16) BÀD-*śu*	
15) e-ga-⸢sì⸣	17) Ì.GUL.GUL	
16) lú-unu.KI-⸢ga-da⸣	18) *in* REC 169	
17) GIŠ.tukul	19) UNU.[KI]	
18) ⸢e⸣-da-sìg	20) [*iš*$_{11}$-*ar*]	
19) TÙN.KÁR[A]	21) [URU.KI]	
20) e-NI-[sì]	22) [SAG.GIŠ.RA]	
21) lug[al-zà-ge-si]	23) [lugal-z]à-ge-si	23–31) captured [Lugal-z]age-si, king of [Ur]uk, in battle and led him off to the gate of the god Enlil in a neck stock.
22) [lugal]-	24) ⸢LUGAL⸣	
23) [unu.KI-ga-da]	25) [UN]U.KI	
24) [GI]Š.tuku[l]	26) *in* REC 169	
25) [e]-d[a-sìg]		
26) ⸢e⸣-ga-dab$_5$	27) ŠU.DU$_8$.A	
27) GIŠ.si-gar-ta	28) *in* SI.GAR-*rìm*	
28) ká-^{d}en-líl-lá-šè	29) *a-na* KÁ	
	30) ^{d}*en-líl*	
29) ⸢e⸣-de$_6$	31) *u-ru-úš*	
30) śar-um-GI	32) *śar-ru*-GI	32–43) Sargon, king of Agade,

10.1 Sum.: 'great governor'.
12–15.1 Sum.: 'He destroyed the city of Uruk and further, tore down its wall'.
17.1 Akk.: Reduplication of verbal root indicates plurality of object, or possibly Gtn form 'kept tearing down'.
16–20.1 Sum.: 'He smote the 'man' of Uruk with weapons and defeated him'.
21–26.1 Sum.: 'He s[mote] Lu[gal-zage-si], k[ing of Uruk], with [w]eapo[ns] and further, captured him'.

31) lugal-	33) LUGAL	was victorious over Ur in battle,
32) [a]g-ge-dè.KI	34) *a-kà-dè*.KI	conquered the city and destroyed
33) lú-úri.KI-ma-da	35) *in* REC 169	its wall.
34) GIŠ.tukul	36) ÚRI.KI	
35) e-da-sìg	37) *iš*$_{11}$*-ar*	
36) TÙN.KÁRA	38) *ù*	
37) ⌈e⌉-NI-sì		
38) uru-ni	39) URU.KI	
39) e-ḫul (after erased ga-ga)	40) SAG.GIŠ.RA	
	41) *ù*	
40) ⌈bàd⌉-bi	42) BÀD-*śu*	
41) e-ga-⌈sì⌉	43) Ì.GUL.GUL	
42) é-^{d}nin-⌈mar⌉.KI	44) *é-nin-mar*.KI	44–58) He conquered Eninmar,
43) e-ḫul	45) SAG.GIŠ.RA	destroyed its walls, and
	46) *ù*	conquered its district and Lagaš
44) bàd-bi	47) BÀD-*śu*	as far as the sea. He washed his
45) e-ga-⌈sì⌉	48) ⌈Ì.GUL.GUL⌉	weapons in the sea.
	49) ⌈*ù*⌉	
46) gú-kalam-bi	50) KALAM.MA.KI-*śu*	
	51) *ù*	
47) lagaš.KI-ta	52) *lagaš*(LA.BUR.ŠIR.RI).KI	
48) ⌈a⌉-ab-ba-šè	53) *a-dì-ma*	
na-x-[n]e-ne	54) *ti-a-am-tim*	
49) e-ḫul	55) SAG.GIŠ.RA	
50) GIŠ.tukul-ni	56) GIŠ.TUKUL-*kí-śu*	
51) a-ab-ba-ka	57) *in ti-a-am-tim*	
52) ì-luḫ	58) Ì.LUḪ	
53) ⌈lú⌉-umma.KI-⌈da⌉	59) UB.ME.KI	59–66) He was victorious over
54) [GIŠ.tukul]	60) ⌈*in* REC 169⌉	Umma in battle, [conquered the
55) [e-da-sìg]	61) [*iš*$_{11}$*-ar*]	city, and destroyed its walls].
56) [TÙN.KÁRA]	62) [*ù*]	
57) [e-NI-sì]	63) [URU.KI]	
58) [uru-ni]	64) [SAG.GIŠ.RA]	
59) [e-ḫul]	65) [*ù* BÀD-*śu*]	
60) [bàd-bi]	66) [Ì.GUL.GUL]	
61) [e-ga-sì]		
62) [*śar-um*-GI]	67) [*śar-ru*-GI]	67–72) [To Sargon], lo[rd] of the
63) ⌈lugal⌉-	68) LUG[AL]	land the god Enlil [gave no]
64) kalam-ma-ra	69) ⌈KALAM⌉.MA.[KI]	ri[val].
65) ^{d}⌈en⌉-líl-le	70) ^{d}*en-*⌈*líl*⌉	
66) lú-é[rim]	71) *ma-*[*ḫi-ra*]	
67) nu-na-⌈sum⌉	72) [*la i-dì-śum*$_{6}$]	
68) a-⌈ab⌉-[ba]-	73) [*ti-a-am-tám*]	73–78) The god Enlil gave to
69) ⌈IGI.NIM⌉-ma-ta	74) [*a-lí-tám*]	him [the Upper Sea and] the
70) a-ab-ba-	75) [*ù*]	[Low]er (Sea),
71) sig-⌈sig⌉-šè	76) [*śa-pil*]*-tám*	
72) ^{d}⌈en-líl-le⌉	77) ⌈^{d}⌉*en-líl*	
73) [mu-na-sum]	78) *i-dì-nu-śum*$_{6}$	
74) [ù]	79) *íś-tum-ma*	79–85) so that from the Lower
75) [a-ab]-ba-	80) *ti-a-am-tim*	Sea <to the Upper Sea>,
76) [sig-sig]-ta	81) *śa-*⌈*pil*⌉*-tim*	citizens of Agade [h]eld the

33–37.1 Sum.: 'He smote the 'man of Ur' with weapons and defeated him'.
38.1 Sum.: 'his city'.
38–41.1 Sum.: 'He destroyed his city and further, tore down its wall'.
42–45.1 Sum.: 'He destroyed E-ninmar and further, tore down its wall'.
46–49.1 Sum.: 'All the land from Lagaš as far as the sea, he destroyed ...'
53–57.1 Sum.: '[He smote] the 'man' of Umma [with weapons and further, defeated him]'.
66.1 Sum.: 'en[emy]'.
68–71.1 Sum.: 'from the Upper Sea to the Lower Sea'.
85.1 Akk.: The verbs in lines 85 and 93 are in present tense to indicate a continuous action in the past.

77) [dumu-dum]u
78) [ag-ge-dè.KI]
79) n[am-énsi]
80) mu-⌈kin(?)⌉-[x]
81) lú-ma-[rí.KI]

82) lú-NIM.[KI]
83) (erasure)
84) igi-*śar-u*[*m*]-⌈GI⌉-
85) lugal-
86) kalam-ma-ka-šè
87) ì-su$_{8}$-ge-éš
88) *śar-um*-GI
89) lugal-
90) kalam-ma-ke$_{4}$
91) kiš.KI
92) ki-bé
93) bí-gi$_{4}$
94) uru-bé
95) ki-DU e-na-ba
96) ⌈lú mu-sar-ra-e⌉

97) ab-ḫa-lam-e-a
98) ^{d}utu
99) suḫuš-a-ni
100) ḫé-bù-re$_{6}$
101) numun-na-ni
102) ḫé-ga-ri-ri-ge

Colophon
1) mu-sar-ra
2) ki-gal-ba

82) DUMU.DUMU
83) *a*-⌈*kà-dè*⌉.KI
84) ÉNSI-*ku$_{8}$-a-tim*
85) [*u*]-*kà-lú*
86) *ma-rí*.KI
87) *ù*
88) NIM.KI
89) *maḫ-rí-íś*
90) *śar*-⌈*ru*-GI⌉
91) LUGAL
92) KALAM.MA.KI
93) *i-za-zu-ni*
94) ⌈*śar-ru*-GI⌉
95) LUGAL
96) KALAM.MA.KI
97) *kiš*.KI
98) *a-ša-rí-śu*
99) *i-ni*
100) URU.KI-*lam*
101) *u-śá-ḫi-śu-ni*
102) *ša* DUB
103) ⌈*śu$_{4}$*⌉-*a*
104) *u-śa-sà-ku-ni*
105) ^{d}UTU
106) SUḪUŠ-*śu*
107) *li-sú-uḫ*
108) *ù* ŠE.NUMUN-*śu*
109) *li-il-qù-ut*

Colophon
1) mu-sar-⌈ra⌉
2) k[i-gal-b]a

Caption 1
1) *śar-ru*-GI
2) LUGAL
3) KALAM.MA.KI
4) ⌈*ma*⌉-[...]
Lacuna

Caption 1′
1) lugal-zà-⌈ge⌉-si
2) LUGAL
3) UNU.KI

Caption 2′
1) mes-é
2) ÉNSI
3) UB.ME.KI

Caption 3′
1) [...]
2) ⌈LUGAL⌉
3) [...]
Lacuna

governorships (of the land).

86–93) Mari and Elam stood (in obedience) before Sargon, lord of the land.

94–101) Sargon, lord of the land, altered the two sites of Kiš. He made the two (parts of Kiš) occupy (one) city.

102–109) As for the one who removes this inscription, may the god Šamaš tear out his foundations and destroy his progeny.

Colophon
1–2) Inscription on its base.

Caption 1
1–4) Sargon, lord of the land, ...
Lacuna

Caption 1′
1–3) Lugal-zage-si, king of Uruk.

Caption 2′
1–3) Mes-e, governor of Umma.

Caption 3′
1–3) ..., king of ...
Lacuna

81–82.1 Sum.: 'the people of Mari and the Elamites'.
91–93.1 Sum.: 'He restored Kiš'.
94–95.1 Sum.: 'He assigned its city *a place to stand*'.
97.1 Sum.: 'who destroys'.

2

This inscription, known from two Old Babylonian Sammeltafeln copies from Nippur, deals with the defeat of Lugal-zage-si and victories over the cities of Ur, Eninmar, Lagaš, and Umma. It is very similar to E2.1.1.1.

CATALOGUE

Ex.	Museum number	Tablet lines preserved	Text lines preserved	cpn
1	CBS 13972	obv. vii 41–61	1–21	c
		obv. viii 2–25, 29–59	23–46, 50–80	
		obv. ix 4–49	86–131	
		obv. ix 50–52	Colophon	
2	Ni 3200	obv. viii 7–25	1–19	p
		obv. ix 5–26	50–71	
		obv. x 6–10, 18–25	108–11, 119–26	

BIBLIOGRAPHY

1914 Poebel, PBS 4/1 pp. 179–82 no. 34 H (ex. 1, frgm. 1, edition)

1914 Poebel, PBS 5 pl. XX no. 34 (ex. 1, frgm. 1, copy)

1923 Legrain, MJ 14 pp. 204, 208, and 211–12 (ex. 1, frgm. 2, photo, copy, edition)

1926 Legrain, PBS 15 pp. 15–16 and pl. XV no. 41 (ex. 1, frgm. 2, copy, edition); pls. II–IV (ex. 1, frgms. 1–2, photo)

1929 Barton, RISA pp. 110–13 Sharrukin 4 (ex. 1, edition)

1961 Gelb, MAD 2[2] p. 193 Sargon Late Copies no. 1 D (ex. 1, study)

1963 Hirsch, AfO 20 pp. 3 and 40–44 Sargon b 6 (exs. 1–2, edition)

1968 Spycket, Statues p. 42 (ex. 1, partial edition)

1990 Gelb and Kienast, Königsinschriften pp. 170–74 and pls. I–III and XI–XII Sargon C 4 (exs. 1–2, photo, edition); p. 140 (ex. 1, copy)

TEXT

1) *śar-ru*-GI
2) LUGAL
3) *a-kà-dè*.KI
4) MAŠKIM.GI$_4$
5) ^{d}INANNA
6) LUGAL KIŠ
7) PA$_4$.ŠEŠ AN
8) LUGAL
9) KALAM.MA.KI
10) ÉNSI
11) ^{d}*en-líl*·

1–11) Sargon, king of Agade, bailiff of the goddess Aštar, king of the world, anointed priest of the god Anum, lord of the land, governor for the god Enlil,

12) *in* ⸢REC 169⸣(KASKAL+[x])
13) UNU.KI
14) *iš*$_{11}$*-ar*

12–14) was victorious over Uruk in battle,

15) *ù*
16) 50 ÉNSI
17) *in* ŠÍTA
18) *ìl-a-ba*$_4$
19) *ù*
20) URU.KI
21) [S]AG.GIŠ.[RA]
22) [*ù*]
23) B[ÀD-*śu*]

15–24) conquered fifty governors with the mace of the god Ilaba, as well as the city (of Uruk), [and] de[stroyed its (Uruk's)] w[alls].

24) ⸢Ì.GUL.GUL⸣
25) *ù*
26) lugal-zà-ge-si
27) LUGAL
28) UNU.KI
29) *in* REC 169
30) ŠU.DU$_{8}$.A
31) *in* SI.GAR-*rì-im*
32) *a-na* KÁ
33) ^{d}*en-líl*
34) *u-ru-úś*
35) *śar-ru*-GI
36) LUGAL
37) *a-kà-dè*.KI
38) ⸢*in*⸣ REC 169
39) ÚRI.KI
40) *iš*$_{11}$*-ar*
41) *ù*
42) URU.KI
43) SAG.GIŠ.⸢RA⸣
44) ⸢*ù*⸣
45) B[ÀD-*śu*]
46) Ì.G[UL.GUL]
47) [*é-nin-mar*.KI]
48) [SAG.GIŠ.RA]
49) [*ù*]
50) BÀD-*śu*
51) Ì.GUL.GUL
52) *ù*
53) KALAM.KI-*śu*
54) *ù*
55) *lagaš*(LA.BUR.ŠIR).KI
56) *a-dì-ma*
57) *ti-a-am-tim*
58) SAG.GIŠ.RA
59) ⸢GIŠ⸣.TUKUL-*kí-śu*
60) *in ti-a-am-tim*
61) Ì.LUḪ
62) UB.ME.KI
63) *in* REC 169
64) *iš*$_{11}$*-ar*
65) *ù*
66) URU.KI
67) SAG.GIŠ.RA
68) *ù*
69) BÀD-*śu*
70) Ì.GU[L.GUL]
71) *ś*[*ar-ru*-G]I
72) [LUGA]L
73) [KALAM.MA].KI
74) [*šu* ^{d}*en-l*]*íl*
75) *m*[*a-ḫi-r*]*a*
76) *la* ⸢*i-dì-nu*⸣*-śum*$_{6}$
77) *ti-a-*⸢*am-tám*⸣
78) *a-lí-*⸢*tám*⸣
79) ⸢*ù*⸣
80) *śa-pi*[*l-tám*]
81) [*i-dì-śum*$_{6}$]
82) [*íś-tum-ma*]
83) [*ti-a-am-tim*]

25–34) Further, he captured Lugal-zage-si, king of Uruk, in battle (and) led him off to the gate of the god Enlil in a neck stock.

35–46) Sargon, king of Agade, was victorious over Ur in battle, conquer[ed] the city and de[stroyed its] w[alls].

47–61) [He conquered Eninmar], destroyed its walls, and conquered its district and Lagaš as far as the sea. He washed his weapons in the sea.

62–70) He was victorious over Umma in battle, conquered the city, and destroy[ed] its walls.

71–76) To S[argo]n, [lor]d of the [lan]d, to wh[om] [the god En]lil gave no r[ival],

77–81) (the god Enlil) [gave] the Upper Sea and the Low[er] (Sea).

82–91) [Further, from the Lower Sea to] the [Up]per [Se]a [citiz]ens of Agade held the

84) [*śa-pil-tim*]
85) [*a-dì-ma*]
86) [*ti-a-am-t*]*im*
87) [*a-lí-tim*]
88) [DUMU.DUM]U
89) *a-kà-*⸢*dè*⸣.KI
90) ÉNSI-*ku*$_{8}$*-a-a-tim*
91) *u-kà-lú*

governorships (of the land).

92) *ma-rí*.KI
93) *ù*
94) NIM.KI
95) *maḫ-rí-íś*
96) *śar-ru*-GI
97) LUGAL
98) KALAM.MA.KI
99) *i-za-zu-ni*

92–99) Mari and Elam stood (in obedience) before Sargon, lord of the land.

100) *śar-ru*-GI
101) LUGAL
102) KALAM.MA.KI
103) [*k*]*iš*.KI
104) ⸢*a*⸣*-ša-rí-śu*
105) ⸢*i*⸣*-ni*
106) *ù*
107) URU.KI-*lam*
108) *u-śá-ḫi-śu-ni*

100–108) Sargon, lord of the land, altered the two sites of Kiš. He made the two (parts of Kiš) occupy (one) city.

109) *ša* DUB
110) *śu*$_{4}$*-a*
111) *u-śa-sà-ku-ni*
112) ^{d}*en-líl*
113) *ù*
114) ^{d}UTU
115) SUḪUŠ-*śu*
116) *li-sú-ḫa*
117) *ù*
118) ŠE.NUMUN-*śu*
119) *li-il-qù-tá*

109–119) As for the one who removes this inscription, may the gods Enlil and Šamaš tear out his foundations and destroy his progeny.

120) *ma-ma-na*
121) DÙL
122) *śu*$_{4}$-⸢*a*⸣
123) *u-a-*⸢*ḫa-ru*⸣
124) ^{d}⸢*en*⸣*-líl*
125) MU-*śu*
126) *li-a-ḫir*$_{x}$(HA+ŠÚ)
127) GIŠ.TUKUL-*śu*
128) *li-iš-bir*$_{5}$
129) *maḫ-rí-íś*
130) ^{d}⸢*en-líl*⸣
131) *e* DU

120–131) As for anyone who sets aside this statue, may the god Enlil set aside his name and smash his weapon. May he not walk before the god Enlil.

Colophon
1) mu-sar-ra ki-gal-ba
2) igi-lugal-zà-ge-si-šè
3) a-ab-sar

Colophon
1–3) Inscription on a socle; it is written in front of Lugal-zage-si.

3

This inscription, found on two Old Babylonian Sammeltafel copies from Nippur, deals with Sargon's defeat of the cities of Uruk, NaGURzam, Ur, Umma, and Lagaš.

CATALOGUE

Ex.	Museum number	Tablet lines preserved	Text lines preserved	cpn
1	CBS 13972	obv. vi 50–59	1–10	c
		obv. vii 1–27, 29–32	15–41, 43–46	
		obv. vii 33–34	Colophon	p
2	Ni 3200	obv. vii 13–24; 25–28 traces	1–15, 16–9 traces	
		obv. viii 1–6	Caption	

COMMENTARY

Too little of the caption of ex. 1 is preserved to give a coherent reading.

BIBLIOGRAPHY

1914 Poebel, PBS 4/1 p. 179 no. 34 E–F (ex. 1, frgm. 1, edition)
1914 Poebel, PBS 5 pl. XX no. 34 (ex. 1, frgm. 1, copy)
1923 Legrain, MJ 14 pp. 204, 208, and 210–11 (ex. 1, frgm. 2, photo, copy, edition)
1926 Legrain, PBS 15 pp. 14–15 and pl. XV no. 34 (ex. 1, frgm. 2, copy, edition); pls. II–IV (ex. 1, frgms. 1–2, photo)
1929 Barton, RISA pp. 110–11 Sharrukin 3 (ex. 1, edition)
1961 Gelb, MAD 2[2] p. 193 Sargon Late Copies no. 1 C (ex. 1, study)
1963 Hirsch, AfO 20 pp. 3 and 39–40 Sargon b 4+5 (exs. 1–2, edition)
1990 Gelb and Kienast, Königsinschriften pp. 167–70 and pls. I–III, XIV–XV Sargon C 3 (exs. 1–2, photo, edition); p. 140 (ex. 1, copy)

TEXT

1) *ìl-a-ba*$_4$
2) *il-śu*
3) *śar-ru*-GI
4) LUGAL
5) KIŠ
6) *in* 9
7) *ki-ṣé-rí*
8) *a-kà-dè*.KI
9) URU.KI
10) UNU.KI
11) SAG.GIŠ.RA
12) *ù*
13) *in* REC 169
14) *iš*$_{11}$*-ar*
15) *ù*
16) ⌜50⌝ ÉNSI
17) *ù*
18) LUGAL

1–2) The god Ilaba (is) his (personal) god.

3–20) Sargon, king of the world, with nine contingents from Agade conquered the city of Uruk, was victorious in battle, captured fifty governors, and (Sargon) personally captured the king (of Uruk).

19) *šu*$_{4}$*-ma*
20) ŠU.DU$_{8}$.A
21) *ù*
22) *in na*-GUR$_{8}$-*za-am*.KI
23) REC 169
24) *iš-ni-a-ma*
25) *íš-ku*$_{8}$*-na-ma*
26) *iš*$_{11}$*-ar*

21–26) Further, on a second occasion he did battle in NaGURzam and was victorious.

27) *ù*
28) ⸢*in*⸣ ÚRI.KI
29) *úš*-x-*tá-lí-ša-ma*
30) *im*$_{4}$*-tá-aḫ-ṣa-ma*
31) *iš*$_{11}$*-ar*

27–31) Further, on a third occasion the two of them fought each other at Ur and he was victorious.

32) *ù*
33) UB.ME.KI
34) *in* REC 169
35) *iš*$_{11}$*-ar*
36) *ù*
37) URU.KI
38) SAG.⸢GIŠ⸣.RA

32–38) Further, he was victorious over Umma in battle and conquered the city.

39) *ù*
40) *lagaš*(LA.BUR.ŠIR).KI
41) *in* REC 169
42) [*iš*$_{11}$*-ar*]
43) ⸢*ù*⸣
44) GIŠ.⸢TUKUL⸣-[*kí-šu*]
45) ⸢*in*⸣ [*ti-a-am-tim*]
46) Ì.[LUḪ]

39–46) Further, he [was victorious] over Lagaš in battle and [washed his] weapon[s] in [the sea].

Colophon
1) ⸢mu⸣-sa[r-ra alan-na]
2) ⸢ki-gal⸣-[bi nu-sar]

Colophon
1–2) Inscrip[tion on a statue; its] base [is not inscribed].

Caption
1′) *il-a-ba*$_{4}$
2′) KALAG.G[A]
3′) *ì-li*
4′) ^{d}*en-líl*
5′) GIŠ.TUKUL
6′) IN.NA.⸢SUM⸣

Caption
1′–6′) The god Ilaba, mighty one of the gods – the god Enlil gave to him (his) weapon(s).

4

A fragmentary mace head inscription from Ur mentions the defeat of the cities of Uruk and Ur. Unfortunately, the name of the king responsible for these actions is not preserved. A tablet copy of a Sargon inscription (E2.1.1.5) gives, in a restored text, the same royal epithet, 'conqueror of Uruk and Ur' that is found in this inscription; it is therefore likely that E2.1.1.4 also belonged to Sargon.

COMMENTARY

The mace head bears the museum number CBS 14396 and the excavation no. U 221. It was found under the Kurigalzu floor of the E-nun-maḫ. The piece is made of green quartzite and measures 9.3 cm in height and 10.6 cm in diameter. The inscription was collated.

BIBLIOGRAPHY

1928 Gadd, UET 1 no. 6 (copy, edition)
1955 Woolley, UE 4 pp. 49 and 168 (study)
1960 Sollberger, Iraq 22 pp. 75–76 no. 90 (study)
1961 Gelb, MAD 2^{2} p. 205 Unknown Kings Original Inscriptions no. 7 (study)
1963 Hirsch, AfO 20 p. 2 Sargon a 2 (study)
1990 Gelb and Kienast, Königsinschriften p. 63 Sargon 2 (edition)

TEXT

1) [*a-na*]
2) [^{d}....]
3) [*śar-ru*-GI]
4) [LUGAL]
5) [*a-kà-dè*.KI]
6) ⌜SAG.GIŠ.RA⌝
7) SAG
8) UN[U.KI]
9) *ù*
10) ÚR[I.KI]
11) A.MU.RU

1–2) [To the god DN],

3–10) [Sargon, king of Agade], conqueror of Uruk and U[r],

11) dedicated (this mace).

5

A Sammeltafel fragment from Nippur bears an inscription that refers to Sargon as 'conqueror of Uruk [and Ur]'.

COMMENTARY

The tablet bears the museum number N 6266. It originally contained copies of at least three separate inscriptions. Col. ii′ lines 4′–8′ contain the beginning of the text that is edited here. Col. i′ has the curse formula of the end of an inscription and is edited in this volume as E2.0.0.1012, and col. iii′ is edited as ex. 3 of E2.1.3.2. The GN of line 5 is restored as ÚRI.KI following line 10 of the previous text. The inscription was collated.

BIBLIOGRAPHY

1980 Michalowski, JCS 32 pp. 242–43 and 245 (photo, transliteration, copy)
1990 Gelb and Kienast, Königsinsinschriften pp. 63–64 and 189–90 Sargon C 14 (edition)

TEXT

1) *śar-ru*-GI
2) LUGAL *a-kà-dè*.KI
3) SAG.GIŠ.RA
4) [SA]G ⌜UNU⌝.KI
5) [*ù* ÚRI.KI]
Lacuna

1–5) Sargon, king of Agade, conqueror of Uruk [and Ur].
Lacuna

6

This inscription, known from one Old Babylonian Sammeltafel copy from Nippur, mentions the defeat of the city of Uruk and the dedication of some object to the god Enlil in Nippur.

CATALOGUE

Ex.	Museum number	Tablet lines preserved	Text lines preserved	cpn
1	CBS 13972	obv. ix 53–61	1–9	c
		obv. x 1–20, 35–57	10–29, 30–52	
		obv. x 21–26	Caption 1	
		obv. x 27–29	Colophon 1	
		obv. x 30–34	Caption 2	
		obv. x 58–59	Colophon 2	

COMMENTARY

CBS 13972 is conventionally designated here as ex. 1; the inscription is not found on Ni 3200. Like Gelb and Kienast, we have numbered the lines of the captions and colophon separately; the lines of the curse formula are numbered as a continuation of the main text. Line 22 of Gelb and Kienast's edition actually corresponds to two lines on the tablet; the same holds true for their line 26. This accounts for the different line numbers in this edition. The inscription was collated.

The first signs of lines 3 and 5 of Caption 2 are clearly *šu*, as B. Foster has indicated (see Gelb and Kienast, Königsinschriften p. 176).

BIBLIOGRAPHY

1914 Poebel, PBS 4/1 p. 183 no. 34 H γ–I (ex. 1, frgm. 1, edition)

1914 Poebel, PBS 5 pl. XX no. 34 (ex. 1, frgm. 1, copy)

1923 Legrain, MJ 14 pp. 204, 208, and 212–13 (ex. 1, frgm. 2, photo, copy, edition)

1926 Legrain, PBS 15 pp. 16–17 and pl. XV no. 41 (ex. 1, frgm. 2, copy, edition); pls. II–IV (ex. 1, frgms. 1–2, photo)

1929 Barton, RISA pp. 112–13 Sharrukin 5 (edition)

1961 Gelb, MAD 2[2] p. 193 Sargon Late Copies no. 1 E (study)

1963 Hirsch, AfO 20 pp. 3–4 and 44–45 Sargon b 7 (edition)

1990 Gelb and Kienast, Königsinschriften pp.140, 174–76 and pls. I, IV–V, Sargon C 5 (photo, copy, edition)

TEXT

1) *śar-ru*-GI
2) LUGAL
3) *a-kà-dè*.KI
4) MAŠKIM.GI$_4$
5) ⸢^{d}INANNA⸣
6) [LUGAL KI]Š
7) [PA$_4$.ŠE]Š ⸢AN⸣
8) ÉNSI
9) ^{d}⸢*en-líl*⸣

1–9) Sargon, king of Agade, bailiff of the goddess Aštar, [king of the worl]d, [ano]inted priest of the god Anum, governor for the god Enlil.

10) *ì*-[*nu*]
11) ⸢^{d}⸣*en-líl*
12) DI.KU$_5$-*śu*
13) *i*-⸢*dì*⸣-*nu*-⸢*ma*⸣
14) *ù*

10–16) Wh[en] the god Enlil rendered a verdict for him and (Sargon) conquer[ed] Uruk,

15) UNU.KI
16) SAG.GIŠ.R[A-*ni*]
17) [...]
18) [...]
19) [...]
20) x [...]
21) x [...]

17–21) (Too broken for translation.)

22) *a*-[*na*]
23) ⌈^{d}⌉[*en-líl*]
24) ⌈A.MU.RU⌉

22–24) he [de]dicated (this object) t[o the god] Enlil,

25) *ù*
26) NIBRU.KI
27) *a-na*
28) ^{d}*en-líl*
29) *u-li-il*

25–29) and purified Nippur for the god Enlil.

Caption 1
1) *śar-ru*-GI
2) LUGAL
3) KALAM.MA.KI
4) *šu* ^{d}*en-líl*
5) *ma-ḫi-ra*
6) *la i-dì-nu-śum*$_{6}$

Caption 1
1–6) Sargon, king of the land, to whom the god Enlil gave no rival.

Colophon 1
1) ⌈mu⌉-[sar-ra]
2) ki-[gal]-⌈la⌉
3) a-ab-sar

Colophon 1
1–3) In[scription] written on a ba[se].

Caption 2
1) lugal-zà-ge-si
2) EN
3) *šu* UNU.KI
4) LUGAL
5) *šu* ÚRI.KI

Caption 2
1–5) Lugal-zage-si, lord, of Uruk, and king, of Ur.

Curse Formula
30) *ša* DU[B]
31) *śu*$_{4}$-⌈*a*⌉
32) *u-śa-sà-k*[*u-ni*]
33) ^{d}*en-lí*[*l*]
34) *ù*
35) ^{d}UTU
36) SUḪUŠ-*śu*
37) *li-sú-ḫ*[*a*]
38) *ù*
39) ŠE.NUMUN-*śu*
40) *li-il-qù-tá*

Curse Formula
30–40) As for the one who remo[ves] this inscription, may the gods Enli[l] and Šamaš tea[r] out his foundations and destroy his progeny.

41) *ma-ma-na*
42) DÙL
43) *śu*$_{4}$-*a*
44) *u*-⌈*a-ḫa*⌉-*ru*
45) ^{d}*en-líl*
46) MU-*śu*
47) *li-a-ḫir*$_{x}$(ḪA+ŠÚ)
48) GIŠ.TUKUL-*śu*
49) *li-iš-bir*$_{5}$
50) *maḫ-rí-íś*
51) ^{d}*en-líl*
52) ⌈*e* DU⌉

41–52) As for anyone who sets aside this statue, may the god Enlil set his name aside (and) smash his weapon. May he not walk before the god Enlil.

Colophon 2
1) mu-sar-ra
2) murgu lugal-zà-ge-si

Colophon 2
1–2) Inscription on the shoulder of Lugal-zage-si.

7

This brief inscription, known from one Old Babylonian Sammeltafel copy, was once inscribed on a statue. It deals with the defeat of the city of Uruk.

CATALOGUE

Ex.	Museum number	Tablet lines preserved	Text lines preserved	cpn
1	CBS 13972	obv. x 58–60	1–3	c
		obv. xi 2–3, 8–34	5-6, 11–37	
		obv. xi 35–36	Colophon	

COMMENTARY

CBS 13972 is conventionally designated here as ex. 1; the inscription is not found on Ni 3200. The inscription was collated. Lines 4–10 are restored from E2.1.1.3 lines 9–15.

BIBLIOGRAPHY

1914 Poebel, PBS 4/1 pp. 184–85 no. 34 K α (ex. 1, frgm. 1, edition)
1914 Poebel, PBS 5 pl. XX no. 34 (ex. 1, frgm. 1, copy)
1923 Legrain, MJ 14 pp. 204, 208, and 213 (ex. 1, frgm. 2, photo, copy, edition)
1926 Legrain, PBS 15 p. 17 and pl. XV no. 41 (ex. 1, frgm. 2, copy, edition); pls. II–IV (ex. 1, frgms. 1–2, photo)
1929 Barton, RISA pp. 112–13 Sharrukin 6 (edition)
1961 Gelb, MAD 2^{2} p. 193 Sargon Late Copies no. 1 F (study)
1963 Hirsch, AfO 20 pp. 4 and 45–46 Sargon b 8 (edition)
1990 Gelb and Kienast, Königinschriften pp. 140, 177–78 and pls. I, IV–V Sargon C 6 (photo, edition, copy)

TEXT

1) *śar-ru*-GI
2) [LU]GAL
3) *a*-⌈*kà*⌉-*dè*.KI
4) [URU.KI]
5) UN[U.KI]
6) [SA]G.GIŠ.RA
7) [*ù*]
8) [*in* REC 169]
9) [*iš*$_{11}$-*ar*]
10) [*ù*]
11) [50 ÉNSI]
12) ⌈*ù*⌉
13) [L]UGAL
14) [*ś*]*u*$_4$-*ma*
15) ŠU.DU$_8$.A
16) *ša* DUB *śu*$_4$-*a*
17) *u-śa-sà-ku*-<*ni*>
18) ^{d}*en-líl*
19) *ù*
20) ^{d}UTU
21) ŠUḪUŠ-*śu*
22) *li-sú-ḫa*

1–3) Sargon, [ki]ng of Agade,

4–9) co[nquered the city] of Ur[uk and was victorious in battle].

10–15) [Further], he [per]sonally captured [fifty gover]nors and the [ki]ng (of Uruk).

16–25) As for the one who removes this inscription, may the gods Enlil and Šamaš tear out his foundations and destroy his progeny.

23) *ù*
24) ŠE.NUMUN-*śu*
25) *li-il-qù-tá*
26) *ma-ma-na*
27) DÙL
28) *śu*$_4$(erasure)-*a*
29) ⸢*u-a-ḫa-ru*⸣
30) ^{d}*en-líl*
31) MU-*śu*
32) *li-a-ḫir*$_x$(ḪA+ŠÚ)
33) GIŠ.TUKUL-*śu*
34) *li-iš-bir*$_5$
35) *maḫ-rí-íś*
36) ^{d}*en-líl*
37) ⸢*e*⸣ DU

Colophon
1) [mu-sar-ra a]lan-na
2) [...] x

26–37) As for anyone who sets aside this statue, may the god Enlil set his name aside (and) smash his weapon. May he not walk before the god Enlil.

Colophon
1) [Inscription on a st]atue.

8

A second major military campaign of Sargon was directed against the forces of Elam and Paraḫšum in the east. This campaign is recorded in at least two inscriptions of the king.

The first inscription is known from an Old Babylonian Sammeltafel copy from Nippur. The captions copied from the original monument identify the various enemy leaders.

CATALOGUE

Ex.	Museum number	Tablet lines preserved	Text lines preserved	cpn
1	CBS 13972	obv. xi 37–55	1–19	c
		obv. xi 56	Colophon 1	
		obv. xi 57–59	Caption 1	
		obv. xii 1–49	Captions 2–18	
		obv. xii 50	Colophon 3	

COMMENTARY

CBS 13972 is conventionally designated here as ex. 1; the inscription is not found on Ni 3200.

BIBLIOGRAPHY

1914 Poebel, PBS 4/1 pp. 185–87 no. 34 K β to γ, ν′ to ψ′ (ex. 1, frgm. 1, edition)
1914 Poebel, PBS 5 pl. XX no. 34 (ex. 1, frgm. 1, copy)
1923 Legrain, MJ 14 pp. 204, 208, and 213–14 (ex. 1, frgm. 2, photo, copy, edition)
1926 Legrain, PBS 15 pp. 17–18 and pl. XV no. 41(ex. 1, frgm. 2, copy, edition); pls. II–IV (ex. 1, frgms. 1–2, photo)
1929 Barton, RISA pp. 114–15 Sharrukin 7 and 8 (edition)
1961 Gelb, MAD 2^2 p. 193 Sargon Late Copies no. 1 G (study)
1963 Hirsch, AfO 20 pp. 4 and 46–47 Sargon b 9 (edition)
1990 Gelb and Kienast, Königsinschriften pp. 140, 178–81 and pls. I, IV–V Sargon C 7 (photo, copy, edition)

TEXT

1) *śar-ru*-GI
2) LUGAL
3) KIŠ
4) [S]AG.GIŠ.RA
5) [NI]M.KI
6) *ù*
7) *pá-ra-aḫ-śum*.KI
8) *ša* DUB
9) *śu*$_4$*-a*
10) *u-śa-sà-ku-ni*
11) ^{d}*en-líl*
12) ^{d}UTU
13) *ù*
14) ^{d}INANNA
15) SUḪUŠ-*śu*
16) *li-sú-ḫa*
17) *ù*
18) ŠE.NUMUN-*śu*
19) *li-il-qù-tá*

1–7) Sargon, king of the world, [c]onqueror of [El]am and Paraḫšum.

8–19) As for the one who removes this inscription, may the gods Enlil, Šamaš, and Aštar tear out his foundations and destroy his progeny.

Colophon 1
1) mu-sar-ra ki-gal-b[a]

Colophon 1
1) Inscription on its base.

Caption 1
1) Á.GÙB [...]
2) ⸢NIM⸣.[KI ...]
3) x [...]

Caption 1
1–3) [On the] left [...], Elamites ...

Caption 2
1) [*śar-ru*-GI]
2) [LUGAL]
3) [KIŠ]
4) [SAG.GIŠ.RA]
5) [NIM].KI
6) *ù*
7) *pá-*⸢*ra*⸣*-aḫ-śum*.KI

Caption 2
1–7) [Sargon, king of the world, conqueror of Elam] and Paraḫšum.

Colophon 2
1) zà-ga-na gub-ba

Colophon 2
1) Standing on the *right side.*

Caption 3
1) NÌ.LA+IB
2) URU×A.KI

Caption 3
1–2) Booty of Arawa

Caption 4
1) *sa*-NAM-*śi-mu-ut*
2) ÉNSI
3) NIM.KI

Caption 4
1–3) SaNAM-šimut, governor of Elam.

Caption 5
1) *lu-uḫ-iš-an*
2) DUMU *ḫi-śi-ib-ra-si-ni*
3) LUGAL
4) NIM.KI

Caption 5
1–4) Luḫʾišʾan, son of Ḫišibrasini, king of Elam.

Caption 6
1) NÌ.LA+IB
2) *sa-li-a-mu*.KI

Caption 6
1–2) Booty of Saliʾamu.

Caption 7
1) NÌ.LA+IB
2) *kàr-dè-d*[*è*.KI]

Caption 7
1–2) Booty of Karded[e].

Caption 8
1) *ul-u*[*l*]
2) GÌR.N[ÍTA]
3) *pá-ra-aḫ-śu*[*m*.KI]

Caption 8
1–3) Ulu[l], gene[ral] of Paraḫšum.

Caption 9
1) *da-gu*
2) ŠEŠ LUG[AL]
3) *pá-ra-aḫ-śum*.K[I]

Caption 9
1–3 Dagu, brother of the kin[g] of Paraḫšum.

Caption 10
1) NÌ.LA+IB
2) ḪÉ-*ni*.KI

Caption 10
1–2) Booty of ḪEni.

Caption 11
1) NÌ.⸢LA⸣+IB
2) *bu-un-ba-an*.KI

Caption 11
1–2) Booty of Bunban.

Caption 12
1) *zi-na*
2) ÉNSI
3) *ḫu-z*[*i*-x x.KI]

Caption 12
1–3) Zina, governor of Ḫuz[i ...].

Caption 13
1) *ḫi-da-rí-da*-[x]
2) ÉNS[I]
3) *gu-ni-la-ḫa*.K[I]

Caption 13
1–3) Ḫidarida-[...], govern[or] of Gunilaḫa.

Caption 14
1) NÌ.LA+IB
2) *sa*-⸢*bum*.KI⸣

Caption 14
1–2) Booty of Sabum.

Caption 15
1) NÌ.LA+IB
2) *a-wa-an*.K[I]

Caption 15
1–2) Booty of Awan.

Caption 16
1) *si*-⸢*id*⸣-*ga-ù*
2) GÌR.NÍTA
3) *pá*-⸢*ra-aḫ-śum*.KI⸣

Caption 16
1–3) Si[d]gaʾu, general of Paraḫšum.

Caption 17
1) *kùn-du-pum*
2) DI.KU$_5$
3) *pá-ra-aḫ-śum*.KI

Caption 17
1–3) Kundupum, judge of Paraḫšum.

Caption 18
1) NÌ.LA+IB
2) *śu-śi-im*.KI

Caption 18
1–2) Booty of Susa.

Colophon 3
1) ki-gal-ba šu-⸢dù-a⸣

Colophon 3
1) ... on its base.

9

This inscription deals with the dedication of some object to the god Enlil on the occasion of the defeat of the forces of Elam and Paraḫšum.

CATALOGUE

Ex.	Museum number	Tablet lines preserved	Text lines preserved	cpn
1	CBS 13972	rev. xvi 6–7, 9	15–16, 18	c
		rev. xvi 23–48	Captions 1′–8′	
		rev. xvi 49–50	Colophon 2	
2	Ni 3200	rev. iii 34–52	1–19	p
		rev. iii 53–54	Colophon 1	
		rev. iv 11–12	Caption 8′	
		rev. iv 13–14	Colophon 2	

COMMENTARY

Gelb and Kienast posited three captions in the broken section following line 12 of rev. xvi of ex. 1. Their Beischriften (d)–(k) correspond to Captions 1′–8′ of this edition.

BIBLIOGRAPHY

1914 Poebel, PBS 4/1 pp. 188–89 no. 34 M ζ′– λ′ (ex. 1, frgm. 1, edition)

1914 Poebel, PBS 5 pl. XXI no. 34 (ex. 1, frgm. 1, copy)

1923 Legrain, MJ 14 p. 204, 208, 215 (ex. 1, frgm. 2, photo, copy, edition)

1926 Legrain, PBS 15 p. 19 and pl. XV no. 41 (ex. 1, frgm. 2, copy, edition); pls. II–IV (ex. 1, frgms. 1–2, photo)

1929 Barton, RISA pp. 116–17 Sharrukin 12 (ex. 1, edition)

1961 Gelb, MAD 2^{2} p. 193 Sargon Late Copies no. 1 I (ex.1, study)

1963 Hirsch, AfO 20 pp. 4 and 51–52 Sargon b 15+16 (exs. 1–2, edition)

1990 Gelb and Kienast, Königsinschriften pp. 187–89 and pls. VI–VIII Sargon C 13 (exs. 1–2, photo, copy, edition); p. 144 (ex. 1, copy)

TEXT

1) ⌈*a*⌉-*na* ^{d}*en-líl*
2) *śar-ru*-GI
3) LUGAL ⌈KIŠ⌉
4) SAG.GIŠ.RA
5) NIM.KI
6) *ù*
7) *pá-ra*-⌈*aḫ*⌉-*śum*.KI
8) *a-na* ^{d}*en-líl*
9) A.MU.RU
10) *ša* DUB *śu*$_{4}$-*a*
11) *u-śa-sà-ku-ni*
12) ^{d}*en-líl*
13) *ù*
14) ^{d}UTU
15) ⌈SUḪUŠ-*śu*⌉
16) *li-sú-ḫa*
17) *ù*
18) ŠE.N[UMUN-*śu*]
19) *l*[*i-il-qù-tá*]

1) For the god Enlil —
2–7) Sargon, king of the world, conqueror of Elam and Paraḫšum,
8–9) dedicated (this object) to the god Enlil.
10–19) As for the one who removes this inscription, may the gods Enlil and Šamaš tear out his foundations and de[stroy] his pro[geny].

Colophon 1
1) [m]u-⌈sar⌉-[ra]
2) [ki-gal-ba]

Colophon 1
1–2) [Inscr]ipt[ion on its base].

Caption 1′
1 ⌈x-*su-uḫ-ru*⌉
2) ÉNS[I]
3) *ši-rí-ḫi-im*.[KI]

Caption 1′
1–3) x-suḫru, govern[or] of Širiḫum.

Caption 2′
1) *si-id-ga*-⌈*ù*⌉
2) GÌR.NÍTA
3) *pá-ra-aḫ*-⌈*śum*⌉.[KI]

Caption 2′
1–3) Sidgaʾu, general of Paraḫšum.

Caption 3′
1) *sa*-NAM-*śi-m*[*u-ut*]
2) GÌR.NÍ[TA]
3) NIM.KI

Caption 3′
1–3) SaNAM-šim[ut], genera[l] of Elam.

Caption 4′
1) *lu-uḫ-iš-an*
2) DUMU *ḫi-śi*-⌈*ib*⌉-[*ra-si-n*]*i*
3) LUGAL
4) NIM.KI

Caption 4′
1–3) Luḫʾišʾan, son of Ḫišib[rasi]ni, king of Elam.

Caption 5′
1) *kùn-du-pum*
2) ⸢DI⸣.[KU$_{5}$]
3) [*pá-ra-aḫ-šum*.KI]

Caption 5′
1–3) Kundupum, j[udge of Paraḫšum].

Caption 6′
1) [...]
2) 8 L[Ú ...]
3) x x x [...]
4) x ⸢GIŠ⸣.TUKUL ⸢GIŠ.ERIN⸣

Caption 6′
1–4) ..., 8 ... men, ..., ... weapons of cedar wood.

Caption 7′
1) *ḫi-ši-ib-ra-si-ni*
2) LUGAL
3) NIM.KI

Caption 7′
1–3) Ḫišibrasini, king of Elam.

Caption 8′
1) x-RA.NE.NE A.AL.DAB$_{5}$
2) ŠU DU$_{10}$.BA A.AB.RI
3) *ib-ba-li*

Caption 8′
1–3) ... captured, ...

Colophon 2
1) šà-bi an-na
2) ki-gal-ba ^{d}en-líl ^{d}inanna

Colophon 2
1–2) Its centre (part) is ... ; on its base (are) the gods Enlil and Aštar.

10

Five fragments of a victory stele of Sargon were found by de Morgan in excavations at Susa. On one side (A) of the largest fragment there are preserved a few lines of the end of a royal inscription; on another side (C) of the same piece there is a depiction of the king, with an adjoining caption that identitifies him as Sargon. The monument, which was deliberately defaced in antiquity, may have been set up in Susa to commemorate Sargon's victory over Elam or, alternatively, may have been a piece of booty brought by the Elamites from Babylonia.

CATALOGUE

Ex.	Museum number	Lines preserved
1	Sb 1 (+)	Side A – inscription Side C – caption
	Sb 10482 (A 6392) (+)	No inscription
	Sb 11388 (6393) (+)	No inscription
	1359 (+)	No inscription
	Sb 11387	No inscription

COMMENTARY

The stele is made of diorite and measures 50 cm in height. For a drawing of the five stele fragments, see J. Börker-Klähn, Bildstelen figs. 18d–18i. The inscription was collated by B. Foster. The bibliography includes references to photos of the monument in addition to text studies.

BIBLIOGRAPHY

1905 Gautier, RT 27 pp. 176–79 (transliteration, study)
1908 Scheil, MDP 10 pp. 4–8 (edition) and pl. 2 nos. 3–4 (photo of squeeze of inscription)
1908 King, PSBA 30 pp. 238–42 (study)
1910 King, Early History pp. 220–22 (study)
1924 Nassouhi, RA 21 pp. 65–74 (photo, copy, edition)
1926 Pézard and Pottier, Catalogue pp. 34–36 nos. 1 and 3 (study) and pl. 1 (photo)
1926 Unger, SuAK p. 35 (study) and p. 88 no. 33 (photo)
1928-29 Meissner, AfO 5 p. 3 fig. 1 (drawing)
1929 Jeremias, HAOG II p. 2 fig. 4 (photo)
1929 Legrain, MJ 20 p. 275 (drawing)
1929 Barton, RISA pp. 118–19 Sharrukin 16 (edition)
1931 Contenau, Manuel 2 pp. 666–67 figs. 462–63 (photo, copy)
1935 Rutten, Encyclopédie 1 p. 212 (photo)
1959 Barrelet, Syria 36 p. 27 fig. 1 (photo, detail)
1960 Parrot, Sumer figs. 207 and 209 (photo, detail)
1961 Gelb, MAD 2^2 p. 193 Sargon Original Inscriptions no. 1 (study)
1962 Strommenger and Hirmer, Mesopotamien pl. 115 (photo)
1963 Hirsch, AfO 20 p. 2 Sargon a 1 (study)
1967 Moortgat, Kunst no. 125 (photo)
1968 Nagel and Strommenger, BJVF 8 p. 172 (partial edition)
1970 McKeon, BMFB 68 p. 234 no. 354 fig. 10 (photo)
1975 Orthmann (ed.), Der alte Orient p. 195 and pl. 99 (photo, study)
1976 Amiet, L'art d'Agadé no. 1 (photo, drawing, edition)
1981 Spycket, Statuaire pp. 146–47 and no. 14(study)
1982 Börker-Klähn, Bildstelen no. 18 (photos, study, drawing)
1990 Gelb and Kienast, Königsinschriften pp. 62–63 Sargon 1 (edition)

TEXT

Side A
Col. i′
Lacuna
1′) [...].⌈KI⌉
2′) [*in* R]EC169
3′) [SAG.G]IŠ.RA-*ni*
4′) [...]
Col. ii′
Lacuna
1′) [SUḪUŠ-*śu*]
2′) [*li-sú*]-⌈*ḫa*⌉
3′) *ù*
4′) ŠE.NUMUN-*śú*
5′) *li-íl-qù-tá*
Side C
1) *śar-ru*-GI
2) ⌈LUGAL⌉

Side A

Lacuna
i 1′–4′) (When Sargon) [con]quered the place ... [in] battle, ...

Lacuna
ii 1′–5′) [May the two gods ... tea]r out [his foundations] and destroy his progeny.

Side C
1–2) Sargon, the king.

11

A campaign of Sargon against the area of the Upper Euphrates and Ebla is recorded in a royal inscription, extant in both Akkadian and Sumerian versions, that is known from two Old Babylonian Sammeltafel copies from Nippur.

CATALOGUE

Sumerian version

Ex.	Museum number	Tablet lines preserved	Text lines preserved	cpn
1	CBS 13972	obv. v 7–50	4–47	c
2	Ni 3200	obv. v 26–27	16–18	p
		obv. vii 1–10	39–48	
		obv. vii 11–12	Colophon 1	

Akkadian version

Ex.	Museum number	Tablet lines preserved	Text lines preserved	cpn
1	CBS 13972	obv. vi 4–47	1–44	c
		obv. vi 48–49	Colophon 2	
2	Ni 3200	obv. vi. 17–26, 28–31	8–17, 19–23	p

COMMENTARY

The translation follows the Akkadian version for lines 1–5 where the Sumerian is broken away; the line count and translation for the remainder of the text follow the Sumerian version. Lines 38–48 are omitted in the Akkadian version. Although Hirsch, and Gelb and Kienast edited ex. 1 obv. xiv and ex. 2 rev. 2 as further exemplars of this text, these are edited separately in this volume (see the commentary to E2.1.1.12).

BIBLIOGRAPHY

1914 Poebel, PBS 4/1 pp. 177–78 no. 34 C and D (ex. 1, frgm. 1, edition)
1914 Poebel, PBS 5 pl. XX no. 34 (ex. 1, frgm. 1, copy)
1923 Legrain, MJ 14 pp. 204, 208, and 210 (ex. 1, frgm. 2, photo, copy, edition)
1926 Gressmann, ATAT[2] p. 338 (ex. 1, partial translation [by Ebeling])
1926 Legrain, PBS 15 pp. 13–14, 19 and pl. XV no. 41 (ex. 1, frgm. 2, copy, edition); pls. II–IV (ex. 1, frgms. 1–2, photo)
1929 Barton, RISA pp. 108–11 Sharrukin 2 (ex. 1, edition)
1961 Gelb, MAD 2[2] p. 193 Sargon Late Copies no. 1 B (ex. 1, study)
1963 Hirsch, AfO 20 pp. 3 and 37–39 Sargon b 2+3 (exs. 1–2, edition)
1969 Oppenheim in ANET[3] p. 268 (ex. 1, translation)
1984 Borger, TUAT 1 p. 354 (ex. 1, partial translation)
1990 Gelb and Kienast, Königsinschriften pp. 163–67 and pls. I–III, XI–XII Sargon C 2 (exs. 1–2, photo, edition); p. 140 (ex. 1, copy)

TEXT

Sumerian	Akkadian	
1) [*śar-um*-GI]	1) ⌈*śar-ru*-GI⌉	1–8) Sargon, king of the world, was victorious (in) 34 battles. He destroyed their (city) walls as far as the shore of the sea.
2) [lugal]-	2) LUGAL	
3) [KIŠ]	3) KIŠ	
4) [34 (x)] SAḪAR-ra	4) 34 REC 169	
5) [TÙN.KÁ]RA bí-sì	5) *iš$_{11}$-ar*	
6) bàd-bi	6) BÀD.BÀD	
7) ì-gul-gul	7) Ì.GUL.GUL	
8) zà-a-ab-ba-ka-šè	8) *a-dì-ma*	
	9) *pu-ti*	
	10) *ti-a-am-tim*	
9) má-me-luḫ-ḫa.KI	11) MÁ *me-luḫ-ḫa*	9–13) He moored the ships of Meluḫḫa, Magan, and Tilmun at the quay of Agade.
10) má-má-gan.KI	12) MÁ *má-gan*.KI	
11) má-tilmun.KI	13) MÁ *tilmun*.KI	
12) kar-ag-ge-dè.KI-ka	14) *in kà-rí-im*	
	15) *ši a-kà-dè*.KI	
13) bí-kéš	16) *ìr-ku-us*	
14) ⌈*śar*⌉-*um*-GI	17) *śar*-⌈*ru*⌉-[G]I	14–19) Sargon, the king, bowed down to the god Dagān in Tuttul.
15) ⌈lugal⌉	18) ⌈LUGAL⌉	
16) du$_{8}$-du$_{8}$-⌈li⌉.KI-a	19) *in tu-tu-li*.KI	
17) ^{d}da-gan-ra	20) *a-na*	
	21) ^{d}*da-gan*	
18) ki-a mu-na-za	22) *úś-kà-en*	
19) šùd mu-⌈na-de$_{6}$⌉	23) *ik-ru-ub*	
20) kalam-IGI.NIM	24) *ma-tá*[*m*]	20–28) He (the god Dagān) gave to him (Sargon) the Upper Land: Mari, Iarmuti, and Ebla as far as the Cedar Forest and
	25) *a-lí-tám*	
21) mu-na-sum	26) *i-dì-śum$_{6}$*	
22) ma-rí.KI	27) *ma-rí-am*.KI	

23) ià-ar-mu-ti.KI	28) *ià-ar-mu-ti-a-am*.KI	the Silver Mountains.
24) eb-la.KI	29) *eb-la*.KI	
25) tir-	30) *a-dì-ma*	
	31) GIŠ.TIR	
26) GIŠ.erin	32) GIŠ.ERIN	
	33) *ù*	
27) ḫur-sag-	34) KUR.KUR	
28) kù-ga-šè	35) KÙ	
29) *śar-um*-GI	36) *śar-ru*-GI	29–37) 5,400 men daily eat in the presence of Sargon, the king to whom the god Enlil gave no rival.
30) lugal	37) LUGAL	
31) ⌈d⌉en-líl-le	38) *šu* ^d^*en-líl*	
32) lú-gaba-ru	39) *ma-ḫi-ra*	
33) nu-mu-NI-tuk	40) *la i-dì-śum*$_6$	
34) 5,400 érin	41) 5,400 GURUŠ	
35) u$_4$-šú-šè	42) *u-um-śum*$_6$	
36) ⌈igi⌉-ni-šè	43) *ma-ḫar-śu*	
37) ninda ì-kú-e	44) NINDA KÚ	
38) lú mu-⌈sar-ra-e⌉		38–48) As for the one who destroys this inscription, may the god Anum destroy his name. May the god Enlil bring his progeny to an end. May the goddess Inanna cut off his ... *offspring*.
39) a[b]-ḫa-lam-e-a		
40) an-né		
41) mu-ni		
42) ḫé-ḫa-lam-e		
43) ^d^en-líl-le		
44) numun-na-ni		Lacuna
45) ḫé-til-le		
46) ^d^inanna-ke$_4$		
47) e x dumu-na-ni		
48) ḫé-ku$_5$-⌈e⌉		
Lacuna		
Colophon 1	Colophon 2	Colophon 1
1) mu-sar-ra	1) ⌈mu-sar-ra alan⌉-na	1–2) Inscription on its base.
2) ki-gal-ba	2) ki-gal-bi nu-sar	Colophon 2
		1–2) Inscription on a statue. Its base is not inscribed.

12

A fragmentarily preserved inscription found on two Old Babylonian Sammeltafeln from Nippur gives another account of the campaign of Sargon in the region of the Upper Euphrates and Ebla.

CATALOGUE

Ex.	Museum number	Tablet lines preserved	Text lines preserved	cpn
1	CBS 13972	obv. xiii 43–48, 50	3–8, 10	c
		obv. xiv 8–14, 20–24	1′–7′, 13′–17′	
2	Ni 3200	rev. ii 17–36	10′–30′	p
		rev. ii 37	Colophon	
		rev. ii 38–49	Captions 1–7	

COMMENTARY

According to our reconstruction of the text, the inscription begins on ex. 1 at obv. xiii 43, continues down to the bottom of that column, and concludes on the top portion of obv. xiv. We reconstruct a text that is distinct from, but similar to, E2.1.1.11.

The small section preserved on the bottom of obv. xiii was considered to be a separate short inscription by Hirsch (Sargon b 12) and Gelb and Kienast (Sargon C 9). The latter authors took the section appearing on obv. xiv to be a second duplicate of the text, which appears here as E2.1.1.11 (Hirsch, Sargon b 13, and Gelb and Kienast, Sargon C 2). However, we would not expect to find an original inscription copied twice on one Sammeltafel.

Of note is the occurrence of the phrase '(Sargon) was victorious in 34 battles' at the beginning of both E2.1.1.11 and 12. It is unclear why captions naming the defeated enemy leaders of Sargon's southern campaign are listed at the end of this inscription. The reading of lines 13′–14′ of ex. 1 is based on Legrain's copy; a small piece of the tablet has now been chipped away. Caption 4 was inadvertently omitted from Gelb and Kienast's edition.

BIBLIOGRAPHY

1914 Poebel, PBS 4/1 p. 187 no. 34 L (ex. 1, frgm. 1, edition)
1914 Poebel, PBS 15 pl. XX no. 34 (ex. 1, frgm. 1, copy)
1923 Legrain, MJ 14 pp. 204, 208, and 214–15 (ex. 1, frgm. 2, photo, copy, edition)
1926 Legrain, PBS 15 p. 19 and pl. XV no. 41 (ex. 1, frgm. 2, copy, edition); pls. II–IV (ex. 1, frgms. 1–2, photo)
1961 Gelb, MAD 2^2 p. 193 Sargon Late Copies nos. 1 B and I (ex. 1, study)
1963 Hirsch, AfO 20 pp. 4 and 48–50 Sargon b 12+13 (exs. 1–2, edition)
1990 Gelb and Kienast, Königinschriften pp. 163–67 and pls. I, IV–V, XVI–XVIII Sargon C 2 exs. Am and Bm (exs. 1–2, photo, partial edition); p. 140 (ex. 1 copy); pp. 183–84 and pls. I, IV–V Sargon C 9 (ex.1, photo, copy, partial edition)

TEXT

1) [*šar-ru*-GI]
2) [LUGAL]
3) [KIŠ]
4) 30+[4 REC 169]
5) *iš*$_{11}$*-a*[*r*]
6) URU.⸢KI⸣.UR[U.KI]
7) *sà-ar-ru-t*[*im*]
8) *u* ID x
9) [...]
10) *u* [...]

1–10) [Sargon, king of] the w[orld], was victorious in 3[4 battles]. He ... the rebel ci[ties ...].

Lacuna
0′) [MÁ *me-luḫ-ḫa*]
1′) M[Á *má-gán*.KI]
2′) M[Á *tilmun*.KI]
3′) *i*[*n kà-rí-im*]
4′) *ši* ⸢*a*⸣-[*kà-dè*.KI]
5′) *ìr*-[*ku-us*]

Lacuna
0′–5′ (Sargon) moo[red] the shi[ps of Meluḫḫa Magan, and Tilmun] a[t the quay of] Ag[ade].

6′) *šar*-[*ru*-GI]
7′) LU[GAL]
8′) [*in tu-tu-li*.KI]
9′) [*a-na*]
10′) ⸢d⸣[*da-gan*]
11′) *ú*[*š-kà-en*]
12′) *ik-ru-u*[*b*]

6′–12′) Sar[gon], the k[ing], bo[wed down to] the god [Dagān in Tuttul].

13′) *ma-tám*
14′) *a-lí*-⸢*tám*⸣
15′) *i-dì-šum*$_6$
16′) *ma-rí-am*.[KI]
17′) *ià-ar-mu-ti-a-am*.<KI>
18′) *eb-la*.KI

13′–21′) He (the god Dagān) gave to him (Sargon) the Upper Land: Mari, Iarmuti, and Ebla as far as the Cedar Forest and the Silver Mountains.

19′) [*a-dì*]-*ma*
20′) ⌈GIŠ⌉.T[IR] ⌈GIŠ.ERIN⌉
21′) *ù* ⌈KUR.KUR⌉ K[Ù]
22′) *śar-ru*-GI
23′) LUGAL KIŠ
24′) *šu* ^{d}*en-líl*
25′) *ma-ḫi-ra*
26′) *la ì-dì-śum*$_6$
27′) 5,400 GURUŠ
28′) *u-um-śum*$_6$
29′) *ma-ḫar-śu*
30′) NINDA KÚ

22′–30′) 5,400 men daily eat in the presence of Sargon, king of the world, to whom the god Enlil gave no rival.

Colophon
1) ⌈mu-sar-ra alan-na⌉

Colophon
1) Inscription on a statue.

Caption 1
1) NÌ.LA+IB UNU.KI

Caption 1
1) Booty of Uruk.

Caption 2
1) lugal-zà-ge-si
2) LUGAL UNU.KI

Caption 2
1–2) Lugal-zage-si, king of Uruk.

Caption 3
1) lú-^{d}nanna
2) LUGAL ŠEŠ.[UNU.KI]

Caption 3
1–2) Lu-Nanna, king of U[r].

Caption 4
1) NÌ.LA+IB Š[EŠ.UNU.KI]

Caption 4
1) Booty of U[r].

Caption 5
1) NÌ.LA+IB UB.[ME.KI]

Caption 5
1) Booty of Um[ma].

Caption 6
1) mes-zi É[NSI]
2) *laga*[*š*](LA.BUR.[ŠIR]).[KI]

Caption 6
1–2) Mes-zi, g[overnor] of Lagaš.

Caption 7
1) mes-[é]
2) ÉN[SI]
3) ⌈UB⌉.M[E.KI]
Lacuna

Caption 7
1–3) Mes-[e], go[vernor] of Umm[a].
Lacuna

13

This inscription, known from two Old Babylonian Sammeltafel copies from Nippur, is too poorly preserved to determine which deed of the king it commemorated.

CATALOGUE

Ex.	Museum number	Tablet lines preserved	Text lines preserved	cpn
1	CBS 13972	obv. xii 51	1	c
		obv. xiii 5–21	10–26	
2	Ni 3200	rev. i 19–31	14–24, 26–27	p
		rev. i 32	Colophon	

COMMENTARY

The line count follows ex. 1.

BIBLIOGRAPHY

1923 Legrain, MJ 14 pp. 204, 208, and 215 (ex. 1, frgm. 2, photo, copy, edition)

1926 Legrain, PBS 15 p. 18 and pl. XV no. 41 (ex. 1, frgm. 2, copy, edition); pls. II–IV (exs. 1, frgms. 1–2, photo)

1929 Barton, RISA p. 114 Sharrukin 9 (ex. 1, edition)

1961 Gelb, MAD 2[2] p. 193 Sargon Late Copies no. 1 G (ex. 1, study)

1963 Hirsch, AfO 20 pp. 4 and 47–48 Sargon b 10 (exs. 1–2, edition)

1990 Gelb and Kienast, Königsinschriften pp. 182–83 and pls. I, IV–V, XVI–XVII Sargon C 8 (exs. 1–2, photo, edition); p. 140 (ex. 1, copy)

TEXT

1) *ś[ar-ru-*GI]
Lacuna of 8 lines
10) x [...] x [...]
11) DA.AN
12) [d]*en-líl*
13) *u-kál-lim*
14) *ma-ma-na*
15) *pá-ni-śu*
16) *ù-la*
17) *u-ba-al*
18) *ti-a-am-tám*
19) *a-lí-tám*
20) *ù*
21) *śa-pil-*[*tám*]
22) *i-dì-śum*$_6$
23) *śar-ru-*GI
24) LUGAL
25) KIŠ
26) ⌈*ra*⌉-x [x x]
27) GÌR.NÍTA]-*ś*[*u*]
Colophon
1) mu-⌈sar⌉-ra ki-gal-b[a]

1) S[argon],
Lacuna

12–13) The god Enlil instructed (him)

14–17) and (Sargon) showed mercy to no one.

18–22) He (the god Enlil) gave to him the Upper Sea and the Low[er] (Sea).

23–27) Sargon, king of the world: PN is hi[s] gene[ral].

Colophon
1) Inscription on [its] base.

14

This fragmentarily preserved inscription, which is known from one Old Babylonian Sammeltafel copy, deals with the fashioning of a statue of Sargon for the god Enlil.

CATALOGUE

Ex.	Museum number	Tablet lines preserved	Text lines preserved	cpn
2	Ni 3200	rev. i 33–46	1–14	p

COMMENTARY

Ni 3200 is conventionally designated here as ex. 2; the inscription is not preserved on CBS 13972. We would expect, based on the parallel provided by E2.1.4.30 iii 32–34: *i-nu-šu* [x] *tám-ši*$_x$(SU$_4$)-*l*[*í*] *ab-ni-*[*ma*] 'At that time I fashioned a statue of myself', that lines 5–8 of this text refer to the fashioning of a statue.

BIBLIOGRAPHY

1963 Hirsch, AfO 20 pp. 4 and 48 Sargon b 11 (edition)

1990 Gelb and Kienast, Königsinschriften pp. 184–85 and pls. XVI–XVIII Sargon C 10 (photo, copy, edition)

TEXT

1) *maḫ-rí-í*[*š*]
2) ^{d}*en-*[*líl*]
3) *šar-ru-*[GI]
4) LUGAL K[IŠ]
5) *ì-n*[*u*]
6) DÙL-*š*[*u*]
7) MU x
8) x x x x
9) *ma-m*[*a-na* DUB *šu*$_4$*-a*]
10) ⌈*u*⌉*-ša-sà-ku-ni*
11) ^{d}*en-líl*
12) *ù* ^{d}UT[U]
13) SUḪUŠ-*š*[*u*]
14) *l*[*i-sú-ḫa*]
15) [*ù* ŠE.NUMUN-*šu*]
16) [*li-il-qù-tá*]
Colophon (not preserved)

1–2) Befor[e] the god En[lil].
3–8) Sar[gon], king of the wo[rld], whe[n] he ... (this) statue of him[self] ...
9–16) As for anyo[ne] who removes [this inscription], may the gods Enlil and Šama[š] [tear out] hi[s] foundations [and destroy his progeny].
Colophon (not preserved)

15

This inscription, known from two Old Babylonian Sammeltafel copies from Nippur, deals with the fashioning of a statue of the king. It mentions the god Enlil's granting of the sceptre to Sargon.

CATALOGUE

Ex.	Museum number	Tablet lines preserved	Text lines preserved	cpn
1	CBS 13972	rev. xv 20–21, 33–36, 43–48	1–2, 15–18, 25–30	c
2	Ni 3200	rev. iii 10–32	10–32	p

COMMENTARY

After *ì-nu* in line 14 we would normally expect a verb in the subjunctive mood. The indicative forms in lines 17 and 19 seem to indicate that we have in line 14 the adverb *inu,* 'then'. Unfortunately, this understanding results in lines 12–13 standing alone, unconnected to what precedes and follows them. The broken nature of the inscription prevents us from gaining a clear understanding of this passage. Since lines 22–29 of this text parallel lines 11–17 of E2.1.1.13, we would expect line 22 of this text to equate to line 11 of E2.1.1.13. In text 13 DA.AN is found; the corresponding line in this text has a sign that could be DA followed by a broken sign whose reading is unclear; AN is excluded.

BIBLIOGRAPHY

1914 Poebel, PBS 4/1 187–88 no. 34 M α ′ (ex. 1, frgm. 1, edition)

1914 Poebel, PBS 5 pl. XXII no. 34 (ex. 1, frgm. 1, copy)

1923 Legrain, MJ 14 pp. 204, 209, and 215 (ex. 1, frgm. 2, photo, copy, edition)

1926 Legrain, PBS 15 p. 19 and pl. XV no. 41 (ex. 1, frgm. 2, copy, edition); pls. V–VII (ex. 1 frgms. 1-2, photo)

1929 Barton, RISA pp. 114–15 Sharrukin 11 (ex. 1, edition)

1961 Gelb, MAD 2^{2} p. 193 Sargon Late Copies no. 1 H (ex. 1, study)

1963 Hirsch, AfO 20 pp. 4 and 50–51 Sargon b 14 (exs. 1–2, edition)

1990 Gelb and Kienast, Königsinschriften pp. 186–87 and pls. VI–VIII, XVI–XVIII Sargon C 12 (exs. 1–2, photo, edition); p. 144 (ex. 1, copy)

TEXT

1) *šar-r*[*u*-GI]	1–3) Sar[gon], ki[ng of the world]:
2) LU[GAL]	Lacuna
3) [KIŠ]	
Lacuna (6 lines)	
10) [*maḫ*]*-rí-*[*íš*]	10–11) [bef]or[e] the god Enlil.
11) ^{d}*en-líl*	
12) *šar-ru*-GI	12–13) Sargon, king of the world.
13) LUGAL KIŠ	
14) *ì-nu*	14–22) Then the god Enlil gave to him the sceptre, made his intelligence surpassing, and *supported* (him) ...
15) ^{d}*en-líl*	
16) GIŠ.GIDRU	
17) *i-dì-šum*$_{6}$-⌈*ma*⌉	
18) GÉŠTU	
19) *u-wa-ti-ir-šum*$_{6}$	
20) [...] x x	
21) *ú*-⌈*ša*⌉-*z*[*i-iz*]	
22) DA-⌈x⌉	
23) *šar-ru*-GI	23) Sargon —
24) ^{d}*en-líl*	24–25) the god Enlil instructed (him)
25) *u-kál-lim*	
26) *ma-ma-na*	26–29) and (Sargon) showed mercy to no one.
27) *pá-ni-šu*	
28) *ù-la*	
29) *u-ba-al*	
30) SUḪUŠ x x x	30–32) The foundation ... the Great Mountain of the Gods (Enlil).
31) ŠA.DÚ *ì-li*	
32 *ra-bí-um*	
Colophon	Colophon
1) mu-sar-ra ⌈alan⌉-na	1) Inscription on a statue.

16

This inscription, known from an inscribed disk and its Old Babylonian tablet copy, both of which were found in excavations at Ur, deals with the fashioning of a socle for the goddess INANNA.ZA.ZA, by En-ḫedu-ana, *entu* priestess of the god Nanna at Ur and daughter of Sargon.

CATALOGUE

Ex.	Museum number	Excavation number	Object	Dimensions (cm)	Provenance	Lines preserved	cpn
1	CBS 16665	U 6612	Alabaster disk	25.6 dia. 7.1 thick	Ur, from the fill at the NE end of the passageway between blocks A and B, and C of the Isin–Larsa levels of the Gipar-ku	1–5, 7–8, 12–13	c
2	IM—	U 7737	Clay tablet	—	Ur, from no. 7 Quiet Sreet; rooms 5–6	1–3, 5, 7, 8–13	n

COMMENTARY

The disk exemplar was apparently defaced in antiquity, but only after the Old Babylonian tablet copy was made, since the copy is complete. The disk was found in several pieces; a heavily restored version of this object is now housed in the University Museum in Philadelphia. The inscription is found on one side of the disk and a carved pictorial relief on the other. The relief depicts En-ḫedu-ana pouring an oblation over an altar in front of a stepped structure. For a possible identification of the DN INANNA.ZA.ZA of this inscription with Semitic Aštar, see W.G. Lambert, MARI 4 (1985) p. 537 and MARI 6 (1990) p. 644. The bibliography includes references to photos of the disk in addition to text studies.

BIBLIOGRAPHY

1926 Woolley, AJ 6 pp. 376–77 and pl. LIV b (photo, study)
1927 Legrain, MJ 18 pp. 237–40 (study, photo)
1928 Gadd, UET 1 no. 23 and pl. C (ex. 1, photo, copy, edition), no. 289 lines 73–83 (ex. 2, copy, edition)
1929 Gadd, History and Monuments of Ur p. 92 and pl. XVII a (ex. 1, photo, study)
1929 Barton, RISA pp. 358–59 Time of Sargon 1 (ex. 1, edition)
1929–30 Jacobsen, AJSL 46 pp. 68–69 (ex. 1, study)
1934 Woolley, UE 2 p. 334 (ex. 1, study)
1935 Woolley, Sumerian Art p. 97 and pl. 54b (ex. 1, photo, study)
1955 Woolley, UE 4 pp. 49, 172 and pl. 41d (ex. 1, photo, study)
1960 Sollberger, Iraq 22 pp. 75–76 no. 86 (ex. 1, study)
1961 Gelb, MAD 2^2 p. 194 Sargon Family no. 2 (ex. 1, study)
1963 Hirsch, AfO 20 p. 9 no. 2 (ex. 1, study)
1967 Moortgat, Kunst p. 54 and pl. 130 (ex. 1, photo, study)
1968 Hallo and van Dijk, Exaltation p. 2 and frontispiece (ex. 1, photo, study)
1969 Sollberger, RA 63 p. 180 no. 16 (ex. 2, edition, exs. 1–2, study)
1971 Sollberger and Kupper, IRSA IIA1d (exs. 1–2, translation)
1976 Amiet, L'Art d'Agadé pp. 14–15 and fig. 10 (ex. 1, copy of relief, study)
1981 Spycket, Statuaire p. 168 and n. 117 (study)
1987 Winter, CRRA 33 pp. 189–95 (ex. 1, photo, translation, study)
1989 Goodnick Westenholz in Studies Sjöberg, p. 540 (ex. 1, edition)
1990 Gelb and Kienast, Königsinschriften pp. 64–65 Sargon A 1 (ex. 1, edition) and p. 190 Sargon C 15 (exs 1–2, edition)

TEXT

1) en-ḫ[é]-du$_7$-an-na
2) MUNUS.NUNUZ.ZI.^{d}NANNA
3) dam-^{d}nanna

1–3) En-ḫ[e]du-ana, *zirru* priestess, wife of the god Nanna,

4) dumu-
5) ⸢*śar-ru*⸣-GI
6) [lugal]-
7) ⸢KIŠ⸣
8) [é-^{d}INAN]NA.ZA.ZA
9) [ur]i$_{5}$.KI-ma-ka
10) [bára]-si-ga
11) [b]í-e-dù
12) bára banšur-an-na
13) mu-šè bi-sa$_{4}$

4–7) daughter of Sargon, [king] of the world,

8–9) in [the temple of the goddess Inan]na-ZA.ZA in [U]r,

10–11) made a [soc]le (and)

12–13) named it: 'dais, table of the god An'.

17

An inscription found on a gypsum stamp from Sippar gives the name of one of Sargon's sons, a certain Šū-Enlil.

COMMENTARY

The stamp is apparently too small to have been used as a brick stamp; it measures about 5×3 cm. The piece was found in excavations of the University of Baghdad expedition to Sippar in the ruins of a temple of the Neo-Babylonian period that lie next to the ziqqurrat. The text of the inscription is given here through the courtesy of Dr. F. Al-Rawi. Another son of Sargon, Ilaba'iš-takal, is mentioned in the Man-ištūšu Obelisk (Side C xiii 22-23).

TEXT

1) *šu*-^{d}*en-líl*
2) DUMU
3) *śar-ru*-GI
4) LUGAL
5) KIŠ

1–5) Šū-Enlil, son of Sargon king of the world.

2001

This dedicatory inscription mentions Sargon's wife, TašLULtum.

COMMENTARY

The text is incised on YBC 2191, an alabaster bowl fragment that measures 5.4×8×0.9 cm. The inscription was collated. The reading of the PN of line 2′ is uncertain. A form *áš-lul-tum* seems to be excluded because no nominal pattern *aprustum* occurs in Akkadian. Gelb MAD 2^{2} p. 212 proposes a reading *tàš-lul-tum*; see also the comments of Fronzaroli in 'The Concord in Gender in Eblaite Theophoric Personal Names', UF 11 (1979) p. 279 and n. 31. Concerning the second sign of the PN, we may note the remarks of Steinkeller, SEL 1 (1984) p. 16 n. 30: 'For iš-LUL-IL/DINGIR, da-áš-LUL-tum, and Da-áš-LUL-^{d}A-a, which

MAD 3, 271, and AHw, 1142, place under *šalālu*, "to carry away", one might consider the reading l u p, since *šalāpu* "to pull out, to extract (as in birth?)", would give a better meaning than *šalālu*'.

BIBLIOGRAPHY

1915 Clay, YOS 1 no. 7 (copy, edition)
1929 Barton, RISA pp. 116–17 Sharrukin 13 (edition)
1957 Hallo, Titles p. 34 n. 1 (study)
1961 Gelb, MAD 2[2] p. 194 Sargon Family no. 1 and p. 212 (study)
1963 Hirsch, AfO 20 p. 9 no. 1 (study)
1971 Sollberger and Kupper, IRSA IIA1c (translation)
1990 Gelb and Kienast, Königsinschriften p. 65 Sargon B 1 (edition)

TEXT

Lacuna
1′) šabra-é
2′) *tàš*-LUL-*tum*
3′) dam-*śar-ru*-GI-
4′) ka-k[e₄]
5′) ⌈nam⌉-[ti-... šè]
6′) [a-mu-ru]

Lacuna
1′–6′ (PN), the majordomo of TašLULtum, wife of Sargon, [dedicated (this object) [for] the [life of ...]

2002

A calcite vase fragment was dedicated to Sargon.

COMMENTARY

The vase is BM 123122 (1932–10–8, 6). It was found in Woolley's excavations at Ur from 'FH, in the relatively late mass of rubbish poured against the queer wall' season X.

BIBLIOGRAPHY

1965 Sollberger, UET 8 no. 10 (copy)
1968 Nagel and Strommenger, BJVF 8 p. 172 n. 41 (edition)
1989 Potts, Iraq 51 p. 126 and n. 12 (study)
1990 Gelb and Kienast, Königsinschriften p. 64 Sargon 3 (edition)

TEXT

1) [*a*]-*na*
2) [*śar-r*]*u*-GI
3) [LU]GAL
4) [KI]Š

1–4) [F]or [Sar]gon, [ki]ng of the [wor]ld.

2003

Two seals and one seal impression mention the *entu* priestess En-ḫedu-ana, Sargon's daughter.

COMMENTARY

The name of a servant of En-ḫedu-ana appears in a seal inscription from Ur. The lapis lazuli seal bearing the inscription is incomplete. It bears the excavation no. U 8988 and museum no. BM 120572 (1928–10–9, 55). It was found in the grave PG/503. In UE 2 p. 540 Woolley lists CBS 16788 along with BM 120572 under the heading U 8988. The inscription was collated by G. Frame.

BIBLIOGRAPHY

1928 Gadd, UET 1 no. 271 (copy, edition)
1934 Woolley, UE 2 p. 358 and pl. 212 no. 308 and p. 540 (photo, transliteration, study)
1954-56 Sollberger, AfO 17 p. 26 (study)
1960 Sollberger, Iraq 22 p. 75 no. 87 (study)
1961 Gelb, MAD 2[2] p. 194 Sargon Family no. 3 (study)
1963 Hirsch, AfO 20 p. 9 no. 2b (study)
1964 Boehmer, Moortgat Festschrift p. 43 no. 2 (edition)
1965 Boehmer, Glyptik no. 194 fig. 56 (photo)
1968 Nagel and Strommenger, BJVF 8 pp. 152–53 and 157 no. 1 (edition, study)
1968-69 Edzard, AfO 22 p. 15 no. 22–1 (transliteration)
1982 Collon, Cylinder Seals 2 no. 64 (photo, edition [by Sollberger], study
1990 Gelb and Kienast, Königsinschriften p. 39 S–1 (edition)

TEXT

1) en-ḫé-du$_7$-an-na
2) dumu-*śar-ru*-GI
3) DINGIR-IGI.D[U]
4) kinda-⸢ni⸣ [(x)]

1–2) En-ḫedu-ana, daughter of Sargon:

3–4) Ilum-pāl[il] (is) her coiffeur.

2004

A seal found in excavations at Ur gives the name of a high official of En-ḫedu-ana.

COMMENTARY

The seal, which is made of a mottled stone (either granite or diorite), bears the excavation no. U 9178 and the museum no. IM 4221. It measures 3.7 cm in length with its copper caps. It was found loose in the soil of the Royal Cemetery at Ur at a depth of about 3.4 m, in association with U 9177 and 9179. The inscription was collated from the published photo.

For the variation PA.É/PA.AL as a designation of a high official in Ur III texts, see the comments of Hallo, JNES 31 (1972) p. 91.

BIBLIOGRAPHY

1928 Gadd, UET 1 no. 272 (copy, edition)
1934 Woolley, UE 2 p. 358 and pl. 212 no. 307 and p. 542 (photo, transliteration, study)
1954–56 Sollberger, AfO 17 p. 26 (study)
1960 Sollberger, Iraq 22 p. 75 no. 89 (study)
1961 Gelb, MAD 2[2] p. 194 Sargon Family no. 5 (study)
1963 Hirsch, AfO 20 p. 9 no. 2a (study)
1964 Boehmer, Moortgat Festschrift p. 43 no. 1 (edition)
1965 Boehmer, Glyptik no. 204 fig. 53 (photo)
1968 Nagel and Strommenger, BJVF 8 pp. 152–53 and 157 no. 0 b (edition, study)
1968–69 Edzard, AfO 22 p. 14 no. 15-2 (edition)
1969 ANEP[2] no. 681 (photo)
1987 Collon, First Impressions no. 527 (photo, translation)
1990 Gelb and Kienast, Königsinschriften p. 39 S–3 (edition)

TEXT

1) ad-da
2) ugula-é/šábra
3) en-ḫé-du$_7$-an-na

1–3) Adda, estate supervisor/majordomo of En-ḫe-du-ana.

2005

A clay sealing found in excavations at Ur gives the name of a servant of En-ḫedu-ana.

COMMENTARY

The seal impression is found on a sealing with the excavation number U 11684 and museum number BM 123668 (1928–10–10, 832). The piece, which measures 4.2×2.5×2 cm, was found loose in the upper soil of the Royal Cemetery at Ur. The inscription was collated from the published photo.

BIBLIOGRAPHY

1934 Woolley, UE 2 p. 358 and pl. 212 no. 309; p. 572 and pl. 191 (photo, copy, edition)
1936 Legrain, UE 3 pl. 31 no. 537 (copy)
1954-56 Sollberger, AfO 17 p. 26 (study)
1960 Sollberger, Iraq 22 p. 75 no. 88 (study)
1961 Gelb, MAD 2[2] p. 194 Sargon Family no. 4 (study)
1963 Hirsch, AfO 20 p. 9 no. 2c (study)
1964 Boehmer, Moortgat Festschrift p. 43 no. 5 (edition)
1965 Boehmer, Glyptik no. 458 fig. 114 (photo)
1968 Nagel and Strommenger, BJVF 8 pp. 152–53 and 158 no. 4 (edition, study)
1968-69 Edzard, AfO 22 p. 16 no. 24-4 (edition)
1979 Moorey, Iraq 41 pp. 106 and 108 no. 537 (copy)
1987 Collon, First Impressions no. 908 (photo, copy, translation)
1990 Gelb and Kienast, Königsinschriften p. 39 S–2 (edition)

TEXT

1) [en]-ḫé-[du$_7$]-⸢an⸣-na
2) [dumu-*śa*]*r-ru*-GI
3) [x]-ki-tuš-du$_{10}$
4) [dub-s]ar
5) [ir$_{11}$-da-n]i

1–2) [En]-ḫe[du]-ana, daughter of Sa]rgon:

3–5) [x]-kituš-du, [scri]be, (is) [h]er [servant].

Rīmuš

E2.1.2

According to the various manuscripts of the Sumerian King List, Rīmuš, Sargon's son, reigned either 9 or 15 years. Th. Jacobsen (SKL p. 111 n. 246) considered the former number to be original; according to Brinkman's chronology the king's dates would then be 2278–2270. A reconstruction of the events of the reign given by B. Foster (Iraq 47 [1985] p. 28) posits that the king's military campaigns fell into two phases: an early period with battles in Sumer against the cities of Adab, Zabala, KI.AN, Umma, Lagaš, Ur, and the Gulf region with a campaign against Kazallu on his return from the south, and a later period with campaigns in the east against Paraḫšum, Zaḫara, and Elam.

I. Year Names and Events of the Reign

(i) The Adab Campaign

(a) mu adab.KI ḫul-a 'The year Adab was destroyed'. UM 29–13–782: A. Westenholz, OSP 1 no. 76.

Although no royal name appears in year name (a), an attribution to Rīmuš is likely in view of inscription E2.1.2.1, which records the defeat of the cities of Adab and Zabala. This is the only year name that we can attribute to Rīmuš.

II. Notes on a Sargonic Inscription Sometimes Attributed to Rīmuš

A limestone fragment now housed in the Yale collections (YBC 2402) bears an inscription of Sargonic date recording the names and dimensions of a number of large tracts of land in the Lagaš region. B. Foster, who published the piece (Iraq 47 [1985] pp. 15–30), argued for its attribution to Rīmuš, and proposed it was a third piece of a Sargonic victory stele whose other pieces, he proposed, are two stone fragments now housed in the Louvre: AO 2679, edited by F. Thureau-Dangin, SAK pp. 170–71, and AO 2678 (the latter contains pictorial relief only). However, P. Steinkeller has recently argued (in Gelb, Land Tenure p. 89) that the Yale piece is more likely to be a land sale document rather than a royal inscription. In view of this uncertainty, the Yale and Louvre fragments have not been included in this corpus.

1

Inscriptions E2.1.2.1–3 commemorate Rīmuš' campaign against the cities of Sumer. The first inscription, known from two Old Babylonian Sammeltafel copies from Nippur, deals with the defeat of Adab and Zabala.

CATALOGUE

Ex.	Museum number	Tablet lines preserved	Text lines preserved	cpn
1	CBS 13972	rev. xx 32–33, 38–55	1–2, 8–25	c
		rev. xxi 3–12, 15–17	31–40, 43–45	
		rev. xxi 18–19	Colophon	
2	Ni 3200	rev. vi 43–52	1–17	p

COMMENTARY

The line count follows ex. 1. Where this text is broken, the line count follows the pattern established by this exemplar. Gelb and Kienast indicated that lines 53–58 of rev. col. vi were found on the Istanbul tablet. However, collation of the tablet photo reveals that rev. col. vi ends at line 52.

Scholars have debated whether the expression *ana karāśim iśkun* of lines 33–35 means 'to place prisoners in a forced labor camp' (so Foster, Umma p. 50), or 'to slaughter, annihilate' (so Gelb, JNES 32 [1973] pp. 73–74, and Steinkeller, WZKM 77 [1987] pp. 188–89). We have opted for the latter possibility in our translation.

BIBLIOGRAPHY

1914 Poebel, PBS 4/1 pp. 194–95 no. 34 R (ex. 1, frgm. 1, edition)
1914 Poebel, PBS 5 pl. XXI no. 34 (ex. 1, frgm. 1, copy)
1923 Legrain, MJ 14 p. 209 and 217 (ex. 1, frgm. 2, copy, edition)
1926 Legrain, PBS 15 p. 22, pl. XV no. 41 (ex. 1, frgm. 2, copy, edition), and pls. V–VII (ex. 1, frgms. 1–2, photo)
1929 Barton, RISA pp. 120–23 Rimush 5 (ex. 1, edition)
1961 Gelb, MAD 2^{2} p. 196 Rîmuš Late Copies no. 1 D (ex. 1, study)
1963 Hirsch, AfO 20 pp. 11–12, 58–59 Rīmuš b 4 (exs. 1–2, edition)
1990 Gelb and Kienast, Königsinschriften pp. 200–201 and pls. VI–VIII, XVI, XIX–XX Rīmuš C 4 (exs. 1–2, photo, edition); p. 144 (ex. 1, copy)

TEXT

1) *rí-mu-úš*
2) LUGAL
3) KIŠ
4) ⌈*in*⌉ REC 169
5) *adab*.KI
6) *ù*
7) ⌈*zàbala*.KI⌉
8) *iš*$_{11}$-⌈*ar*⌉
9) ⌈*ù*⌉
10) 15,720 LAL 2 GURUŠ.GURUŠ
11) *u-śa-am-qí-it*
12) 14,580 LAL 4 LÚ×ÉŠ

1–3) Rīmuš, king of the world,

4–13) was victorious er Adab and Zabala in battle and struck down 15,718 men. He took 14,576 captives.

12.2 LÚ×[x].

13) ŠU.DU$_8$.⸢A⸣

14) *ù*
15) mes-ki-gal-la
16) ÉNSI
17) *adab*.KI
18) ŠU.DU$_8$.A
19) *ù*
20) lugal-gal-zu
21) ÉNSI
22) *zàbala*.KI
23) ŠU.DU$_8$.A

14–23) Further, he captured Mes-kigala, governor of Adab, and Lugal-galzu, governor of Zabala.

24) URU.KI-⸢*šu-ni*⸣
25) ⸢SAG.GIŠ⸣.[RA]
26) [*ù*]
27) [BÀD-*šu-ni*]
28) [Ì.GUL.GUL]

24–28) He conqu[ered] their two cities [and destroyed the walls of both of them].

29) [*ù*]
30) [*in* URU.KI-*šu-ni*]
31) [N GURUŠ GURUŠ]
32) *u*-⸢*šu-ṣí-am*⸣-*ma*
33) *a-na*
34) *kà-ra-ší-i*[*m*]
35) *iš*-⸢*kùn*⸣

29–35) [Further], he expelled [so many men from their two cities] and annihilated them.

36) *ša* DU[B]
37) *šu$_4$-a*
38) ⸢*u*⸣-*ša-sà*-[*ku-ni*]
39) [^{d}]*en-líl*
40) *ù*
41) [^{d}]UTU
42) [SUḪUŠ-*šu*]
43) [*li-sú-ḫa*]
44) *ù*
45) Š[E.NU]MUN-*šu*
46) *l*[*i*]-*il*-⸢*qù*⸣-*tá*

36–46) As for the one who removes this inscripti[on], may the [gods] Enlil and Šamaš [tear out his foundations] and destroy his [pro]geny.

Colophon
1) mùš ki-gal ki-[ta]
2) egir-ra-⸢ni-šè⸣

Colophon
1-2) .. -socle; bel[ow], behind him.

2

This inscription, known from two Old Babylonian Sammeltafel copies from Nippur, deals with the defeat of the cities of Umma and KI.AN.

CATALOGUE

Ex.	Museum number	Tablet lines preserved	Text lines preserved	cpn
1	CBS 13972	rev. xxi 20–31; 37–60	1–12, 18–41	c
		rev. xxii 4–5	Colophon 1	
		rev. xxii 6–25	Captions 1–8	
		rev. xxii 26–27	Colophon 2	
		rev. xxii 28–33	Caption 9	

Ex.	Museum number	Tablet lines preserved	Text lines preserved	cpn
2	Ni 3200	rev. vii 1–12	14–37	p
		rev. vii 14	Colophon 1	
		rev. vii 15–22	Captions 1–8	
		rev. vii 23	Colophon 2	
		rev. vii 24–26	Caption 9	
		rev. vii 27	Colphon 3	

COMMENTARY

The city name that appears in line 16 is not totally clear on the tablet photo; the traces are compatible with a reading ⌈UB.ME⌉.KI. The name of the ruler of this city appears as ⌈*en*⌉-x; the PN may possibly refer to Ennānum, who is known from other sources to have been a governor of Umma in Sargonic times. See the comments to E2.11.2.2001 in this connection. The line count follows ex. 1 where preserved and the pattern established by this exemplar where it is broken. We have given a reconstruction for lines 14–17 which differs from Gelb and Kienast's edition. This accounts for the divergent line numbers in the catalogue.

For the notation after line 37 in ex. 2: áš-bal-bi šu-bi ⌈na⌉-nam, compare the remarks of Reiner, JNES 33 (1974) p. 222, in which she notes the expression šu-bi dil-àm 'the same' found in commentaries. See also the comments of Foster, Umma p. 48, in which he reads the line in the Rīmuš inscription šu bala-bi šu-bi-ma-nam. The sign before the nam in E2.1.2.2.2 is indistinct in the tablet photo used by the author; it probably was na. In the parallel found in E2.1.2.5.2 the photo reveals a reasonably clear na sign before the nam.

BIBLIOGRAPHY

1914 Poebel, PBS 4/1 pp. 195–96 no. 34 S (ex. 1, frgm. 1, edition)
1914 Poebel, PBS 5 pl. XXI no. 34 (ex. 1, frgm. 1, copy)
1923 Legrain, MJ 14 pp. 209, 217–18 (ex. 1, frgm. 1, copy, edition)
1926 Legrain, PBS 15 pp. 22–23, pl. XV no. 41 (ex. 1, frgm. 2, edition), and pls. V–VII (ex. 1, frgms. 1–2, photo)
1929 Barton, RISA pp. 122–23 Rimuš 6 and 7 (ex. 1, edition)
1961 Gelb, MAD 2^2 Rîmuš Late Copies no. 1 E (ex. 1, study)
1963 Hirsch, AfO 20 pp. 12 and 59–61 Rīmuš b 5+6 (exs. 1–2, edition)
1982 Foster, Umma pp. 48–49 (exs. 1–2, edition)
1990 Gelb and Kienast, Königsinschrfiten pp. 202–205 and pls. VI–X, XVI, XIX–XX Rīmuš C 5 (exs. 1–2, photo, edition); p. 144 (ex. 1, copy)

TEXT

1) *rí-mu-úš*	1–3) Rīmuš, [k]in[g] of the wor[ld],
2) [L]UG[AL]	
3) KI[Š]	
4) *in* ⌈REC 169⌉	4–13) was victor[iou]s over Umma and KI.AN in battle and struck down 8,900 men. He [took] 3,540 captives.
5) ⌈UB.ME⌉.KI	
6) ⌈*ù*⌉	
7) KI.AN.KI	
8) *iš*$_{11}$-[*a*]*r*	
9) *ù*	
10) ⌈8,900⌉ GURUŠ.GURUŠ	
11) [*u*]-*śa*-⌈*am*⌉-*qí*-⌈*it*⌉	
12) ⌈3,540⌉ LÚ×KÁR	
13) [ŠU.DU$_8$.A]	
14) *ù*	14–17) Further, he captured En-x, governor of Umma, and Lugal-KA, governor of KI.AN.
15) ⌈*en*⌉-x	
16) ÉNSI ⌈UB.ME⌉.KI	
17) ŠU.DU$_8$.A	
18) *ù*	
19) lugal-KA	
20) ÉNSI	
21) KI.AN.KI	
22) ŠU.DU$_8$.A	
23) *ù*	23–28) Further, he conquered their two cities and

24) URU.KI-*śu-ni*
25) SAG.GIŠ.RA
26) *ù*
27) BÀD-*śu-ni*
28) Ì.GUL.GUL

destroyed the walls of both of them.

29) *ù*
30) *in* URU.KI-*śu-ni*
31) 3,600 GURUŠ.GURUŠ
32) *u-śu-ṣí-am-ma*
33) *a-na*
34) *kà-ra-śi-im*
35) *iś-kùn*

29–35) Further, he expelled 3,600 men from their two cities and annihilated them.

36) *śa* DUB
37) *śu*$_{4}$*-a*
38) *u-śa-sà-ku-ni*
39) ^{d}*en-líl*
40) ⌜*ù*⌝
41) ^{d}[UTU]
42) [SUḪUŠ-*śu*]
43) [*li-sú-ḫa*]
44) [*ù*]
45) [ŠE.NUMUN-*śu*]
46) [*li-il-qù-tá*]

36–46) As for the one who removes this inscription, may the gods Enlil and [Šamaš tear out his foundations and destroy his progeny].

Colophon 1
1) múš ki-gal ki-ta
2) gùb-bu-na

Colophon 1
1–2) .. -socle, below, on his left.

Caption 1
1) *zi-nu-ba*
2) ŠEŠ
3) ÉNSI

Caption 1
1–3) Zinuba, brother of the governor.

Caption 2
1) *a-ša-ar-mu-pi*$_{5}$
2) SUKKAL-*śu*

Caption 2
1–2) Ašarmupi, his vizier.

Caption 3
1) lugal-gal-z[u](*)
2) ÉNS[I]
3) *zàbala*.K[I]

Caption 3
1–3) Lugal-galz[u], governor of Zabala.

Caption 4
1) ur-^{d}EN.ZU
2) SUKKAL-*śu*

Caption 4
1–2) Ur-Sîn, his vizier.

Caption 5
1) lugal-KA
2) É[N]SI
3) KI.AN.KI

Caption 5
1–3) Lugal-KA, gov[er]nor of KI.AN.

Caption 6
1) giš-šà
2) GAL.SUKKAL-*śu*

Caption 6
1–2) Gišša, his grand vizier.

Caption 7
1) ki-tuš-íd
2) ÉNSI
3) *lagaš*(LA.ŠIR.BUR).KI

Caption 7
1–3) Kituš-id, governor of Lagaš.

Caption 8
1) ad-da
2) GÌR.NITA

Caption 8
1–2) Adda, general.

Colophon 2
1) ki-gal ki-ta
2) šub-ba-meš

Colophon 2
1–2) Socle, below; fallen down.

38–46.2 Omits these lines and inserts after line 37: áš-bal-bi šu-bi ⌜na⌝-nam 'its curse is the same'.
Caption 3 1.1 lugal-g[al-x]. **Caption 3 1**.2 Text: lugal-gal-K[U].

Caption 9
1) *rí-mu-úś*
2) LUGAL
3) KIŠ
4) *šu* ^{d}*en-líl*
5) *ma-ḫi-ra*
6) *la i-dì-śum*$_{6}$

Caption 9
1–6) Rīmuš, king of the world, to whom the god Enlil gave no rival.

Colophon 3
1) mu-sar-ra
2) zà-ga-na

Colophon 3
1–2) Inscription on his shoulder.

3

This inscription, known from two Old Babylonian Sammeltafel copies from Nippur, deals with the defeat of the cities of Ur and Lagaš.

CATALOGUE

Ex.	Museum number	Tablet lines preserved	Text lines preserved	cpn
1	CBS 13972	obv. xix 16–35, 38–60	1–20; 23–45	c
2	Ni 3200	rev. vi 2–26	8–47	p
		rev. vi 27	Colophon	

COMMENTARY

The line count follows ex. 1. In Gelb and Kienast's edition a line was inadvertently omitted between their lines 31 and 32. This fact accounts for the different line count in our catalogue.

BIBLIOGRAPHY

1914 Poebel, PBS 4/1 pp. 192–93 no. 34 P (ex. 1, frgm. 1, edition)
1914 Poebel, PBS 5 pl. XXI no. 34 (ex. 1, frgm. 1, copy)
1923 Legrain, MJ 14 pp. 208 and 216–217 (ex. 1, frgm. 2, copy, edition)
1926 Legrain, PBS 15 pp. 21–22 and pl. XV no. 41 (ex. 1, frgm. 2, copy, edition); pls. V–VII no. 41 (ex. 1, frgms. 1–2, photo)
1929 Barton, RISA pp. 120–21 Rimush 3 (ex. 1, edition)
1961 Gelb, MAD 2^{2} p. 196 Rîmuš Late Copies no. 1 B (study)
1963 Hirsch, AfO 20 pp. 11 and 56–57 Rīmuš b 2 (exs. 1–2, edition)
1990 Gelb and Kienast, Königsinschriften pp. 196–98 and pls. VI–VIII, XVI–XVIII Rīmuš C 2 (exs. 1–2, photo, edition); p. 144 (ex. 1, copy)

TEXT

1) *rí-mu-úś*
2) LUGAL
3) KIŠ
4) *in* REC 169
5) ⸢ŠEŠ⸣.UNU.KI
6) *ù*
7) [*lagaš*(LA.ŠIR.BUR)].KI
8) *iš*$_{11}$-⸢*ar*⸣
9) *ù*

1–3) Rīmuš, king of the world,

4–13) was victorious over Ur and [Lagaš] in battle and struck down 8,040 men. He took 5,460 captives.

10) 8,040 ⌜GURUŠ⌝
11) *u-śa-am-qí-it*
12) ⌜5,460⌝ LÚ×ÉŠ
13) ŠU.DU$_8$.A

14) *ù*
15) KA-kù
16) LUGAL
17) ÚRI.KI
18) ŠU.DU$_8$.A
19) *ù*
20) ki-tuš-íd
21) ÉNSI
22) *lagaš*(LA.ŠIR.BUR).KI
23) ŠU.⌜DU$_8$⌝.A

14–23) Further, he captured KA-ku, king of Ur, and Kituš-id, governor of Lagaš.

24) *ù*
25) [UR]U.KI-*śu-ni*
26) SAG.GIŠ.RA
27) *ù*
28) BÀD-*śu-ni*
29) Ì.GUL.GUL

24–29) Further, he conquered their two cities and destroyed the walls of both of them.

30) *ù*
31) *in* URU.KI-*śu-ni*
32) 5,985 GURUŠ
33) *u-śu-ṣí-am-ma*
34) *a-na*
35) *kà-ra-śi-i*[*m*]
36) *íś-kùn*

30–36) Further, he expelled 5,985 men from their two cities and annihilated them.

37) *śa* DUB
38) *śu$_4$-a*
39) *u-śa-sà-ku-ni*
40) ^{d}*en-líl*
41) *ù*
42) ^{d}UTU
43) SUḪUŠ-*śu*
44) *li-sú-ḫa*
45) *ù*
46) ŠE.NUMUN-*śu*
47) *li-il-qù-tá*

37–47) As for the one who removes this inscription, may the gods Enlil and Šamaš tear out his foundations and destroy his progeny.

Colophon
1) mu-sar gùb-ni-šè a-ab-sar

Colophon
1) Inscription written on his left.

4

This inscription, known from two Old Babylonian Sammeltafel copies from Nippur, describes the capture of the king of Ur and the governor of Kazallu.

12.2 LÚ×KÁR.

CATALOGUE

Ex.	Museum number	Tablet lines preserved	Text lines preserved	cpn
1	CBS 13972	rev. xvi 51–53, 55–58, 61	1–3, 5–8, 11	c
		rev. xvii 4–51	18–66	
		rev. xviii 5–23	79–97	
		rev. xviii 24–25	Colophon 1	
		rev. xviii 26–52	98–124	
		rev. xviii 53	Colophon 2	
		rev. xviii 54–56	Caption 1	
		rev. xviii 57–59	Caption 2	
		rev. xix 5–7	Caption 1′	
		rev. xix 8–10	Caption 2′	
		rev. xix 11–13	Caption 3′	
		rev. xix 14–15	Colophon 3	
2	Ni 3200	rev. iv 15–49	1–36	p
		rev. v 3–29	57–97	
		rev. v 30–43	98–121	

COMMENTARY

The line count in general follows ex. 1; lines 9–15 follow ex. 2, which alone is preserved at this point. A colophon appears after line 97; the text then continues with a second curse formula. Here we have numbered the lines of the colophon separately, with the line count resuming with the second curse formula. In line 50 of Gelb and Kienast's edition, the supposed KALAM sign is, in fact, the bottom part of the signs of line 49. This accounts for the different line numbering in this edition. The translation of line 85 follows the suggestion of M. Krebernik in ZA 81 (1991) p. 141.

BIBLIOGRAPHY

1914 Poebel, PBS 4/1 pp. 189–92 no. 34 N and O (ex. 1, frgm. 1, edition)

1914 Poebel, PBS 5 pl. XXI no. 34 (ex. 1, frgm. 1, copy)

1923 Legrain, MJ 14 pp. 209 and 215–216 (ex. 1, frgm. 2, copy, edition)

1926 Legrain, PBS 15 p. 20 and pl. XV no. 41 (ex. 1, frgm. 2, copy, edition); pls. V–VII (ex. 1, frgms. 1–2, photo)

1929 Barton, RISA pp. 118–21 Rimush 1 and 2 (ex. 1, edition)

1961 Gelb, MAD 2^{2} p. 196 Rîmuš Late Copies no. 1 A (ex. 1, study)

1963 Hirsch, AfO 20 pp. 11 and 52–56 Rīmuš b 1 (exs. 1–2, edition)

1990 Gelb and Kienast, Königsinschriften pp. 191–96 and pls. VI–VIII, XVII–XVIII Rīmuš C 1 (exs. 1–2, photo, edition); p. 144 (ex. 1, copy)

TEXT

1) *rí-mu-úš*
2) LUGAL
3) KIŠ
4) *sú-ra-ma*
5) *śar-ru-tám*
6) ^{d}*en-líl*
7) *i-dì-nu-*⸢*śum*$_6$⸣

1–7) Rīmuš, king of the world — the god Enlil did indeed grant kingship to him.

8) REC 169
9) *šu-me-rí-im*
10) *ad ma-dì-íś*
11) 3 *iš*$_{11}$*-ar*
12) 11,322 ⸢GURUŠ.GURUŠ⸣
13) ⸢*u-śa*⸣*-am-q*[*í-it*]
14) [N LÚ×KÁR]
15) ⸢ŠU.DU$_8$.A⸣

8–15) He was fully three (times) victorious over Sumer in battle. He struck do[wn] 11,322 men. He took [N captives].

16) ⸢*ù*⸣
17) KA-k[ù]

16–23) Further, he captured KA-k[u], king of Ur, and his governors.

14.2 The restoration follows the pattern established by ex. 2 (LU×KÁR) since it is the only available source for lines 9–17.

18) LUGAL
19) ÚRI.KI
20) ŠU.DU$_{8}$.A
21) *ù*
22) ÉNSI.ÉNSI-*śu*
23) ŠU.DU$_{8}$.A
24) *ù*
25) *á-ra-ab-śu-nu*
26) *a-dì-ma*
27) *ti-a-am-tim*
28) *śa-pil$_{5}$-tim*
29) *il-qù-ut*

24–29) Further, he took away their tribute (from) as far as the Lower Sea.

30) *ù*
31) 14,100 GURUŠ.GURUŠ
32) *in* URU.KI.URU.KI
33) *šu-me-rí-im*
34) *u-śu-ṣí-am-ma*
35) *a-na*
36) *kà-ra-śi-im*
37) *íś-kùn*

30–37) Further, he expelled 14,100 men from the cities of Sumer and annihilated them.

38) *ù*
39) URU.KI.URU.KI-*śu-nu*
40) SAG.GIŠ.RA
41) *ù*
42) BÀD-BÀD-*śu-nu*
43) Ì.GUL.GUL

38–43) Further, he conquered their cities and destroyed their walls.

44) *u-lum*
45) *in tù-a-rí-śu*
46) *ka-za-lu*.KI
47) *na-ki-ir-ma*
48) SAG.GIŠ.RA
49) ⌈*in qar-bí*⌉
50) *ka-za-lu*.KI
51) 12,052 GURUŠ.GURUŠ
52) *u-śa-am-qi$_{4}$-it*
53) 5,862
54) LÚ×ÉŠ
55) ŠU.⌈DU$_{8}$⌉.A

44–55) Thereupon, on his return, Kazallu revolted. He conquered it and [wi]thin Kazallu (itself) struck down 12,052 men. He took 5,862 captives.

56) ⌈*ù*⌉
57) *a-ša-ré-ed*
58) ÉNSI
59) *ka-za-lu*.KI
60) ŠU.DU$_{8}$.A
61) *ù*
62) BÀD-*śu*
63) Ì.GUL.GUL

56–63) Further, he captured Ašarēd, governor of Kazallu and destroyed its (Kazallu's) wall.

64) ŠU+NÍGIN 54,016 GURUŠ.GURUŠ
65) *a-dì mi-qi$_{4}$-tim*
66) *a-dì* ⌈LÚ×ÉŠ⌉
67) *a-dì* GURUŠ.GURUŠ
68) *šu-ut a-na*
69) *kà-ra-śi-im*
70) *íś-k*[*ùn-ni*]
71) KASKAL.KI
72) *šu-zu*-x

64–72) In total 54,016 men (including) those struck down, captives and men whom he annihil[ated]... the campaign ...

50 Line 50 of Gelb and Kienast's edtion: KA[LAM.MA.KI], is not supported by collation of the tablet.
62.2 BÀD.BÀD-*śu*.
66.2 LÚ×KÁR.

73) ^{d}UTU
74) *ù*
75) *ìl-a-ba$_{4}$*
76) *ú-ma*
77) *la sú-ra-tim*
78) *lu kí-ni-íś-ma*

73–78) By the gods Šamaš and Ilaba I swear that (these) are not falsehoods, (but) are indeed true.

79) *ì-nu*
80) REC 169 *śu$_{4}$-a*
81) DÙL-*śu$_{4}$*
82) *ib-ni-ma*
83) *a-na*
84) ^{d}*en-líl*
85) *śa-lí-mi-śu*
86) A.MU.RU

79–86) At the time of this battle he fashioned a statue of himself and dedicated it to the god Enlil *for his well-being.*

87) *ša* DUB
88) *śu$_{4}$-a*
89) *u-śa-sà-ku-ni*
90) ^{d}*en-líl*
91) *ù*
92) ^{d}UTU
93) SUḪUŠ-*śu*
94) *li-sú-ḫa*
95) *ù*
96) ŠE.NUMUN-*śu*
97) *li-il-qù-tá*

87–97) As for the one who removes this inscription, may the gods Enlil and Šamaš tear out his foundations and destroy his progeny.

Colophon 1
1) ki-gal an-ta igi-ni-šè
2) ⌜a-ab-sar⌝

Colophon 1
1–2) Written on the socle, above, in front of him.

Curse Formula
98) *ma-na-ma*
99) MU
100) *rí-mu-úś*
101) LUGAL
102) KIŠ
103) *u-śa-sà-ku-ni*
104) *al* DÙL
105) *rí-mu-úś*
106) MU-*śu*
107) *i-śa-kà-nu-ma*
108) DÙL-*mi-me*
109) *i-*[*qá-bi*]-⌜*ù*⌝

Curse Formula
98–109) As for anyone who removes the name of Rīmuš, king of the world, and puts his own name on the statue of Rīmuš and s[ay]s, '(This is) my statue',

110) ^{d}*en-líl*
111) *be-al*
112) DÙL *śu$_{4}$-a*
113) *ù*
114) ^{d}UTU
115) SUḪUŠ-*śu*
116) *li-sú-ḫa*
117) *ù*
118) ŠE.NUMUN-*śu*
119) *li-il-qù-tá*
120) ⌜NITA⌝
121) *a i-dì-na-śum$_{6}$*
122) [*m*]*aḫ-rí-íś*
123) [*ì*]-*lí-śu*
124) [*e*] DU

110–124) may the god Enlil, owner of this statue, and the god Šamaš, tear out his foundations and destroy his progeny. May they not grant a male (heir) to him. May he [not] walk [be]fore his (personal) [g]od.

94.2 *li-su-ḫa*.
Colophon 1 1–2.2 Omits.
116.2 *li-su-ḫa*.

Colophon 2		Colophon 2
1)	lu[gal(?) ...]-ni-šè	1) ... at his ...
Caption 1		Caption 1
1)	ᵈ[...]	1–3) The god ..., who go[es] befo[re him].
2)	*á-lí-[ik]*	
3)	*maḫ-[rí-śu]*	
Caption 2		Caption 2
1)	*a-ša-[ré-ed]*	1–3) Aša[rēd], go[vernor] of Ka[zallu].
2)	É[NSI]	Lacuna
3)	⌜*ka*⌝-[*zal-lu*.KI]	
Lacuna		
Caption 1′		Caption 1′
1)	*e[n-...]*	1–3) E[n-...], go[vernor] of Umma.
2)	É[NSI]	
3)	UB.ME.⌜KI⌝	
Caption 2′		Caption 2′
1)	ᵈ*u-um*	1–3) The god Ūm(um), who goes before him.
2)	*á-lí-ik*	
3)	⌜*maḫ*⌝-*rí-śu*	
Caption 3′		Caption 3′
1)	KA-kù	1–3) KA-ku, king of Ur.
2)	LUGAL	
3)	ÚRI.KI	
Colophon 3		Colophon 3
1)	ki-gal-ba egir	1–2) On its socle, behind Lu-Damu.
2)	lú-ᵈda-mu	

5

This inscription, known from two Old Babylonian Sammelftafel copies from Nippur, deals with the defeat of the city of Kazallu.

CATALOGUE

Ex.	Museum number	Tablet lines preserved	Text lines preserved	cpn
1	CBS 13972	rev. xx 5–29	7–31	c
		rev. xx 30–31	Colophon	
2	Ni 3200	rev. vi 27–39	1–22	p
		rev. vi 41–42	Colophon	

COMMENTARY

The line count follows ex. 1.

BIBLIOGRAPHY

1914 Poebel, PBS 4/1 pp. 193–94 no. 34 Q (ex. 1, frgm. 1, edition)
1914 Poebel, PBS 5 pl. XXI no. 34 (ex. 1, frgm. 1, copy)
1929 Barton, RISA pp. 120–21 Rimush 5 (ex. 1, edition)
1961 Gelb, MAD 2² p. 196 Rîmuš Late Copies no. 1 C (ex. 1, study)
1963 Hirsch, AfO 20 pp. 11 and 57–58 Rīmuš b 3 (exs. 1–2, edition)

1990 Gelb and Kienast, Königsinschriften pp. 198–99 and pls. VI–VIII, XVI, XIX–XX Rīmuš C 3 (exs. 1–2, photo, edition); p. 144 (ex. 1, copy)

TEXT

1) *rí-mu-úš*
2) LUGAL
3) KIŠ
4) *ì-nu*
5) *kà-za-lu*.KI
6) SAG.⌜GIŠ⌝.RA-*ni*
7) [*in*] ⌜REC 169⌝
8) *ka-za-lu*.KI
9) 12,052 GURUŠ.GURUŠ
10) *u-śa-am-qí-it*
11) 5,864 LÚ×ÉŠ
12) ŠU.DU$_8$.A
13) *ù*
14) *a-ša-ré-ed*
15) ÉNSI
16) *kà-za-lu*.KI
17) ŠU.DU$_8$.A
18) *ù*
19) BÀD-*śu*
20) Ì.GUL.GUL
21) *ša* DUB
22) *śu*$_4$-*a*
23) *u-śa-sà*-⌜*ku*⌝-*ni*
24) ^d^*en-líl*
25) ⌜*ù*⌝
26) ^d^⌜UTU⌝
27) SUḪUŠ-*śu*
28) ⌜*li-sú*⌝-*ḫa*
29) ⌜*ù*⌝
30) ŠE.NUMUN-⌜*śu*⌝
31) *li-i*[*l*]-⌜*qù-tá*⌝

Colophon
1) mùš ki-gal ki-ta
2) á-zi-da-na

1–3) Rīmuš, king of the world,

4–12) when he conquered Kazallu, [in] the battle with Kazallu he struck down 12,052 men. He took 5,864 captives.

13–17) Further, he captured Ašarēd, governor of Kazallu

18–20) and destroyed its (Kazallu's) wall.

21–31) As for the one who removes this inscription, may the gods Enlil and Šamaš tear out foundations and destroy his progeny.

Colophon
1–2) ... –socle, below, on his right side.

6

After crushing the rebellion of the Sumerian cities of the south, Rīmuš was able to direct his attention to the east, and he campaigned extensively in Elam and Paraḫšum. The war against Elam is recorded in several Rīmuš inscriptions. The longest version of the campaign is known from two Old Babylonian Sammeltafel copies from Nippur.

8.2 *kà-za-lu*KI.
11.2 LÚ×KÁR.
23–31.2 Omits these lines and inserts the remark: áš-bal-bi šu-bi na-nam 'Its curse is the same as the other one'.

CATALOGUE

Ex.	Museum number	Tablet lines preserved	Text lines preserved	cpn
1	CBS 13972	rev. xxii 36–57	1–22	c
		rev. xxiii 9–39	28–57	
		rev. xxiii 46–64	64–85	
		rev. xxiv 9–17	95–103	
		rev. xxiv 18–19	Colophon 1	
		rev. xxiv 20–39	104–23	
		rev. xxiv 43–60	127–44	
		rev. xxiv 61	Colophon 2	
		rev. xxiv 62	Caption 1	
2	Ni 3200	rev. vii 28–50	1–37	p
		rev. viii 2–32	78–144	
		rev. viii 33	Colophon 2	
		rev. viii 34–36	Caption 1	
		rev. viii 37	Colophon 3	

COMMENTARY

The line count follows ex. 1, except lines 24–28, which follow ex. 2. A colophon follows line 105; its lines are numbered separately and the line count resumes with the second curse formula. The edition follows the suggestion of M. Krebernik (ZA 81 [1991] p. 141) to read *in a-ša-ar* URU in Gelb and Kienast's Rīmuš C 6, lines 51–52, as one line. The Sumerian equivalent of the Akkadian expression *lā surrātum lū kīnišma* '(these) are not falsehoods, (but) are indeed true' of lines 82–83 is now known: lul ba-ra-na ḫé-ge-en. For the equation, see the discussion of G. Haayer in Studies Molin pp. 121–25.

BIBLIOGRAPHY

1914 Poebel, PBS 4/1 pp. 197–200 no. 34 U (ex. 1, frgm. 1, edition)

1914 Poebel, PBS 5 pl. XXI no. 34 (ex. 1, frgm. 1, copy)

1923 Legrain, MJ 14 pp. 209 and 218–19 (ex. 1, frgm. 1, copy, edition)

1926 Legrain, PBS 15 pp. 23–25 and pl. XV no. 41 (ex. 1, frgm. 2, copy, edition); pls. V–VI (ex. 1, frgms. 1–2, photo)

1961 Gelb, MAD 2^2 p. 196 Rîmuš Late Copies no. 1 G (ex. 1, study)

1963 Hirsch, AfO 20 pp. 12, 61–65 Rīmuš b 7–8 (exs. 1–2, edition)

1990 Gelb and Kienast, Königsinschriften pp. 205–11 and pls. VI, IX–X, XVI, XIX–XX Rīmuš C 6 (exs. 1–2, photo, edition); p. 144 (ex. 1, copy)

TEXT

1) *rí-mu-úš*
2) LUGAL
3) KIŠ
4) *in* REC 169
5) *a-ba-al-ga-maš*
6) ⌜LUGAL⌝
7) *pá-rạ-aḫ-šum*.KI
8) *iš*$_{11}$*-ar*

1–8) Rīmuš, king of the world, was victorious in battle over Abalgamaš, king of Paraḫšum.

9) *ù*
10) *za-ḫa-ra*.KI
11) *ù*
12) NIM.KI
13) *in qab*$_{x}$(DA)*-lí*
14) *pá-ra-aḫ-šum*.KI
15) *a-na*
16) REC 169
17) *ip-ḫu-ru-ni-im-ma*
18) *iš*$_{11}$*-ar*
19) *ù*
20) 16,212 GURUŠ.GURUŠ

9–23) Zaḫara and Elam had assembled in Paraḫšum for battle, but he (Rīmuš) was victorious (over them) and struck down 16,212 men (and) took 4,216 captives.

21) *u-śa-am-qi*$_4$*-it*
22) 4,216 LÚ×ÉŠ
23) ŠU.DU$_8$.⸢A⸣
24) ⸢*ù*⸣ *e-maḫ*(?)*-si-n*[*i*]
25) LUGAL NIM.KI Š[U.DU$_8$.A]
26) *ù kà-la-ma*
27) x x x NIM.KI ŠU.DU$_8$.A

24–27) Further, he ca[ptured] *Emaḫsin*[*i*], king of Elam, and all the ... of Elam.

28) *ù si-id-ga-ù*
29) GÌR.NÍTA
30) *pá-ra-aḫ-śum*.KI
31) ŠU.DU$_8$.A

28–31) Further, he captured Sidga'u, general of Paraḫšum,

32) *ù*
33) *śar*-GA-PI
34) GÌR.NÍTA
35) *za-ḫa-ra*.KI
36) ŠU.DU$_8$.A

32–36) and Šar-GA-PI, general of Zaḫara,

37) *in ba-rí-ti*
38) *a-wa-an*.KI
39) *ù*
40) *śu-śi-im*.KI
41) *in* ÍD
42) *qáb-lí-tim*

37–42) in between (the cities of) Awan and Susa, by the 'Middle River'.

43) *ù*
44) *bí-ru-tám*
45) *in a-ša-ar* URU
46) *al-*⸢*śu*⸣*-nu*
47) *íś-*⸢*pu*⸣*-uk*

43–47) Further, he heaped up ov[er th]em a burial mound *in the area of the city*.

48) *ù*
49) URU.KI.URU.KI
50) NIM.KI
51) SAG.⸢GIŠ⸣.RA
52) *ù*
53) BÀD.BÀD-*śu-nu*
54) Ì.GUL.GUL
55) *ù*
56) SUḪUŠ
57) ⸢*pá-ra-aḫ-śum*.KI⸣
58) [*in* KALAM]
59) [NIM.KI]
60) [*i-sú-uḫ-ma*]

48–60) Further, he conquered the cities of Elam, destroyed their walls, and tore out the foundations of Paraḫšum [from the land of Elam].

61) [*rí-mu-úś*]
62) [LUGAL]
63) [KIŠ]
64) NIM.[KI]
65) *i-be-al*
66) ^{d}*en-líl*
67) *u-kál-lim*

61–67) [(Thereby) Rīmuš, king of the world,] ruled Elam. The god Enlil showed him (the way).

68) *in śa-an-tim*
69) *śa-lí-íś-tim*
70) *ša-ti*
71) ^{d}*en-líl*
72) *śar-ru*$_x$(URU×A)*-tám*
73) *i-dì-nu-śum*$_6$
74) ŠU+NÍGIN 9,624
75) GURUŠ.GURUŠ
76) *a-dì mi-qi*$_4$*-tim*

68–77) In the third year of Enlil's having granted kingship to him (there was) a total of 9,624 men (whom he defeated) including those struck down (and) captives.

21.2 *u-śa-am-qí-it*.
22.2 Sign inscribed in ⸢LÚ⸣ cannot be determined.

77) *a-dì* LU×ÉŠ

78) ^{d}UTU
79) *ù*
80) *ìl-a-ba*$_{4}$
81) *ú-má*
82) *la sú-ra-tum*$_{8}$
83) *lu kí-ni-íś-ma*

78–83) By the gods Šamaš and Ilaba I swear that (these) are not falsehoods, (but) are indeed true.

84) *ì-nu*
85) REC 169
86) *śu*$_{4}$*-a*
87) DÙL-*śu*
88) *i*[*b-ni*]*-ma*
89) *a-na*
90) ^{d}*en-líl*
91) *śa-lí-mi-śu*
92) A.MU.RU

84–92) At the time of this battle he fa[shion]ed a statue of himself and dedicated it to the god Enlil *for his well-being*.

93) *śa* DUB
94) *śu*$_{4}$*-a*
95) *u-śa-sà-ku-ni*
96) ^{d}*en-líl*
97) *ù*
98) ^{d}UTU
99) SUḪUŠ-*śu*
100) *li-sú-ḫa*
101) *ù*
102) ŠE.NUMUN-*śu*
103) *li-il-qù-tá*

93–103) As for the one who removes this inscription, may the gods Enlil and Šamaš tear out foundations and destroy his progeny.

Colophon 1
1) ki-gal ⸢á-gùb-ni⸣-šè
2) ⸢a-ab⸣-sar

Colophon 1
1–2) Socle, written towards his left side.

Curse formula
104) *ma-na-ma*
105) MU
106) *rí-mu-úś*
107) LUGAL
108) KIŠ
109) *u-śa-sà-ku-ma*
110) *al* DÙL
111) *rí-mu-úś*
112) MU-*śu*
113) *i-śa-kà-nu-ma*
114) DÙL-*mi-me*
115) *i-qá-bì-ù*

Curse formula
104–115) As for anyone who removes the name of Rīmuš, king of the world, puts his own name on the statue of Rīmuš and says '(This is) my statue',

116) ^{d}*en-líl*
117) *be-al*
118) DÙL *śu*$_{4}$*-a*
119) *ù*
120) ^{d}UTU
121) SUḪUŠ-*śu*
122) *li-sú-ḫa*
123) *ù*
124) ŠE.NUMUN-*śu*
125) *li-il-qù-tá*
126) NITA
127) *a i-dì-na-śum*$_{6}$
128) *maḫ-rí-íś*
129) *ì-lí-śu*

116–130) may the god Enlil, owner of this statue, and the god Šamaš tear out his foundations and destroy his progeny. May they not grant a male (heir) to him. May he not walk before his (personal) god.

Colophon 1 1–2.2 Omits.

130) *e* DU
131) 30 MA.NA
132) KÙ.GI
133) 3,600 MA.NA
134) URUDU
135) 300 IR_{11} GÉME
136) *ì-nu*
137) NIM.KI
138) *ù*
139) *pá-ra-*⌈*aḫ*⌉*-śum*.KI
140) SAG.GIŠ.RA-*ni*
141) *u-ru-a-am-ma*
142) *a-na*
143) ᵈ*en-líl*
144) A.MU.RU

131–144) When he conquered Elam and Paraḫšum, he took away 30 minas of gold, 3,600 minas of copper and 300 male and female slaves and dedicated (them) to the god Enlil.

Colophon 2
1) [...-b]i-šè [...s]ar

1) [Wr]itten at [i]ts ... (Var.: inscription on its base).

Caption 1
1) *rí-mu-úś*
2) LUGAL
3) KIŠ
4) *šu* ᵈ*en-líl*
5) *ma-ḫi-ra*
6) ⌈*la*⌉ *i-dì-śum*$_6$

Caption 1
1–6) Rīmuš, king of the world, to whom the god Enlil gave no rival.

Colophon 3
1) mu-sar-ra
2) zà-ga-na

Colophon 3
1–2) Inscription on his shoulder.

7

A shorter version of the campaign against Elam is known from four Old Babylonian tablet copies.

CATALOGUE

Ex.	Museum number	Provenance	Tablet lines preserved	Text lines preserved	cpn
1	CBS 13972	Nippur	rev. xxv 41–61	1–21	p
			rev. xxvi 11–27	37–53	
			rev. xxvi 28	Colophon	
2	Ni 3200	Nippur	rev. ix 2–29	4–53	p
			rev. ix 30	Colophon	
3	CBS 2344 + N3539 + CBS 14547	Nippur	rev. v′ 1′–13′	1–13	c
			rev. v′ 18–20′	18–20	
			rev. v′ 25′–29′	25–29	
4	AO 5476	Unknown	obv. i 1–15	1–15	c
			obv. ii 1–15	16–30	
			rev. i 1–15	31–45	
			rev. ii 1–8	46–53	

COMMENTARY

Ex. 4 was collated by B. Foster. For the type of bowl designated by the term šen-za-ḫum of the colophon, see AHw pp. 1132–33 sub *šaḫu(m)* and CAD Š pp. 105–106 sub *šāḫu*. For another royal inscription incised on a vessel, see E2.1.4.3 v 9, 24, and 28. For the expression found in lines 41–42, see the commentary to E2.1.2.6.

BIBLIOGRAPHY

1911 Thureau-Dangin, RA 8 pp. 135–38 (ex. 4, copy, edition)
1914 Poebel, PBS 4/1 pp. 201–203 no. 34 X (ex. 1, frgm. 1, edition) and p. 215 no. 37 (ex. 3, frgm. 1, edition)
1914 Poebel, PBS 5 pl. XXI no. 34 (ex. 1, frgm. 1, copy) and pl. XXIII no. 36 rev. (ex. 3, frgm. 1, copy)
1923 Legrain, MJ 14 pp. 209 and 220 (ex. 1, frgm. 2, copy, edition)
1926 Legrain, PBS 15 p. 25 and pl. XV no. 41 (ex. 1, frgm. 2, copy, edition); pls. V–VII (ex. 1, frgms. 1–2, photo)
1929 Barton, RISA pp. 124–27 Rimush 12 (ex. 3, edition)
1961 Gelb, MAD 2^2 p. 196 Rîmuš Late Copies no. I (exs. 1, 3–4, study)
1963 Hirsch, AfO 20 pp. 12–13, 66–68 Rīmuš b 11 (exs. 1–2, edition)
1980 Michalowski, JCS 32 pp. 237–38 and 243 (ex. 3, edition; ex. 3, frgm. 2, copy)
1990 Gelb and Kienast, Königsinschriften pp. 213–15 and pls. VI, IX–X, XVI, XIX–XX Rīmuš C 8 (exs. 1–2, photo, edition); p. 144 (ex. 1, copy)

TEXT

1) *rí-m[u-ú]ś*
2) LUGAL
3) K[I]Š
4) *in* REC 169
5) *a-ba-al-ga-maš*
6) LUGAL
7) *pá-ra-aḫ-śum*.KI
8) *iš*$_{11}$*-ar*

1–8) Rīm[u]š, king of the world, was victorious in battle over Abalgamaš, king of Paraḫšum,

9) *ù*
10) *si-id-ga-ù*
11) GÌR.NITA-*śu*
12) ŠU.DU$_8$.A
13) *in ba-rí-ti*
14) *a-wa-an*.KI
15) *ù*
16) *śu-śi-im*.KI
17) *in* ÍD
18) *qab*$_x$(DA)*-lí-tim*

9–18) and captured Sidgaʾu, his general, in between (the cities of) Awan and Susa by the 'Middle River'.

19) *ù*
20) *bí-ru-tám*
21) *in a-ša-ar* URU
22) *al-śu*
23) *íś-pu-uk*

19–23) Further, he heaped up over him a burial mound *in the area of the city*.

24) *ù*
25) SUḪUŠ
26) *pá-ra-aḫ-śum*.KI
27) *in* KALAM
28) NIM.KI
29) *i-sú-uḫ-ma*

24–29) Further, he tore out the foundations of Paraḫšum from the land of Elam and

30) *rí-mu-úś*
31) LUGAL
32) KIŠ
33) NIM.KI
34) *i-be-al*
35) ^{d}*en-líl*
36) *u-kál-lim*

30–36) (thereby) Rīmuš, king of the world, ruled Elam. The god Enlil instructed (him).

37) ^{d}UTU
38) *ù*
39) *ìl-a-ba*$_4$
40) *ú-má*
41) *la sú-ra-tum*$_8$
42) *lu kí-ni-íś-ma*
43) *ša* DUB
44) *sú*$_4$*-a*
45) *u-sá-sà-ku-ni*
46) ^{d}*en-líl*
47) *ù*
48) ^{d}UTU
49) SUḪUŠ-*śu*
50) *li-sú-ḫa*
51) *ù*
52) ŠE.NUMUN-*śu*
53) *li-il-qù-tá*
Colophon
1) mu-sar-ra
2) ŠEN.*za-ḫum*

37–42) By the gods Šamaš and Ilaba I swear that (these) are not falsehoods, (but) are indeed true.

43–53) As for the one who removes this inscription, may the gods Enlil and Šamaš tear out his foundations and destroy his progeny.

Colophon
1–2) Inscription on a *šaḫum* bowl.

8

An inscription giving a variant version of the Elamite campaign is known from an Ur III tablet copy from Nippur.

COMMENTARY

The tablet bears the museum number HS 193 and measures 10.4×4.6×1.7 cm. The text is known from two slightly divergent published editions, one by J. Oelsner and the other by B. Kienast from notes of I. Gelb. According to Oelsner, the beginning lines of the tablet are completely preserved; thus it appears that the first three lines of the original inscription were omitted by the ancient scribe. The line count here follows Oelsner's edition. For the expression of line 31, see the commentary to E2.1.2.6. The colophon is found on lines 37–41 and the left edge. The inscription was not collated.

BIBLIOGRAPHY

1969 Oelsner, WZJ 18 p. 52 no. 7 (study)
1989 Oelsner in Studies Sjöberg pp. 403–404 (edition)
1990 Gelb and Kienast, Königsinschriften pp. 217–19 Rīmuš C 10 (edition)

TEXT

<*rí-mu-úś*>
<LUGAL KIŠ>
<in REC 169>
1) *a-ba-al-ga-maš*
2) LUGAL *pá-ra-aḫ-śum*.KI
3) *iš*$_{11}$*-ar*

<Rīmuš, king of the world, in battle>

1–3) was victorious over Abalgamaš, king of Paraḫšum.

E2.1.2.7 Colophon 1–2.4 Omits.

4) *ù za-ḫa-ar*.KI
5) *ù* NIM.KI
6) ⸢*ù*⸣ [*g*]*u-pi-in*.KI
7) ⸢*ù*⸣ [*me*]-*luḫ-ḫa*.KI
8) *i*[*n qá*]*b-lí*
9) *pá*-[*ra-aḫ*]-*śum*.KI
10) ⸢*a*⸣-[*na*] ⸢REC 169⸣ *ip-ḫu-ru-ni-im-ma*
11) x [...] UD
12) *i*[*n ba-rí-t*]*i* [*a-w*]*a-an*.KI
13) *ù* [*śu-śi-im*].KI
14) *in* Í[D *qáb-l*]*í-tim*
15) *s*[*i-id-ga*]-⸢*ù*⸣ GÌR.NÍTA
16) [*pá-ra-aḫ-śum*].KI
17) [...] x NIM.KI
18) ⸢*ik*⸣-*mi*
19) [*ù bí-ru*]-*tám*
20) *i*[*n a-ša-a*]*r* URU
21) *al*-[*śu-nu í*]*ś-pu-uk*
22) ⸢*ù*⸣ [S]UḪUŠ *pá-ra-aḫ-śum*.KI
23) *in* KALAM(*) NIM.KI
24) *i-sú-uḫ-ma*
25) *rí-mu-úś*
26) LUGAL KIŠ
27) NIM.KI *i-be*-[*al*]
28) ^{d}*en-líl* ⸢*u-kál-lim*⸣
29) ^{d}[UTU]
30) *ù* [*il-a-ba*$_4$]
31) *ú-m*[*á la sú-ra-tum*$_8$ *lu k*]*í*-[*ni-íś-ma*]
32) *š*[*a* DUB *śu*$_4$-*a*]
33) *u-s*[*á-sà-ku-ni*]
34) [^{d}*en-líl ù* ^{d}UT]U
35) SUḪU[Š-*śu li-s*]*ú-ḫa*
36) *ù* [ŠE.NUMUN-*śu li-il-q*]*ù-tá*

Caption
1) ESI
2) DU$_8$.ŠI *ù* NA$_4$.NA$_4$
3) *ša al*!-*qé-ù*
4) SAG NAM.RA.AK
5) *pá-ra-aḫ-śum*.KI

Colophon
1) GIŠ.erin-ta sar-ra é-gu-la

4–11) Zaḫar, Elam, [G]upin, and [Me]luḫḫa assembled in Pa[raḫ]šum for battle, but ...

12–18) he, (Rīmuš) captured S[idgaʾu], general of [Paraḫšum] (and) [the king(?) of] Elam i[n betwe]en (the cities of) [Aw]an and [Susa], by the '[Mid]dle Ri[ver]'.

19–24) [Further], he [h]eaped up over [them] a [burial mo]und *i*[*n*] *the* [*are*]*a of the city*. In addition, he tore out the [fo]undation of Paraḫšum from the land of Elam and

25–28) (thereby) Rīmuš, king of the world, rule[d] Elam. The god Enlil showed (him the way).

29–31) By the gods [Šamaš] and [Ilaba] I swe[ar] that (these) are not falsehoods, (but) are indeed [t]ru[e].
32–36) As for the o[ne who] re[moves this inscription, may the gods Enlil and Šam]aš [te]ar out [his] founda[tion] and [dest]roy [his progeny].

Caption
1–5) Diorite, *dušû*–stone and (various) stones which I took ... as booty of Paraḫšum.

Colophon
1) Inscribed on(?) a cedar board(?). The Egula temple.

9

A short inscription known from two Old Babylonian Sammelftafel copies praises Rīmuš as the king to whom the god Enlil gave all the lands. In the caption to this text, Rīmuš appears with the title 'conqueror of Elam and Paraḫšum'.

E2.1.2.8 23 Text: URU+LIŠ.
E2.1.2.8 26 Reading without KI follows Kienast.
E2.1.2.8 Caption 1 Reading follows Kienast.

CATALOGUE

Ex.	Museum number	Tablet lines preserved	Text lines preserved	cpn
1	CBS 13972	rev. xxv 9–31	6–28	c
		rev. xxv 32	Colophon 1	
		rev.xxv 33–39	Caption 1	
		rev. xxv 40	Colophon 2	
2	Ni 3200	rev. viii 38	1–3	p

BIBLIOGRAPHY

1914 Poebel, PBS 4/1 pp. 200–201 no. 34 V and W (ex. 1, edition)
1914 Poebel, PBS 5 pl. XXI no. 34 (ex. 1, copy)
1929 Barton, RISA pp. 124–25 Rīmush 11 (second part) and 12 (first part) (ex. 1, edition)
1961 Gelb, MAD 2^2 p. 196 Rîmuš Late Copies no. 1 G (end) and H (ex. 1, study)
1963 Hirsch, AfO 20 pp. 12 and 65–66 Rīmuš b 9 and b 10 (exs. 1–2, edition)
1971 Sollberger and Kupper, IRSA IIA2e (exs. 1–2, translation)
1990 Gelb and Kienast, Königsinschriften pp. 211–12 and pls. VI, IX–X, XVI, XIX–XX Rīmuš C 7 (exs. 1–2, photo, edition); p. 144 (ex. 1, copy)

TEXT

1) *[rí]-⸢mu-úš⸣*
2) ⸢LUGAL⸣
3) KIŠ
4) [^{d}*en-líl*]
5) [KALAM.MA.KI]
6) *⸢kà-la-ma⸣*
7) *i-dì-śum*$_6$
8) *ti-a-am-tám*
9) *a-lí-tám*
10) *ù*
11) *⸢śa⸣-pil*$_5$*-tám*
12) *ù*
13) ŚA.DÚ-*e*
14) *kà-la-sú-nu-ma*
15) *a-na*
16) ^{d}*en-líl*
17) *u-kà-al*

1–17) [Rī]muš, king of the world: [the god Enlil] gave to him all [the land]. He holds the Upper Sea and the Lower (Sea) and all the mountain (lands) for the god Enlil.

18) *ša* DUB
19) *śu*$_4$*-a*
20) *u-śa-sà-ku-ni*
21) ^{d}*en-líl*
22) *ù*
23) ^{d}UTU
24) SUḪUŠ-*śu*
25) *li-sú-⸢ḫa⸣*
26) *ù*
27) ŠE.⸢NUMUN⸣-*śu*
28) *li-il-qù-tá*

18–28) As for the one who removes this inscription, may the gods Enlil and Šamaš tear out his foundations and destroy his progeny.

Colophon 1

1) mu-sar-ra [k]i-gal-ba

Colophon 1

1) Inscription on its base.

Caption

1) *rí-mu-⸢úš⸣*
2) LUGAL
3) KIŠ
4) SAG.GIŠ.R[A]
5) N[IM.KI]

Caption

1–7) Rīm[u]š, king of the world, conqueror of E[lam and] Par[aḫšum].

6) [*ù*]
7) ⌈*pá*⌉-*r*[*a-aḫ-śum*.KI]
Colophon 2
1) ⌈zà⌉-g[a-na a-ab-sar]

Colophon 2
1) [Written on his] should[er].

10

A mace head from Nippur is incised with a dedicatory inscription of Rīmuš.

COMMENTARY

The mace head consists of the join of two fragments, CBS 8888 (the lower half) and CBS 8888a (the upper half). It is made of reddish numulite limestone and has a maximum diameter of 16.7 cm. The inscription was collated.

The mace head was found in excavations in area III south-east of the ziqqurrat. Hilprecht published only the lower half of the mace head; the discovery of the upper half confirms his attribution of the piece to Rīmuš. Barton, while mentioning only the piece copied by Hilprecht and erroneously calling it a vase, did give the complete text of the inscription. We can only guess if he knew of the second piece or simply restored the text from parallels.

BIBLIOGRAPHY

1893 Hilprecht, BE I/1 no. 6 (photo, copy [bottom half only])
1907 Thureau-Dangin, SAK pp. 160–61 Uru-mu-uš b (edition [bottom half only])
1929 Barton, RISA pp. 128–29 Rimush 15 (edition)
1963 Hirsch, AfO 20 p. 10 Rīmuš a 5 (edition [bottom half only])
1990 Gelb and Kienast, Königsinschriften pp. 69–70 Rīmuš 4 (edition [bottom half only])

TEXT

1) *a-na*
2) ᵈ*en-líl*
3) *rí-mu-úś*
4) LUGAL
5) KIŠ
6) A.MU.RU

1–2) To the god Enlil,

3–6) Rīmuš, king of the world, dedicated (this mace).

11

A large number of sub-conical bowl or cylindrical vase fragments found in excavations at Nippur bear an inscription indicating they were booty of Elam and Paraḫšum dedicated by Rīmuš to the god Enlil.

CATALOGUE

Ex.	Museum number	Excavation number	Object	Dimensions (cm)	BE 1 pl. III	Gelb and Kienast	Lines preserved	cpn
1	CBS 8832	—	White marble vase fragm.	6.7×9.5	—	—	1–3	c
2	CBS 8840	—	White marble vase fragm.	3.7×3.8	—	—	1–3	c
3	CBS 8842+8891 +8892a+8892b	—	—	—	4+5	B	1, 4–12	n
4	CBS 8843+8890	—	—	9.3×15.4	8	E	1–7	c
5	CBS 8844	—	—	4.0×1.5	—	—	11–13	c
6	CBS 8846	—	—	—	—	—	9–10	c
7	CBS 8847	—	Banded calcite vase frgm.	7.5×13.5	—	—	1–3	c
8	CBS 8848	—	White marble bowl frgm.	6.2×6.5	—	—	1–3	c
9	CBS 8849	—	White marble vase frgm.	4.7×6.5	—	—	1–2	c
10	CBS 8852	—	White marble convex bowl frgm.	15×15.5	—	—	6–13	c
11	CBS 8853	—	—	13.5×11.7	12	I	11–13	c
12	CBS 8854	—	Banded calcite vase frgm.	11.9×11.4	11	H	8–13	c
13	CBS 8855	—	White marble vase frgm.	11.7×10	—	—	12–13	c
14	CBS 8856+8867	—	Banded calcite vase frgm.	13×7	—	—	1–4, 7–9	c
15	CBS 8857	—	White marble vase frgm.	9.8×6.3	—	—	10–13	c
16	CBS 8858	—	Banded calcite vase frgm.	9.2×4.1	10	G	8–13	c
17	CBS 8859	—	White marble vase frgm.	4.9×7.3	9	F	6–9	c
18	CBS 8860	—	White marble vase frgm.	5.5×6.2	—	J	6–8	c
19	CBS 8861	—	White marble vase frgm.	7.2×5.7	—	—	12–13	c
20	CBS 8862	—	White marble vase frgm.	5.4×6.8	—	—	9–11	c
21	CBS 8863	—	White marble vase frgm.	4.8×4.7	—	—	10–11	c
22	CBS 8864	—	Banded calcite vase frgm.	4.2×5.2	—	—	2–4	c
23	CBS 8865	—	Banded calcite vase frgm.	10.5×12.5	7	D	1–15	c
24	CBS 8866	—	White marble vase frgm.	8×7	6	C	1–5	c
25	CBS 8868	—	White marble vase frgm.	5.8×4.5	—	—	2–3	c
26	CBS 8869	—	Vase frgm.	7.8×6.2	—	—	13	c
27	CBS 8871	—	Bowl frgm.	5.2×6.7	—	—	12–13	c
28	CBS 8889	—	Banded calcite vase frgm.	8.7×13.8	—	—	1–4	c
29	CBS 8892	—	White marble vase frgm.	18.2×9.4	—	—	4–12	c
30	CBS 8894	—	Vase frgm.	5.8×5.9	—	—	1	c
31	CBS 8895	—	White marble vase frgm.	4.7×5	—	—	1	c
32	CBS 9280	—	Vase frgm.	3.3×2.4	—	—	7–9	c
33	CBS 9288	—	Vase frgm.	4×3	—	—	1–3	c
34	CBS 9993	—	Vase frgm.	6.2×5	—	—	10–13	c
35	CBS 9996	—	Vase frgm.	—	—	—	8–10	c
36	CBS 10113	—	Vase frgm.	9.8× 11.1	—	—	7–8	c
37	CBS 10114	—	Vase frgm.	4.8×3.7	—	—	9–11	c
38	CBS 10121	—	White marble vase frgm.	4×4.6	—	—	7–9	c
39	CBS 10131	—	Vase frgm.	4×2.8	—	—	1–2	c
40	CBS 10135	—	White marble vase frgm.	3×10.8	—	—	1	c
41	CBS 10139	—	Vase frgm.	2.4×5	—	—	1	c
42	CBS 13149	—	Vase frgm.	4.5×4.2	—	—	1–3	c
43	CBS 14548	—	Cylindrical vase	—	—	—	—	n
44	EŞ1261 (CBS 9793 cast)	—	White marble cylindrical vase	20.6×5.6	—	A	1–8	p
45	HS 1957	—	Vase frgm.	—	—	K	9–13	n
46	—	2N-T445	Vase(?)	—	—	L	—	n
47	IM 70319	9 N 150	White stone bowl frgm.	5.0×4.6×0.9	—	M	11–13	n
48	A 32678	9 N 33	Limestone bowl frgm.	6.8×8×1.4–1.7	—	N	3–5	n

COMMENTARY

When findspots for exs. 1-43 are given in the CBS catalogue, the pieces are said to have come from area III at Nippur on the SE side of the ziqqurrat. Ex. 47 came from the surface and ex. 48 from area I, dump.

BIBLIOGRAPHY

1893 Hilprecht, BE 1/1 no. 5 (composite copy), pp. 20–21 (edition), p. 47 (exs. 3–4, 11–12, 17–18, 23–24, study) and pl. III (exs. 3–4, 11–12, 16–17, 23–24, photo)

1896 Hilprecht, BE 1/2 pl. XX no. 62 (ex. 44, photo)

1900 Radau, EBH p. 128 (edition)

1907 Thureau-Dangin, SAK pp. 162–63 Vase C (edition)

1929 Barton, RISA pp. 128–29 Rimush 14 A (edition)

1947 Poebel, AS 14 p. 33 (edition)

1961 Gelb, MAD 2^2 p. 195 Rîmuš Original Inscriptions no. 1a (study) and no. 1e (ex. 46, study)

1963 Hirsch, AfO 20 p. 10 Rīmuš no. a 1 (study)

1968 Goetze, JAOS 88 p. 54 (ex. 46, study)

1969 Oelsner, WZJ 18 p. 52 no. 6 (ex. 45, study)

1969 Buccellati and Biggs, AS 17 nos. 43–44 (exs. 47–48, copy)

1971 Sollberger and Kupper, IRSA IIA2a (translation)

1989 Potts, Iraq 51 p. 149 Inscription A 1 (exs. 3–4, 11–12, 16–18, 23–24, 43–44, 46–48, translation, study)

1990 Gelb and Kienast, Königsinschriften pp. 6–67 Rīmuš 1 (exs. 3–4, 11–12, 16–18, 23–24, 44–48, edition)

TEXT

1) *a-na*
2) ^{d}*en-líl*
3) *rí-mu-ús*
4) LUGAL
5) KIŠ
6) *ì-nu*
7) NIM.KI
8) ù
9) *pá-ra-aḫ-śum*.KI
10) SAG.GIŠ.RA-*ni*
11) *in* NAM.RA.AK
12) NIM.KI
13) A.MU.RU

1–2) To the god Enlil,

3–5) Rīmuš, king of the world,

6–10) when he conquered Elam and Paraḫšum,

11–13) dedicated (this vessel) from the booty of Elam.

12

A vase inscription from Nippur gives a variant version of the preceding text.

COMMENTARY

The diorite vase bearing this inscription is a join of two fragments, CBS 8842+9321; together they measure 9.3×7.35×0.8 cm. CBS 8842 alone was published as BE 1/1 no. 10; the bibliography items refer to it. The pieces were found in excavations in area III at Nippur, on the SE side of the ziqqurrat. The inscription was collated.

BIBLIOGRAPHY

1893 Hilprecht, BE 1/1 no. 10 (copy)
1929 Barton, RISA pp. 128–29 Rimush 17 (edition)
1961 Gelb, MAD 2^2 p. 196 Rîmuš Original Inscriptions no. 5 (study)
1963 Hirsch, AfO 20 p. 10 Rīmuš a. 4 (study)
1989 Potts, Iraq 51 p. 149 Inscription B (study)
1990 Gelb and Kienast, Königsinschriften p. 69 Rīmuš 3 (edition)

TEXT

1) [*a-na*]
2) [^{d}*en-líl*]
3) [*rí-mu-ús*]
4) [LUGAL]
5) [KIŠ]
6) [*ì-nu*]
7) [NIM.KI]
8) [ù]
9) [*pá-ra-aḫ*]-⸢*śum*⸣.K[I]
10) SAG.GIŠ.RA-*ni*
11) A.MU.RU

1–2) [To the god Enlil],

3–5) [Rīmuš, king of the world],

6–11) [when] he conquered [Elam and Paraḫ]šum, dedicated (this vase).

13

An inscription incised on a mace head and three vase fragments found in excavations at Ur indicates that these objects were dedicated by Rīmuš to the god Sîn as booty of Elam.

CATALOGUE

Ex.	Museum number	Excavation number	Ur provenance	Object	Dimensions (cm)	Lines preserved	cpn
1	CBS 14933	U 206	Under the Kurigalzu floor of the E-nun-maḫ	White calcite mace head frgm.	Height: 19 Dia.: 21	1–13	c
2	IM 3578	U 7807	Under the Nebuchadnezzar pavement of the E-nun-maḫ	White calcite bowl frgm.	—	—	n
3	CBS 16518	U 6333	EH Sq. N8	Calcite vase frgm.	21×23	9–10	n
4	BM 116436 (1923-11-10, 21)	U 263	As ex. 1	White veined yellow calcite vase frgm.	9.9×6	7–10	c

COMMENTARY

Ex. 3 could not be located in the University Museum collections; it is entered in the score from the published photo (AJ 6 pl. LVIII). Ex. 4 was collated by G. Frame; too little of it remains to be sure that it is a duplicate of this text.

BIBLIOGRAPHY

1923 Woolley, AJ 3 p. 323 and pl. XXXII no. 1 (ex. 1, provenance, photo)
1926 Woolley, AJ 6 pl. LVIII (ex. 3, photo)
1928 Gadd, UET 1 no. 10 (ex. 1, photo, edition), no. 22 (ex. 3, copy), and no. 273 (ex. 4, copy)
1955 Woolley UE 4 pp. 167–68, 171, 174 (exs. 1–4, provenance, study)
1960 Sollberger, Iraq 22 pp. 75–76 nos. 94–96 and 99 (exs. 1–4, study)
1961 Gelb MAD 2^{2} p. 195 Rîmuš Original Inscriptions nos. 2a–c (exs. 1, 3–4, study)
1963 Hirsch, AfO 20 p. 10 Rīmuš a 2 (exs. 1, 3–4, study)
1989 Potts, Iraq 51 p. 149 Inscription A 2 (exs. 2–4, study) and p. 153 figs. 1–2 (exs. 2, 4, copy)
1990 Gelb and Kienast, Königsinschriften pp. 67–69 Rīmuš 2 (exs. 1–4, edition)

TEXT

1) *a-na*	1–2) To the god Sîn,
2) ^{d}EN.ZU	
3) *rí-mu-úś*	3–5) Rīmuš, king of the world,
4) LUGAL	
5) KIŠ	
6) *ì-nu*	6–10) when he conquered Elam and Paraḫšum,
7) NIM.KI	
8) *ù*	
9) *pá-ra-aḫ-śum*.KI	
10) SAG.GIŠ.RA-*ni*	
11) *in* NAM.RA.AK	11–13) dedicated (this object) from the booty of Elam.
12) NIM.KI	
13) A.MU.RU	

14

Two bowl fragments found in excavations at Sippar bear an inscription indicating they were dedicated by Rīmuš as booty of Elam.

CATALOGUE

Ex.	Museum number	Registration number	Object	Dimensions (cm)	Lines preserved	cpn
1	BM 42367	81-7-1, 127	Banded calcite vase frgm.	9×3.7	9–11	c
2	BM 91020 (= BM 12162)	82-7-14, 1014	Banded calcite vase frgm.	7.2×4.8	3–7	c

COMMENTARY

No divine name is preserved on either of these fragments. The restoration of the DN as ^{d}UTU is a guess, based on the fact that the pieces come from Sippar. Another possibility for the DN is Bēlat-Aia, the spouse of Šamaš, who appears in E2.1.3.4. Exs. 1 and 2 were collated by G. Frame. The curvature of the two fragments excludes the possibility that they belonged to the same bowl.

BIBLIOGRAPHY

1899 King, CT 7 pl. 4 12162 (ex. 2, copy)
1922 BM Guide 3 p. 83 no. 7 (ex. 2, study)
1929 Barton, RISA pp. 128–29 Rimush 20 (ex.2, edition)
1961 Gelb, MAD 2^2 p. 195 Rîmuš Original Inscriptions no. 1 b (ex. 2, study)
1963 Hirsch, AfO 20 p. 10 Rīmuš a.1 (ex.2, study)
1980 Walker and Collon in de Meyer (ed.), Tell ed-Dēr 3 p. 98 no. 23 (ex. 1, study) and p. 99 no. 29 (ex. 2, study)
1989 Potts, Iraq 51 p. 149 Inscription A.5 (exs. 1–2, study) and p. 154 fig. 4 (ex. 1, copy)
1990 Gelb and Kienast, Königsinschriften pp. 67–69 Rīmuš 2 Texts E and F (exs. 1–2, edition)

TEXT

1) [*a-na*] 2) [^{d}UTU]	1–2) [To the god Šamaš],
3) *r*[*í-mu-úš*] 4) LUG[AL] 5) KI[Š]	3–5) R[īmuš], ki[ng] of the worl[d],
6) *ì*-[*nu*] 7) N[IM.KI] 8) [*ù*] 9) ⸢*pá-ra-aḫ-šum*.KI⸣ 10) SAG.GIŠ.RA-*ni*	6–10) w[hen] he conquered E[lam and] [Pa]ra[ḫ]šum,
11) *in* ⸢NAM.RA⸣.[AK] 12) [NIM.KI] 13) [A.MU.RU]	11–13) [dedicated (this vase)] from the boo[ty of Elam].

15

Two stone bowl fragments found in excavations at Khafajah bear a dedicatory inscription of Rīmuš.

CATALOGUE

Ex.	Excavation number	Khafajah provenance	Object	Lines preserved	cpn
1	Kh II 94	K 45-2, top layer	Alabaster bowl frgm.	1–6	p
2	Kh II 381	K 45, Oval III	Alabaster bowl frgm.	1	p

COMMENTARY

Because both fragments were found not far from the Sîn temple at Khafajah, Jacobsen suggested a restoration of the divine name in line 2 as Sîn.

BIBLIOGRAPHY

1933 Frankfort, OIC 16 pp. 73–74 and fig. 47 (ex. 1, photo, study)
1940 Jacobsen, Temple Oval pp. 147 and 149–50 nos. 8–9 (exs. 1–2, copy, edition)
1961 Gelb, MAD 2^2 p. 195 Rîmuš Original Inscriptions no. 1 c (ex. 1, study)
1963 Hirsch, AfO 20 p. 10 Rīmuš a 2 (exs. 1–2, study)
1989 Potts, Iraq 51 p. 149 Table 1 Inscription A 3 (ex. 1, translation, study)
1990 Gelb and Kienast, Königsinschriften pp. 68–69 Rīmuš 2 Texts G and H (exs. 1–2, edition)

TEXT

1) *a-n*[*a*]
2) ^{d}E[N.ZU]
3) *r*[*í-mu-uš́*]
4) LU[GAL]
5) K[IŠ]
6) ⸢*ì*⸣-[*nu*]
7) [NIM.KI]
8) *ù*
9) [*pá-ra-aḫ-šum*.KI]
10) [SAG.GIŠ.RA-*ni*]
11) [*in* NAM.RA.AK]
12) [NIM.KI]
13) [A.MU.RU]

1–2) T[o] the god S[în],

3–4) Rī[muš], ki[ng of] the wo[rld],

6–10) wh[en he conquered Elam and Paraḫšum],

11–13) [dedicated (this bowl) from the booty of Elam].

16

A vase fragment found in excavations at Tell Brāk bears an inscription indicating it was dedicated by Rīmuš as Elamite booty.

COMMENTARY

The vase fragment, made of banded calcite (according to T. Potts, Iraq 51 [1989] p. 149), was found in room 22 of 'Naram-Sin's palace', excavation number F 1152; its present whereabouts are unknown. The inscription was collated from the published photo.

While the restoration of the royal name of line 3 as Rīmuš is reasonably sure, the name of the divine recipient of line 2 is uncertain. J.-M. Durand, according to D. Charpin in Eichler, Tall al-Hamīdīya 2 p. 68 and n. 7, and Catagnoti and Bonechi in NABU 1992 no. 65, have argued that the ancient name of Tell Brāk was Nagar. Oates (Iraq 47 [1985] pp. 169–72) argues for an identification with ancient Ta'idu.

BIBLIOGRAPHY

1947 Mallowan, Iraq 9 pp. 27, 66, 197, and pl. L no. 4 (photo, translation, study)

1961 Gelb, MAD 2[2] p. 195 Rîmuš Original Inscriptions no. 1 d (study)

1963 Hirsch, AfO 20 p. 10 n. 93 (transliteration, study)

1989 Potts, Iraq 51 p. 149 Inscription A 4 (study)

1990 Gelb and Kienast, Königsinschriften pp. 8–69 Rīmuš 2 Text I (edition)

TEXT

1) *[a-na]* 2) [DN]	1–2) [To the god/goddess ...],
3) *[rí-mu-úš]* 4) [LUGAL] 5) [KIŠ]	3–5) [Rīmuš, king of the world],
6) *[ì-nu]* 7) N[IM.KI] 8) ⌜*ù*⌝ 9) *pá-ra-[aḫ-šum*.KI] 10) SAG.[GIŠ.RA-*ni*]	6–10) [when] he con[quered] E[lam] and Para[ḫšum],
11) *i[n* NAM.RA.AK] 12) N[IM.KI] 13) [A.MU.RU]	11–13) [dedicated (this vase)] fr[om the booty of] E[lam].

17

An inscription of Rīmuš incised on three vases and one mace head refers to the king as 'conqueror of Elam and Paraḫšum'.

CATALOGUE

Ex.	Museum number	Excavation number	Provenance	Object	Dimensions (cm)	Lines preserved	cpn
1	BM 116455 (1923–11–10, 41 [+] 1923–11–10, 41b)	U 231	Ur, under the Kurigalzu floor of the E-nun-maḫ	Black steatite bowl	10.4×8.4	2–7	c
2	IM 1098	U 3291	Ur, from the late temple of Ningal	Diorite bowl	—	—	n
3	UM 31–43–251	U 16532	Diqdiqqah	Frgm. of calcite mace head	9.5×7	1–6	c
4	VA 5298	—	(Purchased from J. E. Gejou)	Dark green steatite vase frgm.	12.5×16.5×1.3	1–7	n

COMMENTARY

As noted by various commentators, the decorative motifs found on exs. 1 and 4 are typical of the steatite/chlorite vessels from Iran. The bibliography includes items that give photos or drawings of the bowls in which the inscription may not be visible or legible. Ex. 1 was collated by G. Frame.

BIBLIOGRAPHY

1920 Meissner, BuA 1 p. 261 and pl. fig. 125 (ex. 4, photo, study)
1923 Woolley, AJ 3 p. 331 and pl. XXXIII (ex. 1, drawing, study)
1928 Gadd, UET 1 no. 9 (ex. 1, copy, edition)
1929 Barton, RISA pp. 358–59 Rimush 3 (ex. 1, edition)
1935 Woolley, Sumerian Art p. 96 and fig. 53 a (ex. 1, photo)
1936 van Buren, AfO 11 pp. 2 and 5 fig. 1 (ex. 4, photo, study)
1939 van Buren, AnOr 18 p. 11 and pl. III fig. 7 (ex. 4, photo, study)
1956 Woolley, UE 4 pp. 168, 171, 185 (exs. 1–3, study), and pl. 36 (ex. 1, photo, drawing)
1960 Sollberger, Iraq 22 pp. 75–76 nos. 97–98 and 100 (exs. 1–3, study)
1961 Gelb, MAD 2^2 p. 196 Rîmuš Original Inscriptions no. 6 (ex. 1, study) and pp. 216–17 notes to p. 196 (exs. 2–3, study)
1963 Hirsch, AfO 20 p. 10 Rīmuš a 3 (ex. 1, study)
1965 Sollberger, UET 8 p. 25 no. 6 (exs. 2–3, study)
1980 E. and H. Klengel, Rocznik Orientalistyczny 41/2 pp. 45–51 (ex. 4, photo, copy, edition)
1983 Klengel and Marzahn, Sumer, pp. 11–13 and 28 (ex. 4, translation, study)
1989 Potts, Iraq 51 p. 149 Inscription C (exs. 1–2, 4, translation, study)
1990 Gelb and Kienast, Königsinschriften p. 70 Rīmuš 5 (exs. 1–4, edition)

TEXT

1) *rí-mu-úš*
2) LUGAL
3) KIŠ
4) SAG.GIŠ.RA
5) NIM.KI
6) *ù*
7) *pá-ra-aḫ-šum*.KI

1–7) Rīmuš, king of the world, conqueror of Elam and Paraḫšum.

18

The remaining inscriptions of Rīmuš (E2.1.2.18-20) make no mention of either the southern or eastern campaigns of the king. The first of these inscriptions, known in a bilingual version found on Old Babylonian Sammeltafel copies, deals with the fashioning of a statue of the king.

CATALOGUE

Sumerian version

Ex.	Museum number	Provenance	Tablet lines preserved	Text lines preserved	cpn
1	CBS 13972	Nippur	Rev. xxviii 8–27	8–25	c
			Rev. xxviii 30 +Rev. xxvii 31	Colophon 1	
2	CBS 2344+N3539+CBS 14547	Nippur	Rev. vii′ 1′–2′	26–27	c
			Rev. vii′ 3′–5′	Colophon 2	
3	AO 5477	Unknown	Obv. i 1′–9′	7–15	c
			Rev. ii 1–10	16–25	

Akkadian Version

Ex.	Museum number	Provenance	Tablet lines preserved	Text lines preserved	cpn
1	CBS 13972	Nippur	Rev. xxvii 8–30	8–30	c
2	CBS 2344+N3539+CBS 15457	Nippur	Rev. vi′ 1′	30	c
			Rev. vi′ 2′–4′	Colophon 2	
3	AO 5477	Unknown	Obv. ii 1′–11′	5–16	c
			Rev. i 1–3	17–30	

COMMENTARY

Exs. 1–2 were collated by the author, ex. 3 by B. Foster. The line numbering and translation follow the Akkadian version of ex. 3. Variants in the translation of the Sumerian are noted in the apparatus.

For the interpretation of NI.UL of line 16 of the Sumerian, see the comments of Krecher, Orientalia NS 54 (1985) p. 171 n. 76. He proposes that the phrase is to be read mu$_5$-ru$_5$ and translated 'middle'. For the reading of line 17 of the Akkadian as DA-*iš* with a translation, following CAD, 'toward, to the side of', see the comments of Krebernik, ZA 71 (1991) p. 137. For the reading of the verb ŠID in line 19 of the Sumerian, see M.-C. Ludwig, Untersuchungen zu den Hymnen des Išme-Dagan von Isin p. 180. The verb of line 25 of the Sumerian: ḫé-PAD.DU-ne has been read, following the generally accepted practice, hé-bu$_x$-re$_6$-ne and taken as a form of the verb bu, 'to tear out'.

For the vessel of Colophon 1, see the commentary to E2.1.2.7.

BIBLIOGRAPHY

1911 Thureau-Dangin, RA 8 pp. 138–42 (ex. 3, copy, edition)

1914 Poebel, PBS 4/1 pp. 203–204 no. 34 Y (ex. 1, edition)

1914 Poebel, PBS 5 pl. XXI no. 34 (ex. 1, copy)

1929 Barton, RISA pp. 126–29 Rimush 13 (edition)

1961 Gelb, MAD 2^2 p. 196 Rîmuš Late Copies no. 1 I (exs. 1–3, study)

1963 Hirsch, AfO 20 pp. 13 and 68–69 Rīmuš b 12 (edition)

1980 Michalowski, JCS 32 pp. 238–39 (ex. 2, study) and p. 243 (ex. 2, frgm. b, copy)

1990 Gelb and Kienast, Königsinschriften pp. 215–17 Rīmuš C 9 (exs. 1–3, edition); p. 114 and pls. VI, IX–X (ex. 1, photo, copy)

TEXT

Sumerian

1) [*rí-mu-úš*]
2) [lugal]-
3) [KIŠ]
4) [u$_4$-ul-lí-a-ta]
5) [^{d}en-líl-ra]
6) [lú na-me]
7) [al]an-a[n-na]
8) nu-ta-dím
9) *rí-mu-úš*
10) lugal-
11) KIŠ
12) alan-na-ni an-na-kam
13) ì-dím
14) igi-^{d}en-líl-lá-šè
15) ì-gub
16) NI.UL-
17) dingir-re-ne-ka
18) me-te-ni
19) ì-ŠID

Akkadian

1) [*rí-mu-úš*]
2) [LUGAL]
3) [KIŠ]
4) [*íš-tum da-ar*]
5) [*a-na* ^{d}*en-líl*]-*l*[*e*](?)
6) [*m*]*a-na-ma*
7) DÙL KÙ.AN
8) *la ib-ni*
9) *rí-mu-úš*
10) LUGAL
11) KIŠ
12) DÙL-*šu*
13) *ša* KÙ.AN
14) *ib-ni-ma*
15) IGI-*me* ^{d}*en-líl*
16) *i-za-az*
17) DA-*íš ì-li*
18) MU-*šu*
19) *u-ša-mi-id*

1–3) [Rīmuš, king of the world:]

4–8) [from ancient times n]o one had fashioned a statue (made) of meteoric iron for the god Enlil.

9–16) (But) Rīmuš, king of the world, fashioned a statue of himself (made) of meteoric iron Enlil and it (now) stands before the god Enlil.

17–19) He placed his name at the side of the gods.

---

7 Sum.: tin.
12 Sum.: tin.
16–19 Sum. 'he recited his ... in the midst of the gods'.

Sumerian	Akkadian	English
20) lú	20) *ša* DUB	20–30) As for the one who removes this inscription, may gods Enlil and Šamaš tear out his foundations and destroy his progeny.
21) im-sar-ra-e	21) *šu*$_4$*-a*	
22) ab-ḫa-lam-me-a	22) *u-ša-sà-ku-ni*	
23) ^{d}en-líl ^{d}utu-bi	23) ^{d}*en-líl*	
	24) *ù*	
	25) ^{d}UTU	
24) suḫuš-sa-ni	26) SUḪUŠ-*šu*	
25) ḫé-bu$_x$(PAD)-re$_6$-ne	27) *li-sú-ḫa*	
	28) *ù*	
26) [numun-na-n]i	29) ŠE.NUMUN-*šu*	
27) ḫé-ri-ri-ge-ne	30) *li-il-qù-tá*	
Colophon 1		Colophon 1
1) ⸢mu-sar-ra URUDU⸣.šen-*za-*⸢*ḫum*⸣		1) Inscription on a *šaḫum* vessel.
Colophon 2	Colophon 2	Colophon 2
1) mu-sar-ra	1) mu-sar-ra	1–3) Inscription — it is a ... of Rīmuš.
2) ti-x-bi-ni	2) ti-x-bi-ni	
3) *rí-mu-úš*-kam	3) *rí-mu-úš*-kam	

19

A stone slab found at Nippur bears a Sargonic inscription that mentions Rīmuš.

COMMENTARY

The limestone slab measures 12.8× 7.35× 5.55 cm and bears the museum number CBS 8841. It was found in excavations at Nippur in area III, inside the great SE temple wall. The inscription mentions the establishment of offerings by(?) Rīmuš for Šamaš and probably for Lugal-marda. It may be that a Sargonic monument similar to this piece served as inspiration for the much later 'Cruciform Monument' of Man-ištūšu. The reading of the DN of iii′ 2′ line follows the GN mar/már-da.KI of pre-Sargonic and Sargonic sources; see Edzard, Rép. Géogr. 1 pp. 114–15. The inscription was collated.

BIBLIOGRAPHY

1893 Hilprecht, BE 1/1 no. 13 (copy) and p. 48 (study)
1907 Thureau-Dangin, SAK pp. 162–163 6d (edition)
1929 Barton, RISA pp. 128–29 Rimush 18 (edition)
1961 Gelb, MAD 2^{2} p. 196 Rîmuš Original Inscriptions no. 7 (study)
1963 Hirsch, AfO 20 p. 11 Rīmuš a 7 (study)
1990 Gelb and Kienast, Königsinschriften pp. 72–73 Rīmuš 7 (edition)

TEXT

Akkadian	English
Col. i′	
Lacuna	Lacuna
1′) [...]	i′ 1′–5′) ... [wh]en [Rīm]uš,
2′) [...]	Lacuna
3′) [...]	
4′) [*i*]*n* UD	
5′) [*rí-m*]*u-úš*	
Lacuna	

E2.1.2.18 22 Sum.: destroys.

Col. ii′

Lacuna

1′) [...]
2′) [...] NINDA
3′) [...K]AŠ GÚ.NIGIN
4′) *a-na*
5′) SÁ.DU$_{11}$.GA
6′) U$_4$ 1
7′) *a-na* BANŠU[R]
8′) ^{d}UTU
9′) KI.G[AR]

Lacuna

Col. iii′

Lacuna

1′) [...]
2′) ^{d}*lu*[*gal*]-*már*-[*da*]
3′) KAS+K[AS ...]
4′) *i*[*n* ...]
5′) *i*[*n* ...]

Lacuna

Lacuna

ii′ 1′–9′) [so much] bread, [so much b]eer, in total, he establi[shed] as regular offerings for one day for the tabl[e] of the god Šamaš.

Lacuna

Lacuna

iii′ 1′–5′) ... the god Lu[gal]-mar[da], ...

Lacuna

20

The standard three-line inscription of Rīmuš giving his title 'king of the world' is found on a variety of objects: vases, bowls, a mace head, a disk, and even a sea shell, from different sites.

CATALOGUE

Ex.	Museum number	Excavation number	Provenance	Object	Dimensions (cm)	Gelb and Kienast	Lines preserved	cpn
1	AO 184	—	Girsu	Banded calcite (?) sub-conical bowl frgm.	13.5 high 11.5 wide	A	1–3	p
2	AO 3282	—	Girsu	Small jar of banded calcite(?)	15 high	B	1–3	p
3	AO 189	—	Girsu	'Onyx' bowl frgm.	—	C	1–3	p
4	—	Kh II 104	Khafajah, J 45:2 in Oval III	'Calcite' vase frgm.	—	D	1–3	p
5	CBS 8839	—	Nippur	'White marble' bowl (?) frgm.	8.5×5.9	F	1–3	c
6	CBS 8870	—	Nippur	Cylindrical vase frgm.	21×16.4	E	1–3	c
7	CBS 8872	—	Nippur	White marble vase frgm.	7×15		2–3	c
8	CBS 8873	—	Nippur	White marble vase frgm.	10.5×13		1–3	c
9	CBS 8874	—	Nippur	Banded calcite(?) vase frgm.	9 wide		3	c
10	CBS 8875	—	Nippur	Banded calcite(?) vase frgm.	8.7×7.2		1–3	c
11	CBS 8876	—	Nippur	White marble bowl frgm.	4.8×6.5		3	c
12	CBS 8877	—	Nippur	Vase frgm.	4.2×5.4		3	c
13	CBS 8878	—	Nippur	White marble bowl frgm.	3.2×4.2		1–2	c
14	CBS 8881	—	Nippur	Banded calcite vase frgm.	4.5×7		2–3	c
15	CBS 8882+8901	—	Nippur	White marble bowl frgm.	9×5.7		1–3	c
16	CBS 8883	—	Nippur	Reddish stone vase frgm.	8.5×1.8		1–3	c
17	CBS 8884	—	Nippur	Reddish stone vase frgm.	6.5×5.5		1–2	c
18	CBS 8886	—	Nippur	Calcite vase frgm.	7.3×8.3		1–3	c
19	CBS 8887	—	Nippur	Reddish stone vase frgm.	7×8.5		2–3	c
20	CBS 8898	—	Nippur	Vase frgm.	4.2×3.6		1–2	c
21	CBS 8899+8770	—	Nippur	Convex bowl frgm.	9.8×.7.8		1–3	c
22	CBS 8900	—	Nippur	Vase frgm.	8.5×5		1–3	c
23	CBS 9285	—	Nippur	White marble bowl frgm.	4×2.3		1–3	c
24	CBS 9286	—	Nippur	White marble bowl frgm.	1.6×5.4		2	c
25	CBS 9287	—	Nippur	White marble bowl frgm.	2×4.2		2–3	c
26	CBS 9289	—	Nippur	White marble bowl frgm.	2×5.3		2–3	c

Ex.	Museum number	Excavation number	Provenance	Object	Dimensions (cm)	Gelb and Kienast	Lines preserved	cpn
27	CBS 9299	—	Nippur	Vase frgm.	16×4.6		1–3	c
28	CBS 10102	—	Nippur	Banded calcite vase frgm.	5.2×8.2		3	c
29	CBS 10110	—	Nippur	Banded calcite cylindrical vase frgm.	10.3×13.8		1–3	c
30	CBS 11916	—	Nippur	Cylindrical vase frgm.	19×14.5		1–3	c
31	—	—	Nippur	'White marble' vase frgm.	13.5 high 15 dia.	G	1–3	n
32	—	5N–T567	Nippur	Calcite vase frgm.	4.6×2.8×1.7	H	1–3	c
33	A 31306 (Chicago)	6N–T1033a	Nippur	Calcite vase frgm.	4.6×2.8×1.7	I	1–2	c
34	IM 70541	9N–77	Nippur, area I dump	Frgm. of 'white stone' bowl	2.5×1.6	J	1	n
35	BM 91019 (= BM 12161) (82–7–14, 1013 +AH 82–9–18A, 26)	—	Sippar, Rassam's excavations	Banded calcite sub-conical bowl	—	K	1–3	c
36	CBS 14932	U 207	Ur, under the Kurigalzu floor of the E-nun-maḫ	Banded calcite mace head	14 high 13 dia.	M	1–3	c
37	BM 116435 (1923–11–10, 20)	U 251+253	Ur, as ex. 36	Calcite vase frgm.	10.5 high 11.5 dia. 13 dia.	L		c
38	IM 113	U 264	Ur, as ex. 36	Banded calcite cylindrical vase	—	N	1–3	c
39	BM 117148	U 1167	Ur, from debris of the E-nun-maḫ	Banded calcite sub-conical bowl	—		1–2	c
40	IM 16702	U 18308	Ur, ziqqurrat terrace high up in filling, room GG Archaic I: (1st Dyansty room FF according to catalogue in UE 4)	Calcite bowl frgm.	—	O	1–3	n
41	IM —	W 15938	Uruk, Pd XVI 1, from a small gutter	Banded calcite(?) bowl(?) frgm.	8×3.4	P	2–3	p
42	VA 5298	Ass 20580	Aššur, in fE6 IV	Hematite mace head	3.7 high	Q	1–3	p
43	BM 127340	F. 1152, 1938/7–27–190	Tell Brak	Banded calcite cylindrical vase	7.7×3.8	R	1–3	c
44	Ash 1937.652	—	Said to be Kiš, purchased by Kiš expedition	Banded calcite sub-conical bowl	5.6×6.0×.9		2–3	n
45	YBC 2189		Unknown	'Grey limestone' cylindrical vase	17.8 high 14.3 dia.	S	1–3	c
46	YBC 2333	—	Unknown	'Grey limestone' jar	10.3 high 8 dia.	T	1–3	c
47	VA 3325	—	Unknown	Alabaster vase frgm.	—	U	1–3	n
48	AO 21404	—	Unknown	Murex shell	11×11	V	1–3	p
49	Likhachev-Collection	—	Unknown	Banded calcite(?) sub-conical bowl	—	W	1–3	p
50	IM 13679 (Mosul museum)	—	Unknown	Vase frgm.	—	X	—	n
51	Pierpont Morgan Library collection	—	Unknown	Lapis lazuli disk	2.15 dia. 82 high		1–3	p
52	BLMJ 118	—	Unknown	Lapis lazuli disk	—	—	1–3	c

COMMENTARY

Exs. 35, 37–39, and 43 were collated by T. Potts; ex. 52 by P. Steinkeller. In the catalogue the dimensions are first given for the height of the piece, then the width. Nippur exemplars 5–31, as far as can be determined, came from the area on the SE side of the ziqqurrat.

BIBLIOGRAPHY

1884–1912 de Sarzec, Découvertes 1 p. 448 (ex. 2, provenance, study); 2 pl. 5 no. 4 (ex. 1, photo), p. LVI (exs. 1, 3, copy), and pl. 44bis no. 2 (ex. 2, photo)

1893 Hilprecht, BE 1/1 nos. 7–9 (exs. 5–6 copy, ex. 31, partial copy); pl. V no. 14 (ex. 6, photo)

1899 King, CT 7 pl. 4 BM 12161 (ex. 35, copy)

1907 Messerschmidt, VS 1 no. 10 (ex. 47, copy)

1907 Thureau-Dangin, SAK pp. 160–61 Vase A (exs. 1, 5–6, 35, edition)

1910 King, Early History p. 204 fig. 56 (ex. 6, copy) and n. 1 (ex. 35, study)

1915 Šileiko, VN pp. 9–10 (ex. 49, photo, edition)

1922 BM Guide 3 p. 83 no. 6 (ex. 35, study)

1923 Woolley, AJ 3 pl. XXXII fig. 1 (ex. 36, photo)

1928 Gadd, UET 1 no. 8 (ex. 37, copy)
1929 Barton, RISA pp. 128–29 Rimush 16 and 19 (exs. 5–6, 35, edition)
1933 Frankfort, OIC 16 pp. 73–74 and fig. 47 (ex. 4, provenance, photo)
1933 Woolley, AJ 13 pp. 373–74 (ex. 40, study)
1936 Lenzen, UVB 7 p. 20 and pl. 25c (ex. 41, photo, study)
1937 Stephens, YOS 9 nos. 97–98 (exs. 45–46, study) and pl. XLIII (ex. 46, photo)
1940 Jacobsen, Temple Oval pp. 147 and 150 no. 10 (ex. 4, provenance, copy, edition)
1954 Preusser, Wohnhäuser p. 6 and pl. 22b (ex. 42, photo, study)
1956 Woolley, UE 4 pp. 167–68 and 189 (exs. 36–38, 40, study)
1960 Sollberger, Iraq 22 pp. 75–76 nos. 91–93 and 101 (exs. 36–40, study)
1961 Gelb, MAD 2[2] pp. 195–96 and 217 Rîmuš Original Inscriptions no. 3 (study)
1963 Hirsch, AfO 20 pp. 10–11 Rīmuš a 6 (edition)
1965 Sollberger, UET 8 p. 25 no. 5 (exs. 36, 38, 40, study)
1966 Aynard, Syria 43 pp. 21–23 (ex. 48, photo, edition)
1968 Goetze, JAOS 88 pp. 54 and 57 (exs. 32–22, copy, study)
1969 Buccellati and Biggs, AS 17 no. 45 (ex. 34, copy, study)
1969 Loretz, in AOAT 1 p. 199 n. 1 (ex. 43, study)
1969 Loretz, AOAT 3/1 no. 83 (ex. 43, copy, study)
1980 Walker and Collon, in de Meyer, (ed.), Tell ed-Dēr 3 p. 98 no. 28 (ex. 35, study)
1985 Finkel, Iraq 47 p. 201 (ex. 43, study)
1989 Potts, Iraq 51 pp. 149–50 Inscription D (study) and pp. 154–56 figs. 5–9 (exs. 35, 37–39, 43, copy)
1990 Gelb and Kienast, Königsinschriften pp. 70–72 Rīmuš 6 (edition)
1990 Pedersén, BiOr 47 689 (ex. 42, transliteration, study)
1992 Porada, CRRA 38 pp. 69–72 (ex. 51, photo, edition, study)

TEXT

1) *rí-mu-úš*
2) LUGAL
3) KIŠ

1–3) Rīmuš, king of the world.

2001

A diorite fragment, probably a chip from the shoulder of a statue, is incised with a votive inscription for the life of Rīmuš.

COMMENTARY

According to notes of I.J. Gelb, the piece was in the possession of E.S. David and was offered for sale to both the Oriental Institute in Chicago and to Yale, but not purchased by either institution; its present whereabouts are not known. The edition follows that given by Gelb and Kienast. The mention of the goddess Sud in line 3′ suggests that the piece may have originally come from Šuruppak. For the reading of the DN in line 5′ cf. the comments of Michalowski, JCS 28 (1976) p. 164: 'It [the DN] is read Nin-gidri here on the basis of the occurrence of this divinity in PBS 5 76, apparently a coronation ritual, recently edited by Å. Sjöberg, OrSuec 21 (1973) 111. In that text Nin-gidri follows Nin-mena (vii 10 and 15ff.), which suggests that the two deities were personifications of the scepter and the crown'. For the reading of second element as gidru, see MSL 14 p. 192 line 314: gi-id-ru PA MIN (= *ge-eš-ṭu-ru-u*) *ḫa-aṭ-ṭu*.

BIBLIOGRAPHY

1990 Gelb and Kienast, Königsinschriften p. 74 Rīmuš B 1 (edition)

TEXT

Lacuna
1′) [...]
2′) šà-zi-pà-da-
3′) [d]sùd-da

Lacuna
1′–3′) ... chosen in the heart of the goddess Sud,

4′) mu-p[à-da]-
5′) ^{d}nin-gidru-k[a]
6′) nam-ti-
7′) lugal-ni
8′) *rí-mu-úś*
Lacuna

4′–5′) called by name by Nin-gidru,

6′–8′) for the life of Rīmuš, his lord ...
Lacuna

Man-ištūšu

E2.1.3

According to the various manuscripts of the Sumerian King List, Man-ištūšu, older brother and successor of Rīmuš, reigned either seven or fifteen years. Assuming that the latter figure of the King List is correct, the king reigned, according to Brinkman's chronology, 2269–2255. Only a handful of royal inscriptions, and no year names, are known for the third Sargonic king. The most imposing monument of his reign is a large four-sided obelisk or pyramid of black diorite stone that is inscribed with a lengthy text recording Man-ištūšu's purchase of eight parcels of land in the region later known as Babylonia. For the most recent edition of the inscription, see Gelb, Land Tenure pp. 116–140 no. 40.

1

The 'Standard Inscription' of Man-ištūšu is known from five original exemplars — fragments of stone statues or steles — and three later (Old Babylonian) tablet copies. The inscription records the king's defeat of Anšan and Širiḫum as well as his crushing of a coalition of thirty-two cities located on the other side of the Gulf, probably in the area that is modern-day Oman.

CATALOGUE

Ex.	Museum number	Excavation/ Registration number	Provenance	Object	Dimensions (cm)	Gelb and Kienast	Original lines preserved	Text lines preserved	cpn
1	Sb 51	—	Susa, excavations of J. de Morgan	Frgm. of a diorite statue base	21×33	1 A	col. i 1′–11′ col. ii 1′–13′	15–25 47–59	c
2	Sb 15566	—	As ex. 1	Stone frgm.	—	1 B	1′–4′	16–19	n
3	CBS 19925 +unnumbered frgm.	—	Nippur, University of Pennsylvania expedition	Frgm. of a diorite stele or statue base	26.0×22.5×3.8	1 E	1′–7′	15–21	c
4	BM 56630	AH 82-7-14, 1023	Sippar, Rassam's excavations	Frgm. of a granite stele	18.3×6.1×6.1	1 D	1′–10′	12–21	c
5	BM 56631	AH 82-7-14, 1024	As ex. 4	Frgm. of a granite stele	19.4×8.9×9.2	1 C 2	1′–10′	12–21 Dedicatory label	c
6	CBS 13972	—	Nippur, University of Pennsylvania expedition	Clay tablet	—	C 1 A	rev. xxvi 29–39 rev. xxvi 41–50 rev. xxvi 53–63 rev. xxvii 53–58 rev. xxvii 59	1–12 14–23 26–36 Dedicatory label Colophon 2	c

Ex.	Museum number	Excavation/ Registration number	Provenance	Object	Dimensions (cm)	Gelb and Kienast	Original lines preserved	Text lines preserved	cpn
7	Ni 3200	—	As ex. 6	Clay tablet	—	C 1 B	rev. ix 31–33	1–5	p
							rev. x 3–8	53–63	
							rev. x 9	Colophon 1	
							rev. x 10–13	Dedicatory label	
							rev. x 14	Colophon 2	
8	IM —	U 7725	Ur, from no. 7 Quiet Street, rooms 5 or 6	Clay tablet	—	C 1 C	rev. iv 8, 13–23	1, 7–17	n
							rev. v 2-5	24–28	
							rev. vi 10–15	57–62	

COMMENTARY

Hirsch considered the six-line dedicatory section that follows the main text in ex. 6, a later tablet copy, as a separate inscription, designated by him as Maništūsu b 2. However, the occurrence of a similar dedicatory inscription on ex. 5, an original monument, suggests that this section should be edited with the main text, as a label. Ex. 1 was collated by B. Foster, exs. 4–5 by G. Frame.

BIBLIOGRAPHY

1900 Jensen, ZA 15 p. 248 n. 1 (exs. 4–5, conflated transliteration)
1902 Scheil, MDP 4 p. 2 and pl. I no. 2 (ex. 2, photo, edition)
1909 Scheil, RA 7 pp. 103–106 (ex. 1, photo, edition)
1910 King, Early History pp. 211–12 (exs. 1, 4–5, study)
1912 King, CT 32 pl. 5 (exs. 4–5, copy)
1913 Scheil, MDP 14 pp. 1–3 and pl. II no. B (ex. 1, photo, edition)
1914 Poebel, PBS 4/1 p. 209 no. 35 (ex. 3, edition) and pp. 205–207 no. 34 Z a–b (ex. 6, edition)
1914 Poebel, PBS 5 pl. XXI no. 34 (ex. 6, copy) and no. 35 (ex. 3, copy)
1926 Thureau-Dangin, RA 23 p. 26 n. 3 (ex. 6, study)
1926 Pézard and Pottier, Catalogue no. 49 bis (ex. 1, study)
1928 Gadd, UET 1 no. 274 (ex. 8, copy, edition)
1929 Barton, RISA pp. 128–31 Manishtusu 1 (ex. 6, edition), pp. 136–37 Manishtusu 5 Fragment C (ex. 4, edition), Manishtusu 5 Fragment D (ex. 5, edition), and Manishtusu 9 (ex. 1, edition)
1961 Gelb, MAD 2^2 p. 197 Man-ištušu Original Inscriptions no. 1 and Late Copies no. 1 (exs. 1, 3–8, study)
1963 Hirsch, AfO 20 p. 14 Maništušu a 1 (exs. 1, 3–5, study) and pp. 15 and 69–71 Maništušu b 1+2 (exs. 6–7, edition)
1965 Sollberger, UET 8 p. 32 no. 33 (ex. 8, study)
1971 Sollberger and Kupper, IRSA IIA3b (exs. 1, 3–8, translation)
1976 Amiet, L'art d'Agadé no. 14 (ex. 1, photo, translation)
1980 Collon and Walker in de Meyer (ed.), Tell ed-Dēr 3 p. 102 nos. 56–57 (exs. 4–5, study)
1982 Heimpel, RA 76 pp. 65–67 (exs. 1–2, study)
1986 Potts, OrAnt 25 p. 273 (study)
1989 Strommenger, RLA 7/5–6 pp. 336 and 338 nos. A 1 and 11–14 (exs. 1–5, study)
1990 Gelb and Kienast, Königsinschriften pp. 5–77 Maništūsu 1 (exs. 1–5, edition); pp. 77–78 Maništūsu 2 (ex. 4, edition); pp. 220–22 Maništūsu C 1 (exs. 6–8, edition); pls. VI, IX–X, XVI, XIX–X (exs. 6–7, photo) and p. 144 (ex. 6., copy)

TEXT

1) *ma-an-íš-tu-šu*	1–3) Man-ištūšu, king of the world:
2) LUGAL	
3) KIŠ	
4) *ì-nu*	4–8) when he conquered Anšan and Širiḫum,
5) *an-ša-an*.KI	
6) *ù*	
7) *ši$_4$-rí-ḫu-um*.KI	
8) SAG.GIŠ.RA-*ni*	
9) *ti-a-am-tàm*	9–12) had ... ships cross the Lower Sea.
10) *ša-pil-tàm*	
11) MÁ.MÁ GIŠ.LA-*e*	
12) *u-ša-bì-ir*	
13) URU.KI.URU.KI	13–19) The cities across the Sea, thirty-two (in number), assembled for battle, but he was victorious (over them).
14) *a-bar-ti*	
15) *ti-a-am-tim*	

16) 32 *a-na*
17) REC 169
18) *ip-ḫu-ru-nim-ma*
19) *iš*$_{11}$*-ar*
20) *ù*
21) URU.KI.URU.KI-*śu-nu*
22) SAG.GIŠ.RA
23) EN.EN-*śu-nu*
24) [*u-ś*]*a-am-*[*q*]*í-it*
25) *ù*
26) *íś-tu*[*m-ma*]
27) *i*[*d-ké-aś-śu-nu-ni-ma*]
28) *a-dì-*⸢*ma*⸣
29) *ḫu-rí* KÙ
30) *íl-qù-ut*
31) ŚA.DÚ-*e*
32) *a-bar-ti*
33) *ti-a-am-tim*
34) *śa-pil-tim*
35) NA$_4$.NA$_4$-⸢*śu*⸣*-nu* GI$_6$
36) *i-pu-*⸢*lam-ma*⸣
37) *in* MÁ.MÁ
38) *i-ṣa-*[*na-ma*]
39) *in kar-rí-*<*im*>
40) *śi a-kà-dè*.KI
41) *ìr-ku*$_8$*-us*
42) DÙL-*śu*
43) *ib-ni*
44) *a-na*
45) [^{d}*en-líl*]
46) A.MU.RU
47) ^{d}UTU
48) *ù*
49) *ìl-a-ba*$_4$
50) *ú-má*
51) *la sú-ra-tum*
52) *lu kí-ni-íś-ma*
53) *śa* DUB
54) *śu*$_4$*-a*
55) *u-sá-sà-ku-ni*
56) ⸢^{d}⸣*en-líl*
57) *ù*
58) ^{d}UTU
59) SUḪUŠ-*śu*
60) *li-sú-ḫa*
61) *ù*
62) ŠE.NUMUN-*śu*
63) *li-il-qù-tá*

Colophon 1
1) mu-s[ar-ra]
2) [ki-gal-b]a

20–24) Further, he conquered their cities, [st]ru[c]k down their rulers

25–30) and aft[er] he [roused them (his troops)], plundered as far as the Silver Mines.

31–41) He quarried the black stone of the mountains across the Lower Sea, loaded (it) on ships, and moored (the ships) at the quay of Agade.

42–46) He fashioned a statue of himself (and) dedicated (it) to the god [Enlil].

47–52) By the gods Šamaš and Ilaba I swear that (these) are not falsehoods (but) are indeed true.

53–63) As for the one who removes this inscription, may the gods Enlil and Šamaš tear out foundations and destroy his progeny.

Colophon 1
1–2) In[scription] on it[s socle].

16.6 33; the 30 is written over an erased KUR sign (collation Sollberger); text copy gives 43.
38.8 Text copy: *i-ṣa-na-ma*; original *i-ṣa-*[...] (collation Sollberger).
45.8 ^{d}EN.ZU.
47.1 ⸢^{d}⸣[...]
56.1 ^{d}UTU.

Dedicatory label	Dedicatory label
1) *ma-an-íš-tu-šu*	1–6) Man-ištūšu, king of the world, dedicated (this object) to the god Enlil.
2) LUGAL	
3) KIŠ	
4) *a-na*	
5) ^{d}*en-líl*	
6) A.MU.RU	
Colophon 2	Colophon 2
1) mu-sar-ra ki-gal-ba	1) Inscription on its socle.

2

This inscription, known from three Old Babylonian tablet copies from Nippur, deals with the god Enlil's granting of the sceptre of kingship.to Man-ištūšu.

CATALOGUE

Ex.	Museum number	Tablet lines preserved	Text lines preserved	cpn
1	CBS 13972	rev. xxvii 31–50, 56-58	1–20, 26–28	c
2	Ni 3200	rev. x 15–27, 29	1–20, 22	p
3	N 6266	col. iii 1′–6′	6–10	c

COMMENTARY

It is not absolutely certain whether ex. 3, of which only parts of six lines remain, is a duplicate of this text.

BIBLIOGRAPHY

1914 Poebel, PBS 4/1 pp. 207–208 no. 34 Z g (ex. 1, edition)
1914 Poebel, PBS 5 pl. XXI no. 34 (ex. 1, copy)
1929 Barton, RISA pp. 130–31 Manishtusu 3 (ex. 1, edition)
1961 Gelb, MAD 2[2] p. 198 Man–ištušu Late Copies no. 3 (ex. 1, study)
1963 Hirsch, AfO pp. 15 and 71–72 Maništūsu b 3 (exs. 1–2, edition, study)
1971 Sollberger and Kupper, IRSA IIA3c (exs. 1–2, translation)
1980 Michalowski, JCS 32 p. 242–43 (ex. 3, copy)
1990 Gelb and Kienast, Königsinschriften pp. 223–25 and pls. VI, IX–X, XVI, XIX–XX Maništūsu C 3 exs. (1–2, photo, edition); p. 144 (ex. 1, copy)

TEXT

1) ^{d}*en-líl*	1–4) The god Enlil, Man-ištūšu, king of the world:
2) *ma-an-íš-tu-šu*	
3) LUGAL	
4) KIŠ	
5) ^{d}*en-líl*	5–12) The god Enlil made him great, called his name and granted to him the sceptre of kingship.
6) *u-ša-ar-bí-šu*	
7) MU-*šu*	
8) *i-bí*	

E2.1.3.1 Dedicatory label 5.5 [^{d}U]TU.
E2.1.3.2 7.3 *šum*$_6$-[*šu*].

9) *ù*
10) [GI]Š.GIDRU
11) *śar-ru-tim*
12) ⸢*i-dí*⸣-*śum*
13) *ša* DUB
14) *śu*$_4$-*a*
15) *u-śa-sà-ku-ni*
16) ^{d}*en-líl*
17) *ù*
18) ^{d}UTU
19) ⸢SUḪUŠ-*śu*⸣
20) [*l*]*i-sú-ḫa*
21) [*ù*]
22) [ŠE.NUMUN]-⸢*śu*⸣
23) [*li-il-qù-tá*]
24) [...]
25) [...]
26) [...] x x
27) [...] x
28) [...] x
Lacuna

13–28) As for the one who removes this inscription, may the gods Enlil and Šamaš tear out his foundations [and destroy] his [progeny] ...
Lacuna

3

A dedicatory inscription of Man-ištūšu appears on a vase that was found at Nippur.

COMMENTARY

The fragment, made of coarse-grained dolerite, measures 12×12.2×1.6 cm. It was found in excavations by the University of Pennsylvania expedition to Nippur in area III on the SE side of the ziqqurrat; it now bears the museum number CBS 9918. The inscription was collated.

BIBLIOGRAPHY

1896 Hilprecht, BE 1/2 no. 118 (copy)
1907 Thureau-Dangin, SAK pp. 162–63 no. 7 b (edition)
1929 Barton, RISA pp. 136–37 Manishtusu 6 (edition)
1961 Gelb, MAD 2^{2} p . 197 Man-ištušu Original I Inscriptions no. 2 (study)
1963 Hirsch, AfO 20 p. 15 Maništušu a 4 (study)
1990 Gelb and Kienast, Königsinschriften p. 79 Maništūsu 4 (edition)

TEXT

1) [*ma-an-iś*]-*t*[*u-śu*]
2) LUGA[L]
3) KIŠ
4) *a-na*
5) ^{d}*en-lí*[*l*]
6) ⸢A.MU⸣.[RU]

1–3) [Man-iš]t[ūšu], kin[g] of the world,

4–6) dedic[ated] (this vase) to the god Enli[l].

4

A mace head found at Sippar bears a votive inscription of Man-ištūšu.

COMMENTARY

The mace head, made of black and white marble, measures 8.8 cm in diameter and 7.1 cm in height. It was found in excavations by H. Rassam at Sippar and now bears the museum number BM 91018 (= BM 12160), with the registration number 82-7-14, 1011. The inscription was collated by G. Frame.

BIBLIOGRAPHY

1887 Winckler, MAOV 1 pp. 15 and 18 no. 5 (copy)
1892 Winckler, KB 3/1 pp. 100–101 no. 3 (edition)
1892 Winckler and Böhden, ABK no. 67 (copy)
1905 King, CT 21 pl. 1 (copy)
1907 Thureau-Dangin, SAK pp. 162–63 no. 7 a (edition)
1910 King, Early History, plate after p. 206, lower right (photo)
1922 BM Guide 3 p. 19 no. 1 and p. 83 no. 12 (copy, study)
1929 Barton, RISA pp. 136–37 Manishtusu 7 (edition)
1961 Gelb, MAD 2^2 p. 197 Man-ištušu Original Inscriptions no. 3 (study)
1963 Hirsch, AfO 20 p. 15 Maništušu a 5 (study)
1968 Solyman, Götterwaffen p. 130 and pl. XXVII no. 209 (photo, study)
1971 Sollberger and Kupper, IRSA IIA3a (translation)
1980 Walker and Collon, in de Meyer (ed.), Tell ed-Dēr 3 p. 100 no. 44 (study)
1990 Gelb and Kienast, Königsinschriften p. 78 Maništūsu 3 (edition)

TEXT

1) *ma-an-íś-tu-śu*
2) LUGAL
3) KIŠ
4) *a-na*
5) ^{d}NIN-*a-a*
6) A.MU.RU

1–3) Man-ištūšu, king of the world,

4–6) dedicated (this mace) to the goddess Bēlat-Aia.

5

A mace head from Isin bears an inscription indicating that Man-ištūšu dedicated the piece to the goddess Ninisina.

COMMENTARY

The mace head is made of a yellowish-red alabaster and measures 11.1 cm in height with a maximum dia. of 11 cm. It was found by the Munich expedition to Isin at 50.50–50.62 N, 94.28–94.40 W, +10.11 m (top level) and bears the excavation no. IB 1878, IM number unknown. Information on the piece was kindly provided by B. Hrouda.

For the reading of the DN in line 5, see Steinkeller, JCS 30 (1978) pp. 168–69.

BIBLIOGRAPHY

1989 Strommenger, RLA 7/5–6 p. 338 no. A 8 (study)
1990 Gelb and Kienast, Königsinschriften p. 79 Maništūsu 5 (edition)
199x Sommerfeldt, in Hrouda (ed.), Isin 4 (edition, [forthcoming])

TEXT

1) *ma-an-íś-tu-śu*
2) LUGAL
3) KIŠ
4) *a-na*
5) ^{d}*nin-isin*$_{x}$(IN)
6) A.MU.RU

1–6) Man-ištūšu, king of the world,

4–6) dedicated (this mace) to the goddess Ninisina.

6

A door socket found at a small tell located near the junction of the al-ʿUẓaim and Tigris rivers bears an inscription of Man-ištūšu.

COMMENTARY

The existence of this door socket was drawn to the attention of the author by J. Black, who kindly provided a transliteration of the piece. It was found at Tell Ghḍairīfe/Tell Dhuhūbe (sites 2–3 on map 21 in the Atlas of the Archaeological Sites in Iraq [Directorate General of Antiquities, Baghdad, 1976]). The inscribed area measures 22.5×4 cm. The inscription is included in the RIM corpus through the courtesy of Dr. F.N.H. Al-Rawi, who will publish the piece in the near future.

TEXT

1) *ma-an-íś-*
2) *tu-śu*
3) LUGAL
4) KIŠ
5) ^{ba}DÍM
6) É
7) ^{d}*nin-ḫur-sag*
8) *in* ḪA.A.KI
9) *ša* DUB
10) *śu*$_{4}$*-a*
11) *u-śa-sà-ku-ni*
12) ^{d}*nin-ḫur-sag*
13) *ù*
14) ^{d}UTU
15) SUḪUŠ-*śu*
16) *li-sú-ḫa*
17) *ù*
18) ŠE.NUMUN-*śu*
19) *li-il-qù-tá*

1–4) Man-ištūšu, king of the world,

5–8) builder of the temple of the goddess Ninḫursag in ḪA.A.

9–19) As for the one who removes this inscription, may the goddess Ninḫursag and the god Šamaš tear out his foundation and destroy his progeny.

7

A bronze bowl bears the name and title of Man-ištūšu.

COMMENTARY

The bowl, which measures about 14 cm in diameter at the rim, is said to have come from Qamišliyyah, a Syrian village near Nuseybin. It is now conserved in the private German collection of K. Frauenberger. The inscription was collated from the published photo in which line 1 is not legible.

BIBLIOGRAPHY

1970 Nagel, APA 1 p. 195 (photo, edition)

TEXT

1) *ma-an-íš-tu-šu*
2) LUGAL
3) KIŠ

1–3) Man-ištūšu, king of the world.

2001

A votive statue from Susa, dated on stylistic grounds to the early phase of the Early Dynastic period, bears a later inscription of a certain Ešpum, servant of Man-ištūšu. For seals mentioning this Ešpum, see E2.16.1.1 and E2.16.1.2001.

COMMENTARY

The statue, of which only the top half remains, is made of alabaster and measures 30 cm in height. It was found in excavations in the area of the Ninḫursag temple on the acropolis at Susa and bears the museum number Sb 82 (Louvre). In line 5 we would expect to find a zu sign at the end, but the photo, from which this inscription was collated, shows a clear su sign instead.

BIBLIOGRAPHY

1908 Scheil, MDP 10 pp. 1–3 and pl. 1 no. 1 (photo, edition, study)
1907 de Morgan, CRAIB pp. 398–99 (drawing, study)
1908 Bork, OLZ 11 322–23 (study)
1910 Scheil, RA 7 p. 103 (study)
1926 Pézard and Pottier, Catalogue no. 74 and pl. XI (photo, study)
1929 Barton, RISA pp. 136–37 Manishtusu 8 (edition)
1931 Contenau, Manuel 2 pp. 673–74 and figs. 467–68 (photo, study)
1959 Strommenger, ZA 53 pp. 29–36 and pls. I–II (photo, study)
1961 Gelb, MAD 2^2 p. 198 Man-ištušu Officials, etc., no. 2a (study)
1960 Strommenger, Bagh. Mitt. 1 pp. 47–48 (study)
1963 Hirsch, AfO 20 p. 16 Maništušu 2 a (study)

1966 Amiet, Elam pp. 184–85 fig. 135 A and B (photo, study)
1968 Nagel and Strommenger, BJVF 8 pp. 171 and 188 (study)
1971 Sollberger and Kupper, IRSA IIA3d (translation)
1976 Amiet, DAFI 6 p. 55 and pl. VII nos. 1–2 (photo, study)
1981 Spycket, Statuaire p. 73 and pl. 48 (photo, study)
1989 Strommenger, RLA 7/5–6 pp. 338–39 no. D1 (study)
1990 Gelb and Kienast, Königsinschriften p. 80 Maništūsu B 2 (edition)

TEXT

1) *ma-an-íś-tu-śu*
2) LUGAL
3) KIŠ
4) *eš*$_4$*-pum*
5) IR$_{11}$-*su*
6) *a-na*
7) ^{d}*na-ru-ti*
8) A.MU.NA.RU

1–3) Man-ištūšu, king of the world:

4–8) Ešpum, his servant, dedicated (this statue) to the goddess Narunte.

2002

A copper spear-point found at Aššur bears the dedicatory inscription of a servant of Man-ištūšu.

COMMENTARY

The object, which was found in the Ištar temple at Aššur, cA7I, bears the excavation number Ass 21340 and the museum number VA 8300, Ass photo 6558. It measures 45.6×1.44 cm. For the name of the deity in line 7, see RIMA 1 p. 8. The inscription was collated.

BIBLIOGRAPHY

1935 Andrae, MDOG 73 pp. 1–2 and fig. 1 (photo, study)
1937 Frankfort, JRAS pp. 335 (study)
1944 Gelb, Hurrians p. 36 and n. 100 (study)
1945–51 Weidner, AfO 15 p. 85 (edition)
1954 Landsberger, JCS 8 p. 109 n. 206 (study)
1961 Borger, EAK 1 pp. 1–2 (study)
1961 Gelb, MAD 2^2 p. 198 Man-ištušu Officials, etc. no. 1 (study)
1963 Hirsch, AfO 20 p. 16 Maništušu d 2 b (study)
1969 Calmeyer, Datierbare Bronzen p. 36 and n. 112 (study)
1972 Grayson, ARI 1 pp. 2–3 (translation)
1987 Grayson, RIMA 1 p. 8 A.0.1002.2001 (edition)
1989 Strommenger, RLA 7/5–6 p. 338 A9 (study)
1990 Gelb and Kienast, Königsinschriften pp. 89–90 Maništūsu B 1 (edition)

TEXT

1) *ma-an-íś-tu-śu*
2) LUGAL
3) KIŠ
4) *a-zu-zu*
5) ⌈ÌR⌉-*su*
6) ⌈*a-na*⌉
7) ⌈^{d}⌉*be-al*-SI.SI
8) A.MU.RU

1–3) Man-ištūšu, king of the world:

4–8) Azūzu, his servant, dedicated (this spear) to the god Be'al-SI.SI.

2003

A cylinder seal in Brussels bears an inscription that mentions Man-ištūšu.

COMMENTARY

The seal, whose provenance is unknown, is made of a dark stone and measures 3.0 cm in length with a diameter of 2.1 cm. It was catalogued as no. 594 in Speleer's Catalogue of the seals of the Musées Royaux du Cinquantenaire. According to Boehmer (Moortgat Festschrift p. 44 n. 11), the seal probably dates to the Ur III period. The inscription was collated from the published photo.

BIBLIOGRAPHY

1917 Speleers, Catalogue pp. 84–85 and 116–17 no. 594 (photo, copy, edition)
1934 van Buren, Studi e Materiali de Storia delle Religioni 10 pp. 171–72 (edition)
1960 Unger, RA 54 pp. 183–85 (copy, edition)
1961 Gelb, MAD 2[2] p. 198 Maniš-tušu Officials, etc. no. 3 (study)
1963 Hirsch, AfO 20 p. 16 Maništušu d 3 (transliteration)
1964 Boehmer, Moortgat Festschrift p. 44 n. 11(study)
1965 Boehmer, Glyptik no. 990 (study)
1968–69 Edzard, AfO 22 p. 17 no. 26–1 (transliteration)
1990 Gelb and Kienast, Königsinschriften p. 40 S–6 (edition)

TEXT

1) ^{d}*ma-ni-íś-ti-śu*
2) *tá-rí-bu*
3) DAM lugal-ezen
4) MU.NA.DÍM

1) (For) the divine Man-ištūšu:
2–4) Tarību, the wife of Lugal-ezen, had (this seal) fashioned.

Narām-Sîn

E2.1.4

In the Sumerian King List, Narām-Sîn, son of Man-ištūšu, is credited with a reign of 56 years. The same figure of 56 years is given for Sargon's reign; since Jacobsen has shown that the two figures of 56 years cannot be accommodated by the dynastic totals for the Akkadian dynasty, there must have been a confusion in the tradition here. There is much greater documentation for the reign of Narām-Sîn than for the earlier Sargonic kings. However, because we lack a date list or chronicle that would enable us to put this historical data in order, the chronology of the reign remains unclear. A prime index for the dating of the inscriptions and year names is the presence or absence of the prefixed divine determinative in the writing of the king's name. We have assumed that those inscriptions and year names in which the divine determinative does not appear date to an early period of the reign.

Undoubtedly the greatest crisis of Narām-Sîn's reign was a general insurrection of his subject cities. Two rebel leaders, the king of Kiš, a certain Ipḫur-Kiš, and the king of Uruk, Amar-Girid, assembled a northern and a southern coalition of cities to oppose the Akkadian king. A third participant in the revolt was the governor of Nippur, Enlil-nizu. While the existence of the revolt has been known for a long time from an Old Babylonian account preserved on a tablet in Geneva (it is now complemented by the evidence of a Mari and a BM exemplar; see Grayson and Sollberger RA 70 [1976] pp. 103–28), a much better understanding of the events of the insurrection is now possible thanks to Kutscher's publication of an Old Babylonian Sammeltafel copy of the original Old Akkadian version of the revolt. The Kutscher text is edited as E2.1.4.6 in this volume. Of note is the writing of Narām-Sîn's name in the Kutscher text *without* the prefixed divine determinative. If we assume a faithful copy by the Old Babylonian scribe, then the writing of the king's name would indicate that, at the time the Nippur stele commemorating the king's triumph was inscribed, the apotheosis of the king had not yet occurred. In the Mari exemplar of the Old Babylonian account of the revolt mention is made of nine military expeditions against the rebel forces: [*i-na ti*]-*bu-ut* [*um-ma-an*(?)] *a-kà-dè*.KI-*ma* 9 *ṣú-ub-bi-*[*i*]*m* [*ú-ša*]-*at-bi-šu-nu-ši-im* '[With the le]vy of [the army] of Agade, he (Narām-Sîn) raised nine military expeditions against them' (Grayson and Sollberger, RA 70 [1976] p. 112 M rev. 3′–4′). The passage is important because it allows us to see the expression: *ša-ir* 10 LAL 1 REC 169 *in* MU 1 'victor in nine battles in one year', which occurs in a number of original Narām-Sîn inscriptions (E2.1.4.9, 11–13; variant formulation in E2.1.4.10) as an allusion to the events of the 'Great Revolt'. We may be reasonably certain that the deification of the king occurred shortly after the 'Great Revolt'. Events dating to this general period are described in E2.1.4.10; the inscription recounts the construction in Agade of a temple dedicated to Narām-Sîn. In the king's remaining inscriptions, that date to the time after the 'Great Revolt', the king's name is consistently written with the prefixed divine determinative. Details of chronology of the latter part of the reign remain to be sorted out. We have grouped these later inscriptions along geographical lines, in the expectation that the king pursued his campaigns in a systematic manner in various regions. Of course, this need not necessarily have been the case. Thus, the following list of year names and inscriptions is offered as a working model for future discussion, and is not meant to imply a rigid chronological order. Details of the schema given in outline here will appear in a forthcoming separate study. In the following list, year names of uncertain attribution are marked with a dagger (†).

I Year Names and Events of the Reign

(i) The Accession of the King

(a)The Coronation of the King in Nippur: [mu] *na-ra-am-*^{d}EN.ZU é-^{d}en-⌈líl⌉-t[a] tukul-an-na [š]u ba-ti-a 'The year Narām-Sîn received a *weapon of heaven/An* fr[om] the temple of the god Enlil'. N 236: Civil, JCS 15 (1961) p. 80.

(ii) Campaigns Preceding the Deification of the King

(b) The Talmus Campaign. Alluded to in E2.1.4.1.
(c) The Defeat of Šimānum. Recorded in E2.1.4.2 col. ii lines 3–6.
(d) The Defeat of the Coalition Army Headed by the King of AB×U/ŠUŠ.KI (= Apišal). Recorded in E2.1.4.2.
(e) The Defeat of Maridabān: mu *na-ra-am-*^{d}EN.ZU ma-ri-da-ba-an.KI mu-ḫul-a. 'The year Narām-Sîn defeated Maridabān'. Ni 2451: Unger, Naram-Sin p. 47 and pl. 5 no. 9.
(f) The Defeat of [...]-ḫunum: [mu] *na-ra-am-*⌈^{d}⌉EN.ZU [...-ḫ]u-num.[KI]-šè [ì-gi]n-na-a [REC 169 b]a-gar 'The year Narām-Sîn [we]nt to [...]-ḫunum (and) [defe]ated it'. CBS 6117: Barton, PBS 9/1 no. 15.
(g) The Defeat of Šabbunum: mu *na-ra-am-*^{d}EN.ZU [š]a-ab-bu-nu-um.KI mu-ḫul-⌈a⌉ 'The year Narām-Sîn defeated Šabbunum'. HS 787: Pohl, TMH 5 no. 37.
(h) A Military Victory Against an Unnamed Foe. Recorded in E2.1.4.3.
(i) The Magan Campaign. Recorded in E2.1.4.4–5.

(iii) Preparations for Grand War, 'The Great Revolt', and the Defeat of Uruk

(j) The Construction of the Wall of Agade: mu bàd-a-ga-dè.KI <ba-dù-a>† 'The year the wall of Agade <was built>'. N 405: Civil, JCS 15 (1961) p. 80 and Westenholz, OSP 2 pp. 171–72 no. 166.
(k) 'The Great Revolt'. Recorded in E2.1.4.6–7; in addition, allusions to the revolt are found in E2.1.4.8–13.
(l) The Defeat of Uruk: mu REC169 unu.KI nag-su.KI-a ba-gar-ra-a† 'The year when a battle against Uruk in Nagsu took place'. Thureau-Dangin, RTC nos. 99, 136 and 176; BM 86299: Sollberger, CT 50 no. 49.

(iv) Temple Constructions and Cultic Installations

(m) The Construction of the Aštar Temple in Agade: ⌈mu é-^{d}inanna⌉ a-ga-dè.KI al-dù-a† 'The year the temple of the goddess Aštar was built in Agade'. NBC 10247: Foster, JCS 35 (1983) pp. 135–36.
(n) The Construction of the Enlil Temple in Nippur and the Aštar Temple in Zabala: *in* 1 MU ^{d}*na-ra-am-*^{d}EN.ZU *úš-ši*$_{11}$ É ^{d}*en-líl* [*i*]*n* NIBRU.KI ⌈*ù*⌉ É ^{d}INANNA *in* ZABALA.KI *íś-ku-nu* 'The year Narām-Sîn laid the foundations of the temple of the god Enlil in Nippur and of the temple of the goddess Aštar in Zabala'. Thureau-Dangin: RTC nos. 86, 106, and 144.
(o) The Designation of the *entu* priestess of the god Enlil: mu en-^{d}en-líl máš-e íb-dab$_5$-ba 'The year the *entu* priestess of the god Enlil was chosen by omens'. HS 757+934+951: Pohl, TMH 5 no. 7+184+201a and Westenholz, Texts Jena no. 7; N 77: Civil, JCS 15 (1961) p. 80; CBS 6216 Westenholz, OSP 2 no. 99. This year name deals with the king's daughter, Tūta-napšum, who appears in E2.1.4.18–20 and 2017.

(o′) *in* 1 MU [N]IN ^{d}*en-líl-«lá»* ‘The year the *entu* priestess of the god Enlil’. AIA 8: Foster, ASJ 4 (1982) p. 23 col. ii lines 9–10.
(p) Construction of the temple of the god Sîn in Ur. Recorded in E2.1.4.17.

(v) Campaigns Following the Deification of the King (a) — The Conquest of Settlements in the Ḫabur Basin and the Area of the Headwaters of the Tigris

(q) The Defeat of Azuḫinnum: *in* 1 M[U] ^{d}*na-ra-*[*am-*^{d}E]N.ZU REC 169 SUBIR.KI *in a-zu-ḫi-nim*.KI *i-ša-ru tá-ḫi-ša-ti-li ik-mi-ù* ‘The ye[ar] Narā[m-S]în was victorious over Subartum at Azuḫinnum and captured Taḫiš-atili’. AIA 8: Foster, ASJ 4 (1982) p. 23 col. iii–iv. See also Lambert, RA 77 (183) p. 95. Azuḫinnum is also mentioned in E2.1.4.21, an inscription which probably narrates a campaign in the eastern Ḫabur region.
(r) The Construction of a Fortress(?) at Tell Brāk. Recorded in E2.1.4.22.
(s) A Hunting Expedition in the Area of Mount Tibar. Recorded in E2.1.4.23.
(t) The Reaching of the Sources of the Tigris and Euphrates Rivers: [*i*]*n* 1 MU ^{d}*na-ra-am-*^{d}EN.ZU *na-gáb* IDIGNA.I$_{7}$ *ù* BURANUN.I$_{7}$ *ik-ś*[*u-dú*] *ù* ⌜REC 169⌝ ⌜*šè-nam*⌝*-in-da-*[*a*.KI] ⌜*iš*$_{11}$⌝*-a-*⌜*ru*⌝ ‘The year Narām-Sîn reached the sources of the Tigris and Euphrates rivers and was victorious in battle over Šenaminda’. A 22025: Gelb, MAD 1 no. 231; A 220390+22032: Gelb, MAD 1 no. 236.
(u) A Military Victory in the Area of Modern Pir Hüseyn. Recorded in E2.1.4.24.
(v) A Campaign Against Abarnium: [*i*]*n* MU REC 448bis LUGAL *in* ʾ*à-mar-nu-um i-li-kà-am*† ‘The year the king went on a campaign in Amarnum’. Umm-el-Jīr 1932, 354: Gelb, MAD 5 no. 76.

(b) The Conquest of Settlements on the Upper Euphrates and in Syria: Ḫaḫḫum, Talḫadum, Eastern Anatolia, the Amanus Mountains (Cedar Forest), Mukiš, Armānum, and Ebla

(w) The Defeat of Ḫaḫḫum. Alluded to in the Old Babylonian version of the ‘Great Revolt’ (see Grayson and Sollberger, RA 70 [1976] p. 115 L I 5′: [...*a*]*n*(?)*-da* LUGAL *ḫa-aḫ-ḫi-i*.KI).
(x) A Campaign Against Talḫadum. Recorded in E2.1.4.25. In this inscription the king’s name appears without the prefixed divine determinative. We have assumed that this omission was a mistake of the ancient copyist. If not, the campaign against Talḫadum would date to the period before the deification of the king.
(y) A Trip to the Cedar Forest/Amanus Mountains: [*i*]*n* 1 [MU] ^{d}*na-*[*ra-am-*^{d}EN.ZU] *a-na* GIŠ.TIR ERIN *i-li-*[*ku*] ‘The [year] Na[rām-Sîn] we[nt] to the Cedar Forest. Adab 404 (Istanbul): See Gelb and Kienast, Königsinschriften p. 50 D–7.
(z) [*in* 1 MU ^{d}*na-ra-am-*^{d}EN.Z]U [REC 169 ...]*-at*.KI [...*ga*]*l-at*.KI [*iš*$_{11}$]*-a-ru* [*ù śu*$_{4}$*-ma*] *in* [KUR *a*]*m-na-an* [GIŠ.ERIN] *ib-tú-qam* ‘[The year Narām-Sî]n was [vic]torious over GN$_{1}$ and GN$_{2}$ [in battle and personally] cut down [cedar timber] in the [A]manus [Mountains]’. Westenholz, OSP 2 p. 203 no. 1.
(aa) The Defeat of Mukiš. Recorded in E2.1.4.1004.
(bb) The Conquest of Armānum and Ebla. Recorded in E2.1.4.26 and alluded to in E2.1.4.27.

(vi) Temple Constructions Employing Cedar from the Amanus; the Digging of a Canal for Nippur

(cc) Construction of the Aštar Temple in Nineveh. Recorded in E2.1.4.28.
(dd) Construction of the Aštar Temple in Babylon(?). Recorded in E2.1.4.29.
(ee) The Digging of a Canal for Nippur: mu ^{d}*na-ra-am-*^{d}EN.ZU-e ka-I$_{7}$.e-erin-na-ka nibru.KI-šè si im-mi-sá-a ‘The year Narām Sîn directed the uptake of the Eʾeriṇa canal straight to Nippur’. CBS 4675: Barton, PBS 9/1 no. 25.

(vii) The Eastern Campaigns: The Conquest of Azuḫinnum, Lullubum, and the Area of Mount Ebiḫ (Simurrum, Ḫašimar, and Niqqum)
(dd) The Defeat of Azuḫinnum. Recorded in E2.1.4.30.
(gg) The Conquest of Lullubum. Recorded in E2.1.4.31.
(hh) The Defeat of Simurrum: *[i]n* 1 MU [^{d}]*na-ra-am-*^{d}⸢EN.ZU⸣ *a-na* KASKAL.⸢KI⸣ *śi-mu-ur*$_4$*-rí-im*.KI *i-li-ku* 'The year Narām-Sîn went on a campaign to Simurrum'. NBC 10920: Cohen, JCS 28 (1976) p. 228.
(ii) *in* 1 MU ^{d}*na-ra-am-*^{d}E[N.ZU] REC 448bis *śi-mu-ur*$_4$*-ri-*[*im*.KI] *in ki-ra-še-ni-we iš*$_{11}$*-a-ru ù ba-ba* ÉNSI *śi-mu-ur*$_4$*-ri-im*.KI *dub-ul* ÉNSI *a-ra-me*.KI *ik-mi-ù* 'The year Narām-Sîn was victorious over Simurrum at Kirašeniwe and captured Baba, governor of Simurrum, (and) Dubul, governor of Arame'. IM ... : Gelb, MAD 1 no. 217; A 22021: Gelb, MAD 1 no. 220.
(jj) A Campaign in the Eastern Mountains: [*in* 1 MU ...] *ti-*[...] [*b*]*í-bí-*[...] *en-a-*[*ru*] *ù* REC 169 ŚA.DÚ*-a-tim* [*in*] *ḫa-śi-ma-ar*.KUR [*iš*$_{11}$*-a-ru*]† '[The year Narām-Sîn(?)] ... defea[ted] [B]ibi-[...], and [was victorious] in battle in the mountains [at] Ḫašimar'. de Genouillac: ITT 5 no. 9265.
(kk) The Defeat of Niqqum. See commentary to E2.1.4.2005.

(viii) The Installation of En-men-ana
(ll) [mu] en-^{d}nanna dumu *na-<ra>-am-*^{d}EN.ZU ⸢maš⸣-e ⸢íb⸣-dab$_5$-ba '[The year] the *entu* priestess of the god Nanna, daughter of Narām-Sîn, was chosen by omens'. Biggs, OIP 97 p. 82 no. 10.

The Family of Narām-Sîn

Several inscriptions are known which mention Narām-Sîn's children; a summary list of these is given below.

Tūta-napšum, his daughter, and *entu* priestess of the god Enlil in Nippur: E2.1.4.20–22 and 2017.

En-men-ana, his daughter and *entu* priestess of the god Nanna in Ur: E2.1.4.32–33 and 2018–2020.

Šumšanī, his daughter, and *entu* priestess of the god Šamaš in Sippar: E2.1.4.48.

ME-Ulmaš, his daughter: E2.1.4.49.

Šar-kali-šarrī, his son, the crown prince: E2.1.4.2021.

Bin-kali-šarrī, his son: E2.1.4.2022.

Lipit-ilī, his son: E2.1.4.13.

Ukīn-Ulmaš, his son: E2.1.4.42.

Nabi-Ulmaš, his son, governor of Tutub, and Līpuš-iā'um, his granddaughter: E2.1.4.43.

Rigmuš-ālšu, his son: E2.1.4.2025.

1

If we were to assume an east to west progression in Narām-Sîn's conquest of Subartum, an early victory of the king would have been his defeat of the city of Talmus, a GN located by scholars at modern Jerahīyah on the Ḫosr river about 40 kms north of Mosul (see Th. Jacobsen, Jerwan p. 39). An inscription of Narām-Sîn known from an imperfectly preserved Old Babylonian tablet copy mentions captives of Talmus, and probably gave an account of the defeat of this city.

COMMENTARY

The inscription is found on AO 5474, a clay tablet of unknown provenance that measures 6×8.2 cm; it was collated by B. Foster, whose improved readings of a number of broken signs of the copy have been incorporated in this edition. Obv. cols. ii–iii and rev. cols. i–iii provide the text; obv. col. i is treated here as a separate inscription (see E2.1.4.1001). The curvature of the tablet suggests that the original had at least four columns per side. If one assumes that a divine dedication and curse formula followed the preserved text of col. i, then at least 14 lines should be allotted to the missing bottom section of the tablet.

For the reading of the GN as Talmus instead of Rīmuš, see the comments of K. Kessler, Nordmesopotamien p. 17 n. 87. The final sibilant of the OAkk. GN is read *-ús*, based on a comparison with the NA writing *tal-mu-si*. Of interest is the fact that most of the PNs of the captives listed in this inscription are Akkadian; no Hurrian PNs are found.

BIBLIOGRAPHY

1912 Thureau-Dangin, RA 9 p. 34 (copy, study)
1944 Gelb, Hurrians p. 36 (study)
1961 Gelb, MAD 2^2 p. 199 Narâm–Sin Late Copies no. 6 (study)
1963 Hirsch, AfO 20 pp. 21–22 b 8 (study)
1990 Gelb and Kienast, Königsinschriften pp. 131 and 251–53 Narāmsîn C 4 (copy, edition)

TEXT

Col. ii	
1′) [*na*]-⸢*ra-am*⸣^{d}E[N.ZU]	ii 1′–7′) [Na]rām-S[în], the mighty, king of Agade, and of the four quarters,
2′) *da-núm*	
3′) LUGAL	
4′) *a-kà-dè*.KI	
5′) *ù*	
6′) *ki-ib-ra-tim*	
7′) *ar-ba-im*	
8′) *mu-ut* ^{d}INANNA-	ii 8′–9′) spouse of the goddess Aštar-Annunītum,
9′) *an-nu-ni-tum*	
10′) *mu-tár-rí*	ii 10′–12′) leader of the troops of the city of the god Ilaba,
11′) ÉRIN URU	
12′) *ìl-a-*ba_4	
13′) *ì-n*[*u*]	ii 13′–15′) whe[n] the goddess Aštar ... [h]im
14′) ^{d}INANNA	Lacuna
15′) *lu im-da*(?)-⸤*š*⸥*u*	
Lacuna	
Col. iii	
1′) ^{m}[...]	iii 1′–14′) (Too broken for coherent translation.)

2′) ⸢*śar*⸣-[...]
3′) *u-má*-[...]
4′) ^{m}⸢*ir*⸣-[...]
5′) *u-pá-ḫi*-[*ir*]
6′) ^{m}*sá*-[...]
7′) ^{m}*ki*-[...]
8′) ^{m}*a*-⸢*bu*⸣-[...]
9′) ^{m}GÀR-[...]
10′) ^{m}*ba*-⸢*si*⸣-[...]
11′) ^{m}*a* x [...]
12′) ^{m}*ḫu*-⸢*ud*⸣-[...]
13′) ^{m}*r*[*i*-...] x [...]
14′) ^{m}[...]
Lacuna

Lacuna

Col. iv
Lacuna
1′) ^{m}[...]
2′) ^{m}BI [...]
3′) ^{m}*la* [...]
4′) ^{m}ÌR [...]
5′) ^{m}x [...]
6′) ^{m}x [...]
7′) ^{m}x [...]
8′) ^{m}x [...]
9′) ^{m}x [...]
10′) *ra* [...]
11′) *šu* [...]
12′) *šu* [...]
Lacuna

Lacuna
iv 1′–12′) (Too broken for coherent translation.)
Lacuna

Col. v
Lacuna
1′) ^{m}*pù*-⸢*su-su*⸣
2′) ŠEŠ-*śu*
3′) ^{m}*du-du*
4′) AB×ÁŠ URU.KI-*lim*(*)
5′) ^{m}*śu-ru-úś*-GI
6′) ŠABRA É
7′) ^{m}ur-^{d}nisaba
8′) DUB.SAR MAḪ
9′) ^{md}EN.ZU-KÁR
10′) UGULA DUB.SAR
11′) ^{m}*śum-śu-pá-luḫ*
12′) ^{m}*mu-mu*
13′) ^{m}*puzur*$_{4}$-*ru-um*
14′) ^{m}*ì-lí-íś-tá-kál*
15′) ^{m}*aš-tár-al-śu*

Lacuna
v 1′–2′) Pususu, his brother,

v 3′–4′) Dudu, elder of the city,

v 5′–6′) Šuruš-kīn, the majordomo,

v 7′–8′) Ur-Nisaba, the chief scribe,

v 9′–10′) Sîn-KÁR, the overseer of the scribes,

v 11′–15′) Šumšu-paluḫ, Mumu, Puzrum, Ilištakal, Aštar-alšu,

Col. vi
Lacuna
1′) *tal-mu-ús*.KI
2′) ⸢LÚ⸣.KAR
3′) KALAM ŠUBUR.KI
4′) *šu-ut* [*i*]*n pá-ni* ŠÍTA-*ì*
5′) *ìl-a-ba*$_{4}$
6′) *ù*
7′) ^{d}INANNA
8′) *a-na*
9′) [x] KALAM

Lacuna
vi 1′–3′) Talmus, (and) merchants of the land of Subartum,

vi 4′–13′) those whom he ... and [l]ed off [be]fore the mace of the gods Ilaba and Aštar to the land of GN, and ...
Lacuna

---

v 4′ Text: PI.

10′) [...]-⌈bí⌉-*im*.KI
11′) ⌈*u*⌉-⌈*sa*⌉-*u*
12′) [*u*]-*ra-am-ma*
13′) [...] x
Lacuna

2

An inscription of Narām-Sîn known from an Old Babylonian Sammeltafel copy from Nippur deals with the defeat of a coalition of Sumerian cities and Amorites headed by the king of a Sumerian city; the toponym appears in the text as REC 349.KI = AB×U/ŠUŠ.KI. This may be a reference to the city of Apišal, known from historiographical and literary texts of the second and first millennium that deal with Narām-Sîn.

COMMENTARY

The inscription is found on obv. i–vi and rev. i–ii 15 of HS 1954+1955+2499+2506, a clay tablet that measures 10.5×12.1×1.4 cm. The remaining lines of the Sammeltafel (rev. i 16–vii) are edited separately as E2.1.4.3 in this volume. The edition follows the editio princeps of B. Foster.

The campaign of Narām-Sîn against Apišal is recorded in an Old Babylonian literary text (see Güterbock, AfO 13 [1939–40] pp. 46-49 no. 11) and in a chronicle (see Grayson, Chronicles p. 154 lines 24–27). Further, the king of Apišal, a certain Rīš-Adad, appears as one of the foes of the king in the Old Babylonian version of the 'Great Revolt' (see Grayson and Sollberger, RA 70 [1976] p. 112 G 31). The defeat of Apišal also figures in the omen tradition (see Foster, ARRIM 8 [1990] p. 41). A hymn to the city AB×ŠUŠ appears in the 'Archaic zà-mì Hymns' (see Biggs, Abū Ṣalābīkh p. 49 line 102) followed by a hymn to the city of Umma. Evidence from Ur III economic tablets indicates that Apišal and Umma were neighbours.

The GN Aśimānum of col. ii line 4, as Foster points out in his edition, is likely to be connected with the Šimānum that is frequently attested in Ur III archival sources and in a Šū-Sîn royal inscription. It has been located by scholars in the mountainous area north of modern Mardin. An identification with modern Sinan on the Tigris River, about 63 kms northeast of Mardin, will be suggested in the author's forthcoming study of the Narām-Sîn chronology. The toponym in rev. v 29 is restored kar-[LAK 159-a-dé-dé.KI], based on a comparison with the GN kar-LAK 159-a-dé-dé that occurs in the archaic zà-mì hymns (Biggs, Abū Ṣalābīkh p. 49 lines 98–99). It is mentioned there three 'hymns' before Umma. In this text it occurs shortly after a mention of Umma (rev. v 23). The sign in rev. vi 36 is copied as by Foster.

BIBLIOGRAPHY

1963 Hirsch, AfO 20 pp. 19–20 Narâm-Sin b 2 (partial transliteration)
1969 Oelsner, WZJ 18 p. 52 no. 8 (study)
1990 Foster, ARRIM 8 (1990) pp. 25–44 (edition)
1990 Gelb and Kienast, Königsinschriften pp. 244–48 Narāmsîn C 2 (edition)

TEXT

Col. i
1) [*a*]-*na*
2) [EN].EN
3) [*a*]-*lí-a-tim*
4) *ù*
5) ÉNSI.ÉNSI
6) ŠUBUR.KI
7) *iś-tap-pá-ar-ma*

i 1–8) (The king of REC 349) kept sending *insulting messages* (about Narām-Sîn) [t]o the lord[s] of the [U]pper (Lands) and the governors of Subartum (saying):

8) *u-ṣe-li-ma*
9) ⌈*ni-al*⌉*-me*
10) [x x]*-me*
11) [x x] x
12) EN.EN
13) [*a*]*-lí-a-tim*
14) *ù*
15) ÉNSI.ÉNSI
16) ŠUBUR.KI
17) *ki-ma*
18) [^{d}]*en-líl*
19) [*i*]*-pá-la-ḫu*
20) [...] x*-ma*
21) [...] x
22) [...]
23) [...]
24) ⌈*it-ma*⌉*-ù-ni-šu*$_4$*-ma*
25) ^{m}lugal-AB
26) LUGAL
27) REC 349.KI
28) *á*(?)*-ru-ur-ma*
29) *lu-li-ik-ma-me*
30) [x]*-ma*
31) [...]*-ir*
32) ⌈*ù*⌉*-lu*
33) *á-mu-ut*
Col. ii
1) *ù-lu*
2) *u-na-áš*
3) *íš-tum*
4) *a-ši-ma-núm*.KI
5) *a-na*
6) *ši-ši-ìl*.KI
7) *in ši-ši-ìl*.KI
8) IDIGNA.I$_7$
9) *i-bi-ir-ma*
10) *íš-tum*
11) *ši-ši-ìl*.KI
12) *a-na*
13) *pu-ti* BURANUN.I$_7$
14) BURANUN.I$_7$*-tám*
15) *i-bi-ir-ma*
16) *a-na*
17) *ba-ša-ar*
18) ŠA.DÚ*-ì*
19) MAR.DÚ.KI
20) šu-bi igi(?) 1(?)-àm
21) *na-*<*ra-am*>-^{d}<EN.ZU>
22) *ma-núm*
23) *íš-ti-šu*$_4$*-ma*
24) *u-lá-*AŠ*-nu-i-e*
25) *a-kà-dè*.KI
26) ŠU.DU$_8$.A*-ma*
27) *a-na*
28) *pá-ni-*⌈*šu*$_4$⌉
29) *ip-du*
30) *i-gu-úš-ma*
31) *ḫa-ab-ša-at*.KI
Col. iii
1) *na-*[*ra-am*]-^{d}EN.[Z]U

i 9–11) (Too broken for translation)

i 12–23) The lords of the [U]pper (Lands) and the governors of Subartum, because they reverenced the [god] Enlil ...

i 24) They swore this (saying):
i 25 – ii 2) 'I(?) have cursed Lugal-AB, the king of REC 349. Let me go and ..., whether I die or keep (myself) alive'.

ii 3–6) He (Narām-Sîn, went) from Ašimānum to Šišil.

ii 7–13) At Šišil he crossed the Tigris River and (went) from Šišil to the *side* of the Euphrates River.

ii 14–20) He crossed the Euphrates River and (went) to Bašar, the Amorite mountain: (scribal notation: it is the same).

ii 21–29) (As for) Na<rām-Sîn>, anyone who held ... of Agade with them released (them) before him.

ii 30–31) He (Narām-Sîn) marched to Ḫabšat.

iii 1–8) Narām-Sîn, (going) fr[om] the Euphrates

2) *íś-t*[*um*]	River, reached Bašar, the Amorite mountain.
3) BURANUN.I$_7$	
4) *a-na*	
5) *ba-śa-ar*	
6) ŚA.DÚ-*ì*	
7) MAR.DÚ.KI	
8) *ik-śu$_4$-ud*	
9) *śu$_4$-ma*	iii 9–13) He personally *decided* to fight; (the two armies) made (battle) and fought one another.
10) REC 169	
11) *íś-im*(?)-*ma*	
12) *íś-ku$_8$-na-ma*	
13) *i-ta-aḫ-za-ma*	
14) *in* DI.[KU$_5$]	iii 14–16) By the ver[dict] of the goddess Aštar (scribal notation: it is the same).
15) ^{d}INANNA	
16) šu-bi ⌜igi⌝ [...]-àm(?)	
(blank)	
17) *na-*<*ra-am*>-^{d}<EN.ZU>	iii 17–24) Na<rām-Sîn>, the migh<ty>, was victorious in battle over REC 349 at Baš[ar], the Amorite mountain.
18) *da-*<*núm*>	
19) *in* REC 169	
20) *in ba-śa-*[*ar*]	
21) ŚA.DÚ-*ì*	
22) MAR.DÚ.KI	
23) REC 349.KI	
24) *iš$_{11}$-ar*	
25) *ù*	iii 25–27) Further, Enlil-zi: (scribal notation: the tablet *is broken*).
26) ^{d}en-líl-zi	
27) DUB ⌜*ḫe*(?)⌝-[*pi*(?)]	
(blank)	
28) ^{m}*du-*[...]	iii 28–29) Du-[...], go[vernor];
29) É[NSI]	
30) ^{m}*a-*[...]	iii 30 – iv 1) A-[...], go[vernor of [GN];
31) É[NSI]	
Col. iv	
Lacuna (about 5 lines)	Lacuna
6) [...]	iv 6) [of the city GN);
7) ^{m}lugal-nu-zu(?) ŠA.GAN.DU	iv 7–9) Lugal-nuzu(?), the captain of Umma;
8) NU.BÀNDA	
9) *umma*.KI	
10) ^{m}a-ba-^{d}en-líl	iv 10–12) Aba-Enlil, captain of Adab.
11) NU.BÀNDA	
12) *adab*.KI	
13) ŠU.NÍGIN 10 LAL 1 GURUŠ	iv 13–18) He struck do<wn> in the campaign a total of 9 chiefs and 4,325 men.
14) *ra-bí-a-ni*	
15) *ù*	
16) (7×600)+(2×60)+5 GURUŠ.GURUŠ	
17) *in* KASKAL	
18) *u-śa-am-*<*qí*/*qi$_4$-it*>	
19) *na-*<*ra-am*>^{d}<EN.ZU>	iv 19–25) Na<rām-Sîn>, the migh<ty>, captured [N] captives [and the kin]g(?) of REC 349 in the campaign.
20) *da-*<*núm*>	
21) [...] ⌜LÚ×KÁR⌝	
22) [*ù* LUGA]L(?)	
23) REC 349.KI	
24) *in* KASKAL	
25) *i-ik-mi*	
26) ^{m}é-e	iv 26–27) E'e, general;
27) GÌR.NITA	
28) ^{m}en-líl-<...> GAL.SUKKAL	iv 28–30) Enlil-<...>, grand vizier (and) city elder of REC 349;
29) AB×ÁŠ URU.KI	
30) REC 349.KI	

31) ^{m}lugal-TE+UNU(?)	iv 31–32) Lugal-TE+UNU(?), grand vizier;
32) GAL.SUKKAL	
33) ^{md}UTU-*mu-da*	iv 33–34) Šamaš-mūda, majordomo;
34) ŠABRA É	
Col. v	
1) ^{m}⸢ur⸣-[...]	v 1–4) Ur-[...], Ur-[...], and Nigin(?) of Nippur;
2) ^{m}⸢ur⸣-^{d}[...]	
3) ^{m}nìgin(?)	
4) NIBRU.KI-*ù*	
5) ^{md}en-líl-le	v 5–14) Enlile, Mir-si, Šeš-lu, ..., Sipade, Ur-Idigna, Uru-ki, Ur-ki, and Ur-gidru of Uruk;
6) ^{m}mir-si	
7) ^{m}šeš-lú	
8) ^{m}x-x	
9) ^{m}sipa-dè	
10) ^{m}ur-^{d}idigna	
11) ^{m}uru-ki	
12) ^{m}ur-ki	
13) ^{m}ur-gidru	
14) UNUG.KI-*ù*	
15) ^{m}*i-bí-ru-um*	v 15–16) Ibirum of Ur;
16) URI$_{5}$.KI	
17) ^{m}*ku-in*	v 17–18) Ku'in of Lagaš;
18) *lagaš*.KI	
19) ^{m}ad-da-tur	v 19–23) Adda-tur, Sag-sig, Lugal-dugani-zi, and E-zi of Umma;
20) ^{m}sag-sig	
21) ^{m}lugal-du$_{11}$-ga-ni-zi	
22) ^{m}é-zi	
23) *umma*.KI-*ù*	
24) ^{m}da-da	v 24–26) Dada and [U]r-gidru, of the city [GN];
25) [^{m}u]r-gidru	
26) x [...].KI-*ù*	
27) ^{m}*šu*-^{d}[...]	v 27–29) Šū-[...], ca[ptain] of Kar-[LAK 159-adede];
28) NU.[BÀNDA]	
29) *kar*-[LAK 159-*a-dé-dé*.KI]	
30) ^{m}NI-[...]	v 30–32) Ni-[...], ca[ptain] of REC 349;
31) NU.[BÀNDA]	
32) REC 349.KI	
33) ^{m}ur-[...] x [...]	v 33–35) Ur-[...] ca[ptain] of Lagaš;
34) NU.BÀ[NDA]	
35) *lagaš*.KI	
Col. vi	
Lacuna (3 lines)	
4) ⸢NU⸣.BÀNDA	vi 4–5) captain of Adab;
5) *adab*.KI	
6) ^{m}lugal-šà-uru	vi 6–8) (and) Lugal-šauru, captain of Nippur
7) NU.BÀNDA	
8) NIBRU.KI	
9) NU.BÀNDA-*ù*	vi 9) (were) the captains.
10) ^{m}*be-lí-lí*	vi 10–12) Belili (and) KIN-u(?)'ua (were) the Amorites.
11) ^{m}KIN-*u*$_{8}$(?)-*ú-a*	
12) MAR.DÚ.MAR.DÚ	
13) *ra-bu*	vi 13–19) Leaders and chiefs, as well as *5,580* captives (whom) he captured in the campaign.
14) *ù*	
15) *ra-bí-a-ni*	
16) *ù*	
17) 3600(?)+(3×600)+(3×60) LÚ×KÁR	
18) *in* KASKAL	
19) *i-ik-mi*	
20) ŠU.NÍGIN 6 GÌR.NITA GÌR.NITA	vi 20) Total: 6 generals.

21) ŠU.NÍGIN 20 LAL 3 ÉNSI ÉNSI	vi 21) Total: 17 governors.
22) ŠU.NÍGIN 60+20 LAL 2 *ra-bí-a-ni*	vi 22) Total: 78 chiefs.
23) ŠU.NÍGIN x+(3×600(?))+60+10 N[U.BÀNDA]	vi 23) Total: N ca[ptains].
Col. vii	
Lacuna (3 lines)	Lacuna
4) x [...] 5) ŠU.NÍGIN [...] 6) [...] 7) LUGAL	vii 4–7) ... (Grand) total: [N] king(s).
8) ŠU.NÍGIN 13 GÌR.NITA GÌR.NITA	vii 8) (Grand) total: 13 generals.
9) ŠU.NÍGIN 23 ÉNSI.ÉNSI	vii 9) (Grand) total: 23 governors.
10) ŠU.NÍGIN (2×600)+10+2 *ra-bí-a-ni*	vii 10) Grand total: 1,212 chiefs.
11) ŠU.NÍGIN ŠU.NÍGIN (2x60,000[?])+36,000(?)+(?)+(7×600[?]) LAL 60(?) GURUŠ GURUŠ	vii 11) Grand total: *137,400* men.
12) ^{d}*en-líl* 13) *u-kál-lim*	vii 12–13) The god Enlil showed (him the way and)
14) *na-*<*ra-am*>-^{d}<EN.ZU> 15) *da-núm* 16) *in* KASKAL 17) *ma-lá-šu*$_4$*-nu* 18) *u-śa-am-*<*qí/qi*$_4$*-it*> 19) *ù* 20) *i-ik-mi*	vii 14–20) Na<rām-Sîn>, the mighty, struck <down> as many as there were in the campaign, and captured (them).
21) *ù* 22) *šu-un-ni-śu*$_4$*-nu* 23) *na-*<*ra-am-*^{d}EN.ZU> 24) *da-núm* 25) *in* KÁ 26) *ì-li-ma* 27) *u-śa-am-ni*	vii 21–27) Nar<ām-Sîn>, the mighty, made an acount of their ... at the gate of the gods.
28) ^{d}⸢*en*⸣-[*líl*(?)] 29) [*ú-má*] 30) [*la sú-ra-tum*$_8$]	vii 28–29) By the god *Enlil* [I swear that (these) are not falsehoods],
Col. viii	
1) *lu kí-ni-íś-ma*	viii 1) (but) are indeed true.
2) KUŠ-*śu*$_4$*-nu* 3) *im-rí*	viii 2–3) He ... their bodies.
4) ^{d}INANNA- 5) *an-nu-ni-tum* 6) *ù* 7) ^{d}*en-*⸢*líl*(?)⸣ 8) *na-*<*ra-am*>-^{d}<EN.ZU> 9) *da-núm* 10) *in* ŠITA 11) *ìl-a-ba*$_4$ 12) *be-lí-śu* 13) *lu i-ik-mi-śu-nu-ma* 14) *lu u-śa-rí-bu-śu*$_4$*-nu* 15) *in kí-nim*	viii 4–15) By the goddess Aštar-Annunītum and the god *Enlil* (I swear) that Na<rām-Sîn>, the mighty, did indeed truly capture them and bring them in by means of the mace of the god Ilaba.

3

An inscription of Narām-Sîn known from two Old Babylonian tablet copies from Nippur deals with a campaign against Magan.

CATALOGUE

Ex	Museum number	Tablet lines preserved	Corresponding lines of ex. 1	cpn
1	HS 1954+1955+2499+2506	Col. viii = rev. ii 16–35	—	c
		Col. ix = rev. iii 1–36	—	
		Col. x = rev. iv 1–36, 39	—	
		Col. xi = rev. v 1–9, 15–34	—	
		Col. xii = rev. vi 1–12, 19–37	—	
		Col. xiii = rev. vii 1–19	—	
2	N 3539+CBS 14547(+)CBS 2344	rev. 1′2′–5′	rev. ii 16–19	c
		rev. ii′ 1′–16′	rev. iii 18–33	
		rev. iii′ 1′–12′	rev. iv 30– rev. v 10	
		rev. iv′ 1′–20′	rev. vi 3–24	

COMMENTARY

The inscription is found on rev. ii 16 – rev. vii 9 of ex. 1, the Jena tablet. This section begins with a listing of the titulary of the king. Since this is normally found at the beginning of a royal inscription, we propose that a new inscription began at this point. If this is true, the Jena tablet would be a Sammeltafel with two inscriptions — the first an account of the crushing of the revolt of the king of REC 349, and the second a narrative of the Magan campaign. We have, however, retained the original line numbers of Foster's edition. As for ex. 2, the curse formula recorded on the reverse of the tablet totally agrees with that found on ex. 1 and is thus considered to be a duplicate of this inscription. The obverse, on the other hand, provides us with a different inscription (E2.1.4.6). Thus the tablet of ex. 2 was, in all likelihood, also a Sammeltafel.

In the chronicle tradition an account of Narām-Sîn's Magan campaign immediately follows a report of his defeat of the king of Apišal (see Grayson, Chronicles p. 154 lines 24–27). Since Narām-Sîn's name is written in this inscription without the prefixed divine determinative, the Magan campaign, in addition to the crushing of the Apišalian revolt, probably predated the events of the 'Great Revolt'.

The reading of rev. ii 34 is unclear. It consists of two identical signs copied as by Foster (ARRIM 8 p. 28). Foster read: ŠU.NÍGIN(!?).ŠU.NÍGIN(!?) and noted (p. 37) that 'the signs do not closely resemble the other ŠU.NÍGIN signs in the same text'. We have understood the line to contain a reduplicated logogram; it likely corresponds to the *bu-ra-a-at* of the Geneva exemplar of the Old Babylonian version of the 'Great Revolt' (see Grayson and Sollberger, RA 70 [1976] p. 111, line 7). Hence, we have given the translation '*sources*' in this edition. The epithet *mūtarrûm* 'leader' (Gtn participle of *warû*[*m*]) of rev. iii 4 also occurs in E2.1.4.1 ii 10′. Unfortunately, the context in which it appears in this text is obscure. For the *kurkurru*(*m*) vessel of v 9, 24, and 28, see Steinkeller, Texts Baghdad, pp. 53–54.

BIBLIOGRAPHY

1914 Poebel, PBS 4/1 pp. 212–14 no. 36 rev. (ex. 2, edition)
1914 Poebel, PBS 5 no. 36 rev. and pl. CI (ex. 2, photo, copy)
1961 Gelb, MAD 2^2 p. 199 Narâm-Sin Late Copies no. 1 (ex. 2, study)
1963 Hirsch, AfO 20 p. 19 Narâm-Sin b 1 (ex. 2, study) and pp. 19–20 Narâm-Sin b 2 (ex. 1, partial transliteration, study)
1969 Oelsner, WZJ 18 p. 52 no. 8 (ex. 1, study)
1973 Gelb, JNES 32 p. 73 (study)
1978–79 Jacobsen, AfO 26 p. 12 (ex. 2, partial edition)
1990 Foster, ARRIM 8 (1990) pp. 1–21 (ex. 1, edition)
1990 Gelb and Kienast, Königsinschriften pp. 234–38, 242–43 Narāmsîn C 1 (latter part) (ex. 2, edition)

TEXT

Rev. col. ii
16) *na-<ra-am>-*^{d}<EN.ZU>
17) *da-núm*
18) *in śi-ip-rí*
19) ^{d}INANNA
20) *il-śu*$_4$
(large wedge)
21) LUGAL
22) *a-kà-dè*.KI
23) *ù*
24) LUGAL
(space)
25) [...] x
26) [...] x
27) [...-*l*]*im*
28) [...] x
29) É[N]SI
30) ^{d}*en-líl*
31) GÌR.NITA
32) *ìl-a-ba*$_4$
33) MAŠKIM.GI$_4$
34) x x
35) *ir-ni-*[*na*.I$_7$]
Rev. col. iii
1) *mu-kí-in*
2) SUḪUŠ.SUḪUŠ
3) *a-kà-dè*.KI
4) *mu-tár-rí*
5) *dú-un-nim*
6) *a-na*
7) GA.NI
8) *in* É
9) ^{d}*en-*⸢*líl*⸣
10) [...]
11) [...]
12) [...].KI
13) [...]-*na*
14) šu-bi igi(?) 2(?)-àm
15) *ì-nu*
16) *ki-ib-*<*ra-tum*$_8$>
17) *ar-*<*ba-um*>
18) *iś-ti-ni-íś* <*i-*KIR*-ni-śu*$_4$>
19) *śar in śar-rí*
20) *ma-na-ma*
21) *la i-mu-ru*
22) *ì-nu*
23) *na-ra-am-*^{d}EN.ZU
24) *da-núm*
25) *in śi-ip-rí*
26) ^{d}INANNA
27) *kà-lu*$_5$*-ma*
28) *ki-ib-ra-*⸢*tum*$_8$⸣
29) *ar-ba-um*
30) *íś-ti-ni-íś*

rev. ii 16–20) Na<rām-Sîn>, the mighty, (who is) on a mission for the goddess Aštar, his (personal) deity is ...,

ii 21–26) king of Agade and king [*of the four quarters*],

ii 27–28) ...,

ii 29–30) gov[er]nor of the god Enlil,

ii 31–32) general of the god Ilaba,

ii 33–35) guardian of the *sources* of the Irni[na River],

rev. iii 1–3) who made firm the foundations of Agade,

iii 4–9) mighty leader for ... in the temple of the god Enlil

iii 10–14) ... (scribal notation: it is the same)

iii 15–18) When the fo<ur> quar<ters> together <revolted against him>,

iii 19–21) (which) no king whosoever had (ever) seen: .

iii 22–26) when Narām-Sîn, the mighty, (was detained[?]) on a mission for the goddess Aštar,

iii 27–32) all the four quarters together revolted against him and confronted (him).

Rev. iii 23.1 *na-*<*ra-am*>-^{d}<EN.ZU>.

31) *i*-KIR$_x$(ḪA)-*ni-šu$_4$-ma*
32) *im-ḫu-ru-nim*
33) ⸢LUGAL(?)⸣-*am*(?)
34) [...]
35) [...]-⸢*ù*⸣
36) [...-DA]M(?)
Rev. col. iv
1) [x]-*iš-ti*
2) [...]-*tim*
3) [*in*] DI.KU$_5$
4) [^{d}*en*]-*líl*
5) [...] NE
6) [x x] x
7) *iḫ*(?)-*ma*(?)-ZI(?)
8) ^{d}[*e*]*n-l*[*íl*]
9) *be-lí-šu*
10) *in* [...]
11) MU [...]
12) [...]
13) [...]
14) [...] ši x [...]
15) [x] *ši-la*
16) [...]-*ù*
17) [...] x
18) [...] UD(?)
19) *ù*
20) *ti-*[*a-am-ti*]*m*
21) *i-in*(?) [x (x)]
22) *iš*-[...]
23) *i*-⸢*bi*⸣-[*ir-m*]*a*
24) *m*[*á-gan*.K]I
25) ⸢*qáb*⸣-*li*
26) *ti-*[*a*]-*am-tim*
27) SAG.GIŠ.RA
28) *ù*
29) GIŠ.TUKUL-*kí-šu$_4$*
30) *i*[*n*] *ti-a-am-tim*
31) *ša-píl-tim*
32) Ì.LUḪ
33) *na-ra-am*-^{d}EN.ZU
34) *da-núm*
35) *in ši-ip-rí*
36) ^{d}INANNA
37) *ì-nu*
38) ^{d}*en-líl*
39) DI.KU$_5$-*šu*
40) *i-dì-nu-ma*
41) *ù*
Rev. col. v
1) *ṣé-ra-at*
2) NI.SI$_{11}$
3) *qá-ti-ís-su*
4) *i-dì-nu*
5) *ù*
6) *na-e*
7) *e-er-tim*

iii 33) The *king*
iii 34 - iv 2 (Too broken for coherent translation)

rev. iv 3–7) [By] the verdict of the god [En]lil he ...

iv 8–9) [of E]nl[il], his lord

iv 10–18) (Too broken for coherent translation)

iv 19–27) Further, he cros[sed] ... the (Lower) S[ea] and conquered M[agan], in the midst of the sea,

iv 28–32) and washed his weapons in the Lower Sea.

iv 33–36) Narām-Sîn, the mighty, (who is) on a mission for the goddess Aštar,

iv 37–40) when the god Enlil determined (this) verdict (for) him,

iv 41–v 4) entrusted the lead-rope of the people into his hands,

rev. v 5–8) and gave him no superior,

Rev. iii 31.2 *i*-KIR-*ni-šu$_4$-ma*.
Rev. iv 31.1 [*ša*]-⸢*píl*⸣-*tim*.
Rev. iv 33.1 *na*-<*ra-am*>-^{d}<EN.ZU>.

8) *la i-dì-nu-śum*$_{6}$
9) DUG(?).KUR.KU.DÙ [Ì]
10) [IGI-*me*] ⸢^{d}*en-líl*⸣
11) [...]
12) [...]
13) [...]
14) [...]
15) [A].MU.RU

v 9–15) [*he set up* before] the god Enlil a *kurkurru* vessel [for oil] and dedicated (it to him).

16) *ma-na-ma*
17) MU
18) *na-*<*ra-am*>*-*^{d}<EN.ZU>
19) LUGAL
20) *a-kà-dè*.KI
21) GÌR.NITA<<DU>>
22) *ìl-a-ba*$_{4}$
23) *u-śa-sà-ku-ni*(!)

v 16–23) As for the one who removes the inscription of Na<rām-Sîn>, king of Agade, general of the god Ilaba,

24) *al* DUG(?).KUR.KU.DÙ Ì
25) *na-*<*ra-am*>*-*^{d}<EN.ZU>
26) MU-*śu*
27) *i-śa-kà-nu-ma*

v 24–27) puts his name on the *kurkurru* vessel for oil of Na<rām-Sîn>, and

28) DUG(?).KUR.KU.DÙ.Ì-*me*
29) *i-qá-bì-ù*

v 28–29) says: '(This is) my *kurkurru* vessel for oil,

30) *ù*
31) LÚ.KAS$_{4}$
32) LÚ-*lam*
33) *ša-ni-am*
34) *u-kál-la-mu-ma*

v 30–34) or shows it to an outsider or stranger and

Rev. col. vi
1) MU-*śu-me*
2) *pi-ší-iṭ-ma*
3) MU-*mi-me*
4) *śu-kù-un*
5) *i-qá-bì-ù*

rev. vi 1–5) says: 'Erase his name and put my name (on it)',

6) ^{d}INANNA--
7) *an-nu-ni-tum*
8) AN
9) ^{d}*en-líl*
10) *ìl-a-ba*$_{4}$
11) ^{d}EN.ZU
12) ^{d}⸢UTU⸣
13) ^{d}[*nergal*]
14) ⸢^{d}⸣*u-um*
15) ⸢^{d}⸣*nin-kar*
16) ⸢*ì*⸣*-lu*
17) *ra-bí-ù-tum*
18) *in* ŠU.NÍGIN-*śu-nu*

vi 6–18) may the goddess Aštar-Annunītum, (and) the gods Anum, Enlil, Ilaba, Sîn, Šamaš, Nergal, Ūm(um), the goddess Ninkar(rak), the great gods in their totality,

19) *ar-ra-tám*
20) [*l*]*a-mu-ut-tám*
21) *li-ru-ru-úś*

vi 19–21) curse him with a terrible curse.

22) GIDRU *a-na*
23) ^{d}*en-líl*
24) *e u-kí-il*

vi 22–24) May he not hold the sceptre (of kingship) for the god Enlil

25) *śar-ru*$_{9}$(URU)*-tám*
26) *a-na*
27) ^{d}INANNA
28) *e iṣ-ba-at*

vi 25–28) (and) may he not seize the kingship for the goddess Aštar.

29) ^{d}*nin-ḫur-sag*

vi 29–35) May the goddesses Ninḫursag and Nintu

Rev. v 9.2 DUG(?).KUR.KU.DÙ
Rev. vi 20.1 [*la-m*]*u-tám*.

30) *ù*
31) ^{d}*nin-tu*
32) NITA
33) *ù*
34) MU
35) *a i-dì-na-šum*$_6$
36) *ra*-x
37) *šar-ru*$_9$(URU)-*šu*
Rev. col. vii
1) ^{d}[IŠKUR]
2) *ù*
3) ^{d}*nisaba*
4) ⌜*ši*$_4$⌝-*rí-iḫ-šu*$_4$
5) *e u-še-ši-ra*
6) ^{d}EN.KI
7) I$_7$-*šu*$_4$
8) *sà-ki-kà-am*
9) *li-im-dú-ud*

not grant him a male (heir) or offspring.

vi 36–37) ... his kingship,

rev. vii 1–5) May the gods [Adad] and Nisaba not let his furrow flourish.

vii 6–9) May the god Ea *block up* his canal with silt.

4

Four vases bear an inscription of Narām-Sîn indicating they were booty of Magan.

CATALOGUE

Ex.	Museum number	Excavation number	Provenance	Object	Dimensions (cm)	Gelb and Kienast	Lines preserved	cpn
1	—	—	Found at Babylon, near the Nil canal(?) by M. Fresnel	Alabaster vase	—	A	1–7	n
2	NBC 2527	—	—	Alabaster vase	6.4 dia.	C	1–7	p
3	BLMJ 929	—	—	Calcite vase	6.3 high 16.6 dia.	D	1–7	c
4	CBS 14951+14952	U 282+283	Ur, under the Kurigalzu floor of the E-nun-mah, room 11	Black steatite cylindrical bowl frgm.	10.3 dia.	—	1–5	c

COMMENTARY

Ex. 1 is known only from a hand copy prepared from a paper squeeze. The original was said by Rawlinson to have been 'lost in the Tigris', an apparent allusion to the 'Qurna disaster' of 1855. However, as W.G. Lambert has pointed out to the author, this may merely be a deduction from the absence of the piece from Paris. No French source states that the piece was lost in the disaster. The possibility exists, then, that ex. 3 could be the piece published by Rawlinson. The inscription found on ex. 2 arranges the text in 6 lines with unusual line breaks; it is certainly a modern forgery. Ex. 3, on the other hand, according to notes of W.G. Lambert and P. Steinkeller, who collated the inscription, is certainly genuine. A further posited duplicate of this inscription is an incised alabaster vase fragment from Susa published by V. Scheil as MDP 4 p. 1 and pl. I no. 1. Unlike the other pieces, the Susa fragment has the king's name written with the prefixed divine determinative and line 5 has what appear to be traces of an *in* sign rather than a BUR sign. Its inscription has been edited in this volume as a separate text (E2.1.4.42). E. Braun-Holzinger has noted (OrAnt 26 [1988] pp. 288–90) that parallels provided by other Sargonic votive inscriptions suggest that BUR of line 5 of ex. 1 may have resulted from a miscopy of an original *in* sign. However since both exs. 3 and 4 (for the latter, see T. Potts [Iraq 51 (1989) p. 132]) give a clear BUR sign, Braun-Holzinger's hypothesis can safely be dismissed.

BIBLIOGRAPHY

1859 Oppert, Expédition II pp. 62 and 327 (ex. 1, provenance, copy)
1861 1 R pl. 3 no. VII (ex. 1, copy)
1872 Smith, TSBA 1 p. 52 (ex. 1, translation)
1875 Ménant, Babylone p. 103 (ex. 1, translation)
1880 Ménant, Manuel p. 314 (ex. 1, copy)
1881 Oppert, Verh. d. fünften Intern. Or.–Köngr. II p. 245 (ex. 1, study)
1883–84 Pinches, PSBA 6 p. 13 (ex. 1, translation)
1884 Hommel, ZK 1 p. 67 (ex.1, edition)
1886 Bezold, Literatur p. 36 § 12 (ex. 1, study)
1892 Winckler, KB 3/1 pp. 98–99 (ex. 1, edition)
1892 Winckler and Böhden ABK no. 63 (ex. 1, copy)
1907 Thureau-Dangin, SAK pp. 164–65 Narâm-sin c (ex. 1, edition)
1929 Barton, RISA pp. 138–39 Naram-Sin 3 (ex. 1, edition)
1937 Stephens, YOS 9 no. 95 (ex. 2, photo, transliteration)
1941–44 Ugnad, AfO 14 pp. 199–200 (exs. 1–2, study, translation)
1955 Woolley, UE 4 p. 168 (ex. 4, frgm. 1, study)
1960 Sollberger, Iraq 22 pp. 77–78 no. 103 (ex. 4, frgm. 1, study)
1961 Gelb, MAD 2^2 p. 199 Narâm-Sin Original Inscriptions nos. 5a and c (exs. 1–2, study)
1963 Hirsch, AfO 20 p. 18 Narâm-Sin a 5 α and γ (exs. 1–2, study)
1965 Sollberger, UET 8 p. 35 no. 42 (ex. 4, transliteration)
1966 Nagel, BJVF 6 pp. 15–17 and figs. 2–31
1974 Woolley, UE 6 p. 88 (ex. 4, frgm. 2, study)
1981 Sweet, in Muscarella, Ladders no. 33 (ex. 3, photo, edition)
1986 Potts, OrAnt 25 pp. 278–80 and pls. XXIIb–XXIV (exs. 1–3, study, translation; exs. 1–2, copy; exs. 2–3, photo)
1987 Braun-Holzinger, OrAnt 26 pp. 285–90 (exs, 1–3, edition, study)
1987 Goodnick Westenholz in Merhav, Treasures no. 18 (ex. 3, photo, translation)
1989 Potts, Iraq 51 pp. 132–34, 152 Inscription A, and 156 fig. 10 (exs. 1, 3, 4 translation, study; ex. 4, photo, copy, transliteration)
1990 Gelb and Kienast, Köngisinschriften p. 98 Narāmsîn 13 Texts A, C, D (exs. 1–3, edition); Narāmsîn 14 Text F (ex. 4, edition [wrong text attribution])

TEXT

1) *na-ra-am-*ᵈEN.ZU
2) LUGAL
3) *ki-ib-ra-tim*
4) *ar-ba-im*
5) BUR
6) NAM.RA.AK
7) *má-gan*.KI

1–4) Narām-Sîn, king of the four quarters:

5–7) a bowl, booty of Magan.

5

An inscription of Narām-Sîn known from two partially preserved Old Babylonian tablet copies from Ur records the dedication of a statue to the god Sîn. The occasion for the dedication may have been the defeat of an enemy leader.

CATALOGUE

Ex.	Museum number	Excavation number	Ur provenance	Tablet lines preserved	Text lines preserved	cpn
1	IM —	U 7736	No. 7 Quiet Street room 5 or 6	col. i 1–33 col. ii 1–32 col. iii 1–2 col. iii 3–5 col. iv Traces	col. ii′ 1–33 col. iii′ 1–32 col. iv′ 1–2 Caption 1′ col. iv′ 3–5 Caption 2′ col. v′ Traces Caption(?)	n
2	IM 85670	U d	—	col. i′ 1′–7′ col. ii′ 1′, 3′, 6′–12′ col. iii′ 1–15 col. iv′ 1–7	col. i′ 1′–7′ col. ii′ 8, 10, 13–19 col. ii′ 20–32 col. iii′ 17–22	n

COMMENTARY

The reconstructed text is a conflated one; the line count and text for col. i′ come from ex. 2; the line count for the remainder of the text comes from ex. 1.

The beginning of this inscription is missing; the extant text records the dedication of a statue of Narām-Sîn to the god Sîn and recounts a curse against anyone who might damage the statue. B. Foster (JANES 14 [1982] pp. 27–28) proposed that the occasion for dedication was the king's victory over the cities of Armānum and Ebla. He took UET 1 276, a text that deals with Narām-Sîn's campaign against Armānum and which is edited as E2.1.4.26 in this volume, to be a direct continuation of UET 1 275. However, there are some difficulties with Foster's hypothesis. In UET 1 275 the royal name is consistently rendered with the prefixed divine determinative, as we would expect, since in contemporary inscriptions referring to the defeat of the Armānum and Ebla the king's name appears with the DINGIR sign. In both exemplars of this inscription, on the other hand, no DINGIR sign appears before the royal name. One of the two preserved captions of this inscription names a certain lugal-uru-si as general of Sumer and Akkad. As far as can be determined, the captions noted in the copies of Sargonic royal inscriptions, apart from those identifying the king, refer to enemy leaders. If this inscription did indeed deal with the defeat of Armānum, then we might expect to find the name of the ruler of Armānum, Rīd-Adad, or of one of his retainers, at the end. The fact that we find a quite different name suggests that this is a different inscription.

In iii′ 29 the A sign is likely a dittography arising from the ÍD sign of the previous line. The parallel passage in E2.1.4.4 rev. vii 7–9 gives I$_{7}$-*šu*$_{4}$ *sà-ki-kà-am li-im-dú-ud* 'May (the god Ea) block up his canal with silt'.

BIBLIOGRAPHY

1928 Gadd, UET 1 no. 276 (ex. 1, copy, edition)
1963 Hirsch, AfO 20 pp. 21, 77–78 and 82 Narâm-Sin b 6 (ex. 1, edition, study)
1965 Sollberger, UET 8 no. 13 (ex. 2, copy); pp. 32–33 no. 35 (ex.1, study)
1961 Gelb, MAD 2^{2} p. 199 Late Copies no. 4 (ex. 1, study)
1982 Foster, JANES 14 pp. 27–36 (exs. 1–2, edition)
1990 Gelb and Kienast, Königsinschriften pp. 253–54, 257–60 sub Narāmsîn C 5 Texts B and C (exs. 1–2, edition)

TEXT

Col. i′
Lacuna
1′) [*a-n*]*a*
2′) [^{d}EN].⸢ZU⸣
3′) [*áš-ru*]*-uk*(*)
4′) [*ma-n*]*a-ma*
5′) [MU]*-mi*
6′) ⸢*a*⸣ *u-ša-sí-ik*
7′) [DÙ]L*-mi*
8′) [*ma-ḫa-ar*]
9′ [^{d}EN.ZU]
10′) [*li-zi-iz*]
Lacuna

i′ 1′–3′) [I (Narām-Sîn) pres]ented (this statue) [t]o [the god Sî]n.

i′ 4′–10′) May no [o]ne remove my [inscription. (Rather), may] my [stat]ue [stand before the god Sîn].
Lacuna

Col.ii′
1) *ma-na-ma*
2) MU*-mi*
3) *na-ra-am-*^{d}EN.ZU
4) *da-nim*(!)
5) LUGAL
6) *ki-ib-ra-tim*
7) *ar-ba-im*
8) *u-ša-sà-ku-ma*

ii′ 1–8) As for the one who removes the name of Narām-Sîn, the mighty, king of the four quarters,

9) *al* DÙL
10) *na-ra-am-*^{d}EN.ZU
11) *da-nim*
12) MU*-šu*
13) *i-ša-kà-nu-ma*

ii′ 9–15) puts his (own) name on the statue of Narām-Sîn, the mighty, and says 'It is my statue',

i′ 3′.2 Text: AZ.

14) DÙL-*mi-me*
15) *i-qá-bi-ù*
16) *ù* LÚ-*lam*
17) *na-kà-ra-am*
18) *u-kál-la-mu-ma*
19) MU-*śu-me*
20) *pi*$_5$-*ši*$_x$(SU$_4$)-*iṭ-ma*
21) MU-*mi*
22) *śu-ku*$_8$-*un*
23) *i-qá-bi-ù*

ii′ 16–23) or shows (it) to a foreigner and says: 'Erase his name and put my name (on it)',

24) ^{d}EN.ZU
25) *be-al*
26) DÙL ⸢*śu*$_4$⸣-*a*
27) *ù* ^{d}INANNA-
28) *an-nu-ni-tum*
29) AN
30) ^{d}*en-líl*
31) *ìl-a-ba*$_4$
32) ⸢^{d}⸣[EN].ZU
33) [^{d}]UTU

Col.iii′

1) ^{d}*nergal*
2) ^{d}*u-um*
3) ^{d}*nin-kar-ak*
4) DINGIR *ra-bí-ù-tum*
5) *in* ŠU.NÍGIN-*su*$_4$-*nu*

ii′ 24 – iii′ 5) may the god Sîn, owner of this statue, the goddess Aštar-Annunītum, (and the gods) Anum, Enlil, Ilaba, [Sî]n, Šamaš, Nergal Ūm(um), Ninkarrak, the great gods in their totality,

6) *ar*(*)-*ra-tám*
7) *la-mu-tám*
8) *li-ru-ru-úś*

iii′ 6–8) curse him with a terrible curse.

9) GIDRU
10) *a-na* ^{d}*en-*⸢*líl*⸣
11) *śar-ru-tám*
12) *a-na* ^{d}INANNA
13) *a u-kí-il*

iii′ 9–13) May he not hold the sceptre (of kingship) for the god Enlil or the kingship for the goddess Aštar.

14) *maḫ-rí-íś*
15) *ì-lí-śu*
16) *a* DU

iii′ 14–16) May he not walk before his (personal) god.

17) ^{d}*nin-ḫur-sag-gá*
18) *ù*
19) ^{d}*nin-tu*
20) NITA *ù*
21) MU
22) [*a*] *i-dì-na-śum*$_6$

iii′ 17–22) May the goddesses Ninḫursag and Nintu [not] grant him a male (heir) or offspring.

23) ⸢^{d}⸣IŠKUR
24) *ù* ^{d}*nisaba*
25) [*ś*]*i-rí-iḫ-śu*
26) *a* ⸢*ù*⸣-*śe-śi-*⸢*ra*⸣

iii′ 23–26) May the gods Adad and Nisaba not let his furrow flourish.

27) ⸢^{d}⸣EN.⸢KI⸣
28) ÍD-*śu*
29) <<A>> *li-im-dú-ud*
30) *ù* GIŠ.TÚG.PI(*)
31) *a u+ra*(*)-*pí*-IŠ(*)
32) *u-rí-*⸢IŠ⸣

iii′ 27–32) May the god Ea *block up* his canal and not increase (his) wisdom ...

---

ii' 26.2 DÙL *šu-a*.
iii' 6.1 Text: Ù.
iii' 17.2 [^{d}*nin-ḫur-sag*]-⸢*gá*(?)⸣.
iii' 30.1 Text: KAM.
iii' 31.1 *ra*(*) Text: SIKIL; IŠ(*) Text: MA.

Col. iv′
Caption 1′
1) [AN.TA (x)] NE
2) ⌈*im-li*⌉-*ik*
Caption 2′
1) KI.[TA] GÌR.NITA
2) KI.EN.GI KI.URI
3) lugal-uru-si
Col. v′
(Traces)

Caption 1′
1–2) [Above ...], *Imlik.*

Caption 2′
1-3) Below, the general of the land of Sumer and Akkad, Lugal-uru-si.

v′
(Traces)

6

An inscription of Narām-Sîn known from two Old Babylonian tablet copies from Nippur deals with his crushing of the 'Great Revolt'. The inscription informs us that two grand coalitions rebelled against the Sargonic king: a confederacy of northern cities led by Ipḫur-Kiš, king of Kiš, and a league of southern Sumerian cities headed by Amar-Girid, king of Uruk. A third antagonist of Narām-Sîn was probably Enlil-nizu of Nippur.

CATALOGUE

Ex.	Museum Number	Dimensions (cm)	Tablet lines preserved	Text lines preserved	cpn
1	BT 1	8.0×19.0×2.7	col. i 1′–20′, 1″-21″ col. ii 1′–22′, 24′-43′ col. iii 1′–45′ col. iv 1′–45′ col. v 2′–25′, 27′–39′ col. vi Traces	col. i 1′–20′, 1″-21″ col. ii 1′–22′, 24′-43′ col. iii 1′–45′ col. iv 1′–45′ col. v 2′–25′, 27′–39′ col. vi Traces	p
2	N 3539+CBS 15474(+)CBS 2344	—	col. i 1–10 col. ii 1–6 col. iii 1–5 col. iii 1′–5′ col. iv 1′–6′ col. v 1′–20′ col. vi 1′–17′ col. vi 1′–13′	col. i 1–10 col. i 13″–18″ col. ii 29′–34′ 5 unplaced lines col. iii 27′–32′ col. iv 20′–39′ col. v 15′–31′ col. vi 1′–13′	c

COMMENTARY

The line count follows ex. 1, except for col. vi, which follows ex. 2. Since considerable lacunae remain in the text, a consecutive numbering is not given in this edition. The edition uses as its basis the editio princeps of Kutscher. Original photos of the tablets were examined by A. Westenholz, who kindly communicated the results of his collations to the author in a letter dated January 22, 1990. The tablet itself was examined by P. Steinkeller in December 1992, at which time it was on loan to the Bible Lands Museum in Jerusalem; Steinkeller kindly communicated his collations to the author.

In i 5 the translation 'clan (god)' follows the suggestion of Kutscher, Brockmon tablets p. 28. See also Hirsch, WZKM 81 (1991) p. 286. In i 3′ and 8′ we find the rare adverbial ending *-śum*, for which see von Soden, GAG § 67 g. Thus we translate *śar-ru*$_x$*-śúm* 'to kingship'. The lines preceding i 1′, following J. Goodnick Westenholz (in Vogelzang and Vanstiphout, Epic Literature, p. 140) may possibly be restored '[When the four quarters together revolted against him]'. For the translation 'Amorite highlanders' for the expression [ŚA].DÚ-*ì* MAR.DÚ.KI of i 1″–2″, see the comments of the author in BiOr 48 (1991) p. 386.

BIBLIOGRAPHY

1914 Poebel, PBS 4/1 pp. 209–12 no. 36 (ex. 2, frgm. 3, edition) and p. 215 no. 37 (ex. 2, frgm. 2, edition)
1914 Poebel, PBS 5 no. 36 (obv. only) and pl. CI (ex. 2, frgm. 3, photo, copy) and no. 37 (ex. 2, frgm. 2, copy)
1961 Gelb, MAD 2^{2} p. 199 Narâm-Sin Late Copies no. 1 (ex. 2, frgm. 3 study)
1963 Hirsch, AfO 20 p. 19 Narâm-Sin b 1 (ex. 2, frgm. 3, study) and p. 20 Narâm-Sin b 3 (ex. 2, frgm. 2, study)
1973 Gelb, JNES 32 p. 73 (study)
1980 Michalowski, JCS 32 pp. 233–37, 243, and 245 (ex. 2, frgm. 1, photo, copy, edition); (ex. 2, study)
1989 Kutscher, Brockmon Tablets pp. 13–34, 118 and pl. I (ex. 1, photo, copy, edition)
1990 Gelb and Kienast, Königsinschriften pp. 226–43 Narāmsîn C 1 first part, lines 1–318 (exs. 1–2, edition)

TEXT

Col. i
1) ^{d}*en-líl*
2) *il-śu*
3) *ì-a-ba*$_{4}$
4) KALAG *ì-li*
5) [*il*]-⌜*la*⌝-*at-śú*
6) [*na*]-*ra-am*-[^{d}]EN.ZU
7) [*d*]*a-núm*
8) [LU]GAL
9) [*ki-ib-r*]*a-tim*
10) [*ar-ba-im*]
Lacuna
1′) [*in kiš*.KI]
2′) ⌜*ip-ḫur*⌝-*kiš*
3′) *śar-ru*$_{x}$(URU×A)*súm*(ZUM)
4′) *i-śi*$_{11}$-⌜*ù*⌝
5′) *ù*
6′) *in* UNU.KI
7′) amar-gírid
8′) *śar-ru*$_{x}$(URU×A)-*súm*(ZUM)-*ma*
9′) *i-śi*$_{11}$-*ù*
10′) *ip-ḫur-kiš*
11′) LUGAL
12′) *kiš*.KI
13′) *u-ṣa-bi-àm-ma*
14′) 1 *kiš*.KI
15′) 1 *gú-du*$_{8}$-*a*.KI
16′) 1 A.ḪA.KI
17′) 1 ZIMBIR(AN.UB.KIB.NUN).KI
18′) 1 *ka-zal-lu*.KI
19′) 1 *gir*$_{13}$-*tab*.KI
20′) [1 *a-pi*$_{5}$]-*ak*.KI
21′) [1 ... .K]I
Lacuna (3 lines missing)
1″) [ŚA].DÚ-*ì*
2″) MAR.DÚ.KI
3″) *in ba-rí-ti*
4″) A.ḪA.KI
5″) *ù*
6″) ÚR×Ú.KI
7″) *in* SIG$_{7}$-*rí*
8″) ^{d}EN.ZU
9″) *íś-dú-ud-ma*
10″) REC 169
11″) *u-qá-e*
12″) *na-ra-am*-^{d}EN.ZU

i 1–2) The god Enlil (is) his (personal) deity (and)

i 3–5) the god Ilaba, mighty one of the gods, is his clan (god).

i 6–10) [Na]rām-Sîn, the [m]ighty, [ki]ng of the [fou]r [quar]ters, ...
Lacuna

i 1′–4′) [In Kiš] they elevated Ipḫur-Kiš to kingship

i 5′–9′) and in Uruk they elevated Amar-Girid likewise to kingship.

i 10′–13′) Ipḫur-Kiš, king of Kiš, went to war

i 14′–21′) and [rallied] (the cities of) Kiš, Kutha, TiWA, Sippar, Kazallu, Kiritab, [Api]ak, GN

Lacuna
i 1″–2″) ... (and) Amorite [hi]ghlanders.

i 3″–11″) In between the cities of TiWA and Urum, in the field of the god Sîn, he drew up (battle lines) and awaited battle.

i 12″–18″) Narām-Sîn, the mighty, ... his young

13″) *da-núm*
14″) GURUŠ.GURUŠ-*šu*
15″) É-*ba-at*
16″) *-ma*
17″) *a-kà-dè*.KI

men (there), and he held Agade.

18″) ŠU.DU$_8$.A-*ma*
19″) *a-na* ^{d}UTU
20″) *è-dì-ìl*
21″) ^{d}UTU-*šu*
22″) *kiš*.KI-*ši-um*

i 19″–22″) He *closed off* (the city) for the god Šamaš. (He said): 'O Šamaš, the Kišite, ...'

Col. ii
Lacuna

Lacuna

1′) [...*š*]*u*-⸢*nu*⸣
2′) *u-šá-zé*
3′) *ù*
4′) *bí-bí-in-na-at-su-nu*
5′) *u-gal-li-ib*

ii 1′–5′) He ... their ... and shaved their heads.

6′) *e*-NI
7′) *i-tá-kir*$_9$
8′) *sá-bi-a*

ii 5′–8′) ... became hostile ...

9′) *in* SIG$_7$-*rí*
10′) ^{d}EN.ZU
11′) REC 169
12′) *íš-ku*$_8$*-na-ma*
13′) *i-tá-aḫ-za-ma*

ii 9′–13′) In the field of the god Sîn the two of them engaged in battle and grappled with each other.

14′) *in* DI.KU$_5$
15′) ^{d}INANNA-
16′) *an-nu-ni-tum*
17′) *na-ra-am*-^{d}EN.ZU
18′) *da-núm*
19′) *in* REC 169
20′) *in* A.ḪA.KI
21′) [*k*]*iš*.KI-[*š*]*i-am*
22′) [*iš*$_{11}$*-a*]*r*

ii 14′-22′) By the verdict of the goddess Aštar-Annunītum, Narām-Sîn, the mighty, [was vict]orious over the Kišite in battle at TiWA.

23′) [*ù*]
24′) ^{m}*ì*-⸢*lí*⸣*-ré-ṣí*
25′) GÌR.NÍTA
26′) ^{m}DINGIR-*mu-da*
27′) ^{m}*i-bí*-^{d}*za-ba*$_4$*-ba*$_4$
28′) ^{m}*im*$_4$*-tá-lik*
29′) ^{m}*puzur*$_4$-^{d}ASAR
30′) NU.BÀNDA-*ù*
31′) *kiš*.KI
32′) *ù*
33′) ^{m}*puzur*$_4$-^{d}*nin-gal*
34′) ÉNSI
35′) A.ḪA.KI
36′) ^{m}DINGIR-SIPA
37′) NU.BÀNDA-*šu*
38′) ^{m}*ku*$_8$*-lí-zum*
39′) NU.BÀNDA
40′) *éreš*.KI
41′) ^{m}*e-dam-u*(*)
42′) NU.BÀNDA
43′) *gú-du*$_8$*-a*.KI

ii 23′–43′) [Further], Ilī-rēṣī, the general; Ilum-mūda, Ibbi-Zababa, Imtalik, (and) Puzur-Asar, captains of Kiš; and Puzur-Ningal, governor of TiWA; Ilī-rēʾa, his captain; Kullizum, captain of Ereš; Edamʾu, captain of Kutha,

---

i 15″ Kutscher took É-*ba-at* to be a form of *ebēṭu*(*m*) 'to gird', but since its thematic vowels are i-i, this is not possible.
ii 41′.1 Text: ^{m}*e*-SAL.DA-*u*.

Col. iii

Lacuna

1′) ^{m}DINGIR-⸢*dan*⸣
2′) ÉNSI
3′) BAR.KI
4′) ^{m}*da-da*
5′) ÉNSI
6′) *a-pi*$_5$*-ak*.KI
7′) ŠU.NÍGIN 300 GURUŠ
8′) *ra-bí-a-ni*
9′) *ù*
10′) 4,932 LÚ×ÉŠ
11′) *in* REC 169
12′) *i-ik-mi*

Lacuna

iii 1′–12′) Ilum-dān, governor of Borsippa; Dada governor of Apiak — in total 300 officers and 4,932 captives — he captured in battle.

13′) *ù*
14′) *a-dì-ma*
15′) *kiš*.KI
16′) *ìr-da-šu*$_4$*-ma*
17′) *ù*
18′) *al le-ti*
19′) *kiš*.KI
20′) KÁ
21′) ^{d}*nin-kár*
22′) REC 169
23′) *iš*$_{11}$*-ni-a-ma*
24′) *íš-ku*$_8$*-na-ma*
25′) [*i-tá*]*-aḫ-*⸢*za-ma*⸣

iii 13′–25′) Further, he (Narām-Sîn) pursued him (Ipḫur-Kiš) to Kiš, and right beside Kiš, at the gate of the goddess Ninkarrak, the two of them engaged in battle for a second time, and grappled with each other.

26′) *in* DI.[KU$_5$]
27′) *an-nu-ni-tum*
28′) *ù*
29′) AN-*nim*
30′) ⸢*na-ra-am*⸣-^{d}EN.ZU
31′) *da-núm*
32′) *in* REC 169
33′) *in kiš*.KI
34′) *kiš*.KI*-ši-am*
35′) *iš*$_{11}$*-ar*

iii 26′–35′) By the verdict of the goddess Annunītum and the god Anum, Narām-Sîn, the mighty, was victorious over the Kišite in battle at the Kiš.

36′) *ù*
37′) ^{m}*puzur*$_4$-^{d}*nu-muš-da*
38′) ÉNSI
39′) *ka-zal-lu*.KI
40′) ^{m}*da-núm*
41′) NU.BÀNDA
42′) BAR.KI
43′) ^{m}*pu*-BALA
44′) NU.BÀNDA
45′) *a-pi*$_5$*-ak*.KI

iii 36′–45′) In addition, Puzur-Numušda, governor of Kazallu; Dannum, captain of Borsippa; Pû-palîm, captain of Apiak,

Col. iv

Lacuna

1′) ^{m}*i-*⸢*dì*⸣-[DINGIR]
2′) ÉNSI
3′) *gú-du*$_8$*-a*.KI
4′) ^{m}⸢*ì-lí-íš*⸣*-tá-*⸢*kál*⸣
5′) ÉNSI
6′) ZIMBIR(AN.UD.KIB.NUN).KI
7′) ^{m}*šá-lim-be-lí*

Lacuna

iv 1′–24′) Iddi(n)-[Ilum], governor of Kutha; Iliš-takal, governor of Sippar; Šalim-bēlī, governor of Kiritab; Qīšum, governor of Ereš; Ita-Ilum, governor of Dilbat; and Imtalik captain of TiWA — in total 1,000 officers and 2,015 captives — he captured in battle.

---

iii 10′ Hand copy LU×ÉŠ; published photo indistinct.
iii 21′ Collation Westenholz.
iii 27′ 2 ⸢*an-nu*⸣-[*ni-tum*]..

8′) ÉNSI
9′) *gir*$_{13}$*-tab*.KI
10′) ^{m}*qì-šum*$_{6}$
11′) ÉNSI
12′) *éreš*.KI
13′) ^{m}*i-tá*-DINGIR
14′) ÉNSI
15′) *dal-ba-at*.KI
16′) ^{m}*im*$_{4}$*-tá-lik*
17′) NU.BÀNDA
18′) A.ḪA.KI
19′) ŠU.NÍGIN 10 ME GURUŠ
20′) *ra-bí-a-ni*
21′) *ù*
22′) 2,015 LÚ×ÉŠ
23′) *in* REC 169
24′) *i-ik-mi*
25′) *ù*
26′) *a-na*
27′) [U]D.KIB.NUN.⸢I$_{7}$⸣-*tim*
28′) *u-ma-li-šu-*⸢*nu*⸣
29′) *ù*
30′) URU.KI-*lam*
31′) *kiš*.KI
32′) SAG.GIŠ.RA
33′) *ù*
34′) BÀD-*šu*
35′) Ì.GUL.GUL

iv 25′–35′) Further, he filled the Euphrates River with their (bodies), conquered the city of Kiš, and destroyed its wall.

36′) *ù*
37′) I$_{7}$
38′) *in qer-bí-šu*
39′) *u-šu-ṣí*
40′) *ù*
41′) *qè-ré-eb*
42′) URU.KI-*lim*
43′) 2,525 GURUŠ.GURUŠ
44′) *u-ša-am-qì-it*
45′) *ù*

iv 36′–45′) Further, he made the river/canal go forth in its (the city's) midst and struck down 2,525 men within the city. Further ...

Col. v
Lacuna
1′) [...]
2′) *da*-[...]
3′) ⸢*ù*⸣
4′) *kiš*.[KI]-*š*[*i*(?)-x]
5′) DU [...]
6′) ^{m}[amar-gírid]
7′) L[UGAL]
8′) UNU.⸢KI⸣
9′) *u-ṣa-b*[*i*]*-àm-ma*
10′) 1 UNU.KI
11′) 1 ÚRI.[KI]
12′) 1 *lagaš*.KI
13′) 1 *umma*.KI
14′) 1 *adab*.KI
15′) 1 *šuruppak*.KI
16′) 1 IN.KI

Lacuna
v 1′–21′) ... [Amar-Girid], ki[ng] of Uruk, went to war and rallied (the cities of) Uruk, Ur, Lagaš, Umma, Adab, Šuruppak, Isin, and Nippur, and (settlements) from (the province of) the Lower Sea.

---

iv 22′ Number is only partially preserved.
iv 24′.2 *i-ik-mi* (contra Gelb and Kienast).

17′)	1 NIBRU.K[I]	
18′)	*íš-tum-ma*	
19′)	*ti-a-am-tim*	
20′)	*ša-pil-tim*	
21′)	*id-ké-áš-šu-nu-ma*	
22′)	*ba-rí-ti*	v 22′–28′) In between the cities of URU×UD and Ašnak he drew up battle lines and awaited battle.
23′)	URU×UD.KI	
24′)	*ù*	
25′)	*áš-na-ak*.KI	
26′)	*íš-dú-ud-ma*	
27′)	REC 169	
28′)	*u-qá-e*	
29′)	*na-ra-am-*^{d}EN.ZU	v 29′–38′) Narām-Sîn, the mighty, heard about him and hast[ened] to [his] side fr[om] Kiš. The two of them engaged in battle [and] grappled with each other. By the ver[dict of the goddess Aštar-Annunītum ...]
30′)	*da-núm*	
31′)	*íš-má-šu*$_4$-⸢*ma*⸣	
32′)	*íš-t*[*um*]	
33′)	*kiš*.[KI]	
34′)	DA-*í*[*s-su*]	
35′)	*ig-r*[*u-úš*]-*m*[a]	
36′)	⸢REC 169⸣	
37′)	*íš-k*[*u*$_8$]-*na*-[*ma*]	
38′)	*i-tá*-[*aḫ*]-*za*-[*ma*]	
39′)	*in* DI.[KU$_5$]	
Col. vi		
Lacuna		Lacuna
1′)	*u*-[...]	vi 1′–9’) ..., and made the ... river/canal go forth (in its midst). ...
2′)	x [...]	
3′)	*ša a*[*l*-...] x x	
4′)	*ša* [...]	
5′)	I$_7$ x [...]	
6′)	*u-šu*-[*ṣí*]	
7′)	*ù*	
8′)	*ma* x [x]	
9′)	⸢*ù*⸣	vi 9′–13′) Further, Luga[l-nizu], governor of [N]ippur, ...
10′)	^{m}luga[l-nì-zu]	
11′)	ÉNS[I]	Lacuna
12′)	[NI]BRU.[KI]	
13′)	[x] x x [x]	
Lacuna		

7

A Sargonic school exercise tablet from Ešnunna bears an excerpt of a historical-literary text that mentions both Lugal-ane and Ipḫur-Kiš.

COMMENTARY

The tablet, with excavation number TA 1931,729, was found in room 14 of the private house XIX in sector H/J (= H 18:14), stratum IVb, that is, the Akkadian level, Tell Asmar. The tablet, which is now in Chicago (no A number assigned), measures 9.2x5.0 cm and contains many erasures. Due to its broken nature, a secure translation of much of it is not possible. The inscription was collated by G. Frame.

For -súm of line 11, see the commentary to E2.1.4.6. The translation of lines 3–11, in general, follows that given in the cited study of Goodnick Westenholz. For the subjunctive *-a* of line 6, see Gelb, MAD 2 pp. 170–71.

BIBLIOGRAPHY

1952 Gelb, MAD 1 p. 92 no. 172 (transliteration)
1961 Gelb, MAD 2[2] p. 202 Narâm-Sin Late Legends no. 4b (study)
1967 Delougaz, Private Houses p. 219 (provenance)
1974–77 Westenholz, AfO 25 pp. 96–97 no. 7 (copy, study)
1978–79 Jacobsen, AfO 26 pp. 1–3 (edition, study)
1990 Gelb and Kienast, Königsinschriften pp. 272–73 Narāmsîn C 15 (transliteration)
1992 Goodnick Westenholz, in Vogelzang and Vanstiphout, Epic Literature pp. 140–41 (partial study)

TEXT

1) [...] x
2) [...]-*śí*-⸢*in*⸣
3) [...] x [... *k*]*iš*.KI
4) x *bu*(?) *na na-śe*$_{11}$*-nim*

1–4) ... , their ..., ... [K]iš, ... *was elevated* (*to kingship*).

---

5) [*i*]*p-ḫur-kiš*.KI
6) [*na*] *śi*$_{11}$*-ʾa*$_{x}$(NI)*-ma* lugal-an-né
7) [*i*]*g*(?)*-ru-śa-am* LUGAL [(x)]
8) (Erasure) ŠEŠ.AB.K[I]

5–8) [(When) I]pḫur-Kiš, *was elevated* (*to kingship*), Lugal-ane [h]astened there, the king of Ur.

---

9) ⸢*ù*⸣ *la ma-al-ku*[*m*]
10) [*u*]*r-ki-um i-dì-ís-s*[*u* (x)]
11) [*ś*]*ar-ru*$_{x}$(URUxA)*-ús-súm ù* ⸢x⸣ [x]
12) (Erasure) KALAM-*śu*
13) *íś-ku*-(erasure)-*un*

9–13) And that non-(entity of a) king, the *Urukean*, ... to h[is side], for [k]ingship. And he established the ... of his land.

---

14) DU/SUḪUŠ(?) [...]
15) 10(?) URU(?) [...]
16) BALA x [...]
(Reverse illegible)

14–16) (Too broken for translation)

8

Fragments of two carnelian foundation tablets in the Böhl Collection bear an inscription that alludes to the 'Great Revolt'. An attribution of the pieces to Narām-Sîn is likely.

CATALOGUE

Ex.	Museum number	Dimensions (cm)	Tablet lines preserved	Text lines preserved	cpn
1	LB 16a	2.9×2×3×1.4	obv. i′ 1′–4′	ii 4′–7′	n
			obv. ii′ 1′–2′	iii 3′–4′	
			rev. i′ 1–5	vi 4–8	
			rev. ii′ 1–5	vii 1–5	
2	LB 16b	2.5×3.4×1.4	obv. i′ 1′–5′	iii 2′–6′	n
			obv. ii′ 1′–6′	iv 1′–6′	
			rev. i 1–5	v 1–5	
			rev. ii 1–6	vi 1–6	

COMMENTARY

While Gelb and Kienast edited these two pieces as separate inscriptions, the fact that two lines of our reconstructed text for col. iii, and probably three lines for col. vi, duplicate one another, coupled with the similarity in the script and the identity of the type of stone, raises the distinct possibility that the two tablets were duplicate copies. We have thus given a conflated edition here. Assuming a similar arrangement between this inscription and E2.1.5.5, another foundation tablet, we have reconstructed an original text with four columns per side and at least eight lines per column. Ex. 1 preserves part of cols. ii–iii and vi–vii; ex. 2 preserves part of cols. iii–vi. In van Driel's copy of ex. 1, LB 16[a] (Symbolae Böhl p. 106), the rev. is depicted on the top, the obv. on the bottom. Since no royal name appears in the extant text, its attribution is uncertain. However, a number of parallels can be seen between this text and inscriptions of Narām-Sîn. Compare, for example, ii 1′-7′ with lines 5–11 of E2.1.4.11, and iv 4′ – v 1 with lines 16–18 of E2.1.4.9. The mention of the making fast of the ships of Agade is worthy of note.

BIBLIOGRAPHY

1933 Böhl, Leiden Coll. 1 pp. 11–12 (exs. 1–2, transliteration)
1963 Hirsch, AfO 20 p. 33 no. 4 (exs. 1–2, study)
1971 Kupper, OrAnt 10 p. 102 n. 45 (exs. 1–2, study)
1973 van Driel, Symbolae Böhl pp. 105–106 (exs. 1–2, copy, study)
1990 Gelb and Kienast, Königsinschriften p. 94 Narāmsîn 6 (ex.1, edition) and pp. 95–96 Narāmsîn 7 (ex.2, edition)

TEXT

Col. i (not preserved)
Col. ii
Lacuna
1′) [*ì-nu*]
2′) [*ki-ib-ra-tum*]
3′) [*ar-ba-um*]
4′) [*íś-ti-ni-í*]*ś*
5′) [*i*-KIR-*ni*]-*śu*$_4$
6′) [*in rí-m*]*a*-[*t*]*i*
7′) [x N]UM
Col. iii
Lacuna
1′) [*ki-ib-ra-tum*]
2′) [*ar-ba-um*]
3′) *í*[*ś-t*]*i-ni-íś*
4′) *im*$_4$*-ḫu-ru-ni-śu*$_4$*-ma*
5′) [*íś-t*]*e*$_4$
6′) [^{d}*en-l*]*íl*
Col. iv
Lacuna
1′) [*kà-la-śu*]-*nu-m*[*a*]
2′) *iš*$_{11}$*-ar*
3′) *ù*
4′) *śar-rí-śi-in*
5′) *šu-ut in ra-m*[*a*-x]-*at*
6′) *i*-[*śi*$_{11}$*-ù-nim*]
Col. v
1) *ik-mi*-[*ma*(?)]
2) *in* GIŠ.SI.GAR-*im*
3) *maḫ-rí-íś*
4) ^{d}*en-líl*
5) *a-bí-śu*
6) [*u-śá-rí-ib*]
Lacuna
Col. vi
1) [MÁ.GUR$_8$].MÁ.GUR$_8$
2) [*a-kà-d*]*è*.KI
3) [URU.KI-*l*]*í-śu*
4) *u-kí-in-nu*

Lacuna
ii 1′–7′) [When the four quarters togethe]r [revolted] against him, [through the lo]ve ...

Lacuna
iii 1′–4′)[The four quarters] to[ge]ther confronted him,

iii 5′–6′) [wi]th (the help of) [the god En]lil

Lacuna
iv 1′–2′) he was victorious over [all] their [...]

iv 3′ v 1) Further, their kings, whom they [had raised (against him)] in ..., he captured.

v 2–6) [He brought them] in a neck stock before the god Enlil, his father.
Lacuna

vi 1–4) He/they made fast the ship[s] of [Agad]e, his [ci]ty,

5) *ù*
6) *ki-i*[*b-ra-t*]*im*
7) *a*[*r-ba-im*]
8) x [...]
Lacuna
Col. vii
1) [*a-k*]*à-dè*.KI
2) [U]RU.KI-*lí-šu*
3) ⌈*ù*⌉
4) [*ki-i*]*b-ra-tum*
5) [*ar-b*]*a*-⌈*um*⌉
Lacuna
Col. viii (not preserved)

vi 5–8) and the f[our] qu[arters] ...
Lacuna

vii 1–2) ... of [Ag]ade, his [ci]ty.

vii 3–5) Further, the [fo]ur [qua]rters
Lacuna

viii (not preserved)

9

The royal epithet *ša-ir* 10 LAL 1 REC 169 *in* MU 1 'victor in nine battles in one year' appears in four inscriptions of Narām-Sîn; it apparently alludes to the king's crushing of the 'Great Revolt'. As noted, a parallel to this phrase is found in the Old Babylonian version of the 'Great Revolt' (see Grayson and Sollberger, RA 70 [1976] p. 112 M rev. 3′–4′): [*i-na ti*]*-bu-ut* [*um-ma-an*] *a-kà-dè*.KI-*ma* 9 *ṣú-ub-bi-*[*i*]*m* [*ú-ša*]*-at-bi-šu-nu-ši-im* '[with the l]evy [of the army] of Agade he [mo]unted nine campaigns against them'.

The first text that employs this epithet is found on four door sockets from Wannat al-Saʿdūn (ancient Marad). It deals with the construction of the temple of the god Lugalmarda at Marad by Lipit-ilī, governor of the city and son of Narām-Sîn. In this inscription and the two following, the king's name is written without the prefixed divine determinative. Thus these three texts probably date to the time period shortly after the 'Great Revolt' but before the apotheosis of the king. The unnamed three rebel kings mentioned in this inscription were in all likelihood Iphur-Kiš of Kiš, Amar-Girid of Uruk, and Enlil-nizu of Nippur.

CATALOGUE

Ex.	Museum number	Dimensions (cm)	Lines preserved	cpn
1	YBC 2164	Upper face dia.: 29.5 Lower face dia.: 36 14 thick	1–38	c
2	Draper Collection no. 24, New York Public Library,	31.5 high, 9 wide	1–38	c
3	AO 6782	14x33	1–38	c

COMMENTARY

Ex.3, donated to the New York Public Library by Mrs. Draper in 1914, was collated by M. Van De Mieroop. It is the only Narām-Sîn door socket now housed in that museum. Ex. 3 was collated by B. Foster.

BIBLIOGRAPHY

1914 Clay, OLZ 17 110–12 (ex. 1, edition)
1914 Scheil, RA 11 p. 193 (exs. 1, 3 study)
1914 Thureau-Dangin, RA 11 pp. 88–91 no. 24 (ex. 3, photo, edition)
1915 Clay, YOS 1 no. 10 (exs. 1–2, edition, study; ex. 1, photo; ex. 2, copy)
1927 Ungnad, Babylonisch-Assyrisches Keilschriftlesebuch pp. 80 and 86 (ex. 2, copy, study)
1929 Barton, RISA pp. 138–39 Naram-Sin 7 (ex. 1, edition)
1915 Banks, The Open Court 29 p. 746ff.
1961 Gelb, MAD 2^{2} p. 199 Narâm-Sin Original Inscriptions nos. 6a–c (exs. 1–3, study)
1963 Hirsch, AfO 20 pp. 17–18 Narâm-Sin a 3 (exs. 1–3, study)
1971 Sollberger and Kupper, IRSA IIA4c (exs. 1–3, translation)
1990 Gelb and Kienast, Königsinschriften pp. 102–103 Narāmsîn A 1 (exs. 1–3, edition)

TEXT

1) *na-ra-am-*^{d}EN.ZU
2) *da-núm*
3) LUGAL
4) *ki-ib-ra-tim*
5) *ar-ba-im*
6) *ša-ir*
7) 10 LAL 1 REC 169

1–7) Narām-Sîn, the mighty, king of the four quarters, victor in nine battles in one year:

8) *in* MU 1
9) *íś-tum*
10) REC169.REC 169
11) *śu*$_{4}$*-nu-ti*
12) *iš*$_{11}$*-ar-ru*
13) *ù*
14) *śar-rí-śu-nu* 3
15) *i-ik-mi-ma*
16) *maḫ-rí-íś*
17) ^{d}*en-líl*
18) *u-śa-rí-ib*

9–18) After he was victorious in those battles, he captured their three kings and brought (them) before the god Enlil,

19) *in u-mi-śu*
20) *li-pi*$_{5}$*-it-ì-li*
21) DUMU-*śu*
22) ÉNSI
23) *már-da*.KI
24) É
25) ^{d}*lugal-már-da*
26) *in már-da*.KI
27) *ib-ni*

19–27) At that time, Lipit-ilī, his son, governor of Marad, built the temple of the god Lugalmarda at Marad.

28) *ša* DUB
29) *śu*$_{4}$*-a*
30) *u-śa-sà-ku-ni*
31) ^{d}UTU
32) *ù*
33) ^{d}*lugal-már-da*
34) SUḪUŠ-*śu*
35) *li-sú-ḫa*
36) *ù*
37) ŠE.NUMUN-*śu*
38) *li-il-qù-tá*

28–38) As for the one who removes this inscription, may the gods Šamaš and Lugalmarda tear out his foundation and destroy his progeny.

10

A second inscription referring to the nine victories in one year is incised on a statue base of a *laḫmu* from Bāseṭkī, a village located on the road between Mosul and Dohuk, about 70 kms northwest of Mosul. The inscription deals primarily with the deification of the king and the construction at Agade of a temple dedicated to him.

COMMENTARY

The statue base, which is made of copper (see al-Fouadi, Sumer 32 [1976] p. 68), measures 67 cm in diameter, and the inscription 34.5x13.5 cm. The piece bears the museum number IM 77823; its inscription was collated from the published photo.

BIBLIOGRAPHY

1976 al-Fouadi, Sumer 32 pp. 63–76 and 2 plates following p. 76 (photo, edition)

1976 Madhloom, Sumer 32 (Arabic section) pp. 41–48 and pls. 1–8 and 17 (photo, study)

1976 Rashid, Sumer 32 (Arabic section) pp. 49–58 and 2 plates following p. 58 (photo, edition)

1978–79 Jacobsen, AfO 26 p. 12 n. 45 (study)

1979 Oates, Babylon fig. 17 (photo)

1983 Farber, Orientalia NS 52 pp. 67–72 (edition)

1983–84 Hirsch, AfO 29–30 pp. 58–61 (study)

1984 Braun-Holzinger, Bronzen pp. 23–24 and pl. 13 no. 61 (photo, study)

1986 M. Tanret, Histoire et archéologie. Dossiers 103 (March 1986) p. 21 (photo)

1988 Hecker TUAT 2/4 pp. 485–86 (translation)

1990 Gelb and Kienast, Königsinschriften pp. 81–83 Narāmsîn 1 (edition)

TEXT

1) *na-ra-am-*^{d}EN.ZU	1–4) Narām-Sîn, the mighty, king of Agade,
2) *da-núm*	
3) LUGAL	
4) *a-kà-dè*.KI	
5) *ì-nu*	5–9) when the four quarters together revolted against him,
6) *ki-ib-ra-tum*	
7) *ar-ba-um*	
8) *íś-ti-ni-íś*	
9) *i-*KIR*-ni-śu*$_{4}$	
10) *in rí-ma-ti*	10–12) through the love which the goddess Aštar showed him,
11) ^{d}INANNA	
12) *tár-a-mu-śu*$_{4}$	
13) 10 LAL 1 REC 169	13–19) he was victorious in nine battles in one year, and the kings whom they (the rebels[?]) had raised (against him), he captured.
14) *in* MU 1	
15) *iš*$_{11}$*-ar-ma*	
16) *ù*	
17) LUGAL-*rí*	
18) *šu-ut i-śi*$_{11}$*-<ù>-nim*	
19) *i-ik-mi*	
20) *al ši in pu-uš-qí-im*	20–23) In view of the fact that he protected the foundations of his city from danger,
21) SUḪUŠ.SUḪUŠ	
22) URU.KI-*lí-śu*	
23) *u-kí-nu*	
24) URU.KI-*śu*	24–51) (the citizens of) his city requested from Aštar

25) *íś-te*$_{4}$
26) ^{d}INANNA
27) *in é-an-na-ki-im*
28) *íś-te*$_{4}$
29) ^{d}*en-líl*
30) *in* NIBRU.KI
31) *íś-te*$_{4}$
32) ^{d}*da-gan*
33) *in tu-tu-li*.KI
34) *íś-te*$_{4}$
35) ^{d}*nin-ḫur-sag*
36) *in kèš*.KI
37) *íś-te*$_{4}$
38) ^{d}EN.KI
39) *in eridu*.KI
40) *íś-te*$_{4}$
41) ^{d}EN.ZU
42) *in* ÚRI.KI
43) *íś-te*$_{4}$
44) ^{d}UTU
45) *in* ZIMBIR(DINGIR.UD.KIB.NUN).KI
46) *íś-te*$_{4}$
47) ^{d}*nergal*
48) *in gú-du*$_{8}$*-a*.KI
49) *ì-li-íś* URU.KI-*śu-nu*
50) *a-kà-dè*.KI
51) *i-tár-śu-ni-íś-ma*
52) *qáb-li-*
53) *ma*

in Eanna, Enlil in Nippur, Dagān in Tuttul, Ninḫursag in Keš, Ea in Eridu, Sîn in Ur, Šamaš in Sippar, (and) Nergal in Kutha, that (Narām-Sîn) be (made) the god of their city, and

54) *a-kà-dè*.KI
55) É-*śu*
56) *ib-ni-ù*
57) *ša* DUB

54–57) they built within Agade a temple (dedicated) to him.

58) *śu*$_{4}$*-a*
59) *u-śa-sà-ku-ni*
60) ^{d}UTU
61) *ù*
62) ^{d}INANNA
63) *ù*
64) ^{d}*nergal*
65) MAŠKIM
66) LUGAL
67) *ù*
68) ŠU.NÍGIN *ì-lí*
69) *á-ni-ù-ut*

58–70) As for the one who removes this inscription, may the gods Šamaš, Aštar, Nergal, the bailiff of the king, namely all those gods (mentioned above)

70) SUḪUŠ-*śu*
71) *li-sú-ḫa*
72) *ù*
73) ŠE.NUMUN-*śu*
74) *li-il-qù-tu*

70–74) tear out his foundations and destroy his progeny.

11

The epithet 'victor in nine battles in one year' is also found in an inscription known from an Old Babylonian tablet copy from Nippur.

COMMENTARY

The inscription is found on rev. col. v′ lines 7–20 of BT 1 = lines 1–14 of our reconstructed text. The four additional lines to Kutscher's original edition result from a collation of the tablet by P. Steinkeller. Gelb and Kienast (Königsinschriften pp. 267–68 Narāmsîn C 9) edited this inscription as a duplicate of N 202+4007+4930, a Nippur tablet published by P. Michaloswski (JCS 32 [1980] pp. 239–240, 244, and 246). In this volume, the two inscription are edited separately.

BIBLIOGRAPHY

1989 Kutscher, Brockmon Tablets pp. 27–29, 36, 111, and 119 (photo, copy, edition)

1990 Gelb and Kienast, Königsinschriften pp. 267–68 Narāmsîn C 9 Text B (edition)

TEXT

1) *na-ra-am*-dE[N.ZU]
2) [*da-núm*]
3) [LUGAL]
4) *ki-ib-r*[*a-tim*]
5) *ar-ba-im*
6) *ša-ir*
7) 10 LAL 1 REC 169
8) *in* MU 1
9) *a-na*
10) d⸢*en*⸣-*líl*
11) [A.MU].RU
12) [*ša* D]UB
13) [*su*$_4$]-*a*
14) [*u-ša-sà-ku*]-*ni*
Lacuna

1–8) Narạm-S[în], [the mighty, king] of the four quart[ers], victor in nine battles in one year,

9–11) [dedic]ated (this object) to the god Enlil.

12–14) Whoever [remo]ves [th]is [in]scription
Lacuna

12

The epithet 'victor in nine battles in one year' also occurs in an inscription of Narām-Sîn known from an Old Babylonian tablet copy from Nippur.

COMMENTARY

The inscription is found on N 202+4007+4930, the upper half of a four-column tablet. The inscription begins at the bottom of col. i (now broken away), = lines 1–5 of our reconstructed text, and continues on col. ii, lines 1–7 = lines 6–12 of our reconstructed text. The inscription was collated.

BIBLIOGRAPHY

1980 Michalowski, JCS 32 pp. 239–40, 244, and 246 (photo, edition, copy)

1990 Gelb and Kienast, Königsinschriften pp. 267–68 Narāmsîn C 8 (edition)

TEXT

1) [(^{d})*na-ra-am*-^{d}EN.ZU]
2) [*da-núm*]
3) [LUGAL
4) [*ki-ib-ra-tim*]
5) [*ar-ba-im*]
6) *š*[*a-ir*] 10 LA[L 1] ⸢REC 169⸣
7) *in* MU 1
8) *a-na*
9) ⸢^{d}⸣*en-líl* <A.MU.RU>
10) [*š*]*a* DUB
11) [*š*]*u*$_{4}$*-a*
12) [*u*]-⸢*ša*⸣-*s*[*à-ku-ni*]
Lacuna

1–5) [Narām-Sîn, the mighty, king of the four quarters],

6–7) vic[tor] (in) nine battles in one year,

8–9) <dedicated> (this object) to the god Enlil.

10–12)[Who]ever [r]emo[ves] [th]is inscription ...
Lacuna

13

A fifth inscription alluding to Narām-Sîn's nine victories in one year is found on a statue base from Susa. Its incompletely preserved text records Narām-Sîn's defeat of Magan and the capture of its ruler, Manium.

COMMENTARY

The statue base, found in excavations on the acropolis at Susa, is numbered Sb 52 in the Louvre collections. The piece measures 47×64 cm. Its inscription was collated by B. Foster.

In contrast to the other inscriptions alluding to the 'Great Revolt', in this text the king's name appears with the prefixed divine determinative. It is probably the earliest example in the extant Narām-Sîn corpus to do so. It suggests that the apotheosis of the king occurred shortly after the events of the 'Great Revolt'. For a summary of the various suggested readings of the name of the ruler of Magan, see Potts, OrAnt 23 (1986) pp. 276–77. Since the god Šamaš normally appears together with the city god in Sargonic curse formulae, his name is restored in ii 23. In ii 25 we might expect a restoration [^{d}INANNA *a-kà-d*]*è*.KI, since Aštar is well known as tutelary deity of Agade; the spacing, however, does not support this restoration. Kupper (OrAnt 10 [1971] p. 98 n. 27) suggested [AN *a-kà-d*]*è*.KI, a reading also given in Gelb and Kienast's edition. The bibliography includes items of a non-textual nature including photos or discussions of the form of the statue fragment. In only some of the photos is the inscription legible.

BIBLIOGRAPHY

1905 Scheil, MDP 6 pp. 2–5 and pl. 1 no. 1 (photo, edition)
1907 Thureau-Dangin, SAK pp. 166–67 Narâm-sin h (edition)
1926 Pézard and Pottier, Catalogue no. 50 (study)
1929 Barton, RISA pp. 142–43 Naram-Sin 14 (edition)
1960 Parrot, Sumer fig. 216 (photo)
1960 Strommenger, Bagh. Mitt. 1 p. 51 and pl. 12 no. 2 (photo)
1961 Gelb, MAD 2^{2} p. 199 Narâm-Sin Original Inscriptions no. 10 (study)
1963 Hirsch, AfO 20 p. 17 Narâm-Sin a 2 (study)
1967 Moortgat, Kunst pl. 152 (photo)
1971 Kupper, OrAnt 10 pp. 97–98 (study)
1975 Orthmann (ed.), Der alte Orient pl. 51b (photo)
1976 Amiet, L'art d'Agadé no. 29 (photo, translation, study)
1981 Spycket, La Statuaire p. 155 n. 64 (study)
1986 Potts, OrAnt 25 pp. 275–76 (translation [by Westenholz], study)
1990 Gelb and Kienast, Königsinschriften pp. 89–90 Narāmsîn 3 (edition)

TEXT

Col. i	
1) ^{d}*na-ra-am-*^{d}EN.ZU	i 1–8) Narām-Sîn, the mighty, king of the four quarters, victor in nine battles [i]n one year,
2) *da-núm*	
3) LUGAL	
4) *ki-ib-ra-tim*	
5) *ar-ba-im*	
6) *ša-ir*	
7) 10 LAL 1 REC 169	
8) [*i*]*n* MU 1	
9) [*í*]*š-tum*	i 9–12) [af]ter he was [vic]torious in [th]ose [ba]ttles,
10) [RE]C 169.REC 169	
11) [*šu*$_4$]*-nu-ti*	
12) [*iš-a*]*r-ru*	
13) ⌈*ù*⌉	i 13–18) [he captured] the[ir] three [kings], [and brought them before the god Enlil].
14) [*šar-rí*]*-šu-*[*nu*] ⌈3⌉	Lacuna
15) [*i-ik-mi-ma*]	
16) [*maḫ-rí-íš*]	
17) [^{d}*en-líl*]	
18) [*u-ša-rí-ib*]	
Lacuna	
1′) [...]-⌈*šú*⌉	1′–2′) (Too broken for translation)
2′) ⌈*ù*⌉	
Col. ii	
1) *má-gan*.KI	ii 1–4) He conquered Magan and captured Maniu[m], the rul[er] of Magan.
2) SAG.GIŠ.RA	
3) ⌈*ù*⌉	
4) *ma-ni-u*[*m*]	
5) E[N]	
6) *má-gan*.[KI]	
7) ŠU.DU$_8$.[A]	
8) *in* ŠA.DÚ*-šu-nu*	ii 8–14) In their mountains he quarried diorite stone and brought it to Agade, his city, and
9) NA$_4$.NA$_4$.*e-ši*$_{11}$*-i*[*m*]	
10) *i-pu-lam-ma*	
11) *a-na*	
12) *a-kà-dè*.KI	
13) URU.KI*-šu*	
14) *u-bí-lam-ma*	
15) DÙL*-šu*	ii 15–16) fashioned a statue of himself.
16) ⌈*ib*⌉*-ni*	
17) [*a-na*]	ii 17–19) [He dedicated it to the god DN].
18) [^{d}x]	
19) [A.MU.RU]	
20) [*ša* D]UB	ii 20–22) [As for the one who remov]es [this in]scription,
21) [*šu*$_4$*-a*]	

22) [*u-śa-sà-ku*]-*ni*
23) [^{d}UTU]
24) ⸢*ù*⸣
25) [DINGIR(?) *a-kà*]-*d*[*è*].KI
26) [SUḪ]UŠ-*śu*
27) [*l*]*i-sú-ḫa*
28) *ù*
29) ŠE.NUMUN-*śu*
30) *li-il-qù-tá*

ii 23–30) [may the god Šamaš] and [*the god* of Agad]e tear out his [foun]dation and destroy his progeny.

14

Year name (n) of Narām-Sîn in our compilation commemorates the (re)laying of the foundations of the temples of the god Enlil at Nippur and of the goddess Aštar at Zabala. Work on the Enlil temple is commemorated in two of the king's inscriptions (E2.1.4.14–15).

COMMENTARY

The first inscription, according to notes of Haynes, studied by Westenholz, was stamped on a brick. Its present whereabouts are unknown (it may be in Istanbul). The text was established by Westenholz from a paper squeeze. While Westenholz, followed by Gelb and Kienast, suggested a restoration for the first column now broken away, in view of its tentative nature it has not been included in this edition. The attribution of the piece to Narām-Sîn is based on the occurrence of the names of two officials, Šuʾāš-takal and Uruna-badbi, who are known from other sources to be contemporaries of the king (see Westenholz, OSP 2 p. 55). Uruna-badbi is also named in E2.6.1.2001.

BIBLIOGRAPHY

1987 Westenholz, OSP 2 p. 55 no. 40 (copy, edition)
1990 Gelb and Kienast, Königsinschriften pp. 107–108 Narāmsîn B 3 edition)

Col. i
(missing)
Col. ii
1) é-^{d}en-líl-ka
2) ì-si
3) u$_4$-ba *śu$_4$-a-áš-tá-kál*
4) šabra-é-lugal
5) lú á-<ág>-gá-bi
6) uru-na-bàd-bi
7) sanga-^{d}en-líl-lá-kam

i) (missing)

ii 1–2) deposited (the foundation inscription?) in the temple of the god Enlil.
ii 3–5) At that time, Šuʾāš-takal, majordomo of the king, was director (of the work)

ii 6–7) (and) Uruna-badbi was *šangû* priest of the god Enlil.

15

As part of his reconstruction of the Ekur temple, Narām-Sîn laid out an extensive courtyard terrace around the ziqqurrat tower. Many of the bricks from the platform bear a three-line building inscription of the king. Curiously, the same inscription is found on bricks from the northeast city wall.

CATALOGUE

Ex.	Museum number	Excavation number	Nippur provenance	Dimensions (cm)	Lines preserved	cpn
Stamps						
1	HS 1990 (old HS 26)	—	—	—	—	n
2	HS 1978 (old HS 27)	—	—	—	—	n
3	CBS 8755	—	—	11.75×12.08×2	1–3	p
4	CBS 8764	—	—	11×11×2	1–3	c
5	CBS 12210	—	—	11.4×12	1–3	c
6	CBS 15540	—	—	10.5×11.6	1–3	c
7	UM 51-6-314	2 N 520	—	9.3×4.6	1–3	c
8	A 32681 (Chicago)	9 N 37	Pennsylvania dump west of Šaṭṭ-en-Nil	6×5.5×2.7	2–3	c
9	IM —	11 N 128	WA 50c, level X, 3	—	2–3	n
10	L-29-6-319	—	—	11.3×11.8	1–3	c
11	L-29-6-320	—	—	11.4×10.3	1–3	c
12	Philadelphia (number unknown)	—	—	11.4×9.7	1–3	c
Bricks						
13	CBS 16204a	—	—	39×40×7	—	n
14	CBS 16204b	—	—	39×39×7.5	1–3	c
15	CBS 16204c	—	—	40×40×7.5	1–3	c
16	UM 84-26-21	—	—	30×30×8	1–3	c
17	UM 84-26-22	—	—	39×20×7	1–3	c
18	UM 84-26-23	—	—	38×20×8	1–3	c
19	UM 84-26-24	—	—	38×39×7.6	1–3	c
20	UM 84-26-25	—	—	39×39×8	1–3	c
21	EŞ 1544	—	—	37×37.5×7.5	1–3	c
22	EŞ 8922	—	—	39×39×7.7	1–3	c
23	EŞ 8923	—	—	38×39×7.5	1–3	c
24	EŞ 8924	—	—	39×39×8	—	n
25	EŞ 8925	—	—	39×26×8	—	n
26	(Philadelphia)	2N-T737	—	31×19×7.7	1–3	c
27	IM 56104	2 N —	—	—	—	n

COMMENTARY

The Narām-Sîn bricks with this inscription fall into two groups: full bricks measuring 38.5–40 cm square and half-bricks measuring about 40×20 cm. According to Westenholz (OSP 2 p. 28), the pavement of full bricks was laid above a pavement of half-bricks, the latter, strangely enough, often bearing an inscription of Šar-kali-šarrī. Apparently, some of the bricks in the terrace were fired a red colour, and others yellow; they may have been laid out in a decorative rug-like pattern. A similar alternation of red and yellow bricks of Narām-Sîn was found in room 17 of the structure designated by the excavators as the En temple (see McCown, Nippur 1 p. 4).

The available documentation does not allow us to determine which bricks came from the courtyard terrace and which from the city wall.

Ex. 8 was collated by G. Frame; exs. 10–11 are on loan to the University Museum from the Philadelphia Art Museum.

BIBLIOGRAPHY

1893 Hilprecht, BE 1/1 no. 4 and p. 18 (ex. 3, photo, copy, edition)
1897 Peters, Nippur 1 p. 276 and 2 pp. 123, 159, 205, and 212 (provenance)
1903 Hilprecht, Explorations pp. 388–89 (provenance, translation)
1907 Thureau-Dangin, SAK pp. 164–65 Narâm-sin a (ex. 3, edition)
1907 Fisher, Nippur I p. 30 (provenance, translation)
1929 Barton, RISA pp. 136–37 Naram-Sin 1 (ex. 3, edition)
1934 Jacobsen, AS 6 p. 27 (ex. 3, edition)
1961 Gelb, MAD 2[2] p. 198 Narâm-Sin Original Inscriptions no. 1a (ex. 3, study)
1963 Hirsch, AfO 20 pp. 18–19 Narâm-Sin a 10 α (ex. 3, edition)
1967 McCown, Nippur I pp. 3–4 (provenance)
1969 Oelsner, WZJ 18 p. 52 no. 9 (exs. 1–2, study)
1969 ANEP[2] no. 252 (ex. 4, photo)
1969 Buccellati and Biggs, AS 17 p. 11 (ex. 8, study)
1971 Sollberger and Kuper, IRSA, IIA4a (ex. 3, translation)
1975 Civil in Gibson, OIC 22 p. 136 no. 36 (ex. 9, edition)
1975–76 Basmachi, Treasures p. 205 (ex. 27, study)
1985 Behrens, JCS 37 p. 230 no. 2 (exs. 13–20, 26, study)
1987 Westenholz, OSP 2 p. 28 (provenance)
1990 Gelb and Kienast, Königsinschriften pp. 100–1 Narāmsîn 17 (exs. 1–3, 8–9, 13–20, 26, edition)

TEXT

1) [d]*na-ra-am-*[d]EN.ZU
2) *ba*DÍM
3) É [d]*en-líl*

1–3) Narām-Sîn, builder of the temple of the god Enlil.

16

Two brick stamps with an inscription recording Narām-Sîn's construction of the temple of the goddess Aštar were found by Banks at Bismāyā.

CATALOGUE

Ex.	Museum number	Provenance	Dimensions (cm)	Lines preserved	cpn
1	A 458 (Chicago)	Bismāyā, from just below	11.0×11.3×3.5	1–3	c
2	Kalamazoo Public Library 32.1198	As ex. 1(?)	12×11×2.5	—	n

COMMENTARY

E.J. Banks reports finding three brick stamps with this inscription; only two of them could be located. Information on ex. 2 was kindly provided by P. Metzner, registrar of the Kalamazoo Public Library; its existence was communicated to the author by M. Stolper. Ex. 1 was collated by G. Frame.

We might expect that these brick stamps were connected with Aštar's E-šar temple in Adab (for the E-šar, see C. Wilcke, RLA 5 p. 78). A number of votive objects dedicated in this temple were found in excavations at mound V (see Luckenbill, Adab nos. 5, 7–9, 10, 11, and 28–31); mound V apparently marked the site of the E-šar temple. The Narām-Sîn bricks, on the other hand, came from mound IV. Yang (Sargonic Inscriptions p. 107) suggests that they may be strays from the neighbouring city of Zabala, where Narām-Sîn, according to year name (n) in our compilation, built the temple of the goddess Ištar. This hypothesis is supported by the find of a fragmentary brick from Adab recording Ḫammu-rāpi's construction of the temple of the goddess Aštar at Zabala (see E4.3.6.15).

BIBLIOGRAPHY

1912 Banks, Bismya pp. 317, 321, and 342 (ex. 1, provenance, photo, translation)
1930 Luckenbill, Adab no. 27 (ex. 1, copy)
1961 Gelb, MAD 2^2 p. 198 Narâm-Sin Original Inscriptions no. 2 (study)
1963 Hirsch, AfO 20 pp. 18–19 Narâm-Sin a 10 γ (ex. 1, edition)
1971 Sollberger and Kupper, IRSA p. 106 n. 2 to IIA4a (ex. 1, study)
1986 Yang, Sargonic Archive p. 19 no. 4 (ex. 1, edition)
1989 Yang, Sargonic Inscriptions p. 107 (ex. 1, study)
1990 Gelb and Kienast, Köngisinschriften p. 101 Narāmsîn 19 (ex. 1, edition)

TEXT

1) [d]*na-ra-a*[*m*]-[d]EN.Z[U]
2) *ba*DÍM
3) É [d]INANNA

1–3) Narā[m]-Sî[n], builder of the temple of the goddess Aštar.

17

An inscription of Narām-Sîn known from two brick stamps deals with the construction of the temple of the god Sîn.

CATALOGUE

Ex.	Museum number	Excavation number	Registration number	Provenance	Dimensions (cm)	Lines preserved	cpn
1	BM 103040	—	1909-12-9, 1	Said to have come from Telloh	Originally 10.6×10.2	1–3	p
2	BM 116454	U 79	1923-11-10, 40	Ur, found on the surface, Season 1	—	2–3	n

COMMENTARY

Ex. 1 is said to have come from Telloh; it might possibly be a stray from the city of Ur, since a duplicate of this text (ex. 2) comes from that city. According to Hibbert (OrAnt 21 [1982] p. 257 sub CBI 3), BM 116454 is not a duplicate of this text. This assertion, however, is based on a misunderstanding. Hibbert takes no. 43 of Sollberger's catalogue on p. 35 of UET 8 to refer to the piece copied on pl. VII of the same volume. However, it is clear from Sollberger's description of the piece that it cannot be the item copied on pl. VII; rather pl. VII gives a copy of the item catalogued as no. 43 on p. 9, a fragment of a black steatite tablet of Ur III date.

BIBLIOGRAPHY

1909 King, PSBA 31 pp. 286–88 and pl. XLI (ex. 1, photo, edition)
1922 BM Guide p. 58 no. 11 (ex. 1, study)
1961 Gelb, MAD 2^2 p. 198 Narâm-Sin Original Inscriptions no. 1b (ex. 1, study)
1963 Hirsch, AfO 20 p. 19 Narâm-Sin a 10 β (ex. 1, study)
1965 Sollberger, UET 8 p. 35 no. 43 (ex. 2, transliteration)
1971 Sollberger and Kupper, IRSA p. 106 n. 2 to IIA4a (exs. 1–2, study)
1981 Walker, CBI no. 3 (exs. 1–2, transliteration)
1990 Gelb and Kienast, Königsinschriften p. 101 Narāmsîn 18 (exs. 1–2, edition)

TEXT

1) [(^{d})*na-ra*]-*am*-[^{d}EN].ZU
2) [*ba*D]ÍM
3) [É] ⌈^{d}⌉EN.ZU

1–3) [Nar]ām-[S]în, [bui]lder of the [temple] of the god Sîn.

18

Three inscriptions of the princess Tūta-napšum (E2.1.4.18–20) and a seal inscription of one of her servants (E2.1.4.2017) are known. The first inscription is found on a stone plaque now conserved in Jena.

As noted in our introductory comments for Narām-Sîn, a year name of Sargonic date in Sumerian (year name [o]) records the oracular designation of the *entu* priestess of the god Enlil: mu en ^{d}en-líl máš-e íb-dab$_5$-ba. This is almost certainly a reference to Tūta-napšum. What may be the Akkadian form of the same year name (year name [o′]) appears on a tablet published by Foster: *in* 1 MU [NI]N ^{d}*en-líl-*<<*lá*>>. An identity of the two year names, although likely, cannot be proved, because the end of the Akkadian example was not given by the ancient scribe. On the tablet published by Foster a succeeding year name, likely the one that fell two years after Tūta-napšum's designation or installation, deals with Narām-Sîn's campaign against the city of Azuḫinnum. This may be a reference to the city that lay in the Ḫabur region.

COMMENTARY

The fragmentary plaque, is made of dark grey slate, and measures 15.5×14.0×1.9–2.0 cm. It was found in excavations at Nippur and bears the museum number HS 194b (formerly HS 32). The inscription was collated from the published photo.

Despite the comments of Kutscher (Brockmon Tablets p. 34) and Gelb and Kienast (Königsinschriften p. 105 Narāmsîn A 6), it is by no means certain that inscription E2.1.4.20 is a duplicate of this text. For that reason we have not restored the end of the inscription.

BIBLIOGRAPHY

1963 Hirsch, AfO 20 pp. 22–23 Narâm-Sin d 1 δ (transliteration)
1969 Oelsner, WZJ 18 p. 52 no. 10 (transliteration)
1981 Michalowski, RA 75 p. 174 (transliteration, study)
1983 Westenholz and Oelsner, AoF 10 pp. 212–16 (photo, edition, study)
1983 A. and J. Westenholz, AoF 10 pp. 387–88 (study)
1990 Gelb and Kienast, Königsinschriften p. 105 Narāmsîn A 6 (edition)

TEXT

1) ^{d}*na-r*[*a-am*]-^{d}EN.Z[U]
2) LUGA[L]
3) *ki-ib-ra-t*[*im*]
4) *ar-ba-*[*im*]
5) *tu-t*[*á-na*]-*a*[*p-šum*$_6$]
Lacuna

1–4) Nar[ām]-Sî[n], kin[g] of the fou[r] quarter[s]:

5) Tū[ta-n]a[pšum]
Lacuna

19

A second inscription of Tūta-napšum is also conserved in Jena.

COMMENTARY

The inscription is incised on a bowl fragment made of a grey stone that measures 8.5×3.7×0.9–1.2 cm, original diameter about 25 cm. It was found in excavations at Nippur, and bears the museum number HS 1960 (formerly HS 55). The restoration of the text, although not entirely certain, is likely. The inscription was collated from the published photo.

BIBLIOGRAPHY

1969 Oelsner, WZJ 18 p. 53 no. 24 (transliteration, study)
1983 Westenholz and Oelsner, AoF 10 pp. 215–16 (photo, edition, study)
1990 Gelb and Kienast, Königsinschriften p. 106 Narāmsîn A 7 (edition)

TEXT

1) *t*[*u-tá-na-ap-šum*$_6$]
2) NIN.DINGIR [^{d}*en-líl*]

1–2) T[ūta-napšum], *entu* priestess [of the god Enlil].

20

A third inscription mentioning Tūta-napšum is known from an Old Babylonian tablet copy from Nippur.

COMMENTARY

The inscription is found on rev. col. 3′ 5–13 of BT 1 (= lines 1–9 of our reconstructed text). The end of the inscription is missing. The inscription was collated by P. Steinkeller.

BIBLIOGRAPHY

1989 Kutscher, Brockmon Tablets, pp. 26, 29, 34–35, 111, and 119 (photo, copy, edition)
1990 Gelb and Kienast, Königsinschriften pp. 274–75 Narāmsîn C 18 (edition)

TEXT

1) ^{d}[*na*]-*ra-am*-^{d}EN.ZU
2) LUGAL
3) *ki-ib-ra-tim*
4) *ar-ba-im*
5) *tu-tá-na-ap-šum*$_{6}$
6) EN NIN.⌈DINGIR(?)⌉
7) ^{d}*en-líl*⌉.<<KI>>
8) DUMU.MUNUS-*su*
Lacuna

1–4) [Na]rām-Sîn, king of the four quarters:

5–8) Tūta-napšum, *entu priestess* of the god Enlil, (is) his daughter.
Lacuna

21

Two Sargonic royal inscriptions, and possibly a third, record activities of Narām-Sîn in the Ḫabur region. In all inscriptions and year names dating from this period, as far as can be determined, the king's name is written with the prefixed divine determinative.

The first inscription, a stone fragment, perhaps a piece of a stele, is now housed in the Nies Babylonian Collection. It bears an inscription in classic Sargonic script which gives an apparent itinerary of cities in the Ḫabur region. In view of its monumental nature, it likely was a royal inscription; the piece apparently recounts a campaign of a Sargonic king in the Ḫabur district. As noted, one of the toponyms of the text, Azuḫinnum, is mentioned in year name (q) of Narām-Sîn: in 1 M[U] ^{d}*na-ra-*[*am*-^{d}E]N.ZU REC 169 SUBIR.KI *in a-zu-ḫi-nim*.KI *i-ša-ru tá-ḫi-ša-ti-li ik-mi-ù* 'The ye[ar] Narā[m-Sîn] was victorious over Subartu at Azuḫinnum and captured Taḫiš-atili'. If the Yale fragment be indeed a fragment of a royal inscription, then Narām-Sîn would likely be its author.

COMMENTARY

The inscription is incised on NBC 11428, a limestone fragment of unknown provenance. It measures 8 cm in height and its two preserved columns meet at an exterior angle of 12½°. A study and transliteration of the text were kindly provided to the author for inclusion in the RIM edition by B. Foster in advance of its publication.

Although Foster emended the text to read KUR for PA$_{4}$ at the end of i′ 2′ and 6′, we prefer an unemended text, and see in the cited lines a reference to a hydronym. Now, an apparent PN *ḫa-ra*-NE, probably to be read as *ḫa-ra-bí*, occurs in connection with the city of Nagar in an archival text from Ebla cited by Archi (in Fronzaroli, Studies Ebla p. 231). Since hydronyms are sometimes found as components of PNs, as, for example, in the Sargonic RN Šū-Turul, there may be a connection between the PN *ḫa-ra-bí* of the Ebla text and a restored hydronym, [*ḫa*]-*ra-bí*.PA$_{4}$ of the Foster fragment. In this connection we may note that Oates (Iraq 47 [1985] p. 170) has shown that the Wādi Jaghjagh, the stream that flows by modern Tell Brāk, corresponds to the ancient hydronym Ḫarmiš; the name also equates with the Hirmas of medieval Arab geographers. Bearing in mind the fact that *iš* serves as an element of toponym formation in Hurrian toponyms, coupled with the frequent alternation between b and m in foreign toponyms (for the latter, see Steinkeller, Aula Orientalis 2 [1984] p. 142), we propose that the [*ḫa*]-*ra-bí*.PA$_{4}$ of the Foster fragment corresponds to the river name Ḫarmiš. If this be true, it would indicate that the ancient city of Naḫur lay not far from the Ḫarmiš river.

The GN Azuḫinnum of ii′ 5′ is likely a reference to the city that appears in the Old Babylonian texts from Mari and Tell al-Rimāḥ, and which, according to Charpin (RA 84 [1990] p. 94), was situated: 'au nord du Sinjar, mais à l'ouest du Tigre, non loin de Razamâ'. Of importance to the question of Azuḫinnum's location is a 'Cappadocian' tablet (CCT 1, 26b) that mentions Uzuḫinnum, presumably a variant spelling of Azuḫinnum, together with Daraqum. Daraqum was situated in the area southeast of Tell Leilān, possibly at Tell Çilpārat, about 40–55 kms southeast of Tell Leilān (see Nashef, Rép. Géog. 4 p. 114), or at Tell Hādi (see Eidem, NABU 1988 no. 1).

We propose a restoration of the GN of ii′ 4′ as *kùr-[da*.KI] following the second suggestion given by Foster (CRRA 38 p. 74). According to Charpin (in Eichler, Tall al-Hamīdīya 2 p. 72 n. 22) ancient Kurda lay north of Karanā a distance that could could be traversed in a single day. Charpin (in Durand, Mohammed Diyab pp. 97–102) further indicates a location for the ancient city just south of the Jebel Sinjar. The units of length employed in this text have no exact English equivalents. We have translated DA.NA as 'stage' following Powell (RLA 7/8 p. 476). The DA.NA is thought to have measured about 10.8 kms. We have assumed, perhaps erroneously, that the unit of measurement [ÉŠE].GÍD, which Foster restores in this text, correlates to the unit of length ÉŠE/*ašlu*(*m*) 'rope'. It may be that it was a longer measure, perhaps equivalent to the UŠ (= 6 ÉŠE).

BIBLIOGRAPHY

1992 Foster, CRRA 38 pp. 73–76 (copy, edition, study)

TEXT

Col. i′
Lacuna
1′) [...]
2′) [*a-na ḫa*]*-ra-*[*b*]*í*.PA$_4$
3′) [N D]A.NA [N ÉŠE].GÍD
4′) [1 UD] ⸢Ì⸣.GIN
5′) [*íš*]*-tum*
6′) [*ḫa-ra*]*-bí*.PA$_4$
7′) [*a-na n*]*a-ḫur*.KI
8′) [N DA].NA 1 [ÉŠE.GÍD]
9′) [1 UD Ì.GIN]
Lacuna

Lacuna
i′ 1′–4′ [... to] the stream [Ḫa]ra[b]i, [N st]ages and N 'ro[pes]' he went [in one day].

i′ 5′–9′) [Fr]om the stream [Ḫara]bi [to N]aḫur, [N st]ages and [N 'ropes' he went in one day].
Lacuna

Col. ii′
Lacuna
1′) 2(?) D[A.NA] 12+x [ÉŠE.GÍD]
2′) 1 UD Ì.[GIN]
3′) *íš-t*[*um*]
4′) *kùr-*[*da*.KI]
5′) *a-na a-z*[*u*]*-ḫi-núm*.[KI]
6′) 1½ DA.NA 3 [ÉŠE].GÍD
7′) 1 ⸢UD⸣ [Ì.GIN]
Lacuna

Lacuna
ii′ 1′–2′) Two(?) st[ages] 12+x ['ropes'] he went in one day.
ii′ 3′–7′) Fr[om] Kur[da] to Az[u]ḫinnum, one and one-half stages and three ['ro]pes' [he went] in one day.
Lacuna

22

Having defeated the Subarian forces at Azuḫinnum (see E2.1.4.21), Narām-Sîn may have sought to consolidate his hold over the Ḫabur region by the construction of fortress at Tall Brāk. Seven stamped bricks with an inscription of Narām-Sîn were found during excavations of that structure.

CATALOGUE

Ex.	Museum number	Excavation number	Photo number	Dimensions (cm)	Lines preserved	cpn
1	—	—	M (allowan)	—	1–2	n
2	Institute of Archaeology, London (lower half only)	—	M 901	—	—	n
3	BM 126497 (1939-2-8, 133)	—	M 902	37.5×22.5×8.0	1–2	n
4	—	—	M 903	—	1–2	n
5	Institute of Archaeology, London (right half only)	—	M 904	—	1–2	p
6	—	Tell Brāk 84.1453	—	36.0×36.0×8.0	1–2	p
7	—	Tell Brāk 84.1454	—	32.5×32.5×8.0	1–2	p

COMMENTARY

In ex. 7, the DINGIR sign lacks a vertical wedge.

BIBLIOGRAPHY

1938 Mallowan, ILN October 15 p. 697 fig. 3 (ex. 5, photo)
1947 Mallowan, Iraq 9 p. 66 and pl. LXIV (ex. 5, copy, study)
1961 Gelb, MAD 2[2] p. 199 Narâm-Sin Original Inscriptions no. 12 (ex. 5, study)
1963 Hirsch, AfO 20 p. 19 Narâm-Sin a 11 (ex. 5, transliteration)
1981 Walker, CBI no. 4 (ex. 3, transliteration)
1985 Finkel, Iraq 47 pp. 189–90 and pl. XXXIII (exs. 1–7, study; exs. 6–7, photo, copy)
1990 Gelb and Kienast, Königsinschriften pp. 101–102 Narāmsîn 20 (exs. 1–7, edition)

TEXT

1) ^{d}*na-ra-am*-^{d}EN.ZU

1) Narām-Sîn.

23

An inscription of Narām-Sîn known from two Old Babylonian tablet copies deals with the king's slaying of a wild bull at Mount Tibar and the dedication of an image to the god Enlil at Nippur.

CATALOGUE

Ex.	Museum number	Provenance	Dimensions (cm)	Tablet lines preserved	Text lines preserved	cpn
1	AO 5475	Unknown, probably Nippur	8.5x10	obv. col. i 1–10 obv. col. ii 1–9 rev. col. i 1–10	1–10 11–18, 20 21–31	c
2	BT 1	Nippur	8.0×9.0×2.7	rev. col iv 1–22	8–29	p

COMMENTARY

Mount Tibar has been identified with the modern Jebel ʿAbd al-ʿAzīz, situated just west of the Ḫabur river (see Stol, Trees pp. 25–30). Of note is the lack of subjunctive verbal forms in lines 7 and 14; they are expected after the conjunction *inu* in line 5.

BIBLIOGRAPHY

1911 Thureau-Dangin, RA 8 pp. 199–200 (ex. 1, copy, edition)
1929 Hrozny, ArOr 1 pp. 75–76 (ex. 1, study)
1957 Hallo, Titles p. 6 (ex. 1, study)
1957 Kupper, Nomades pp. 113–14 (ex. 1, study)
1961 Gelb, MAD 2^2 p. 199 Narâm-Sin Late Copies no. 5 (ex. 1, study)
1963 Hirsch, AfO 20 p. 21 Narâm-Sin b 7 (ex. 1, study)
1970 Sollberger, RA 64 p. 173 (ex. 1, study)
1971 Sollberger and Kupper, IRSA IIA4f (ex. 1, translation)
1974 Barnett, CRRA 19 p. 441 (ex. 1, study)
1989 Kutscher, Brockmon Tablets pp. 26–27, 29, 35–36, 111, and 119 (ex. 2, photo, copy, edition)
1990 Gelb and Kienast, Königsinschriften pp. 265–66 Narāmsîn C 6 (exs. 1–2, edition)

TEXT

1) [(^{d})*na-ra-am*-^{d}]EN.ZU	1–4) [Narām]-Sîn, [kin]g of the four [quarter]s,
2) [LUGA]L	
3) [*ki-ib-ra-ti*]*m*	
4) ⸢*ar-ba-im*⸣	
5) *ì-nu*	5–14) when he defeated ḪARšamat and personally felled a wild bull at Mount Tiba[r],
6) ḪAR-*ša-ma-at*.KI	
7) *en*-⸢*a*⸣-[*r*]*a-am*	
8) *ù*	
9) AM	
10) *in qab*$_{x}$(DA)-*lá*-NI	
11) *ti-ba-a*[*r*]	
12) ŚA.DÚ-*im*	
13) *śu*$_{4}$-*ma*	
14) *u-śa-am-qí-it-śu*	
15) *tám-ši-il-śu*	15–19) he fashioned an image of himself and dedicated it to the god Enlil, his fa[th]er.
16) *ib-ni-ma*	
17) *a-na*	
18) ^{d}*en-líl*	
19) *a-b*[*í*]-*śu*	
20) A.MU.RU	
21) *ša* DUB	21–31) As for the one who removes this inscription, may the gods Enlil and Šamaš tear out his foundations and destroy his progeny.
22) *śu*$_{4}$-*a*	
23) *u-śa-sà-ku-ni*	
24) ^{d}*en-líl*	
25) *ù*	
26) ^{d}UTU	
27) SUḪUŠ-*śu*	
28) *li-sú-ḫa*	
29) *ù*	
30) ŠE.NUMUN-*śu*	
31) *li-il-qù-tám*	

15.2 *tám-ši*$_{x}$(SU$_{4}$)-*il-śu*.

19.1 Omits.

23.2 *u-śa-sà-k*[*u-ni*] collation of tablet photo (Westenholz).

24

In the first phase of Narām-Sîn's campaigns after the deification of the king, the king's objective may have been to extend Akkadian control over the settlements of the Tigris basin from the area of Šimānum, where he had campaigned early in his reign before the outbreak of the hostilities of the 'Great Revolt', to the headwaters of the Tigris. Three events enable us to mark the king's progress in this region. The first was his taking of the city of Šenaminda, recorded in year name (t). Another battle may have taken place in the vicinity of modern Pir Hüseyn, a village about 25 kms northeast of Diyarbakır, since a victory stele of the king was found there. However, as noted below, Pir Hüseyn may not have been the original provenance of the stele. Finally, year name (t) records the king's reaching the source of the Tigris and Euphrates rivers.

A victory stele found at Pir Hüseyn commemorates Narām-Sîn's defeat of a foe whose name is not preserved.

COMMENTARY

The stele fragment was found by the well of a country home just east of Pir Hüseyn. Naab (in Unger, Naram-Sin p. 33) indicates that it originally came from the vicinity of the village of Ambar-Chai. Börker-Klähn (Bildstelen p. 133) gives an original provenance of Miyafarkin, a village about 75 km northeast of Diyarbakir. The stele fragment measures at its maximum extent 57×42×20 cm and is made of basalt (Jastrow-Hilprecht) or diorite (Unger). The inscribed portion measures 19.1×18.4 cm; the piece now bears the museum number EŞ 1027. The inscription was collated from the published photo. Photos or drawings of the stele have appeared frequently in studies on the art of Mesopotamia; the bibliography contains only a selection of these items. For a complete list, see Börker-Klähn, Bildstelen p. 134.

Despite the comments of Börker-Klähn, Bildstelen p. 134, the inscription is almost certainly not a building inscription, but rather commemorates a military victory of the king. Col. ii 1: for the logographic spelling of the god Ea's name in Old Akkadian (and Old Babylonian) texts see the comments of J. and A. Westenholz, Orientalia NS 46 (1977) p. 204. Ea's role of allowing no rivals to the king (ii 1–6) is uniquely attested for the Sargonic period in this inscription. Perhaps the god appears here because of his role as guardian of the sources of the rivers. For the restoration of ii 1′ – iii 1, see Steinkeller, WZKM 77 (1987) pp. 188–89. For iii 3: KI.GAL = sur_7 = *birūtam* 'burial mound', see Westenholz, AfO 23 (1970) pp. 28–29 and Kienast, OrAnt 19 (1980) p. 259 and nn. 24–25. The restoration of iii 8–12 assumes at least three divine names because the verb forms of the curse are plural, not dual; curses mentioning two gods are more commonly found in the Sargonic royal inscriptions.

BIBLIOGRAPHY

1893 Maspero, RT 15 pp. 65–66 (study)
1893 Scheil, RT 15 pp. 62–64 and plate following p. 64 (photo, edition)
1895 Maspero, Histoire Ancienne 1 p. 602 (drawing)
1896 Hilprecht, BE I/2 no. 120 (copy, photo)
1898 Hilprecht, Recent Research pp. 87–88 (photo, study)
1900 Scheil, MDP 2 p. 55 (edition)
1906 Meyer, Sumerier und Semiten pl. III (photo)
1907 Thureau-Dangin, SAK pp. 166–67 Narâm-Sin f (edition)
1910 King, Early History pp. 244–46 and fig. 59 (drawing, study)
1929 Barton, RISA pp. 140–41 Naram-Sin 12 (edition)
1934 Unger, Naram-Sin pp. 16–18, 39–41, and pl. 1 (photo, edition)
1935 Zervos, L'art p. 164 (photo)
1937 Rigg, JAOS 57 p. 417 (study)
1940 Christian, Altertumskunde 1 pl. 365 no. 3 (photo)
1960 Parrot, Sumer fig. 211 (photo)
1961 Gelb, MAD 2^2 p. 199 Narâm-Sin Original Inscriptions no. 7 (study)
1963 Hirsch, AfO 20 p. 18 Narâm-Sin a 7 (study)
1964 Borger, JCS 18 p. 54 (study)
1967 Moortgat, Kunst pl. 153 (photo)
1975 Orthmann (ed.), Der alte Orient pl. 105 (photo)
1976 Amiet, L'art d'Agadé p. 31 fig. 21 (photo)
1976 Uzunoğlu, IESEM p.25 no. 4 b and fig. 32 (study, photo)
1982 Börker-Klähn, Bildstelen no. 25 (drawing, study)
1990 Gelb and Kienast, Königsinschriften pp. 92–93 Narāmsîn 5 (edition)

TEXT

Col. i
1) [^{d}*na-r*]*a-am*-[^{d}EN].ZU
2) [*da-n*]*úm*
Lacuna

i 1–2) [Nar]ām-Sîn, the [migh]ty,
Lacuna

Col. ii
1) ^{d}EN.KI
2) *in ki-ib-ra-tim*
3) *ar-ba-im*
4) *na-e*
5) [*i*]*r-tim*
6) [*ul i-d*]*ì*-[-*śum*$_6$]
Lacuna

ii 1–6) The god Ea [ga]v[e him no] rival in the four quarters.
Lacuna

1′) [*ana*]
2′) [*karāšim*]
Col. iii
1) *íś-ku-un*
2) *ù*
3) KI.GAL
4) *íś-pu-uk*

ii 1′– iii 4 He *an*[*nihilated* ...] and heaped up a burial mound.

5) *ša* DUB
6) *śu*$_4$*-a*
7) ⸢*u*⸣-*śa-sà-ku-ni*
8) [^{d}IN]ANNA
9) [*ù*]
10) [^{d}X]
11) [*ù*]
12) [^{d}Y]
Lacuna

iii 5–12) As for the one who removes this inscription, may the goddess Aštar [and the gods X and Y]
Lacuna

1′) [SUḪUŠ-*śu*]
Col. iv
1) *li-sú*-⸢*ḫu*⸣
2) *ù*
3) ŠE.NUMUN-*śu*
4) *li-il-qù-t*[*u*]

iii 1′ – iv 4) tear out [his foundations] and destroy his progeny.

5) NIT[A]
6) *ù*
7) ⸢MU⸣
8) [*a i-d*]*ì*-[*nu-súm*$_6$]

iv 5–8) [May they not gr]ant [him] a ma[le] (heir) or offspring.

9) [*maḫ-rí-íś*]
10) [*i-lí-śu*]
11) [*a* DU]
Lacuna

iv 9–11) [May he not walk before his (personal) deity].
Lacuna

25

A Narām-Sîn inscription known from two Old Babylonian tablet copies alludes to a campaign against the city of Talḫadum. This city has generally been equated by scholars with the GN Tilḫad. Talḫad is mentioned in the Old Assyrian tablets from Kül Tepe; it was an important way station on the way to Kaniš (see Nashef, Rép. Géogr. 4 p. 119). The city has been identified with classical Δολίχη; a location at modern Tell

Dülük about 11 km north of ʿAintāb/Gazian Tepe has been proposed (see Lewy, Orientalia 21 [1952] p. 425).

CATALOGUE

Ex.	Museum number	Excavation number	Provenance	Dimensions (cm)	Tablet lines preserved	Text lines preserved	cpn
1	IM—	U 7725	Ur, from no. 7 Quiet Street room 5 or 6	—	i 1–19 ii 1–21 iii 4–23 iv 1–7	1–19 20–40 45–64 65–71	n
2	Ni 2435	—	Nippur	10×6×2	i 1–8	1–8	p

COMMENTARY

We believe, based on geographical considerations, that this inscription dates to a period late in Narām-Sîn's Subarian campaigns, by which time the king had been deified. However, no DINGIR sign appears before the royal name in either exemplar 1 or 2. The divine determinative may have been omitted by the ancient copyist. The mention of the Cedar Forest in lines 15–16 accords well with the fact that Talḫadum/Düluk Tepe lies a scant 70 kms east of the Amanus Mountains. Lines 33–37 parallel lines 2–6 of E2.1.4.2. For the reading of the DN of line 52, cf. Diri VII 59: ^{d}nin-EZENxLA = ni-in-gu-ub-la-ga(quoted in Owen, JNES 33 [1974] p. 176). Cf. also MSL 14 p. 117: [g]u-ba-la-ag! EZENxLA.

BIBLIOGRAPHY

1928 Gadd, UET 1 no. 274 (ex. 1, copy, edition)
1929 Langdon, JRAS p. 372 (ex. 1, study)
1929–30 Jacobsen, AJSL 46 p. 70 (ex.1, study)
1931 Landsberger, OLZ 34 130–31 (ex.1, study)
1934 Unger, Naram-Sin p. 48 and pl. V no. 10 (ex. 2, photo, edition)
1937 Goetze, JAOS 57 p. 107 (ex.1, study)
1944 Gelb, Hurrians p. 35 and n. 88 (exs. 1–2, study)
1948 Kraus, Iraq 10 p. 91 (exs. 1–2, study)
1961 Gelb, MAD 2^2 p. 199 Narâm-Sin Late Copies nos. 2a –b (exs.1–2, study)
1963 Hirsch, AfO 20 pp. 20 and 72–73 Narâm-Sin b 4 (study, edition)
1965 Sollberger, UET 8 p. 32 no. 33 (ex. 1, study)
1971 Sollberger and Kupper, IRSA IIA4d (exs. 1–2, translation)
1990 Gelb and Kienast, Königsinschriften pp. 249–51 Narāmsîn C 3 (exs. 1–2, edition)

TEXT

1) *na-ra-am-*^{d}EN.ZU
2) LUGAL
3) *a-kà-dè*.KI
4) *śa-pí-ir*
5) KIŠ MI KAM
6) KALAM
7) NIM.KI
8) *kà-lí-śa-ma*
9) *a-dì-ma*
10) *pá-ra-aḫ-śum*.KI
11) *ù*
12) KALAM
13) [Š]UBUR$^{\textit{śu-bar-tim}}$.KI
14) *a-dì-ma*
15) GIŠ.TIR
16) [GI]Š.ERIN

1–16) Narām-Sîn, king of Agade, commander ... of all the land of Elam, as far as Paraḫšum, and the land of [S]ubartum as far as the Cedar Forest.

5.1 Gadd's copy suggests that MI is a gloss. In ex. 2 the MI sign is written in full size.

17) *ù*
18) [*ì*]-*nu*
19) [*a*]-*na*
20) *tal-ḫa-dim*.[K]I
21) *i-lí-ku*
22) KASKAL.KI *šu*$_{4}$-*a*
23) *śar in śar-rí*
24) *ma-na-ma*
25) *la i-lí-ik*
26) *na-ra-am*-^{d}EN.ZU
27) LUGAL
28) *a-kà-dè*.KI
29) *i-lí-ik-ma*
30) ^{d}INANNA
31) *ma-ḫi-ra*
32) *la id-dì-šum*$_{6}$

17–32) Now, [wh]en he went [t]o Talḫadum — no king (previously) had gone on such a campaign — Narām-Sîn, king of Agade, went there and the goddess Aštar gave him no rival.

33) ÉNSI.ÉNSI
34) ŠUBUR.KI
35) (erasure) *ù*
36) EN.EN
37) <KUR.KUR> *a-lí-a-tim*
38) NIDBA-*š*[*u-nu*]
39) [*m*]*aḫ-rí*-[*šu*]
40) *u-ša-r*[*í-bu*]

33–40) The governors of Subartum and the lords of the Upper <Lands> bro[ught] th[eir] offerings before [him].

41) [...]
42) [...]
43) [...]
44) N[AM(?)-...]
45) *a-l*[*a*-...]]
46) *i*-R[I-x-*a*]*m*

41–46) (Too broken for translation)

47) *na-ra-am*-^{d}EN.ZU
48) LUGAL
49) *a-kà-dè*.KI
50) *a-na*
51) ^{d}*nin-gublaga*
52) A.MU.RU

47–52) Narām-Sîn, king of Agade, dedicated (this statue) to the god Ningublaga.

53) *ša* DUB
54) *u-ša-sà-ku-ni*
55) ^{d}*nin-gublaga*
56) *be-al*
57) DÙL *šu*$_{4}$-*a*
58) *ù*
59) ^{d}UTU
60) SUḪUŠ-*šu*
61) *li-sú-ḫa*
62) ŠE.NUMUN-*šu*
63) *li-il-qù-tá*
64) NITA-[*šu*]
65) ⸢*ù*⸣
66) [M]U-*šu*
67) [*a*] ⸢*i*⸣-*dì-na-šum*$_{6}$
68) *maḫ-rí-iš*
69) [*i*]-*lí-šu*
70) [*a*] DU

53–70) As for the one who removes this inscription, may the god Ningublaga, the owner of this statue, and the god Šamaš, tear out his foundations. May they destroy his progeny. May they [not] grant to him [his] male (heir) or his off[spring]. May he [not] walk before his (personal) [g]od.

26

The climax of Narām-Sîn's Subarian campaigns may have been his taking of the cities of Armānum and Ebla. The former event is described in an inscription known from an Old Babylonian tablet copy.

COMMENTARY

The clay tablet with this inscription, IM 85461, was found at Ur, from either room 5 or 6, no. 7 Quiet Street. It was given the excavation number U 7756. The text follows B. Foster's edition, which benefited from collations by E. Sollberger and J. Black. Unlike Foster, however, who considered UET 1 no. 276 to contain the end of this inscription, we have edited that text along with UET 8 no. 13 as a separate inscription (see the comments to E2.1.4.5). The text is noteworthy for its detailed description of the city walls of Armānum; as far as can be determined, no comparable description is found in a royal inscription of the third millennium. If we assume a faithful copy by the ancient and modern copyists, the name of the king of Armānum would appear in two slightly variant writings: *ri-da-*ᵈIŠKUR (iii 2) and *ri-id-*ᵈIŠKUR (iii 28); the name has been normalized following the second writing. It has been compared with the PN Rīš-Adad, king of Apišal, known from the later chronicle and omen tradition (see Grayson, Chronicles p. 154). Since the name type *Rīš*-DN is found in Old Akkadian and Old Babylonian texts, a reading *Rīš-Adad* would not be unexpected; it would, however, require an emendation of the text, as far as it can be determined from the available sources. Collation of the relevant lines is, unfortunately, not possible at present. Since the name belonged to the king of Armānum, it need not have been Akkadian. For the translation 'undermined' for v 16, see W.G. Lambert, BWL p. 130, line 96.

A notation at the end of the text indicates that the statue bearing this inscription stood beside one erected by king Sîn-irībam; the latter is probably a reference to the statue which figures in the name of the second year of the Larsa king (see UET 5 no. 196).

Thanks to the excavations of the Italian team headed by P. Matthiae, the identification of ancient Ebla with Tell Mardīkh is secure; the location of Armānum, on the other hand, is less certain.

BIBLIOGRAPHY

1928 Gadd, UET 1 no. 275 (copy, edition)
1929 Langdon, JRAS p. 372 (study)
1929–30 Jacobsen, AJSL 46 pp. 70–71 (study)
1931 Landsberger, OLZ 34 131 (study)
1948 Kraus, Iraq 10 pp. 81–92 (study)
1961 Gelb, MAD 2^2 p. 199 Narâm-Sin Late Copies no. 3 (study)
1963 Hirsch, AfO 20 pp. 20–21 and 73–77 Narâm-Sin b 5 (edition)
1969 Oppenheim, in ANET^3 p. 268 (partial translation)
1965 Sollberger, UET 8 p. 32 no. 34 (study)
1971 Sollberger and Kupper, IRSA IIA4e (partial translation)
1982 Foster, JANES 14 pp. 27–36 (edition)
1984 Borger, TUAT 1 pp. 354–55 (partial translation)
1990 Gelb and Kienast, Königsinschriften pp. 253–64 Narāmsîn C 5 Text A only (edition)

TEXT

Col. i
1) *ša iś-tum*
2) *da-ar*
3) *śi-ki-ti*
4) NI.ŚI$_{11}$(*)
5) *śar in* ⸢*śar*⸣*-rí*
6) *ma-na-ma*
7) *ar-ma-nam*.KI

i 1–10) Whereas, for all time since the creation of mankind, no king whosoever had destroyed Armānum and Ebla,

i 4 Text: ÁB.

8) *ù*
9) *eb-la*.KI
10) *la u-śa-al-pi$_5$-tu*
11) *in* GIŠ(?).TUKUL(?)-*ki*
12) ^{d}*nergal*
13) *pá-da-an*
14) ^{d}*na-ra-am*-^{d}EN.ZU
15) *da-nim$_4$*
16) *ip-te-ma*
17) *ar-ma-nam*.KI
18) *ù*
19) *eb-la*.KI
20) *i-dì-śum$_6$*
21) *ù*
22) *a-ma-nam*
23) ŚA.DÚ
24) GIŠ.ERIN
25) *ù*
26) *ti-a-am-tám*
27) *a-lí-tám*
28) *i-qí-íś-śum$_6$*
29) *-ma*
30) *in* GIŠ.TUKUL-*ki*
31) ^{d}*da-gan*
32) *mu-śa-ar-bí-ì*
Col.ii
1) *śar-ru$_9$-ti-śu$_4$*
2) ^{d}*na-ra-am*-^{d}EN.ZU
3) *da-núm*
4) *ar-ma-nam*.KI
5) *ù*
6) *eb-la*.KI
7) *en-ar*
8) *ù*
9) *íś-tum-ma*
10) *pu-ti*
11) BURANUN.I$_7$
12) *a-dì-ma*
13) *u-li-śi-im*.KI
14) NI.SI$_{11}$(*)
15) *ša-at*
16) ^{d}*da-gan*
17) BÍL-*íś*
18) *i-qí-śu-śum$_6$*
19) *u-ra-iš-ma*
20) GIŠ.DUSU
21) *ìl-a-ba$_4$*
22) *ì-lí-śu*
23) *na-śi$_{11}$*(*)-<*ù*>-*nim*
24) *ù*
25) *a-ma-nam*
26) ŚA.DÚ
27) GIŠ.ERIN
28) *i-ig-mu-ur*
(Space)
29) *ì-nu*
30) ^{d}*da-gan*

i 11–20) the god Nergal, by means of (his) weapons opened the way for Narām-Sîn, the mighty, and gave him Armānum and Ebla.

i 21–29) Further, he gave to him the Amanus, the Cedar Mountain, and the Upper Sea.

i 30 – ii 1) By means of the weapons of the god Dagān, who magnifies his kingship,

ii 2–7) Narām-Sîn, the mighty, conquered Armānum and Ebla.

ii 8–19) Further, from the *side* of the Euphrates River as far as (the city of) Ulišum, he smote the people whom the god Dagān had given to him for the first time,

ii 20–23) so that they perform service for the god Ilaba, his god.

ii 24–28) Further, he totally (conquered) the Amanus, the Cedar Mountain.

ii 29 – iii 6) When the god Dagān determined the verdict (for) Narām-Sîn, the mighty, delivered into

ii 14 Text: ÁB.
ii 23 Text: ÁB.

31) DI.KU$_5$
32) ^{d}*na-ra-am*-^{d}EN.ZU
33) *da-nim*
Col. iii
1) *i-dì-nu-ma*
2) *rí-da*-^{d}IŠKUR
3) LUGAL
4) *ar-ma-nim*.KI
5) *qá-ti-ís-su*
6) *i-dì-nu-ma*
7) *šu*$_4$*-ma*
8) *qab*$_x$(DA)*-li*
9) *na-ra-ab-ti-šu*
10) *i-ik-mi-ù-šu*$_4$(*)
11) *in* E.SI
12) DÙL-*šu*
13) *ib-ni-ma*
14) *a-na*
15) ^{d}EN.ZU
16) A.MU.RU
17) *en-ma*
18) ^{d}*na-ra-am*-^{d}EN.ZU
19) *da-núm*
20) LUGAL
21) *ki-ib-ra-tim*
22) *ar-ba-im*<<KI>>
23) ^{d}*da-gan*
24) *ar-ma-nam*
25) *ù*
26) *eb-la*.KI
27) *i-dì-nam-ma*
28) *rí-id*-^{d}IŠKUR
29) LUGAL
30) *ar-ma-nim*.K[I]
31) *ak-mi-m*[*a*]
32) *i-nu-šu* [x]
33) *tám-ši*$_x$(SU$_4$)*-l*[*í*]
34) *ab-ni-*[*ma*]
Col. iv
1) *a-*[*na*]
2) ^{d}EN.Z[U]
3) *áš*(*)*-ru-*⸢*uk*⸣
4) *ma-na-ma*
5) MU-*mi*
6) *a*(*) *u-ša-sí-ik*
7) DÙL-*mi*
8) *ma-ḫa-ar*
9) ^{d}EN.ZU
10) *li-zi-iz*(*)
11) *ù*
12) *ša il-šu*
13) *i-na-di*(*)*-nu-šum*$_6$
14) *li-li-*⸢*ik*⸣(?)*-šu*$_4$
15) *ši-pí-ir*

his hands Rīd-Adad, king of Armānum,

iii 7–10) and (when) he (Narām-Sîn) personally captured him in the midst of his (palace) entryway,

iii 11–16) he (Narām-Sîn) fashioned a statue of himself (made) of diorite and dedicated (it) to the god Sîn.

iii 17–31) Thus says Narām-Sîn, the mighty, king of the four quarters: 'The god Dagān gave me Armānum and Ebla and I captured Rīd-Adad, king of Armānum.

iii 32 – iv 3) At that time I fashioned an image of myself and I(*)(Text: he) dedicated (it) to the god Sîn.

iv 4–6) May no one remove my inscription, (but rather)

iv 7–10) may my statue stand before the god Sîn.

iv 11–19) Further, that which his god will give to him, may it be pleasing to him — (but) the deed which I performed ...

iii 10 Text: SI.
iv 3 Text: *íš*.
iv 6 Text: DIŠ.
iv 10 Text: ID.
iv 13 Text: ID.

16) *al-li-ku*
17) *a-na*
18) *u-su$_4$-a-im*
19) *a-ti-ir*
(Space)
20) *íś-tum*
21) BÀD *da-ni-im*
22) *a-na*
23) BÀD.GAL
24) 60+60+10 KÙŠ SUKUD
25) ŚA.DÚ-*im*
26) 44 KÙŠ SUKUD BÀD

iv 20–26) From the fortification wall to the great wall: 130 cubits is the height of the hill (and) 44 cubits is the height of the wall.

Col. v
1) *íś-tum*
2) BÀD *kà-rí-im*
3) *a-na*
4) BÀD *da-ni-im*
5) 180 KÙŠ SUKUD
6) ŚA.DÚ-*im*
7) 30 KÙŠ SUKUD BÀD

v 1–7) From the quay wall to the fortification wall: 180 cubits is the height of the hill (and) 30 cubits is the height of the wall.

(Space)
8) ŠU.NÍGIN 404
9) x KÙŠ SUKUD
10) *íś-tum*
11) *qá-qá-rí-im*
12) *a-na*
13) SAG BÀD

v 8–13) Total: 404 cubits in height, from ground (level) to the top of the wall.

14) URU.KI-*lam*
15) *ar*(*)-*ma-num*.KI
16) KI-*śu e-ni*

v 14–16) He undermined the city Armānum.

(Space)
17) *ša i-di* É.KISAL.GIBIL$_4$
(Space)

v 17) (Inscription) on the side (of the monument facing) the chapel of the 'New Court'.

Col. vi
1) *íś-tum*
2) I$_7$
3) *a-na*
4) BÀD
5) *kà-rí-im*
6) 196 KÙŠ SUKUD
7) ŚA.DÚ-*im*
8) 20 KÙŠ SUKUD
9) BÀD

vi 1–9) From the river to the quay wall: 196 cubits is the height of the hill (and) 20 cubits is the height of the wall.

(Space)
10) *íś-tum*
11) BÀD *kà-rí*(*)-*im*
12) *a-na*
13) BÀD *da-ni-im*
14) 156 KÙŠ SUKUD
15) ŚA.DÚ-*im*
16) 30 KÙŠ SUKUD
17) BÀD

vi 10–17) From the quay wall to the fortification wall: 156 cubits is the height of the hill (and) 30 cubits is the height of the wall.

(Space)
18) *ša a-na i-di*
19) ALAM ^{d}EN.ZU-*i-ri-ba-am*
20) GU.LA

vi 18–20) (Inscription) on the side (of the monument facing) the great statue of Sîn-irībam.

---

v 15 Text: SI+KU.
vi 11 Text: GAL.

27

Narām-Sîn's title 'smiter of Armānum and Ebla' appears in an inscription found on a marble lamp, a stone plaque, and a copper bowl.

CATALOGUE

Ex.	Museum number	Provenance	Object	Dimensions (cm)	Lines preserved	cpn
1	Musée de Cinquantenaire Brussels, O.710	Telloh	Polychrome marble lamp	14×15	1–9	n
2	AO 3291	Telloh	Plaque made of slate like material	29×26.5	1–7	c
	Israel Museum, Jeruslaem, no. 74.49.99	Luristan(?)	Copper bowl	8 high; 13 dia.	1–9	c

COMMENTARY

Ex. 2 was collated by B. Foster. The present location of ex. 4 was pointed out to the author by P. Steinkeller. Its inscription was collated by J. Goodnick Westenholz.

BIBLIOGRAPHY

1884–1912 de Sarzec, Découvertes 1 p. LVII and pl. 26bis no. 1 (ex. 2, photo, copy)
1899 Thureau-Dangin, CRAIB p. 348 pl. I (ex. 2, edition)
1900 Radau, EBH p. 162 (ex. 2, edition)
1907 Thureau-Dangin, SAK pp. 166–67 Narâm-Sin d (ex. 2, edition)
1913 de Genouillac, RA 10 pp. 101–102 no. 1 (ex. 1, copy, translation)
1925 Speleers, Receuil no. 7 (ex. 1, copy)
1929 Barton, RISA pp. 138–39 Naram-Sin 8 (ex. 1, edition); pp. 140–41 Naram-Sin 10 (ex. 2, edition)
1934 Unger, Naram-Sin pp. 43–46 (exs. 1–2, edition)
1940 Christian, Altertumskunde 1 pl. 350 no. 2 (ex. 1, photo)
1948 Parrot, Tello pp. 134–36 and fig. 32g (ex. 2, copy, translation)
1961 Gelb, MAD 2^{2} p. 198 Narâm-Sin Original Inscriptions no. 4a–b (exs. 1–2, study)
1963 Hirsch, AfO 20 p. 18 Narâm-Sin a 6 (exs. 1–2, study)
1969 Calmeyer, Datierbare Bronzen p. 28 no. 12 B (ex. 3, translation, study); p. 160 no. 3 (transliteration)
1971 Sollberger and Kupper, IRSA IIA4b (exs. 1–2, translation)
1971 Boese, Weihplatten pp. 125–27 and 202–3 no. T 14 (ex. 2, study)
1990 Gelb and Kienast, Königsinschriften p. 97 Narāmsîn 11 (exs. 1–3, edition)

TEXT

1) ^{d}*na-ra-am*-^{d}EN.ZU
2) *da-núm*
3) LUGAL
4) *ki-ib-ra-tim*
5) *ar-ba-im*
6) SAG.GIŠ.RA
7) *ar-ma-nim*.KI
8) *ù*
9) *eb-la*.KI

1–4) Narām-Sîn, the mighty, king of the four quarters,

6–9) conqueror of Armānum and Ebla.

28

Two similar inscriptions (E2.1.4.28–29) commemorate construction work by Narām-Sîn on temples of the goddess Aštar. The first text likely refers to her temple in Nineveh; the second to her temple in Babylon.

A diorite foundation tablet pieced together from five fragments found in excavations in the area between the Nabû and Ištar temples at Nineveh, and from a sixth fragment that had been incorporated into the foundations of the mosque at Nabi Yunus, bears an inscription that, as far as preserved, duplicates inscriptions of Narām-Sîn (E2.1.4.29) and Šar-kali-šarrī (E2.1.5.5) that deal with construction work on temples of the goddess Aštar. In view of the fragments' provenances, the tablet likely commemorated work on the goddess' temple at Nineveh. The name of the king in line 1 is almost completely broken away. We have tentatively assigned the inscription to Narām-Sîn; an attribution to Šar-kali-šarrī, in view of the existence of E2.1.5.5, cannot be excluded.

CATALOGUE

Ex.	Museum number	Registration number	Nineveh provenance	Tablet lines preserved	Text lines preserved	cpn
1	Thompson, Archaeologia 79 no. 49	—	Thomspon's excavations 1927–28, V 7, in area	Ob. i 1′–4′	1–4	p
	+ Lehmann-Haupt, Materialien no. 2 (frgm. 2)	—	In foundations of the mosque at Nabi Yunus	Obv. ii 1′–4′	9–12	p
	+ BM 98917 (frgm. 3)	(Th. 1905-4-9, 423)	Thompson's excavations 1903–4, in area of the Nabû temple	Obv. iii 1′–4′	18–21	c
	(+) BM 98918 (frgm. 4)	(Th. 1905-4-9, 424)	As frgm. 3	Obv. iv 1′–6′	27–32	c
	(+) BM 98919 (frgm. 5)	(Th. 1905-4-9, 425)	As frgm. 3	Rev. i 1′–5′	37–41	c
	(+) BM 128215 (frgm. 6)	(Th. 1929-10-12, 871)	As frgm. 1	i′ 1–2	Not placed	c

COMMENTARY

The line count for this reconstructed text comes from E2.1.5.5, a tablet inscribed with a Neo-Babylonian copy of an inscription of Šar-kali-šarrī. As far as can be determined, the text of E2.1.5.5 agrees, even to the extent of its column divisions, with this text; the only variance is the substitution of the RN Šar-kali-šarrī for Narām-Sîn. Thus the Šar-kali-šarrī inscription is an important source for the textual restorations of this text. For the reading of lines 13–14, see the comments to E2.1.5.5, lines 13–14.

Fragments 1 and 2 have not been located. It is virtually certain that fragment 5 belongs to this inscription; its reddish hue, size of script, and width of column divisions perfectly match the other pieces. Its text, however, could not be placed within the inscription.

A cylinder inscription known from numerous fragments found in excavations by Thompson in the area of the Ištar temple at Nineveh records Šamšī-Adad's construction of a temple for the goddess Ištar at Nineveh (see Grayson, RIMA 1 A.0.39.2). In the inscription (i 7–13 and ii 21) the Old Babylonian king relates that the temple had been built previously by Man-ištūšu. The evidence of E2.1.4.28, if interpreted correctly here, indicates that work on the temple was also undertaken by Narām-Sîn.

BIBLIOGRAPHY

1907 Lehmann-Haupt, Mat. pp. 6–7 no. 2 (frgm. 2, photo, edition)
1912 King, CT 32 pl. 5 BM 98917 and 98918 (frgms. 3, 4, copy)
1915 Meissner, OLZ 18 173–74 (frgm. 2, study)
1929 Barton, RISA pp. 134–137 Manishtusu 5 Fragments A and B (frgms. 3–4, edition)
1929 Thompson, Archaeologia 79 pl. XLIII no. 49 (frgm. 1, copy)
1931–32 Weidner, AfO 7 p. 280 (frgms. 1–2, study)
1934 Unger, Naram-Sin pp. 41–42 (frgms. 1–2, edition) and pl. IV nos. 6 (frgm. 2, photo) and 7 (frgm. 1, copy)
1961 Gelb, MAD 2^2 p. 199 Narâm-Sin Original Inscriptions no. 8 (frgms. 1–2, study) and p. 206 Unknown Kings nos. 10–11 (frgms. 3–4, study)
1963 Hirsch, AfO 20 p. 18 Narâm-Sin a 4 (frgms. 1–2, study) and p. 33 no. 5 (exs. 3–4, study)
1984 Frayne, ARRIM 2 pp. 23–27 (frgms. 1–6, edition; frgms. 5–6, copy)
1990 Gelb and Kienast, Königsinschriften pp. 84–88 Narāmsîn 2 (frgs. 1–6, copy, edition)

TEXT

1) [^{d}*na-ra-am-*^{d}EN].Z[U](?)
2) [*d*]*a-núm*
3) [L]UGA[L]
4) [*a-k*]*à-dè*.[KI]
5) [^{ba}DÍM]
6) [ki.sanga$_x$(REC 170)-x-x]
7) [É ^{d}INANNA]
8) [*in zabala*$_5$.KI]
9) [*ì-n*]*u*
10) [*ki-i*]*b-ra-tum*
11) *ar-ba-um*
12) *íś-ti-ni-*[*íś*]
13) [*i-*KIR*-ni-śu*$_4$]
14) [*íś-tum-ma*]
15) [*a-bar-ti*]
16) [*ti-a-am-tim*]
17) [*śa-píl-tim*]
18) ⸢*a*⸣-[*dì-ma*]
19) *t*[*i*]-⸢*a*⸣*-am-tim*
20) *a-lí-tim*
21) [NI.Ś]I$_{11}$
22) [*ù*]
23) [ŚA.DÚ-*e*]
24) [*kà-la-śu-nu-ma*]
25) [*a-na*]
26) [^{d}*en-líl*]
27) [*u-ra-í*]*ś*
28) ⸢*ù*⸣
29) *śar-rí-śi-in*
30) *in kà-mi-e*
31) *ú-śá-rí-ib*
32) ⸢*maḫ-rí-íś*⸣
33) [^{d}*en-líl*]
34) [^{d}*na-ra-am-*^{d}EN.ZU]
35) [*da-núm*]
36) [*in* NAM.NIR x x]
37) [^{d}]⸢*en*⸣*-lí*[*l*]
38) [*i*]*n* REC 169.REC 169
39) ⸢*śu*$_4$*-nu*⸣-[*ti*]
40) *ma-*[*na-ma*]
41) *pá-n*[*i-śu*]
42) [*ù-la*]
43) [*ù-ba-al*]

Lacuna

1–8) [Narām-S]î[n], the [m]ighty, [k]in[g] of [Ag]ade, [builder of the ... of the temple of the goddess Aštar in Zabala].

9–13) [Wh]en the four [qu]arters togeth[er revolted against him],

14–27) [from beyond the Lower Sea] as fa[r as] the Upper Sea [he smo]te [the peo]ple [and all the Mountain Lands for the god Enlil],

28–33) and brought their kings in fetters before [the god Enlil].

34–43) [Narām-Sîn, the mighty, by the ... authority of the god] Enli[l, showed mercy to no] on[e i]n tho[se] battles.

Lacuna

29

A Sargonic inscription known from a later tablet copy from Babylon commemorates construction work by Narām-Sîn on the temple of the goddess Aštar; it likely refers to her temple in Babylon.

COMMENTARY

The tablet, which measures 12.0×7.2×2.8 cm, was found by Koldewey in sounding 31, that is, about 50 m northeast of the Ninurta temple E-ḫursag-tila. Its excavation number is BE 13380 and its photo number Bab. 1210. It bears the museum number VAT 17018. A transliteration and copy of the tablet were provided by H. Neumann, who kindly permitted its inclusion in the RIM corpus in advance of his own publication of the piece. The line count follows the Berlin tablet; line numbers corresponding to the reconstructed text of E2.1.5.5 (and E2.1.4.28) are also given.

The tablet was found in a locus that yielded about 160 tablets. Neumann suggests an Old Babylonian date for the copy, while raising the possibility (in a letter of June 6, 1991, and in his publication of the piece) that it might have been a later (Neo-Babylonian?) copy.

The text itself does not tell us where the Aštar temple, whose construction it commemorated, was located. In view of its provenance, we might expect that it was the temple of Aštar in Babylon. Several data support this hypothesis. We know, for example, that Šar-kali-šarrī continued work on many temples whose construction had been begun by his father Narām-Sîn. Now, a year name of Šar-kali-šarrī (year name [k]) records the king's laying of the foundations of the temples of the goddess Annunītum and of the god Ilaba in Babylon. As Kutscher has pointed out (Brockmon Tablets p. 47), in Sargonic times Annunītum was 'a designation for the goddess Inanna and not the name of a separate goddess'. We propose, then, that Narām-Sîn began work on the Aštar temple in Babylon, and commemorated the deed in E2.1.4.29 and possibly in an as yet unattested year name. The work was apparently continued by Šar-kali-šarrī, who, as noted, recorded the construction in his year name (k) and in a royal inscription (E2.1.5.5). Of interest is Neumann's suggestion that this copy might date from Neo-Babylonian times. We know that the Neo-Babylonian kings, Nabonidus, in particular, took care to find and copy foundation inscriptions of their distant Sargonic predecessors. Indeed, Nabonidus is known to have rebuilt E-mašdari, the temple of the goddess Ištar of Agade in Babylon (see Berger, Neubabylonische Königsinschriften p. 360 Nabonid Zylinder II, 3 and Al-Rawi, ARRIM 9 [1991] pp. 7–10 nos. 6–7); perhaps the tablet copy E2.1.4.29 was made in conjunction with this work. Certainly, the Šar-kali-šarrī inscription E2.1.5.5, which is a virtual duplicate of E2.1.4.29, clearly dates to Neo-Babylonian times. We may note that the ductus of E2.1.4.29 is an entirely faithful copy of Sargonic script. Had we not been aware of the copy's stratigraphic context, it would have almost certainly been taken for an original Sargonic inscription.

A crux in the interpretation of this text is the reading of the RN in line 1. According to Neumann, the first line is now broken away from the tablet. The excavation photo, he discloses, reveals the traces of two signs indicating a restoration: [^{d}*n*]*a-r*[*a-am*-^{d}EN.ZU].

Concerning the temple name of line 3: ki-šanga$_x$(REC 170) [x x], we may note the comments of Civil in Cagni, Il bilinguismo p. 95: 'In text no. 51 the sign is LAGAB×LAK 175, a variant of the sign ancestor of sanga$_{2-6}$, to be transliterated preferably as šanga$_x$ (Diri VI ii 25f.; the form with s – is from Sb). This sign is known in Ur III in the title šanga$_x$ ^{d}en-lí̄l-lá (Owen, NATN 155 and unpubl. Nippur tablets); its form differs slightly from LAK 175: . Its rare occurrences in OB texts are often misinterpreted, see Steible, *Hāja*, ad UET 6,101:19'. The interpretation of rev. 9′ is uncertain. As Hirsch, WZKM 81 (1991) p. 285 points out, we would expect in this line a form x-*íś*, where x, presumably an infinitive, would be derived from a root primae š. The verb *šapāku(m)* is excluded from consideration here because the required form would be written *śa-pá-kí-íś* in Old Akkadian. Hirsch suggests a connection with the entry *ši-ib-qu* = *ri-kis sip-pi* of Malku I 248ff.

BIBLIOGRAPHY

1990 Neumann, JCS 42 pp. 202–210 (copy, edition)

TEXT

Obv.	E2.1.5.5		
1)	1	[^{d}*n*]*a-r*[*a-am*-^{d}EN.ZU]	1-4) [N]ar[ām-Sîn, the migh]ty, king of A[gade,
2)	2-4	[*da-n*]*úm* LUGAL *a-k*[*à-dè*.KI]	bui]lder of the ... of the temple of the goddess Aštar
3)	5-6	[^{b}]^{a}DÍM ki.sanga$_{x}$(REC 170) [x (x)]	in Zabala.
4)	7-8	⌈É-^{d}⌉INANNA *in zabala*$_{5}$.KI	
5)	9-10	*ì-nu ki-ib-ra-tum*$_{8}$	5-7) When the four quarters together revolted
6)	11-12	*ar-ba-*[*u*]*m íš-ti-ni-*[*í*]*š*	against him,
7)	13	*ì*-KIR-<*ni*>-*su*$_{4}$	
8)	15	[*íš*]*-tum-ma*	8-15) [fr]om [bey]ond the [Lo]wer Sea as far as the
9)	16-17	[*a-bar-t*]*i ti-*⌈*a*⌉*-a*[*m*]*-tim*	Upper [S]ea, he [smote the people] and [all] the
10)	18-19	[*ša-p*]*íl-tim a-dì-ma*	Mountain Lands [for the god E]nli]l].
11)	20-21	[*ti-a-a*]*m-tim a-lí-tam*	Lacuna
12)	22-24	[NI.SI$_{11}$] ⌈*ù*⌉ ŠA.DÚ-*e*	
13)	25	[*kà-la*]*-šu-n*[*u-ma*]	
14)	26-27	[*a-na* ^{d}*e*]*n-lí*[*l*]	
15)	28	[*u-ra-íš*]	
Lacuna			
Rev.			
Lacuna			Lacuna
1′)	41	[*ma-na-ma*]	1′-2′) [he showed mercy to] no [one].
2′)	42-44	[*pá-ni-šu*] ⌈*ù*⌉*-l*[*a ù-bạ-al*]	
3′)	45-46	[... *n*]*a-g*[*áb*]	3′-7′) He [reach]ed the [s]ource of the [Tigris]
4′)	47	[IDIGNA].⌈I$_{7}$⌉	River [and] the [so]urce of the [Euph]rates River
5′)	48-50	[... *n*]*a-g*[*áb*]	and
6′)	51	[BURA]NUN.KI.I$_{7}$	
7′)	52	[*ik-šu-u*]*d-ma*	
8′)	53-54	[GIŠ.ERIN *in a*]*-ma-nim*	8′-10′) [c]ut down [cedar wood in the A]manus
9′)	55-56	[*ša*]-B[A-K]I-[*í*]*š* É ^{d}INANNA	(Mountains) in order to ... the temple of the
10′)	57	[*i*]*b-*⌈*tu*⌉*-qám*	goddess Aštar.
11′)	58-59	[*ša* D]UB *šu*$_{4}$*-a*	11′-12′) [As for the one who rem]o[ves] this
12′)	60	[*u-ša-sà-k*]*u-*[*ni*]	[in]scription
Lacuna			Lacuna

30

A campaign of a Sargonic king in the area bordering on Azuḫinnum is recorded in an inscription known from two Old Babylonian tablet copies from Nippur. While no royal name appears in the extant text, the partially preserved epithet '[king] of the four qua[rters]' makes an attribution to Narām-Sîn virtually certain; he alone of all the Sargonic kings used that title. Although only three lines of exs. 1 and 2 overlap, it is reasonably certain they were copies of the same inscription.

CATALOGUE

Ex.	Museum number	Dimensions (cm)	cpn
1	UM 29-16-103	8.2×5	c
2	N 3580 (+) UM 29-13-559	7×6.2	c

COMMENTARY

A crux in our understanding of this text is whether the *a-zu-ḫi-núm*.K[I] of ex. 2 col. iv lines 8–9 refers to the 'western' Azuḫinnum that, according to Charpin (RA 84 [1990] p. 94), was located 'au nord du Sinjar, mais à l'ouest du Tigre, non loin de Razamâ' or the 'eastern' Azuḫinnum, for which a location at modern Gök Tepe, about 32 kms northwest of modern Kirkuk, has been proposed (see Speiser, AASOR 8 p. 41; Fadhil, Arraphe p. 77). The author will provide arguments in his forthcoming study of the Narām-Sîn chronology that this text refers to the eastern Azuḫinnum.

In ex. 1 col. i 11′ the expected form would be *kà-lí-i-ša* if this line refer to Subartum.

BIBLIOGRAPHY

1986 Michalowski, ZA 76 pp. 4–11 and 4 pls. following p. 8 (exs. 1–2, edition, photo; ex. 1, copy)

1990 Gelb and Kienast, Königsinschriften pp. 284–91 Fragment C 5 and C 6 (exs. 1–2, edition)

TEXT

Ex. 1 Obv. Col. i	
Lacuna	Lacuna
1′) [^{d}*na-ra-am*-^{d}EN.ZU]	i 1′–5′) [Narām-Sîn, the mighty, king] of the fou[r] qua[rters],
2′) [*da-núm*]	
3′) [LUGAL]	
4′) ⸢*ki*⸣-*i*[*b-ra-tim*]	
5′) *ar-ba-i*[*m*]	
6′) SAG.GIŠ.RA	i 6′–7′) conqueror of UŠ.GI,
7′) UŠ.GI	
8′) *ša-bir*$_{5}$	i 8′11′) who smashed the weapon of all of (the land of) Subartum,
9′) GIŠ.TUKUL	
10′) ŠUBUR.KI	
11′) *kà-lí-i-šu*	
12′) *mu-kí-in*	i 12′–14′) who made firm the foundations of the *army camps*,
13′) SUḪUŠ.SUḪUŠ	
14′) *um-ma-nim*.KI	
Ex. 2 Col. i′	
(Traces of the last signs of five lines)	
Ex. 1 Obv. Col. ii	
Lacuna	Lacuna
1′) x [...]	ii′ 1′–4′) ..., Ab[u-...] revol[ted and] went to war.
2′) *a-b*[*u-*...]	
3′) *úš-ba-al-k*[*i-it-ma*]	
4′) *u-ṣa-ab-bi-à*[*m*]	
5′) *íš-tum-*[*ma*]	ii′ 5′–9′) After Tutu[šše] and [its] territory ...
6′) *tu-tu-*[*uš-šè*.KI]	
7′) *ù*	
8′) KALAM.K[I-*šu*]	
9′) *ur-k*[*i-*...]	
Lacuna	Lacuna
Ex. 2 Col. ii′	
1) x x.KI	ii′ 1–8) GN and its territory, Ḫaḫun and <its territory> as far as the land of ⸢GN⸣,
2) *ù*	
3) ⸢KALAM⸣.KI-*šu*	
4) *ḫa-ḫu-un*.KI	
5) *ù* <KALAM.KI-*šu*>	
6) *a-dì-ma*	
7) ⸢KALAM(?)⸣.KI	

8) [...] x x
Lacuna
1′) [...].KI
2′) *ù*
3′) [KALAM.K]I-*šu*
4′) [...].KI
5′) [...].KI
6′) [*ù* KALA]M.KI-*šu*
7′) [x] *im*(?)-*ul*(?).KI
8′) x *ùḫ*(?)-*ḫu*(?).KI
9′) ⸢ḪAR(?)⸣-*a-núm*.KI
10′) ⸢*ù*⸣ KALAM.KI-*šu*
11′) *gal*(?)-*áš*.KI
12′) ḪAR-*ba-ak*(?).KI
13′) ⸢*a*⸣-*li-we*.KI
14′) [*ḫ*]*a*(?)-*šu-an-šè*.KI
15′) [x]-*in-šè*.KI
16′) [*ù* K]ALAM.KI-*šu*

Lacuna
ii′ 1′–16′) ⸢GN⸣ and its [terri]tory, [GN] and [GN] and their territory, [x]-im-x, x-uḫḫu, ḪAR-ānum and its territory, Galaš, ḪAR-bak, Aliwe, [Ḫ]ašu'anše, [x]-inše and its territory,

Ex. 2 Col. iii′ and ex. 1 Rev.
1) *ù a*-⸢*dì*⸣-*m*[*a*]
2) KALAM.K[I]
3) *ki*-x-*e-na-á*[*š*].⸢KI⸣
4) LAGAB×TIL-*šè*.KI
5) *ù* KALAM.KI-*šu*
6) *tu-tu-uš-šè*.K[I]
7) *ù* KALAM.K[I-*šu*]
8) *ne-ri*-x-[....KI]
9) *ù*
10) KALAM.K[I-*šu*]
11) [x] ⸢x⸣ [...]

iii′ 1–11) and as far as the land of Ki-x-ena[š], LAGAB×TIL-še and its territory, Tutušše and its territory, Neri-[...], and [its] territory, ...

Lacuna
1′) *ù*
2′) *ga*-[...]
3′) SIPA(?)
4′) *šu*-x [...] x [...]
5′) *ši*-x-NI-[... .KI]
6′) *ša-ak-nu* [...]

Lacuna
iii′ 1′–6′) and the cities Ga-[...], SIPA-[...], Šu-x-[...], Ši-x-NI, [...] were situated.

7′) x-*tir-šè*.KI
8′) *zum-ḫi-in-núm*.KI
9′) *ù* KALAM.KI-*šu*

iii′ 7′–9′) x-tirše, Zumḫinnum and its territory,

10′) *nin*$_9$(SAL+KU)-*li-in-su*-⸢*è*⸣.K[I]
11′) *mu-luḫ*.⸢KI⸣
12′) AB×U-*sig*-⸢*ge*⸣.K[I]
13′) *su-ùḫ*-[...]

iii′ 10′-13′) Ninlinsuʾe, Muluḫ, AB×U-sigge, Suḫ-[...]

Ex. 2 Col. iv'
1) *kum*(?)-*ti*-x [...]
2) *ù* KALA[M.KI-*šu*]
3) *šè-wi-i*[*n* ... .KI]
4) *šu-un*-x-[... .KI]
5) *ù* KALAM.K[I-*šu*]

iv′ 1–5) Kumti-x-[...] and its territory, Šewin-[...], Šun-x-[...] and its territory,

6) *šu-a-we*.K[I]
7) *ù* KALAM.KI-*šu*

iv′ 6-7) Šuʾawe and its territory,

8) *a-zu-ḫi-núm*.K[I]
9) ⸢*ù*⸣ KALAM.KI-*šu*

iv′ 8-9) Azuḫinnum and its territory.

10) *iš-tum-ma*
11) SAG.GIŠ.RA-*ù-š*[*u*]
12) *ba-al-<ṭú>-ti-šu*
13) 14 ⸢BÀD⸣
14) ⸢*a-na*⸣ [...]

iv′ 10–14) After he smote it, its *survivors* ..., fourteen fortresses, for/to ...,

Lacuna	Lacuna
1′) ḪAR(?)-NE [... .KI] 2′) *ku-um-ra-at*.KI 3′) *ìr-in-da*.KI 4′) *ù* KALAM.MA.<KI>-*šu*	iv′ 1′–4′) ḪAR-NE [...], Kumrat, Irʾinda, and its territory,
5′) *àm-mi-ra*.KI 6′) *ù* KALAM.KI-*šu*	iv′ 5′-6′) Ammira and its territory,
Ex. 2 Col. v′ 1) [x] x x x.KI 2) [*ù* KALA]M.⌜KI-*šu*⌝ 3) [...]-x-*šè*.KI 4) [...]-*in-núm*.KI	v′ 1-4)) ⌜GN⌝ and its [territ]ory, [...]-x-šè, ... [...]-innum [
5) [*ù* K]ALAM.KI-*šu* 6) [...] x KI 7) [*ù* KAL]AM.KI-*šu* 8) [...]-⌜*we*⌝.KI 9) [*ù* KA]LAM.KI-*šu*	v′ 5-9) [and] its [ter]ritory, ⌜GN⌝ and its [te]rritory, [...]-we [and its terr]itory,
10) [...].KI 11) [*ù* KAL]AM.KI-*šu*	v′ 10-11) [GN and its ter]ritory,
12) [...-*š*]*è*.KI 13) [...].KI 14) [...].KI 15) [...] x	v′ 12-15) [...-š]e, GN, GN, ...
Lacuna 1′) [*ù* KALAM.K]I-*šu*	Lacuna v′ 1′and its [territory].
2′) [*a-d*]*i-ma* 3′) [...].KI 4′) [*ù*] URU.KI.URU.KI 5′) [*a*]-*bar-ti* 6′) [I]DIGNA.I$_7$	v′ 2′-6′) [As fa]r as [GN and] the cities [ac]ross the [T]igris River.

31

A stele found by J. de Morgan on the acropolis at Susa depicts Narām-Sîn's defeat of the Lullubu people. The monument, known today as the 'Victory Stele' of Narām-Sîn, had been taken from Sippar by the Elamite king Šutruk-Naḫḫunte, who added his own inscription to the piece.

COMMENTARY

The stele is made of limestone and measures 200 cm in height and 105 cm in width. It bears the museum number Sb 4; the inscription was collated by B. Foster. A select bibliography is given for this object; for a complete bibliography, see Börker-Klähn, Bildstelen p. 135.

Here *si-du*[*r*-x] of i 2′ is taken to be the name of the Lullubean leader. The evidence of the stele, in naming Sidu[r-x] as the Lullubean leader, is at variance with the Old Babylonian account of the 'Great Revolt'. In the London exemplar of this composition the name of the Lullubean leader appears in a broken context (see Grayson and Sollberger RA 70 [1976] p. 115 L I 4′: [...]-*a-el*); this may perhaps be connected with the PN ^{m}*la-pa-na-i-la* of the corresponding lines of the Hittite version (see Güterbock, ZA 44 [1938] p. 68 line 10′).

BIBLIOGRAPHY

1900 de Morgan, MDP 1 pl. X (photo)
1900 Scheil, MDP 2 pp. 53–55 and pl. 11 (photo, copy, edition)
1900 Scheil, RT 22 pp. 27–29 (photo, edition)
1907 Thureau-Dangin, SAK pp. 166–67 Narâm-sin g (edition)
1926 Pézard and Pottier, Catalogue pp. 36–39 no. 4 and pl. II (photo, study)
1929 Barton, RISA pp. 142–43 Naram-Sin 13 (edition)
1931 Contenau, Manuel 2 pp. 674–76 and fig. 469 (photo, study)
1935 Zervos, L'art p. 165 (photo)
1941 Rutten, Syria 22 pl. IX (photo)
1954 Frankfort, Art and Architecture pl. 44 (photo)
1960 Parrot, Sumer fig. 213 (photo)
1961 Gelb, MAD 2^2 p. 199 Narâm-Sin Original Inscriptions no. 9 (study)
1963 Hirsch, AfO 20 p. 17 Narâm-Sin a 1 (study)
1962 Strommenger and Hirmer, Mesopotamien pls. 122–23 (photo)
1967 Moortgat, Kunst pl. 155 (photo)
1969 ANEP^2 no. 309 (photo)
1971 Hrouda, Vorderasien 1 pl. 50 (photo)
1975 Orthmann (ed.), Der alte Orient pl. 104 (photo)
1976 Amiet, L'art d'Agadé no. 27 (photo, translation, study)
1982 Börker-Klähn, Bildstelen no. 26 (photo, copy, study)
1988 Haas, Hurriter fig. 2 (photo)
1990 Gelb and Kienast, Königsinschriften pp. 90–92 Narāmsîn 4 (edition)

TEXT

Col. i
1) ^{d}[*na-r*]*a-am*-^{d}EN..ZU
2) *da-núm*
Lacuna
1′) *a*-[...]
2′) *si-du*[*r*-x]
3′) ŚA.DÚ-*ì*
4′) *lu-lu-bi-i*[*m*.KI]
5′) *ip-ḫu-ru-n*[*im-ma*]
Col. ii
1) ⸢REC 169⸣
2) *i*[*m*-x x] x [x]
3) ⸢*a*⸣-*na*
Lacuna
1′) ŚA.[DÚ-*ì*]
Lacuna
Col. iii
1) [*iś-pu-u*]*k*
2) [...] x ŠÈ [...] ZU
3) [*a-na*]
4) [^{d}DN]
5) A.⸢MU.RU⸣
Lacuna

i 1–2) [Nar]ām-Sîn, the mighty,

Lacuna
i 1′–5′) ..., Sidu[r-x] (and) the highlanders of Lullubum assembled together ...

ii 1–3) ... bat[tle]. For/to
Lacuna

ii 1′) the high[landers ...]
Lacuna

iii 1) [heap]ed up [a burial mound over them].
iii 2–5) ... (and) dedicated (this object) [to the god ...]
Lacuna

32

As noted, year name (ii) of Narām-Sîn records the Sargonic king's defeat of the city of Simurrum and the capture of its ruler, a certain Baba. This same Baba, in all likelihood, appears in an inscription carved on a now fragmentarily preserved mace head; it was probably dedicated by Narām-Sîn.

COMMENTARY

The mace head fragment is made of alabaster and originally measured about 20 cm in diameter. The piece was excavated by Rassam at Sippar and bears the museum number BM 22462 (82-7-14, 1015). The inscription was collated by G. Frame.

BIBLIOGRAPHY

1893 Winckler, AOF 1 p. 545 no. 3 (copy)
1978 Hallo, RHA 36 p. 73 (study)
1980 Walker and Collon, in de Meyer (ed.) Tell ed-Dēr 3 p. 100 and pl. 26 no. 40 (copy, study)
1990 Gelb and Kienast, Königsinschriften pp. 124–25 Fragment 4 (edition)

TEXT

Lacuna
1′) [*i*]-*nu*
2′) [*ba*]-*ba*
3′) [PA.T]E.SI
4′) [*śi-m*]*u-ur*$_4$-[*ri-i*]*m*.KI
Lacuna

Lacuna
1′–4′) [wh]en Ba]ba, [gov]ernor of [Sim]ur[r]um
Lacuna

33

Year name (11) of Narām-Sîn commemorates the oracular designation of his daughter as *entu* priestess of the god Nanna (at Ur). This priestess, known from other sources to be En-men-ana, appears in two inscriptions. The first is found on a clay tablet fragment from Ur.

COMMENTARY

The fragment, whose exact findspot at Ur is not known, was given the excavation number U c by Sollberger; its museum number is IM 85669. The inscription was not collated.

BIBLIOGRAPHY

1965 Sollberger, UET 8 no. 12 (copy)
1968 Nagel BJVF 8 pp. 181–82 and n. 62 (transliteration, study)
1971 Sollberger and Kupper, IRSA IIA4g (translation)
1990 Gelb and Kienast, Königsinschriften p. 273 Narāmsîn C 16 (edition)

TEXT

1) [^{d}*na-ra-am-*^{d}EN.ZU]
2) [LUGAL]
3) [*ki-ib-ra-tim*]
4) ⌈*ar*⌉-[*ba-im*]

1–4) [Narām-Sîn, king of the] f[our quarters]:

5) en-men-a[n-na]
6) MUNUS.NUNUZ.ZI.^{d}N[ANNA]
7) DAM ^{d}N[ANNA]
8) EN
9) ^{d}EN.ZU
10) *in* URI$_{5}$.K[I]
11) DUMU.MUNUS-*su*

5–11) En-men-a[na], *zirru* priestess of the god Nanna, spouse of the god N[anna], *entu* priestess of the god Sîn at Ur, (is) his daughter.

34

En-men-ana's name also appears on a door socket from Ur.

COMMENTARY

The door socket, made of limestone, was found in the Gipar-ku; it was reused in room 52 of the Kassite period building. Its excavation number is U 6703 and its museum number IM 1131.

BIBLIOGRAPHY

1928 Gadd, UET 1 no. 69 (copy, edition)
1954–56 Sollberger, AfO 17 p. 27 (transliteration, study)
1965 Woolley, UE 8 pp. 40–41 and 104 (provenance)
1976 Woolley and Mallowan, UE 7 pp. 52 and 224 (provenance)
1961 Gelb, MAD 2^{2} p. 200 Narâm-Sin Family no. 4 (study)
1960 Sollberger, Iraq 22 pp. 77–78 no.107 (study)
1963 Hirsch, AfO 20 p. 27 Familie Narâm-Sins no. 1 (study)
1990 Gelb and Kienast, Königsinschriften p. 103 Narāmsîn A 2 (edition)

TEXT

1) en-men-an-na

1) En-men-ana.

35

Four inscriptions of Narām-Sîn record the dedication of various objects — vases and mace heads — to the gods. The first inscription, which is incised on an alabaster vase fragment, tells us that the piece was dedicated to the god Enlil.

COMMENTARY

The piece was found at Nippur during the third season of excavations of the University of Pennsylvania expedition. It now bears the museum number CBS 10111; the inscription was collated. While no royal name is preserved in the extant text, the title 'king of the four quarters' makes an attribution to Narām-Sîn virtually certain.

BIBLIOGRAPHY

1926 Legrain, PBS 15 no. 18 (copy, edition)
1929 Barton, RISA pp. 138–39 Naram-Sin 6 (edition)
1941–44 Ungnad, AfO 14 p. 200 (translation)
1961 Gelb, MAD 2^2 p. 205 Unknown Kings Original Inscriptions no. 4 (study)
1963 Hirsch, AfO 20 p. 18 Narâm-Sin a 9 (study)
1990 Gelb and Kienast, Königsinschriften p. 96 Narāmsîn 9 (edition)

TEXT

1) [(ᵈ)*na-ra-am*-ᵈEN.ZU]
2) LUGAL
3) *ki-ib-ra-*[*tim*]
4) *ar-ba-i*[*m*]
5) [*a-na*]
6) ᵈ*en-lí*[*l*]
7) *in* NI[BRU.KI]
8) [A].M[U.RU]

1–4) [Narām-Sîn], king of the four quarter[s],

5–8) [ded]ic[ated (this vase) to] the god Enli[l] at Nip[pur].

36

This inscription is found on a mace head fragment; the piece was dedicated to the god Ištaran.

COMMENTARY

The calcite mace head, which measures 8.7×6.4 cm, bears the museum number UM 31-43-250 and the excavation number U 16531. It was found at Ur, House II, Pavement I, in the NW court of the main Isin-Larsa and later residential quarter, season IX. The inscription was collated.

BIBLIOGRAPHY

1955 Woolley, UE 4 p. 185 (study)
1960 Sollberger, Iraq 22 pp. 77–78 no. 105 (study)
1961 Gelb, MAD 2^2 p. 217 no. 15 (study)
1965 Sollberger, UET 8 no. 11 (copy)
1990 Gelb and Kienast, Königsinschriften p. 97 Narāmsîn 10 (edition)

TEXT

1) *na-ra-am*-ᵈEN.ZU
2) LUGAL
3) *ki-ib-ra-tim*
4) *ar-ba-im*
5) *a-na*
6) ⸢ᵈKA⸣.DI
7) A.[M]U.⸢RU⸣

1–4) Narām-Sîn, king of the four quarters,

5–7) dedicated (this mace) to the god [I]štaran.

37

A small mace head from the Inanna temple at Nippur bears a votive inscription of Narām-Sîn.

COMMENTARY

The mace head is made of a variegated stone and measures 11.1 cm in diameter and 5.4 cm in height. It was found at locus SB 75, in fill below level II, that is, in the fill of the Parthian platform (information courtesy R. Zettler), excavation number 6N-128, museum number A 30975 (Chicago). The inscription was collated by R. Biggs.

BIBLIOGRAPHY

1959 Crawford, Archaeology 12 p. 79 (study)
1965 Hansen, in Ehrich, Chronologies p. 209 (study)
1968 Goetze, JAOS 88 p. 55 no. 2 (copy, edition)
1990 Gelb and Kienast, Königsinschriften p. 96 Narāmsîn 8 (edition)

TEXT

1) [d]*na-r*[*a-am*]-[d]EN.ZU	1–4) Nar[ām]-Sîn, king of the four quarters,
2) LUGAL	
3) *ki-ib-ra-tim*	
4) *ar-ba-im*	
5) *a-na*	5–8) dedicated (this mace) to the goddess Aštar at Nip[pur].
6) [d]INANN[A]	
7) *in* NIB[RU.KI]	
8) A.MU.RU	

38

A mace head fragment in the Yale collections bears a dedicatory inscription to the goddess Nisaba of Ereš. The title 'king of the four quarters' in lines 2–4 argues for an attribution of the piece to Narām-Sîn.

COMMENTARY

The mace head fragment is made of brecciated rock and measures 10 cm in diameter; it bears the museum number NBC 2566.

BIBLIOGRAPHY

1991 Foster, ASJ 13 pp. 181–3 no. 5 (copy, edition)

TEXT

1) [(ᵈ)*na-ra-am*-ᵈEN.ZU] 2) ⌜LUGAL⌝ 3) *ki-ib-ra-tim* 4) *ar-ba-im*	1–4) [Narām-Sîn], king of the four quarters,
5) *a-na* 6) ᵈ*nisaba* 7) *in éreš*.KI 8) A.MU.RU	5–8) dedicated (this mace) to the goddess Nisaba at Ereš.

39

A fragment of a mace head from Ur gives the beginning of a Narām-Sîn inscription.

COMMENTARY

The mace head is made of white calcite and measures 8 cm in height with a preserved width at the base of 4.3 cm. It was found under the Kurigalzu floor of the E-nunmaḫ, excavation number U 284; it now bears the museum number CBS 14937. The inscription was collated.

BIBLIOGRAPHY

1956 Woolley, UE 4 p. 168 (study)
1960 Sollberger, Iraq 22 pp. 77–78 no. 104 (study)
1961 Gelb, MAD 2[2] p. 217 no. 14 (study)
1990 Gelb and Kienast, Königsinschriften p. 100 Narāmsîn 16 (study)

TEXT

1) ⌜*na*⌝-*ra-am*-[ᵈEN.ZU] Lacuna	1) Narām-[Sîn] Lacuna

40

A number of objects are known which are inscribed simply with the name of Narām-Sîn and his titles; these are edited as E2.1.4.40–45 in this volume. The first inscription is found on a bowl fragment from Khafajah.

COMMENTARY

The bowl fragment is made of alabaster, and was found in K 45 in Oval III at Khafajah. It bears the excavation number Kh. II 79.

BIBLIOGRAPHY

1940 Jacobsen, Temple Oval pp. 147 and 149 no. 7 (copy, edition)
1990 Gelb and Kienast, Königsinschriften p. 100 Narāmsîn 15 (edition)

TEXT

1) [dn]*a-ra-am*-[d]⌈EN⌉.[ZU]	1) [N]arām-S[în]
Lacuna	Lacuna

41

This inscription, found on a variety of objects, gives Narām-Sîn's name and his title 'king of the four quarters'.

CATALOGUE

Ex.	Museum number	Excavation number	Provenance	Object	Dimensions (cm)	Lines preserved	cpn
1	AO 74	—	Telloh	Vase	19 high	1–4	p
2	EŞ 5207	—	Tell Drehem(?)	Albaster vase	16.5 high	1–4	p
3	YBC 2386	—	Purchased from David, June, 1936	Red marble dish	2.2 high; 8.2 dia.	1–4	c
4	BM 118553 (1927-5-27, 26)	U 6355	Ur, from under the Isin period pavement of room C.25 of the Gipar-ku.	Granite cup	16×14	1–4	c
5	Teheran, Foroughi Collection	—	Luristan	Bronze bowl	8 high; 13.3 dia.	1–4	p
6	BM 104418 (89–1–12, 7)	—	—	Alabaster vase frgm.	4.5×4.8	1–3	c
7	AO 197	—	Telloh	Alabaster vase frgm.	—	1–4	n
8	AO 8536	—	—	Alabaster vase frgm.	—	1–4	n

COMMENTARY

Exs. 4 and 6 were collated by G. Frame. Text F of Gelb and Kienast's edition of this inscription is a duplicate of the 'Magan bowl inscription' and is edited as ex. 4 of E2.1.4.4 in this volume. On ex. 4 there is also incised a text of Šulgi; see Steible and Behrens NBW2, sub Šulgi 66.

BIBLIOGRAPHY

1884–1912 de Sarzec, Découvertes 1 p. 118 (ex. 1, study); 2 pl. 44 and p. LVII no. 1 (ex. 1, photo, copy)
1907 Thureau-Dangin, SAK pp. 164–65 Narâm-sin b (ex.1, edition)

1912 King, CT 32 pl. 8 (ex. 6, copy)
1925 Nassouhi, RA 22 p. 91 (ex. 2, photo, edition)
1926 Woolley, AJ 6 p. 377 (ex. 4, study)
1928 Gadd, UET 1 no. 24A (ex. 4, photo, copy, edition)
1929 Barton, RISA pp. 138–39 Naram-Sin 2 and 5 (exs. 1–2, edition) and 358–59 Naram-Sin 4 (ex. 4, edition)
1937 Stephens, YOS 9 no. 96 (ex. 3, photo)
1941–44 Ungnad, AfO 14 p. 200 (exs 1–2, 6, translation, study)
1960 Sollberger, Iraq 22 pp. 77–78 and 86–87 no. 102 (ex. 4, study)
1961 Gelb, MAD 2[2] p. 198 Narâm-Sin Original Inscriptions no. 3 a–e (exs. 1–4 and 6, study)
1961 Ghirshman, Sept mille no. 488 (ex. 5, study)
1962 Dossin, IrAnt 2 p. 163 and pl. XXXI no. 28 (ex. 5, photo, edition)
1962 Ghirshman, Kunstschätze no. 205 (ex. 5, study)
1963 Hirsch, AfO 20 p. 18 Narâm-Sin a 5 δ (ex. 6, study) and a 8 (exs. 1–4, translation, study)
1963 Ghirshman, Perse fig. 340 (ex. 5, photo)
1969 Calmeyer, Datierbaren Bronzen p. 28 no. 12A and p. 161 no. 2 (ex. 5, transliteration, study)
1986 Potts, OrAnt 25 p. 279 no. 4 (ex. 6, study)
1990 Gelb and Kienast, Königsinschriften p. 99 Narāmsîn 14 (exs. 1–8, edition)

TEXT

1) ^{d}*na-ra-am*-^{d}EN.ZU
2) LUGAL
3) *ki-ib-ra-tim*
4) *ar-ba-im*

1–4) Narām-Sîn, king of the four quarters.

42

A cylindrical vase fragment found by de Morgan in excavations at Susa bears an inscription of Narām-Sîn.

COMMENTARY

The vase was said to be alabaster, but, as Potts suggests, it may be banded calcite. The piece bears the museum number Sb 17825. After the standard titulary of Narām-Sîn, line 5, according to Potts (Iraq 51 [1989] p. 132, n. 37a) has indistinct traces of one sign, possibly *in*. The inscription likely ended in the phrase: *in* NAM.RA.AK GN A.MU.RU 'he dedicated it from the booty of GN'.

BIBLIOGRAPHY

1902 Scheil, MDP 4 p. 1 and pl. 1 no. 1 (photo, edition)
1907 Thureau-Dangin, SAK pp. 164–65 Narâm-sin b, note m (study)
1929 Barton, RISA Naram-Sin 3 n. 2 (study)
1961 Gelb, MAD 2[2] 199 Narâm-Sin Original Inscriptions no. 5b (study)
1963 Hirsch, AfO 20 p. 18 Narâm-Sin a 5 β (study)
1986 Potts, OrAnt 25 p. 279 no. 2 and n. 28 (study)
1987 Braun-Holzinger, OrAnt 26 p. 286 no. 2 (transliteration)
1989 Potts, Iraq 51 pp. 132–33 and 152 Inscription B (translation, study)
1990 Gelb and Kienast, Königsinschriften p. 98 Narāmsîn 13 Text B (edition)

TEXT

1) ^{d}[*na-ra-am*]-^{d}E[N.ZU]
2) LUGA[L]
3) *ki-ib-ra-ti*[*m*]
4) *ar-ba-i*[*m*]
5) [(x)] ⸢x⸣ [(x)]

1–5) [Narām]-S[în], kin[g] of the fou[r] quarte[rs], ...

E2.1.4.41 1.5 *na-ra-am*-^{d}EN.ZU.

43

An inscription incised on an alabaster vase fragment adds the title 'the mighty' to the title 'king of the four quarters' found in the previous inscription.

COMMENTARY

The piece was 'brought in' and given the excavation number U 7843; its original provenance is not known. The text breaks off after line 5. The text may have been a simple label which ended at that point; another possibility is that it continued after line 5 with a dedication to some deity.

BIBLIOGRAPHY

1928 Gadd, UET 1 no. 277 (copy, edition)
1960 Sollberger, Iraq 22 pp. 77–78 no. 109 (study)
1961 Gelb, MAD 2[2] p. 198 Narâm-Sin Original Inscriptions no. 4c (study)
1963 Hirsch, AfO 20 p. 19 Narâm-Sin a 12 (edition)
1990 Gelb and Kienast, Königsinschriften p. 98 Narāmsîn 12 (edition)

TEXT

1) [(d)*na-ra-am*-dEN.ZU]
2) [*da-n*]*úm*
3) [LUG]AL
4) [*ki-ib-r*]*a-tim*
5) [*ar-ba-im*]
(Lacuna)

1–5) [Narām-Sîn], the [migh]ty, [ki]ng of the [four] [quarte]rs:
(Lacuna)

44

A duck weight bears an inscription of Narām-Sîn.

COMMENTARY

The duck weight is a black-coloured calcium carbonate stone and measures 11.7 cm in length and 6.8 cm in height. It is no. MM 740.004 in the collection of the monastery of Montserrat (Barcelona). The piece was purchased from an antiquities dealer in Baghdad; it is said to have come from Sippar. The inscription was collated from the published photo.

BIBLIOGRAPHY

1989 Molina, Aula Orientalis 7 pp. 125–27 (photo, edition, study)

TEXT

1) *na-ra-am-*
2) ^{d}EN.ZU
3) LUGAL

1–3) Narām-Sîn, the king.

45

A fragmentarily preserved Sargonic school tablet gives various titles of Narām-Sîn.

COMMENTARY

The tablet was found in excavations at Tell Asmar, in J 27:1, 'Akkadian house', second stratum. It measures 4.8×5.5 cm and bears the excavation number TA 1933, 17. The inscription, which is now in Chicago (no A number assigned), was collated by G. Frame.

BIBLIOGRAPHY

1952 Gelb, MAD 1 no. 194 (obv. 1–3, transliteration)
1974–77 Westenholz, AfO 25 p. 103 no. 14 (copy)
1990 Gelb and Kienast, Königsinschriften pp. 271–72 Narām-Sîn C 14 (edition)

TEXT

1) ⸢*zi*⸣-[*m*]*e* [(x)]
2) *da*-⸢*núm*⸣
3) LUGAL *a-k*[*à*]*-a-d*[*è*.KI]
4) [L]UGAL⸣[...]
Lacuna
Reverse
Lacuna
1′) ⸢*ki*⸣-[*ib-ra-tim*]
2′) ⸢*ar-ba*⸣-[*im*]
3′) ^{d}⸢ÉZINU⸣
Frgm. from reverse
Lacuna
1′) [*na-ra*]-⸢*am*⸣-^{d}⸢EN⸣.ZU x [(x)]
2′) [...] ⸢*ib*⸣(?)⸣[(x)]
Lacuna

1–4) ..., the mighty, king of Agad[e], king of ...
Lacuna

Lacuna
rev. 1′–3′) (of) the fou[r] q[uarters], the goddess A[šnan] ...

Lacuna
rev. frgm. 1′–2′) [Narā]m-[S]în, ...
Lacuna

46

An Old Babylonian tablet from Mari has the copy of a stele inscription of Narām-Sîn.

COMMENTARY

The tablet bears the excavation number M 7624. The inscription was collated from the published photo.

BIBLIOGRAPHY

1984 Charpin, MARI 3 pp. 65–66, 72, 80 (photo, copy, edition)
1990 Gelb and Kienast, Königinschriften p. 271 (edition)

TEXT

Obv.
1) *na-ra-am-*[^{d}EN.ZU][
2) LUGAL *ki-ib-ra-a*[*t*]
3) *ar-ba-i*[*m*]
4) [...] x
5) [...] x
Lacuna
Rev.
Lacuna
1′) ⌈*ì*⌉*-li-su*
2′) *ša ku-ra-ri-di*
3′) *n*[*a*]*-ru-ú ša* ⌈*a-*⌉[*ku-ṣ*]*í*.KI

obv. 1–5) Narām-[Sîn], king of the fou[r] quarter[s],
...
Lacuna

Lacuna
rev. 1′–3′) ...-ilišu, ... Stele of A[kus]um.

47

An Old Babylonian copy of a Narām-Sîn inscription is found on the Narām-Sîn Sammeltafel in the Brockmon Collection in Haifa. Two little of the text is preserved to determine which royal deed it commemorated.

COMMENTARY

The inscription is found on rev. ii 1 – iii 4 of BT 1.

BIBLIOGRAPHY

1989 Kutscher, Brockmon Tablets pp. 26, 111, and 119 (photo, copy, edition)

1990 Gelb and Kienast, Königsinschriften p. 274 Narām-Sîn C 17 (edition).

TEXT

1) *^{d}na-ra-am-*^{d}EN.ZU 2) *da-núm* 3) LUGAL 4) *ki-i[b-r]a-tim* 5) *[ar-ba-im]* 6) [...] x Lacuna	1–6) Narām-Sîn, the mighty, king of the [four] qu[ar]ters Lacuna
1′) *ù* 2′) ŠE.NUMUN-*šu* 3′) *li-il-qù-tá*	1′–3′) and may they (the two gods) destroy his progeny.
Colophon 1) [mu-sar-r]a ki-gal-ba	Colophon 1) [Inscripti]on on its socle.

48

The end of a probable Narām-Sîn inscription is preserved on the Sammeltafel of Narām-Sîn inscriptions in the Brockmon Collection.

COMMENTARY

The inscription is found on rev. v′ 1–6 of BT 1; the line numbering of a reconstructed text is given here. The inscription was collated by P. Steinkeller.

BIBLIOGRAPHY

1989 Kutscher, Brockmon Tablets pp. 27, 111, and 119 (photo, copy, edition)

1990 Gelb and Kienast, Königsinschriften p. 275 Narām-Sîn C 19 (edition)

TEXT

Lacuna 0) *[a-na]* 1) *^{d}en-líl* 2) *in* NIBRU.KI 3) A.MU.RU	Lacuna 0–3) [He] dedicated (this object) to the god Enlil in Nippur.
Colophon 1) mu-sar-ra zà-ga-na 2) alam-bi 3) x-x-e DU.DU	Colophon Inscription on his shoulder. Its statue *stands* at ...

49

An Old Babylonian tablet from Nippur bears an Old Babylonian copy of the beginning of a Narām-Sîn inscription.

COMMENTARY

The inscription, which is preserved on col. i of N202+4007+4930, was collated.

BIBLIOGRAPHY

1980 Michalowski, JCS 32 pp. 239, 244, 246 (photo, copy, edition)

1990 Gelb and Kienast, Königinschriften p. 267, Narāmsîn C 8 (edition)

TEXT

1) ^{d}*na-ra-am-*^{d}EN.ZU
2) *da-núm*
3) [LU[GAL
4) [*ki-ib-r*]*a-*⸢*tim*⸣
Lacuna

1–4) Narām-Sîn, the mighty, [k]ing of [the four qu]ạrters
Lacuna

50

An Old Babylonian tablet from Nippur gives the beginning section of a Narām-Sîn inscription.

COMMENTARY

The inscription is found on obv. cols. iii–iv of N202+4007+4930. The inscription was collated.

BIBLIOGRAPHY

1980 Michalowski, JCS 32 pp. 240, 244, 246 (photo, copy, edition)

1990 Gelb and Kienast, Königinschriften Narāmsîn C 10 (edition)

TEXT

Col. ii
1) [^{d}*na-ra-a*]*m*-[^{d}]EN.[Z]U
2) *da-núm*
3) LUGAL
4) *a-*⌜*kà-dè*⌝.[KI]

ii 1–4) [Nara]m-[S]în, the mighty, king of Agade

Col. iii
1) *tám-s*[*i*$_{4}$*-il*]*-ś*[*u*]
2) *ib-ni-ma*
3) *a-na*
4) ^{d}*en-líl*
5) [*a-bí-ś*]*u*
6) [A.MU.RU]

iii 1–6 fashioned an image of himself and [dedicated] it to the god Enlil, [h]is [father].

51

Four inscribed objects are known that once belonged to children of Narām-Sîn; their inscriptions are edited here as E2.1.4.51–54. Seal inscriptions of servants of the royal children are edited as E2.1.4.2017, 2019–2015.

Narām-Sîn installed his daughter Šumšanī as *entu* priestess of the god Šamaš in Sippar. Her name appears on a bronze bowl from Mari.

COMMENTARY

The bowl was found in excavations at Mari, in the 'maison rouge', sector R. 28, in a level that was assigned by the excavator, on the basis of this and other inscriptional finds, to the Akkadian period. It bears the excavation number M 3250. The transliteration results from the combined evidence of a small published drawing and a photo of the bowl. Line 6 is restored from the parallel provided by E2.1.4.2017.

BIBLIOGRAPHY

1955 Parrot, Syria 32 pp. 195, 201, and pl. XVI no. 2 (photo, study)
1955 Parrot, ILN Aug. 6, 1955 p. 228 fig. 6 (photo)
1961 Gelb, MAD 2[2] p. 200 sub 8 (study)
1968 Nagel and Strommenger, BJVF 8 p. 146 n. 11 (edition)
1969 Calmeyer, Datierbare Bronzen p. 28 no. 12c (study)
1974 Parrot, Mari capitale fabuleuse p. 90 fig. 46 (drawing)
1990 Gelb and Kienast, Königsinschriften p. 112 Narāmsîn B 10 (edition)

TEXT

1) *na-ra-am-*^{d}EN.ZU
2) LUGAL
3) *ki-ib-ra-tim*
4) *ar-ba-im*

1–4) Narām-Sîn, king of the four quarters:

5) *śum*$_{6}$*-śa-ni*
6) ⌜EN⌝*-na-at*
7) ^{d}UTU
8) *in* ⌜ZIMBIR.KI⌝
9) DUMU.MUNUS-*su*

5–9) Šumšanī, *entu* priestess of the god Šamaš in Sippar, (is) his daughter.

52

The name of another daughter of Narām-Sîn is inscribed on a bronze bowl from Mari.

COMMENTARY

The bowl was found in excavations of the 'maison rouge', sector R. 28, in a level assigned by the excavator to the Akkadian period. It bears the excavation number M 3255. The inscription was collated from the published photo. For other Old Akkadian PNs with the initial element ME, see Gelb, MAD 3 p. 167. The sign may have been read phonetically, to judge from the spelling of the hydronym I_7.*me-e-ku-bi* (VAS 13 no. 87 line 5).

BIBLIOGRAPHY

1955 Parrot, Syria 32 pp. 195, 201, and pl. XVI no. 1 (photo, study)
1955 Parrot, ILN Aug. 6, 1955 p. 228 fig. 4 (photo)
1954–56 Parrot, AfO 17 p. 424 and fig. 15 (study, photo)
1961 Gelb, MAD 2[2] p. 200 Narâm-Sin Family no. 8 (study)
1968 Nagel and Strommenger, BJVF 8 p. 146 n. 11 (edition)
1969 Calmeyer, Datierbare Bronzen p. 28no. 12d (translation)
1971 Sollberger and Kupper, IRSA IIA4j (translation)
1974 Parrot, Mari capital fabuleuse p. 90 fig. 46 (drawing)
1990 Gelb and Kienast, Königsinschriften pp. 104–105 Narāmsîn A 5 (edition)

TEXT

1) *na-ra-am-*ᵈEN.ZU
2) LUGAL
3) *ki-ib-ra-tim*
4) *ar-ba-im*
5) ME-*ùl-maš*
6) DUMU.MUNUS-*su*

1–4) Narām-Sîn, king of the four quarters:
5–6) ME-Ulmaš (is) his daughter.

53

A seal of a son of Narām-Sîn is in Fribourg.

COMMENTARY

The seal is made of serpentine and measures 3.94×2.73 cm. The piece was formerly in the Sarre Collection, but is now housed in the Institut Biblique in Fribourg (no. 54). The inscription was collated from the published photo.

BIBLIOGRAPHY

1920 Weber, AO 17–18 no. 229 (photo, study)
1926 Unger, RLV 4/2 pl. 157a (photo)
1926 Unger, SuAK fig. 39 (photo)
1930 Unger in Bossert (ed.), Kunstgewerbes 3, p. 421 no. 4 (photo)
1957 Lambert, RA 51 p. 33 fig. 4 (copy)
1961 Gelb, MAD 2[2] p. 200 Narâm-Sin Family no. 9 (study)
1963 Hirsch, AfO 20 p. 23 d 2 α (edition)
1964 Boehmer, Moortgat Festschrift p. 48 and pl. 11 no. 15 (photo, edition)
1965 Boehmer, Glyptik no. 763 and fig. 256 (photo)
1968 Nagel and Strommenger, BJVF 8 pp. 152–53 and 163 no. 14 (edition, study)
1968–69 Edzard, AfO 22 p. 15 nos. 20–21 (transliteration)
1987 Collon, First Impressions no. 528 (photo, translation)
1990 Gelb and Kienast, Königsinschriften p. 41 S–9 (edition)

TEXT

1) [d]*na-ra-am*-[d]EN.ZU
2) DINGIR *a-kà-dè*.KI
3) *u-kí-in-ul-maš*
4) DUMU-*śú*

1–2) Narām-Sîn, god of Agade:

3–4) Ukīn-Ulmaš (is) his son.

54

The names of a son and granddaughter of Narām-Sîn occur together in an inscription carved on a stone plaque from Girsu.

COMMENTARY

The plaque, which is made of slate, measures 27×24.5×4 cm and bears the museum number AO 3296. It was found by de Sarzec in the 'Tell des Tablettes'.

The inscription was collated by B. Foster. As noted, the Nabi-ulmaš of this inscription appears in an archival text dated to year name (ii) of Narām-Sîn.

BIBLIOGRAPHY

1884–1912 de Sarzec, Découvertes 2 p. LVII and pl. 26bis no.2 (photo, copy)
1899 Thureau-Dangin, CRAIB 1899 pp. 346–48 and pl. 1 (copy, edition, study)
1900 Radau, EBH pp. 173–74 (edition)
1907 Thureau-Dangin, SAK pp. 166–67 Narâm-sin e (edition)
1914 Poebel, PBS 4/1 p. 132 (study)
1929 Barton, RISA pp. 140–41 Naram-Sin 11 (edition)
1948 Parrot, Tello pp. 134–36 and fig. 32g (drawing)
1961 Gelb, MAD 2[2] p. 200 Narâm-Sin Family no. 7 (study)
1963 Hirsch, AfO 20 p. 27 Familie Narâm-Sins no. 2 (study)
1971 Sollberger and Kupper, IRSA IIA4k (translation)
1971 Boese, Weihplatten pp. 125–27, 203 and pl. XXXII T 15 (drawing, study)
1990 Gelb and Kienast, Königsinschriften pp. 103–104 Narāmsîn A 3 (edition)

TEXT

1) DUMU [d]*na-ra-am*-[d]EN.ZU
2) *da-nim*
3) *na-bí-ùl-maš*
4) ÉNSI
5) *tu-tu*.KI

1–5) The son of Narām-Sîn, the mighty, (is) Nabi-Ulmaš, governor of (the city of) Tutu:

6) *li-pu-uš-ià-a-um*
7) BALAG.DI
8) dEN.ZU
9) DUMU.MUNUS-*sú*

6–9) Līpuš-iāʾum, the lyre player of the god Sîn (is) his daughter.

1001

An inscription of a Sargonic ruler known from an Old Babylonian Sammeltafel copy deals with the fashioning of a statue of the king.

COMMENTARY

The inscription is found on obv. i of AO 5474, a clay tablet of unknown provenance that measures 6×8.2 cm. The inscription was collated by B. Foster.

No royal name is found in the preserved portion of this inscription. However, its attribution to Narām-Sîn is probable because the following inscription on the Sammeltafel belongs to Narām-Sîn (see E2.1.4.1). The occurrence of a third fem. singular verb in line 3′ (*taddinšumma*) makes a restoration of the divine name in line 1′ as Aštar likely. Narām-Sîn seems to have had an especially close relationship with this goddess; she figures in many of his royal inscriptions.

BIBLIOGRAPHY

1912 Thureau-Dangin, RA 9 p. 34 (copy, study)
1961 Gelb, MAD 2[2] p. 199 Narâm-Sin Late Copies no. 6 (study)
1963 Hirsch, AfO 20 pp. 21–22 Narâm-Sin b 8 (study)
1990 Gelb and Kienast, Königsinschriften pp. 131 and 266–67 Narāmsîn C 7 (copy, edition)

TEXT

Lacuna
1′) ⌈d⌉x [...]
2′) *ma-ḫi-ra*
3′) *la tá-ad-dì-in-šum₆-ma*
4′) DÙL KÙ.GI
5′) *ša da-rí⌈ri⌉-a-ti*
6′) *dú-un-ni-šu*
7′) *ù*
8′) REC 169-*e*
9′) *iš₁₁-a-ru-ni*
10′) *tám-ši-il-šu*
11′) *ib-ni-ma*
12′) x [x] x
Lacuna

Lacuna
1′–3′) The goddess [*Aštar*] gave him no rival.

4′–12′) He fashioned an image of himself, a golden eternal statue (depicting) his might and the battles in which he had been victorious, ...
Lacuna

1002

A tablet fragment found in excavations at Nippur contains the end of an inscription of a Sargonic king, probably Narām-Sîn.

COMMENTARY

The tablet, in the University Museum in Philadelphia, bears the museum number N202+4007+4930. The inscription began on a part of obv. iv now broken away and continued to rev. i–ii. The fact that two Narām-Sîn inscriptions are recorded on the obv. of this Sammeltafel makes an attribution of this text to Narām-Sîn likely. The inscription was collated.

The restoration of rev. col. ii of this text follows Michalowski's edition rather than the edition of Gelb and Kienast.

BIBLIOGRAPHY

1980 Michalowski, JCS 32 pp. 240–41, 244, and 246 (photo, copy, transliteration)

1990 Gelb and Kienast, Königsinschriften pp. 269–70 Narāmsîn C 11 (edition)

TEXT

Rev. col. i
Lacuna
1′) [*a-lí*]-*t*[*im*]
2′) *ù*
3′) *ša-píl-tim*
4′) *ù*
5′) *kà-la*
6′) NI.SI$_{11}$
Rev. col. ii
1) [*šu*$_{4}$-*a*]
2) [*u-ša-sá-ku-ni*]
3) [^{d} ...]
4) [*ù*]
5) [^{d} ...]
6) [SUḪUŠ-*šu*]
7) *li-sú-ḫa*
8) *ù*
9) ŠE.NUMUN-*šu*
10) *li-i*[*l-qù-t*]*á*
Lacuna

Lacuna
rev. i 1′–6′) ... the [Upp]er and Lower [Lands/Seas] and all the people.

rev. i 7′ – ii 10) [As for the one who removes this] inscription, [may the gods X and Y] tear out [his foundations] and de[stro]y his progeny.
Lacuna

1003

The previously mentioned tablet also contains the end of a dedicatory inscription of a Sargonic king, probably Narām-Sîn.

COMMENTARY

The inscription is found on rev. iii of the tablet N202+4007+4930 in the University Museum, Philadelphia. A reconstructed text is given that follows Michalowski's edition; the restoration is based on parallels from other Sargonic royal inscriptions, in particular E2.1.4.35.

BIBLIOGRAPHY

1980 Michalowski, JCS 32 pp. 241, 244, and 246 (photo, copy, edition)

1990 Gelb and Kienast, Königsinschriften pp. 270–71 Narāmsîn C 12 (edition)

TEXT

1) [(d)*na-ra-am*-dEN.ZU]	1–4) [Narām-Sîn, king of the four quarters],
2) [LUGAL]	
3) [*ki-ib-ra-tim*]	
4) [*ar-ba-im*]	
5) [*in*]	5–7) [from the booty of GN]
6) [NAM.RA.AK]	
7) [x].KI	
8) [*a*]-*na*	8–11) de[dicated (this object) t]o [the god Enlil in Nippur].
9) [d*en*]-⸢*líl*⸣	
10) [*in* NIBRU.KI]	
11) A M[U.RU]	

1004

An Old Babylonian tablet copy of an apparent royal inscription in Sumerian names several toponyms in the regions to the northwest and southeast of Mesopotamia. Since many of the toponyms appearing in the text — Ebla, Abarnum, the Cedar Forest, and Magan, for example — are all known to have been areas where Narām-Sîn campaigned, an attribution of the inscription to the Sargonic king is likely.

COMMENTARY

The inscription is found on the reverse of Ni 9654, a tablet fragment in Istanbul. The edition follows the copy of Kramer and the transliteration of Civil which were published by Civil in JCS 21 (1967) pp. 27 and 37. According to our understanding, Ni 9654 is a fragment of a Sammeltafel that contained inscriptions of both Šū-Sîn and Narām-Sîn. It is unlikely that the reverse of Ni 9654 gives the text of a Šū-Sîn inscription; if this were the case, we would expect to find some year names of the Ur III king commemorating his victories in the regions mentioned in Ni 9654. It turns out that the furthest west the king seems to have travelled in his campaigns was to the city of Simānum, whose defeat is commemorated in the name of the king's third year. Civil's proposal to see Ni 9654 as part of the same tablet that contained Ni 9662, the latter a tablet fragment with a Šū-Sîn inscription that was published by Edzard in AfO 19 (1959–60) pp. 28–31 and pl. 4, is not supported by our proposed attribution of this text to Narām-Sîn.

BIBLIOGRAPHY

1967 Civil, JCS 21 pp. 27 and 37–38 (copy [by Kramer], transliteration, study)

TEXT

Lacuna
1′) GÁ x x [...] P[U ...]
2′) ⌈ma⌉-ḫa-z[u-um.KI ...]
3′) pu-u[š.KI ...]
4′) x [x x x] da aš(?) gi(?) KU x [(x)]
5′) e[b-l]a.KI ma-rí.KI tu-tu-ul.KI ma-x [(x)]
6′) ur-gi$_4$-iš.KI mu-x-⌈gi$_4$⌉-iš EZEN(x X?).NI-^{d}IŠKUR
7′) x-x-la.KI a-bar-nu-um.KI
8′) ù kùr GIŠ.erin-ku$_5$ ma-da-ma-d[a-bi]
9′) kur šubur-r[a] gaba-gaba-a-ab-[ba I]GI.NIM-ma x [x]
10′) ù má-gan.KI ma-da-[ma-da-bi] kur x [...]
11′) bal-a-ri a-[ab-ba ...]
Lacuna

Lacuna
1′–11′) ..., Māḫāz[um], Pu[š], ... E[bl]a, Mari, Tuttul, ..., Urkiš, Mukiš, ..., ..., Abarnum, and the land where the cedars are cut down, along with their provinces. The land of Subartum on the shores of the [Up]per Se[a], and Magan, along with [its] province[s] ... the other side of the se[a ...]
Lacuna

2001

The names of several high officials of the administration of Narām-Sîn are known from inscriptions found on objects dedicated to the king, or from seal legends. These inscriptions are edited here as E2.1.4.2001–2018.

The first official noted here is Uruna-badbi, who was *šangû* priest of the god Enlil at Nippur.

COMMENTARY

The inscription is found on a large circular slab of yellowish marble, 62.5 cm in diameter and 8.5 cm thick. The slab has one rough inscribed side and one very smoothly polished side; Haynes suggested that it might have served as a table. This theory is supported by the fact that the piece is similar in form to the calcite disk of En-ḫedu-ana (here inscription E2.1.1.16), which, according to its inscription, served as a table for the god An. The Nippur piece was excavated in the fourth season of the University of Pennsylvania expedition, probably from the area of the ziqqurrat; it now bears the museum number CBS 16202. Its Sumerian text was collated from the published photo. Uruna-badbi also appears in inscriptions E2.1.4.14 and E2.6.1.2001.

BIBLIOGRAPHY

1903 Hilprecht, Explorations p. 474 (study)
1926 Legrain, PBS 15 no. 81 (edition, copy)
1929 Barton, RISA pp. 390–91 Naram-Sin 1 (edition)
1957 Hallo, Titles p. 49 (transliteration)
1961 Gelb, MAD 2^2 p. 200 Narâm-Sin Officials, etc. no. 7 (study)
1963 Hirsch, AfO 20 p. 22 Narâm-Sin d 1 β (study)
1971 Sollberger and Kupper, IRSA IIA4n (translation)
1987 Westenholz, OSP 2 no. 41 (photo, edition, study)
1990 Gelb and Kienast, Königsinschriften p. 108 Narāmsîn B 4 (edition)

TEXT

1) *na-*⌈*ra-am*⌉*-*dEN.ZU
2) lugal-
3) a-ga-dè.KI
4) lugal-
5) an-ub-límmu-ba
6) uru-na-⌈bàd⌉-bi
7) sanga-
8) ⌈den-líl⌉
9) ir_{11}-zu

1–3) Narām-Sîn, king of Agade, king of the four quarters:

6–8) Uruna-badbi, *šangû* priest of the god Enlil, (is) your servant.

2002

A statue fragment now in the Louvre bears a dedicatory inscription of Šuʾāš-takal, the majordomo.

COMMENTARY

The fragment is made of diorite and measures 19×15.5 cm. It was found in excavations by de Morgan on the acropolis at Susa and bears the museum number Sb 53. The inscription was collated from the published photo. For the reading of the DN in line 2 see the comments of P. Steinkeller, ZA 77 (1987) p. 164 n. 18a. His proposed identification of the DN with the god Erra is not certain. For the reading of the PN in line 11, see Westenholz, OSP 2 p. 55.

BIBLIOGRAPHY

1905 Scheil, MDP 6 p. 6 and pl. 1 no. 2 (photo, edition)
1907 Thureau-Dangin, SAK pp. 168–69 Narâm-sin 1 (edition)
1926 Pézard and Pottier, Catalogue no. 51 (study)
1929 Barton, RISA pp. 142–43 Naram-Sin 15 (edition)
1959 Strommenger, ZA 53 p. 43 pl. VIII (photo)
1960 Strommenger, Bagh. Mitt. 1 pp. 50–51 and pl. 13 (photo, study)
1961 Gelb, MAD 2^2 p. 200 Narām-Sîn Officials, etc. no. 4 (study)
1963 Hirsch, AfO 20 p. 22 Narâm-Sin d 1 γ (translation)
1966 Boehmer, Orientalia NS 35 pl. XLVII no. 10 (photo)
1967 Moortgat, Kunst figs. 150–51 (photo)
1971 Sollberger and Kupper, IRSA IIA4l (translation)
1976 Amiet, L'art d'Agadé no. 28 (photo, translation, study)
1975 Orthmann (ed.), Der alte Orient pls. 51a–b photo)
1981 Spycket, Statuaire p. 156 and n. 65 (study)
1987 Westenholz, OSP 2 p. 55 sub no. 40 commentary to ii 3 (study)
1987 Steinkeller, ZA 77 p. 164 n. 18a (study)
1990 Gelb and Kienast, Königsinschriften pp. 106–107 Narāmsîn B 2 (edition)

TEXT

1) *a-na*
2) dNIN.KIŠ.UNU
3) *a-na*
4) ⌈*na-ʾà-ši*⌉
5) d*na-ra-am-*dEN.⌈ZU⌉
6) *da-nim*
7) *ru-ì-*⌈*šu*⌉
8) LUGAL
9) *ki-ib-ra-tim*
10) *ar-ba-im*

1–2) To the god NIN.KIŠ.UNUG,

3–10) for the life of Narām-Sîn, the mighty, his (the god's) friend, king of the four quarters,

11) ⸢*šu*$_4$*-a-áš*⸣*-tá-kál*
12) DUB.SAR
13) ŠABRA É
14) DÙL-*šu*
15) ⸢A.MU.RU⸣

11–13) Šuʾāš-takal, scribe (and) majordomo,

14–15) dedicated his (Narām-Sîn's) statue.

2003

A clay bulla found in excavations of de Sarzec at Telloh bears a seal impression of Šarriš-takal, the scribe.

COMMENTARY

The bulla was catalogued as AOTb 382 and now bears the museum number AO 24032. The inscription was collated by B. Foster.

BIBLIOGRAPHY

1897 Thureau-Dangin, RA 4 pp. 76–77 and pl. VII no. 23 (copy, edition)
1903 Thureau-Dangin, RTC no. 170 (copy)
1907 Thureau-Dangin, SAK pp. 168–69 Narâm-sin m (edition)
1910 Delaporte, Bibliothèque Nationale p. XXVII no. 12 (study)
1920 Delaporte, Louvre 1 T. 57 (photo, edition)
1929 Barton, RISA pp. 142–43 Naram-Sin 18 (edition)
1961 Gelb, MAD 2^2 p. 200 Narâm-Sin Officials, etc. no. 3 (study)
1963 Hirsch, AfO 20 p. 23 Narâm-Sin d 2 γ (translation)
1964 Boehmer, Moortgat Festschrift p. 47 and pl. 11 no. 11 (photo, edition)
1965 Boehmer, Glyptik no. 603 and fig. 172 (photo)
1968 Nagel and Strommenger, BJVF 8 pp. 152-53 and 161 no. 9 (edition, study)
1968–69 Edzard, AfO 22 p. 16 no. 24–10 (transliteration)
1971 Sollberger and Kupper, IRSA IIA4m (translation)
1976 Amiet, L'art d'Agadé no. 69 (photo, edition)
1990 Gelb and Kienast, Königsinschriften p. 42 Narāmsîn S-16 (edition)

TEXT

1) ^{d}*na-ra-am-*^{d}EN.ZU
2) DINGIR *a-kà-dè*.KI
3) *šar-rí-íš-tá-kál*
4) DUB.SAR
5) IR$_{11}$*-sú*

1–2) Narām-Sîn, god of Agade:

3–5) Šarriš-takal, scribe (is) his servant.

2004

Four clay bullae found in excavations of de Sarzec at Telloh bear seal impressions of Lugal-ušumgal, governor of Lagaš.

COMMENTARY

The bullae are numbered AOTb. 380, 380bis, 380ter, and 380^{quater}; they are subsumed under the museum number AO 24062. The inscription was collated from the published photo. For a seal inscription of Lugal-ušumgal as governor under Šar-kali-šarrī, see E2.1.5.2004.

BIBLIOGRAPHY

1884–1912 de Sarzec, Découvertes 1 pp. 285–86 figs. E–F (copy, translation)
1897 Heuzey, RA 4 pp. 10-11 (copy, translation)
1903 Thureau-Dangin, RTC nos. 165–66 (copy)
1906 Meyer, Sumerer und Semiten pp. 60–61 (copy)
1907 Thureau-Dangin, SAK pp. 168–69 Narâm-sin k (edition)
1910 Ward, Seals pp. 26–27 nos. 7–8 figs. 50–50a (copy)
1920 Delaporte, Louvre 1 T. 105 (photo, edition)
1929 Barton, RISA pp. 142–43 Naram-Sin 16 (edition)
1961 Gelb, MAD 2^2 p. 200 Narâm-Sin Officials, etc. no. 1 (study)
1963 Hirsch, AfO 20 p. 23 Narâm-Sin d 2 β (translation)
1964 Boehmer, Moortgat Festschrift p. 49 no. 18 (copy, edition)
1965 Boehmer, Glyptik no. 1045 and fig. 431 (photo, drawing)
1968 Nagel and Strommenger, BJVF 8 pp. 152–53 and 159–60 no. 8 (edition, study)
1968–69 Edzard, AfO 22 p. 16 no. 24–14 (transliteration)
1971 Sollberger and Kupper, IRSA IIA4p (translation)
1976 Amiet, L'art d'Agadé no. 83 (photo, copy, edition)
1987 Collon, First Impressions p. 125 sub no. 537 (translation)
1990 Gelb and Kienast, Königsinschriften p. 42 S-3 (edition)

TEXT

1) ^{d}*na-ra-am-*^{d}EN.ZU
2) *da-núm*
3) DINGIR *a-kà-dè*.KI
4) LUGAL
5) *ki-ib-ra-tim*
6) *a*[*r*]*-ba-im*
7) lugal-ušumgal
8) DUB.⌜SAR⌝
9) ÉNS[I]
10) *la*[*gaš*.KI]

1–6) Narām-Sîn, the mighty, king of Agade, king of the four quarters:

7–10) Lugal-ušumgal, scribe, gover[nor] of La[gaš].

2005

Two inscriptions mentioning Karšum, governor of the city of Niqqum and servant of Narām-Sîn, are known. One is incised on stone mace heads (E2.1.4.2005) and the other on a bronze mace head (E2.1.4.2006).

CATALOGUE

Ex.	Museum number	Dimensions (cm)	Lines preserved	Lambert, OrNS 37 (1968) pls. 8–9	cpn
1	—	—	1–16	Fragm. a	p
2	—	—	14–18	Fragm. b	p
3	—	—	17–19	Fragm. ct	p
4	Israel Museum, no. 74.49.95	26×17	6–11	—	c

COMMENTARY

The first inscription is found on five or six stone mace heads that were shown to the Louvre by a private collector, but which were not acquired by that institution. The text is established from the three exemplars published in photo by M. Lambert, and from a fourth now housed in the Israel Museum. The existence of ex. 4 was pointed out to the author by P. Steinkeller; its inscription was collated by J. Goodnick Westenholz. The provenance of the pieces is said to be Luristan. For a location of the city of Niqqum on the Upper Diyala River, see D. Frayne, Early Dynastic List, § 3.2.5.

BIBLIOGRAPHY

1968 Lambert, Orientalia NS 37 pp. 85–86 and pls. VIII–IX (photo, edition)
1969 Calmeyer, Datierbare Bronzen p. 162 nos. 4a–f (study)
1971 Sollberger and Kupper, IRSA IIA4q (translation)
1990 Gelb and Kienast, Königsinschriften pp. 110–11 Narāmsîn B 7 (edition)

TEXT

1) *a-na* 2) *ìl-a-ba*$_4$	1–2) To the god Ilaba,
3) [d]*na-ra-am-*[d]EN.ZU 4) *da-núm* 5) LUGAL 6) *ki-ib-ra-tim* 7) *ar-ba-im* 8) SAG.GIŠ.RA 9) *ar-ma-nim*.KI 10) *ù* 11) *eb-la*.KI 12) *ù* 13) NIM.KI	3–13) Narām-Sîn, the mighty, king of the four quarters, conqueror of Armānum, Ebla, and Elam,
14) A.MU.RU	14) dedicated (this mace).
15) *kàr-šum* 16) *šu* SUKKAL-*li* 17) ÉNSI 18) *ni-qum*.KI 19) IR$_{11}$-*sú*	15–19) Karšum, the one (who is in charge of) the messengers, governor of Niqqum, (is) his servant.

2006

A bronze mace head bears a different inscription of Karšum, the governor of Niqqum.

COMMENTARY

The mace head, which measures 16.5 cm high, was in the collection Foroughi in Teheran. Its probable provenance is Luristan.

BIBLIOGRAPHY

1962 Dossin, IrAnt 2 pp. 158–59 and pl. XXV no. 15 (photo, copy, edition)
1961 Ghirshman, Sept mille no. 278 (study)
1962 Ghirshman, Kunstschätze no. 128 (study)
1963 Nagel, Altorientalisches Kunsthandwerk p. 42 and pl. LXXIII no. 7 (study, drawing)
1968 Lambert, Orientalia NS 37 p. 86 (study)
1969 Calmeyer, Datierbare Bronzen p. 26 no. 10 A, p. 161 no. 4, and pl. 2 no. 1 (photo, transliteration, study)
1971 Sollberger and Kupper, IRSA IIA4r (translation)
1990 Gelb and Kienast, Königsinschriften pp. 109–10 Narāmsîn B 6 (edition)

TEXT

1) ^{d}*na-ra-am-*^{d}EN.ZU
2) *da-núm*
3) LUGAL
4) *ki-ib-ra-tim*
5) *ar-ba-im*
6) *kàr-šum*
7) *šu* SUKKAL-*li*
8) ÉNSI
9) *ni-qum*.KI
10) IR$_{11}$-*sú*
11) *a-n*[*a*] x x
12) ^{d}*ba-*⸢*li*⸣*-ḫi-lí*
13) A.MU.RU

1–5) Narām-Sîn, the mighty, king of the four quarters:

6–10) Karšum, the one (who is in charge of) the messengers, governor of Niqqum, (is) his servant.

11–13) He dedicated (this mace) to the god ...

2007

The inscription of a Mama-šadûm, servant of Narām-Sîn, appears on a hemispherical bowl.

COMMENTARY

The copper bowl, which reportedly comes from Luristan, measures 6.8 cm in height and 12.4 cm in diameter. It is now in the Bible Lands Museum (Jerusalem), BLMJ 937. The inscription was collated by P. Steinkeller. For Old Akkadian PNs composed with *šadûm* (written ŚA.DÚ), see Gelb MAD 3 p. 264. For a seal inscription containing the title UGULA *šu-ti* GIŠ.TUKUL 'overseer of the men-at-arms', see Weber, AO 17–18 (1920) p. 43 no. 195.

BIBLIOGRAPHY

1981 Sweet in Muscarella, Ladders no. 32 (photo, edition, study)
1987 Goodnick Westenholz in Merhav, Treasures no. 17 (photo, translation)
1990 Gelb and Kienast, Königsinschrften p. 111 Narāmsîn B 8 (edition)

TEXT

1) ^{d}*na-ra-am-*^{d}EN.ZU
2) DINGIR *a-kà-dè*.KI

1–2) Narām-Sîn, god of Agade:

3) *ma-ma*-ḪUR.SAG
4) UGULA *šu-ti* GIŠ.TUKUL
5) IR_{11}-*sú*

3–5) Mama-šadûm, overseer of the men-at-arms, (is) his servant.

2008

A clay bulla found in excavations of de Sarzec at Telloh bears the seal impression of Šū-ilišu, judge and servant of Narām-Sîn.

COMMENTARY

The bulla, now housed in the Louvre, bears the museum no. AOTb. 378; the inscription was collated from the published photo.

BIBLIOGRAPHY

1897 Thureau-Dangin RA 4 pp. 77–78 and pl. VII no. 24 (copy, edition)
1903 Thureau-Dangin, RTC no. 168 (copy)
1907 Thureau-Dangin, SAK pp. 168–69 Narâm-sin o (edition)
1910 Delaporte, Bibliothèque Nationale p. XXVII no. 9 (study)
1920 Delaporte, Louvre 1 T. 44 (photo, edition)
1929 Barton, RISA pp. 144–45 Naram-Sin 20 (edition)
1961 Gelb, MAD 2^2 p. 200 Narâm-Sin Officials, etc. no. 5 (study)
1963 Hirsch, AfO 20 p. 23 Narâm-Sin d 2 δ (translation)
1964 Boehmer, Moortgat Festschrift pp. 48–49 and pl. 11 no. 16 (photo, edition)
1965 Boehmer, Glyptik no. 669 and fig. 203 (photo, study)
1968 Nagel and Strommenger, BJVF 8 pp. 152–53 and 157 no. 2 (edition, study)
1968–69 Edzard, AfO 22 p. 16 no. 24–12 (transliteration)
1990 Gelb and Kienast, Königsinschriften p. 43 S–17 (edition)

TEXT

1) [*na-ra-a*]*m*-^{d}EN.ZU]
2) ⌈LUGAL⌉
3) *a-kà-dè*.KI
4) *šu-ì*-[*lí-šu*]
5) $DI.KU_5$ [...]
6) ⌈IR_{11}⌉-[*sú*]

1–3) Narām-Sîn, king of Agade:

4–6) Šū-ilišu, judge, (is) [his] servant.

2009

A clay bulla found in excavations of de Sarzec at Telloh bears the seal impression of a servant of Narām-Sîn.

COMMENTARY

The bulla bears the museum number AO 24059 (formerly AOTb. 381). The inscription was collated from the published photo.

BIBLIOGRAPHY

1884–1912 de Sarzec, Découvertes 1 p. 287 fig. G (copy)
1903 Thureau-Dangin, RTC no. 171 (copy)
1906 Meyer, Sumerer und Semiten p. 27 (copy)
1909 Gressmann ATBAT fig. 143 (copy)
1910 Delaporte, Bibliothèque Nationale p. XXVII no. 11 (study)
1910 Thureau-Dangin, in Cros, Tello p. 173 (copy)
1910 Ward, Seals fig. 386 (copy)
1913 Jeremias HAOG 1 fig. 89 (copy)
1920 Delaporte, Louvre 1 T. 103 (photo, copy, edition, study)
1928-29 Meissner, AfO 5 pl. 1 no. 6 (copy)
1926 Unger, RLV 4/2 pl. 199b (copy)
1939 Frankfort, Cylinder Seals p. 116 and fig. 32 (copy)
1961 Gelb, MAD 2[2] p. 200 Narâm-Sin Officials, etc. no. 2 (study)
1963 Hirsch, AfO 20 p. 23 Narâm-Sin d 2 ε (translation)
1964 Boehmer, Moortgat Festschrift p. 50 no. 19 (copy, edition)
1965 Boehmer, Glyptik no. 1267 and fig. 542 (copy, study)
1968 Nagel and Strommenger, BJVF 8 pp. 152–53 and 162 no. 11 (edition, study)
1968 Spycket, Statues pp. 24–25 and fig. 12 (translation, study, drawing)
1968–69 Edzard, AfO 22 p. 16 no. 24–15 (transliteration)
1970 Barrelet, Orientalia NS 39 pl. XIII fig. 21 (photo, copy)
1976 Amiet, L'art d'Agadé no. 89 (photo, copy, edition, study)
1990 Gelb and Kienast, Königsinschriften p. 42 S–5 (edition)

TEXT

1) *na-ra-am*-^{d}EN.ZU 2) DINGIR *a-kà-dè*.KI	1–2) Narām-Sîn, god of Agade:
3) *na*-x 3) MUḪALDIM LU[GAL] 4) IR$_{11}$-[*sú*]	3–5) Na-x, ro[yal] cook, is [his] servant.

2010

A fragment of gold leaf found in excavations at Adab is inscribed with the name of a servant of the king.

COMMENTARY

In an unpublished report (see Yang, Sargonic Archive p. 21), E.J. Banks said the fragment came from a chamber of the temple of mound V at Bismāyā, 1.5 metres below the surface of the hill. The piece measures 13.7×4.9 cm and bears the museum number A 1217 (Chicago). The inscription was collated by G. Frame.

BIBLIOGRAPHY

1912 Banks, Bismya p. 145 (copy, study)
1913 Hommel, OLZ 16 (transliteration)
1949 Nestmann, Excavations p. 66 fig. 13 (photo)
1961 Gelb, MAD 2[2] p. 200 Narâm-Sin Officials, etc. no. 6 (study)
1963 Hirsch, AfO 20 p. 22 Narâm-Sin d 1 α (study)
1986 Yang, Sargonic Archive pp. 21, 23 no. 3, and 52 no. 3 (transliteration, study)
1989 Yang, Sargonic Inscriptions p. 107 (study)
1990 Gelb and Kienast, Königsinschriften p. 111 Narāmsîn B 9 (edition)

TEXT

1) *na-ra-am-*[d]EN.ZU
2) LUGAL
3) *a-kà-dè*.KI
4) [I]R_{11}(?)-[d]*en-líl*
5) [x]-*bum*
6) [LU]GAL
Lacuna

1–3) Narām-Sîn, king of Agade:

4–6) [Wa]rad(?)-Enlil, ... [of the ki]ng,
Lacuna

2011

A clay sealing found in excavations at Adab bears the end of a seal inscription of a servant of Narām-Sîn.

COMMENTARY

The sealing, which measures 3.5×3.5 cm, was found in Mound III at Bismāyā by Banks. It now bears the museum number A 889 (Chicago). The inscription was collated from the published photo.

BIBLIOGRAPHY

1912 Banks, Bismya p. 301 (lower middle) (photo)
1986 Yang, Sargonic Archive p. 15 no. 6 b (study) and p. 451 (photo)
1989 Yang, Sargonic Inscriptions p. 345 (transliteration)

TEXT

1) [([d])*na-ra-am-*[d]EN.ZU]
2) [LUGAL]
3) [*ki-ib-ra-tim*]
4) *ar-ba-im*
5) ur-mes
6) DUB.⸢SAR⸣
7) IR_{11}-⸢*sú*⸣

1–4) [Narām-Sîn, king of] the four [quarters]:

5–7) Ur-mes, scribe, (is) his servant.

2012

A clay bulla found in two pieces during excavations of de Sarzec at Telloh bears seal impressions of a cupbearer whose name is not preserved.

COMMENTARY

The pieces bear the museum numbers AO 24060 and AO 24061 (formerly AOTb 383 and 383bis). The inscription was collated from the published photo.

BIBLIOGRAPHY

1884–1912 de Sarzec, Découvertes 1 pp. 284–85 and fig. D (copy, study)
1897 Heuzey, RA 4 pp. 9–10 (copy, study)
1903 Thureau-Dangin, RTC no. 174 (copy)
1907 Thureau-Dangin, SAK pp. 168–69 Narâm-sin q (edition)
1910 Delaporte, Bibliothèque Nationale p. XXVIII no. 15 (study)
1910 Ward, Seals p. 26 no. 6 and p. 27 fig. 49 (copy, study)
1920 Delaporte, Louvre 1 T. 104 (photo, edition, study)
1929 Barton, RISA pp. 144–45 Naram-Sin 22 (edition)
1961 Gelb, MAD 2[2] p. 201 Narâm-Sin Officials, etc. no. 11 (study)
1963 Hirsch, AfO 20 p. 23 Narâm-Sin d 2 ε (translation)
1964 Boehmer, Moortgat Festschrift p. 48 and pl. 11 no. 14 (photo, edition)
1965 Boehmer, Glyptik no. 645 and fig. 194 (photo, study)
1968 Nagel and Strommenger, BJVF 8 pp. 152–53 and 159 no. 5 (edition, study)
1968–69 Edzard, AfO 22 p. 16 no. 24–11 (transliteration)
1976 Amiet, L'art d'Agadé no. 70 (photo, edition)
1990 Gelb and Kienast, Königsinschriften p. 43 S–9 (edition)

TEXT

1) *na-ra-am-*^{d}EN.ZU
Lacuna
1′) SAGI
2′) IR_{11}-*sú*

1) Narām-Sîn,
Lacuna
1′–2′) cupbearer, (is) his servant.

2013

A clay bulla found in excavations of de Sarzec at Telloh bears the seal impression of a servant of Narām-Sîn whose name is broken away.

COMMENTARY

The clay bulla is numbered AOTb 385 in the Louvre collections. It was collated from the published photo.

BIBLIOGRAPHY

1897 Thureau-Dangin, RA 4 p. 76 and pl. VII no. 22 (copy, edition)
1903 Thureau-Dangin, RTC no. 172 (copy)
1910 Delaporte, Bibliothèque Nationale p. XXVIII no. 17 (study)
1920 Delaporte, Louvre 1 T. 35 (photo, edition, study)
1961 Gelb, MAD 2[2] p. 201 Narâm-Sin Officials, etc. no. 10 (study)
1963 Hirsch, AfO 20 p. 23 Narâm-Sin d 2 ζ (translation)
1964 Boehmer, Moortgat Festschrift p. 49 and pl. 11 no. 17 (photo, edition)
1965 Boehmer, Glyptik no. 695 and fig. 221 (photo, study)
1968 Nagel and Strommenger BJVF 8 pp. 152–53 and 162 no. 10 (edition, study)
1968–69 Edzard, AfO 22 p. 16 no. 24–13 (transliteration)
1990 Gelb and Kienast, Königsinschriften p. 44 S–22 (edition)

TEXT

1) ^{d}*na-ra-am-*^{d}EN.ZU
2) DINGIR *a-kà-dè*.KI
3) x [...]
4) x [...]
5) I[R$_{11}$-*sú*]

1–2) Narām-Sîn, god of Agade:

3–5) ... (is) [his] se[rvant].

2014

A clay bulla found in excavations of de Sarzec at Telloh bears the seal impression of a servant of a Sargonic king, probably Narām-Sîn.

COMMENTARY

The bulla is numbered AOTb. 403 in the Louvre collections; the inscription was collated from the published photo. Narām-Sîn is the only Sargonic king known to have adopted the title DINGIR *a-kà-dè*.KI 'god of Agade' and for that reason this inscription has been attributed to that ruler.

BIBLIOGRAPHY

1897 Thureau-Dangin, RA 4 p. 78 and pl. VIII no. 26 (copy, translation)
1903 Thureau-Dangin, RTC no. 173 (copy)
1907 Thureau-Dangin, SAK pp. 168–69 Narām-sîn n (edition)
1910 Delaporte, Bibliothèque Nationale p. XXVII-XXXVIII no. 13 (study)
1920 Delaporte, Louvre 1 T. 64 (photo, edition)
1929 Barton, RISA pp. 144–45 Naram-Sin 19 (edition)
1961 Gelb, MAD 2^{2} p. 205 Unknown Kings Original Inscriptions no. 6 (study)
1963 Hirsch, AfO 20 p. 23 Narâm-Sin d 2 ι (translation)
1964 Boehmer, Moortgat Festschrift p. 51 and pl. 12 no. 23 (photo, edition)
1965 Boehmer, Glyptik no. 604 (study)
1968 Nagel and Strommenger, BJVF 8 pp. 154–55 and 163 no. 17 (edition, study)
1968–69 Edzard, AfO 22 p. 16 no. 24–34 (transliteration)
1990 Gelb and Kienast, Königsinschriften p. 43 S–18 (edition)

TEXT

1) <^{d}*na-ra-am-*^{d}EN.ZU>
2) DINGIR *a-kà-dè*.KI
3) ur-da
4) DUB.SAR
5) IR$_{11}$-*sú*

1–2) <Narām-Sîn>, god of Agade:

3–5) Urda, the scribe, (is) his servant.

2015

A seal impression on an Old Assyrian tablet and tablet envelope gives the name of Narām-Sîn and one of his servants.

COMMENTARY

The tablet and envelope are in the Musée d'Art et d'Histoire, Geneva, and bear the museum numbers MAH 15,962 and MAH 16,213 respectively. Gelb and Sollberger (JNES 16 pp. 173–75) thought the tablet came from Aššur. The seal impression measures 2.1 cm in height. The inscription was not collated.

BIBLIOGRAPHY

1957 Gelb and Sollberger, JNES 16 pp. 170, 172, and pl. XXIX (photo, transliteration)
1963 Hirsch, AfO 20 pp. 23–24 n. 253 (transliteration)
1964 Boehmer, Moortgat Festschrift pp. 47–48 and pl. 11 no. 12 (edition)
1965 Boehmer, Glyptik no. 643 and fig. 193 (photo, study)
1968 Nagel and Strommenger, BJVF 8 pp. 152–53 and 159 no. 7 (edition, study)
1990 Gelb and Kienast, Königsinschriften p. 44 S–21 (edition)

TEXT

1) [d]*na-ra-am*-[d]EN.ZU	1–4) Narām-Sîn, king of the four quarters:
2) LUGAL	
3) *ki-ib-ra-tim*	
4) *ar-ba-im*	
5) x-[d]ASAR	5–7) ...–Asar, ...
6) Traces	
7) Traces	

2016

A clay bulla found in excavations of de Sarzec at Telloh gives the beginning of a seal inscription of a servant of Narām-Sîn.

COMMENTARY

The bulla is numbered AOTb. 384 in the Louvre collections. The inscription was collated from the published photo.

BIBLIOGRAPHY

1903 Thureau-Dangin, RTC no. 167 (copy)
1907 Thureau-Dangin, SAK pp. 168–69 Narâm-sin p (edition)
1910 Delaporte, Bibliothèque Nationale p. XXVIII no. 16 (study)
1920 Delaporte, Louvre 1 T. 101 (photo, edition)
1929 Barton, RISA pp. 144–45 Naram-Sin 21 (edition)
1961 Gelb, MAD 2[2] p. 201 Narâm-Sin Officials, etc. no. 9 (study)
1963 Hirsch, AfO 20 p. 23 Narâm-Sin 2 d θ (translation)
1964 Boehmer, Moortgat Festschrift p. 51 and pl. 12 no. 22 (photo, edition)
1965 Boehmer, Glyptik no. 1511 and fig. 656 (photo, study)
1968 Nagel and Strommenger, BJVF 8 pp. 152–53 and 159 no. 6 (edition, study)
1990 Gelb and Kienast, Königsinschriften p. 43 S–20 (edition)

TEXT

1) ^{d}*n*[*a*]-*ra*-[*am*]-^{d}EN.ZU
2) LUGAL
3) *ki-ib-ra-t*[*im*]
4) [*ar-ba-im*]
Lacuna

1–4) N[a]rām-Sîn, king of the [four] quar[ters]:
Lacuna

2017

A seal which was in the Marquis of Lorne Collection bears the inscription of a servant of the *entu* priestess Tūta-napšum; its present location is unknown.

COMMENTARY

The inscription was collated from the published photo.

The seal design depicts Tūta-napšum seated on a throne with a pointed diadem on her head. Her servant, presumably Aman-Aštar, stands in front of her presenting some kind of musical instrument. For the expression MUNUS.Ú.ḪÚB of line 3, cf. MSL 12 p. 52 lines 542–43: ú-ḫub, munus-ú-ḫub, and p. 142 col. iv line 14′ ú-ḫub = *su-uk-ku* 'deaf'. In line 4 *ṣa-bi-rí-im* is understood to be a *parīsu*(*m*) form of *ṣabāru*(*m*) 'to be voluble, to prattle'.

BIBLIOGRAPHY

1899 Ball, Light p. 153 (photo of seal impression)
1910 Ward, Seal p. 81 and fig. 217 (copy)
1961 Gelb, MAD 2[2] p. 7 sub no. 2 (study)
1967 Renger, ZA 58 p. 137 with n. 183 (study)
1981 Michalowski, RA 75 p. 174 (study)
1983 Westenholz and Oelsner, AoF 10 pp. 214–16 and fig. 4 (photo of seal impression, edition)
1987 Collon, First Impressions no. 530 (photo, study)
1990 Gelb and Kienast, Königsinschriften p. 41 Narāmsîn S-12 (edition)

TEXT

1) *tu-tá-na-ap-šum*$_6$
2) EN-*na-at* ^{d}*en-líl*
3) *a-ma-an-aš-tár* MUNUS.Ú.ḪÚB
4) *ša-at ṣa-bi-rí-im*
5) GÉME-*sà*

1–2) Tūta-napšum, *entu* priestess of the god Enlil:

3–5) Aman-Aštar, the deaf lady, the *prattler*, (is) her female servant.

2018

An inscription incised on a stone plaque, and two seal inscriptions, mention servants of En-men-ana, the *entu* priestess of the god Nanna at Ur. The first of these inscriptions gives the name of her majordomo, Išṭup-Ilum.

COMMENTARY

The Sumerian inscription is found on a stone plaque which probably came from courtyard 2 of the palace built by Nabonidus at Ur for his daughter. It was given the excavation number U 16002 and bears the museum no. BM 122935 (reg. no. 1931-10-10, 3). The inscription was collated by G. Frame.

BIBLIOGRAPHY

1931 S. Smith, BMQ 6 p. 81 (study)
1954–56 Sollberger, AfO 17 pp. 27–28 (copy, edition, study)
1960 Sollberger, Iraq 22 pp. 77–78 no. 106 (study)
1961 Gelb, MAD 2² p. 200 Narâm-Sin Family no. 6 (study)
1963 Hirsch, AfO 20 p. 23 Narâm-Sin d 1 ε (translation)
1965 Sollberger, UET 8 p. 3 sub no. 12 (study)
1971 Boese, Weihplatten p. 126 n. 603a (study)
1971 Sollberger and Kupper, IRSA IIA4h (translation)
1990 Gelb and Kienast, Königsinschriften p. 106 Narāmsîn B 1 (edition)

TEXT

1) ᵈnin-gublaga
2) a-sug-giš-dù-a-ka-ra
3) nam-ti-
4) ᵈ*na-ra-am*-ᵈEN.ZU
5) dingir-a-ga-dè.KI-ka-šè
6) nam-t[i]-
7) en-men-an-[na]-k[a-šè]
8) *iš-ṭu*[*p*-DINGIR]
9) šabr[a-é]-k[a-ni]
10) a mu-[na-ru]

1–2) To the god Nin-gublaga of Asuggišdua,

3–5) for the life of Narām-Sîn, god of Agade,

6–7) (and) for the li[fe] of En-men-an[a],

8–10) Išṭu[p-Ilum], [her] major[domo], ded[icated (this plaque)].

2019

The seal of Ursi, servant of En-men-ana, was found at Ur.

COMMENTARY

The seal is made of green marble and measures 3.1×2.1 cm. It was found in grave PG/719 at Ur and bears the excavation number U 9844. Its present whereabouts are unknown. The inscription was collated from the published photo.

BIBLIOGRAPHY

1934 Woolley, UE 2 pp. 314, 350–51, 550, pl. 191 and pl. 206 no. 198 (photo, copy, edition, study)
1954–56 Sollberger, AfO 17 p. 27 (edition)
1961 Gelb, MAD 2² p. 200 Narâm-Sin Family no. 5 (study)
1963 Hirsch, AfO 20 p. 27 Familie Narâm-Sins 1 (transliteration)
1964 Boehmer, Moortgat Festschrift p. 50 and pl. 12 no. 20 (photo, edition)
1965 Boehmer, Glyptik no. 1287 and fig. 548 (photo, study)
1968 Nagel and Strommenger, BJVF 8 pp. 154–55 and pl 167 no. 26b (edition, study)
1968–69 Edzard, AfO 22 p. 17 no. 25-1 (transliteration)
1990 Gelb and Kienast, Königsinschriften p. 41 Narāmsîn S-11 (edition)

TEXT

1) en-men-an-na
2) ur-si
3) ì-du_8
4) ir_{11}-da-ni

1) En-men-ana:
2–4) Ursi, door-keeper, (is) her servant.

2020

A seal impresssion of a servant of En-men-ana is found on a clay bulla that was found in excavations of de Sarzec at Telloh.

COMMENTARY

The bulla, now in the Archaeological Museum in Istanbul, bears the inventory number L. 1094 and measures 5.2×3.2 cm. The inscription was collated from the published photo.

BIBLIOGRAPHY

1897 Scheil, RT 19 p. 187 (partial copy, edition)
1910 Thureau-Dangin, ITT 1 no. 1094 (copy)
1954–56 Sollberger, AfO 17 p. 27 no. c (edition)
1961 Gelb, MAD 2^2 p. 200 Narâm-Sin Family 3 (study)
1963 Hirsch, AfO 20 p. 23 Narâm-Sin d 2 κ (translation)
1964 Boehmer, Moortgat Festschrift p. 50 and pl. 12 no. 21 (photo, edition)
1965 Boehmer, Glyptik no. 1694 and fig. 725 (photo, copy, study)
1968 Nagel and Strommenger, BJVF 8 pp. 154–55 and 164 no. 18 (edition, study)
1968–69 Edzard, AfO 22 p. 17 no. 25–3 (transliteration)
1971 Sollberger and Kupper, IRSA IIA4i (translation)
1975 Orthmann (ed.), Der alte Orient p. 238 and fig. 44e (study, copy)
1983 Selz, Bankettszene 1 pp. 576–77 and 2 p. K72 no. 578 (edition, study)
1990 Gelb and Kienast, Königsinschriften p. 41 Narāmsîn S–10 (edition)

TEXT

1) ^{d}*na-ra-am*-^{d}EN.ZU
2) dingir-a-ga-dè.KI
3) en-men-an-na
4) e[n ^{d}nanna]
5) dumu-[ni]
6) LU-x [...]
7) dub-[sar]
8) ir_{11}-⌜da⌝-[ni]

1–2) Narām-Sîn, god of Agade.

3–5) En-men-ana, *e*[*n*]*tu* priestess [of the god Nanna], (is) [his] daughter:

6–8) Lu-x-[...] scr[ibe], (is) [her] servant.

2021

A seal found during excavations at Nippur bears the inscription of a servant of the crown prince Šar-kali-šarrī.

COMMENTARY

The seal, which was found in the fill of an Old Babylonian drain in WA near the southeast corner of Mound I, bears the excavation number 13N 336. Its inscription was collated from the published photo. The interpretation of the PN in line 3 is not absolutely certain; here we follow the reading of Civil. Westenholz (OSP 2 p. 24 and n. 18) read ḪI.PÙ.URU.KI.IM, comparing it to the Hurrian PN ḪI.PÙ.ŠÈ.NAM. Šar-kali-šarrī apparently served in a high administrative post at Nippur, possibly as governor of the city, prior to his accession to the throne.

BIBLIOGRAPHY

1977 Gibson, Archaeology 30 pp. 29–32 (photo, translation, study)
1978 Gibson, Sumer 34 pp. 116–117, fig. 10 and p. 121 n. 4 (photo, edition, study)
1982 Gibson, BSMS 3 pp. 18–19 (study)
1987 Westenholz, OSP 2 p. 24 and n. 18 (edition)
1990 Gelb and Kienast, Königsinschriften p. 46 S–33 (edition)

TEXT

1) *śar-kà-lí*-LUGAL-*rí*
2) DUMU LUGAL
3) DU_{10}-*pù*-URU.KI-*im*
4) DUB.SAR
5) IR_{11}-*sú*

1–2) Šar-kali-šarrī, son of the king:

3–5) Ṭāb-pû-ālim, scribe, (is) his servant.

2022

Seal inscriptions of three servants of Bin-kali-šarrī, son of Narām-Sîn, are known. The first is found on a cylinder seal whose present whereabouts are unknown.

COMMENTARY

The piece, which measures 3.8 cm in height, was said by Ménant to be housed in the 'Musée de New-York'. It is not, however, part of the Metropolitan Museum of Art's present holdings (information courtesy of Dr. J. Aruz, Assistant Curator, Department of Near Eastern Art, Metropolitan Museum). For the interpretation of the PN of line 3 as *isinnum* 'festival', see Gelb, MAD 3 p. 69.

BIBLIOGRAPHY

1883 Ménant, Glyptique 1 pp. 75–76 and pl. 1 no. 1 (photo, copy of seal design, translation)
1888 Hommel, Geschichte p. 299 (drawing)
1892 Winckler and Böhden, ABK no. 66 (copy)
1900 Radau, EBH p. 173 (edition)
1907 Thureau-Dangin, SAK pp. 168–69 Bingâni-šar-ali a (edition)
1910 Ward, Seals p. 20 fig. 27; p. 21 no. 2; p. 69; p. 70 fig. 183 (copy, translation, study)
1920 Weber, AO 17–18 no. 125 (photo)
1926 Unger, RLV 4/2 pl. 157b (photo)
1926 Unger, SuAK p. 94 fig. 41 (photo)
1929 Barton, RISA pp. 148–49 Bingani–sharri 1 (edition)
1961 Gelb, MAD 2² p. 199 Narâm-Sin Family no. 1 (study)
1963 Hirsch, AfO 20 p. 31 Binkališarrī 1 (translation)
1964 Boehmer, Moortgat Festschrift p. 47 and pl. 11 no. 10 (photo, edition)
1965 Boehmer, Glyptik no. 553 and fig. 165 (photo, study)
1968 Nagel and Strommenger BJVF 8 pp. 152–53 and 163 no. 13 (edition, study)
1968–69 Edzard, AfO 22 p. 16 no. 24–1 (transliteration)
1990 Gelb and Kienast, Königsinschriften p. 40 S–8 (edition)

TEXT

1) *bi-in-kà-lí*-LUGAL-*rí* 2) DUMU LUGAL	1–2) Bin-kali-šarrī, the prince:
3) *i-sí-núm* 4) DUB.SAR 5) IR$_{11}$-*sú*	3–5) Isinnum, the scribe, (is) his servant.

2023

A clay bulla from Telloh bears a seal inscription of a second servant of Bin-kali-šarrī.

COMMENTARY

The bulla is in the Louvre, number AOTb. 386; the impression measures 3.2 cm in height. The inscription was collated from the published photo.

BIBLIOGRAPHY

1884–1912 de Sarzec, Découvertes 1 pp. 288–89 and fig. H (copy, translation)
1897 Thureau-Dangin, CRAIB p. 190 (translation)
1903 Thureau-Dangin, RTC no. 169 (copy)
1907 Thureau-Dangin, SAK pp. 168–69 Narâm-sin 1 (edition)
1920 Delaporte, Louvre 1 T. 36 (photo, edition, study)
1929 Barton, RISA pp. 142–43 Naram-Sin 17 (edition)
1961 Gelb, MAD 2² p. 199 Narâm-Sin Family no. 2 (study)
1963 Hirsch, AfO 20 p. 23 Narâm-Sin d 2 λ (translation)
1964 Boehmer, Moortgat Festschrift p. 48 and pl. 11 no. 13 (edition)
1965 Boehmer, Glyptik no. 644 (study)
1968 Nagel and Strommenger, BJVF 8 pp. 152–53 and 162 no. 12 (edition, study)
1968–69 Edzard, AfO 22 p. 16 no. 24–9 (transliteration)
1990 Gelb and Kienast, Königsinschriften p. 40 S–7 (edition)

TEXT

1) ^{d}*na-ra-am*-^{d}EN.ZU 2) DINGIR *a-kà-dè*.KI	1–2) Narām-Sîn, god of Agade:
3) *bi-in-kà-lí*-LUGAL-*rí* 4) DUMU-*šú*	3–4) Bin-kali-šarrī (is) his son.

5) *a-bí-i-śa*[*r*]
6) DUB.SAR
7) IR_{11}-*sú*

5–7) Abī-išar, scribe, (is) his servant.

2024

A seal of a third servant of Bin-kali-šarrī is in the British Museum.

COMMENTARY

The seal is made of quartz of the chaldedony variety (green jasper) and measures 4.1×2.7 cm. It bears the museum number BM 136842 (reg. no. 1977-6-11, 1). The inscription was collated from the published photo.

BIBLIOGRAPHY

1982 Collon, Cylinder Seals 2 no. 116 (photo, edition [by Sollberger], study)

TEXT

1) *bi-in-kà-lí*-LUGAL-*rí*
2) DUMU LUGAL
3) á-su
4) IR_{11}-*sú*

1–2) Bin-kali-šarrī, son of the king:

3–4) Asu (is) his servant.

2025

A copper bowl bears the inscription of a servant of Rigmuš-ālšu, 'son of the king'.

COMMENTARY

The bowl, which measures 5.4 cm in height and 7.5 cm in diameter, was in the Foroughi Collection in Teheran. For the reading of the princely name and its probable identification with a son of Narām-Sîn, see the comments of Gelb and Kienast, Königsinschriften p. 104 sub Narāmsîn A 4.

BIBLIOGRAPHY

1961 Ghirshman, Sept milles no. 486 (study)
1962 Dossin, IrAnt 2 p. 164 and pl. XXXIV no. 32 (photo, edition)
1962 Ghirshman, Kunstschätze no. 203 (study)
1969 Calmeyer, Datierbare Bronzen p. 28 no. 12 G (study)
1990 Gelb and Kienast, Königsinschriften p. 104 Narāmsîn A 4 (edition)

TEXT

1) *rí-ig-*⌈*mu*⌉*-úš-*⌈*al-šu*⌉
2) DUMU LUGAL
3) *iš-kà*(?)*-ru-um*
4) BA.[x]
5) IR_{11}-[*sú*]

1–2) Rigmuš-ālšu, son of the king:

3–5) Iškarum, the ..., (is) [his] servant.

Šar-kali-šarrī

E2.1.5

The Sumerian King List relates that Šar-kali-šarrī, son of Narām-Sîn, reigned 25 years. According to J.A. Brinkman's chronology, this would be 2217–2192. While over half the year names of this king are extant, relatively few royal inscriptions survive. In the following list the order of year names is unsure; it is likely, however, that year names (d) to (g), all of which deal with the construction of the Enlil temple in Nippur, are consecutive. Year names of uncertain attribution are marked with a dagger. For an inscription of Šar-kali-šarrī dating to the time when he was prince, see E2.1.4.2021.

I Year Names and Events of the Reign

(i) The Accession of the King
(a) mu lugal-a-ga-dè.KI ba-tuš-a† 'The year the king of Agade sat (on his throne)'. L. 11146: Çığ, Kramer Anniversary pp. 76 and 80 no. 4.
(b) [mu *śar-kà-lí*-LUGAL-*rí* ki-en:gi.KI-šè im-ta-e$_{11}$-da x sag-gá] ['The year Šar-kali-šarrī went down to Sumer ...'] Reconstructed from year name (c).
(c) mu *śar-kà-lí*-LUGAL-*rí* ki-en:gi.KI-šè ⸢im⸣-ta-e$_{11}$-da x sag-gá [m]u-ús-bi 'The year after Šar-kali-šarrī went down to Sumer ...' CBS 15202: Poebel, PBS 5 no. 38 and Westenholz, OSP 2 no. 100. For the connection of year names (b) and (c) with the accession of the king, see the commentary section below.

(ii) Construction of the Enlil Temple in Nippur
(d) [mu *śar-kà-lí*-LUGAL-*rí puzur$_4$-eš$_4$-tár* GÌR.NÍTA é-^{d}en-líl dù-da bí-gub-ba-a] ['The year Šar-kali-šarrī installed Puzur-Aštar as military governor to build the temple of the god Enlil'.] Reconstructed from year name (e).
(e) mu *śar-kà-lí*-LUGAL-*rí puzur$_4$-eš$_4$-tár* GÌR.NÍTA é-^{d}en-líl dù-da bí-gub-ba-a mu ab-ús-a 'The year after Šar-kali-šarrī installed Puzur-Aštar as military governor to build the temple of the god Enlil'. 6N-T662 = NBC 10619: Goetze, JAOS 88 (1968) pp. 56 and 58.
(f) [*i*]*n* 1 MU *śar-kà-lí*-LUGAL-*rí* [*úś*]-⸢*śi*$_{11}$⸣ É -^{d}*en*-⸢*líl*⸣ [*in*] NIBRU.[KI] [*íś-ku-nu*] 'The year Šar-kali-šarrī [laid the foun]dations of the temple of the god Enlil [in] Nippur'. Thureau-Dangin, RTC no. 87 (Akkadian version).
(f′)[mu] ús é-[^{d}en]-líl-ka ki ab-gar 'The [year] the foundations of the temple of [the god En]lil were laid'. N 248: Westenholz, OSP 2 no. 94 (Sumerian version).
(g) mu ús é-^{d}e[n-l]íl-ka ⸢ki⸣ ab-⸢gar-ra mu ab⸣-ús-a 'The year after the foundations of the temple of the god E[nli]l were laid'. N 6182+: Westenholz, OSP 2 no. 96.
(h) mu lugal *śar-kà-lí*-⸢LUGAL⸣-*rí* x é-^{d}⸢en-líl-ke⸣$_4$ ì-⸢DU⸣-[...] 'The year the king Šar-kali-šarrī ... the ... of the temple of the god Enlil'. Thureau-Dangin, ITT 1 no. 1114.

(iii) The Trip to the Source of the Tigris and Euphrates Rivers, the Cutting Down of Cedar Timber in the Amanus Mountains, and the Construction of the Temples of the Gods Ilaba and Annunītum in Babylon

(i) The Trip to the Source of the Tigris and Euphrates rivers. Recorded in E2.1.5.4–5.

(j) *i*[*n*] 1 MU [^{d}*śa*]*r-kà-lí*-[LU]GAL-*rí* [x].ZU.GAL [ÉŠ].DÉ.A KÙ.GI [GIŠ.ER]IN É ^{d}*en-líl* [*ib*]-*tu-qú* 'The year [Ša]r-kali-[ša]rrī ... (fashioned) a golden [*eš*]*da* vessel (and) [c]ut down [ced]ar [timber] (for) the temple of the god Enlil'. A 651 (Chicago): Luckenbill, Adab no. 117; Adab 177 (Istanbul): see Gelb and Kienast, Königsinschriften p. 55 D–33.

(k) [*i*]*n* 1 MU [^{d}*śar-k*]*à-lí*-LUGAL-*rí* [*úś-śi*$_{11}$] ⸢É⸣ *an*-⸢*nu*⸣-*ni-tim ù* ⸢É⸣ *il*-⸢*a*⸣-*ba*$_4$ *in* KÁ.DINGIR.KI *íś-ku-nu ù* ^{m}*śar-la-ak* LUGAL *gu*$_5$-*ti-im*.KI *ik-mi-ù* 'The year [Šar-k]ali-šarrī laid [the foundations] of the temple of the goddess Annunītum and of the temple of the god Ilaba in Babylon, and captured Šarlak, king of Gutium'. Thureau-Dangin, RTC no. 118; RA 4 (1898) pl. V no. 13. Adab 405 (Istanbul), see Gelb and Kienast, Königsinschriften p. 54 D–27. The construction of the Annunītum temple in Babylon is likely commemorated in E2.1.5.5.

(iv) Military Campaigns of the King

The Victory over the Amorites

(l) *in* 1 MU *śar-kà-*<*lí*>-LUGAl-<*rí*> REC 169 MAR.DÚ *iš*$_{11}$-*a-ru* 'The year Šar-kali-šarrī was victorious in battle over the Amorites. IM —: Gelb, MAD 1 no. 268.

(l′) [*i*]*n* 1 MU *śar-kà-lí*-LUGAL-*rí* MAR.DÚ-*am in ba-śa-ar*.KUR [*iš*$_{11}$-*a-ru*] 'The year Šar-kali-šarrī [was victorious over] the Amorites at Mount Bašar'. Thureau-Dangin, RTC no. 124.

(l″) ⸢*in*⸣ 1 MU *śar-kà-lí*-LUGAL-*rí* MAR.DÚ-*am* 'The year Šar-kali-šarrī (was victorious over) the Amorites'. Thureau-Dangin, RTC no. 85; RA 4 (1898) pl. VI no. 17.

The Defeat of the Elamites

(m) *in* 1 MU *śar-kà-lí*-LUGAL-*rí* REC 169 NIM.KI *ù za-ḫa-ra*.KI *in pu-ti* UD.⸢ÚḪ.KI⸣ *ù* SAG.LI *íś-ku-*[*nu*] *iš*$_{11}$-*a-*[*ru*] 'The year Šar-kali-šarrī did battle with Elam and Zaḫar opposite Akšak and ... (and) was victor[ious] (over them)'. Thureau-Dangin, RTC no. 130; RA 4 (1898) pl. VI no. 16. ITT 1 no. 1097.

(m′) ⸢*in*⸣ 1 MU *śar-kà-lí*-LUGAL-⸢*rí*⸣ ⸢REC 169⸣ NI[M.KI] *ù za-ḫa-ra*.⸢KI⸣ *iš*$_{11}$-*a-r*[*u*] 'The year Šar-kali-šarrī was victor[ious] in battle over Ela[m] and Zaḫara'. Thureau-Dangin, ITT 1 no. 1115.

Clashes with the Gutians

(n) mu REC 169 gu-ti-um.(KI) ba-gar-ra-a 'The year Gutium was defeated'. Thureau-Dangin, ITT 1 nos. 1048, 1052, 1053; RTC no. 88; RA 4 (1889) pl. V no. 15. See also year name (k) above.

(vi) Fragmentarily Preserved Year Names

(o) [*in* 1 MU] *śar-kà-lí*-L[UGAL-*rí*] ⸢x⸣ SAG x [...] '[The year] Šar-kali-š[arrī] ...' de Genouillac, ITT 2 no. 3078.

(p) [*in*] 1 MU [*śar*]-*kà-lí*-LUGAL-*rí* [x]-⸢x⸣-NI *a-kà-dè*.KI 'The year Šar-kali-šarrī, ... Agade'. L. 11143: Çığ, Kramer Anniversary pp. 76 and 79 no. 1.

(q) [*i*]*n* 1 MU ^{d}*en-líl* [^{d}*śar-k*]*à-lí*-LUGAL-*rí* [x] SU x [...]; *in* 1 MU ^{d}*en-líl* ^{d}*śar-kà-lí*-LUGAL-*rí* SU x x x x SU 'The year the god Enlil, Šar-kali-šarrī ...' Sollberger, CT 50 nos. 50–51.

(r) mu *śar-kà-lí*-⸢LUGAL⸣-*rí* lugal-a-ga-dè.KI 'The year Šar-kali-šarrī, king of Agade' NBC 10097; see Gelb and Kienast, Königsinschriften p. 57 D–40.

(s) [*i*]*n* 1 MU [*śar-kà-lí*-L]UGAL-[*rí* ...] 'The year [Šar-kali]-šarrī ...' SMN 4104: Meek, HSS 10 no. 40. This restoration is not absolutely certain; an alternative reading would be [*i*]*n* 1 MU [L]UG]AL [...]; in this case no certain attribution would be possible.

II Commentary

(i) The Accession of the King

The attribution of year name (a), in which no royal name appears, is uncertain. M. Çığ, who published the one tablet bearing this date, read its verb as ba-dab$_5$-a and understood the year name to refer to the capture of an Akkadian king, presumably Šar-kali-šarrī. However, since the Sumerian verb dab$_5$, as far as can be determined, is always complemented with -ba rather than -a, a preferred reading would be ba-tuš-a. If this be correct, the year name would likely refer to the enthronement of an Akkadian king. Since the script dates the tablet to late Sargonic times, we have tentatively assigned it to Šar-kali-šarrī, whose coronation ceremony is abundantly attested in contemporary archival sources (see below).

Year name (b), restored from (c), its mu-ús-bi formula, deals with a trip that Šar-kali-šarrī made to Sumer. The broken end of the year name has elicited various restorations from scholars. Westenholz (OSP 2 p. 203 no. 2) read: [2]-sag-gá and translated 'for the first time'. This interpretation was repeated by Volk, ZA 82 (1992) p. 23 and n. 9. Foster (JANES 12 [1980] p. 40) offered: [men?] sag-gá '(and) [the crown] upon (his) head', and Kienast (Königsinschriften p. 56 D–35) gave: ⸢ḫur?⸣-sag-gá, without translation. Foster (JANES 12 [1980] pp. 36–42) has collected and discussed numerous references in the economic texts of the period that refer to a trip Šar-kali-šarrī made to Nippur/Sumer; he has plausibly connected these references with year name (b). Foster argues that the occasion for the trip was the king's coronation as the ruler of Sumer and Akkad in Nippur. This idea is supported by Steinkeller's observation (Steinkeller, Texts Baghdad pp. 56–57) that three of the four tablets from Umma recording disbursements for the king's journey to Sumer/Nippur are dated to year 1 in the 'mu iti' dating system. He proposes that these dates refer not a local era of the city governor, as Foster argued, but rather to regnal years of the Sargonic king. By Steinkeller's understanding, the disbursements at Umma for the king's trip to Nippur would have dated to the first year of Šar-kali-šarrī.

(ii) The Construction of the Enlil Temple at Nippur

Perhaps Šar-kali-šarrī's most notable achievement was his completion of the construction work on the temple of the god Enlil at Nippur; the work begun by his father apparently lay unfinished on Narām-Sîn's death. Inscriptions E2.1.5.1–3 deal with this work. According to Westenholz (OSP 2 pp. 24–29), an archive of administrative texts from Nippur is connected with the Enlil temple's rebuilding. The task was deemed so important by Šar-kali-šarrī that he named one of his years (year name [d] in our compilation) for the installation of the military governor of Nippur responsible for the deed. The official, Puzur-Aštar, may possibly be the same man who appears as the addressee of an Old Akkadian letter published by Thureau-Dangin (RA 23 [1926] pp. 25–29). The sender of the letter, a certain Iškun-Dagān, is likely to have been a high official resident at Adab. In the letter Iškun-Dagān invokes the gods Ašgi and Ninḫursag, tutelary deities of Adab, in addition to the imperial deities Aštar and Ilaba. He is probably to be identified with the queen's majordomo at Adab, whose seal legend is edited as E2.1.5.2001 in this volume. He may be the same person whose tablet archive was found at Adab (see Yang, Sargonic Inscriptions p. 122).

Year name (h) also deals with the Enlil temple at Nippur, but its broken nature prevents us from determining what specific deed it commemorated.

(iii) The Trip to the Source of the Tigris and Euphrates Rivers, the Cutting Down of Cedar Timber in the Amanus Mountains, and the Construction of the Temples of the Gods Ilaba and Annunītum in Babylon

Šar-kali-šarrī followed in his father's footsteps by journeying to the sources of the Tigris and Euphrates rivers; the trip is mentioned in E2.1.5.4–5. He also emulated his father actions in cutting down cedar timber in the Amanus Mountains, since year name (j) in our compilation, according to a plausible restoration, records the king's cutting down of cedar trees for the Enlil temple. A similar logging expedition is described in E2.1.5.5; there the locale is specified as the Amanus Mountains, with the final destination of the wood apparently being the Aštar temple in Babylon.

The full name of the golden object which appears in a broken context at the beginning of year name (j) is uncertain. Based on the writing eš-dé found in the Nanše Hymn (Heimpel, JCS 33 [1981] p. 84 line 48), we propose a restoration [ÉŠ].DÉ.A in the year name and see here a reference to one of the large ritual vessels that were routinely constructed by the kings as lavers for the gods. The particular vessel has been discussed at some length by van Dijk (Sumerische Götterlieder pp. 127–30); he gives the various spellings of the word: šita$_x$ (REC 316), URUDU.éš-da, eš-da, to which we may add the Nanše hymn's eš-dé and the year name's [EŠ].DÉ.A. As noted, Šar-kali-šarrī journeyed to the sources of the Tigris and Euphrates rivers and, according to the evidence of E2.1.5.4, dedicated some object, apparently a commemorative of his trip, to the god Enlil on his return. The exact nature of the votive object is not known since the late tablet copy does not record its name. However, the occurrence in the inscription of the royal epithet 'cupbearer of the god Enlil' (lines 6–7) is of note. As far as can be determined, it occurs in no other Šar-kali-šarrī inscription and it may give a clue as to the nature of the object dedicated by the king. In Gudea Cylinder B (col. xvii lines 9–11) the *ešda* vessel is described in metaphorical terms: éš-da-bi da-ba gub-ba-bi I$_7$.idigna I$_7$.buranun-bi-da ḫé-gál túm-túm-àm 'its *ešda* that stands beside it is the Tigris and Euphrates rivers bringing abundance'. It would appear, then, that an *ešda* vessel would have been an apt symbol to commemorate the king's trip to the sources of the two rivers. Further, we have evidence that the *ešda* vessels were sometimes fashioned of gold; a passage from the literary composition 'Enmerkar and the Lord of Aratta' (Cohen, Enmerkar pp. 77–78 lines 315–16) reads: lugal-e eš-da kù.GI-ga-ke$_4$ en-me-er-kár dumu-^{d}utu-ke$_4$ du$_{10}$ mu-un-bad-bad-du 'The king — since the *ešda* vessels were of gold — he, Enmerkar, the son of Utu, set them wide apart'. We propose that Šar-kali-šarrī fashioned a golden *ešda* vessel to commemorate his trip to the sources of the rivers, incised the vessel with the inscription edited as E2.1.5.4 in this volume, and commemorated the event in year name (j).

Year name (k), that deals with the laying of the foundations of the temples of the gods Annunītum and Ilaba in Babylon, is likely to be connected with E2.1.5.5, an inscription that records construction work on the temple of Aštar. The equation is based on Kutscher's observation (Kutscher, Brockmon Tablets p. 47) that in Sargonic times Annunītum 'is a designation for Inanna and not the name of a separate goddess'. While E2.1.5.5 does not relate the locale of the Aštar temple whose construction it commemorates, the fact that the Neo-Babylonian tablet copy comes from Babylon suggests that the temple was located in that city. The Šar-kali-šarrī text may be compared with an almost identical inscription of Narām-Sîn (E2.1.4.29) that records construction work on an Aštar temple in an unspecified city; this text, as well, is known from tablet copy from Babylon. It too, in all likelihood, commemorated work on the Aštar temple in Babylon. As was the case for the Enlil temple at Nippur, the rebuilding of the temple was begun by Narām-Sîn and finished by his son Šar-kali-šarrī.

(iv) Military Campaigns of the King

The end of Šar-kali-šarrī's reign was a troubled period, as the Sargonic king faced ever increasing opposition from both within and outside his realm. Concrete evidence of his difficulties is found in several year names which record campaigns of the king against foreign enemies. Just as his father Narām-Sîn had confronted a coalition of Amorites and Sumerians mustered in the area of Mount Bašar to do battle against him (see E2.1.4.2 iii 1–13, vi 10–12), so year name (l) of Šar-kali-šarrī records a campaign against the Amorites in the very same area, their mountain stronghold. A greater threat, as it turned out, came from the east, where the growing menace of the Gutians had to be met. A major confrontation is recorded in year name (k); it commemorates the Sargonic king's defeat of the Gutian ruler Šarlak, a figure who may, in all likelihood, be identified with the Šarlagab of the Sumerian King List. Further battles against the Gutians are recorded in year name (n); although no royal name appears in the available exemplars of this date, it is almost certainly to be assigned to Šar-kali-šarrī. An idea of the havoc caused by the Gutian incursions at this time is provided by an Old Akkadian letter (Smith, JRAS 1932 pp. 295–30; improved translation in Oppenheim, Letters pp. 71–72). It refers to apparently frequent cattle raids made by the Gutians and the urgent measures that were taken to counter them. The Sargonic king's problems in the east were compounded by the activities of the Elamites; a battle with them in the neighbourhood of Akšak is recorded in year name (m) of Šar-kali-šarrī. Their intervention at this time is not at all unexpected; throughout Mesopotamian history Akkad's eastern neighbour was quick to extend its influence over the Diyala region when the central power was weak. Evidence of internal dissension during the latter part of Šar-kali-šarrī's reign is provided by a Sumerian letter from Lagaš edited by Volk (ZA 82 [1992] pp. 24–27). The letter, according to a probable restoration of the PN Puzur-Mama in line 3, contains an appeal of Puzur-Mama (who is elsewhere attested as governor of Lagaš in RTC 181) to Šar-kali-šarrī(?) to guarantee the territorial integrity of Lagaš in an apparent boundary dispute between that city and Ur. Subsequently, perhaps at the time of Šar-kali-šarrī's death, Puzur-Mama declared Lagašite independence; in a royal inscription issued by the erstwhile governor, he uses the title 'king of Lagaš' (E2.12.5.1). The usurpation of the power of the central authority by local governors was likely repeated in other cities of the south; unfortunately, our lack of sources for this period prevents us from clearly documenting this process. Šar-kali-šarrī was simply unable to hold together the empire that his father had managed, through brute force, to maintain as one entity. He left to the succeeding Sargonic kings a small rump state whose centre lay at the confluence of the Diyala and Tigris rivers.

1

Three inscriptions of Šar-kali-šarrī deal with work on the Enlil temple at Nippur. The first is inscribed on two diorite door sockets from Nippur.

CATALOGUE

Ex.	Museum number	Nippur provenance	Dimensions (cm)	Lines preserved	cpn
1	Philadelphia, number	Area III beneath the rooms of the Enlil temple	58×41	1–24	c
2	Istanbul(?)	In rubbish below the Ur-Nammu platform	—	1–24	n

COMMENTARY

According to Westenholz, two examples of this door socket were found; for the details concerning their findspots, see Westenholz, OSP 2 p. 23 fig. 1 nos. 42A and 42B. Ex. 1 was located on display in Philadelphia and its inscription collated; however, no museum number could be determined for it. Ex. 2 is known from Westenholz's transliteration of Haynes' field photograph IV A 31. According to Scheil (RT 15 p. 64) a tablet bearing this inscription was in Istanbul. This may possibly be a mistaken reference to exemplar 2, since Scheil does not mention actually seeing the piece. BE 1/1 pl. I gives a photo of E2.1.5.2, not E2.1.5.1; the photo is mislabelled.

BIBLIOGRAPHY

1893 Hilprecht, BE 1/1 no. 1 (ex. 1, copy)

1893 Scheil, RT 15 p. 64 (ex. 2 [?], copy, edition)

1897 Peters, Nippur 2 p. 242 (ex. 1, photo)

1907 Thureau-Dangin, SAK pp. 162–63 Šargâni-šar-ali c (exs. 1–2, edition)

1910 Radau, EBH pp. 167–69 (ex. 1, edition)

1929 Barton, RISA pp. 144–45 Sharganisharri 1 (exs. 1–2, edition)

1961 Gelb, MAD 2[2] p. 202 Šar-kali-šarrī Original Inscriptions no. 1 (ex. 1, study)

1963 Hirsch, AfO 20 p. 28 Šarkališarrī a 2 (ex. 1, study)

1987 Westenholz, OSP 2 pp. 56–57 no. 42 (exs. 1–2, edition, study)

1990 Gelb and Kienast, Königsinschriften pp. 113–14 Šarkališarrī 1 (exs. 1–2, edition)

TEXT

1) [d]*en-líl*
2) *u-kál-lim*
3) *śar-kà-lí*-LUGAL-*rí*
4) *da-núm*
5) LUGAL
6) *a-kà-dè*.KI
7) [ba]DÍM
8) *é-kur*
9) É
10) [d]*en-líl*
11) *in* NIBRU.KI
12) *ša* DUB
13) *śu*₄-*a*
14) *u-śa-sà-ku-ni*
15) [d]*en-líl*
16) *ù*
17) [d]UTU
18) *ù*
19) [d]INANNA
20) SUḪUŠ-*śu*
21) *li-sú-ḫu*
22) *ù*
23) ŠE.NUMUN-*śu*
24) *li-il-qù-tu*

1–2) The god Enlil instructed (him).

3–11) Šar-kali-šarrī, the mighty, king of Agade, builder of Ekur, temple of the god Enlil at Nippur.

12–24) As for the one who removes this inscription, may the gods Enlil, Šamaš, and Aštar tear out his foundations and destroy his progeny.

2

An inscription known from four exemplars gives a variant account of Šar-kali-šarrī's building of the Ekur temple at Nippur. For details on the provenance of the two door sockets with this inscription, see Westenholz, OSP 2 p. 23 nos. 43A and 43B.

CATALOGUE

Ex.	Museum number	Nippur provenance	Object	Dimensions (cm)	Lines preserved	cpn
1	CBS 8751	Area III beneath the rooms of the Enlil	Diorite door socket	75×41.5×17.5	1–23	c
2	Istanbul(?)	From a trench not far from ex. 1	Diorite door socket	13.2 long	—	n
3	National Museum, Copenhagen	Said to have come from Nippur	Piece of gold foil	—	1–23	p
4	CBS 14226+N 537	—	Clay tablet	7.6×4.2×1.7	1–23	c

COMMENTARY

The present location of ex. 2 is uncertain. Scheil, in a note dated at Constantinople (RT 15 pp. 86–87), refers to this inscription; in all likelihood he saw a door socket that was housed in the Imperial Ottoman Museum. We have, as yet, been unable to identify this piece in the collections of the Eşki Şark Müzesi.

BIBLIOGRAPHY

1893 Hilprecht, BE 1/1 pp. 1, 47 and pl. 2 no. 2 (exs. 1–2, composite copy, study); pl. 1 no. 1 (ex. 1, photo)
1893 Oppert, RA 3 p. 22 (exs. 1–2, edition)
1893 Scheil RT 15 pp. 86–87 (ex. 2, partial edition)
1900 Radau, EBH pp. 169–70 (exs. 1–2, edition)
1907 Thureau-Dangin, SAK Šargâni-šar-ali d (exs. 1–2, edition)
1922 Legrain, PBS 13 no. 14 (ex. 4, frgm. 1, copy, edition)
1924 Poebel, OLZ 27 265 (ex. 4, frgm. 1, study)
1929 Barton, RISA pp. 146–47 Sharganisharri 2 (exs. 1–2, edition) and 5 (ex. 4, frgm. 1, edition)
1934 Jacobsen, AS 6 pp. 26–27 (exs. 1–2 and 4, frgm. 1, edition)
1939 Jacobsen, Copenhagen no. 80 (ex. 3, photo, study)
1961 Gelb, MAD 2² p. 203 Šar-kali-šarrī Original Inscriptions no. 2 (exs. 1–4, study)
1961 Civil, JCS 15 p. 80 (ex. 4, copy)
1963 Hirsch, AfO 20 p. 28 Šarkališarrī a 3 (exs. 1–4, study)
1971 Sollberger and Kupper, IRSA IIA5a (exs. 3–4, edition)
1987 Westenholz, OSP 2 no. 43 (exs. 1–4, edition, study)
1990 Gelb and Kienast, Königsinschriften pp. 114–15 Šarkališarrī 2 (exs. 1–3, edition); pp. 281–82 Šarkališarrī C 3 (ex. 4, edition)

TEXT

1) ᵈ*šar-kà-lí*-LUGAL-*rí*
2) DUMU *da-dì* ᵈ*en-líl*
3) *da-núm*
4) LUGAL
5) *a-kà-dè*.KI
6) *ù*
7) *bù-ú-la-ti*
8) ᵈ*en-líl*
9) ᵇᵃDÍM
10) *é-kur*
11) É ᵈ*en-líl*
12) *in* NIBRU.KI

1–12) Šar-kali-šarrī, beloved son of the god Enlil, the mighty, king of Agade and of the subjects of the god Enlil, builder of Ekur, temple of the god Enlil at Nippur.

13) *ša* DUB
14) *šu*$_{4}$*-a*
15) *u-ša-sà-ku-ni*
16) ^{d}*en-líl*
17) *ù*
18) ^{d}UTU
19) SUḪUŠ-*šu*
20) *li-sú-ḫa*
21) *ù*
22) ŠE.NUMUN-*šu*
23) *li-il-qù-tá*

13–23) As for the one who removes this inscription, may the gods Enlil and Šamaš tear out his foundations and destroy his progeny.

3

Numerous brick stamps and two bricks from Nippur record the construction of Enlil's temple by Šar-kali-šarrī.

CATALOGUE

Ex.	Museum number	Excavation number	Nippur provenance	Object	Dimensions (cm)	Lines preserved	cpn
Bricks							
1	EŞ 1263	—	Found out of place on the SE side of the ziqqurrat	Stamped brick	23.5×18×8	1–2	c
1a	CBS 8637	—	As ex 1	Gypsum cast of ex. 1	As ex. 1	1–2	c
2	IM 61764	6N-T1123	At the south end of the street which runs along the west side of the ziqqurrat	Stamped brick	—	1–6	n
Stamps							
3	CBS 7165	—	—	Brick stamp	13.2×9.2	1–6	c
4	EŞ 1936		Area III, close to the SE wall of the ziqqurrat	Brick stamp	9.45×13.55×2	1–6	p
4a	CBS 8754	—		Gypsum cast of ex. 4	As ex. 3	1–6	c
5	EŞ —	—	—	Brick stamp	5.8×4.6×1.8	1	n
5a	CBS 8756	—	—	Gypsum cast of ex. 5	As ex. 5	1	c
6	CBS 8777	—	—	Brick stamp	14.0×9.4	1–6	c
7	CBS 15539	—	—	Brick stamp	14.3×9.6×1.7	1–6	c
8	UM 29-13-325	—	—	Brick stamp	14.2×9.4×1.7	1–6	c
9	L-29-306	—	—	Brick stamp	—	1–6	c
10	L-29-309	—	—	Brick stamp	14.2×9.5×1.8	1–6	c
11	HS 1968	—	—	Brick stamp	—	—	n
12	HS 1969	—	—	Brick stamp	—	—	n
13	HS 1970	—	—	Brick stamp	—	—	n
14	HS 1971	—	—	Brick stamp	—	—	n
15	HS 1972			Glazed terracotta copy of a brick stamp			
16	HS 1973	—	—	Brick stamp	—	—	n
17	HS 1974	—	—	Brick stamp	—	—	n
18	HS 1975	—	—	Brick stamp	—	—	n
19	HS 1976	—	—	Brick stamp	—	—	n
20	HS 1979	—	—	Brick stamp	—	—	n
21	HS 1980	—	—	Brick stamp	—	1–6	n
22	HS 1981	—	—	Brick stamp	—	1–6	n
23	HS 1982	—	—	Brick stamp	—	—	n
24	HS 1983	—	—	Brick stamp	—	—	n
25	HS 1984	—	—	Brick stamp	—	—	n
26	HS 1985	—	—	Brick stamp	—	—	n
27	HS 1986+1993	—	—	Brick stamp	—	—	n
28	HS 1987	—	—	Brick stamp	—	—	n

15.1 *<u>-ša-sà-ku-ni.*

Ex.	Museum number	Excavation number	Nippur provenance	Object	Dimensions (cm)	Lines preserved	cpn
29	HS 1988	—	—	Brick stamp	—	—	n
30	HS 1989	—	—	Brick stamp	—	—	n
31	HS 1992	—	—	Brick stamp	—	—	n
32	HS 1994	—	—	Brick stamp	—	—	n
33	HS 1995	—	—	Brick stamp	—	—	n
34	HS 1996	—	—	Brick stamp	—	—	n
35	HS 1997	—	—	Brick stamp	—	—	n
36	HS 1998	—	—	Brick stamp	—	—	n
37	HS 1999	—	—	Brick stamp	—	—	n
38	IM 55855	2N-382	En 18 VI 1c	Brick stamp	9.5×8.2	3–6	p
39	IM 55856	2N-469	En 13 VI 2a,	Brick stamp	7.6×4.6	—	n
40	—	2N-473	En 13 VI 1c	Brick stamp	—	—	n
41	IM 55854	2N-511	En 10 VI 2b	Brick stamp	5.8×5.5	—	n
42	—	2N-512	En 13 VI 1 b	Brick stamp	—	—	n
43	—	2N-526	En 13 VI 1b	Brick stamp	—	—	n
44	A 32679	9N-35	Pennsylvania dump west of Shaṭṭ-en-Nil	Brick stamp	8.0×9.0	—	n
45	IM 70313	9N-38	Area I dump	Brick stamp	5.4×6.2	—	n
46	Ägyptologische Staatsammlung München ÄS 5880	—	—	Brick stamp	—	—	n
47	Ägyptologische Staatsammlung München ÄS 5881	—	—	Brick stamp	—	—	n

COMMENTARY

Ex. 1a is a gypsum cast of a brick, and exs. 4a and 5a casts of brick stamps. The originals are in Istanbul, the casts in Philadelphia. Ex. 5 has not been located. Exs. 9–10, now housed in the University Museum, Philadelphia, are on loan from the Philadelphia Art Museum.

BIBLIOGRAPHY

1893 Hilprecht, BE 1/1 pp. 15 and 47 no. 3 (ex. 4, copy, edition); pl. II no. 2 (ex. 4, photo of handle)

1896 Hilprecht, BE I/2 pl. XXI no. 63 (ex. 1, photo)

1897 Peters, Nippur 2 p. 374 and facing plate (provenance, photo)

1903 Hilprecht, Explorations p. 333 (provenance)

1903 Hilprecht, Bêl-Tempel p. 52, fig. 34 (ex. 4, copy)

1907 Thureau-Dangin, SAKIpp. 162–63 Šargâni-šar-ali a) (edition)

1929 Barton, RISA pp. 146–47 Sharganisharri 3 (edition)

1934 Jacobsen, AS 6 p. 27 (edition)

1951 McCown, UMB 16/2 pl. VI (ex. 34, photo [in situ])

1961 Gelb, MAD 2[2] p. 203 Šar-kali-šarrī Original Inscriptions no. 3 (study)

1963 Hirsch, AfO 20 p. 28 Šarkališarrī a 4 (translation)

1967 McCown, Nippur I p. 25 (exs. 38–43, study)

1968 Goetze, JAOS 88 p. 55 (ex. 2, edition)

1969 Buccellati and Biggs, AS 17 p. 11 nos. 35 and 38 (exs. 44–45, study)

1969 Oelsner, WZJ 18 p. 52 no. 11 (exs. 11–37, study)

1969 ANEP[2] no. 251 (ex. 6, photo)

1976 Uzunoğlu, IESEM p. 50 no. 5 and fig. 64 a–b (ex. 4, photo, study)

1981 Michalowski, RA 75 p. 175 n. 14 (ex. 39, study)

1985 Behrens, JCS 37 p. 230 no. 3 (ex. 1a, study)

1990 Gelb and Kienast, Königsinschriften pp. 115–16 Šarkališarrī (edition) and p. 117 Šar–kališarrī 6 Text C (ex. 1, edition)

TEXT

1) *śar-kà-lí*-LUGAL-*rí*
2) LUGAL
3) *a-kà-dè*.KI
4) ^{ba}DÍM
5) É
6) ^{d}*en-líl*

1–6) Šar-kali-šarrī, king of Agade, builder of the temple of the god Enlil.

4

This inscription records the dedication of a cult object to the god Enlil on the occasion of the king's return from a trip to the sources of the Tigris and Euphrates rivers.

COMMENTARY

The inscription is found on HS 195, a reddish-brown baked tablet that measures 9.0×4.8×2.8 cm, with an original width of 6.5–7.0 cm. According to Oelsner, the tablet is probably a Neo-Babylonian copy inscribed in an archaising script. The tablet was one of a group of antiquities that were deposited in a vase; it was found during excavations of the University of Pennsylvania in the Neo-Babylonian stratum of 'Tablet Hill'. The copy gives a bilingual version in two columns, with the Sumerian on the left and the Akkadian on the right. Unfortunately, most of the Akkadian text is broken away.

The line numbering and translation follow the Sumerian version. The line count in this edition differs from that given by Oelsner. Here the text commences with line 1, and lines 4–5, 9–10, 15–16, 25–26, and 28–29 of Oelsner's edition are treated as single lines.

As noted in the comments of the introductory section for Šar-kali-šarrī, this inscription may be connected with the fashioning of a golden *ešda* vessel mentioned in year name (k).

BIBLIOGRAPHY

1903 Hilprecht, Explorations pp. 518–19 (provenance)
1969 Oelsner, WZJ 18 p. 52 no. 12 (study)
1989 Oelsner in Studies Sjöberg pp. 404–407 no. 2 (edition)

TEXT

Sumerian	Akkadian	
1) ^{d}en-líl-le	1 [^{d}*en-líl*]	1–2) The god Enlil decreed (it to him).
2) bí-du$_{11}$	2) [...]	
3) ^{d}*šar-kà-lí*-LUGAL-*rí*	3) ⸢^{d}⸣[*šar-kà-lí*-LUGAL-*rí*]	3–12) Šar-kali-šarrī, mighty king, cupbearer of the god Enlil, king of Agade, king of the subjects of the god Enlil.
4) lugal-	4) *d*[*a*!-*núm*]	
5) kalag-ga	5) [...]	
6) sagi-	6) [SAGI]	
7) ^{d}en-líl-lá	7) [^{d}*en-líl*]	
8) lugal-	8) [LUGAL]	
9) a-ga-dè.KI	9) *a-kà*-[*dè*.KI]	
10) lugal	10) *ù*	
11) un!-	11) [*bù-ú-la-ti*]	
12) ^{d}en-líl-lá	12) [^{d}*en-líl*]	
13) igi en-na	13) [...]	13–14) (The god Enlil) ... *as far as* ... *from* ...
14) x LAGAB-ta	14) [...]	
15) nigin-ta	15) x [...]	15-16) gave to him *in its entirety*.
16) in-na-an-sum	16) ⸢*i*⸣-[*dì-šum*$_6$]	
17) u$_4$ *nag-bu*	17) [*ì-nu na-gáb*]	17–22) After he reached the sources of the Tigris and Euphrates rivers,
18) i$_7$-	18) [IDIGNA].	
19) idigna	19) [I$_7$]	
20) i$_7$-	20) [*ù* BURANUN].	

8–12 Akk.: '[king of Aga]de and [of the subjects of the god Enlil]'.

Sumerian	Akkadian	Translation
21) buranun-na-bi-da	21) [I$_7$]	
22) sá-du$_{11}$-ga	22) [*ik-śu-dú*]	
23) a-né ^{d}en-líl-ra	23) *a*-[*na* ^{d}*en-líl*]	23–25) he personally dedicated (this object) to the god Enlil in Nippur.
24) nibru.KI	24) *in* [NIBRU.KI]	
25) a-mu-ru	25) A.M[U.RU]	
Colophon	Colophon	Colophon
1) 6-àm ŠID-bi	1) mu-sar-[ra]	Sum.: Its 'count' is 6.
	2) *ša* ⌜^{d}⌝[*śar-kà-lí*-LUGAL-*rí*]	Akk.: Inscription of [Šar-kali-šarrī].

5

A Neo-Babylonian tablet from Babylon gives a copy of a Šar-kali-šarrī inscription that commemorates construction work on the temple of Aštar.

COMMENTARY

The tablet, BM 38302 (80-11-12, 184), measures 9.3×6.0 cm; it was collated from a museum photo. The piece is registered as having come from Babylon. However, Sollberger has pointed out that this designation could stand for Babylonia in general in the early registers. The text shows striking similarities to E2.1.4.28 and E2.1.4.29, inscriptions of Narām-Sîn that likewise record work on the Aštar temple. As noted in the introductory section for Šar-kali-šarrī, this inscription may be connected with year name (k) of Šar-kali-šarrī.

For the reading of the temple name of line 6, see the commentary to E2.1.4.29.

BIBLIOGRAPHY

1982 Sollberger, in Studies Diakonoff pp. 345–48 (edition)
1984 Frayne, ARRIM 2 pp. 23–27 (study)
1990 Gelb and Kienast, Königsinschriften pp. 276–79 Šarkališarrī C 1 (edition)

TEXT

1) *śar-kà-lí*-LUGAL-*rí*	1–8) Šar-kali-šarrī, the mighty, king of Agade, builder of the ... of the temple of the goddess Aštar at Zabala.
2) *da-núm*	
3) LUGAL	
4) *a-kà-dè*.KI	
5) ^{ba}DÍM	
6) ⌜ki⌝.sanga$_x$(REC 170)-x-[x]	
7) É ⌜^{d}INANNA⌝	
8) *in zabala$_5$*.KI	
9) [*i*]-*nu*	9–13) [W]hen the four quarters together revolted against him,
10) *ki*-⌜*ib-ra-tum*⌝	
11) *ar-ba*-⌜*um*⌝	
12) *íś-ti-ni-íś*	
13) *i*-KIR-*ni-śu$_4$*	
14) (Traces)	14) (Traces)
15) [*íś*]-*tum-ma*	15–28) [fr]om beyond the Lower Sea as far as the Upper [S]ea, he smote the people and all the Mountain Lands for the god Enlil
16) *a-bar-ti*	
17) *ti-a-am-tim*	

14. Sollberger read: ⌜*i-nu-mi-su*⌝ for line 14. Collation of the tablet photo reveals only indistinct traces at this point. In view of the fact that *i-nu-mi-śu* does not appear in the parallel text (see E2.1.4.29 lines 7–8), we have not adopted Sollberger's reading for this line.

18) *śa-píl-tim*
19) *a-dì-ma*
20) [*t*]*i-a-am-tim*
21) ⸢*a-lí*⸣*-tim*
22) NI.ŚI$_{11}$
23) *ù*
24) ŚA.DÚ-*e*
25) *kà-la-śu-nu-ma*
26) ⸢*a-na*⸣
27) ^{d}*en-líl*
28) *u-ra-íś*

29) ⸢*ù*⸣
30) ⸢*śar-rí*⸣*-śi-in*
31) *i*[*n*] ⸢*kà-mi*⸣-[*e*]
32) *ú-śá-*⸢*rí-ib*⸣
33) *maḫ-rí-íś*
34) ^{d}*en-líl*

29–34) and brought their kings i[n] fette[rs] before the god Enlil.

35) *śar-kà-lí*-LUGAL-*rí*
36) *da-núm*
37) *in* [NAM].NIR x x x
38) ^{d}*en-líl*
39) *in* REC 169.REC 169
40) *śu$_{4}$-nu-ti*
41) *ma-na-ma*
42) *pá-ni-śu*
43) *ù-la*
44) ⸢*ú*⸣-[*ba-al*]

35–44) Šar-kali-šarrī, the mighty, by the ... au]thority of the god Enlil, sh[owed] mercy to no one in those battles.

45) *ḫa*-x-*la*-(erasure)-*áš*
46) *na-gáb*
47) IDIGNA.I$_{7}$
48) *ù*
49) NI U x
50) *na-gáb*
51) BURANUN.⸢I$_{7}$⸣
52) *ik-śu-*⸢*ud*⸣*-ma*

45–52) He reached ... the source of the Tigris River and ... the source of the Euphrates River and

53) GIŠ.⸢ERIN⸣
54) *in* ⸢*a-ma-nim*⸣
55) *ša*-BA-KI-*íś*
56) É ^{d}INANNA
57) *ib-tu-qù*

53–57) cut down cedar wood in the Amanus (Mountains) in order to ... the temple of the goddess Aštar.

58) *ša* DUB
59) *śu$_{4}$-a*
60) *u-śa-sà-ku-ni*
61) ^{d}*en-líl*
62) *ù*
63) ^{d}UTU
64) *ù*
65) ^{d}INANNA
66) SUḪUŠ-*śu*
67) *li-sú-ḫu*
68) *ù*
69) ŠE.NUMUN-*śu*
70) *li-il-qù-tu*

58–70) As for the one who removes this inscription, may the gods Enlil, Šamaš, and Aštar tear out his foundations and destroy his progeny.

Colophon
1) *a-na pí-i* NA$_{4}$.NA.RÚ.A
2) *ša* NA$_{4}$.*mar-ḫuš-za*
3) *ša ab-nam*

Colophon
1–4) According to the text of a stele of *marḫuša* stone.

37 Collation of the tablet photo reveals a clear NIR sign.

4) *ša-aṭ-ru*
5) ^md^U.GUR-*šu-mi-ib-ni*
6) DUMU LÚ *iš-šá-ak-ku*
7) *za-am-ra-am*
8) *iš-ṭú-ur*

5–8) That which was written (on) the stone, Nergal-šumī-ibni of the Iššakku family wrote out quickly.

6

An inscription known from an incompletely preserved Ur III tablet copy deals with Šar-kali-šarrī's construction of some cult object, possibly a statue, for the god Enlil.

COMMENTARY

The tablet bears the excavation number 6N-T658 and measures 5.2×7.2 cm. It was found at Nippur, locus SB 76. The tablet bears the museum number IM 61619. A cast of the original was collated by G. Frame and R. Biggs in Chicago.

Charpin (MARI 3 p. 64) suggested a restoration of iii 7 as ⌈*u-šè*⌉*-ra-bu-šu* 'who brings it in'. However, there is not sufficient space before the *ra* to accommodate ⌈*u-šè*⌉ (collation Frame and Biggs). Further, the *šu* at the end of the verb cannot be the pronominal suffix; it is written *śu* elsewhere in this text. We are presumably dealing with a verbal root r b/p š; its meaning is unclear.

BIBLIOGRAPHY

1968 Goetze, JAOS 88 pp. 55–57 (copy, edition)
1984 Charpin, MARI 3 p. 64 (study)
1990 Gelb and Kienast, Königsinschriften pp. 279–81 Šarkališarrī C 2 (edition)

TEXT

Col. i
1) ^d^*en-líl*
2) LUGAL
3) *ì-li*

i 1–3) For the god Enlil, king of the gods.

4) ^d^*śar-kà-lí*-LUGAL-*rí*
5) ⌈DUMU *da*⌉*-dì-śu*
Lacuna

i 4–5) Šar-kali-šarrī, his beloved son,
Lacuna

1′) [*maḫ-rí-íś*]
2′) [^d^*en-líl*]

1′–2′) [before the god Enlil],

Col. ii
1) *a-bí*-⌈*śu*⌉
2) *a-na* NIBRU.KI
3) *è-la-kam*
4) *al-śu*
5) *i-za-az**

ii 1–5) his father — he used to go to Nippur and *stand beside* him.

6) *ma-na-ma*
7) *śi-ṭì-i*[*r-ti*]
8) É ^d^[*en-líl*]

ii 6–11) As for the one who remo[ves my] inscript[ion] (from) the temple of the god [Enlil] and [p]u[ts] [his] name (instead, or)

ii 5 Text: AD.

9) *u-śa-*[*sà-ku-ma*]
10) ⸢MU⸣-[*śu*]
11) [*i-sá-kà-nu-ma*]
12) [*a-na* LÚ *na-ak-rí-im*]
13) [MU]
Col. iii
1) [*śar-kà-lí*]-LUG[AL-*rí*]
2) *śu-sí-i*[*k*]
3) *śu-mi*
4) *śu-ṭur*
5) *i-qá-ab-*[*bi*]-⸢*ù*⸣
6) *ù lu in na-ab-šè-ì-śu*
7) ⸢x⸣-*ra-bu-šu*
8) ^{d}*en-líl*
9) LUGAL
10) ⸢*ì*⸣-*li*
Col. iv
1) [...] x
2) [...] x
3) [...]
4) [*di-in*]-*sú*
5) [*li-dì*]-*na*
6) [ŠE.NUMUN-]*śu*
7) *li-il-qù-*[*t*]*á*(?)
Colophon
1) DU.DU-ta ⸢sar⸣-[ra]
2) ^{d}*śar-kà-*⸢*lí*⸣-LUGAL-⸢*rí*⸣

ii 12 – iii 7) who says [to a foreigner]: 'Remove [the name of Šar-kali]-šar[rī] and write my name (instead)', or who ... in his storehouse,

iii 8 – iv 7) may the god Enlil, king of the gods, [and the god DN dec]ide his [case] (and) destroy [hi]s [progeny].

Colophon
1–2) Written on (its) base: Šar-kali-šarrī.

7

A brick stamp bears the three-line standard inscription of Šar-kali-šarrī.

COMMENTARY

The terracotta brick stamp measures 9.2×6.9×1.9 cm and bears the museum number YBC 2310. While Gelb and Kienast included the brick fragment published as BE 1/2 pl. XXI no. 63 as a further exemplar of this inscription (their Text C), we have listed the brick instead as a duplicate of E2.1.5.3. The inscription was collated.

BIBLIOGRAPHY

1937 Stephens, YOS 9 no. 7 (copy)
1961 Gelb, MAD 2^{2} p. 203 Šar-kali-šarrī Original Inscriptions no. 6 (study)
1963 Hirsch, AfO 20 p. 28 Šarkališarrī a 5 (transliteration)
1988 Beckman, ARRIM 6 p. 1 (study)
1990 Gelb and Kienast, Königsinschriften p. 117 Šarkališarrī 6 Text A (edition)

TEXT

1) *śar-kà-lí-*LUGAL-*rí*
2) LU[G]AL
3) ⸢*a*⸣-*kà-dè*.KI

1–3) Šar-kali-šarrī, ki[n]g of Agade.

8

A vase and a bowl bear the standard three-line inscription of Šar-kali-šarrī.

CATALOGUE

Ex.	Museum number	Provenance	Dimensions (cm)	Lines preserved	cpn
1	Allard Pierson Museum B	Unknown	—	1–3	n
2	Bible Lands Museum (Jerusalem)	Unknown	3.6 high 6.8 dia.	1–3	p

BIBLIOGRAPHY

1973 Stol, in van Voss, et al., Van Beitel tot Penseel p. 6 no. M5 (ex. 1, transliteration)
1981 Sweet, in Muscarella, Ladders no. 34 (ex. 2, photo, edition)
1987 Westenholz in Merhav, Treasures no. 19 (ex. 2, photo, translation)
1990 Gelb and Kienast, Königsinschriften p. 117 Šarkališarrī 6 Text B (ex. 1, edition)

TEXT

1) *śar-kà-lí*-LUGAL-*rí*
2) LUGAL
3) *a-kà-dè*.KI

1–3) Šar-kali-šarrī, king of Agade.

9

A mace head with a votive inscription of Šar-kali-šarrī was found in excavations at Sippar.

COMMENTARY

The pink marble mace head bears the museum number BM 91146 and the registration number 83-1-18, 700. It measures 6.6 cm in height and 5.7 cm in diameter. The inscription was collated by G. Frame.

BIBLIOGRAPHY

1883–84 Pinches, PSBA 6 pp. 11–12 (copy in typescript, edition)
1883–84 Rylands, PSBA 6 p. 68 (copy)
1885 Pinches, TSBA 8 p. 348 (copy in typescript, edition) and pl. 4 facing p. 182 no. 1 (photo)
1892 Winckler, KB 3/1 pp. 100–101 no. 1 (edition)
1892 Winckler and Böhden, ABK no. 64 (copy)
1897 Rassam, Asshur p. 277 note at page bottom (study)
1899 Ball, Light pp. 51–52 (photo, copy, translation)
1905 King, CT 21 pl. 1 BM 91146 (copy)
1907 Thureau-Dangin, SAK pp. 162–63 Šargâni-šar-ali b (edition)
1910 King, Early History p. 218 and pl. facing, top (photo, study)
1922 BM Guide[3] p. 19 no. 2 (copy) and p. 83 no. 13 (photo)

1929 Barton, RISA pp. 146–47 Sharganisharri 6 (edition)
1961 Gelb, MAD 2² p. 203 Original Inscriptions no. 4 (study)
1963 Hirsch, AfO 20 p. 28 Šarkališarrī a 1 (study)
1968 Solyman, Götterwaffen no. 239 (photo)
1971 Sollberger and Kupper, IRSA IIA5b (translation)
1980 Walker and Collon in de Meyer, (ed.), Tell ed-Dēr 3 pp. 100–101 no. 45 (study)
1990 Gelb and Kienast, Königsinschriften p. 115 Šarkališarrī 3 (edition)

TEXT

1) *śar-kà-lí*-LUGAL-*rí*	1–3) Šar-kali-šarrī, king of Agade,
2) LUGAL	
3) *a-kà-dè*.KI	
4) *a-na*	4–6) for the god Šamaš at Sippar
5) ^{d}UTU	
6) *in* ZIMBIR(AN.UD.KIB.NUN).KI	
7) A.MU.RU	7) dedicated (this mace).

10

A Neo-Babylonian clay tablet bearing the impression of an original inscription of Šar-kali-šarrī is in the University Museum, Philadelphia.

COMMENTARY

The tablet, a purchased piece of unknown provenance, measures 6.2×4.2×1.2 cm and bears the museum number CBS 16106. The inscription was collated. The tablet colophon indicates that the original, apparently round, object from which the impression was made came from the palace of Narām-Sîn in the city of Agade. The size of the impression indicates that the original object was too big to be a seal and too small to be a door socket. A scribe by the name Nabû-zēru-līšir dates to the time of Nabonidus (see Joannès, NABU 1988 no. 55; Beaulieu, Nabonidus pp. 141–42). As Joannès and Beaulieu have pointed out, he likely was the scribe mentioned in this inscription. The impression of the original inscription, as one would expect, appears in 'mirror writing', the colophon in normal writing. The meaning of *asarru* in line 2 of the colophon is uncertain.

BIBLIOGRAPHY

1903 Hilprecht, Explorations p. 517 (photo of obv., study)
1912 Clay, MJ 3 pp. 23–25 (photo, edition)
1914 Clay, Art and Archaeology I pp. 29–31 (photo, translation, study)
1914 Poebel, PBS 4/1 p. 198 n. 1 (partial edition)
1927 Unger, AuBK p. 95 fig. 5f (photo)
1933 Unger, RLA 2/1 p. 25 (study)
1961 Gelb, MAD 2² p. 203 Šar-kali-šarrī Original Inscriptions no. 5 (study)
1963 Hirsch, AfO 20 p. 30 Šarkališarrī B b (study)
1971 Sollberger and Kupper, IRSA IIA5c (translation)
1990 Gelb and Kienast, Königsinschriften pp. 116–17 Šarkališarrī 5 (edition)
1989 Beaulieu, Nabonidus, pp. 141–42 (study)

TEXT

1) ^{d}*śar-kà-lí*-LUGAL-*rí*	1–5) Šar-kali-šarrī, the mighty, king of the subjects of the god Enlil.
2) *da-núm*	
3) LUGAL	
4) *bù-ú-la-ti*	
5) ^{d}*en-líl*	

Colophon
1) [*z*]*i-i-pa a-gur-ru* NA$_4$.ESI
2) *ša a-sa-ar-ru pa-li-su-tim*
3) *ša i-na* É.GAL ⌈*a*⌉*-sa-ar-ru*
4) *ša* ^{d}*na-ra-am-*^{d}EN.ZU LUGAL
5) *i-na qé-er-ba a-kà-dè*.KI
6) ^{md}AG-ŠE.NUMUN-SI.SÁ DUB.SAR *i-mu-ru*

Colophon
1–6) Impression from a diorite slab of the *asarrus* which Nabû-zēru-līšir, scribe, found in the *asarru* palace of Narām-Sîn, the king, in Agade.

2001

Various Sargonic archival sources provide us with the name of Šar-kali-šarrī's queen, Tūta-šar-libbiš ('She has found the king of her heart' — presumably an assumed marriage name). Impressions of the seals of three of her majordomos are known. The first of these belongs to Iškun-Dagān; his seal impression is conserved in the Yale collections.

COMMENTARY

The clay tag, which has two impressions of the seal, bears the museum number NBC 4142. The inscription was collated from the published photo. For the possible identification of this Iškun-Dagān as the sender of an Old Akkadian letter, see the introductory remarks for Šar-kali-šarrī, comments to section (ii).

BIBLIOGRAPHY

1971 Hallo, RLA 3/9 p. 710 (study)

1981 Buchanan and Hallo, Early Near Eastern Seals no. 429 (photo, edition)

TEXT

1) ^{d}*śar-kà-lí*-LUGAL-*rí*
2) LUGAL
3) *bù-u-la-ti*
4) ^{d}*en-líl*
5) *tu-tá-śar-li-bí-íś*
6) NIN
7) *íś-ku-un-*^{d}*da-gan*
8) DUB.[SAR]
9) ŠABRA [É]-*ti*-[*śa*]
10) ÌR-[*sà*]

1–4) Šar-kali-šarrī, king of the subjects of the god Enlil.

5–6) Tūta-šar-libbiš, the queen:

7–10) Iškun-Dagān, scr[ibe] and her major[d]omo, (is) [her] servant.

2002

The impression of a seal of the majordomo of queen Tūta-šar-libbiš appears twice on a clay bulla from ancient Adab.

COMMENTARY

The bulla was found during excavations of Banks in mound III at Bismāyā. It now bears the museum number A 1167 (Chicago); the inscription was collated.

BIBLIOGRAPHY

1910 Ward, Seals p. 26 no. 5 and fig. 48 (copy, study)
1912 Banks, Bismya p. 302 (study)
1961 Gelb, MAD 2² p. 203 Šar-kali-šarrī Family no. 2 (study)
1964 Boehmer, Moortgat Festschrift p. 52 and pl. 13 no. 28 (copy, edition)
1965 Boehmer, Glyptik no. 560 (study)
1968 Nagel and Strommenger, BJVF 8 pp. 154–55 and 166 no. 24 (edition, study)
1968 Edzard, AfO 22 p. 16 nos. 24–25 (transliteration)
1977 Zettler in Gibson and Biggs, Seals pp. 36 and 38 n. 5 (translation, transliteration, study)
1981 Michalowski, RA 75 p. 176 (edition)
1986 Yang, Sargonic Archive pp. 16 and 49 n. 50 (edition)
1990 Gelb and Kienast, Königsinschriften p. 44 S–23 (edition)

TEXT

1) [*ś*]*ar-kà-lí*-LUGAL-*rí*
2) [L]UGAL
3) *a-kà-dè*.KI
4) *tu-tá-śar* ⸢*li-bí-íś*⸣
5) NIN
6) ⸢*i-śar-be-lí*⸣
7) ⸢ŠABRA⸣ [É]-*ti*-⸢*śa*⸣
8) ⸢IR₁₁-*sà*⸣

1–3) Šar-kali-šarrī, king of Agade.

4–5) Tūta-šar-libbiš, the queen:

6–8) Išar-bēlī, [her] majordomo, (is) [her] ser[vant].

2003

A clay bulla from Telloh is impressed with the seal of Dada, a third majordomo of Tūta-šar-libbiš.

COMMENTARY

The bulla, which has an impression of the seal on the front and the back, bears the museum number AOTb 375 (Louvre). It measures 4.2 cm in height. The inscription appears in four separate boxes, as is indicated in the edition; it was collated from the published photo.

BIBLIOGRAPHY

1884–1912 de Sarzec, Découvertes 1 pp. 281–83 and fig. B (copy, study) and 2 pl. 32bis no. 6 (photo)
1898 Heuzey, RA 4 pp. 4–7 (copy, study)
1903 Thureau-Dangin, RTC no. 161 (copy)
1907 Thureau-Dangin, SAK pp. 164–65 Šargâni-šar-ali e (edition)
1910 Delaporte, Bibliothèque Nationale pp. XXV–XVI no. 1 (study)
1910 Ward, Seals p. 26 no. 2 and fig. 45 (copy, study)
1920 Delaporte, Louvre 1 T. 107 (photo, edition, study)
1928–29 Meissner, AfO 5 pl. VII no. 2 (copy)
1929 Barton, RISA pp. 146–47 Sharganisharri 7 (edition)
1961 Gelb, MAD 2² p. 203 Šar-kali-šarrī Family no. 1 (study)
1963 Hirsch, AfO 20 p. 29 Šarkališarrī d 2 α (translation, study)
1964 Boehmer, Moortgat Festschrift p. 54 and pl. 14 no. 34 (photo, edition)
1965 Boehmer, Glyptik no. 1513 and fig. 657 (photo, copy, study)
1968 Nagel and Strommenger, BJVF 8 pp. 154–55 and 165 no. 23 (edition, study)
1968–69 Edzard, AfO 22 p. 16 no. 24–23 (transliteration)
1990 Gelb and Kienast, Königsinschriften p. 44 S–24 (edition)

TEXT

(Middle)
1) *śar-kà-lí*-LUGAL-*rí*
2) *da-núm*
3) LUGAL
4) *a-kà-dè*.KI
(Bottom)
5) *tu-tá-śar-li-bí-íś*
(Top)
6) [*na*]-*ra-ma-at*
7) [L]UGAL
(Right)
8) da-da
9) ŠABRA
10) É-x [(x)]
11) ⌜IR$_{11}$⌝-x

1–4) Šar-kali-šarrī, the mighty, king of Agade,

5) Tūta-šar-libbiš,

6–7) [be]loved of the [k]ing:

8–11) Dada, ... majordomo, (is) [her(?)] servant.

2004

The impression of the seal of Lugal-ušumgal, governor of Lagaš under Šar-kali-šarrī, is found on five clay bullae from Telloh.

COMMENTARY

The bullae bear the museum numbers AOTb 377, 377bis, 377ter, 390, and 930bis. The inscription was collated from the published photos. For a seal inscription of Lugal-ušumgal as governor under Narām-Sîn, see E2.1.4.2004.

BIBLIOGRAPHY

1884–1912 de Sarzec, Découvertes 1 pp. 283–84 and fig. C (copy, translation, study)
1898 Heuzey, RA 4 pp. 8–9 (copy)
1903 Thureau-Dangin, RTC no. 162 (copy, translation)
1907 Thureau-Dangin, SAK pp. 164–65 Šargâni-šar-ali f (edition)
1910 Ward, Seals p. 26 no. 3 and fig. 46 (copy, study)
1913 Jeremias, HAOG p. 56 and fig. 30 (study, drawing)
1920 Delaporte, Louvre 1 T. 106 (photo, edition, study)
1929 Barton, RISA pp. 146–47 Sharganisharri 8 (edition)
1939 Frankfort, Cylinder Seals pp. 9 and 99 fig. 31 (copy, translation)
1961 Gelb, MAD 2^2 p. 203 Officials, etc. no. 6 (study)
1963 Hirsch, AfO 20 pp. 29–30 Šarkališarrī d 2 β (translation, study)
1964 Boehmer, Moortgat Festschrift pp. 53–54 and pl. 13 no. 33 (photo, edition)
1965 Boehmer, Glyptik no. 1046 and fig. 432 (photo, study)
1968 Nagel and Strommenger, BJVF 8 pp. 154–55 and 164 no. 19 (edition, study)
1968–69 Edzard, AfO 22 p. 16 no. 24–21 (transliteration)
1987 Collon, First Impressions no. 537 (copy, translation)
1990 Gelb and Kienast, Königsinschriften p. 46 no. S–32 (edition)

TEXT

1) [*śa*]*r-kà-lí*-LUGAL-*rí*
2) *da-núm*
3) LUGAL
4) *a-kà-dè*.KI
5) ⌜lugal⌝-ušumgal
6) ÉNSI
7) *lagaš*.KI
8) ÌR$_{11}$-*sú*

1–4) [Ša]r-kali-šarrī, the mighty, king of Agade:

5–8) Lugal-ušumgal, governor of Lagaš, (is) his servant.

2005

Impressions of a seal of Lugal-giš, governor of Adab under Šar-kali-šarrī, are found on three clay bullae from Adab.

COMMENTARY

The bullae bear the museum numbers Adab 767, 768, and 774 (Istanbul). The first two were collated from the published photos. For impressions of seals of servants of Lugal-giš that may date to a period of Adab independence, see E2.9.2.2001–2002. There is no conclusive evidence (contra Gelb and Kienast, Königsinschriften p. 46 S–30) to indicate that the Lugal-giš whose name appears in a seal inscription on a bulla from Girsu (Thureau-Dangin, RTC no. 177) was a functionary of Šar-kali-šarrī.

BIBLIOGRAPHY

1947 Kraus, JCS 1 p. 101 (study)
1952 Gelb, MAD 2² p. 203 Šar-kali-šarrī Officials, etc. no. 5 (study)
1964 Boehmer, Moortgat Festschrift p. 53 and pl. 13 no. 30 (photo, edition)
1965 Boehmer, Glyptik no. 688 and fig. 214 (photo, edition, study)
1968 Nagel and Strommenger, BJVF 8 pp. 154–55 and 166 no. 26 (edition, study)
1968–69 Edzard, AfO 22 p. 16 no. 24–20 (transliteration)
1986 Yang, Sargonic Archive p. 49 and n. 49 (edition, study)
1989 Yang, Sargonic Inscriptions p. 30 and n. 53 (edition, study)
1990 Gelb and Kienast, Königsinschriften p. 46 S–29 (edition)

TEXT

1) [*š*]*ar-kà-lí*-LUGAL-*rí*
2) DINGIR UR.SAG
3) *a-kà-dè*.KI
4) lugal-giš
5) DUB.SAR
6) É[NSI]
7) *ad*[*ab*.KI]
8) IR_{11}-[*sú*]

1–3) [Š]ar-kali-šarrī, god, hero of Agade:

4–8) Lugal-giš, scribe and go[vernor] of Ad[ab, (is) his] servant.

2006

A stone bowl fragment bears an inscription informing us that the *šangû* priest of the city of Niqqum dedicated it for king Šar-kali-šarrī.

COMMENTARY

The bowl fragment was purchased by Frankfort; it is reported to have come from Khafajah. The piece now bears the museum number A 7162 (Chicago). The inscription was collated by R. Biggs.

BIBLIOGRAPHY

1939 Feigin, JAOS 59 pp. 107–108 (partial study, edition)
1961 Gelb, MAD 2[2] p. 204 Šar-kali-šarrī Officials, etc. no. 10 (study)
1963 Hirsch, AfO 20 p. 29 Šarkališarrī d 1 α (study)
1990 Gelb and Kienast, Königsinschriften pp. 117–18 Šarkališarrī B 1 (edition)

TEXT

1) *śar-kà-lí*-LUGAL-*rí*
2) ⸢LUGAL⸣
3) [*a-kà-dè*.KI]
4) [...]
5) [...]
6) [...]
7) [...]
8) [SA]NGA ⸢*ni*⸣-*q*[*um*.KI]
9) [A].MU.RU
10) [*i*]*n ni-qum*.KI

1–6) Šar-kali-šarrī, king [of Agade]: ...

7–10) [PN, *šan*]*gû* priest of (the city of) Niqq[um], dedicated (this bowl), [i]n Niqqum.

2007

The impression of a seal of a servant of Šar-kali-šarrī, whose name is not entirely preserved, but which is probably to be read as Lipit-ilī, is found on a clay bulla that was found in excavations of de Sarzec at Telloh.

COMMENTARY

The bulla, which bears the museum number AOTb 376, measures 3.1 cm across. The inscription was collated from the published photo.

BIBLIOGRAPHY

1884–1912 de Sarzec, Découvertes 1 p. 281 and fig. A (copy, translation, study)
1898 Heuzey, RA 4 pp. 3–4 (copy, translation, study)
1903 Thureau-Dangin, RTC no. 163 (copy)
1907 Thureau-Dangin, SAK pp. 164–65 Šargâni-šar-ali g (edition)
1910 Ward, Seals pp. 25–26 no. 1 and fig. 44 (copy, study)
1920 Delaporte, Louvre 1 T. 38 (photo, edition, study)
1929 Barton, RISA pp. 148–49 Sharganisharri 9 (edition)
1961 Gelb, MAD 2[2] p. 203 Šar-kali-šarrī Officials, etc. no 4 (study)
1963 Hirsch, AfO 20 p. 30 Šarkališarrī d 2 γ (translation, study)
1964 Boehmer, Moortgat Festschrift p. 53 and pl. 13 no. 32 (photo, edition)
1965 Boehmer, Glyptik no. 747 and fig. 248 (photo, study)
1967 Boehmer, ZA 58 p. 306 fig. 5 (photo)
1968 Nagel and Strommenger, BJVF 8 pp. 154–55 and 165 no. 22 (edition, study)
1968–69 Edzard, AfO 22 p. 16 no. 24–22 (transliteration)
1990 Gelb and Kienast, Königsinschriften p. 45 S–28 (edition)

TEXT

1) *śar-kà-lí*-LUGAL-*rí*
2) LUGAL
3) ⸢*a-kà-dè*⸣.KI

1–3) Šar-kali-šarrī, king of Agade:

4) [l]i-⌈pi₅⌉-[i]t-⌈i⌉-li
5) DUMU śum₆-ᵈma-li[k]
6) GÌR.NÍT[A]
7) IR₁₁-[sú]

4–7) Lipit-ilī, son of Šum-Mali[k], the gener[al], (is) [his] servant.

2008

A clay bulla from Telloh was impressed with the the seal of Adda, scribe and servant of Šar-kali-šarrī.

COMMENTARY

The bulla bears the museum number AOTb 379; two of its sides are impressed with the seal. The inscription was collated from the published photo.

BIBLIOGRAPHY

1897 Thureau-Dangin, RA 4 p. 76 and pl. VII no. 21 (copy, edition)
1903 Thureau-Dangin, RTC no. 164 (copy)
1920 Delaporte, Louvre 1 T. 39 (photo, edition, study)
1961 Gelb, MAD 2² p. 203 Šar-kali-šarrī Officials, etc. no. 9 (study)
1963 Hirsch, AfO 20 p. 30 Šarkališarrī d 2 δ (translation)
1964 Boehmer, Moortgat Festschrift p. 52 and pl. 13 no. 29 (photo, edition)
1965 Boehmer, Glyptik no. 647 (study)
1968 Nagel and Strommenger, BJVF 8 pp. 154–55 and 165 no. 21 (edition, study)
1968–69 Edzard, AfO 22 p. 16 no. 24–26 (transliteration)
1990 Gelb and Kienast, Königsinschriften p. 45 S–25 (edition)

TEXT

1) śa[r-kà]-⌈lí-LUGAL-rí⌉
2) LUGAL
3) [a-k]à-⌈dè.KI⌉
4) ad-⌈da DUB.SAR⌉
5) ⌈IR₁₁-sú⌉

1–3) Ša[r-ka]li-šarrī, king of [Ag]ade:

4–5) Adda, the scribe, (is) his servant.

2009

The name of a servant of Šar-kali-šarrī appears on a clay sealing found in excavations of Banks at Bismāyā.

COMMENTARY

The sealing bears the museum number A 917 (Chicago). Concerning the provenance of the piece, we may note the comments of R. Zettler (in Gibson and Biggs, Seals p. 38): 'In a popular account of the excavations, Bismya or the Lost City of Adab (New York, 1912) the excavator, Edgar James Banks, states that this bulla came from a brick-paved floor in the so-called Semitic Quarter (cf. pp. 300–301 of that book). Banks, in a report (dated March 1, 1904) to R.F. Harper, states that the sealing was found on February 28, 1904, and that it came from 'the court of Palace III less than a meter below the surface ...' (The III here apparently refers to Mound III on the site plan published on page 152 of his book). The inscription was collated by R. Biggs who indicates that there is a clear *kir* sign in line 4; some commentators had read the sign as *ši*. For other examples of the PN of line 4, see Gelb, MAD 3 p. 150.

BIBLIOGRAPHY

1910 Ward, Seals p. 26 no. 4 and fig. 47 (copy, study)
1961 Gelb, MAD 2[2] p. 203 Šar-kali-šarrī Officials, etc. no. 3 (study)
1964 Boehmer, Moortgat Festschrift p. 52 and pl. 13 no. 27 (copy, edition)
1965 Boehmer, Glyptik no. 646 (study)
1968 Nagel and Strommenger, BJVF 8 pp. 154–55 and 164 no. 20 (edition, study)
1968–69 Edzard, AfO 22 p. 16 no. 24–24 (transliteration)
1977 Zettler, in Gibson and Biggs, Seals pp. 33 and 38 n. 2 (provenance, translation, study)
1986 Yang, Sargonic Archive pp. 16 and 49 (edition)
1989 Yang, Sargonic Inscriptions p. 350 (transliteration)
1990 Gelb and Kienast, Königsinschriften p. 45 S–27 (edition)

TEXT

1) *śar-kà-lí*-LUGAL-*rí*
2) LUGAL
3) *a-kà-dè*.KI
4) *kir-ba-núm*
5) DUB.SA[R]
6) IR_{11}-*s*[*ú*]

1–3) Šar-kali-šarrī, king of Agade:

4–6) Kirbānum, the scri[be], (is) h[is] servant.

2010

The seal of Ibni-šarrum, servant of Šar-kali-šarrī, which was formerly in the Collection de Clercq, is now conserved in the Louvre.

COMMENTARY

The seal measures 4.0×2.6 cm; it bears the museum number AO 22303. The inscription was collated from the published photo.

BIBLIOGRAPHY

1877 Menant, CRAIB pp. 330–32 (copy, edition)
1883–84 Pinches, PSBA 6 p. 12 (copy in typescript, edition)
1883 Ménant, Glyptique 1 pp. 73–75 and fig. 34 (copy, translation, study)
1885 Pinches, TSBA 8 p. 349 (copy in typescript, edition)
1888 de Clercq, Collection 1 pp. 49–50 no. 46 (copy, edition, study)
1892 Winckler, KB 3/1 pp. 100–101 no. 2 (edition)
1892 Winckler and Böhden, ABK no. 65 (copy)
1907 Thureau-Dangin, SAK pp. 164–65 Šargâni-šar-ali h (edition)
1910 King, Early History pp. 217–18 (study)
1910 Ward, Seals p. 20 fig. 26 and p. 21 no. 1 (copy, study)
1927 Dussaud, RHR 95 pp. 17–18 (drawing, study)
1929 Barton, RISA pp. 148–49 Sharganisharri 10 (edition)
1929 Jeremias, HAOG[2] fig. 13 (photo)
1939 Frankfort, Cylinder Seals pl. XVII c (photo)
1961 Gelb, MAD 2[2] p. 203 Šar-kali-šarrī Officials, etc. no. 1 (study)
1963 Hirsch, AfO 20 p. 30 Šarkališarrī d 2 ε (translation)
1964 Boehmer, Moortgat Festschrift p. 53 and pl. 13 no. 31 (photo, edition)
1965 Boehmer, Glyptik no. 724 and fig. 232 (photo, study)
1968 Nagel and Strommenger BJVF 8 pp. 154–55 and 166 no. 25 (edition, study)
1968–69 Edzard, AfO 22 p. 16 no. 24–19 (transliteration)
1969 Frankfort, Art and Architecture[4] pl. 45 d (photo)
1969 ANEP[2] no. 682 (photo)
1971 Sollberger and Kupper, IRSA IIA5f (translation)
1976 Amiet, L'art d'Agadé no. 73 (photo, edition, study)
1982 André-Leicknam, Naissance de l'écriture no. 273 (photo, translation)
1987 Collon, First Impressions no. 529 (photo, translation, study)
1990 Gelb and Kienast, Königsinschriften p. 45 S–26 (edition)

TEXT

1) ᵈ*śar-kà-lí*-LUGAL-*rí*
2) LUGAL
3) *a-kà-dè*.KI
4) *ib-ni*-LUGAL
5) DUB.SAR
6) IR$_{11}$-*sú*

1–3) Šar-kali-šarrī, king of Agade:

4–6) Ibni-šarrum, the scribe, (is) his servant.

2011

A poorly preserved cylinder seal bears an inscription that should be attributed to a servant of Šar-kali-šarrī.

COMMENTARY

The seal is made of shell and measures 2.5 cm in diameter. It is numbered 237 in the Morgan Collection of Seals and Tablets. The inscription was collated from a photo kindly provided by D. Logie.

BIBLIOGRAPHY

1920 Ward, Morgan p. 54 and pl. XIII no. 90 (photo, study)
1948 Porada, Corpus no. 237 (photo, edition, study)
1965 Boehmer, Glyptik no. 954 (study)
1968–69 Edzard, AfO 22 p. 16 no. 24–27 (transliteration)

TEXT

1) ⌜*śar*⌝(?)-*k*[*à*(?)-*lí*]
2) LU[GAL-*rí*]
3) LU[GAL (x)]

1–3) Šar-k[ali]-ša[rrī], ki[ng (x)].

2012

A votive inscription of a servant of Šar-kali-šarrī is incised on a bronze bowl in the Metropolitan Museum, New York.

COMMENTARY

The bowl, which was formerly in the possession of Kelekian in New York, now bears the museum number MMA 48.178.2. Muscarella (Bronze and Iron, p. 337) points out that the claimed provenance of the bowl, Luristan, is uncertain. The bowl measures 5.4 cm in height. In line 5, *ir-śa-tim* is understood to be the plural of *eršu*(*m*) 'bed'. The inscription, which was collated from the published photo, may be a first millennium copy.

BIBLIOGRAPHY

1934 Pope, Bulletin of the American Institute for Persian Art and Archaeology 7 p. 20
1938–39 Langdon, in Pope, Survey 1 p. 281 no. II and fig. 69 (copy, drawing, edition)
1941 Herzfeld, Iran in the Ancient East p. 115 and fig. 227
1957 Hallo, Royal Titles pp. 59–60 (study)
1961 Gelb, MAD 2² p. 203 Šar-kali-šarrī Officials, etc. no. 2 (study)
1969 Calmeyer, Datierbare Bronzen p. 29 no. 12 J and fig. 28 (drawing, translation, study) and p. 162 no. 6 (transliteration)
1971 Sollberger and Kupper, IRSA IIA5e (translation)
1988 Muscarella, Bronze and Iron no. 468 (photo)
1990 Gelb and Kienast, Königsinschriften p. 119 Šarkališarrī B 4 (edition)

TEXT

1) ᵈ*śar-kà-lí*-LUGAL-*rí*
2) *da-núm*
3) DINGIR *ma-ti* URI(*).KI
4) *i-śar*-DI.KU₅-*ni*
5) *šu ir-śa-tim*
6) IR₁₁-*sú*

1–3) Šar-kali-šarrī, the mighty, god of the land of *Akkad*:

4–6) Išar-daiiānī, the *chamberlain*, (is) his servant.

2013

A hemispherical bowl is incised with a votive inscription of a servant of Šar-kali-šarrī.

COMMENTARY

The bronze or copper bowl was found at Piravend about five miles north of Tak-i-Bostan in Iran, and is now in Philadelphia, museum number UM 30-38-59. The bowl measures 12 cm in diameter and 6.5 cm in height. The inscription was collated. For the PN of line 4, see Gelb, MAD 3 p. 137.

BIBLIOGRAPHY

1931 Legrain, UMB 2/6 p. 199 (translation)
1931–32 Weidner, AfO 7 p. 138 (study)
1932 Pope, ILN Oct. 29. p. 667 fig. 9 (photo)
1932–33 Weidner, AfO 8 pp. 258–259 and fig. 6a (copy, edition)
1934 Legrain, Luristan Bronzes p. 19 and pl. XXIII no. 61 (photo, edition)
1935–36 Sarre, AfO 10 pp. 293–94 (study)
1938–39 Langdon, in Pope, Survey 1 p. 280 no. I (edition)
1938–39 Pope, Survey 7 pl. 25A (photo)
1961 Gelb, MAD 2² p. 203 Šar-kali-šarrī Officials, etc. no. 8 (study)
1963 Hirsch, AfO 20 p. 29 Šarkališarrī d 1 γ (translation)
1969 Calmeyer, Datierbare Bronzen p. 28 no. 12 E (translation, study) and p. 162 no. 5 (transliteration)
1990 Gelb and Kienast, Königsinschriften p. 118 Šarkališarrī B 3 (edition)

TEXT

1) *śar-kà-lí*-LUGAL-*rí*
2) LUGAL
3) *a-kà-dè*.KI
4) *ša-ki-be-lí*
5) IR₁₁-*sú*

1–3) Šar-kali-šarrī, king of Agade:

4–5) Ša-ki-bēlī (is) his servant.

2012 3 The sign appears to be an URI sign with its right portion greatly elongated so as to resemble the 'feet' of a NÁ sign.

2014

The name of a servant of Šar-kali-šarrī is inscribed on an alabaster cup.

COMMENTARY

The cup, a piece of unknown provenance, is now housed in the Gallery of Fine Arts, Yale University (number 1915.24) and measures 10.7 cm in height and 8.2 cm in diameter. It was collated by P.-A. Beaulieu. The inscription is probably a fake.

BIBLIOGRAPHY

1937 Stephens, YOS 9 no. 8 (photo, copy)
1957 Hallo, Royal Titles p. 24 n. 2 (study)
1961 Gelb, MAD 2[2] p. 203 Šar-kali-šarrī Officials, etc. no. 7 (study)
1963 Hirsch, AfO 20 p. 29 Šar-kali-šarrī d 1 β (translation)
1990 Gelb and Kienast, Königsinschriften p. 118 Šarkališarrī B 2 (edition)

TEXT

1) lú-[d]šára
2) <DUMU> é-da TIBIRA
3) IR_{11} *śar-kà-lí*-LUGAL-*rí*

1–3) Lu-šara, <son> of Eda, the metalworker, (is) the servant of Šar-kali-šarrī.

2015

A fragment of a clay sealing from Nippur mentions Šar-kali-šarrī.

COMMENTARY

The present location of the sealing is not known; it may be in Istanbul. It was copied by Westenholz from a field photograph taken by J.H. Haynes (Ni–III 394; UM neg. no. 5701). The first sign in line 1′ is unclear in the tablet photo; Westenholz read it as GAL(?). He also indicated that there was a second column of the impression now broken away. However, there are no traces of this in the tablet photo and we have taken line 2′ here to be the end of the inscription.

BIBLIOGRAPHY

1987 Westenholz, OSP 2 no. 37 (photo, copy, edition)
1990 Gelb and Kienast, Königinschriften p. 47S–34 (edition)

TEXT

Lacuna
1′) x [...]
2′) ^{d}*śar-kà*-[*lí*]-LUGAL-[*rí*]

Lacuna
1′–2′) ... of Šar-ka[li-]šar[rī].

Period of Confusion

E2.1.6–9

The Sumerian King List gives the names of four kings who reigned in the period of confusion following the collapse of the Sargonic empire on the death of Šar-kali-šarrī: (a) Igigi (variant: Irgigi), (b) Nanum, (c) Imi, and (d) Elulu. They are said to have reigned a total of three years (2192–2190). One of these, Elulu, has sometimes been equated with the RN LI-*lu-ul*-DAN that is found on a spear point and bronze bowl of late Sargonic date (E2.1.12.1), but the equation is uncertain.

Dudu

E2.1.10

The Sumerian King List gives the names of two kings who reigned at Agade following the Period of Confusion: Dudu and Šū-Turul. The first of these is said to have ruled for 21 years (2189–2169). The only historical event known for Dudu's reign is a campaign the king directed against the regions of Girsu, Umma, and Elam. For the attack on Girsu, which was probably undertaken to crush the independence asserted by Puzur-Mama, see E2.1.10.2; for the campaign against Umma and Elam, see Wilcke, AfO 25 (1974–77) p. 84 and pl. IV Böllinger 1, lines 7–9. An allusion to the attack on Umma by Dudu is likely found in the inscription of the Umma ruler Lugal-ana-tuma (see E2.11.13 lines 4–7).

A seal of a servant of Dudu published by R. Opificius (Geschnittene Steine no. 23) was listed by Borger (HKL 3 p. 3) under the heading 'Dudu von Akkad'. However, the inscription on the seal is of a type PN_1 + ÌR PN_2, which, according to Hallo (Buchanan and Hallo, Early Near Eastern Seals p. 442, type 20), is characteristic of the Ur III period.

1

The first inscription of Dudu is found on two vases.

CATALOGUE

Ex.	Museum number	Provenance	Object	Lines preserved	cpn
1	CBS 10119	Nippur	Vase frgm.	1–4	c
2	AO 6773	Unknown	Alabaster vase	1–4	n

COMMENTARY

W. Hallo (Royal Titles p. 67 n. 11) listed Adab 769 (Istanbul) as a third vase exemplar of this inscription. However, the piece is actually a seal impression of a servant of Dudu; it is edited in this volume as E2.1.10.2001.

BIBLIOGRAPHY

1914 Poebel, PBS 4/1 pp. 133 and 216 no. 39 (ex. 1, edition, study)

1914 Poebel, PBS 5 no. 39 and pl. XCVIII (ex. 1, photo, copy)

1918 Thureau-Dangin, Chronologie pp. 62–63 (ex. 2, copy, edition)
1925 Meissner, WZKM 32 p. 303 (ex. 2, study)
1935 Weissbach, RLA 2/3 p. 237 (exs. 1–2, study)
1947 Kraus, JCS 1 p. 101 (transliteration)
1957 Hallo, Royal Titles p. 67 and n. 11 (study)
1961 Gelb, MAD 2[2] p. 205 Dudu Original Inscriptions no. 1 (exs. 1–2, study)
1963 Hirsch, AfO 20 p. 31 Dudu and n. 348 (exs. 1–2, transliteration, study)
1971 Sollberger and Kupper, IRSA IIA7a (translation)
1990 Gelb and Kienast, Königsinschriften p. 121 Dudu 1 (exs. 1–2, edition)

TEXT

1) *du-du*
2) *da-núm*
3) LUGAL
4) *a-kà-dè*.KI

1–4) Dudu, the mighty, king of Agade.

2

A votive inscription of Dudu is known from an Ur III Sammeltafel copy from Nippur.

COMMENTARY

The inscription is preserved on NBC 10736, a clay tablet measuring 5.5×5.1 cm. The tablet was found in SB 67 of the Inanna temple at Nippur, and given the excavation number 6N-T264. The inscription begins after a blank line on the obverse and continues on the reverse. As a result of collation, the royal name Dudu could be identified in the traces of reverse line 1.

BIBLIOGRAPHY

1968 Goetze, JAOS 88 pp. 54 and 57 (copy, edition)
1985 Foster, Iraq 47 p. 27 (study)
1990 Gelb and Kienast, Königinschriften pp. 150 and 283 Fragment C 2 (copy, edition)

TEXT

1) *a-*[*na*]
2) ⌈d⌉INA[NNA]
3) ⌈*du*⌉-[*du*]
4) LU[GAL]
5) *a-kà-d*[*è*.KI]
6) *ì-nu gír-*[*su*.KI]
7) *en-a-*[*ru*]
8) *in* NAM.RA.[AK]
9) [*gí*]*r-su*.[KI]
10) [A.MU.RU]

1–2) T[o] the goddess Aš[tar],

3–5) Du[du, ki[ng of] Agad[e],

6–7) when he con[quered] Gir[su],

8–10) [dedicated] (this object) from the boot[y] of [Gi]rsu.

3

A vase in the collection of J. Mariaud de Serres, Paris, bears a votive inscription of Dudu to Nergal, tutelary deity of the city of Apiak.

COMMENTARY

The vase is made of alabaster and measures 10.4 cm in height and 6.2 cm in diameter; the inscription, 7.5×3.9 cm. It numbers A 51 in the de Serres collection. The inscription was not collated; the edition follows Grégoire's copy.

BIBLIOGRAPHY

1981 Grégoire, MVN 10 no. 3 (copy, edition)
1990 Gelb and Kienast, Königsinschriften p. 121 Dudu 2 (edition)

TEXT

1) *du-du* 2) *da-núm* 3) LUGAL 4) *a-kà-dè*.KI	1–4) Dudu, the mighty, king of Agade
5) *a-na* 6) [d]*nergal* 7) *a-pi₅-ak*.KI 8) A.MU.RU	5–8) dedicated (this vase) to the god Nergal of Apiak.

2001

The seal inscription of a servant of Dudu is found on a clay bulla from Adab.

COMMENTARY

The bulla was excavated by Banks at Bismāyā and bears the museum number Adab 769 (Istanbul). The inscription was collated from the published photo. This piece was erroneously listed by Gelb and Kienast (Königsinschriften p. 121 Dudu 1 Text C) as a duplicate of E2.1.4.10.1.

BIBLIOGRAPHY

1951 Kraus, JCS 1 p. 101 (study)
1957 Hallo, Royal Titles p. 67 and n. 11 (study)
1961 Gelb, MAD 2^2 p. 205 Dudu, Officials, etc. no. 1 (study)
1964 Boehmer, Moortgat Festschrift p. 54 and pl. 14 no. 35 (photo, edition)
1965 Boehmer, Glyptik no. 1457 and fig. 641a (photo, edition, study)
1968 Nagel and Strommenger, BJVF 8 pp. 154–55 and 167 no. 27 (edition, study)
1968–69 Edzard, AfO 22 p. 16 no. 24–3 (transliteration)
1990 Gelb and Kienast, Königsinschriften p. 47 S-36 (edition)

TEXT

1) *du-du*	1–4) Dudu, the mighty, king of Agade:
2) *da-núm*	
3) LUGAL	
4) *a-kà-dè*.KI	
5) amar-MÙŠ	5–7) Amar-MUŠ, the scribe, (is) his servant.
6) DUB.SAR	
7) [I]R$_{11}$-⸢*sú*⸣	

Šū-Turul

E2.1.11

Šū-Turul, the son of Dudu, is credited with a reign of 15 years in the Sumerian King List (2168–2154). For the reading of the second component of the RN, see the comments of Leemans, JCS 20 (1966) pp. 36–37 and note 4, and Borger, AfO 23 (1970) p. 1. The ancient river name Túr-ùl/Túr-an/Túr-na-at corresponds to the modern Diyālā.

A 1 mana weight stone belonging to an official of Šū-Turul was found, according to a local resident, at the mound of Titriş Höyük, a tell located about 17 kms southeast of Samsat in the Euphrates basin of southeastern Turkey (see Algaze, Kurban Höyük 2 pp. 344–45 and the same author in Mār Šipri 5/2 [1992] p. 3). The piece is now housed in the Urfa Museum; its inscription has not yet been published.

1

A copper axe bears a four-line inscription of Šū-Turul.

COMMENTARY

The axe, which measures 17 cm in length, was purchased for the Foroughi Collection from among a group of Luristan bronzes. The inscription was collated from the published photo.

BIBLIOGRAPHY

1961 Ghirshman, Sept milles no. 27 (study)
1962 Dossin, IrAnt 2 p. 156 and pl. XXII no. 11 (photo, edition)
1966 Dürr, Trésors no. 296 (study)
1969 Calmeyer, Datierbare Bronzen p. 27 no. 11 C and fig. 25; p. 162 no. 9 (drawing, transliteration, study)
1971 Sollberger and Kupper, IRSA IIA8a (translation)
1990 Gelb and Kienast, Königsinschriften p. 122 Šū-DUR.ÙL 1 (edition)

TEXT

1) *šu-túr-ùl*
2) *da-núm*
3) LUGAL
4) *a-kà-dè*.KI

1–4) Šū-Turul, the mighty, king of Agade.

2001

A clay bulla from Kiš bears a seal inscription that mentions Šū-Turul.

COMMENTARY

The bulla measures 2.6×3.0 cm; it was found during excavations of de Genouillac at Kiš. The present location of the piece is not known. The edition follows the copy of de Genouillac.

BIBLIOGRAPHY

1925 de Genouillac, Kich 2 p. 23 P. 111 and pl. 54 no. 9 (copy, study)
1961 Gelb, MAD 2² p. 205 Šu-Turul Original Inscriptions no. 1 (study)
1963 Hirsch, AfO 20 p. 32 Šu-DUR.ÙL 2 (study)
1964 Boehmer, Moortgat Festschrift p. 54 and pl. 14 no. 36 (copy, edition)
1965 Boehmer, Glyptik no. 770 and fig. 261 (copy, study)
1968 Nagel and Strommenger, BJVF 8 pp. 154–55 and 167 no. 28 (edition, study)
1968–69 Edzard, AfO 22 p. 16 no. 24–29 (transliteration)
1990 Gelb and Kienast, Königsinschriften p. 47 S-37 (edition)

TEXT

1) [*šu*]-*túr-ùl*
2) [*d*]*a-núm*
3) LU[GAL]
4) *a*-[*kà-dè*.KI]
Lacuna

1–4) [Šū]-Turul, the [m]ighty, ki[ng] of A[gade]:
Lacuna

2002

A clay sealing bears a fragmentarily preserved seal inscription of a servant of Šū-Turul.

COMMENTARY

The sealing measures 3×5.5 cm and was found in the 'Houses Dump' at Tell Asmar; excavation number As 31:627 (TA 701). Its present whereabouts are not known. The inscription was collated from the published photo.

BIBLIOGRAPHY

1955 Frankfort, Stratified Cylinder Seals p. 49 and pl. 65 no. 701 (photo, copy, study; edition [by Jacobsen])
1957 Hallo, Royal Titles p. 67 n. 12 (study)
1961 Gelb, MAD 2^2 p. 205 Šu-Turul Officials, etc. no. 2 (study)
1963 Hirsch, AfO 20 p. 32 Šu-DUR.ÙL 3 (study)
1964 Boehmer, Moortgat Festschrift p. 55 and pl. 14 no. 37 (photo, edition)
1965 Boehmer, Glyptik no. 771 and fig. 262 (photo, copy, study)
1968 Nagel and Strommenger, BJVF 8 pp. 154–55 and 168 no. 29 (edition, study)
1968–69 Edzard, AfO 22 p. 16 no. 24–28 (transliteration)
1990 Gelb and Kienast, Königsinschriften pp. 47–48 S–38 (edition)

TEXT

1) [*š*]*u-túr-ùl*
2) [*d*]*a-núm*
3) [LU]GAL
4) [*a-kà*]-*dè*.KI
5) [...] MAḪ
6) [...] x
7) [IR$_{11}$-*sú*]

1–4) [Š]ū-Turul, the [m]ighty, [ki]ng of [Aga]de:

5–7) ... [(is) his servant].

2003

A hammer head in the British Museum bears a votive inscription for the life of Šū-Turul.

COMMENTARY

The hammer head is made of dark green marble and measures 10.3×3.8 cm; it bears the museum number BM 114703. The inscription was collated by G. Frame.

BIBLIOGRAPHY

1912 Pognon, CRAIB pp. 416–17 (translation, study)
1913 Pognon, JA 1913/1, pp. 418–26 (copy, edition, study)
1914 Poebel, PBS 4/1 p. 134 (translation by Pognon)
1918 Thureau-Dangin, Chronologie p. 63 (edition)
1921 Gadd, Early Dynasties pp. 29–30 and pl. 3 (copy, edition, study)
1922 Poebel, OLZ 25 507 (study)
1925 Meissner, WZKM 32 p. 303 (study)
1961 Gelb, MAD 2^2 pp. 99 and 205 Šu-Turul Officials, etc. no. 1 (study)
1963 Hirsch, AfO 20 p. 32 Šu-DUR.ÙL 1 (study)
1971 Sollberger and Kupper, IRSA IIA8b (translation)
1990 Gelb and Kienast, Königsinschriften pp. 122–23 Šū-DUR.ÙL B 1 (edition)

TEXT

1) *a-na*	1–2) To the god Nergal,
2) ^{d}*nergal*	
3) *a-na*	3–7) for the life of Šū-Turul, king of Agade,
4) *na-ʾà-śi*	
5) *šu-túr-ùl*	
6) LUGAL-*rí*	
7) *a-kà-dè*.KI	
8) *la-ba-áʾ-śum*$_6$	8–10) Lā-baʾšum, the majordomo, dedicated (this hammer).
9) ŠABRA É	
10) A.MU.RU	

LI-*lu-ul*-DAN

E2.1.12

1

A three-line inscription of a certain LI-*lu-ul*-DAN, king of Agade, is found on a copper spear point and a bronze bowl. Gelb (AJSL 53 [1936–37] p. 38) proposed to read the RN i_x(LI)-*lu-ul-dan* and Jacobsen (SKL p. 114) suggested e_x-*lu-ul-dan*; both saw a connection with the *E-lu-lu* of the Sumerian King List. However, as noted, the correlation is uncertain. LI-*lu-ul*-DAN does not appear in the section of the Sumerian King List dealing with the dynasty of Agade; we have arbitarily placed his sole inscription at the end of our Akkad section. The name is certainly not to be connected with the supposed *E-lu-lu-me-eš* of the Gutian section of the Sumerian King List; a collation of the relevant line in both the Weld-Blundell prism and a Nippur fragment in Philadelphia (Michalowski, JAOS 103 [1983] pp. 246–48) reveals *si-lu-lu-me-eš*/*si-lu-lu-e*.

CATALOGUE

Ex.	Museum number	Provenance	Object	Dimensions (cm)	Lines preserved	cpn
1	IM 8912	Diyala region, possibly Ishchali	Copper spear point	33×1.7	1–3	p
2	Foroughi Collection, Teheran	Luristan	Bronze bowl	6 high., 12 dia.	1–3	p

BIBLIOGRAPHY

1935–36 Levi, AfO 10 p. 281 (ex. 1, photo, copy, edition)
1939 Jacobsen, SKL p. 114 n. 266a (transliteration, study)
1961 Gelb, MAD 2² p. 204 Lilul-dan Original Inscriptions no. 1 (ex. 1, study)
1961 Ghirshman, Sept milles no. 437 (ex. 2, study)
1962 Ghirshman, Kunstschätze no. 204 (ex. 2, study)
1962 Dossin, IrAnt 2 p. 163 and pl. XXXI no. 29 (ex. 2, photo, edition)
1963 Hirsch, AfO 20 p. 31 (ex. 1, transliteration, study)
1969 Calmeyer, Datierbare Bronzen p. 28 no. 12F and fig. 27; p. 162 no. 7 (ex. 2, copy, edition)
1971 Sollberger and Kupper, IRSA IIA6a (exs. 1–2, translation)
1990 Gelb and Kienast, Königsinschriften p. 120 Eluldān 1 (exs. 1–2, edition)

TEXT

1) LI-*lu-ul*-DAN	1–3) LI-*lu-ul*-DAN, king of Agade.
2) LUGAL	
3) *a-kà-dè*.KI	

GUTIUM

E2.2

The Sumerian King List places a dynasty of 21 Gutian kings between its Uruk V and VI dynasties. Of the 20 RNs in the list only a handful can be identified with rulers known from contemporary inscriptions. Curiously, the longest extant inscriptions of a Gutian ruler belong to Erridu-pizir, whose name does not even appear in the list. We have, following Jacobsen (SKL p. 117), identified him with the 'king without a name' who heads the list and have accorded him the number E2.2.1.

The reading of many of the Gutian kings' name is uncertain and the order of the kings varies widely in the manuscripts of the Sumerian King List. Here they are listed according to the normalized forms and order given in Jacobsen's edition. Those kings for whom royal inscriptions or servant seals are extant, or who are mentioned in other inscriptions, are marked with a dagger(†).

Borger (HKL p. 9), citing an inscribed seal from Ur (Legrain, PBS 14 no. 237), identified a certain Puzur-Sîn/Suen as a third millennium ruler of Ur. One might have been tempted to connect this Puzur-Sîn/Suen with the ruler by the same name who appears as the eighteenth king in the Gutian section of the Sumerian King List. However, as P. Steinkeller pointed out to me, the identification of the Puzur-Sîn/Suen named in this seal as a ruler of Ur is based on Legrain's erroneous reading of the seal inscription. Lines 2–3 actually read: ENGAR(?) *tá-ra-am*-ŠE[Š].AB.KI 'ploughman(?) of Tarām-Uri'. The reference is likely to a servant of a wife of Ur-Nammu (see M. Civil, RA 56 [1962] pp. 213–14).

The Tiriga who is given a reign of 40 days as the twenty-first king in the Sumerian King List can plausibly be identified with the Tirigan who appears as the opponent of Utu-ḫegal in inscription E2.13.6.3.

E2.2.1	'A king without a name' Erridu-pizir	E2.2.11	Iarla<ngab>
E2.2.2	Imtʾa	E2.2.12	Kurum
E2.2.3	Inkišuš	E2.2.13	Ḫabil-kīn
E2.2.4	Sarlagab	E2.2.14	Lā-ʾarābum†
E2.2.5	Šulmeʾ	E2.2.15	Irarum
E2.2.6	Elulumeš	E2.2.16	Ibranum
E2.2.7	Inimabakeš	E2.2.17	Ḫablum
E2.2.8	Igešauš	E2.2.18	Puzur-Sîn
E2.2.9	Iarlagab	E2.2.19	Iarlaganda†
E2.2.10	Ibate	E2.2.20	Si'u(m)†
		E2.2.21	Tiriga(n)†

Erridu-pizir

E2.2.1

1–3

An Old Babylonian tablet from Nippur contains copies of three statue inscriptions of the Gutian king Erridu-pizir. As noted, this king's name does not appear in the Sumerian King List, and exactly where Erridu-pizir is to be placed in its sequence of Gutian rulers cannot be determined from the sources available at present. Jacobsen (SKL p. 117 n. 285) proposed that Erridu-pizir might be the king who appears as the 'king without a name' in the king list. Following this suggestion we have edited Erridu-pizir's inscriptions at the head of the Gutian section, bearing in mind that his dates are uncertain.

COMMENTARY

The original tablet, restored from 20 fragments and once containing about nine-tenths of the inscription, measured 20×13.6 cm. It was found in excavations of the University of Pennsylvania on 'Tablet Hill' during the fourth season of excavations. R. Kutscher found two pieces of this tablet (BT 2 and 3) containing six columns on each side in the Brockmon Collection in Haifa. BT 2 is composed of a join of three fragments and measures 11.8×13.5 cm and BT 3 measures 7.2×8.2 cm. Kutscher suggests that two lines are missing between the two fragments. This edition benefited from collations of a tablet photo of a superior quality to the published photo that were kindly communicated by A. Westenholz — his photo collations are marked with an asterisk — and collations of the tablet itself by P. Steinkeller. For conciseness the general information on the tablet and the bibliography will be given here only under the rubric E2.2.1.1–3. Since the text still contains many lacunae we have not given a consecutively numbered line count of a reconstructed text as is our usual custom. Rather, column and line numbers of the original tablet are indicated. The lines of the colophons and captions are not numbered separately from the rest of the text.

BIBLIOGRAPHY

1910 Hilprecht, Deluge Story pp. 3 and 20–24 (study)
1914 Poebel, PBS 4/1 p. 134 (study)
1938 Weissbach, RLA 2/5 p. 471 (study)
1939 Jacobsen, SKL p. 117 n. 285 (study)
1971 Sollberger and Kupper, IRSA IIJ1 (study)
1971 Hallo, RLA 3/9 p. 712 (study)
1989 Kutscher, Brockmon Tablets pp. 49–70, 112–13 and 120–21 (photo, copy, edition)
1990 Gelb and Kienast, Königsinschriften pp. 310–16 Gutium C 1–3 (edition)

1

The first inscription is found on BT 2+3, cols. i – iii 24.

COMMENTARY

For the translation 'clan (god)' in i 11, see the commentary to E2.1.4.6.

TEXT

Col. i
1) [...-*i*]*m*
2) [...] x
3) [...] x
4) [...] x
5) [^{d}INANN]A
6) [*an-nu-ni-t*]*um*
7) [x] x x ⸢*id*⸣(*)-*śu*
8) *ù*
9) *ìl-a-ba*$_4$
10) KALAG *ì-li*
11) *il-la-at-śu*

i 1–11) [The god ... is his (personal) god], [the goddess Eštа]r-[Annunī]tum (is) his ..., (and) the god Ilaba, the mighty one of the gods, is his clan (god).

12) *e-er-ri-du-pi-zi-ir*
13) *da*(*)-*núm*
14) LUGAL
15) *gu-ti-im*
16) *ù*
17) *ki-ib-ra-tim*
18) *ar-ba*-⸢*im*⸣
19) *a*-[x]

i 12–19) Erridu-pizir, the mighty, king of Gutium and of the four quarters: ...

20) ^{m}*ù*-[x x]
21) GÌR.[NÍTA-*ś*]*u*
22) ⸢*ma*(?)⸣-[*a*]*d*-[*ga*].KI
23) [...]-BI
24) [...]-*im*
25) [...] x
Lacuna

i 20–25) U-[...], his gen[eral], *Madga* ...
Lacuna

1′) [*e-er-ri-du*]-*pi-zi-i*[*r*]
2′) *da-núm*
3′) LUGAL
4′) *gu-ti-im*
5′) *ù*
6′) *ki-ib-ra-tim*
7′) *ar-ba-im*
8′) DA-*ís-su*
9′) *ig-ru-úś*

i 1′–9′) [Erridu]-pizi[r], the mighty, king of Gutium and the four quarters, hastened (to confront) him.

10′) *ip-la-aḫ-śú*-⸢*ma*⸣
11′) *e-tá-ra-ab*
12′) *śa-dú-śum*$_6$

i 10′–17′) (Since the ruler of Madga) feared him he entered (his own) mountain (land), and (Erridu-pizir) hunted him down, captured him (and) he, the king,

---

i 7 Collation Westenholz.
i 13 Text: DU.

13′) *e-ṣú-ud-śú-*⸢*ma*⸣
14′) *ik-mi-śu*

led him away (and) ... him.

15′) LUGAL
16′) *ù-ru-a-šu-ma*
17′) *um-ma*(?)*-ni-śu*
18′) ⸢*e*⸣*-er-ri-du-*[*pi*]*-zi-ir*
Col. ii
1) *da-*[*núm*]
2) ⸢LUGAL⸣
3) *gu-ti-im*
4) *ù*
5) *ki-ib-ra-tim*
6) *ar-ba-im*

i 18′ – ii 6) Erridu-[pi]zir, the migh[ty], king of Gutium and the four quarters

7) *in* KÁ
8) DINGIR *gu-ti-im*
9) *im-si*$_4$(*)
10) *il-pu-ut-su-ma*
11) SAG.GIŠ.RA-*śu*
12) LUGAL(*)

ii 7–12) took (him) away by force through the gate of the god of Gutium, struck him, and killed him, the king (of Madga).

13) *en-ma*
14) *e-er-ri-du-pi-zi-ir*
15) *da-núm*
16) LUGAL
17) *gu-ti-*⸢*im*⸣
18) [*ù*]
19) [*ki*]*-*⸢*ib-ra*⸣*-tim*
20) [*a*]*r-ba-im*

ii 13–20) Thus (says) Erridu-pizir, the mighty, king of Gutium [and] of the [f]our [qua]rters:

21) *in u-mi-śu*
22) DÙL-*mì*
23) *ab-ni-ma*
24) *in na-pá-áś*(*)*-ti-śu*
25) *sa-ab-śu*
26) ⸢*íś*⸣*-ku-un*
27) [...] ⸢x x⸣ [...]
Lacuna

ii 21–27) 'At that time I fashioned a statue of myself and I(*) set a ... on its neck ...
Lacuna

1′) [...]⸢
2′) ⸢x⸣-[...]
3′) *lu-ub-ś*[*a*(?)*-am*(?)]
4′) ZA.GÌN *ša* [...]
5′) *la áś-ku-*⸢*nu*⸣(*)
6′) *a-na*
7′) ^{d}*en-líl*
8′) *in* NIBRU.KI
9′) DÙL-*śu*
10′) A.MU.RU

ii 1′–10′) ... *a garment* ... lapis lazuli, *which I did not set,* and dedicated a statue of myself(*) to the god Enlil in Nippur.

11′) *ša* DUB
12′) *śu*$_4$*-a*
13′) *u-śa-sà-ku-ni*
14′) ^{d}UTU
15′) ^{d}INANNA

ii 11′–iii 15′) As for the one who removes this inscription, may the gods Šamaš, Aštar,

---

ii 9 Westenholz: 'vielleicht SI statt SU$_4$'; Steinkeller: 'clear SI$_4$/SU$_4$.
ii 12 Collation Westenholz and Steinkeller.
ii 24 Collation Westenholz and Steinkeller.
ii 26 Text: he.
ii 4' Collation Steinkeller.
ii 5' Collation Westenholz.
ii 9' Text: himself.

Col. iii
1) [*ù*]
2) *il-a-*[*ba*$_4$]
3) ⸢SUḪUŠ⸣-*šu*
4) *li-sú-ḫu*
5) *ù*
6) Š[E].NUMUN-*šu*
7) *li-il-qú-tu*

iii 1–3) [and] Ila[ba] tear out his foundations and destroy his [p]rogeny.

Colophon 1
8) mu-sar-ra ki-gal-ba

Colophon 1
iii 8) Inscription on its base.

Caption 1
9) *e-er-ri-du-pi-zi-ir*
10) *da-núm*
11) LUGAL
12) g[*u*]*-ti-im*
13) *ù*
14) ⸢*ki*⸣*-ib-ra-tim*
15) [*a*]*r*-⸢*ba*⸣*-i*[*m*]
16) [*a-na*]
17) [^{d}*e*]*n*-[*líl*]
18) *in* N[IBRU.KI]
19) A.MU.[RU]

Caption 1
iii 9–19) Erridu-pizir, the mighty, king of Gutium and the four quarters, dedicat[ed] (this statue) [to the god E]n[lil] in N[ippur].

Colophon 2
20) mu-sar-ra x [x x]
21) alam-bi x [x x] i[m-x x]

Colophon 2
iii 20–21) Inscription ... its image ...

Caption 2
22) ^{m}*ù*-[...]
23) GÌR.[NÍTA]
24) *m*[*a-ad-ga*.KI.]
Lacuna

Caption 2
iii 22–24) U-[...], gen[eral] of M[adga].
Lacuna

2

A copy of a second statue inscription of Erridu-pizir is found on BT 2+3 cols. iii 1′ – viii 7′.

COMMENTARY

Vii 13′–14′ is emended to read: *si*-<DAR>-*ki-šu* based on the following parallels: *a-dì si*-DAR-*ki-šu* (Sollberger, CRRA 15 [1967] p. 106 line 6′) and *a-dì si*-DAR-*ki-šu* (Nassouhi, AfO 3 [1926] p. 112 line 22). Durand (MARI 4 [1985] pp. 151–52) read the Sollberger passage: *a-dì ší-ṭár* ki-*šu* and translated 'jusqu'à (faire disparaître) la mention écrite de sa résidence'. Von Soden (AHw p. 1251) compares *si*-DAR-*ki* with Hurrian šitarni- 'curse'. The meaning of the expression is uncertain.

TEXT

Col. iii
1′) ⸢*e*⸣-[*er-ri-du*]*-pi-*[*zi-ir*]
2′) *da-*[*núm*]
3′) ⸢LUGAL⸣
4′) *gu-ti-im*

iii 1′–7′) E[rridu]-pi[zir], the migh[ty], king of Gutium and of the four quarters:

5′) *ù*
6′) *ki-ib-ra-tim*
7′) *ar-ba-im*
8′) *in u-mi*
9′) ᵐKA-*ni-iš-ba*
10′) *ni-ku-ur-tám*
Col. iv
1) [*íš*]-*ku-nu*
2) [*a*]-*bi*
3) [*e*]*n-ri-da-pi-zi-ir*
4) *da-nim*
5) LUGAL
6) *gu-ti-im*
7) *ù*
8) *ki-ib-ra-tim*
9) *ar-ba-im*
10) ⌈*è*⌉-*zi-bu*
11) ŠA.DÚ-*e*
12) *ù*
13) URU.KI.⌈URU⌉.KI(*)
14) *u-úš-ba-al-ki-tu*
15) *ù*
16) *a-dì-ma*
17) KALAM
18) [*lu*]-*l*[*u*]-*bi-im*.KI
19) [x]-NI.KI
20) ⌈x⌉-x.KI
21) [x].⌈KI⌉
22) [(x)] ⌈KI⌉
Lacuna
1′) x [...]
2′) DA-[*ís-su*]
3′) *ig*-[*ru-úš*]
4′) ÍL-[...]
5′) GIŠ [...]
6′) *ti*-[...]
Col. v
1) *ù*
2) ᵈINANNA
3) *in a-kà-dè*.KI
4) ÉRIN-*am*
5) *íš-ku-un*
6) *ip-ḫur-šum*$_{6}$
7) *um-ma-núm*
8) *kà-lu*$_{5}$-*ša*
9) *a-na*
10) *ši-mu-ur*$_{4}$-*rí-im*.KI
11) *è-ru-úš*
12) ŠITA(*) LAM×KUR(*)
13) *è-ru-ub*
14) *in a-kà-dè*.KI
15) *u-ra-ṣi*
16) *ra-bí-ù-tim*
17) <*a-na*> *ì-li*
18) ⌈*ú*⌉-*qá-ra-ab*
Lacuna

iii 8′ – iv 1) when KA-Nišba (king of Simurrum) [in]itiated hostilities,

iv 2–10) ignored (the orders of) my [fa]ther, Enrida-pizir, the mighty, king of Gutium and of the four quarters,

iv 11–14) caused the mountain lands and cities to revolt,

iv 15–22) (and) as far as the land of [Lu]llubum (and the lands) ...
Lacuna

iv 1′–6′) ... he has[tened] (to confront) [him] ...

v 1–5) Further, the goddess Aštar had stationed troops in Agade.

v 6–11) The whole army assembled for him (Erridu-pizir) (and) went to Simurrum.

v 12–18) He (Erridu-pizir) entered ... (while) it (the army?) was making offerings of large male goats <to> the gods in Agade.
Lacuna

iv 13 Collation Westenholz and Steinkeller.
v 12 Ibid.

Col. vi

1) *u-śa-a[m]-*qi_4*-it*
2) *a-ar-*⸢NAM⸣(*)
3) ⸢*ù*⸣
4) *ba-al-ṭù-*<*ti*>*-śú-nu*(*)
5) NIDBA-*śu-nu*(*)
6) *íl-qá-ù-ni[m]*(*)
7) ANŠE.*sí-s[í]-śu-nu*(*)
8) GU_4-*śu-*⸢*nu*⸣(*)
9) *ù*
10) UDU-*śu-nu*(*)
11) *sa-bi*
12) DINGIR *gu-ti-im*
13) *ù*
14) *en-ri-da-pi-zi-ir*
15) *è-ḫu-zu*
16) *be-al* NI-*me*
17) *li-*[...]

Lacuna

vi 1) he struck down.

vi 2–6) As for ... and their *survivors*, their offerings they took,

vi 7–11) their hors[es], their large cattle, and their sheep ...

vi 12–16) the god of Gutium and Enrida-pizir took hold of (them) ...

Lacuna

Col. vii

1′) [...] ⸢*ù*⸣
2′) *śar-ru-tám*
3′) *a-na*
4′) ^{d}*en-líl*
5′) GIDRU
6′) *a-na*
7′) ^{d}INANNA
8′) *a u-ki-il*
9′) ^{d}*nin-ḫur-sag*
10′) *ù*
11′) ^{d}*nin-tu*
12′) ŠE.NUMUN-*śu*
13′) *a-na*
14′) <*śi*>-DAR-*ki-śu*
15′) *li-il-*⸢*qù-tá*⸣
16′) DINGIR [...]
17′) ⸢x⸣-[...]

Lacuna

vii 1′–8′) ... and may he not hold the kingship for the god Enlil or the sceptre for the goddess Aštar.

vii 9′–17′) May the goddesses Ninḫursag and Nintu destroy his progeny ...

Col. viii

Lacuna

1′) x [...]
2′) DÙL-⸢*śu*⸣
3′) *a-na*
4′) ^{d}*en-líl*
5′) A.MU.RU

Colophon

6′) mu-sar-ra zà-ga-na
7′) alam-bi ugu-kišib-ba gìr an-ús

Lacuna

viii 1′–5′) ... He (Erridu-pizir) dedicated a statue of himself to the god Enlil.

Colophon

viii 6′–7′) Inscription on its shoulder. Its image: (his) foot treading on the ...

---

vi 2 Collation Steinkeller.
vi 4 Ibid.
vi 5 Collation Westenholz and Steinkeller.
vi 6 Ibid.
vi 7 Ibid.
vi 8 Ibid.
vi 10 Ibid.

3

A copy of a third statue inscription of Erridu-pizir is found on BT 2+3 cols. viii 8′ – xii 8.

TEXT

Col. viii
8′) KA-*ni-iš-ba*
9′) LUGAL
10′) *śi-mu-ur$_4$-rí-im*.KI
11′) UN
12′) *śi-mu-ur$_4$-rí-im*.KI
13′) *ù*
14′) *lu-lu-bi-im*.KI
15′) <<*tu*>>-*uś-ba-al-ki-*⸢*it*⸣*-ma*

viii 8′–15′) KA-Nišba, king of Simurrum, instigated the people of Simurrum and Lullubum to revolt and

Col. ix
1) ⸢*sa*⸣-[*bi*]
2) DINGIR *gu-*[*ti-im*]
3) *da-*[...]
4) ᵐ ⸢x⸣-[...]
Lacuna
1′) x [...]
2′) x [...]
3′) *ì-n*[*u*]
4′) ᵐ⸢*am*⸣-[NI]-*li*
5′) [GÌR].NÍTA
6′) *šè-*⸢*ru*(?)⸣-[x]-*im*
7′) ⸢x⸣-[...]-ZÉ
8′) [...] ⸢x⸣.KUR
8′) *u-*[*na*]*-ak-*[*ki*]-⸢*ru*(?)⸣*-ma*
9′) *ù*
10′) *śar-*⸢x⸣-[(x)]*-ma*
11′) *e-*⸢*ḫu*(?)⸣-(x)-*śu*
12′) *e-er-*[*r*]*i-du-*[*pi-zi*]*-ir*
13′) [*da-n*]*úm*
14′) [LUGAL]
15′) [*gu-ti-im*]
16′) [*ù*]
17′) [*ki-ib-ra-tim*]
18′) [*ar-ba-im*]

ix 1–4) the ... of the god of Gu[tium] . .
Lacuna

ix 1′–11′) ... whe[n] *Amnili*, [gen]eral of ... made the land ... rebel and ...

ix 12′–18′) Er[r]idu-[piz]ir, [the migh]ty, [king of Gutium and of the four quarters]

Col. x
1) DA-*íś-śu*
2) *ig-ru-úś*
3) *è-ku-uš-ma*
4) ŚA.DÚ-*e*
5) *ni-iš-ba* .KUR
6) *in* 6 UD
7) *ḫa-me-me-*x*-pi-*[*ir*.KUR]
8) *na-*[*ra-ab-tám*(?)]
9) [SAG.GIŠ.RA]
Lacuna

x 1–2) hastened (to confront) him.

x 3–5) He proceeded (through) the peaks of Mount Nišba.

x 6–9) In six days [he conquered] the *p*[*ass*] at [Mount] Ḫameme-x-pi[r].
Lacuna

1′) ⌈x⌉ [...]
2′) *na-r*[*a*]-*a*[*b*]-*ti-śu*
3′) *è-ru-ub*
4′) ⌈*e-er-ri*⌉-*du*-[*pi-z*]*i-ir*
5′) *d*[*a*]-*núm*
6′) *ìr-da-śu*$_4$-*ma*
7′) *nu-úḫ-pi-ir*.KUR
8′) *na-ra-ab-tám*
9′) SAG.GIŠ.RA-*ma*
10′) *ù*
11′) ^{m}*am*-NI-*li*
12′) ḪUR-*nam*
13′) *in ra-śi-śu*
14′) *u*-[*śa-a*]*m*-[*qi*$_4$-*it*]
15′) x [...]
Lacuna
Col. xi
1) *in* 1 UD
2) *u-śu-rí-id*
3) *ù*
4) *mu-ma-am*.KUR
5) *na-ra-ba-at*
6) *ur-bi-lum*.KI
7) SAG.GIŠ.RA
8) *ù*
9) ^{m}*ni-ri-iš-ḫu-ḫa*
10) ÉN[SI]
11) *ur-bi*-[*lum*.KI]
Lacuna
1′) [*a-na*]
2′) [^{d}*en-líl*]
3′) [*in* NIB]RU.KI
4′) [A].MU.RU
5′) *ša* DUB
6′) *śu*$_4$-*a*
7′) *u-śa-sà-ku*-<*ni*>
8′) ⌈^{d}⌉*en-líl*
9′) *ù*
10′) ^{d}UTU
11′) SUḪUŠ-*śu*
12′) *li-sú-ḫa*
Colophon 1
13′) mu-sar-ra ki-gal-ba
Caption 1
14′) *e-er-ri-du-pi-zi-ir*
15′) *da-núm*
16′) LUGAL
17′) *gu-ti-im*
18′) *ù*
19′) *ki-ib-ra-tim*
20′) *ar-ba-im*
21′) *a-na*
Col. xii
1) [^{d}*en*]-*líl*
2) [*in* NI]BRU.KI
3) ⌈A⌉.MU.RU
Colophon 2
4) mu-sar-ra
5) zà-ga-na
Space

x 1′–3′) ... en[te]red its pass.

x 4′–6′) Erridu-[pizi]r, the m[i]ghty, pursued him and

x 7′–9′) conquered the pass at Mount Nuḫpir.

x 10′–15′) Further, he [st]ru[ck] down [*A*]*mnili*, the ..., on its summit ...
Lacuna

xi 1–7) In a single day he brought .... down and conquered the pass of Urbillum at Mount Mumum.

xi 8–11) Further, he [*captured*] Nirišḫuḫa, the gover[nor] of Urbi[llum].
Lacuna

xi 1′–4′) He [ded]icated (this statue) [to the god Enlil in Nipp]ur.

xi 5′–12′) As for the one who removes this inscription, may the gods Enlil and Šamaš tear out his foundations.

Colophon 1
xi 13′) Inscription on its base.
Caption 1
xi 14′ – xii 3) Erridu-pizir, the mighty, king of Gutium and of the four quarters, dedicated (this statue) to the god [En]lil [in Nip]pur.

Colophon 2
xii 4–5) Inscription on its [sh]oulder.

Summary colophon (refers to the entire tablet containing the text of E2.2.1.1–3)
6) dub mu-sar-ra
7) 3 alam
8) *e-er-ri-du-pi-zi-ir*

Summary colophon

xii 6–8) Inscribed tablet with three statue (inscriptions) of Erridu-pizir.

Lā-ʾarāb

E2.2.14

1

A mace head bears an inscription of Lā-ʾarāb, king of Gutium. He is probably to be identified with the [...]-*ra-bu-um* who is named as the fourteenth king in the Sumerian King List; there he is given a reign of two years. The name is normalized following Gelb, MAD 3 p. 61.

COMMENTARY

The inscription is found on an albaster mace head that measures 19.7 cm in diameter and 16.8 cm in height; it came from Rassam's excavations at Sippar. The piece bears the museum number BM 90852 and registration number AH 82-7-14, 1041. The inscription was collated by G. Frame.

In lines 9′ following (as pointed out to me by W.G. Lambert), it looks as if the name of 'the god of Gutium' was mechanically added to the head of a stock Old Akkadian curse formula that invoked the deities Aštar and Sîn. This would account for the grammatically incorrect dual verbal forms in lines 14′ and 17′.

BIBLIOGRAPHY

1889 Winckler, ZA 4 p. 406 and following pl. (copy, study)
1893 Jensen ZA 8 pp. 238–39 (edition)
1907 Thureau-Dangin, SAK pp. 170-74 Lasirab, König von Gutiu (edition)
1910 King, Early History p. 250 and pl. facing p. 206 (photo, study)
1929 Barton, RISA pp. 170–71 Lasirab (edition)
1939 Jacobsen, SKL 11 p. 119 n. 305 (study)
1961 Gelb, MAD 2^2 p. 7 no. 1 (study)
1971 Sollberger and Kupper, IRSA IIJ2a (translation)
1971 Hallo, RLA 3/9 pp. 711–12 (study)
1980 Walker and Collon in de Meyer, (ed.), Tell ed-Dēr 3 p. 100 no. 42 (study)
1990 Gelb and Kienast, Königsinschriften pp. 294–95 Gutium 1 (edition)

TEXT

1) *la*-⸢*ʾà*⸣-*r*[*a-a*]*b*
2) ⸢*da*⸣-[*núm*]
3) [LU]GAL
4) [*g*]*u-ti-im*
Lacuna (about 7 lines)
1′) [...]
2′) *ib*-[*ni-m*]*a*
3′) A.MU.RU
4′) *ša* DUB
5′) *šu*$_4$*-a*
6′) *u-ša-sà-ku-ni*
7′) *ù*(*) *šum*$_6$*-šu*
8′) *i-ša-ṭa-ru*
9′) DINGIR *gu-ti-im*
10′) ^{d}INANNA
11′) *ù*
12′) ^{d}EN.ZU
13′) SUḪUŠ(*)-*šu*
14′) *li-sú-ḫa*
15′) *ù*
16′) ŠE.NUMUN-*šú*
17′) *li-il-qù-tá*
18′) *ù*
19′) KASKAL(*).KI-(x)-*šú*
20′) *a i-ši-ir*

1–4) Lā-ʾarāb, the mig[hty, ki]ng of [G]utium,
Lacuna

1′–3′) ... fash[ioned] and dedicated (this mace).

3′–8′) As for the one who removes this inscription and writes his own name (instead),

9′–20′) may the god of Gutium, Aštar, and Sîn tear out his foundations and destroy his progeny. Further, may his campaign not succeed.

Iarlagan

E2.2.19

The Iarlaganda who is assigned a reign of seven years as the nineteenth Gutian king in the Sumerian King List is probably to be identified with the Iarlagan, king of Gutium, mentioned in an inscription of Nammaḫni, governor of Umma (see E2.11.12.1); the name is normalized here in accordance with the Umma inscription.

7′ Text: GIŠ.
13′ Text: DU.
19′ The sign consists of two crossed rectangles similar to a KIB sign, and thus differs from a normal KASKAL sign.

Si'um

E2.2.20

The Si'u who is assigned a reign of seven years as the twentieth Gutian king in the Sumerian King List is probably to be identified with the Si'um, king of Gutium, who is mentioned in an inscription of Lugal-ana-tuma, ruler of Umma (see E2.11.13.1). The name is normalized here to agree with the Umma inscription.

2001

A seal inscription dated to late Sargonic times names Ilulu as a servant of a certain *Si-a-um*; the latter PN may possibly refer to the Gutian ruler Si'um.

COMMENTARY

The seal is made of serpentine and measures 2.93 cm in length and 1.77 cm in diameter. The piece, which was obtained through the antiquities trade, is of unknown provenance; it now bears the museum number VA 2929. The inscription was collated from the published photo.

BIBLIOGRAPHY

1920 Weber, AO 17–18 no. 230 (photo)
1940 Moortgat, VAR no. 186 (photo, edition, study)
1965 Boehmer, Glyptik no. 753 and fig. 252 (photo, study)
1971 Nagel, APA 2 p. 3 and fig. 6 (photo, edition)
1971 Hallo, RLA 3/9 p. 712 (study)
1987 Rost, Das Vorderasiatische Museum fig. 127 (photo)

TEXT

1) *ì-lu-lu*
2) IR$_{11}$ *si-a-um*

1–2) Ilulu, servant of Si'ā'um.

MARI

E2.3

The history of Mari during Sargonic times is obscure because of the relative lack of sources for this period. In contrast, a long series of independent rulers is known for the preceding Early Dynastic period, from contemporary building and votive inscriptions, from a list of rulers of Mari in the Sumerian King List, and from the extensive epigraphic finds from ancient Ebla, Mari's rival. Mari's independence was brought to an end by the incursions of a Sargonic king. According to a recent analysis by M. Lebeau (MARI 4 [1985] p. 135), the archaeological record clearly shows a massive destruction in the level 'P(alais) P(résargonique) 1' and a reoccupation of the site in the early or middle Sargonic period. Sargon, the first Sargonic king, claimed that the lands of Mari and Elam stood before him (see E2.1.1.1 lines 81–87), a probable reference to his defeat of those two regions. Further, a year name dealing with the destruction of Mari is probably to be assigned to Sargon. While we have no evidence from archival or monumental sources for Akkadian control over Mari during the reigns of Sargon's successors Rīmuš and Maništūšu, the discovery of a pair of copper bowls inscribed with the names of two daughters of Narām-Sîn (see E2.1.4.48–49) suggests that Narām-Sîn may have controlled the city. Further, the city of Mari appears in an inscription, of probable attribution to Narām-Sîn, that apparently lists various lands and cities conquered by the Sargonic king (E2.1.4.1004 line 5). The period of Akkadian domination over Mari was remembered by the city's later inhabitants; they maintained a cult of the dead kings (*kispum*) for Sargon and Narām-Sîn.

A handful of building inscriptions of various *šakkanakku*s 'military governors' of the city are to be dated to the Sargonic-Gutian period. Until recently, the order of these rulers and their relative date with respect to the rulers of Sumer and Akkad have been obscure. However, the publication by J.-M. Durand of a list of Mari *šakkanakku*s has shed valuable light on this subject. Durand provides a list of six rulers whom he dates to the period from Narām-Sîn down to the end of the Gutian period. The seventh *šakkannaku* in the list, Apil-kīn, is known from other sources to have been a contemporary of Ur-Nammu of Ur. These rulers of Mari may date to a period of independence which resulted from the overthrow of Akkad's yoke, possibly late in the reign of Narām-Sîn.

Ididiš

E2.3.1

Ididiš appears as the first *šakkanakku* in the list published by J.-M Durand; he is assigned there a reign of 60 years. No inscriptions are known at present for this ruler.

BIBLIOGRAPHY

1985 Durand, MARI 4 pp. 152 and 158 (study)

Šū-Dagān

E2.3.2

According to the *šakkannaku* list, Ididiš was succeeded by his son, Šū-Dagān, who reigned five years. No inscriptions are known at present for this ruler.

BIBLIOGRAPHY

1985 Durand, MARI 4 p. 152 (study)

Išma-Dagān

E2.3.3

According to *šakkanakk* list, Šū-Dagān was succeeded by a ruler Išmaḫ-Dagān, who is said to have reigned 45 years. His name appears in the form Išma-Dagān in inscriptions of his son. As yet, no inscriptions of this ruler himself have come to light.

BIBLIOGRAPHY

1985 Durand, MARI 4 p. 152 (study)

Niwār-Mēr

E2.3.4

According to the *šakkanakku* list, Išmaḫ-Dagān was succeeded by his son, Nūr (=Niwār)-Mēr, who reigned five years.

1

An inscription known from four bronze foundation tablets records Niwār-Mēr's construction of the temple of the goddess Ninḫursag at Mari.

CATALOGUE

Ex.	Excavation number	Mari provenance	Lines preserved	cpn
1	M 1781	From a corner of the Ninḫursag temple	1–6	n
2	M 1782	As ex. 1	1–6	n
3	M 1783	As ex. 1	1–6	n
4	M 1784	As ex. 1	1–6	n

COMMENTARY

The writing *ᵈnin-ḫur-sag* of the DN of line 5 in this Akkadian text may be compared with the writing *ᵈnin-ḫur-sag-gá* found in the so-called 'Nouvelle Pantheon de Mari' published by Talon in Akkadica 20 (1980) p. 13 line 6. Talon's text, as far as can be determined, always gives the Akkadian forms of the divine names.

BIBLIOGRAPHY

1940 Parrot, Syria 21 pp. 5–7 and pl. II nos. 1 and 2 (provenance, photo of foundation deposits 3 and 4, translation)
1940 Dossin, Syria 21 pp. 152–59 (ex. 3, copy; exs. 1–4, edition)
1961 Gelb, MAD 2² p. 16 no. 1b (study)
1971 Sollberger and Kupper, IRSA IIIE6a (translation)
1974 Parrot, Mari capitale fabuleuse p. 98 (translation)
1985 Durand, MARI 4 p. 151 (exs. 1–4, edition)
1990 Gelb and Kienast, Königsinschriften pp. 362–63 MŠ 8 (exs. 1–4, edition)

TEXT

1) *ni-wa-ar-me-er*
2) GÌR.NÍTA
3) *ma-rí*.KI
4) É
5) *ᵈnin-ḫur-sag*
6) *ib-ni*

1–6) Niwār-Mēr, military governor of Mari, built the temple of the goddess Ninḫursag.

Ištup-Ilum

E2.3.5

According to the *šakkanakku* list, Nūr-Mēr was succeeded by his brother, Ištup-Ilum, who reigned 11 years. Three inscriptions are known for this ruler.

1

A statue found at Mari bears a brief inscription of Išṭup-Ilum.

COMMENTARY

The statue is made of a black basaltic stone and measures 152 cm in height including the socle, 138 cm excluding it. It was found lying on its back in the throne room (room 65) of the palace of Zimrī-Līm and was given the excavation number M 800. The statue is at present in the Archeological Museum in Aleppo. The inscription is located on the right shoulder of the statue and was collated from the published photo.

BIBLIOGRAPHY

1936 Parrot, Syria 17 pp. 24–25 and pl. VII (provenance, photo)
1936 Parrot, Mari, une ville perdue pp. 180–85 (provenance)
1953 Parrot, Mari figs. 104–105 (photo)
1959 Parrot, MAM 2/3 pp. 2–5 and figs. 1–3 (photo, edition, study)
1960 Parrot, Sumer figs. 331–33 (photo)
1961 Gelb, MAD 2[2] p. 16 no. 1 b (study)
1967 Moortgat, Kunst pl. 177 (photo)
1971 Sollberger and Kupper, IRSA IIIE4a (translation)
1974 Parrot, Mari, capitale fabuleuse fig. 66 and pls. XXIV 2 and XXVIII 1 (photo, drawing)
1975 Orthmann (ed.), Der alte Orient pl. 66 (photo)
1981 Spycket, La Statuaire pp. 209–10 and pl. 142 (photo, study)
1990 Gelb and Kienast, Königsinschriften p. 362 MŠ 7 (edition)

TEXT

1) *íš-ṭup*-DINGIR
2) GÌR.NÍTA
3) *ma-rí*.KI

1–3) Išṭup-Ilum, military governor of Mari.

2

Foundation deposits from the southwest, southeast and northwest corners of the 'Temple aux lions' at Mari yielded nine foundation tablets that record, in two slightly variant versions, the construction of the temple of the god Bēl-mātim by Išṭup-Ilum. The first version comes from the southwest and southeast corners of the temple.

CATALOGUE

Ex.	Excavation number	Mari provenance	Object	Lines preserved	cpn
1	M —	From the SW corner of the 'Temple aux lions'	White limestone tablet	1–10	n
2	M —	As ex. 1	Bronze tablet	1–10	n
3	M —	As ex. 1	Schist tablet	1–10	n
4	M 1842	From the SE corner of the 'Temple aux lions'	White limestone tablet	1–10	p* (obv. only)
5	M 1846	As ex. 4	Bronze tablet	1–10	n
6	M 1841	As ex. 4	Schist tablet	1–10	p* (obv. only)

COMMENTARY

The reading of the divine name in line 9 as *bēl-mātim* is based on the correlation of the entry ^{d}L[UGAL-*ma-tin*] of the 'Pantheon of Ur III' with ^{d}*be-el-ma-tim* of the 'New Pantheon of Mari' noted by J.-M. Durand in MARI 4 (1985) p. 163. W.G. Lambert, on the other hand (MARI 4 p. 529 n. 4), argues that the name would appear to be Šar-mātim; he notes the Old Assyrian writing *šar-*(*ra*)*-ma-tí-in*/*in*$_4$ (Hirsch, AfO Beiheft 13/14 p. 26).

BIBLIOGRAPHY

1940 Parrot, Syria 21 pp. 20–21 and fig. 15 (exs. 1–3, copy, translation) and pl. X no. 1 (exs. 4–6, photo)
1940 Dossin, Syria 21 pp. 161, 163 (exs. 4–6, provenance, composite copy, edition)
1961 Gelb, MAD 2[2] p. 16 no.1 b (study)
1971 Sollberger and Kupper, IRSA IIIE4b (translation)
1974 Parrot, Mari, capitale fabuleuse pp. 102–103 and fig. 56 (exs. 1-3, copy, translation)
1985 Durand, MARI 4 p. 151 (ex. 4, edition)
1990 Gelb and Kienast, Königsinschriften p. 362 MŠ 6 (exs. 4–6, edition)

TEXT

1) *íš-má-*^{d}*da-gan*	1–3) Išma-Dagān, military governor of Mari:
2) GÌR.NÍTA	
3) *ma-rí*.KI	
4) *iš-ṭup*-DINGIR	4–7) Ištup-Ilum, military governor of Mari, his son,
5) GÌR.NÍTA	
6) *ma-rí*.KI	
7) DUMU-*šu*	
8) É	8–10) built the temple of the god Bēl-mātim.
9) ^{d}LUGAL-*ma-tim*	
10) *ib-ni*	

3

A variant version of the building inscription dealing with the temple of Bēl-mātim was found on three tablets from the northwest corner of the 'Temple aux lions'.

CATALOGUE

Ex.	Excavation number	Object	Lines preserved	cpn
1	M 1877	White limestone tablet	1–9	p* (obv. only)
2	M 1880	Bronze tablet	1–9	n
3	M 1876	Schist tablet	1–9	p* (obv. only)

BIBLIOGRAPHY

1940 Parrot, Syria 21 p. 22 and pl. X no. 2 (exs. 1–3, photo, study)
1940 Dossin, Syria 21 pp. 161–62 (exs. 1–3, composite copy)
1961 Gelb, MAD 2[2] p. 16 no. 1b (study)
1971 Sollberger and Kupper, IRSA IIIE4b (exs. 1–3, translation)
1985 Durand, MARI 4 p. 151 (ex. 4, edition)
1990 Gelb and Kienast, Königsinschrifkten p. 361 MŠ 5 (exs. 1–3, edition)

TEXT

1) *íš-ṭup*-DINGIR 2) GÌR.NÍTA 3) *ma-rí*.KI	1–3) Išṭup-Ilum, military governor of Mari,
4) DUMU *íš-má-*[d]*da-gan* 5) GÌR.NÍTA 6) *ma-rí*.KI	4–6) son of Išma-Dagān, military governor of Mari,
7) É 8) [d]LUGAL-*ma-tim* 9) *ib-ni*	7–9) built the temple of the god Bēl-mātim.

Iškun-Adad

E2.3.6

Durand (MARI 4 p. 152) tentatively read the PN which follows Išṭup-Ilum in the *šakkanakku* list as Išgum-Adad (*iš-gum-*[d]IŠKUR); a reading *iš-kùn-*[d]*da-gan* is much more likely. No inscriptions of this ruler, who is said to have reigned eight years, have as yet appeared.

BIBLIOGRAPHY

1985 Durand, MARI 4 p. 152 (study)

AŠŠUR

E2.4

Relatively little is known about the history of the city of Aššur in Sargonic times. While there is no evidence at present for Sargon's control over the city, the discovery of a mace head with an inscription of Rīmuš (E2.1.2.19 ex. 42) and a spear point with the name of a servant of Man-ištūšu (E2.1.3.2002) suggests that Agade held the city during the early part of the Sargonic period. Man-ištūšu is known from a later inscription of Šamšī-Adad I (RIMA 1 A.0.39.2) to have built the temple of the goddess Aštar at Nineveh, a city not far upstream, and the discovery at Aššur of an alabaster vase fragment with a votive inscription of a Sargonic king to the goddess Aštar (E2.0.0.1005) shows a similar concern for her cult in that city. The GN Aššur occurs frequently in the late Sargonic period archive from nearby Gasur and is also mentioned in a text of probable Sargonic origin (known from a later tablet copy [UET 8 no. 14]) that gives a list of city governors.

ITITI

E.2.4.1

1

A stone plaque found at Aššur gives the name of a seemingly independent ruler of Aššur named Ititi.

COMMENTARY

The plaque was found in the Ištar temple, eA7IISE, and bears the excavation number Ass 20377 and the museum number VA 8831a. It is shown in Assur photo 6253. The plaque measures 25×21.1 cm; the inscription was collated. Another fragment of the plaque without writing is Ass 19882 = VA 8831b.

BIBLIOGRAPHY

1912 Jordan, MDOG 49 p. 27 (study)
1922 Andrae, AIT pl. 64a–b (photo)
1922 Schroder, KAH 2 no. 1 (copy)
1926 Meissner, IAK I 1 (edition)
1926 Luckenbill, ARAB 1 §§ 17–18 (translation)
1926–27 Luckenbill, AJSL 43 pp. 209–10 (study)
1935 Meek, HSS 10 p. x (study)
1938 J. Lewy, JAOS 58 pp. 451 and 460 (study)
1942 Poebel, JNES 1 pp. 259–60 (edition)
1955 Gelb, OAIC p. 334 (study)
1959 Weidner, RLA 3/2 p. 151 (study)
1961 Borger, EAK 1 p. 1 (study)
1967 Seux, ERAS p. 358 and n. 5 (study)
1971 Boese, Weihplatten pp. 127–29, 207–208 and pl. XXXV 1 AR 1 (copy, study)
1972 Grayson, ARI 1 p. 2 (translation)
1976 Larsen, City-State pp. 31–32 (study)
1977 Edzard, Rép. Géogr. 1 p. 54 (study)
1987 Grayson, RIMA 1 p. 7 A.0.1001.1 (edition)
1990 Gelb and Kienast, Königsinschriften p. 369 Varia 2 (edition)

TEXT

1) *i-ti-ti*
2) PA
3) DUMU *i-nin-la-ba*
4) *in śa-la-ti*
5) *ga-sur*$_{x}$(SAG).KI
6) *a-na*
7) [d]INANNA
8) A.MU.RU

1–8) Ititi, the ruler, son of Innin-labba, dedicated (this plaque) from the booty of Gasur to the goddess Aštar.

GASUR

E2.5

Very little of the political history of Gasur, later Nuzi, a small town not far from modern Kirkuk, is known for the Sargonic period. The administrative texts discovered there were dated by Meek to the early Sargonic period, but a reconsideration of their chronology by B. Foster (OrAnt 21 [1982] p. 39) suggests a date to the time of Narām-Sîn or later. One fragmentarily preserved year name in the Gasur archive (HSS 10 no. 40) may belong to Šar-kali-šarrī; it is so badly broken that the attribution is not certain. The name of a Sargonic period governor of Gasur is found on a bulla found at Tell Brāk.

Itbe-labba

E2.5.1

1

The seal of Itbe-labba, governor of Gasur, was impressed on a clay bulla found in excavations at Tell Brāk.

COMMENTARY

The bulla, which measures 5.5×4 cm, was found in the fill immediately overlying the lower Akkadian building, site FS. It bears the registration number 2204; locus FS 392; excavation number TB 8014. The inscription was collated from the published photo. The style of the seal motif on this impression is designated as Akkadisch III by Boehmer (Glyptik p. 34–46); he dates this style to the time of Narām-Sîn to Šū-Turul. This fact provides a rough indication for the date of Itbe-labba's governorship at Gasur.

BIBLIOGRAPHY

1987 Oates, Iraq 49 p. 190 and pl. XXXVIII a–b (photo, study)

1988 Illingworth, Iraq 50 pp. 98–99 no. 22 (copy, edition)

TEXT

1) *it-be-la-*⸢*ba*⸣
2) ÉNS[I]
3) *ga-súr*.KI

1–3) Itbe-labba, govern[or] of Gasur.

NIPPUR

E2.6

Nippur, Sumer's religious capital, was an important prize for the Sargonic kings and it is significant that Sargon's first act after defeating Lugal-zage-si was to take the captive king in a neck stock to Nippur, the city which not long before had recognized the Uruk ruler himself as king of the land.

There is abundant evidence for the Akkadian kings' reverence toward the god Enlil and his cult city. Excavators have found, for example, many pieces of booty, generally vases, that were dedicated by the Sargonic kings to Enlil in Nippur. Sargon's daughter En-ḫedu-ana recognized the importance of the city by placing the hymn to Nippur second in her compilation of 'Sumerian Temple Hymns'. Narām-Sîn installed his daughter Tūta-napšum as *entu* priestess of Enlil at Nippur (see E2.1.4.18–20) and appointed his son and heir Šar-kali-šarrī to some high administrative post in the city (see E2.1.4.2021). Narām-Sîn began a massive rebuilding of the Ekur temple (see E2.1.4.18–19); this project was apparently completed during the reign of his successor (see E2.1.5.1–3).

The reaction of the Nippur authorities to the imposition of Akkadian rule was twofold. On the one hand, as a result of the political reality of their times, they duly recognized the Akkadian kings' claim to the kingship of the land. In inscription E2.1.1.3, for example, Sargon relates that it was the god Enlil who granted his weapon to him. In inscription E2.1.2.5, Rīmuš tells how the god Enlil gave him kingship, and, in E2.1.2.10, relates how the same god entrusted all the lands to him for safekeeping. In inscription E2.1.3.2, Man-ištūšu refers to the god Enlil's gift of the sceptre of kingship. As noted, year name (a) of Narām-Sîn apparently deals with the king's receiving of some symbol of kingship from the temple of Enlil at Nippur. In their inscriptions both Narām-Sîn and Šar-kali-šarrī refer to the god Enlil as their father and the latter king even adopted the title 'beloved son of Enlil' (E2.1.5.2). Like his father, Šar-kali-šarrī made a ceremonial trip to Nippur at the beginning of his reign and was apparently crowned king of the land in that city (see the introductory comments to Šar-kali-šarrī, section I i).

On the other hand, Nippur, as the ancient religious capital of Sumer, must have chafed under the imposition of Akkadian rule, and it is not surprising that on at least two separate occasions the city participated in major revolts against the Akkadian king. The first rebellion took place early in the reign of Narām-Sîn, when Nippur joined a league of Sumerian cities led by the king of AB×U/ŠUŠ (possibly Apišal) in an unsuccessful bid to rid themselves of their Akkadian overlords. A second rebellion broke out later in the same reign; in this case one of the enemy leaders seems to have been a governor of Nippur, Enlil-nizu. His name can be restored with reasonable certainty in text E2.1.4.6. The second revolt, like the first, was successfully put down and Nippur appears to have been a loyal vassal until the collapse of the empire during the reign of Šar-kali-šarrī.

Six inscriptions are presently known from the Sargonic period that give the names of local potentates of Nippur.

Uruna-badbi

E2.6.1

2001

A dedicatory inscription for the life of Uruna-badbi, *šangû* priest of the god Enlil, is found on a vase fragment from Nippur. For a dedicatory inscription of Uruna-badbi for Narām-Sîn, see E2.1.4.2001 above.

COMMENTARY

The vase fragment is gray calcite stalagmite and presently measures 17.1×11×1.35 cm; its original diameter was 17.3 cm at the centre. The actual inscription measures 10×3 cm. The vase comes from the third season of the University of Pennsylvania's excavations and bears the museum number CBS 9330. The inscription was collated. In line 6 the sign after dub-sar is an AB sign with an inscribed single diagonal wedge.

BIBLIOGRAPHY

1896 Hilprecht, BE 1/2 no. 113 and pp. 49–50 n. 4 (copy, edition)
1907 Thureau-Dangin, SAK pp. 158–59 Patesis und sonstige Beamte von Nippur no. 9 (edition)
1926 Legrain, PBS 15 p. 48 sub no. 81 (study)
1929 Barton, RISA pp. 8–9 Urunabadbi (edition)
1961 Gelb, MAD 2^2 p. 201 Narâm-Sin Officials, etc. no. 8 (study)
1971 Sollberger and Kupper, IRSA IIA4o (translation)
1990 Gelb and Kienast, Königsinschriften pp. 108–109 Narāmsîn B 5 (edition)

TEXT

1) ^{d}nin-líl-ra	1) To the goddess Ninlil,
2) uru-na-bàd-bi	2–4) in order that Uruna-badbi, *šangû* priest of the god Enlil, might live,
3) sanga-^{d}en-líl	
4) ḫé-ti-la-šè	
5) ur-sa_6-ga	5–7) Ur-saga, ... scribe of the temple of the god Enlil,
6) dub-sar-AB×LAK 178	
7) é-^{d}en-líl-ka-ke_4	
8) ga-ti-la-šè	8) as an ex-voto,
9) nam-ti-	9–10) for the life of Amaʾabzi
10) ama-áb-zi-šè	
11) nam-ti-	11–12) (and) for the lives of his wife (and) children,
12) dam-dumu-na-šè	
13) a mu-na-ru	13) dedicated (this vase).

Lugal-nizu

E2.6.2

1

A number of bricks stamped with a three-line inscription of Lugal-nizu, governor of Nippur and *šangû* priest of the god Enlil, were found, for the most part, in the area of the Ekur temple in Nippur.

The fact that one of the bricks (exemplar 3) was coloured with a distinct reddish hue (see H. Behrens, JCS 37 p. 237 no. 36) suggests that Lugal-nizu's pavement, like that of Narām-Sîn, was composed of a pattern of red and yellow bricks (see commentary to E2.1.4.15).

CATALOGUE

Ex.	Museum number	Excavation number	Nippur provenance	Dimensions (cm)	Lines preserved	cpn
1	CBS 16201a	—	—	37×35×7.5	1–3	c
2	CBS 16201b	—	—	38.5×38.5×7.0	1–3	c
3	UM 84-26-19	—	—	38.0×19.0×7.5	1–3	c
4	Istanbul, number unknown	—	—	—	1–3	p
5	—	—	Out of context in the talus of Mount VI	39.3×19.0×18.7	—	n
6	—	—	As ex. 5	—	—	n
7	—	2 N-T488	En 13, floor 2a, slightly below the level of the Akkadian pavement	—	—	n

COMMENTARY

The PN of line 1 was read lugal-nì-ba by Legrain, but collation of exs. 1–3 reveals a clear zu sign at the end of the line.

BIBLIOGRAPHY

1903 Hilprecht, Explorations pp. 475–76 (provenance, translation)
1926 Legrain, PBS 15 no. 82 (ex. 1, copy, edition)
1951 McCown, UMB 16/2 pl. VI (ex. 7, photo [in situ])
1967 McCown, Nippur 1 p. 25 (ex. 7, findspot)
1981 Michalowski, RA 75 p. 175 n. 14 (exs 1,7 study)
1985 Behrens, JCS 37 p. 237 no. 36 (exs. 1–3, study)
1987 Westenholz, OSP 2 p. 28 (exs. 5–7, study)
1991 Steible, NSBW 2 p. 340 Lugalnigzu 1 (exs. 1–2, 7, edition)

TEXT

1) lugal-nì-zu
2) énsi-nibru.KI
3) sanga-^{d}en-líl

1–3) Lugal-nizu, governor of Nippur, *šangû* priest of the god Enlil.

Nammaḫ-abzu

E2.6.3

Two tablets from Nippur dated by a year name of Šar-kali-šarrī (see Goetze, JAOS 88 [1968] p. 58) mention a certain Nammaḫ as governor of Nippur. His name appears in a fuller writing, Nammaḫ-abzu, in a votive inscription (E2.6.3.2001) and a seal inscription of one of his servants (E2.6.3.2002). The Nammaḫ, governor of Nippur, whose name appears on a bowl fragment from Nippur published by Buccellati and Biggs (AS 17 no. 5), on the other hand, is apparently not the governor of Sargonic times, for the script of that inscription clearly dates to ED III times. For archival texts mentioning the Nammaḫ-(abzu) of Sargonic times, see Westenholz, OSP 2 nos. 93 and 98.

2001

A Sumerian inscription incised on the rim of a small cup indicates that the object was dedicated for the life of Nammaḫ-abzu.

COMMENTARY

The cup fragment is made of alabaster and bears the museum number AO 4637. The edition follows the reading established by Steible.

BIBLIOGRAPHY

1909 Scheil, RT 31 p. 134 (edition)
1910 Thureau-Dangin, RT 32 p. 44 (copy)
1929 Barton, RISA pp. 10–11 no. 8 Nammakhabsu (edition)
1982 Steible, ASBW 2 p. 225 sub Nammaḫ 1 (edition)
1991 Steible, NSBW 2 p. 341 Nammaḫabzu 1 (edition)

TEXT

1) ^{d}nin-é-gal
2) nam-ti-
3) nam-maḫ-abzu
4) énsi-nibru.KI-šè
5) igi-^{d}en-líl-šè
6) ir_{11}-da-né
7) a m[u-na-r]u

1) For the goddess Nin-egal,
2–4) for the life of Nammaḫ-abzu, governor of Nippur,
5–7) Igi-Enlilše, his servant, de[dica]ted (this cup).

2002

The impression of a seal of a servant of Nammaḫ-abzu is found on clay tag from Nippur.

COMMENTARY

The clay tag measures 3.4×2.3 cm and bears the museum number N 7718. (Philadelphia). The edition follows the reading provided by Westenholz.

BIBLIOGRAPHY

1987 Westenholz, OSP 2 no. 187 (edition)

TEXT

1) nam-maḫ-abzu
2) énsi-nibru.KI
3) un-íl
4) dumu nita-zi
5) ugula-é
6) ìr-[zu]

1–2) Nammaḫ-abzu, governor of Nippur:

3–6) Un-il, son of Nita-zi, the chief administrator of the temple, (is) [your] servant.

ISIN

E2.7

Although recent archaeological work at Isin has revealed that the city was indeed occupied in Sargonic times, we do not yet know how important the city was at that time. Sargonic royal inscriptions from Isin are rare; only two (E2.1.3.5 and E2.0.0.1013) are known at present. Archival texts of Sargonic date, on the other hand, are more plentiful (see Foster, ZA 72 [1982] pp. 6–7).

Lu-dingirana

E2.7.1

2001

A seal of a servant of a *šangû* priest of the city of Isin, dated on the basis of its seal design to the Sargonic period, is in the Newell Collection.

COMMENTARY

The seal is made of limestone and measures 2.8×1.9 cm. It bears the registration number NCBS 96 and is part of the Newell Collection of Babylonian Seals currently housed at Yale. The inscription was collated from the published photo. The last sign of the inscription appears before the foreleg of the lion in design of the seal.

BIBLIOGRAPHY

1934 von der Osten, Newell no. 96 (photo, edition, study)
1965 Boehmer, Glyptik no. 634 and fig. 189 (photo, study)
1968–9 Edzard, AfO 22 p. 16 no. 24–8 (transliteration)
1977 Zettler in Gibson and Biggs, Seals p. 36 (translation)
1981 Buchanan and Hallo, Early Near Eastern Seals no. 423 (photo, edition, study)

TEXT

1) lú-dingir-ra-⸢na⸣
2) ⸢sanga⸣ IN.KI
3) lú-dingir-ra
4) dub-sar ir_{11}-<da>
5) -ni

1–2) Lu-dingirana, *šangû* priest of Isin:

3–5) Lu-dingira, the scribe, (is) his servant.

ŠARRĀKUM

E2.8

The city of Šarrākum was an important centre in Early Dynastic and Sargonic times; its influence declined considerably, however, in the succeeding Ur III and Old Babylonian periods. For a proposed location of the city on the Iturungal canal north of the city of Adab, see D. Frayne, Early Dynastic List §2.2.6. The city was probably part of the domains of Lugal-zage-si of Uruk and passed to Akkadian control when Sargon defeated the Uruk ruler. As part of the Sargonic realm its shrine was celebrated by En-ḫedu-ana in her famous collection of temple hymns. Unlike the other cities of the south, there is no evidence of any campaigns of the Akkadian kings against Šarrākum, nor any record of revolts of the city against its northern masters. It is probable that Šarrākum became independent in late Sargonic-Gutian times. To be dated to this period is the rule of a certain ŠAR-A-TI-GU-BI-SI-IN (reading of name uncertain), known from two inscriptions. The evidence of one of these, E2.8.2002, indicates that ŠAR-A-TI-GU-BI-SI-IN's father, whose name is still unknown, had already adopted the title LUGAL 'king' and thus, like his son, was apparently an independent ruler of Šarrākum.

ŠAR-A-TI-GU-BI-SI-IN

E2.8.1

2001

A fragmentarily preserved plaque bears a dedicatory inscription in Sumerian for the life of ŠAR-A-TI-GU-BI-SI-IN.

COMMENTARY

The plaque is made of limestone and measures 20×26×2.1 cm. It is said to have come from Jōkha, ancient Umma; the contents of the inscription would suggest an original provenance of Šarrākum. The piece, acquired by the Louvre in 1911, bears the museum number AO 4799; its inscription was collated by B. Foster. Collation indicates that the broken DN of line 1 is composed with the EZEN×KUR sign; its reading is unknown. For the reading of the GN of line 7 as a compound logogram pronounced Šarrākum, or the like, see the comments of P. Steinkeller in Vicino Oriente 6 (1986) p. 35 n. 39. The interpretation of the RN of line 11 is uncertain. Jacobsen (SKL 11 p. 120 n. 308) proposed a reading *mú-a-ti-gu-bi-si-in* with translation 'Mu'ati (has heard) their wail'. Gelb, in MAD 3 p. 224 proposes, with reservation: 'O king, I gave their (the sisters') laments'. While the existence of components of the PN that could be explained as Akkadian *šar*, *adi*, and *-šin* suggests that the name was Akkadian, an understanding of the name as a whole is not clear. Perhaps it was a Gutian name.

BIBLIOGRAPHY

1912 Thureau-Dangin, RA 9 pp. 74–76 (photo, edition)
1929 Barton, RISA pp. 170–71 Sharratiguisin (edition)
1939 Jacobsen, SKL p. 120 n. 308 (study)
1952 Gelb, MAD 2[2] p. 174 n. 19 (study)
1957 Gelb, MAD 3 pp. 224 and 287 (study)
1965 Boehmer, Glyptik p. 41 n. 170 (study)
1971 Boese, Weihplatten pp. 129–33, 208–209 and pl. XXXVI UM 1 (copy, study)
1971 Nagel, APA 2 p. 1 (study)
1971 Sollberger and Kupper, IRSA IIF1a (translation)
1976 Amiet, L'art d'Agadé no. 65 (photo, translation, study)
1983 Selz, Bankettszene 1 pp. 571–74 (edition, study) and 2 p. K 61 no. 478 (edition, study)
1990 Gelb and Kienast, Königsinschriften pp. 297–99 Gutium 4 (edition)

TEXT

1) ᵈnin-EZEN×KUR 2) lugal 3) ḫul-gál ra	1–3) To the god Nin-EZEN×KUR, the king who smites the evil-doer,
4) nì-du$_7$-pa-è 5) dub-sar 6) pisan-dub-ba 7) URU.SAG.RIG$_7$.KI	4–7) Nidu-pae, scribe (and) archivist of the city of Šarrākum,
8) dumu-ur-GIŠ.kiri$_6$ 9) dub-sar-ra-ke$_4$	8–9) son of Ur-kiri, scribe,

10) nam-ti-
11) ŠAR-A-TI-GU-BI-SI-IN
12) lugal-la-na-šè
13) nam-ti-la-ni-šè
14) nam-ti-
15) dam-dumu-na-šè
16) a mu-na-ru
Caption 1
1) nin-geštin/ nin-abzu-a/ nam-šita-du$_{11}$-du$_{11}$/ géme-^{d}in[anna]
Caption 2
1) géme-mug-sag-gá-na
2) dam-ni
Caption 3
1) sig$_4$-kalam-ì-tu
2) lugal-u$_4$-an-na
Caption 4
1) *puzur$_4$-é-a*
2) ur-⸢d⸣ištaran

10–12) for the life of ŠAR-A-TI-GU-BI-SI-IN, his lord,

13–15) (and) for his own life (and) for the lives of his wife (and) children,

16) dedicated (this plaque).
Caption 1
1) Nin-geštin/ Nin-abzua/ Namšita-dudu/ Geme-In[anna].
Caption 2
1–2) Geme-mug-sagana, his wife.

Caption 3
1) Sig-kalam-itu,
2) Lugal-u-ana.
Caption 4
1) Puzur-Ea,
2) Ur-Ištarana.

2002

A seal in the British Museum bears the inscription of a servant of ŠAR-A-TI-GU-BI-SI-IN.

COMMENTARY

The seal is made of dolomite and measures 3.3×2.2 cm. It came from the Oscar Raphael bequest; its original provenance is unknown. The piece bears the museum number BM 130691 (1945-10-15, 18). The inscription was collated from the published photo. Boehmer indicates a post-Akkadian period date for this seal.

BIBLIOGRAPHY

1965 Boehmer, Glyptik no. 798 and fig. 271 (copy, edition, study)
1966 Boehmer, Orientalia NS 35 pl. LV no. 22 (copy)
1968–69 Edzard, AfO 22 p. 16 no. 24–18 (transliteration)
1971 Nagel, APA 2 p. 1 (edition)
1971 Sollberger and Kupper, IRSA pp. 123–24 n. 2 to IIF1a (translation)
1982 Collon, Cylinder Seals 2 no. 103 (photo, edition, study)
1990 Gelb and Kienast, Königsinschriften p. 299 (edition)

TEXT

1) ŠAR-A-TI-GU-BI-SI-IN
2) DUMU LUGAL
3) ur-sa$_6$
4) DUB.SAR
5) ⸢IR$_{11}$⸣-*sú*

1–2) ŠAR-A-TI-GU-BI-SI-IN, son of the king:

3–5) Ursa, the scribe, (is) his servant.

ADAB

E2.9

Adab was an important centre in late Early Dynastic and Sargonic times; according to Adams (Heartland of Cities p. 160), 'The Adab region thus became particularly densely occupied, and it is arguably the largest urban concentration yet known within the Old Akkadian realm'. The importance of the city at this time is also indicated by the large number of archival texts of Sargonic date found by E.J. Banks at Bismāyā (see Foster, ZA 72 [1982] pp. 4–5). The city may well have been independent for a least some part of the Early Dynastic period, since a dynasty from Adab figures in the Sumerian King List and inscriptions of such rulers as Lugal-da-lu and Me-ba-dur, who styled themselves 'king' (lugal), are known. This independence was certainly brought to an end by the conquest of the city by Lugal-zage-si of Uruk, who confirmed Mes-kigal as city governor (see commentary to E.2.9.1.2001). The city, in turn, passed to Sargonic control when Sargon defeated Lugal-zage-si. As part of the Sargonic realm its temple was honoured by the *entu* priestess En-ḫedu-ana in hymn 29 of her 'Collection of Temple Hymns'. An uprising by the city against Sargonic rule was crushed early in the reign of Rīmuš when the city governor Mes-kigala was captured (see E2.1.2.1). The city of Adab supported two more widespread rebellions during the reign of Narām-Sîn, the first led by the king of the city AB×ŠUŠ (see E2.1.4.2) and the second led by the king of Uruk (see E2.1.4.6); both rebellions were quelled by Narām-Sîn. Adab remained firmly under Akkadian control during the remainder of Narām-Sîn's reign and into the reign of Šar-kali-šarrī, when Lugal-giš served as governor and vassal of the Akkadian king (see E2.1.5.2005). Seals or seal impressions that mention four Akkadian period rulers of Adab are also known.

Mes-kigal

E2.9.1

2001

A statue fragment is incised with a dedicatory inscription for the life of Mes-kigal, governor of Adab.

COMMENTARY

The broken alabaster statue consists of three joined pieces that together measure 88 cm in height; they now bear the museum number IM 5572. The statue was purchased from I. Gegou and is said to have come from Bismāyā. The inscription was not collated.

On the basis of its stylistic features, Strommenger and Nagel date the statue to the Fara/Ur I period, that is, to ED III times. An economic tablet (Hackman, BIN 8 no. 26) indicates that Mes-kigala, presumably a variant writing for Mes-kigal, served as governor of Adab during the time of Lugal-zage-si of Uruk. He apparently continued in that position through the reign of Sargon and into the reign of Rīmuš, since, as noted, Mes-kigala was defeated by Rīmuš. The exact date of his statue inscription is unknown; it is edited here, for convenience, among the inscriptions of the Sargonic period governors of Adab.

BIBLIOGRAPHY

1934 Meissner, MAOG 8 1/2 pp. 28–31 and fig. 19 (photo of statue [inscription not visible], study)

1966 Iraq Directorate General of Antiquities, Iraq Museum Guide p. 22 no. 26

1968 Nagel and Strommenger, BJVF 8 p. 177 (transliteration [by Sollberger], study)

1970 Rowton, CAH 1/1 p. 220 and n. 1 (study)

1981 Spycket, Statuaire p. 85 (study)

1986 Yang, Sargonic Archive pp. 51–52 and n. 55 (transliteration)

TEXT

1) ^{d}nin-šubur
2) sukkal-an-ra
3) nam-ti-
4) [mes]-ki-gal
5) [én]si-
6) [adab.KI]
Lacuna

1–2) To the god Ninšubur, vizier of the god An,

3–6) for the life of [Mes]-kigal, [gov]ernor of [Adab, PN dedicated (this statue)].

Lugal-giš

E2.9.2

2001

According to inscription E2.1.5.2005, Lugal-gis served as governor of Adab during the reign of Šar-kali-šarrī. An impression of a seal of a servant of this Lugal-giš is found on a clay bulla from Bismāyā.

COMMENTARY

The bulla was found in excavations of Banks in the 'school room' of Mound IV and now bears the museum number A 813 (Chicago). The inscription was collated by R. Biggs.

BIBLIOGRAPHY

1912 Banks, Bismya p. 301 (photo; A 813 appears in upper left)
1986 Yang, Sargonic Archive pp. 18 and 48–49 (edition, study)
1989 Yang, Sargonic Inscriptions pp. 30 and 334 (edition)

TEXT

1) ⌜lugal-giš⌝
2) ÉNSI
3) ⌜UD⌝.NUN.KI
4) x [...]
5) DUB.SAR
6) IR$_{11}$-*s*[*ú*]

1–3) Lugal-giš, governor of Adab:

4–6) [PN], scribe, (is) h[is] servant.

2002

A seal of a servant of Lugal-giš is now in Brussels.

COMMENTARY

The seal is made of rock crystal and measures 3 cm in length and 2.1 cm in diameter. The piece is said to have come from Kiš; it now bears the inventory number 866 in the collection of the Musées Royaux d'Art et d'Histoire, Brussels. The inscription was collated from the published photo.

BIBLIOGRAPHY

1943 Speleers, Catalogue Suppl. pp. 68 and 186 no. 866 (photo, copy, edition)
1965 Boehmer, Glyptik no. 711 and fig. 548 (photo, study)
1968 Nagel and Strommenger, BJVF 8 pp. 154–55 and 167 no. 26a (edition, study)
1990 Gelb and Kienast, Königsinschriften p. 46 no. S–31 (edition)

TEXT

1) ur-^{d}iškur dub-sar
2) ir$_{11}$ -lugal-giš

1–2) Ur-Iškur, the scribe, (is) the servant of Lugal-giš.

2003

A cylinder seal in the Atarashi Collection in Tokyo bears the Sumerian inscription of a servant of Lugal-giš.

COMMENTARY

The seal is made of 'greenstone schist' and measures 3.02 cm in length. The diameter of the piece ranges from 1.88–1.90 cm at the ends, and 1.69–1.75 cm at the middle. The inscription was collated from the published photo.

BIBLIOGRAPHY

1992 Kuga, ASJ 14 pp. 103–123 (photo, edition, study)

TEXT

(Column i)
1) lugal-giš
2) énsi
3) adab.KI
(Column ii)
4 nam-tar-ré
(Column iii a)
5) dub-sar
6) sanga
(Column iii b)
7) ^{d}en-ki
8) ir$_{11}$-da-ni

1–3) Lugal-giš, governor of Adab:

4–8) Namtarre, the scribe, *šangû* priest of the god Enki, (is) his servant.

Ur-TUR

E2.9.3

1

A seal of Ur-TUR, governor of Adab, was found in excavations of Banks at Bismāyā.

COMMENTARY

The seal is made of lapis lazuli and measures 3.7×2.5 cm. It was found by E.J. Banks at Mound III, the 'Semitic Quarter', and bears the museum number A 526 (Chicago). The style of the design is assigned by Boehmer (Entwicklung p. 160 no. 655) to his 'Akkadisch III' type. The inscription was collated from the published photo.

BIBLIOGRAPHY

1910 Ward, Seals p. 51 and fig. 135b (copy, translation [by Price])
1912 Banks, Bismya pp. 301–303 (photo, copy, translation)
1927–28 Williams, AJSL 44 p. 239 and pl. 1 no. 16 (photo, edition, study)
1965 Boehmer, Glyptik no. 655 and fig. 197 (photo, study)
1968–69 Edzard, AfO 22 p. 15 no. 17–2 (transliteration)
1986 Yang, Sargonic Archive pp. 15 and 51 (transliteration, study)
1989 Yang, Sargonic Inscriptions p. 32 (transliteration)

TEXT

1) ur-^{d}TUR
2) énsi-
3) adab.KI

1–3) Ur-TUR, governor of Adab.

[...]-AB

E2.9.4

2001

The partially preserved name of a governor of Adab appears on a clay bulla.

COMMENTARY

The bulla was found in excavations of Banks at Bismāyā; it bears the museum number Adab 771 (Istanbul). The edition follows the transliteration of Boehmer. The style of the seal design is assigned by Boehmer (Entwicklung p. 157 no. 562) to his 'Akkadisch III' group. For the PN in line 3, see the comments of Gelb, MAD 3 p. 104.

BIBLIOGRAPHY

1947 Kraus, JCS 1 p. 101 (study)
1965 Boehmer, Glyptik no. 562 (edition, study)
1968–69 Edzard, AfO 22 p. 17 no. 24–38 and n. 50 (transliteration)
1986 Yang, Sargonic Archive p. 51 (transliteration)
1989 Yang, Sargonic Inscriptions p. 32 (transliteration)

TEXT

1) [...]-AB
2) [ÉN]SI *adab*.KI
3) [a]-ba-an-da-sá
4) DUB.SAR
5) IR$_{11}$-*sú*

1–2) [...]-AB, [go]vernor of Adab:

3–5) [A]ba-andasa, the scribe, (is) his servant.

Unknown Governor

E2.9.5

2001

A clay bulla bears the seal impression of a servant of a governor of Adab whose name is largely broken away.

COMMENTARY

The bulla was found in excavations of E.J. Banks at Bismāyā and bears the museum number Adab 773 (Istanbul). The style of the seal design is assigned by Boehmer (Entwicklung p. 157 no. 562) to his 'Akkadisch III' group. The edition follows that given by Boehmer.

BIBLIOGRAPHY

1947 Kraus, JCS 1 p. 101 (study)
1965 Boehmer, Glyptik no. 561 (edition, study)
1968–69 Edzard, AfO 22 p. 17 no. 24–37 (transliteration)

TEXT

1) [...] 2) [ÉN]SI 3) [*ad*]*ab*.KI	1–3) [PN, go]vernor of [Ad]ab:
4) LUGAL-x-x 5) [...] 6) IR_{11}-[*sú*]	4–6) Lugal-x-x, ..., (is) [his] servant.

ŠURUPPAK

E2.10

Although archaeological evidence attests to some occupation of Šuruppak during the Sargonic period (H. Martin, Fara p. 116), virtually nothing is known of its history during this time. The city does not appear as the target of any military campaign of the Sargonic kings. It is named, however, as one of the Sumerian cities which supported the king of Uruk in his rebellion against Narām-Sîn (E2.1.4.6).

An inscription of Ḫala-adda, governor of Šuruppak (E2.10.1), may possibly date to late Sargonic or Gutian times.

Ḫala-adda

E2.10.1

1

A clay cone found at Fara provides a Sumerian inscription of Ḫala-adda, city governor of Šuruppak.

COMMENTARY

The cone bears the excavation number F. 1035 and the museum number VA 6705. It was found by Koldewey on the western side of the mound, Graben XI cg; 1.20 metres 'in Wehschicht'. It measures 11.3 cm in length and and 6.3 cm in diameter. Information on the cone was kindly provided by J. Marzahn.

E. Sollberger (IRSA p. 123 IIE1a n. b) connects the ad-uš of line 8 with Akkadian *aduššu* 'a synonym for wall', which appears in the late synonym list Malku = šarru (see CAD A/1 p. 137). The word appears in the form *adaššu*(*m*), with the meaning 'exterior enclosure wall of a city' in OB texts from Mari (Dossin, RA 66 [1972] pp. 111–30). Whether there is a connection of this term with Sum. ad-uš of this inscription is uncertain.

BIBLIOGRAPHY

1903 Koldewey and Delitzsch, MDOG 16 pp. 13–14 (copy, translation)
1907 Thureau-Dangin, SAK pp. 150–51 Ḫa-la-ad-da (edition)
1929 Barton, RISA pp. 10–11 Khaladda (edition)
1931 Heinrich, Fara pp. 4–5 (photo, copy, study)
1932 Kramer, JAOS 52 p. 116 (study)
1961 Salonen, Türen p. 136 (study)
1971 Sollberger and Kupper, IRSA IIE1a (translation)
1988 Martin, Fara p. 129 (study)

TEXT

1) da-da 2) énsi- 3) šuruppak.KI	1–3) Dada, governor of Šuruppak:
4) ḫa-la-ad-da 5) éns[i]- 6) šuruppak.KI 7) dumu-ni	4–7) Ḫala-adda, gover[nor] of Šuruppak, his son,
8) ad-uš-abul(KÁ.GAL)- 9) ^{d}sùd-da-ke$_4$ 10) bí-in-ús	8–10) *laid* the ... of the city gate of the goddess Sud.

UMMA

E2.11

The city of Umma, marked today by the extensive tell named Jōkha, was, along with Adab, one of the largest regional centres in the area northeast of Uruk in Sargonic times. The importance of the city at this time is indicated by its extensive archives; B. Foster (ZA 72 [1982] pp. 5–6) estimates that almost 500 economic texts of Sargonic date derive from Umma.

The combined evidence of the archival texts and the royal inscriptions of both native Umma rulers and Sargonic kings provides us with the names of thirteen Sargonic-Gutian period rulers of Umma. In the list below, those rulers for whom we have actual inscriptions or who are named in seal legends are marked with a dagger.

RIM no.	Umma Governor	Sargonic / Gutian King	Source
E2.11.1	mes-é	Sargon	E2.1.1.1
E2.11.2	*en-na-núm*†	Rīmuš	E2.1.2.4 Foster Umma p. 154 no. a
E2.11.3	$IŠ_{11}$.RU-bi	—	Foster, Umma p. 154 no. b
E2.11.4	pa_4-šeš	Man-ištūšu	Obelisk of Man-ištūšu A 12 22 Foster, Umma p. 154 no. c
E2.11.5	*śu-ru-úš*-GI†	Man-ištūšu	Obelisk of Man-ištūšu A 12 21 Foster, Umma p. 154 no. d
E2.11.6	lú-^{d}utu†		Foster, Umma p. 154 no. e
E2.11.7	en-an-na-tum		Foster, Umma p. 154 no. f
E2.11.8	ŠU.DU-*ni-ì-lí*		Foster, Umma p. 154 no. g
E2.11.9	me-ság	Narām-Sîn/ Šar-kali-šarrī	Foster, Umma p. 154 no. h
E2.11.10	lú-šára		Foster, Umma p. 154 no. i
E2.11.11	šul†	—	—
E2.11.12	nam-maḫ-ni†	Iarlagan	Foster, Umma p. 154 no. j
E2.11.13	lugal-an-na-tum†	Si᾿um	Foster, Umma p. 154 no. k

Ennānum

E2.11.2

2001

In inscriptions E2.1.2.2 and E2.1.2.4 of Rīmuš the broken name of a ruler of Umma appears; only the first sign of his name, EN, is preserved. The name is probably to be restored *en*-[*na-núm*], since a governor of Umma by this name is known from various archival texts (see Foster, Umma p. 154 no. a and Frayne, ARRIM 7 [1989] no. 1). Here we have not adopted Foster's proposal to read the name Ennalum (Umma p. 154). A seal of a servant of Ennānum is now housed in the Bible Lands Museum in Jerusalem.

COMMENTARY

The seal is made of serpentine and measures 3.5×2.5 cm.; it bears the museum number BLMJ 2512. The inscription was collated by P. Steinkeller.

BIBLIOGRAPHY

1981 Williams-Forte in Muscarella, Ladders no. 40 (photo, transliteration [by Sweet])

1987 Noveck in Merhav, Treasures no. 27 (photo, translation)

TEXT

1) ⌜x-DU(?)⌝
2) ir_{11}-*è-na-núm*

1–2) PN, servant of Ennānum.

Šuruš-kīn

E2.11.5

1

An inscription of Šuruš-kīn, governor of Umma, was found at Jōkha. As noted, Šuruš-kīn appears as the son of Pašeš, governor of Umma, in the Obelisk of Man-ištūšu: PN_1 PN_2 2 DUMU *śu-ru-úś*-GI *ši* pa_4-šeš ÉNSI *umma*.KI (see Scheil, MDP 2 pl. III A xii 21–24). For the construction PN_1 DUMU PN_2 *ši* PN_3, see the comments of Gelb, MAD 3 p. 250.

COMMENTARY

The inscription is found on a large tenon made of a bituminous substance; it was probably once inserted in a wall. The piece measures 38 cm in length with a diameter of 22 cm; it bears the museum number AO 4798. For other examples of this kind of object see Jéquier, in de Morgan, MDP 7 p. 31 figs. 19 and 20. The inscription was collated from the published photo.

BIBLIOGRAPHY

1912 Thureau-Dangin, RA 9 p. 76 no.19 (copy, edition)
1929 Barton, RISA pp. 302–303 Shurushgi (edition)
1961 Gelb, MAD 2^2 p. 7 (study)
1963 Hirsch, AfO 20 pp. 21 n. 217 and 33 Verschiedene Inschriften no. 5 (study)
1971 Sollberger and Kupper, IRSA IID1a (translation)
1990 Gelb and Kienast, Königsinschriften p. 48 S–41 (edition)

TEXT

1) *śu*$_4$*-ru-úś*-GI	1–2) Šuruš-kīn, governor of Umma.
2) énsi-umma.KI	

Lu-Utu

E2.11.6

1

A cone inscription in Sumerian deals with Lu-Utu's construction of the temple of the goddess Ninḫursag.

CATALOGUE

Ex.	Museum number	Registration number	Dimensions (cm)	Lines preserved	cpn
1	BM 15782	96-6-12, 2	15.6 long, 4.4 wide	1–12	c
2	BM 15781	96-6-12, 1	17 long, 4.8 wide	1–8	c
3	BM 15783	96-6-12, 3	16.8 long, 4.5 wide	1–12	c
4	Formerly in the private collection of V. Scheil	—	—	1–8	n

COMMENTARY

The inscriptions of exs. 1–3 were kindly collated by A.R. George. Exs. 2 and 4 omit lines 9–12. For a discussion of the expression temen ... si of line 10, see Dunham, Foundations pp. 341–64.

BIBLIOGRAPHY

1896 King, CT 1 pl. 50 (ex. 3, copy; exs. 1–2, variants)
1899 Scheil, RT 21 p. 125 (ex. 4, copy in NA typeface, translation)
1907 Thureau-Dangin, SAK pp. 150–51 Galu-babbar (exs. 3–4, edition)
1929 Barton, RISA pp. 92–93 Lu-Utu 1 (exs. 3–4, edition)
1943 Jacobsen, JNES 2 p. 119 (study)
1971 Sollberger and Kupper, IRSA IID2a (exs. 3–4, translation)
1980 Dunham, Foundations pp. 342–43 (ex. 3, edition)
1986 Dunham, RA 80 p. 41 (ex. 3, edition)
1991 Steible, NSBW 2 pp. 345-46 Lu'utu 3 (exs. 1, 3, edition) and Lu'utu 4 (exs. 2, 4, edition)

TEXT

1) ^{d}nin-ḫur-sag
2) ama-dingir-re-ne-ra
3) lú-^{d}utu
4) énsi-
5) umma.KI-ke$_4$
6) nam-ti-la-ni-šè
7) tillà-ki-ág-na
8) é mu-na-dù

1–2) For the goddess Ninḫursag, mother of the gods,
3–5) Lu-Utu, governor of Umma,
6) for his (own) life,
7–8) built a temple for her in her beloved square.

9) uš-bi mu-du$_{10}$
10) temen-bi mu-si
11) me-bi šà-bi-a
12) si im-ma-ni-sá

9–12) He improved its foundation, drove in its *foundation pegs*, (and) saw after everything that was necessary within it.

2

A cone inscription in Sumerian deals with Lu-Utu's construction of the temple of the goddess Ereškigal.

CATALOGUE

Ex.	Museum number	Registration number	Dimensions (cm)	Lines preserved	cpn
1	BM 109930	1914-4-6, 833	15.5 long, 4.8 wide	1–11	c
2	BM 109931	1914-4-6, 834	16.3 long, 4.8 wide	1–11	c
3	YBC 2148	—	15.2 long, 5 wide	1–4, 6–11	c

COMMENTARY

Exs. 1–2 were kindly collated by A.R. George. All exemplars were purchased pieces which presumably originally came from Jōkha. The line count follows ex. 1.

For the translation 'sunset' for u$_4$-šu$_4$, cf. OBGT 1 line 818 (MSL 4 p. 59): u$_4$-šú = *e-re-eb* UTU-*i*[*m*]. The translation 'drain' in line 11 is uncertain; it follows Steible, NSBW 2 pp. 343–44 Lu'utu 1.

BIBLIOGRAPHY

1915 Clay, YOS 1 no. 14 (ex. 3, copy, edition)
1921 Gadd, CT 36 pl. 3 BM 109930 (ex. 1, copy)
1929 Barton, RISA pp. 94–95 Lu-Utu 2 (ex. 1, edition) and 3 (ex. 3, edition)
1971 Sollberger and Kupper, IRSA IID2b (exs. 1–3, translation)
1974 Postgate, Sumer 30 p. 208 (study)
1991 Steible, NSBW 2 pp. 343–44 Lu'utu 1 (ex. 3, edition) and Lu'utu 2 (exs. 1–2, edition)

TEXT

1) ^{d}ereš-ki-gal
2) nin-ki-u$_4$-šu$_4$-ra
3) lú-^{d}utu
4) énsi-umma.KI
5) dumu-^{d}nin-in-sín-ka-ke$_4$
6) nam-ti-la-ni-šè
7) ki-^{d}utu-è
8) ki-nam-tar-re-da
9) é mu-na-dù

1–2) For the goddess Ereškigal, the Lady of the West (lit. the place where the sun sets),
3–5) Lu-Utu, governor of Umma, son of Nin-isina,
6) for his own life,
7–8) (facing?) the east, the place where destinies are decided,
9) built a temple for her.

E2.11.6.1 9–12 Omitted by exs. 2 and 4.
E2.11.6.2 4.3 Written in two lines; adds -ke$_4$ at end.
E2.11.6.2 5.3 Omits.

10) gaba-ba a bí-in-gi
11) mu-bi pa bí-in-è

10) On its (the temple's) front he fixed a *drain*
11) (and) made its (the temple's) name resplendent.

Šul

E2.11.11

2001

A seal in the British Museum bears the inscription of a servant of Šul, governor of Umma. The governor is otherwise unattested.

COMMENTARY

The seal is made of lapis lazuli and measures 2.75×1.6 cm. The piece, which was purchased, bears the museum number BM 12285 (94-10-22, 1).

BIBLIOGRAPHY

1922 BM Guide 1922 p. 234 no. 12 (study)
1982 Collon, Cylinder Seals 2 no. 109 (photo, edition [by Sollberger], study)

TEXT

1) šul ÉNSI
2) *umma*.KI
3) nir-gál-^{d}/an-⌜x⌝
4) IR_{11}-*sú*

1–2) Šul, governor of Umma:
3–4) Nirgal-... (is) his servant.

E2.11.6.2 10.3 Written in two lines with -a at beginning of the second; bí-in-gi-in.
E2.11.6.2 11.3 Written in two lines.

Namaḫni

E2.11.12

1

A Sumerian inscription deals with Namaḫni's construction of the temple of the goddess Ninura.

COMMENTARY

The piece is a cylindrical object which is apparently not a cone; it measures 4.7 in length and 4.1 cm in diameter. The piece was acquired through purchase; it bears the museum number YBC 2149. The inscription was collated. The Iarlagan, king of Gutium, of this inscription is likely to be identified with the Iarlaganda who appears as the nineteenth Gutian king of the Sumerian King List. Ninura and Šara were the tutelary deities of Umma.

BIBLIOGRAPHY

1915 Clay, YOS 1 no. 13 (copy, edition)
1916 Johns, PSBA 38 pp. 199–200 (study)
1920 Deimel, Orientalia 2 p. 54 (study)
1929 Barton, RISA pp. 300–303 Nammakhni 1 (edition)
1939 Jacobsen, SKL p. 120 n. 305a (study)
1939 Deimel, Šumerische Grammatik² p. 128 (copy, edition)
1954–56 Sollberger, AfO 17 p. 35 (study)
1961 Gelb, MAD 2² p. 7 no. 1 (study)
1963 Kramer, Sumerians p. 325 no. 32 (translation)
1971 Sollberger and Kupper, IRSA IID3a (translation)
1990 Gelb and Kienast, Königsinschriften p. 296 Gutium 2 (edition)

TEXT

1) ᵈnin-ur₄-ra
2) ama-umma.KI-ra
3) nam-maḫ-ni
4) énsi-
5) umma.KI-ke₄
6) é-ù-la-ni
7) mu-na-dù
8) ki-bé mu-na-gi₄
9) u₄-ba *ià-ar-la-ga-an*
10) lugal-*gu-ti-um*-kam

1–2) For the goddess Ninura, mother of Umma,
3–5) Namaḫni, governor of Umma,
6–7) built her E-ula temple
8) (and) restored it.
9–10) At that time Iarlagan was king of Gutium.

Lugal-ana-tuma

E2.11.13

1

A Sumerian inscription deals with Lugal-ana-tuma's construction of the E-gidru temple in Umma.

COMMENTARY

The inscription is incised on a marble tablet that was said by its seller to have come from 'Yôkha'; it was donated by V. Scheil to the Académie des Inscriptions et Belles-Lettres. Its present whereabouts are unknown. The inscription was collated from the published photo.

The attack on Umma alluded to in lines 4–5 is probably to be connected with the defeat of Umma by the late Sargonic king Dudu (see Wilcke, AfO 25 [1974–77] p. 84 no. 1 lines 7–9).

BIBLIOGRAPHY

1911 Scheil, CRAIB pp. 318–27 (photo, edition, study)
1914 Poebel, PBS 4/1 pp. 134–35 (study)
1939 Jacobsen, SKL p. 120 n. 306 (study)
1957 Hallo, Titles p. 142 and n. 2 (study)
1961 Gelb, MAD 2^2 p. 7 no. 1 (study)
1966 Falkenstein, Inschriften Gudeas p. 16 n. 1 (edition)
1971 Sollberger and Kupper, IRSA IID4a (translation)
1980 Dunham, Foundations pp. 343–44 (edition)
1986 Dunham, RA 80 pp. 41–42 (edition)
1990 Gelb and Kienast, Königsinschriften pp. 296–97 Gutium 3 (edition)

TEXT

1) lugal-an-na-túma 2) énsi- 3) umma.KI-ke$_4$	1–3) Lugal-ana-tuma, governor of Umma —
4) umma.KI 5) ba-ba-a 6) 35 mu 7) zal-la-ba	4–7) 35 years having past since (the territory of) Umma was divided up —
8) é-gidru umma.KI 9) ì-dù	8–9) built the E-gidru at Umma,
10) temen-bi 11) ki-a ì-si-si	10–11) drove into the earth its *foundation pegs*,
12) me-bi šà-ba 13) si ba-ni-sá	12–13) (and) saw after everything that was necessary therein.
14) u$_4$-ba *si-ù-um* 15) lugal-*gu-ti-um*-kam	14–15) At that time, Si'um was king of Gutium.

LAGAŠ

E2.12

Although many economic texts of Sargonic date were unearthed by the French excavators of Telloh, ancient Girsu, relatively little is known of the history of the region in Sargonic imes. Lagaš was one of the main targets of Sargon's campaign against the south. The defeat of the city is recorded in inscriptions E2.1.1.1–3, and a caption accompanying inscription E2.1.1.12 gives us the name of the defeated governor of Lagaš: Mes-zi. A later attack on the city by Rīmuš is narrated in E2.1.2.3; from this source we learn the name of the contemporary city governor: Kituš-id. Lagaš participated in both major revolts of the reign of Narām-Sîn. Having finally pacified the city, Narām-Sîn installed Lugal-ušumgal as city governor; he served in that role into the reign of Šar-kali-šarrī. Lugal-ušumgal's two personal seal inscriptions are edited in this volume as E2.1.4.2004 and E2.1.5.2004; the seal legend of one of his servants as E2.12.4.2001. He may have been succeeded by the governor Ur-e who is mentioned in a Sumerian letter (RTC no. 83) discussed by Volk (ZA 82 [1992] pp. 24–25). The same letter names Puzur-Mama, Ur-e's probable successor, as governor of Lagaš. Puzur-Mama apparently began a period of independence for Lagaš; it was probably suppressed by the Sargonic king Dudu. Booty from Dudu's attack on Girsu was dedicated by the king in Nippur (E2.1.10.2). Not long after this a certain Ur-Ningirsu instituted once again a period of independence for Lagaš; it was to endure until the city's defeat at the hands of Ur-Nammu of Ur. An edition of the inscriptions of Ur-Ningirsu and his successors is planned for a future RIM volume.

RIM number	Lagaš governor	Sargonic king	Source
E2.12.1	Mes-zi	Sargon	E2.1.1.12
E2.12.2	Kituš-id	Rīmuš	E2.1.2.3
E2.12.3	Lugal-ušumgal	Narām-Sîn	E2.1.4.2004
		Šar-kali-šarrī	E2.1.5.2004
		Šar-kali-šarrī	E2.12.4.2001
E2.12.4	Ur-e	Šar-kali-šarrī(?)	RTC no. 83
E2.12.5	Puzur-Mama	Šar-kali-šarrī	RTC nos. 83, 181; E2.12.5.2001–2002
E2.12.5	Puzur-Mama (king)	Dudu	E2.12.5.1

Lugal-ušumgal

E2.12.3

2001

A seal inscription of a servant of Lugal-ušumgal, governor of Lagaš under Narām-Sîn and Šar-kali-šarrī, occurs on a number of clay bullae found in excavations of de Sarzec at Telloh.

COMMENTARY

The seal inscription measures 3.2 cm in height; it is found on bullae numbered AOTb. 402 1–6 (Louvre). The inscription was collated from the published photos.

BIBLIOGRAPHY

1898 Thureau-Dangin, RA 4 p. 78 and pl. VIII no. 25 (copy, translation)
1903 Thureau-Dangin, RTC no. 179 (copy)
1920 Delaporte, Louvre 1 T. 58 (photo, edition)
1961 Gelb, MAD 2² p. 200 Officials, etc. sub no. 1 (study)
1964 Boehmer, Moortgat Festschrift p. 51 and pl. 12 no. 25 (photo, edition)
1965 Boehmer, Glyptik no. 617 and fig. 182 (photo, study)
1968 Nagel and Strommenger, BJVF 8 pp. 154–55 and 163 no. 15 (edition, study)
1968–69 Edzard, AfO 22 p. 16 no. 23–4 (transliteration)
1976 Amiet, L'art d'Agadé p. 34 fig. 22 (copy)
1990 Gelb and Kienast, Königsinschriften p. 42 S–14 (edition)

TEXT

1) sipa-an-né
2) gal_5-lá-gal
3) ir_{11}-lugal-ušumgal
4) énsi-
5) lagaš.KI-ka

1–5) Sipa-anne, chief of police, (is) the servant of Lugal-ušumgal, governor of Lagaš.

Puzur-Mama

E2.12.5

Puzur-Mama is named as governor of Lagaš in a Sumerian letter (RTC no. 83) discussed by Volk (ZA 82 [1992] pp. 24–26) and in an economic text from Girsu (RTC no. 181). The name appears in the so-called 'Rulers of Lagaš' text edited by Sollberger (JCS 21 [1967] p. 291 line 183). According to the historical reconstruction offered by Volk (ZA 82 [1992] p. 27), Puzur-Mama served as governor at Lagaš during the latter part of the reign of Šar-kali-šarrī. At some point, perhaps in the confused period that followed the death of Šar-kali-šarrī, he declared independence for Lagaš; the title 'king' appears in his royal inscription edited here as E2.12.5.1 and in the economic text ITT 5 no. 6758.

1

A Sumerian royal inscription of Puzur-Mama is incised on two clay bowls.

CATALOGUE

Ex.	Museum number	Excavation number	cpn
1	AO 4597	—	n
2	AO 14537	TG 4409	n

COMMENTARY

The PN of i 1′, if restored correctly, would refer to the Elamite king Kutik-Inšušinak. If this be true, the text would provide an important synchronism between Lagaš and Elam. For the toponym of i 4′, see Edzard, Rép. Géogr. 2 p. 51 sub GAR-NE.NE.

BIBLIOGRAPHY

1930 de Genouillac, RHR 101 pp. 220–21 (ex. 1, copy)
1954–56 Sollberger, AfO 17 p. 17 and n. 118 (ex. 1, study)
1990 Volk, ZA 82 (1992) pp. 22–29 (ex. 1, partial edition, study)
1991 Steible, NSBW2 pp. 336–37 Puzur-Mama 1 (exs. 1–2, edition)

TEXT

Col. i	
Lacuna	Lacuna
1′) [PUZ]UR$_4$-[^{d}MÙŠ.ER]IN	i 1′–6′) [Ku]tik-[Inšuši]nak of [Su]sa, [...]-šè(?)-ga-AN of [G]àr-NE.[NE], ⸢x⸣-da of GN,
2′) [MÙŠ].ERIN.KI	
3′) [...]-šè(?)-ga-AN	Lacuna
4′) [g]àr-NE.[N]E.KI	
5′) ⸢x⸣-da	
6′) [...].[K]I	
Lacuna	
Col. ii	
Lacuna	Lacuna
1′) [mu pà-da]	ii 1′–2′) [called by name] by [the god Enlil],
2′) [^{d}en-líl-lá]-ke$_4$	
3′) ⸢á⸣-sum-ma	ii 3′–4′) granted power by the god Ningirsu,
4′) ⸢^{d}⸣nin-gír-su-ka-⸢ke$_4$⸣	
5′) géštu-sum-ma-	ii 5′–6′) granted intelligence by the god Enki,
6′) ^{d}en-ki-ka-ke$_4$	
7′) ga-zi-kú-a	ii 7′–8′) suckled with 'true' milk by the goddess Ninḫursag,
8′) ^{d}nin-ḫur-sag-ka-ke$_4$	
9′) mu-du$_{10}$-sa$_4$-a-	ii 9′–10′) called with a good name by the goddess Inanna,
10′) ^{d}inanna-ka-ke$_4$	
11′) [dumu]-tu-da-	ii 11′–12′) natural [son] of the goddess [Ga]tum[d]u,
12′) [^{d}g]á!-tùm-[d]u$_{110}$-[ka-k]e$_4$	
13′) [...] ⸢x⸣	ii 13′) ...
Lacuna	Lacuna
Col. iii	
Lacuna	Lacuna
1′) ⸢x⸣ [...]	iii 1′) ...
2′) am[a-tu]-d[a-ni]	iii 2′-3′) [his natur]al moth[er] is the goddess Ninšubur,
3′) ^{d}nin-šubur-kam	
4′) dingir-ra-ni	iii 4′–5′) his personal god is the god Šul-utula.
5′) šul-utul$_{12}$-àm	
6′) puzur$_4$-^{d}ma-ma	iii 6′–8′) Puzur-Mama, king of Lagaš
7′) lugal-	Lacuna
8′) lagaš.[KI-kam]	
Lacuna	

2001

A seal of a son of the governor Puzur-Mama is housed in the Vatican collections.

COMMENTARY

This haematite cylinder seal measures 2.3×1.1 cm and bears the museum number Museo Profano no. 6183. The seal apparently dates to the time before Puzur-Mama adopted the title 'king'. The inscription was collated from the published photo.

The design carved on the seal is a 'presentation scene'. For a discussion of Sargonic examples of this seal motif, see M. Haussperger, Die Einführungsszene pp. 120–40.

BIBLIOGRAPHY

1942 van Buren, AJA 46 pp. 362–63 (photo, edition)

TEXT

1) *śar-ru-ì-li*
2) dumu puzur-ma-ma
3) énsi

1–3) Šarru-ilī, son of Puzur-Mama the governor.

URUK

E2.13

The Sumerian King List places a dynasty of five kings from Uruk, conventionally designated by modern historians as the Uruk IV dynasty, between its list of Sargonic and Gutian rulers. In total they are said to have reigned thirty years. Following the Gutian kings, it places another Uruk dynasty (Uruk V), whose sole member, Utu-ḫegal, is credited with a reign of seven years; in all likelihood, he ruled immediately after the last Uruk IV king. The synchronism between Utu-ḫegal and Tirigan, the last Gutian king, which is provided by inscription E2.13.6.4, indicates that the Uruk IV and V kings date to late Gutian times. The royal inscriptions of the two dynasties are edited together in this section.

Ur-nigina

E2.13.1

1

According to the Sumerian King List, Ur-nigina, first king of the Uruk IV dynasty, reigned seven years. One inscription dating to the period of his reign is known.

COMMENTARY

The cone was found in the mausolea of Šulgi and Amar-Suena, in the filling of houses, top level, in season IX. It was given the excavation number U 16003 and now bears the museum number UM 31-43-247. Although the cone is actually an inscription of the prince Ur-gigira, it dates to the time when Ur-nigina ruled as king, and hence is edited here under the rubric of the father's name.

The inscription records the construction of a temple to the goddess Nin-šeše-gara; the DN may be compared with the temple name é-šeš-šeš-e-gá-ra which appears in a Šulgi inscription dedicated to the goddess Nanše (Kärki, KDDU pp. 34–35 Šulgi 13). The epithet 'military governor of the god Dumuzi' of lines 2–3 suggests control by the kings of the Uruk IV dynasty over Bad-tibira; Dumuzi was the tutelary deity of that city. This is not an unlikely proposition in view of the fact that the mound marking the site, Tell Madā'in, lies a scant 12 miles northeast of Uruk.

The reading of line 8 is uncertain. SAL.ME by itself has a reading lukur 'woman dedicated to a god'. On the other hand, F. Wiggermann has proposed (ZA 78 [1988] pp. 225–40) that SAL.ḪÚB is to be read lagar$_x$ and that it denotes either an official with a function similar to that of the sukkal 'vizier' or a female devotee of the god. In the lexical list Proto-Ea line 437 (see MSL 14 p. 49), la-ga-ar is equated with the logogram SAL.ME, variant SAL.ḪÚB. Perhaps SAL.ME.ḪÚB in line 8 combines both traditions.

BIBLIOGRAPHY

1965 Sollberger, UET 8 no. 15 (copy [by Legrain], study)
1966 Falkenstein, BiOr 23 p. 165 (study)
1967 Pettinato, Orientalia NS 36 p. 452 (edition)
1971 Sollberger and Kupper, IRSA IIK1a (translation)
1991 Steible, NSBW 2 p. 321–22 Urnigin 1 (edition)

TEXT

1) ur-GIŠ.gigir 2) GÌR.NÍTA 3) ^{d}dumu-zi-da	1–3) Ur-gigira, viceroy of the god Dumuzi,
4) dumu-ur-nìgin 5) nita-kalag-ga 6) lugal- 7) unu.KI-ga-ka-ke$_4$	4–7) son of Ur-nigina, mighty man, king of Uruk,
8) ù ama-SAL.ME.ḪÚB 9) ama-ni	8–9) and Ama-SAL.ME.ḪÚB, his mother,
10) ^{d}nin-šeš-e-gar-ra 11) nin-a-ni	10–11) for the goddess Nin-šeše-gara, his lady,
12) é-šeš-⸢e⸣-gar-[ra] 13) é-ki-á[g]-⸢gá⸣-ni 14) ⸢e⸣-ti-bí-ra.KI-k[a] 15) mu-na-dù	12–15) built the E-šeše-gar[a], her beloved temple in E-tibira.

Ur-gigira

E2.13.2

According to the Sumerian King List, Ur-gigira, Ur-nigina's son, reigned six (variant: seven) years.

2001

A mace head from Warka is incised with a dedicatory inscription for the life of Ur-gigira, king of Uruk.

COMMENTARY

The mace head is made of onyx and measures 8.7 cm in height and 7.2 cm in diameter; it bears the museum number AO 8663. The inscription was collated from the published photo.

BIBLIOGRAPHY

1923 Thureau-Dangin, RA 20 pp. 5–7 (photo, edition)
1965 Sollberger, UET 8 p. 3 sub no. 15 (study)
1968 Solyman, Götterwaffen no. 225 (photo, study)
1971 Sollberger and Kupper, IRSA IIK2a (translation)
1991 Steible, NSBW 2 p. 322 Urgigir 1 (edition)

TEXT

1) [^{d}DN]
2) nam-ti-
3) ur-GIŠ.gigir
4) nita-kalag-ga
5) lugal-unu.KI-ga
6) lugal-an-na-túm
7) išib-an-na-ke$_4$
8) a mu-na-⌈ru⌉

1) [For DN],
2–5) for the life of Ur-gigira, mighty man, king of Uruk,
6–8) Lugal-ana-tum, purification priest of the god An, dedicated (this mace).

Kuda

E2.13.3

According to the Sumerian King List, Kuda, Ur-gigira's successor, reigned six years. One inscription is known that may belong to this ruler.

1

A bowl fragment in the Yale collection has a dedicatory inscription of Kuda, *šangû* priest of the goddess Inanna.

COMMENTARY

The bowl fragment, a portion of a rim, is made of dark green steatite and measures 7.5×6.0×0.6 cm. The piece was acquired by purchase in December 1933; it may have originally come from Ur. The inscription was collated.

If the identification of the Kuda of this inscription with the Kuda of the Sumerian King List be correct, the inscription would date to a time when the prince of Uruk served as *šangû* priest prior to his enthronement. A second personal name in line 5 is probably to be restored as [U]r-Utu. A connection with the fifth king of the Uruk IV dynasty (Sollberger, UET 8 p. 3 sub no. 15) is tempting, albeit uncertain, since the broken text does not allow us to determine the relationship between Kuda and Ur-Utu. Further, the Sumerian King List does not indicate whether or not Kuda's successors Puzur-ilī and Ur-Utu were his sons. Another possibility is that [U]r-Utu is to be connected with the Ur-Utu named as governor of Ur in the Sumerian letter discussed by K. Volk, ZA 82 (1992) pp. 24–26.

BIBLIOGRAPHY

1937 Stephens, YOS 9 no. 10 (copy, study)
1965 Sollberger, UET 8 p. 3 sub no. 15 (study)
1966 Hallo, JCS 20 p. 137 n. 60 (study)
1991 Steible, NSBW pp. 323–23 (edition)

TEXT

1) ^{d}nin-gal
2) ^{d}nin-uri$_{5}$.KI-ma-ra
3) ku$_{5}$-da
4) [s]anga-^{d}inanna
5) [u]r(?)-^{d}utu-k[e$_{4}$]
6) [x (x)] KI [x]
Lacuna

1–2) For the goddess Ningal, the (divine) lady of Ur,

3–6) Kuda, [*š*]*angû* priest of the goddess Inanna, (and) [U]r(?)-Utu, ...
Lacuna

1001

A seal of Nin-ès-sá, *entu* priestess of the god Pisangunu and daughter of Lugal-TAR, dates to Sargonic times.

COMMENTARY

The seal is made of agate and measures 3.1×1.8 cm. The piece was acquired by purchase; it was formerly in the de Clercq collection and is now housed in the Louvre, museum number AO 23309. The inscription was collated from the published photo.

For the reading of the DN of line 2, see the most recent discussion by A. George (Babylonian Topographical Texts pp. 322–23). Since Pisangunu was a god with apparent origins at or near Uruk, there is a distinct possibility that the seal belonged to a daughter of a ruler of that city. The interpretation of the last line of the inscription is uncertain.

If the TAR sign is actually part of the inscription, then the PN of line 3 should be read Lugal-TAR. At first glance this name would appear to be connected with the Lugal-TAR who appears as *ensi* of Uruk in a fragmentary royal inscription published by van Dijk (Sumer 15 [1959] pp. 5–8 and pl. 1 following p. 14). However, the script of the van Dijk text firmly dates the royal inscription to pre-Sargonic times, whereas the seal design is dated by Boehmer (Glyptik p. 187 no. 1594) to the period Akkadisch (II)/III, that is, to Sargonic times. If we were to read the name on line 3 of the seal as lugal-ku₅ a connection with the Uruk king Kuda would be possible.

BIBLIOGRAPHY

1883 Ménant, Glyptique 1 pp. 105–106 fig. 59 (copy)
1888 de Clercq, Collection 1 no. 82 (copy, edition, study)
1910 Ward, Seals fig. 216 (drawing)
1970 Rowton, CAH 1/1 p. 223 (study)
1965 Boehmer, Glyptik no. 1594 and fig. 670 (photo, study)
1968–69 Edzard, AfO 22 p. 15 no. 16–7 (transliteration)
1976 Amiet, L'art d'Agadé no. 116 (photo, edition, study)

TEXT

1) nin-ès-sá
2) en-^{d}MES^{sanga}-unu.KI
3) dumu-lugal-TAR

1–3) Nin-ès-sá, *entu* priestess of the god Pisangunu, daughter of Lugal-TAR.

Puzur-ilī

E2.13.4

According to the Sumerian King List, Puzur-ilī, Kuda's successor, reigned five years. No inscriptions are known at present for this ruler.

Ur-Utu

E2.13.5

The Ur-Utu who appears as the fifth king of the Uruk IV dynasty is given a reign of six years in the Sumerian King List.

2001

A seal of a servant of Ur-Utu is now housed in the Iraq Museum.

COMMENTARY

The seal is made of shell and measures 3.1×1.6 cm. It was found in excavations of the 'Tell de l'Est' at Telloh and given the excvation number T 488. It is currently part of the Iraq Museum collections (museum number unknown). The inscription was collated from the published photo.

BIBLIOGRAPHY

1954 Parrot , Glyptique mésopotamienne no. 123 (photo, study, copy, edition [by M. Lambert])

1965 Boehmer, Glyptik no. 1306 (study)

1968–69 Edzard, AfO 22 p. 16 no. 23–1 (transliteration)

1971 Nagel, APA 2 p. 2 and fig. 2 (photo, edition)

TEXT

1) ba-za utul
2) ir$_{11}$-ur-^{d}utu

1–2) Baza, the cowherd, (is) the servant of Ur-Utu.

Utu-ḫegal

E2.13.6

In all likelihood there was a considerable expansion of Uruk's power and influence during the seven-year reign of Utu-ḫegal. Noteworthy is the king's adoption of the title 'king of the four quarters' last used by Narām-Sîn and the Gutian ruler Erridu-pizir. Further, the king may have received special recognition by the Nippur authorities. In a text dealing with his expulsion of the Gutians (E2.13.6.4), Utu-ḫegal relates that it was the god Enlil who had commissioned him to drive out the foreigners. We may also note that the same composition is known from at least one Nippur tablet copy; thus, it was apparently transmitted in the Nippur schools. T. Maeda (ASJ 10 [1988] pp. 28–31) has argued that two year names of late Gutian or early Ur III date found on Girsu tablets (mu lú-maḫ-^{d}inanna maš-e ì-pà 'The year the *lumaḫ* priest of the goddess Inanna was chosen by omens' and mu éš-gán-lugal šà gír-su.KI-ke$_4$ ba-ta-è 'The year the royal measuring rope was brought out in Girsu') should be attributed to Utu-ḫegal. If Maeda is correct, then the year names' existence would indicate control by the king of Uruk, for at least a short period of time, over part of the Lagaš region. A reflection of Utu-ḫegal's control over this area may be found in the appearance of the name Ḫengal in the so-called 'Rulers of Lagaš' text edited by Sollberger (JCS 21 [1967] p. 291 lines 189 and 191).

In JSOR 10 (1926) p. 286 no. 9, S. Mercer published a clay cone inscription which purportedly recorded the dedication of a royal palace to the god Ningirsu by Utu-ḫegal. Since this text displays a number of unusual features, its authenticity has been in doubt. Utu-ḫegal's title 'king of the Amnānum (tribe)', for example, is totally unexpected for a pre-Ur III king of Uruk. Further, it is unclear why the king of Uruk would have built a palace in Girsu. An examination of the cones of the former Mercer collection now housed in the Royal Ontario Museum reveals that this inscription does not exist; it resulted from Mercer's erroneous conflation of two cone inscriptions: one, the Utu-ḫegal inscription dealing with the restoration of the Lagaš boundary for the god Ningirsu (ROM 967.287.70, here edited as ex. 8 of E2.13.6.3), and the other the Sîn-kāšid inscription recording the construction of a royal palace in Uruk (ROM 910x209.208, ex. 41 of E4.4.1.2, see RIME 4, p. 442).

1

An inscription recorded on clay cones found in the vicinity of Lagaš recounts Utu-ḫegal's restoration of the border of the Lagaš city-state for the goddess Nanše.

CATALOGUE

Ex.	Museum number	Registration number	Dimensions (cm)	Lines preserved	cpn
1	BM 117836	1925-10-17,2	8.3 long, 4.2 dia.	1–9	c
2	NBC 6109	—	8.1 long, 4.0 dia.	1–9	c
3	YBC 2325	—	8.1 long, 4.3 dia.	1–9	c
4	IM 20857	—	—	—	n
5	IM 20859	—	—	—	n
6	IM 20860	—	—	—	n
7	Eames Collection no. FF–5	—	6.9 long, 4.8 dia.	1–9	c
8	Eames Collection no. FF–4	—	8.5 long, 3.8 dia.	1–9	c
9	ROM 967.287.71	—	8.5 long, 4.7 dia.	1–9	c
10	Collection Kurth, Archäologisches Museum, Martin-Luther-Universität Halle-Wittenberg	—	8.0 long, 4.5 dia.	1–9	n
11	LB 971	—	8.2 long, 4 dia.	1–9	n

COMMENTARY

Ex. 1 was kindly collated by A.R. George; exs. 7–8 by M. Van De Mieroop. Ex. 9 was formerly in the private collection of S. Mercer. The provenance of these cones is uncertain. Gadd (JRAS [1926] p. 684) writes concerning ex. 1: 'Internal evidence of the inscriptions makes it clear that they were found at Telloh, from which also a number of statues have recently been obtained by illicit digging'.

The demarcation of a new boundary for Lagaš by Utu-ḫegal was necessary because of the earlier raid on the region by the forces of Ur-Nammu; the details of that incursion will be set out in the forthcoming Ur III volume in the RIM series. By fixing a new boundary for Lagaš, Utu-ḫegal was acting in a role analogous to that played much earlier by king Me-silim of Kiš (see Sollberger and Kupper, IRSA IC7i, I 1–12); in that case the dispute was between the rival city states of Umma and Girsu. In addition to the commemoration in this royal inscription, the demarcation of the Lagaš boundary may also have been recorded in a year name: mu éš-gána-lugal šà-gír-su.KI-ke$_4$ ba-ta-è 'The year the royal measuring rope was brought out in Girsu'. As noted above, Maeda has argued that this year name may belong to Utu-ḫegal.

BIBLIOGRAPHY

1926 Gadd, JRAS pp. 684–88 (ex. 1, copy, edition)
1937 Stephens, YOS 9 nos. 20 and 112 (ex. 2, copy; ex. 3, study)
1940 Schwartz, BNYPL 44 p. 808 nos. 16–17 (exs. 6–7, study)
1954-56 Sollberger, AfO 17 p. 12 n. 7 (exs. 1–3, study)
1957 Edzard, Sumer 13 p. 175 no. 2 (exs. 4–6, study)
1962 Grégoire, Lagash pp. 36–37 (edition)
1966 Hallo, JCS 20 p. 137 and n. 61 (study)
1971 Sollberger and Kupper, IIK3b n. 1 (study)
1973 Kampman, in Symbolae Böhl p. 219 no. 10 (ex. 11, study)
1976 Neumann, Wissenschaftliche Zeitschrift der Martin-Luther-Universität Halle-Wittenberg 25 G, Heft 3 p. 86 and fig. 3 (ex. 10, copy, edition)
1991 Steible, NSBW 2 pp. 324–25 Utuḫegal 1 (exs. 1–8, 10–11, edition)

TEXT

1) ^{d}nanše
2) nin-uru$_{16}$
3) nin-in-dub-ba-ra
4) ^{d}utu-ḫé-gál
5) lugal-an-ub-da-limmu$_5$-ba-ke$_4$
6) ki-sur-ra-lagaš.KI
7) lú-uri$_5$.KI-ke$_4$
8) inim bí-gar
9) šu-na mu-ni-gi$_4$

1–3) For the goddess Nanše, the mighty lady, the lady of the boundary,

4–5) Utu-ḫegal, king of the four quarters,

6–9) restored into her (Nanše's) hands the border of Lagaš on which the man of Ur had laid a claim.

3.1, 11 omit -ra.
6.1 ⌜x⌝ at end of line. **6**.2, 8 ki-sur-ra-lagaš.KI-ka. **6**.10 ki-sur-ra-lagaš.KI-[k]a(?). **6**.11 ki-sur-<ra>-lagaš.KI-ka.
7.1 Omits line. 7.3 lú-ŠEŠ.<AB>.KI-ke$_4$. **7**.4 omits -ke$_4$. **7**.11 lú-uri$_5$-ma.

2

A cone inscription deals with Utu-ḫegal's demarcation of a new boundary for the god Ningirsu.

COMMENTARY

The inscription is found on YBC 2294; the cone measures 7.7 cm in length and 4.1 cm in diameter The inscription was collated.

BIBLIOGRAPHY

1937 Stephens, YOS 9 no. 19 (copy) and 113 (ex.3, study)
1962 Grégoire, Lagash p. 36 (edition)
1991 Steible, NSBW 2 pp. 325–26 Utuhegal 2 (edition)

TEXT

1) ki-sur-ra
2) [d]nin-gír-su
3) ur-sag-kalag-ga
4) [d]en-líl-lá-ka
5) [d]utu-ḫé-gál
6) lugal-an-ub-da-limmu$_5$-ba-ke$_4$
7) šu-na mu-ni-gi$_4$

1–4) The border of Ningirsu, mighty champion of the god Enlil,
5–7) Utu-ḫegal, king of the four quarters, returned into his (the god Ningirsu's) hands.

3

A variant version of the previous inscription is found on a number of cones from the Lagaš region.

CATALOGUE

Ex.	Museum number	Dimensions (cm)	Lines preserved	cpn
1	BM 117837 (1925-10-17, 3)	7.3 long, 4.2 dia.	1–9	c
2	NBC 6108	9 long, 4.1 dia.	1–9	c
3	YBC 2328	8.9 long, 4.0 dia.	1–9	c
4	IM 20861	—	—	n
5	IM 23093/1	—	—	n
6	IM 23093/2	—	—	n
7	Collection Hoza, Camberg, Germany	9.8 long, 4.7 dia.	1–9	n
8	ROM 967.287.70	8.3 long, 4.5 dia.	1–9	c
9	FLP 2634.1	—	—	n
10	FLP 2634.2	—	—	n
11	FLP 2643.3	—	—	n
12	FLP 2643.4	—	—	n
13	FLP 2643.5	—	—	n

Ex.	Museum number	Dimensions (cm)	Lines preserved	cpn
14	FLP 2643.6	—	—	n
15	FLP 2643.7	—	—	n
16	FLP 2635.1	—	—	n
17	FLP 2635.2	—	—	n
18	FLP 2635.3	—	—	n
19	FLP 2635.4	—	—	n
20	FLP 2635.5	—	—	n
21	FLP 2635.6	—	—	n
22	FLP 2635.7	—	—	n
23	FLP 2635.8	—	—	n
24	FLP 2635.9	—	—	n

COMMENTARY

Ex. 1 was kindly collated by A.R. George. Ex. 8 was formerly in the private collection of S. Mercer. A defective copy and edition of the piece were published by Mercer in JSOR 10 (1926) p. 286 no. 9; see the introductory comments for Utu-ḫegal above. IM 23093/1–2 could be duplicates of either this inscription or of E2.13.6.1. They are arbitrarily listed here.

BIBLIOGRAPHY

1926 Gadd, JRAS pp. 684–88 (ex. 1, copy, edition)
1926 Mercer, JSOR 10 p. 286 no. 9 and plate following p. 286 (ex. 8, copy, edition)
1937 Stephens, YOS 9 no. 18 (ex. 2, copy) and 113 (ex. 3, study)
1954-56 Sollberger, AfO 17 p. 12 n. 7 (exs. 1–3, study)
1951 Smick, Cuneiform Documents no. 74 (copy, translation)
1957 Edzard, Sumer 13 p. 175 (exs 4–6, study)
1962 Grégoire, Lagash p. 36 (edition)
1966 Hallo, JCS 20 p. 137 and n. 61 (study)
1971 Sollberger and Kupper, IRSA IIK3b (exs. 1–2, translation)
1981–82 Waetzoldt, AfO 28 pp. 132–33 and fig. 1 (ex. 7, copy, edition)
1991 Steible, NSBW2 pp. 326–27 Utuhegal 3 (exs. 1–7, 9–24, edition)

TEXT

1) ^{d}nin-gír-su
2) ur-sag-kalag-ga
3) ^{d}en-líl-lá-ra
4) ^{d}utu-ḫé-gál
5) lugal-an-ub-da-limmu$_5$-ba-ke$_4$
6) ki-sur-ra-lagaš.KI
7) lú-uri$_5$.KI-ke$_4$
8) inim bí-gar
9) šu-na mu-ni-gi$_4$

1–3) For the god Ningirsu, mighty champion of the god Enlil,

4–5) Utu-ḫegal, king of the four quarters,

6–9) restored into his (Ningirsu's) hands the border of Lagaš on which the man of Ur had laid a claim.

4

An Utu-ḫegal inscription known from three Old Babylonian tablet copies commemorates the Uruk king's defeat of Tirigan, king of the Gutians, and the return of autonomy to Sumer.

6.2 la[gaš.KI]-ka. **6**.7 lagaš.KI-ka.
7.8 lú-uri$_5$.<KI>-ke$_4$.
9.8 šu-na mu-<ni>-gi$_4$.

CATALOGUE

Ex.	Museum number	Provenance	Dimensions (cm)	Lines preserved	cpn
1	AO 6018	—	13.3×6.7	1–92, 95–129	n
2	AO 6314	—	—	41–58, 60–90	n
3	Ni 4167	Nippur	—	3–7, 33–39, 87–99, 111, 113–23 Caption 1′–18′	n

COMMENTARY

Many scholars have classified this text as a literary-historical composition rather than a royal inscription. The decision to include it in this corpus was made because of the importance of the text for the reconstruction of the history of the late Gutian period. Not surprisingly, the text displays more textual variants than are commonly found in the royal inscriptions edited in this volume. For the convenience of the reader, the author has inserted the scores for this text immediately after the edition. The master text is ex. 1. In it we often find several lines of text enclosed between rulings. Jacobsen points out (SKL pp. 139–40 n. 11) that the irregularity of the ruling of ex. 1 is best explained by the assumption that it reflects the case divisions of an original monument on which the text columns were arranged around reliefs. The fact that ex. 3 comes from Nippur suggests that such a monument once stood in Nippur. In Kramer's copy of ex. 3 (ISET 2 pl. 124) the side designated the obverse is actually the reverse, and vice versa.

The meaning of the compound giš ... dù in lines 52, 74, 76, and 85 is uncertain. Thureau-Dangin, followed by Kramer and Sollberger, took the expression to be related to giš ... tag, and consequently translated 'to make a sacrifice'. Since Sum. dù is equated with Akk. *zaqāpu*(*m*) or *retû*(*m*), the expression would appear to deal with the setting up of some object. Edzard suggested to the author that the term might refer to the driving in of tent pegs; if so, a translation 'erected his tents, camped' would be called. For the translation of line 99, we may note CAD G p. 107: 'The possibility remains that *gišparru* is a free variant of *gišburru*'.

BIBLIOGRAPHY

1912 Thureau-Dangin, RA 9 pp. 111–20 (ex. 1, copy, edition)
1913 Thureau-Dangin, RA 10 pp. 98–100 (ex. 2, copy, transliteration)
1913–23 Witzel, Babyloniaca 7 pp. 57–62 (study)
1924 Gadd, Reading-book pp. 64–73 (exs. 1–2, conflated copy, edition)
1934 Güterbock, ZA 42 pp. 14–15 (exs. 1–2, study)
1939 Jacobsen, SKL pp. 138–40 n. 11 (exs. 1–2, study)
1967 Sauren, RA 61 pp. 75–79 (exs. 1–2, study)
1970 Komoróczy, Sumer pp. 247ff. (exs. 1–2, translation)
1971 Sollberger and Kupper, IRSA IIK3a (exs. 1–2, translation)
1971 Hallo, RLA 3/9 pp. 714–15 (study)
1963 Kramer, Sumerians pp. 325–26 no. 33 (exs. 1–2, translation)
1976 Kramer, ISET 2 pl. 124 (ex. 3, copy)
1984 Römer, TUAT 1/4 pp. 316–19 (exs. 1–3, translation)
1985 Römer, Orientalia NS 54 pp. 274–88 (exs. 1–3, edition)

TEXT

1) ^{d}en-líl ⌜*gu*⌝-[*ti-um*.KI]
2) muš-GÍR-ḫur-sag-[gá]
3) lú-á-zi(*)-ga-dingir-⌜e!-e-ne⌝
4) lú nam-lugal-
5) ki-en-gi-rá
6) kur-šè ba-de$_6$-a
7) ki-en-gi-rá
8) nì-a-ne-ru bí-i[n-s]i-a
9) dam-tuk dam-ni
10) ba-an-da-kar-ra
11) dumu-tuk dumu-ni
12) ba-an-da-kar-ra
13) nì-a-ne-ru nì-á-zi
14) kalam-ma mi-ni-in-gar-ra

1–14) The god Enlil — (as for) Gu[tium], the *fanged* serpent of the mountain, who acted with violence against the gods, who carried off the kingship of the land of Sumer to the mountain land, who fi[ll]ed the land of Sumer with wickedness, who took away the wife from the one who had a wife, who took away the child from the one who had a child, who put wickedness and evil in the the land (of Sumer) —

3.1 Text: NAM.

15) ^{d}en-líl lugal-kur-kur-ra-ke$_4$
16) mu-bi ḫa-lam-e-dè
17) ^{d}utu-ḫé-gál
18) nita-kalag-ga
19) lugal-unu.KI-ga
20) lugal-an-ub-da-limmu$_5$-ba
21) lugal du$_{11}$-ga-na nu-gi$_4$-gi$_4$-da
22) ^{d}en-líl lugal-kur-kur-ra-ke$_4$
23) á-bi mu-da-an-ág

15–23) the god Enlil, lord of the foreign lands, commissioned Utu-ḫegal, the mighty man, king of Uruk, king of the four quarters, the king whose utterance cannot be countermanded, to destroy their name.

24) ^{d}inanna nin-a-ni
25) mu-na-an-gin
26) šùd mu-na-de$_6$

24–26) (Thereupon) he (Utu-ḫegal) went to the goddess Inanna, his lady (and) prayed to her, (saying):

27) nin-mu pirig-mè
28) kur-kur-da du$_7$-du$_7$
29) ^{d}en-líl-le nam-lugal-ki-en-gi-ra
30) ⌜šu⌝-ba gi$_4$-gi$_4$-dè
31) ⌜á⌝-[bi mu-da-an-ág]
32) ⌜á⌝-[daḫ-mu ḫé-me]

27–32) 'My lady, lioness of battle, who butts the foreign lands, the god Enlil has com[missioned me] to bring back the kingship of the land of Sumer. [May you be my] a[lly]'.

33) ugni[m lú]-kúr-kúr-ra
34) ⌜ki⌝ ḫ[é-ni]-ús-ú[s]
35) *ti-rí-[ga-a-an]*
36) ⌜lugal⌝-*gu-ti-um*.<KI>-ke$_4$
37) ka-bi ba-[š]i(?)-ba
38) lú nu-mu-ši-è
39) I$_7$.idigna gú-min-a-ba
40) bí-in-dab$_5$
41) sig-šè ki-en-gi-rá
42) gána bí-kešda
43) IGI.NIM-šè gìr ì-kešda
44) kaskal-kalam-ma-ke$_4$
45) ú-gíd-da bí-in-mú

33–45) The enemy hordes had trampled (everything). Tiri[gan], the king of Gutium, had ..., (but) no one set out against him. He had seized both banks of the Tigris River. In the south, in Sumer, he had blocked (water from) the fields. In the north, he had closed off the roads (and) caused tall grass to grow up along the highway(s) of the land.

46) lugal ^{d}en-líl-le
47) á-sum-ma
48) ^{d}inanna-ke$_4$ šà-ge-pà-da
49) ^{d}utu-ḫé-gál nita-kalag-ga
50) unu.KI-ta mu-ši-è
51) é-^{d}iškur-ka
52) giš bí-dù
53) dumu-uru-na-ke$_4$-ne
54) gù mu-ne-dé-e

46–54) (But), the king granted power by the god Enlil, the one chosen in the heart of the goddess Inanna — Utu-ḫegal — the mighty man, went forth from Uruk (and) set up ... in the temple of the god Iškur. He called out to the citizens of his city, (saying):

55) *gu-ti-um*.KI
56) ^{d}en-líl-le ma-an-sum
57) nin-mu ^{d}inanna
58) á-daḫ-mu-um

55–64) 'The god Enlil has given Gutium to me. My lady, the goddess Inanna, is my ally. The god Dumuzi-ama-ušumgal-ana has declared 'It is a matter for me'. The god Gilgameš, son of the

36.1 [*g*]*u-ti-*[*um*.KI]; cf. 104.1.
37.3 sag-bi ba-⌜x⌝-[...].
38.3 nu-mu-u[n(?)]-ši (Text: PI)-UD(?).D[U(?)].
41.2 ki-e[n-g]i-ra.
42.2 giš bí-[kešda].
43.2 i-in-[kešda].
44.2 -kalam-ma-ka.
48.2 šà-kù-ge-pà-da.
50.2 mu-un-ši-è.
51.2 ⌜é-^{d}iškur⌝-ra-ta.
52.2 bí-in-dù.
53.2 [dumu-ur]u-[n]a-ke$_4$-ne-er.
54.2 mu-un-na-dé-e.
58.2 á-daḫ-mu.

59) ^{d}dumu-zi-
60) ama-ušumgal-an-na-ke$_4$
61) nam-mu bí-⸢du$_{11}$⸣
62) ^{d}GIŠ.⸢bil⸣-ga-mes
63) dumu-^{d}nin-sún-na-ke$_4$
64) maškim-šè ma-an-sum

goddess Ninsun, has assigned him (Dumuzi) to me as bailiff'.

65) dumu-unu.KI-ga
66) dumu-kul-aba$_4$.KI-ka
67) šà-ḫúl-la ba-an-gar
68) uru-ni lú-aš-gin$_7$
69) egir-ra-né ba-ab-ús
70) ka-kešda igi-bar-ra
71) si bí-⸢sá⸣

65–71) He made the citizens of Uruk (and) Kullab happy. His city followed him as if they were (just) one person. He (Utu-ḫegal) arranged in correct array his select elite troops.

72) é-^{d}iškur-ka zi-ga-ni
73) u$_4$-limmu$_5$-kam-ma nag-su I$_7$.EN-ùri-gal-ka
74) giš bí-dù

72–74) After he (Utu-ḫegal) departed (from) the temple of the god Iškur, on the fourth day he set up ... in the city of Nagsu on the Iturungal canal.

75) u$_4$-5-kam-ma bára-*ì-lí*-TAB.⸢BA⸣-*e*-ka
76) giš bí-dù

75–76) On the fifth day he set up ... in the shrine Ilī-tappê.

77) ur-^{d}nin-a-zu
78) *na-bi-*^{d}*en-líl*
79) GÌR.NÍTA-*ti-rí-ga-a-an*
80) ki-en-gi-šè kin-gi$_4$-a
81) im-gi$_4$-éš
82) in-dab$_5$-dab$_5$ šu-ba giš ì-⸢gar⸣

77–82) He captured Ur-Ninazu (and) Nabi-Enlil, generals whom he (Tirigan) had sent as envoys to the land of Sumer, (and) put handcuffs on them.

83) bára-*ì-lí*-TAB.⸢BA⸣-*e*-ka zi-ga-ni
84) u$_4$-6-kam-ma-ka karkar.KI-ka
85) giš bí-dù
86) ^{d}iškur-ra mu-na-⸢an-gin⸣
87) šùd mu-na-de$_6$

83–87) After he departed (from) the shrine Ilī-tappê, on the sixth day he set up ... at Karkar. He proceeded to the god Iškur (and) prayed to him, (saying):

88) ^{d}iškur GIŠ.tukul ^{d}en-líl-⸢le⸣ ma-an-sum
89) á-daḫ-mu ḫé-me

88–89) 'O god Iškur! The god Enlil has given me (his) weapon. May you be my ally'.

90) šà-gi$_6$-ba-⸢šè⸣[...] im-ma-an-[zi]
91) IGI.NIM-adab.[KI]
92) ^{d}utu-è(?)-[a]
93) mu-⸢na-an⸣-[gin]
94) šùd m[u-n]a-[de$_6$]

90–94) In the middle of that night he [got up], and at daybreak [proceeded] (to a point) upstream from Adab. He pra[yed] to him (Utu), (saying):

95) ^{d}utu *gu-ti-um*.KI
96) ^{d}en-líl-le ma-an-sum
97) á-daḫ-mu ḫé-me

95–97) 'O god Utu! The god Enlil has given Gutium to me. May you be my ally'.

98) ki-bé bar-*gu-ti-um*.KI
99) giš mu-na-bar
100) éren mu-na-laḫ$_5$

98–100) In that place, against the Gutians, he laid a trap (and) led (his) troops against them.

101) ^{d}utu-ḫé-gál nita-kalag-ga
102) GÍN.KÁR im-mi-sì
103) GÌR.NÍTA-bi u$_4$-ba *ti-rí-ga-a-an*

101–108) Utu-ḫegal, the mighty man, defeated their generals. Then Tirigan, king of Gutium, fled alone on foot. In the place where he (tried) to save his life

---

60.2 [am]a-ušumgal-an-na-<ke$_4$>.
61.2 nam-x-mu bí-du.
66.2 -kul-aba$_4$.KI-ra.
72.2 zi-ga-a-⸢ni⸣.
73.2 [u$_4$-limmu$_5$-kam]-ma-k[a g]ú-I$_7$.ÉRIN.NUN.NA-ka.
74.2 ⸢bí⸣-in-dù.
75.2 [u$_4$]-⸢5-kam-ma⸣-ka bára-*ì-lí-tap-pé-e*-ka.
76.2 bí-in-dù.
79.2 *ti-rí-ga*.
81.2 ⸢in⸣-gi$_4$-gi$_4$-eš-a.
82.2 giš šu-na mi-ni-gar.
83.2 bára-*ì-lí-*[*tap*]*-pé-e-*⸢ta⸣ zi-ga-a-ni.
85.2 bí-in-dù.
87.2 mu-un-na-an-de$_6$.
88.1 <GIŠ>.⸢tukul⸣. **88**.3 <GIŠ>.tukul (Copy: UR).
89.1 ḫ[é-me]; restoration from 97.1.

104) lugal-*gu-ti-um*.KI
105) aš-a-ni gìr ba-da-an-kar
106) ki zi-ni
107) ba-da-an-kar-ra
108) *dab$_6$-ru-um*.KI-ma ba-an-⌜sa$_6$⌝

— Dabrum — he (at first) was safe.

109) lú-*dab$_6$-ru-um*.<KI>-ma-ke$_4$
110) ^{d}utu-ḫé-gál
111) bar lugal ^{d}en-líl-le á-sum-ma
112) ì-me-a ì-zu-a-ke$_4$-éš
113) *ti-rí-ga-a-an*-ra
114) šu nu-ni-ba

109–114) (But) since the citizens of Dabrum realized that Utu-ḫegal was the king to whom the god Enlil had granted power, they did not let Tirigan go.

115) lú-kin-gi$_4$-a ^{d}utu-ḫé-gál
116) *ti-rí-ga-a-an*
117) ù dam-dumu-ni
118) *dab$_6$-ru-um*.KI-ma m[u-un]-dab$_5$
119) šu-na g̃iš b[í(?)]-gar
120) igi-na túg bí-si
121) ^{d}utu-ḫé-gál igi-^{d}u[tu]-šè
122) gìr-ni-šè mu-ná
123) gú-na gìr bí-gub

115–123) The envoys of Utu-ḫegal captured Tirigan along with his wife (and) children at Dabrum. They put handcuffs and a blindfold on him. Utu-ḫegal made him lie at the feet of the god U[tu] and placed his foot on his neck.

124) *gu-t[i-u]m*.KI ⌜muš-GÍR-ḫur⌝-sag-gá
125) ⌜ki⌝-i[n-du-a] ⌜bí⌝-nag
126) x [...] x
127) g̃iš ⌜bí(?)⌝-x
128) x má-gíd zà-ba im-ta-gar
129) nam-lugal-ki-en-gi-ra šu-ba im-mi-gi$_4$

124–129) Gutium, the *fanged* serpent of the mountain — ... drank water (from[?]) the *watercourses*. ... (Utu-ḫegal) removed ... He brought back the kingship of the land of Sumer.

SCORES

1 0 ^{d}en-líl ⌜*gu*⌝-[*ti-um*.KI]
1 1 ^{d}en-líl ⌜*gu*⌝-[...]
1 2 [...]
1 3 [...]

2 0 muš-GÍR-ḫur-sag-[gá]
2 1 muš-GÍR-ḫur-sag-[gá]
2 2 [...]
2 3 [...]

3 0 lú-á-zi(Text: NAM)-ga-dingir-⌜re!-e-ne⌝
3 1 lú-á-zi(Text:NAM)-ga-dingir-⌜re!-e-ne⌝
3 2 [...]
3 3 [...-n]e

4 0 lú nam-lugal-
4 1 lú nam-lugal-
4 2 [...]
4 3 [...-luga]l-

5 0 ki-en-gi-rá
5 1 ki-en-gi-rá
5 2 [...]
5 3 [... -r]á

6 0 kur-šè ba-de$_6$-a
6 1 kur-šè ba-de$_6$-a
6 2 [...]
6 3 [...]-a

7 0 ki-en-gi-rá
7 1 ki-en-gi-rá
7 2 [...]
7 3 [... -r]á

8 0 nì-a-ne-ru bí-i[n-s]i-a
8 1 nì-a-ne-ru bí-i[n-s]i-a
8 2 [...]
8 3 [...]

114.3 nu-ni-bar.
115.3 ^{d}utu-ḫé-gál-ke$_4$.
118.1 *dab$_6$-ru-um*.<KI>-ma. **118**.3 [*d*]*ab$_6$-ru-um*.KI-ta.
121.3 ^{d}utu-ḫé-[gá]l-e.
122.3 ì-[(x)]-ná.

9 0 dam-tuk dam-ni
9 1 dam-tuk dam-ni
9 2 [...]
9 3 [...]

10 0 ba-an-da-kar-ra
10 1 ba-an-da-kar-ra
10 2 [...]
10 3 [...]

11 0 dumu-tuk dumu-ni
11 1 dumu-tuk dumu-ni
11 2 [...]
11 3 [...]

12 0 ba-an-da-kar-ra
12 1 ba-an-da-kar-ra
12 2 [...]
12 3 [...]

13 0 nì-a-ne-ru nì-á-zi
13 1 nì-a-ne-ru nì-á-zi
13 2 [...]
13 3 [...]

14 0 kalam-ma mi-ni-in-gar-ra
14 1 kalam-ma mi-ni-in-gar-ra
14 2 [...]
14 3 [...]

15 0 ^{d}en-líl lugal-kur-kur-ra-ke$_4$
15 1 ^{d}en-líl lugal-kur-kur-ra-ke$_4$
15 2 [...]
15 3 [...]

16 0 mu-bi ḫa-lam-e-dè
16 1 mu-bi ḫa-lam-e-dè
16 2 [...]
16 3 [...]

17 0 ^{d}utu-ḫé-gál
17 1 ^{d}utu-ḫé-gál
17 2 [...]
17 3 [...]

18 0 nita-kala-ga
18 1 nita-kala-ga
18 2 [...]
18 3 [...]

19 0 lugal-unu.KI-ga
19 1 lugal-unu.KI-ga
19 2 [...]
19 3 [...]

20 0 lugal-an-ub-da-limmu$_5$-ba
20 1 lugal-an-ub-da-limmu$_5$-ba
20 2 [...]
20 3 [...]

21 0 lugal du$_{11}$-ga-na nu-gi$_4$-gi$_4$-da
21 1 lugal du$_{11}$-ga-na nu-gi$_4$-gi$_4$-da
21 2 [...]
21 3 [...]

22 0 ^{d}en-líl lugal-kur-kur-ra-ke$_4$
22 1 ^{d}en-líl lugal-kur-kur-ra-ke$_4$
22 2 [...]
22 3 [...]

23 0 á-bi mu-da-an-ág
23 1 á-bi mu-da-an-ág
23 2 [...]
23 3 [...]

24 0 ^{d}inanna nin-a-ni
24 1 ^{d}inanna nin-a-ni
24 2 [...]
24 3 [...]

25 0 mu-na-an-gin
25 1 mu-na-an-gin
25 2 [...]
25 3 [...]

26 0 šùd mu-na-de$_6$
26 1 šùd mu-na-de$_6$
26 2 [...]
26 3 [...]

27 0 nin-mu pirig-mè
27 1 nin-mu pirig-mè
27 2 [...]
27 3 [...]

28 0 kur-kur-da du$_7$-du$_7$
28 1 kur-kur-da du$_7$-du$_7$
28 2 [...]
28 3 [...]

29 0 ^{d}en-líl-le nam-lugal-ki-en-gi-ra
29 1 ^{d}en-líl-le nam-lugal-ki-en-gi-ra
29 2 [...]
29 3 [...]

30 0 ⸢šu⸣-ba gi$_4$-gi$_4$-dè
30 1 ⸢šu⸣-ba gi$_4$-gi$_4$-dè
30 2 [...]
30 3 [...]

31 0 ⸢á⸣-[bi mu-da-an-ág]
31 1 ⸢á⸣-[...]
31 2 [...]
31 3 [...]

32 0 ⸢á⸣-[daḫ-mu ḫé-me]
32 1 ⸢á⸣-[...]
32 2 [...]
32 3 [.á-da]ḫ [...]

33 0 ugni[m lú]-kúr-kúr-ra
33 1 ug[nim ...]
33 2 [...]
33 3 ugni[m lú-]-kúr-kúr-ra

34 0 ⸢ki⸣ ḫ[é-...]-ús-ú[s]
34 1 ⸢ki⸣ ḫ[é-...]
34 2 [...]
34 3 [...]-ús-ú[s]

35 0 *ti-r[í-ga-a-an]*
35 1 *ti-rí*-[...]
35 2 [...]
35 3 *ti-r[í*-...]

36 0 ⸢lugal⸣-*gu-ti-um*.<KI>-k[e$_4$]
36 1 ⸢lugal⸣-[*g*]*u-ti*-[*um*.KI]
36 2 [...]
36 3 [lugal]-*g*[*u*]-⸢*ti*⸣-*um*.<KI>-k[e$_4$]

37 0 ka-bi b[a-š]i(?)-ba
37 1 ka-bi b[a-š]i(?)-ba
37 2 [...]
37 3 sag-bi ba-⸢x⸣-[...]

38 0 lú nu-mu-ši-è
38 1 lú nu-mu-ši-è
38 2 [...]
38 3 lú nu-mu-u[n]-ši(Text: PI)-UD.D[U]

39 0 I$_7$.idigna gú-min-a-ba
39 1 I$_7$.idigna gú-min-a-ba
39 2 [...] x [...]
39 3 ⸢I$_7$⸣.idig[na ...]

40 0 bí-in-dab$_5$
40 1 bí-in-dab$_5$
40 2 [...]
40 3 [...]

41 0 sig-šè ki-en-gi-rá
41 1 sig-šè ki-en-gi-rá
41 2 sig-šè ki-e[n-g]i-ra
41 3 [...]

42 0 gána bí-kešda
42 1 gána bí-kešda
42 2 giš bí-[kešda]
42 3 [...]

43 0 IGI.NIM-šè gìr ì-kešda
43 1 IGI.NIM-šè gìr ì-kešda
43 2 IGI.NIM-šè gìr i-in-[kešda]
43 3 [...]

44 0 kaskal-kalam-ma-ke$_4$
44 1 kaskal-kalam-ma-ke$_4$
44 2 kaskal-kalam-ma-ka
44 3 [...]

45 0 ú-gíd-da bí-in-mú
45 1 ú-gíd-da bí-in-mú
45 2 ú-gíd-da bí-i[n-x]
45 3 [...]

46 0 lugal ^{d}en-líl-le
46 1 lugal ^{d}en-líl-le
46 2 lugal ^{d}en-líl-le
46 3 [...]

47 0 á-sum-ma
47 1 á-sum-ma
47 2 á-sum-⸢ma⸣
47 3 [...]

48 0 ^{d}inanna-ke$_4$ šà-ge pà-da
48 1 ^{d}inanna-ke$_4$ šà-ge pà-da
48 2 ^{d}inanna-ke$_4$ šà-kù-ge pà-da
48 3 [...]

49 0 ^{d}utu-ḫé-gál nita-kala-ga
49 1 ^{d}utu-ḫé-gál nita-kala-ga
49 2 ^{d}utu-ḫé-⸢gál⸣ [nit]a-kala-ga
49 3 [...]

50 0 unu.KI-ta mu-ši-è
50 1 unu.KI-ta mu-ši-è
50 2 unu.KI-ta mu-un-ši-è
50 3 [...]

51 0 é-^{d}iškur-ka
51 1 é-^{d}iškur-ka
51 2 ⸢é-^{d}iškur⸣-ra-ta
51 3 [...]

52 0 giš bí-dù
52 1 giš bí-dù
52 2 giš bí-in-dù
52 3 [...]

53 0 dumu-uru-na-ke$_4$-ne
53 1 dumu-uru-na-ke$_4$-ne
53 2 [dumu-ur]u-[n]a-ke$_4$-ne-er
53 3 [...]

54 0 gù mu-ne-dé-e
54 1 gù mu-ne-dé-e
54 2 gù mu-un-na-dé-e
54 3 [...]

55 0 *gu-ti-um*.KI
55 1 *gu-ti-um*.KI
55 2 [....K]I/[*u*]*m*
55 3 [...]

56 0 ^{d}en-líl-le ma-an-sum
56 1 ^{d}en-líl-le ma-an-sum
56 2 ^{d}en-líl-le ma-an-sum
56 3 [...]

57 0 nin-mu ^{d}inanna
57 1 nin-mu ^{d}inanna
57 2 nin-mu ^{d}inanna
57 3 [...]

58 0 á-daḫ-mu-um
58 1 á-daḫ-mu-um
58 2 á-daḫ-mu
58 3 [...]

59 0 ^{d}dumu-zi-
59 1 ^{d}dumu-zi-
59 2 [...]
59 3 [...]

60 0 ama-ušumgal-an-na-ke$_4$
60 1 ama-ušumgal-an-na-ke$_4$
60 2 [am]a-ušumgal-an-na-<ke$_4$>
60 3 [...]

61 0 nam-mu bí-⸢du$_{11}$⸣
61 1 nam-mu bí-⸢du$_{11}$⸣
61 2 nam-x-mu bí-du
61 3 [...]

62 0 ^{d}GIŠ.⸢bil⸣-ga-mes
62 1 ^{d}GIŠ.⸢bil⸣-ga-mes
62 2 [...]-ga-mes
62 3 [...]

63 0 dumu-^{d}nin-sún-na-⸢ke$_4$⸣
63 1 ⸢dumu⸣-^{d}nin-sún-na-⸢ke$_4$⸣
63 2 dumu-^{d}nin-sú[n-...]
63 3 [...]

64 0 maškim-šè ma-an-sum
64 1 maškim-šè ma-an-sum
64 2 maš[ki]m-šè ma-an-s[um]
64 3 [...]

65 0 dumu-unu.KI-ga
65 1 dumu-unu.KI-ga
65 2 [...-g]a
65 3 [...]

66 0 dumu-kul-aba$_4$.KI-ka
66 1 dumu-kul-aba$_4$.KI-ka
66 2 dumu-kul-aba$_4$.KI-ra
66 3 [...]

67 0 šà-ḫúl-la ba-an-gar
67 1 šà-ḫúl-la ba-an-gar
67 2 šà-⸢ḫúl⸣-la ba-an-⸢gar⸣
67 3 [...]

68 0 uru-ni lú-aš-gin$_7$
68 1 uru-ni lú-aš-gin$_7$
68 2 [... l]ú-aš-gin$_7$
68 3 [...]

69 0 egir-ra-né ba-ab-ús
69 1 egir-ra-né ba-ab-ús
69 2 egir-ra-né ba-⸢ab⸣-ús
69 3 [...]

70 0 ka-kešda igi-bar-ra
70 1 ka-kešda igi-bar-ra
70 2 [...]-ra
70 3 [...]

71 0 si bí-⸢sá⸣
71 1 si bí-⸢sá⸣
71 2 si bí-[sá]
71 3 [...]

72 0 é-^{d}iškur-ka zi-ga-ni
72 1 é-^{d}iškur-ka zi-ga-ni
72 2 [...-k]a zi-ga-a-⸢ni⸣
72 3 [...]

73 0 u$_4$-limmu$_5$-kam-ma nag-su I$_7$.EN-ùri-gal-ka
73 1 u$_4$-limmu$_5$kam-ma nag-su I$_7$.EN-ùri-gal-ka
73 2 [...]-ma-k[a(?) g]ú-I$_7$.ÉRIN.NUN.NA-ka
73 3 [...]

74 0 giš bí-dù
74 1 giš bí-dù
74 2 giš ⸢bí⸣-in-dù
74 3 [...]

75 0 u$_4$-5-kam-ma bára-*ì-lí*-TAB.⸢BA⸣-*e*-ka
75 1 u$_4$-5-kam-ma bára-*ì-lí*-TAB.⸢BA⸣-*e*-ka
75 2 [u$_4$]-⸢5-kam-ma⸣-ka bára-*ì-lí-tap-pé-e*-ka
75 3 [...]

76 0 giš bí-dù
76 1 giš bí-dù
76 2 giš bí-in-dù
76 3 [...]

77 0 ur-^{d}nin-a-zu
77 1 ur-^{d}nin-a-zu
77 2 [u]r-^{d}nin-[x-x]
77 3 [...]

78 0 *na-bi-^{d}en-líl*
78 1 *na-[b]i-^{d}en-líl*
78 2 *[n]a-bi-^{d}en-líl*
78 3 [...]

79 0 GÌR.NÍTA-*ti-rí-ga-a-an*
79 1 GÌR.NÍTA-*ti-rí-ga-a-an*
79 2 GÌR.NÍTA-*ti-rí-ga*
79 3 [...]

80 0 ki-en-gi-šè kin-gi$_4$-a
80 1 ki-en-gi-šè kin-gi$_4$-a
80 2 ki-en-gi$_4$-ra ⸢kin⸣-gi-a
80 3 [...]

81 0 im-gi$_4$-éš
81 1 im-gi$_4$-éš
81 2 ⸢in⸣-gi$_4$-gi$_4$-eš-a
81 3 [...]

82 0 in-dab$_5$-dab$_5$ šu-ba giš ì-⸢gar⸣
82 1 in-dab$_5$-dab$_5$ šu-ba giš ì-⸢gar⸣
82 2 in-dab$_5$-dab$_5$ giš šu-na mi-ni-gar
82 3 [...]

83 0 bára-*ì-lí*-TAB.⸢BA⸣-*e*-ka zi-ga-ni
83 1 [b]ára-*ì-lí*-TAB.⸢BA⸣-*e*-ka zi-g[a]-ni
83 2 bára-*ì-lí-[tap]-pé-e*-⸢ta⸣ zi-ga-ani
83 3 [...]

84 0 u$_4$-6-kam-ma-ka karkar.KI-ka
84 1 u$_4$-6-kam-ma-⸢ka⸣ karkar.KI-ka
84 2 u$_4$-6-kam-ma-ka k[arkar.K]I-⸢ka⸣
84 3 [...]

85 0 giš bí-dù
85 1 giš bí-dù
85 2 giš bí-in-dù
85 3 [...]

86 0 ^{d}iškur-ra mu-na-⸢an-gin⸣
86 1 ^{d}⸢iškur-ra⸣ mu-na-⸢an-gin⸣
86 2 ^{d}iškur-ra mu-na-a[n-gi]n
86 3 [...]

87 0 šùd mu-na-de$_6$
87 1 šùd mu-na-⸢de$_6$⸣
87 2 ⸢šùd⸣ mu-un-na-an-de$_6$
87 3 šùd ⸢mu⸣-[...]

88 0 ^{d}iškur GIŠ.tukul ^{d}en-líl-l[e] ma-an-sum
88 1 ^{d}⸢iškur⸣ <GIŠ>.⸢tukul⸣ ^{d}en-⸢líl⸣-l[e] m[a-...]
88 2 ^{d}iškur GIŠ.tukul ^{d}en-líl-[le ...]-sum
88 3 ^{d}iškur <GIŠ>.tukul(? Copy: UR) ^{d}en-líl [(x)] ma-an-[sum]

89 0 á-daḫ-mu ḫé-me
89 1 á-daḫ-mu ḫ[é-me]
89 2 ⸢á-daḫ⸣-mu ḫé!-me-en
89 3 á-daḫ-mu x [...]

90 0 šà-gi$_6$-ba-ka [...] im-ma-an-[zi]
90 1 šà-⸢gi$_6$⸣-ba-⸢ka⸣ [...]
90 2 ⸢šà-g]i$_6$-[...] x [...]
90 3 šà-gi$_6$-ba-k[a] im-ma-an-[x]

91 0 IGI.NIM adab.[KI]
91 1 IG[I....]
91 2 [...]
91 3 IGI.NIM adab.[KI]

92 0 ^{d}utu-è(?)-[a]
92 1 ⸢^{d}⸣[...]
92 2 [...]
92 3 ^{d}utu-è(?)-[a]

93 0 mu-⸢na-an⸣-[gin]
93 1 [...]
93 2 [...]
93 3 mu-⸢na-an⸣-[x]

94 0 šùd m[u-n]a-[de$_6$]
94 1 [...]
94 2 [...]
94 3 šùd m[u-n]a-[x]

95 0 ^{d}utu *gu-ti-um*.KI
95 1 ^{d}utu *gu-ti-um*.KI
95 2 [...]
95 3 ^{d}u[tu] *gu-ti-[um*.KI]

96 0 ^{d}en-líl-le ma-an-sum
96 1 ^{d}en-líl-le ma-an-sum
96 2 [...]
96 3 ⌈^{d}⌉en-líl-l[e] ma-an-[x]

97 0 á-daḫ-mu ḫé-me
97 1 á-daḫ-mu ḫé-me
97 2 [...]
97 3 á-daḫ-m[u ...]

98 0 ki-bé bar-*gu-ti-um*.KI
98 1 ki-bé bar-*gu-ti-um*.KI
98 2 [...]
98 3 ki-bé [...]

99 0 giš mu-na-bar
99 1 giš mu-na-bar
99 2 [...]
99 3 x x

100 0 éren mu-na-laḫ$_{5}$
100 1 éren mu-na-laḫ$_{5}$
100 2 [...]
100 3 [...]

101 0 ^{d}utu-ḫé-gál nita-kala-ga
101 1 ^{d}utu-ḫé-gál nita-kala-ga
101 2 [...]
101 3 [...]

102 0 GÍN.KÁR im-mi-sì
102 1 GÍN.KÁR im-mi-sì
102 2 [...]
102 3 [...]

103 0 GÌR.NÍTA-bi u$_{4}$-ba *ti-rí-ga-a-an*
103 1 GÌR.NÍTA-bi u$_{4}$-ba *ti-rí-ga-a-an*
103 2 [...]
103 3 [...]

104 0 lugal-*gu-ti-um*.KI
104 1 lugal-*gu-ti-um*.KI
104 2 [...]
104 3 [...]

105 0 aš-a-ni gìr ba-da-an-kar
105 1 aš-a-ni gìr ba-da-an-kar
105 2 [...]
105 3 [...]

106 0 ki zi-ni
106 1 ki zi-ni
106 2 [...]
106 3 [...]

107 0 ba-da-an-kar-ra
107 1 ba-da-an-kar-ra
107 2 [...]
107 3 [...]

108 0 *dab$_{6}$-ru-um*.KI-ma ba-an-⌈sa$_{6}$⌉
108 1 *dab$_{6}$-ru-um*.KI-ma ba-an-⌈sa$_{6}$⌉
108 2 [...]
108 3 [...]

109 0 lú-*dab$_{6}$-ru-um*.<KI>-ma-ke$_{4}$
109 1 lú-*dab$_{6}$-ru-um*.<KI>-ma-ke$_{4}$
109 2 [...]
109 3 [...]

110 0 ^{d}utu-ḫé-gál
110 1 ^{d}utu-ḫé-gál
110 2 [...]
110 3 [...]

111 0 bar lugal ^{d}en-líl-le á-sum-ma
111 1 bar lugal ^{d}en-líl-le á-sum-ma
111 2 [...]
111 3 [...] ⌈á⌉-[...]

112 0 ì-me-a ì-zu-a-ke$_{4}$-éš
112 1 ì-me-a ì-zu-a-ke$_{4}$-éš
112 2 ì-me-[a] ì-zu-a-ke$_{4}$-éš
112 3 [...]

113 0 *ti-rí-ga-a-an*-ra
113 1 *ti-rí-ga-a-an*-ra
113 2 [...]
113 3 *ti-rí-ga-a-an*-ra

114 0 šu nu-ni-ba
114 1 šu nu-ni-ba
114 2 [...]
114 3 šu nu-ni-bar

115 0 lú-kin-gi$_{4}$-a ^{d}utu-ḫé-gál
115 1 lú-kin-gi$_{4}$-a ^{d}utu-ḫé-gál
115 2 [...]
115 3 lú-kin-gi$_{4}$-a ^{d}utu-ḫé-gál-ke$_{4}$

116 0 *ti-rí-ga-a-an*
116 1 *ti-rí-ga-a-an*
116 2 [...]
116 3 *ti-rí-ga-a-an*

117 0 ù dam-dumu-ni
117 1 ù dam-dumu-ni
117 2 [...]
117 3 ⌈ù⌉ dam-dumu-ni

118 0 *dab$_6$-ru-um.*<KI>-ma m[u-un]-dab$_5$
118 1 *dab$_6$-ru-um.*<KI>-ma m[u-un-da]b$_5$
118 2 [...]
118 3 *[d]ab$_6$-ru-um.*KI-ta [...]-dab$_5$

119 0 šu-na giš b[í(?)]-gar
119 1 šu-na giš [...]
119 2 [...]
119 3 šu-na giš b[í(?)]-gar

120 0 igi-na túg bí-si
120 1 igi-na túg b[í-si]
120 2 [...]
120 3 ⸢igi⸣-na túg bí-si

121 0 ^{d}utu-ḫé-gál igi-^{d}u[tu]-šè
121 1 ^{d}utu-ḫé-gál [igi]-⸢^{d}⸣[utu]-⸢šè⸣
121 2 [...]
121 3 ^{d}utu-ḫé-[gá]l-e! igi-^{d}u[tu]-šè

122 0 gìr-ni-šè mu-ná
122 1 gìr-ni-šè mu-⸢ná⸣
122 2 [...]
122 3 gìr-ni-šè ì-[(x)-n]á

123 0 gú-na gìr bí-gub
123 1 gú-na gìr bí-gub
123 2 [...]
123 3 [...-gu]b

124 0 *gu-t[i-u]m.*KI ⸢muš-GÍR ḫur⸣-sag-gá
124 1 *gu-t[i-u]m.*KI ⸢muš-GÍR ḫur⸣-sag-gá
124 2 [...]
124 3 [...]

125 0 ⸢ki⸣-i[n-du-a] ⸢bí⸣-nag]
125 1 ⸢ki⸣-i[n-du-a] ⸢bí⸣-nag
125 2 [...]
125 3 [...]

126 0 x [...] x
126 1 x [...] x
126 2 [...]
126 3 [...]

127 0 giš ⸢bí(?)⸣-x
127 1 giš ⸢bí(?)⸣-x
127 2 [...]
127 3 [...]

128 0 x má-gíd zà-ba im-ta-gar
128 1 x má-gíd zà-ba im-ta-gar
128 2 [...]
128 3 [...]

129 0 nam-lugal ki-en-gi-ra šu-ba im-mi-gi$_4$
129 1 nam-lugal ki-en-gi-ra šu-ba im-mi-gi$_4$
129 2 [...]
129 3 [...]

5

An Old Babylonian Sammeltafel gives a copy of an apparent royal inscription of Utu-ḫegal.

COMMENTARY

The inscription is found on rev. col. iii′ of Ni 4167 (ex. 3 of E2.13.6.4); it is erroneously marked as being on the obverse of the tablet in Kramer's copy.

The inscription begins (lines 1′–12′) with what appear to be epithets of a deity. If the restoration of lines 2′–3′ [nita-dam-ki]-ág-[^{d}]inanna, following Frayne, RIME 4 p. 276 line 3, be correct, it would argue for an identification of the missing DN as Dumuzi. We may note, in this connection, that lines 62–64 of E2.13.6.4 relate how the god Dumuzi-ama-ušumgal-ana served as maškim 'bailif' for Utu-ḫegal in his war against the Gutians. This inscription may have been a dedicatory label on the monument inscribed with the account of Utu-ḫegal's war against the Gutians

BIBLIOGRAPHY

1976 Kramer, ISET 2 pl. 124 (ex. 3, copy)
1985 Römer, Orientalia NS 54 p. 288 (transliteration)

TEXT

Lacuna
1′ [...] x
2′ [nita-dam-ki]-ág-
3′ [d]inanna
4′ [...]] x ga/bi
5′ [...]-da
6′ [...]-ba
7′ [...-du_{11}-g]a-na
8′ [nu-gi_4-gi_4]-da
9′ [...]
10′ [...]
11′ [...] x
12′ [lugal(?)]-a-ni-ir
13′ [d]utu-ḫé-gál
14′ [nit]a-kala-ga
15′ [lugal]-unu.KI-ga
16′ [lugal]-⸢an-ub⸣-da-
17′ [$limmu_5$-b]a-ke_4
18′ [...]-⸢ni⸣
Lacuna

Lacuna
1′–6′) (For) [DN, be]loved [husband] of [the goddess] Inanna, ...

7′–11′) whose [utteran]ce can[not be countermanded ...],

12′) his [lord(?)],
13′–18′) Utu-ḫegal, the mighty [ma]n, [king] of Uruk, [king of the fou]r quarters, ...
Lacuna

6

An inscription incised on a bronze bowl gives the titles of Utu-ḫegal and a curse formula.

COMMENTARY

The bowl measures 15 cm in height, with a diameter of 9.5 cm at the lip, 15.5 cm at the widest point, and 7.4 cm at the base. The object, formerly in the Erlenmeyer Collection (Basle), was sold at Christie's in London in December 1988 and was resold at Christie's in December 1992. The edition benefited from collations of I. Finkel kindly conmunicated to the author, and of H. Steible published in NSBW2 p. 330. For the restoration of line 17, compare Kärki, KDDU p. 65 Šulgi 61 line 14.

BIBLIOGRAPHY

1969 Calmeyer, Datierbare Bronzen pp. 37 no. 17 and 162 no. 14 (study)
1971 Erlenmeyer, APA 2 pp. 255–56 (photo, copy, study)
1988 Christie's (London), Ancient Near Eastern Texts from the Erlenmeyer Collection pp. 32–33 no. 61 (photo, copy, study)
1989 Michalowski and Walker in Studies Sjöberg p. 392 (edition)
1991 Steible, NSBW 2 pp. 330–32 (edition)

TEXT

1) dutu-ḫé-gál
2) nita-kalag-ga
3) lugal-unu.KI-ga

1–6) Utu ḫegal, mighty man, king of Uruk, king of the four quarters.

4) lugal-an-ub-da-limmu$_5$-ba-ka
5) lú mu-sar-ra-na
6) šu-ni bí-in-⸢ùr⸣-a
7) mu-ni bí-⸢íb⸣-sar-a
8) ⸢áš⸣-ba-lá-a-⸢ke$_4$-éš⸣
9) lú-kúr-ra ⸢ḫé-ni⸣-in-dab$_5$
10) íb-zi-⸢ra⸣-a
11) bala-a-ni
12) ⸢ḫé-ku$_5$⸣
13) ⸢numun-a⸣-ni ⸢ḫé⸣-til
14) an lugal-d[ingir-re-n]e
15) ⸢^{d}⸣inanna ⸢nin⸣-[un]u.KI-g[a]
16) in-x-(x)-x-⸢na⸣
17) ⸢nam ḫa-ba⸣-d[a-kuru$_5$]-ne

7–10) As for the one who erases the inscription (and) writes his (own) name there (or) who on account of the curse has someone else take hold of it (and) remove it,
11–12) may his reign be cut (short),

13) (and) may his progeny come to an end.
14–17) May An, king of the go[d]s, and the goddess Inanna, lady of [Ur]uk, ... cu[rse] him.

2001

A stele fragment from Ur bears a dedicatory inscription of Ur-Nammu, military governor of Ur, to the goddess Ningal for the life of Utu-ḫegal.

COMMENTARY

The stele fragment is made of diorite and measures 22.5×19.5 cm. It was found under the pavement near the doorway of room 6 of the Neo-Babylonian period temple of Ningal. The piece was given the excavation number U 3158 and now bears the museum number IM 1048. For the translation 'servant' for ama-[a-tu] of line 13, see the comments of C. Wilcke in CRRA 19 p. 193 n. 67. The edition follows the copy of Gadd.

BIBLIOGRAPHY

1925 Woolley, AJ p. 371 (provenance)
1928 Gadd, UET 1 no. 30 (copy, edition)
1929 Barton, RISA pp. 360–61 Utu-Khegal 1 (edition)
1939 Jacobsen, SKL p. 202 n. 30 (study)
1955 Woolley, UE 4 p. 170 (study)
1962 Grégoire, Lagash p. 39 n. 182 (edition)
1966 Hallo, JCS 20 p. 137 (study)
1971 Sollberger and Kupper, IRSA IIK3c (translation)
1974 Wilcke, CRRA 19 p. 193 n. 67 (transliteration, study)
1991 Steible, NSBW 2 pp. 329–30 Utuḫegal 6 (edition)

TEXT

1) [^{d}nin-g]al
2) [dam-ki-á]g-
3) [^{d}EN].ZU-na
4) [nin]-a-ni
5) ⸢nam⸣-ti-
6) ^{d}utu-ḫé-gál
7) nita-kalag-g[a]
8) lugal-unu.KI-ga
9) lugal-a[n-ub]-da-l[ímmu$_5$-ba-ka-šè]

1–4) For the [goddess Ning]al, [belov]ed [wife] of [the god S]în, his [lady],

5–9) for the life of Utu-ḫegal, mighty man, king of Uruk, king of the f[our] qua[rters],

---

E2.13.6.5 6 -⸢ùr⸣-a, collation Finkel.
E2.13.6.5 9 ⸢ḫé-ni⸣-in-dab$_5$, collation Finkel.
E2.13.6.5 10 íb-zi-⸢ra⸣-a, reading follows Steible.
E2.13.6.5 15 ⸢nin⸣-[un]u.KI-g[a], reading follows Steible.

10) ur-[^{d}nammu]
11) GÌR.[NÍTA]
12) uri$_5$.K[I-ma]
13) ama-[a-tu]
14) é-k[iš-nu]-gá[l-la]
15) š[eš-a-né]
Lacuna

10–15) Ur-[Nammu], military go[vernor] of Ur, ser[vant] of the Ek[išnu]ga[l, his] br[other]
Lacuna

2002

An inscription incised on a stele fragment from Ur indicates that the piece was dedicated for the life of Utu-ḫegal; the names of both the dedicator and the divine recipient are now broken away. The piece probably belonged to Ur-Nammu and was dedicated to the god Nanna.

COMMENTARY

The stele fragment is made of white limestone and measures 40×40×17 cm. It was found in the surface soil near the Neo-Babylonian temple of Ningal. The piece was given the excavation no. U 3173, and now bears the museum no. BM 119064. The inscription was collated from the published photo. The presence of a large lunar crescent on the top of the stele provides a strong argument that the stele was dedicated to the god Nanna.

BIBLIOGRAPHY

1925 Woolley, AJ 5 p. 398 (provenance)
1928 Gadd, UET 1 no. 31 (copy, edition)
1929 Barton, RISA pp. 360–61 Utu-Khegal 2 (edition)
1955 Woolley, UE 4 p. 170 (study)
1966 Hallo, JCS 20 p. 137 (study)
1977 Dyson, Expedition 20/1 p. 17 fig. 21 (photo)
1991 Steible, NSBW 2 pp. 327–28 Utuhegal 5 (edition)

TEXT

1) ⸢^{d}⸣[nanna]
2) lugal-a-[nun-na-ke$_4$-ne]
3) lugal-a-[ni]
4) nam-[ti]-
5) ⸢^{d}⸣utu-ḫé-[gál]
6) ⸢nita⸣-kalag-[ga]
7) [lu]gal-un[u.KI-ga]
8) lugal-a[n-ub]-da-limmu$_5$-ba-[ka-šè]
Lacuna

1–3) To the god [Nanna, k]ing of the A[nunnaku gods, his] lord,

4–8) for the li[fe] of Utu-ḫe[gal], mighty [man, ki]ng of Ur[uk], king of the four quar[ters],
Lacuna

BÀD.KI

E2.14

Two inscriptions of Sargonic date refer to a certain Puzur-Šullat, *šangû* priest of the city BÀD.KI. The identification of this toponym is uncertain.

Puzur-Šullat

E2.14.1

2001

A bronze bowl of Sargonic date found in excavations at Tell Munbāqa in northern Syria bears the inscription of a daughter of a *šangû* priest of the city BÀD.KI.

COMMENTARY

The bowl in question was found in the hoard of stone and metal objects from the flooring H5/H6 of a house in quadrant 26/35 NW and bears the excavation number MBQ 26/35–62 (= 71 MBQ 59). It measures 6.65 cm in height with a maximum diameter of 8.7 cm. The inscription was collated from the published photo.

P. Steinkeller's proposed identification of Tell Munbāqa with ancient BÀD.KI (RA 78 [1984] pp. 83–84) is uncertain. Since portable objects such as this bowl can easily travel, their discovery is not good evidence for site identifications. According to the tablets found at Tell Munbāqat, the city was called Ekalte in late Old Babylonian times (see Mayer, MDOG 122 [1990] pp. 49–51). The city name appears in the writing *ia-k*[*a-a*]*l-tim*.KI in a Mari letter (see W. Yuhong, NABU 1992 no. 51). Of course, this need not be the Sargonic name of the city. The PN in line 3 apparently contains the dual pronominal suffix, for which, see Whiting, JNES 31 (1972) pp. 331–37.

BIBLIOGRAPHY

1974 Wäfler, MDOG 106 p. 43 (study)
1980 Wäfler, MDOG 112 pp. 9–11 (photo, copy, edition, study)
1983 Boese, Damas Mitt. 1 pp. 9–16 and fig. 1 (copy, study)
1984 Steinkeller, RA 78 pp. 83–4 (edition, study)

TEXT

1) *puzur*$_4$-^{d}*šúllat*
2) SANGA ⌈BÀD.KI⌉
3) ME-*šu-ni*
4) DUMU.MUNUS-*sú*

1–2) Puzur-Šullat, *šangû* priest of BÀD.KI:

3–4) MEšunī (is) his daughter.

2002

A cylinder seal of Puzur-Šullat is now housed in the British Museum.

COMMENTARY

The seal, which is made of quartz, measures 3.6×2.3 cm. It was acquired in 1825 as part of the Rich collection and bears the museum number BM 89147. The inscription was collated from the published photo. The bibliography includes items which give the seal design without the inscription.

BIBLIOGRAPHY

1842–43 Cullimore, Oriental Cylinders no. 41 (drawing)
1844 Micali, Monumenti pl. I no. 11
1847 Lajard, Mithra pl. XIX no. 6
1876 G. Smith, Chaldean Genesis frontispiece (photo [detail])
1883 Ménant, Glyptique 1 pp. 79–80 and fig. 39 (drawing [detail], study)
1884 Perrot and Chipiez, Chaldée et Assyrie p. 502 fig. 225 (drawing [detail])
1885 Hommel, Geschichte p. 350 (drawing)
1885 Pinches, JBAA 43 p. 403 and pl. I no. 1
1887 Reber, ZA 2 pp. 12 and 40 no. 1 (drawing, study)
1890–94 Roscher, Lexikon II/1 col. 786 (drawing [detail])
1891 Middleton, Engraved Gems p. 4 (drawing [detail])
1892 Middleton, Lewis Collection p. 14 fig. 1
1895 Maspéro, Histoire 1 p. 591 (drawing [detail])
1899 Ball, Light p. 44 no. 1 (photo, translation)
1900 Fürtwängler, Gemmen, pl. I no. 1 (photo)
1910 Ward, Seals fig. 159 (drawing)
1910 King, Early History pl. facing p. 76 (photo)
1920 Weber, AO 17–18 fig. 138 (photo, study)
1922 BM Guide p. 234 no. 25 (study)
1926 Unger, RLV 4 pl. 157c (photo)
1926 Unger, SuAK p. 94 fig. 40 (photo)
1939 Frankfort, Cylinder Seals pl. XVIIa (photo [detail])
1954 Frankfort, Art and Architecture pl. 45A (photo [detail])
1959 Wiseman and Forman, Seals no. 35 (photo)
1960 Parrot, Sumer p. 187 no. 225 (photo [detail])
1962 Strommenger and Hirmer, Mesopotamien pl. 113 (photo)
1965 Boehmer, Glyptik no. 728 and fig. 236 (photo, study)
1966 Boehmer, Orientalia NS 35 pp. 363–364 and pl. XLV no. 4 (photo, study)
1966 Unger, Siegelbildforschung p. 60 (study)
1968–69 Edzard, AfO 22 p. 16 no. 24–17 (transliteration)
1982 Collon, Cylinder Seals 2 no. 114 (photo, edition [by Sollberger], study)
1983 Boese, Damas. Mitt. 1 p. 11 fig. 2 (copy)
1984 Steinkeller, RA 78 pp. 83–84 (edition)
1987 Collon, First impressions no. 955 (photo, translation)

TEXT

1) *puzur*$_4$-^{d}*šúllat*
2) SANGA BÀD.KI
3) *šag-gul-lum*
4) DUB.SAR
5) IR$_{11}$-*sú*

1–2) Puzur-Šullat, *šangû* priest of BÀD.KI:

3–5) Šaggullum, the scribe, (is) his servant.

Ur

E2.15

Sargon's conquest of Ur, part of his campaign against Sumer, was one of the most notable achievements of his reign, and he commemorated the deed in three monuments set up in Nippur; their inscriptions are known from later Old Babylonian tablet copies (E2.1.1.1–3). In one of the captions accompanying another inscription, E2.1.1.12, we learn the name of the defeated ruler of Ur: Lu-Nanna. Of interest is the fact that Lu-Nanna, like Lugal-zage-si of Uruk, is given the title LUGAL 'king'. It may be that Lu-Nanna presided over a small independent kingdom centred at Ur in late pre-Sargonic times. Probably late in the reign of Sargon, Ur rebelled. The revolt was led by Kaku, 'king of Ur', and was quelled by Sargon's successor Rīmuš (E2.1.2.4). Rīmuš apparently bore no lasting malice toward the rebel city, since he later deposited pieces of booty from his Elamite campaign — vases and a mace — (E2.1.2.12 and E2.1.2.16) in the city's temples. His successors, Man-ištūšu and Narām-Sîn, both set up monuments in Ur to commemorate their military victories. The latter king, however, was not able to hold the fealty of the local populace; Ur participated in the two major revolts of Narām-Sîn's reign. The status of the city in late Sargonic-Gutian times is unclear; we may note, for example, that no inscription from Ur is known that mentions Šar-kali-šarrī. It may be that Ur, like Lagaš, declared its independence in the troubled period that followed the death of Šar-kali-šarrī; the cone inscription of Lu-saga, governor of Ur (E2.15.1), may date to this period. Later, the city was apparently under the domination of Lagaš; Ur-Baba's installation of his daughter as *entu* priestess of the god Nanna (UET 1 no. 25) clearly attests to this fact. The discovery of inscriptions of Gudea at Ur (UET 1 nos. 27 and 28), however, is not unequivocal proof of Lagašite control over the city; the inscriptions could be stray pieces from Lagaš. Further, there is clear evidence indicating control over Ur by the last king of the Uruk IV dynasty. In a votive inscription Ur-Nammu, 'military governor of Ur', acknowledges Utu-ḫegal as his overlord (E2.14.6.2001). Shortly thereafter, Ur-Nammu declared his independence by adopting the title 'king of Ur', and founded a dynasty that was to dominate Sumer and Akkad for over one hundred years.

RIM number	Ur king	Ur governor	Sargonic king	Source
	Lu-Nanna		Sargon	E2.1.1.12 Caption 3
	KA-ku		Rīmuš	E2.1.2.4
		Ur-Utu	Narām-Sîn	RTC no. 83
E2.15.1		Lu-saga		

Lu-saga

E2.15.1

1

A cone inscription of Lu-saga, a seemingly independent governor of Ur, records his declaration of the border of Ur for the god Nanna.

CATALOGUE

Ex.	Museum number	Excavation number	Registration number	Ur Provenance	Dimensions (cm)	Lines preserved	cpn
1	IM 9227	U 17822	—	—	—	1–8	n
2	IM 92758	U 8839	—	'Loose in soil' in the Royal Cemetery area, season V	—	1–8	n
3	IM 92757	U 10109	—	From the 'top filling' in the Royal Cemetery, season VI	—	—	n
4	IM 92749	U 11674	—	Royal Cemetery area, season VII	—	—	n
5	BM 138344	—	1935-1-13,747	—	5 long, 5 wide	1–8	c
6	BM 138345	—	1935-1-13,748	—	6 long, 5.2 wide	1–8	c

COMMENTARY

Exs. 2–6 were all found in excavations of Woolley in the Royal Cemetery area at Ur. Exs. 5–6 were kindly collated by A.R. George. While Steible (NSBW 2 p. 347) edited a vase inscription that mentions a certain Lu-saga (Clay, YOS 1 no. 9) as a second inscription of Lu-saga of Ur, there is no evidence that the Yale vase actually refers to the governor of Ur; lú-sa$_6$-ga is a common Sumerian name.

BIBLIOGRAPHY

1928 Gadd, UET 1 no. 309 (ex. 2, copy, transliteration)
1957 Edzard, Sumer 13 pp. 181–82 and pl. 2 following p. 188 (ex. 1, copy, edition)
1965 Sollberger, UET 8 p. 35 no. 40 (exs. 1–4, study; ex. 2, transliteration)
1966 Falkenstein, Inschriften Gudeas p. 12 n. 6 and p. 14 (study)
1966 Hallo, JCS 20 p. 137 (study)
1971 Sollberger and Kupper, IRSA IIB1a (exs. 1–4, translation)
1991 Steible, NSBW 2 pp. 347–348 Lušaga 2 (exs. 1–6, edition)

TEXT

1) ^{d}nanna 2) lugal-a-ni	1–2) For the god Nanna, his lord,

2.1 lú-a-ni.

3) lú-sa$_6$-ga
4) énsi-
5) uri$_5$.KI-ma-ke$_4$
6) ki-sur-ra-ni
7) KA-ta mu-na-ta-è
8) bára mu-na-si

3–8) Lu-saga, governor of Ur, declared his (Nanna's) boundary (and) set up a shrine for him.

7.1,5,6 are divided into two parts by a crossed-out line that runs between KA-ta mu-na- and ta-è.
8.1 mu-si.

ELAM

E2.16

The fertile plain of Susiana and the neighbouring highland areas of Elam and Paraḫšum were a tempting target for the Sargonic kings, and the history of the period is marked by their almost constant warfare in the east. As noted in the introductory remarks for Sargon, a first step in the conquest of Elam was Sargon's defeat of the city of Arawa (Sargon year name [a]); the city was a western outpost of Elamite control. The conquest of Elam (NIM.KI) — presumably a reference to Susiana — followed soon after this (Sargon year name [b]). The later conquest of Paraḫšum marked the final stage in Sargon's eastern wars. The Elamite campaign is commemorated in a victory stele, known from a later Old Babylonian tablet copy that was erected by Sargon in Nippur (E2.1.1.8). Its captions reveal the names of a number of defeated enemy cities; chief among these were Susa and Awan. Also given are the names of various Elamite leaders. Heading the list are SaNAM-Šimut, governor of Elam, and Luḫʾišʾan, son of Ḫišibrasini, king of Elam. The latter name, in all likelihood, is to be connected with the ᵐ*lu-uḫ-ḫi-iš-šà-*⌜*an*⌝, immediate predecessor of ᵐ*ḫi-še-*⌜*ep*⌝*-ra-te-*⌜*ep*⌝, in an Old Babylonian tablet copy of a list of kings of Awan (Scheil, RA 28 [1931] p. 2 lines 8–9). The victory over Elam is further alluded to in E2.1.1.1, which describes the lands of Elam and Mari as standing before Sargon. The conquest of Elam was apparently not complete at Sargon's death, since his son and successor, Rīmuš, continued to campaign in the east. Tablet copies of three separate accounts of his Elamite war are known (E2.1.2.6–8). One of these (E2.1.2.6 line 24), gives the name of the governor of Elam defeated by the Akkadian king: *e-maḫ*(?)*-si-n*[*i*]. As victor, Rīmuš was able to claim the title 'conqueror of Elam and Paraḫšum' found in two of his inscriptions (E2.1.2.9 and E2.1.2.17). Archaeologists have unearthed a large number of pieces of Elamite booty dedicated by Rīmuš to the various city gods of Sumer and Akkad; the inscriptions on them are edited as E2.1.2.11–16 in this volume. The victory of Rīmuš ushered in a period of Akkadian control over the area of lowland Elam. This is attested by the appointment by Man-ištūšu of Ešpum as governor of Elam. The latter is known from a statue inscription in which Ešpum acknowledges his Sargonic overlord (E2.1.3.2001), from Ešpum's own seal inscription (E2.16.1.1), and from a seal inscription of one of his servants (E2.16.1.2001). With Elam pacified, Man-ištūšu was able to direct his attentions further east and claimed in his 'standard inscription' (E2.1.3.1) to have defeated Anšan (modern Tell Malyan in Fars) and Širiḫum, as well as thirty-two cities along the Gulf coast. His son, Narām-Sîn, claimed hegemony over Elam; in inscription E2.1.4.25 the king styles himself 'commander ... of all the land Elam as far as Paraḫšum'. Evidence of Sargonic control over the region is attested by the tenure of an Sargonic vassal, Epir-mupi, as governor of Susa and viceroy of Elam. Inscriptions mentioning Epir-mupi appear in this volume as E2.16.2.1 and E2.16.2.2001–2002. Probably early in the reign of Narām-Sîn the Sargonic king concluded a treaty with a ruler of Elam whose name is unfortunately broken away from the extant text of the accord (see Hinz, ZA 58 [1967] pp. 66–96). The existence of this document argues for a degree of autonomy for Elam, for at least part of the region, which would not have been apparent from the evidence of the Sargonic sources alone. While the Old Babylonian version of the Narām-Sîn 'Great Revolt' text names [m]*ḫu-up-šum-ki-pí* and [...-*š*]*ar* as his Marḫašean and Elamite rivals, respectively, the original Old Akkadian version of this text (E2.1.4.6), at least in the extant portion, makes no mention of Elamite participation in the revolt. That Narām-Sîn did, in fact, campaign in Elam is suggested by the title 'conqueror of Armānum, Ebla, and Elam' found in a mace head inscription of a servant of the king (E2.1.4.2005). Probably to be dated to the latter part of the reign of Narām-Sîn, or to the reign of Šar-kali-šarrī, is the rule of Ilī-išmāni, 'viceroy of Elam', who is known from an inscription incised on an axe (E2.16.3.1). The various correlations between the Elamite kings and governors, and the Sargonic kings, are summarized in the following table. The relative placement of the Elamite kings Ḫelu and Ḫita of the Scheil king list with respect to the Sargonic kings is uncertain.

Sargonic king	Elam/Susa	Scheil King List (RA 28 [1913] pp. 1–8)
Sargon	SaNAM-Šimut, governor of Elam (E2.1.1.8)	
	Luḫ'iš'an, son of Hišibrasini, king of Elam (E2.1.1.8)	Luḫ'iš'an
		Ḫišipratep
Rīmuš	Emaḫ(?)sin[i] (E2.1.2.6)	
Man-ištūšu	Ešpum(E2.1.3.2001, E2.16.1.1 and E2.16.1.2001)	(Helu)
Narām-Sîn	Ešpum (E2.1.3.2001, E2.16.2.2001 and E2.16.2.2002)	(Hita)
	Ilī-išmāni (E2.16.3.1)	
Šar-kali-šarrī		

Ešpum

E2.16.1

1

A clay sealing from Susa gives the name and title of Ešpum.

COMMENTARY

The sealing, which measures 3.0 cm in height, bears the museum number AS 10083 (Louvre), formerly S 471. The inscription was collated from the published photo.

BIBLIOGRAPHY

1913 Scheil, MDP 14 p. 4 and pl. III no. 1 (photo, copy, edition)
1920 Delaporte, Louvre 1 p. 58 S 471 (photo, copy, edition, study)
1961 Gelb, MAD 2[2] p. 198 Man-ištušu Officials, etc. no. 2b (study)
1963 Hirsch, AfO 20 p. 16 n. 161 (study)
1964 Boehmer, Moortgat Festschrift p. 45 and pl. 10 no. 9 (photo, edition)
1965 Boehmer, Glyptik no. 876 and fig. 330 (photo, study)
1968 Nagel and Strommenger, BJVF 8 pp. 152–53 and 160 no. 8c (edition, study)
1968–69 Edzard, AfO 22 p. 15 no. 17-1 (transliteration)
1990 Gelb and Kienast, Königsinschriften p. 39 S-4 (edition)

TEXT

1) *eš$_4$-pum*
2) ÉNSI
3) NIM.KI

1–3) Ešpum, governor of Elam.

2001

The seal inscription of a servant of Ešpum is known from several clay sealings found in excavations at Susa.

CATALOGUE

Ex.	Museum number	Lines preserved	cpn
1	As 10097	1–2	p
2	As 10098	1–4	p
3	As 10099	1–4	p
4	As 10100	(only seal design visible)	p
5	As 10101	1–4	p
6	Sb 2244	1–4	p

COMMENTARY

Exs. 1–5 come from the excavations of de Morgan, ex. 6 from those of de Mecquenem.

BIBLIOGRAPHY

1911 Pézard, in Soutzo, MDP 12 p. 117 fig. 125 (drawing)
1913 Scheil, MDP 14 p. 4 (copy, edition)
1920 Delaporte, Louvre 1 S. 443 (photo, copy, edition)
1961 Gelb, MAD 2[2] p. 198 Man-ištušu Officials, etc. no. 2c (study)
1963 Hirsch, AfO 20 p. 16 n. 161 (study)
1965 Boehmer, Glyptik p. 142 no. XXVIII a and pl. II figs. 10a–b (photo, copy, study)
1968–69 Edzard, AfO 22 p. 16 no. 23–2 (transliteration)
1972 Amiet, MDP 43 no. 1469 (ex. 6, photo, edition)
1990 Gelb and Kienast, Königsinschriften p. 40 S-5 (exs. 1–6, edition)

TEXT

1) *e-gi-gi*
2) ŠABRA É
3) IR_{11}
4) *eš$_4$-pum*

1–4) Egigi, the major-domo, (is) the servant of Ešpum.

Epir-mupi

E2.16.2

A tablet found in excavations at Susa (Scheil, MDP 14 p. 5 no. 1) names a certain Epir-mupi as governor of Susa. Hallo (Royal Titles p. 66) proposed that this same Epir-mupi appears in a royal inscription of Rīmuš. However, a collation of the relevant passage by Foster (Umma p. 48) yields the PN *a-ša-ar-mu-pi$_5$* instead of *e-pir$_6$-mu-pi$_5$* (see E2.1.2.2 Caption 2).

Epir-mupi's own seal inscription and the seal inscriptions of two of his servants are found on clay bullae from Susa.

1

In Epir-mupi's personal seal inscription he appears with the title 'military governor of Elam'.

COMMENTARY

The bulla with this seal inscription measures 2.2 cm across and bears the museum number As 10080 (Louvre). The inscription was collated from the published photo.

BIBLIOGRAPHY

1913 Scheil, MDP 14 p. 6 no. 3 (copy, edition)
1920 Delaporte, Louvre 1 S. 475 (photo, edition)
1929 Barton, RISA pp. 154–55 Enammune 3 (edition)
1963 Hirsch, AfO 20 p. 33 Verschiedene Inschriften 4 g (translation)
1964 Boehmer, Moortgat Festschrift p. 45 and pl. 10 no. 6 (photo, edition)
1965 Boehmer, Glyptik no. 1456 and fig. 640 (photo, study)
1967 Boehmer, ZA 58 pp. 302–310 and fig. 2 (photo, translation, study)
1968 Nagel and Strommenger, BJVF 8 pp. 152–53 and 158 no. 3 (edition, study)
1968–69 Edzard, AfO 22 p. 15 no. 18–1 (transliteration)
1990 Gelb and Kienast, Königsinschriften p. 319 Epirmupi c (edition)

TEXT

1) *e-pír₆-mu-pi₅*
2) GÌR.NÍTA
3) *ma-ti*
4) NIM.KI

1–4) Epir-mupi, military governor of the land of Elam.

2001

A clay bulla from Susa is impressed with several impressions of a seal of a servant of Epir-mupi.

COMMENTARY

The bulla measures 4.8×1.8 cm and bears the museum number Sb 6673 (Louvre). The inscription was collated from the published photo.

BIBLIOGRAPHY

1911 Janneau, Les rois d'Ur p. 35 (copy, edition)
1913 Scheil, MDP 14 pp. 5–6 no. 2 (copy, edition)
1915 Scheil, RA 12 pp. 59–60 (copy, edition)
1929 Barton, RISA pp. 154–55 Enammune 2 (edition)
1963 Hirsch, AfO 20 p. 33 Verschiedene Inschriften 4 b (translation)
1964 Boehmer, Moortgat Festschrift p. 45 and pl. 10 no. 7 (copy, edition)
1965 Boehmer, Glyptik no. 483 and fig. 128 (copy, study)
1966 Amiet, Elam fig. 159
1967 Boehmer, ZA 58 pp. 302–310 and figs. 4a–c (photo, translation, study)
1968 Nagel and Strommenger, BJVF 8 pp. 152–53 and 160 no. 8a (edition, study)
1968–69 Edzard, AfO 22 p. 16 no. 24–5 (transliteration)
1990 Gelb and Kienast, Königsinschriften p. 319 Epirmupi b (edition)

TEXT

1) *e-pir*$_6$*-mu-pi*$_5$
2) *da-núm*
3) *li-bur-be-lí*
4) SAGI
5) ⌜IR$_{11}$-*sú*⌝

1–2) Epir-mupi, the mighty:

3–5) Libūr-bēlī, the cup-bearer, (is) his servant.

2002

A seal in the British Museum bears the inscription of a servant of Epir-mupi.

COMMENTARY

The seal, which was purchased by Budge and has no known provenance, measures 2.7×1.7 cm. It bears the museum number BM 89119 (91-5-9, 2560). The inscription was collated from the published photo.

BIBLIOGRAPHY

1922 BM Guide p. 235 no. 51 (study)
1931 Jean, Religion p. 123 n. 7 and fig. 55 (photo, study)
1960 Hirsch, AfO 20 p. 32 Verschiedene Inschriften 4 a (edition)
1964 Boehmer, Moortgat Festschrift p. 45 and pl. 10 no. 8 (photo, edition)
1965 Boehmer, Glyptik no. 880 and fig. 332 (photo, study)
1967 Boehmer, ZA 58 pp. 302–10 and fig. 3 (photo, translation, study)
1968 Nagel and Strommenger, BJVF 8 pp. 152–53 and 160 no. 8b (edition, study)
1968–69 Edzard, AfO 22 p. 16 no. 24–6 (transliteration)
1976 Amiet, L'art d'Agadé no. 68 (photo, edition, study)
1982 Collon, Cylinder Seals 2 no. 135 (photo, edition [by Sollberger], study)
1987 Collon, First Impressions no. 516 (photo, translation)
1990 Gelb and Kienast, Königsinschriften p. 319 Epirmupi a (edition)

TEXT

1) *e-pir*$_6$*-mu-pi*$_5$
2) *da-núm*
3) ME-DU
4) IR$_{11}$-*sú*

1–2) Epir-mupi, the mighty:

3–4) ME-DU (is) his servant.

Ilī-išmāni

E2.16.3

1

A bronze axe from Susa bears the inscription of Ilī-išmāni, military governor of Elam.

COMMENTARY

The axe is numbered Sb 14243 in the Louvre collections. Its inscription was collated from the published photo.

BIBLIOGRAPHY

1979 Lambert, JA 217 pp. 12–13 (copy, edition)
1986 Amiet, L'âge des échanges inter-iraniens p. 273 fig. 79 (drawing)
1990 Gelb and Kienast, Königsinschriften p. 320 Elam 1 (edition)

TEXT

1) *ì-lí-íš-ma-ni*
2) DUB.SAR
3) GÌR.NÍTA
4) *ma-ti*
5) NIM.KI

1–5) Ilī-išmāni, scribe, military governor of the land of Elam.

Unattributed

E2.0.0

1001

A Sargonic cylinder seal in the British Museum bears the inscription of a servant of Ūbil-Aštar, brother of the king.

COMMENTARY

The seal is made of diorite and measures 3.32×2.05 cm. It was purchased by Layard in Hillah before 1852 and now bears the museum number BM 89137 (N 1208). The reading of the PN in line 3 is uncertain.

BIBLIOGRAPHY

1853 Layard, Nineveh and Babylon p. 538 (copy)
1860 King, Antique Gems p. 126 no. 1
1872 King, Antique Gems and Rings II pl. 1 no. 6
1885 King, Handbook pl. 3 no. 6 (copy)
1876 G. Smith, Chaldean Genesis p. 188 (copy)
1883 Ménant, Glyptique 1 p. 104, fig. 58, and pl. III no. 1 pl. 3 (photo, copy)
1885 Pinches, JBAA 41 pl. 1 no. 2
1885 Hommel, Geschichte pp. 206 and 300 (translation, copy)
1885 King, Handbook pl. 3 no. 6
1887 Reber, ZA 2 pp. 15 and 40 no. 2 (copy, study)
1892 Winckler, KB 3/1 pp. 84–85 BIL-GUR-aḫi (edition)
1895 Maspéro, Histoire 1 p. 723 (drawing)
1899 Ball, Light p. 45 no. 3 (photo, translation)
1900 Fürtwängler, Gemmen pl. 1 no. 3 (photo)
1905 King, CT 21 pl. 1 (copy)
1906 Meyer, Sumerier und Semiten pp. 72–74 (photo, translation, study)
1907 Thureau-Dangin, SAK pp. 168–69 Ûbil-ištar (edition)
1910 King, Early History p. 246 and facing plate (photo, study)
1910 Ward, Cylinders p. 21 no. 3 and fig. 28 (copy, study)
1913 Curtius, HBKWS 1 p. 268 and pl. 8 no. 3 (photo, study)
1922 Contenau, Glyptique Syro-Hittite pl. 1 no. 2 (copy)
1928–29 Meissner, AfO 5 p. 5 and pl. II no. 5 (photo, study)
1929 Barton, RISA pp. 148–49 Ubil-Aštar (edition)
1930 Unger, in Bossert, Geschichte des Kunstgewerbes aller Zeiten und Völker 3 pp. 424 and 427 (photo, study)
1939 Frankfort, Cylinder Seals pl. XXIV c (photo)
1940 Christian, Altertumskunde 1 pl. 359 no. 2 (photo)
1961 Gelb, MAD 2^2 p. 205 Unknown Kings no. 3 (study)
1963 Hirsch, AfO 20 p. 32 Verschiedene Inschriften 1, Ubil-Ištar (translation)
1962 Strommenger and Hirmer, Mesopotamien pl. 113a (photo)
1965 Boehmer, Glyptik no. 1686 and fig. 717 (photo, study)
1966 Unger, Siegelbildforschung p. 60 (study)
1968 Nagel and Strommenger, BJVF 8 pp. 152–53, 156 no. 0a and pl. 30 no. 1 (photo, edition, study)
1968–69 Edzard, AfO 22 p. 16 no. 24–31 (transliteration)
1969 Barnett and Wiseman, Fifty Masterpieces no. 39 (photo, translation, study)
1982 Collon, Cylinder Seals 2 no. 141 (photo, edition, study)
1990 Gelb and Kienast, Königsinschriften p. 48 S–39 (edition)

TEXT

1) *u-bil-eš₄-tár*
2) ŠEŠ LUGAL
3) KAL KI
4) DUB.SAR
5) IR₁₁-*sú*

1–2) Ūbil-Aštar, brother of the king:

3–5) KAL.KI, the scribe, (is) his servant.

1002

A stele fragment inscribed with an Old Akkadian text gives the end of a royal inscription. Unfortunately, the king's name is not preserved; stylistic considerations noted by Amiet (see bibliography) suggest that it may have belonged to Sargon.

COMMENTARY

The fragment is made of diorite; it measures 54.7 cm in height and 26 cm in width. The piece was found in excavations of de Morgan at Susa at a point about 50 metres from where the Sargon stele (E2.1.1.10) was found. It now bears the museum number AO 6053 (formerly Sb 2). The inscription was collated from the published photo.

BIBLIOGRAPHY

1905 Gautier, RT 27 pp. 178–79 (transliteration, study)
1908 Scheil, MDP 10 pp. 7–8 (study)
1924 Nassouhi, RA 21 pp. 70–72 figs. 5–7 (photo, copy)
1926 Pézard and Pottier, Catalogue no. 2 (study)
1926 Unger, SuAK p. 35 and fig. 34 (photo, study)
1928–29 Meissner, AfO 5 p. 5 fig. 2 (copy)
1945–46 Spycket, RA 40 p. 152 and fig. 1 (copy, translation)
1961 Moscati, Atti dell'accademia nazionale dei lincei 358 pl. 16 (photo)
1966 Liverani, Il protagonisti della storia universale LVII: Sargon di Akkad p. 10 fig. 1 (photo)
1967 Moortgat, Kunst pls. 126–27 (photo)
1969 ANEP[2] fig. 307 (photo)
1975 Orthmann (ed.), Der alte Orient pl. 100 (photo)
1976 Amiet, L'art d'Agadé no. 6 (photo, edition, copy, study)
1982 Börker-Klähn, Bildstelen no. 19 (copy, study)

TEXT

Col. i′
Lacuna
1′) ⌈*ù*⌉
2′) [*i*]*l-a-ba*$_4$
3′) [SU]ḪUŠ-*śu*
Lacuna

Lacuna
1′–3′) [may the gods ...] and Ilaba [tear out] his foundations.
Lacuna

1003

A vase fragment bears the inscription of a Sargonic king.

COMMENTARY

The vase fragment, made of white marble, measures 10×12.5×6.2 cm and bears the museum number CBS 1128. Although Hilprecht indicated that the piece came 'presumably from the neighbourhood of Babylon', the mention of the god Šamaš in i 2′ suggests a Sippar provenance; many of the pieces with low CBS numbers came from that city. The inscription bears many similarities to inscription E2.1.1.15 of Sargon.

The translation of this fragmentary text is uncertain; the verbs in i 3′ and 5′ are apparently dual forms, so we would expect a divine pair, Šamaš and another deity, as subject. Col. ii is restored from a parallel passage in E2.1.1.15.

BIBLIOGRAPHY

1893 Hilprecht, BE 1/1 no. 12 (copy)
1961 Gelb, MAD 2^2 p. 205 Unknown kings no. 1 (study)
1990 Gelb and Kienast, Königsinschriften p. 124 Fragment 3 (edition)

TEXT

Col. i
Lacuna
1′) [...] x
2′) ⸢^{d}⸣UTU
3′) *u-śa-za-za-śu*$_4$
4′) GÉŠTU
5′) ⸢*ú*⸣*-wa-ti-*[*r*]*a-śum*$_6$
Lacuna
Col. ii
Lacuna
1′) *u-k*[*ál-lim*]
2′) *m*[*a-ma-na*]
3′) *p*[*á-ni-śu*]
4′) ⸢*ù*⸣-[*la*]
5′) [*u-ba-al*]
Lacuna

Lacuna
i 1′–5′) [The god DN] (and) the god Samaš *support* him. They made his intelligence surpassing.
Lacuna

Lacuna
ii 1′–5′) [The god DN] ins[tructed (him), (and) he (the king)] sh[owed mercy to] n[o one].
Lacuna

1004

A diorite statue fragment contains the end of a royal inscription that is probably to be attributed to a Sargonic king.

COMMENTARY

The fragment was found in excavations of de Morgan in the acropolis area at Susa. It measures 28.5 cm in height and 38 cm in width; it now bears the museum number Sb 9097. The inscription was collated from the published photo.

BIBLIOGRAPHY

1926 Pézard and Pottier, Catalogue no. 49 (study)
1960 Strommenger, Bagh. Mitt. 1 p. 49 and pl. 10 (photo, study)
1967 Moortgat, Kunst pl. 144 (photo)
1976 Amiet, L'art d'Agadé no. 16 (photo, edition, study)
1981 Spycket, Statuaire p. 154 and n. 60 (study)
1990 Gelb and Kienast, Königsinschriften pp. 126–27 Fragment 8 (edition)

TEXT

Lacuna
1′) ŠE.NUMUN-*śu*
2′) [*li-i*]*l-*[*qù*]*-tá*

Lacuna
1′–2′) [May the gods DN$_1$ and DN$_2$] de[str]oy his progeny.

1005

A fragment of an alabastron ('an elongated narrow-necked flask used as a perfume or unguent container') bears a dedicatory inscription in Old Akkadian script for the goddess Aštar-Annunītum. It likely was offered by a Sargonic king.

COMMENTARY

The alabastron fragment was found at Aššur in deep levels between the Aššur temple and the great ziqqurrat in hE51. It was given the excavation no. Ass 4938, and is shown in Ass ph 568.

In light of Man-ištūšu's known construction work on Aštar's Emenue shrine in Nineveh (see A.O.39.2 in RIMA 1), Weidner suggested that this piece might be evidence of a similar concern of the Sargonic monarch for the cult of Aštar in Aššur. Borger indicates, on the other hand, that an attribution to Narām-Sîn is equally possible. Further, the possibility of a dedication by a private individual cannot be excluded. The edition follows the transliteration of Weidner.

BIBLIOGRAPHY

1945–51 Weidner, AfO 15 p. 95 n. 65 (transliteration, study)
1963 Hirsch, AfO 20 p. 16 Maništušu b 2 g (study)
1961 Borger, EAK 1 p. 2 (study)
1961 Gelb, MAD 2[2] p. 206 Unknown Kings Original Inscriptions no. 13 (study)
1973 Gödecken, UF 5 pp. 142 and 144 (study)
1990 Gelb and Kienast, Königsinschriften p. 123 Fragment 1 (edition)
1990 Pedersén, BiOr 47 669 (transliteration, study)

TEXT

Lacuna
1′) *a*-[*na*]
2′) dINANNA-
3′) *an-nu-ni-tim*
4′) A.MU.RU

Lacuna
1′–4′) [RN/PN] dedicated (this vase) t[o] the goddess Aštar-Annunītum.

1006

A statue fragment in the Yale Collections that is dated on stylistic grounds to the general time period of Man-ištūšu bears a partially preserved inscription; it probably belonged to a Sargonic king.

COMMENTARY

The fragment, YBC 2299, is made of diorite and consists of the back portion of a statue. It measures 11 cm in length and 7.5 cm in width. The piece was acquired through purchase; its original provenance is unknown. The inscription was collated.

BIBLIOGRAPHY

1937 Stephens, YOS 9 no. 9 (photo, copy, study)
1959 Strommenger, ZA 53 pp. 32 and 37 pl. V a (photo, study)
1960 Strommenger, Bagh. Mitt. 1 p. 53 (study)
1961 Gelb, MAD 2[2] p. 206 Unknown Kings Original Inscriptions no. 9 (study)
1963 Hirsch, AfO 20 p. 33 Verschiedene Inschriften 6 (study)
1981 Spycket, Statuaire p. 154 n. 60 (study)
1989 Strommenger, RLA 7'5–6 p. 357 no. 3B (study)
1990 Gelb and Kienast, Königsinschriften p. 126 Fragment 7 (edition)

TEXT

Col. i′
Lacuna
1′) [...] x [...] x
2′) [...] x

Lacuna
i′ 1′–2′) (No translation possible)

Col. ii′
Lacuna
1′) [...] x
2′) [SUḪ]UŠ-*šu*
3′) [*l*]*i-sú-ḫa*
4′) *ù*
5′) ŠE.NUMUN-*šu*
6′) *li-il-qù-tá*

Lacuna
ii′ 1′–6′) [May DN_1 and D]N_2 tear out his [foun]dation and destroy his progeny.

1007

A statue fragment (lower portion), which is dated on stylistic grounds to the general time of Man-ištūšu, depicts a royal figure trampling four enemy leaders. On the prostrate foes are inscribed their names.

COMMENTARY

The statue fragment is made of limestone and measures 134 cm in height and 72.5 cm in width. It was found in excavations of de Morgan in the area of the acropolis at Susa in the pavement of the Inšušinak temple, and is probably a piece of booty from the city of Agade or its vicinity. It bears the museum no. Sb 48 (Louvre).

As Kienast, (Königsinschriften p. 128) points out, the PN in fragment 1 is probably to be read *a-ku-ku-ià*. The name is possibly Elamite; see Zadok, Elamite Onomasticon p. 61 sub *a-ku-ku-ni*. This Akukuʾia may be the same figure who appears as *a-ku-ki* in three Old Babylonian liver omens (see Goetze, JCS 1 [1947] pp. 263–64 nos. 44 and 45 and Nougayrol, JAOS 70 [1950] p. 113). According to the omens 'all the land brought tribute to him'. The supposed brick inscription of AkukuNI (Scheil, MDP 28 p. 4 no. 2) is non-existent; its existence was based on a misunderstanding of earlier notes, as was pointed out by M. Lambert (RA 59 [1965] p. 178). The bibliography includes items showing a photo of the statue fragment as a whole; in many of these photos the inscription is illegible.

BIBLIOGRAPHY

1905 Scheil, MDP 6 p. 15 (transliteration)
1920 Meissner, BuA 1 pl. 223 (photo)
1926 Pézard and Pottier, Catalogue no. 47 (study)
1931 Contenau, Manuel 2 pp. 670–71 and fig. 466 (photo)
1939 Scheil, MDP 28 p. 4 no. 2 (partial copy, transliteration)
1957 Gelb, MAD 3 p. 25 (study)
1959 Strommenger, ZA 53 p. 35 pl. IV (photo)
1960 Strommenger, Bagh. Mitt. 1 p. 52 (study)
1965 Lambert, RA 59 pp. 177–82 (copy, edition)
1967 Moortgat, Kunst p. 50 and pl. 142 (photo, study)
1967 Orthmann, Der alte Orient pl. 44 (photo, study)
1972 Amiet, RA 66 pp. 103–105 and fig. 7 (photo)
1976 Amiet, L'art d'Agadé no. 15 (photo, edition)

1981 Spycket, Statuaire pp. 152–54 and nn. 49–50 and pl. 101 (photo, study)
1989 Strommenger, RLA 7/5–6 p. 337 no. B 4 (study)
1990 Gelb and Kienast, Königsinschriften pp. 127–28 Fragment 10 (edition)

TEXT

Inscription A	
1) *a-ku-ku-ià*	A 1–2) Akuku'ia, the governor.
2) ÉNSI	
Inscription B	
1) KUR [...]	B 1) The land [...].
Inscription C	
1) [x]⌈d⌉[*i*]-*śum*$_6$	C 1–3) [x-I]šum, the [go]vernor of Nirrab.
2) [É]NSI	
3) *nir-ra-ab*.KI	
Inscription D	
1) *i-mì-id*	D 1–2) Imid, the door-keeper
2) Ì.DU$_8$	

1008

A vase fragment from Khafajah gives a few lines of an inscription of Sargonic date.

COMMENTARY

The fragment is made of black stone; it was found in K 45 in Oval III and was given the excavation number Kh II 162. Its present whereabouts are unknown. The edition follows the copy of Jacobsen.

BIBLIOGRAPHY

1940 Delougaz, Temple Oval pp. 147 and 150 no. 11 (copy, edition)
1961 Gelb, MAD 2[2] p. 206 Unknown Kings Original Inscriptions 12 (study)
1963 Hirsch, AfO 20 p. 33 Verschiedene Inschriften 7 (study)
1990 Gelb and Kienast, Königsinschriften p. 125 Fragment 5 (edition)

TEXT

Lacuna	Lacuna
1′) [...]	1′–5′) ... [Ag]ade ...
2′) [...] *a r*[*í* ...]	Lacuna
3′) [... *a-k*]*à-dè*.K[I]	
4′) [...] *uz* [...]	
5′) [...]	
Lacuna	

1009

A tablet of Ur III date found in excavations at Nippur has copies of dedicatory inscriptions of two Sargonic kings. The first inscription, which is edited here, occurs on lines 1–6 of the obverse. In it the royal name is totally missing. In the second inscription, the traces of the royal name can be restored to read Dudu (see E2.1.10.2).

COMMENTARY

The clay tablet measures 5.5×5.1 cm and was found in SB 67 of the Inanna temple at Nippur; it was given the excavation number 6N-T264. It now bears the museum number NBC 10736. The inscription was collated. The occurrence of the royal title LUGAL KIŠ 'king of the world' means that this inscription should be attributed to one of the early Sargonic kings: Sargon, Rīmuš, or Maništūšu; the title was not used by Narām-Sîn or his successors. The most likely restoration of the DN in line 2 is Inanna, since the goddess is named in the second inscription on the Sammeltafel (see E2.1.10.2).

BIBLIOGRAPHY

1968 Goetze, JAOS 88 pp. 54 and 57 (copy, edition)

1990 Gelb and Kienast, Königinschriften p. 283 Fragment C 1 (edition)

TEXT

1) [*a-na*]
2) [DN]
3) [RN]
4) [LUGAL]
5) (Erasure) KIŠ.[KI]
6) A.MU.RU

1–6) [To the god(dess) DN, RN king] of the world, dedicated (this object).

1010

A vase fragment preserves the end of a dedicatory inscription of a Sargonic king.

COMMENTARY

The vase is made of white calcite and measures 4.8×8.4×1 cm. It was found by the expedition of the University of Pennsylvania to Nippur in the area SE of the ziqqurrat in the third season and was given the museum number CBS 9331. The inscription was collated. The title 'king of Agade' appears in inscriptions of Sargon, Narām-Sîn, and Narām-Sîn's successors.

BIBLIOGRAPHY

1896 Hilprecht, BE 1/2 no. 119 (copy)
1907 Thureau-Dangin, SAK pp. 170–71 Unbekannte Könige a (edition)
1929 Barton, RISA pp. 146–47 Sharganisharri 4 (edition)
1961 Gelb, MAD 2^{2} p. 205 Unknown Kings Original Inscriptions no. 2 (study)
1963 Hirsch, AfO 20 p. 33 no.m 3 (study)
1990 Gelb and Kienast, Königsinschriften p. 123 Fragment 2 (edition)

TEXT

Lacuna
1′) [LUGAL]
2′) *a-kà-dè*.KI
3′) *a-na*
4′) ^{d}*en-líl*
5′) A.MU.RU

Lacuna
1′–5′) [king] of Agade, dedicated (this vase) to the god Enlil.

1011

A fragment of an Old Babylonian Sammeltafel has preserved the curse formula of a Sargonic royal inscription.

COMMENTARY

The tablet bears the museum number N 6266. Column i′ has the text of E2.0.0.1011; column ii′ the text of E2.0.0.1012 and E2.1.1.5, and column iii′ the text of E2.1.3.2.3.

BIBLIOGRAPHY

1980 Michalowski, JCS 32 pp. 242–43 and 245 (photo, copy, transliteration)
1990 Gelb and Kienast, Königsinschriften pp. 149 and 284 Fragment C 3 (edition)

TEXT

Col. i′
Lacuna
1′) [*ša* DUB]
2′) [*šu*$_{4}$*-a*]
3′) [*u-ša-sà*]-⸢*ku*⸣-[*ni*]
4′) [^{d}*e*]*n-líl*
5′) [*ù*] ⸢^{d}⸣UTU
6′) [SUḪUŠ]-*šu*
7′) [*li-sú*]-*ḫa*
8′) [*ù* ŠE.NU]MUN-*šu*
9′) [*li-il-qù-t*]*á*

Lacuna
1′–3′) [As for the one who rem]ov[es this inscription],
4′–9′) [may the gods E]nlil [and] Šamaš [tear] out his [foundations] and [destr]oy his [prog]eny.

1012

An Old Babylonian tablet fragment gives the very end of a Sargonic royal inscription.

COMMENTARY

The inscription, which is found on column ii of N 6266, was collated.

BIBLIOGRAPHY

1980 Michalowski, JCS 32 pp. 242–43 and 245 (photo, copy, transliteration)
1990 Gelb and Kienast, Königinschriften p. 284 Fragment C 4 (edition)

TEXT

Col. ii′
1′) ŠE.NUM[UN-*šu*]
2′) *li-i*[*l-qù-tá*]

ii′ 1′ – 2′) [May they] destroy his progeny.

1013

A small fragment of a Sargonic period statue or stele was found in recent excavations at Isin.

COMMENTARY

The fragment was found in court B of the Gula temple, under the asphalt layer near the supporting wall of Meli-Šipak. It was given the excavation number IB 1005; its Iraq Museum number is not known. The piece is made of diorite and measures 4.2×6.3×1.8 cm. A copy of the inscription was kindly provided by C. Wilcke in advance of its publication.

BIBLIOGRAPHY

1981 Walker and Wilcke, in Hrouda, Isin 2 p. 92 B 6 b (study)
1990 Gelb and Kienast, Königsinschriften p. 128 Fragment 11(edition)

TEXT

Col. i	
(not preserved)	
Col. ii	
Lacuna	Lacuna
0′) [*ša* DUB *śu*$_4$-*a*]	ii 1′–4′) [As for the one who] removes [this inscription, may] the gods Ša[maš] and [DN]
1′) *u-śa-sà-ku-n*[*i*]	
2′) ^{d}U[TU]	
3′) ⌈*ù*⌉	
4′) [DN]	
Lacuna	Lacuna

1014

A clay sealing found in excavations at Nippur bears the seal inscription of a servant of a Sargonic king.

COMMENTARY

The sealing was found in En 20 VI 2b and bears the field number 2 ND 822; its present location is unknown. The edition follows the transliteration of Westenholz.

BIBLIOGRAPHY

1967 McCown, Nippur 1 p. 22 and pl. 31 no. 2 (provenance, photo)

1987 Westenholz, OSP 2 no. 38 (edition)

1990 Gelb and Kienast, Königsinschriften p. 48 S–40 (edition)

TEXT

1) [RN]	1–3) [RN], king of [Aga]de:
2) LUGAL	
3) [*a-kà*]-*dè*.KI	
4) [PN]	4–6) [PN, ...], (is) his servant.
5) [...]	
6) ⌈IR$_{11}$⌉-*sú*	

1015

An axe in the Teheran Museum bears an inscription of Bēlī-išar.

COMMENTARY

The Bēlī-išar of this inscription, as far as can be determined, is unattested in historical sources. The fact that he styles himself 'the mighty' indicates that he was an independent ruler. Gelb and Kienast (Königsinschriften p. 377) suggest he was a petty prince of the Gutian period.

No details of the axe's material composition, dimensions, or museum number are available at present. The inscription is known only from a poor, small handcopy. While various scholars have read line 3 [LU]GAL K]I[Š], this reading is not supported by Godard's copy.

BIBLIOGRAPHY

1962 Godard, L'art de l'Iran pp. 71–73 and fig. 94 (copy, translation)
1969 Calmeyer, Datierbare Bronzen pp. 33–34 no. 14 E and fig. 33, and p. 162 no. 8 (copy, edition)
1990 Gelb and Kienast, Königsinschriften p. 377 Varia no. 8 (edition)1

TEXT

1) *be-lí-i-śar*
2) *da-núm*
3) x x x

1–3) Bēlī-išar, the mighty, ...

Index of Museum Numbers

Haifa, University of Haifa (Brockmon Collection)

No.	E2.	No.	E2.	No.	E2.	No.	E2.
BT 1	1.4.6	BT 1	1.4.20	BT 1	1.4.47	BT 2+3	2.1.1–3
BT 1	1.4.11	BT 1	1.4.23	BT 1	1.4.48		

Istanbul, Arkeoloji Müzeleri

No.	E2.	No.	E2.	No.	E2.	No.	E2.
Adab 767	1.5.2005	EŞ 8923	1.4.15.23	Ni 3200	1.1.7.2	Ni 3200	1.2.3.2
Adab 768	1.5.2005	EŞ 8924	1.4.15.24		1.1.8.2		1.2.4.2
Adab 769	1.10.2001	EŞ 8925	1.4.15.25		1.1.9.2		1.2.5.2
Adab 771	9.4.2001	Ni 1263	1.5.3.1		1.1.11.2		1.2.6.2
Adab 773	9.5.2001	Ni 1936	1.5.3.4		1.1.12.2		1.2.7.2
Adab 774	1.5.2005	Ni 2435	1.4.25.2		1.1.13.2		1.2.9.2
EŞ 1027	1.4.24	Ni 3200	1.1.1.2		1.1.14.2		1.3.1.7
EŞ 1544	1.4.15.21		1.1.2.2		1.1.15.2		1.3.2.2
EŞ 5207	1.4.41		1.1.3.2		1.2.1.2	Ni 9654	1.4.1004
EŞ 8922	1.4.15.22		1.1.6.2		1.2.2.2		

Jena, Hilprecht Sammlung of the University of Jena

No.	E2.	No.	E2.	No.	E2.	No.	E2.
HS 194b		HS 1970	E2.1.5.3.13	HS 1980	E2.1.5.3.21	HS 1990	
(old HS 32)	1.4.18	HS 1971	E2.1.5.3.14	HS 1981	E2.1.5.3.22	(old HS 26)	1.4.15.1
HS 195	E2.1.5.4	HS 1972	E2.1.5.3.15	HS 1982	E2.1.5.3.23	HS 1992	E2.1.5.3.31
HS 1954+1955		HS 1973	E2.1.5.3.16	HS 1983	E2.1.5.3.24	HS 1994	E2.1.5.3.32
+2499+2506	1.4.2	HS 1974	E2.1.5.3.17	HS 1984	E2.1.5.3.25	HS 1995	E2.1.5.3.33
HS 1954+1955		HS 1975	E2.1.5.3.18	HS 1985	E2.1.5.3.26	HS 1996	E2.1.5.3.34
+2499+2506	1.4.3	HS 1976	E2.1.5.3.19	HS 1986+1993	E2.1.5.3.27	HS 1997	E2.1.5.3.35
HS 1960	1.4.19	HS 1978		HS 1987	E2.1.5.3.28	HS 1998	E2.1.5.3.36
HS 1968	E2.1.5.3.11	(old HS 27)	1.4.15.2	HS 1988	E2.1.5.3.29	HS 1999	E2.1.5.3.37
HS 1969	E2.1.5.3.12	HS 1979	E2.1.5.3.20	HS 1989	E2.1.5.3.30		

Jerusalem, Bible Lands Museum

No.	E2.	No.	E2.	No.	E2.
BLM 929	1.4.4.3	BLM 937	1.4.2007	BLM 2512	11.2.2001

Leiden, de Liagre Böhl Collection

No.	E2.	No.	E2.
LB 16a	1.4.8.1	LB 16b	1.4.9.2

London, British Museum

Munich, Ägyptische Staatssammlung

New Haven, Yale University

New York, Allard Pierson Museum

Paris, Collection J. Mariaud de Serres

Paris, Louvre

Philadelphia, John Frederick Lewis Collection of the Free Library

Philadelphia, University Museum

Philadelphia, University Museum (continued)

Teheran, Foroughi Collection (without numbers)

Index of Excavation Numbers

Aššur (Qalʿat Širqāt)

Tell Brāk

Ešnunna (Tell Asmar)

Isin (Išān Baḥrīyāt)

Mari (Tell Harīrī)

Tell Munbāqa

Nippur (Nuffar)

Šušina (Susa)

Tutub (Ḫafājī)

Ur (Tell al-Muqayyar)

Uruk (Warka)

Concordances of Selected Publications

Barton, RISA

No.		E2.
Nippur		
p. 8ff.:	5. Urunabadbi	6.1.2001
Dynasty of Agade and Kish:		
1. Sharrukin		
pp. 100–107:	1. Inscription AB	1.1.1.1
pp. 108–111:	2. Inscription CD	1.1.11.1
pp. 110f.:	3. Inscription E	1.1.3
pp. 110–13:	4. Inscription F	1.1.2.1
pp. 112f.:	5. Inscription G	1.1.6
	6. Inscription H	1.1.7.1
pp. 114f.:	7. Inscription I	1.1.8.1
	8. Inscription J	1.1.8 .1 Caption
	9. Inscription K	1.1.13.1
	10. Inscription L xiii	—
	10. Inscription L xiv	1.1.12.1
	11. Inscription M xv	1.1.15.1
	Inscription M xvi	1.1.9.1
pp. 116f.:	12. Inscription N	1.1.9.1 Captions
	13. Votive Fragment	1.1.2001
pp. 118f.:	16. Stele	1.1.10
2. Rimush:		
pp. 118–121:	1. Inscription A	1.2.4.1
	2. Inscription B	1.2.4.1 Captions
	3. Inscription C	1.2.3.1
	4. Inscription D	1.2.5.1
pp. 120–23:	5. Inscription E	1.2.1.1
pp. 122f.:	6. Inscription F	1.2.5.1
	7. Inscription G	1.2.5.1 Captions 1–8
	8. Inscription H	1.2.5.1 Caption 9
	9. Inscription I	1.2.6.1 lines 1–2
pp.122–25:	10. Inscription J	1.2.6.1 lines 128–130
pp. 124f.:	11. Inscription K xxiv	1.2.6.1 lines 131–44
	11. Inscription K xxv	1.2.9.1
pp. 124–27:	12. Inscription L	1.2.7.1
pp. 126–29:	13. Inscription M	1.2.18.1
pp. 128f.:	14.Vase A	1.2.11.3
	15. Vase B	1.2.10
	16. Vase C+D	1.2.20.5–6
	17. Vase E	1.2.12
	18. Fragment of stone slab	1.2.19
	19. Fragment A	1.2.20.35
	20. Fragment B	1.2.14.2
3. Manishtusu:		
pp. 128–31:	1. Inscription A	1.3.1.6
pp. 130f.:	2. Inscription B	1.3.1.6 Dedicatory label
	3. Inscription C	1.3.2.1
pp. 134–37:	5. Monolith Fragment A	1.4.28.1 frgm. 5

No.		E2.
3. Manishtusu:		
pp. 134–37:	5. Monolith Fragment B	1.4.28.1 frgm. 4
	5. Monolith Fragment C	1.3.1.4
pp. 134–37:	5. Monolith Fragment D	1.3.1.5
pp. 136f.:	6. Vase	1.3.3
pp. 136ff.:	7. Mace Head	1.3.5
	8. Bust	1.3.2001
	9. Broken Statue	1.3.1.1
4. Narāmsîn:		
pp. 136f.:	1. Brick Stamp	1.4.15.3
pp. 138f.:	2. Vase A	1.4.41.1
	3. Vase B	1.4.4.1
	4. Vase C	1.4.41.6
	5. Vase D	1.4.41.2
	6. Vase E	1.4.35
	7. Door-socket	1.4.9
	8. Marble Fragment	1.4.27.1
pp. 140f.:	10. Perforated Disc A	1.4.27.2
	11. Perforated Disc B	1.4.54
	12. Stele A	1.4.24
pp. 142f.:	13. Stele B	1.4.31
	14. Statue A	1.4.13
	15. Statue B	1.4.2002
pp. 142f.:	16. Seal A	1.4.2004
	17. Seal B	1.4.2023
	18. Seal C	1.4.2003
pp. 144f.:	19. Seal D	1.4.2014
	20. Seal E	1.4.2008
pp. 144f.:	21. Seal F	1.4.2016
	21. Seal G	1.4.2012
	21. Seal H	1.4.2009
5. Sharganisharri:		
pp. 144f.:	1. Door-socket A	1.5.1
	2. Door-socket B	1.5.2
	3. Brick Stamp	1.5.3
	4. Vase A	0.0.1010
	5. Clay Tablet	1.5.2
	6. Mace Head	1.5.9
	7. Seal A	1.5.2003
	8. Seal B	1.5.2004
pp. 148f.:	9. Seal C	1.5.2007
	10. Seal D	1.5.2010
6. Bingani-sharri:		
pp. 148f.:	1. Seal A	1.4.2022
	2. Seal B	1.4.2013
7. Ubil-Astar (Ubileštar):		
pp. 148f :	1. Seal	1.11.2002
8. Unknown Kings:		
pp. 148f.:	1. Vase	0.0.1010

Barton, RISA (continued)

No.		E2.
Kings of Guti:		
pp. 170f.:		
1. Sharratigu-bisin	1. Votive plaque	8.1.2001
2. Lasirab:	2. Scepterhead	2.14.1
pp. 170ff.:		
Later Rulers of Umma:		
1. Nammahni:		

No.		E2.
pp. 300f.:	1. Tablet	2.11.12.1
Appendix II–III:		
pp. 358f.:	2. Time of Sargon	1.1.16
	3. Rimush	1.2.17.1
pp. 358ff.:	4. Naram-Sin	1.4.41.4
pp. 390f.:	1. Naram-Sin	1.4.2001

Calmeyer, Datierbare Bronzen

No.		E2.
Katalog pp. 161f.:		
No. 2.	Narāmsin	1.4.41.5
No. 3.	Narāmsin	1.4.27.3
No. 4.	Narāmsin	1.4.2006
No. 4 a–f.	Narāmsin	1.4.2005
No. 5.	Šarkališarrī	1.5.2013

No.		E2.
No. 6.	Šarkališarrī	1.5.2012
No. 7.	LI-*lu-ul-dan*	1.12.1.1
No. 8.	*be-lí-i-šar*	0.0.1015
No. 9.	*šu-dur-ùl*	1.11.1
No. 13.	*ri-ig-*[*m*]*u* (?)	1.4.2025

Gelb, MAD 2^2

No.		E2.
Sargonic Sources:		
pp. 6ff.:	No. 1b (governors of Susa)	17
	No. 1c (seal of Šuruš-kîn)	11.5.1
	No. 1d kings of Gutium:	2
	(Enridawazir/ Erriduwazir)	2.1.1–3
	(Lâ-ʾarab)	2.14.1
	(Jarlagan)	2.19
	(Šiʾum)	2.20
Sargon, Original Inscriptions:		
p. 193:	No. 1	1.1.10
Late Copies:		
p. 193:	No. 1Aa+b	1.1.1.1
	No. 1Ba–c	1.1.11.1
	No. 1C	1.1.3.1
	No. 1D	1.1.2.1
	No. 1E	1.1.6.1
	No. 1F	1.1.7–8.1
	No. 1G	1.1.12–14.1
	No. 1H	1.1.15.1
	No. 1I	1.1.9.1
Family:		
p. 194:	No. 1 Tašlultum	1.1.2001
	No. 2 Enḫeduanna	1.1.16
	No. 3 Enḫeduanna (Seal)	1.1.2003
	No. 4 Enḫeduanna (Seal)	1.1.2005
	No. 5 Adda	1.1.2004
Rîmus, Original Inscriptions:		
pp. 195:	No. 1a	1.2.11.1–43
	No. 1b	1.2.14.2
	No. 1c	1.2.15.1

No.		E2.
p. 195	No. 1d	1.2.16
Rîmus, Original Inscriptions:		
	No. 1e	1.2.11.46
	No. 2a	1.2.13.1
p. 195:	No. 2b	1.2.13.3
	No. 2c	1.2.13.2
	No. 3a	1.2.20.6
	No. 3b	1.2.20.5
	No. 3c	1.2.20.31
	No. 3d	1.2.20.35
p. 195:	No. 3e	1.2.20.1
	No. 3f	1.2.20.3
p. 196:	No. 3g	1.2.20.2
	No. 3h	1.2.20.37
	No. 3i	1.2.20.36
	No. 3j	1.2.20.47
	No. 3k	1.2.20.45
	No. 3l	1.2.20.46
	No. 3m	1.2.20.49
	No. 3n	1.2.20.4
	No. 3o	1.2.20.41
	No. 3p	1.2.20.42
	No. 4	1.2.10
	No. 5	1.2.12
	No. 6	1.2.17.1
	No. 7	1.2.19
Late Copies:		
p. 196:	No. 1A	1.2.4.1
	No. 1B	1.2.3.1
	No. 1C	1.2.5.1
	No. 1D	1.2.1.1
	No. 1E	1.2.2.1
	No. 1F	1.2.2.1 Caption 1
	No. 1G	1.2.6.1; 1.2.9.1
	No. 1H	1.2.9.1 Caption 1

Gelb, MAD 2[2] (continued)

No.		E2.
Man-ištušu, Original Inscriptions:		
p. 197:	No. 1 Ia–d	1.2.7.1, 2 and 4
	No. 1Ja–d	1.2.18
	No. 1a	1.3.1.1
	No. 1b	1.3.1.4
	No. 1c	1.3.1.5
	No. 1d	1.3.1.3
	No. 1e	1.3.1.2
	No. 2	1.3.3
	No. 3	1.3.4
	No. 4	1.3.1
Late Copies:		
p. 197:	No. 1a	1.3.1.6
	No. 1b	1.3.1.8
p. 198:	No. 2	1.3.1.6 (label)
Man-ištušu Late Copies:		
	No. 3	1.3.2.1
Officials, etc.		
p. 198:	No. 1	1.3.2002
	No. 2a	1.3.2001
	No. 2b	16.1.1
	No. 2c	16.1.2001
	No. 3	1.3.2003
Naram-sin, Original Inscriptions:		
p. 198:	No. 1a	1.4.15
	No. 1b	1.4.17
	No. 2	1.4.16
	No. 3a	1.4.41.4
	No. 3b	1.4.41.6
	No. 3c	1.4.41.1
	No. 3d	1.4.41.2
	No. 3e	1.4.41.3
	No. 4a	1.4.27.1
	No. 4b	1.4.27.2
	No. 4c	1.4.43
p. 199:	No. 4d	1.4.6.2
	PBS 5 No. 37	1.4.6.2
	Nos. 5a–c	1.4.4.1–2
	No. 6a	1.4.9.1
	No. 6b	1.4.9.3
	No. 6c	1.4.9.2
p. 199:	No. 7	1.4.24
	No. 8	1.4.28
	No. 9	1.4.31
	No. 10	1.4.13
	No. 12	1.4.22.5
Late Copies:		
p. 199:	No. 1	1.4.6.2
	No. 2a	1.4.25.1
	No. 2b	1.4.25.2
	No. 3	1.4.26
	No. 4	1.4.5.2
	No. 5	1.4.23.1
	No. 6	1.4.1; 1.4.1001
Family:		
p. 199:	No. 1	1.4.2022
	No. 2	1.4.2023
p. 200:	No. 3	1.4.2020
	No. 4	1.4.34
	No. 5	1.4.2019
	No. 6	1.4.2018
	No. 7	1.4.51
	No. 8	1.4.49
	No. 9	1.4.50
Officials, etc.:		
p. 200:	No. 1a	1.4.2004
	No. 1b	12.4.2001
	No. 2	1.4.2009
	No. 3	1.4.2003

No.		E2.
p. 200:	No. 4	1.4.2002
	No. 5	1.4.2008
	No. 6	1.4.2010
	No. 7	1.4.2001
	No. 8	6.1.2001
	No. 9	1.4.2016
	No. 10	1.4.2013
Šar-kali-šarrī, Original Inscriptions:		
	No. 11	1.4.2012
p. 202:	No. 1	1.5.1.1
p. 203:	No. 2a	1.5.2.1
	No. 2b	1.5.2.3
	No. 2c	1.5.2.4
	No 3	1.5.3.
	No. 4	1.5.9
	No. 5	1.5.10
Šar-kali-šarrī, Original Inscriptions:		
	No. 6	1.5.7
Family:		
p. 203:	No.1	1.5.2003
	No. 2	1.5.2002
Officials, etc.		
p. 203:	No. 1	1.5.2010
	No. 2	1.5.2012
	No. 3	1.5.2009
	No. 4	1.5.2007
	No. 5	1.5.2005
	No. 6	1.5.2004
	No. 7	1.5.2014
	No. 8	1.5.2013
	No. 9	1.5.2008
p. 204:	No . 10	1.5.2006
Lilul-dan (= Êlul-dan? = Elulu?), Original Inscriptions:		
p. 204:	No. 1	1.12.1.1
Dudu, Original Inscriptions:		
p. 205:	No. 1a-b	1.10.11–2
Officials, etc.		
p. 205:	No. 1	1.10.2001
Šu-turul, Original Inscriptions:		
p. 205:	No. 1	1.11.2001
Officials, etc.,		
p. 205:	No. 1	1.11.2003
	No. 2	1.11.2002
Unknown kings, Original Inscriptions:		
p. 205:	No. 1	0.0.1003
	No. 2	0.0.1010
	No. 3	0.0.1001
	No. 4	1.4.35
	No. 5	see E2.1.2
	No. 6	1.4.2014
	No. 7	1.1.4
p. 206:	No. 8	1.4.8
	No. 9	0.0.1006
	No. 10	1.4.28.1 (frgm. 3)
	No. 11	1.4.28.1 (frgm. 4)
	No. 12	0.0.1008
	No. 13	0.0.1005
Late Copies:		
p. 206:	No.1	1.1.
	No. 3	1.4.25.2
Additions and Corrections: (pp. 206 und 216f.)		
to p. 195:	U 263	1.2.13.4
to p. 196:	U 207	1.2.20.36
	U 3291	1.2.17.2
	U 16532	1.2.17.4
	U 18306	1.2.20.40
to p. 199:	U 282+283	1.4.4
	U 284	1.4.39
	U 16531	1.4.36

Gelb and Kienast, Königsinschriften

	No.	E2.
Die Inschriften		
III. Die Originalinschriften der Könige von Akkade		
2. Die Siegellegenden		
p. 39.:	S-1	1.1.2003
	S-2	1.1.2005
	S-3	1.1.2004
	S-4	16.1.1
p. 40:	S-5	16.1.2001
	S-6	1.3.2003
	S-7	1.4.2023
	S-8	1.4.2022
p. 41:	S-9	1.4.53
	S-10	1.4.2020
	S-11	1.4.2019
	S-12	1.4.2017
p. 42:	S-13	1.4.2004
	S-14	12.4.2001
	S-15	1.4.2009
	S-16	1.4.2003
p. 43:	S-17	1.4.2008
	S-18	1.4.2014
	S-19	1.4.2012
	S-20	1.4.2016
p. 44:	S-21	1.4.2015
	S-22	1.4.2013
	S-23	1.5.2002
	S-24	1.5.2003
p. 45:	S-25	1.5.2008
	S-26	1.5.2010
	S-27	1.5.2009
	S-28	1.5.2007
p. 46:	S-29	1.5.2005
	S-30	—
	S-31	9.2.2002
	S-32	1.5.2004
	S-33	1.4.2021
p. 47:	S-34	1.5.2015
	S-35	1.10.2001
	S-36	1.10.2001
	S-37	1.11.2001
	S-38	1.11.2002
p. 48:	S-39	0.0.1001
	S-40	0.0.1014
	S-41	11.5.1
Die Inschriften des Sargon		
pp. 62ff.:	Sargon 1	1.1.10
	Sargon 2	1.1.4
	Sargon 3	1.1.2002
	Sargon A1	1.1.16
	Sargon B1	1.1.2001
Die Inschriften des Rīmuš		
pp. 66ff.:	Rīmuš 1	1.2.11
	Rīmuš 2	1.2.13
	Rīmuš 3	1.2.12
	Rīmuš 4	1.2.10
	Rīmuš 5	1.2.17
	Rīmuš 6	1.2.20
	Rīmuš 7	1.2.19
	Rīmuš B 1	1.2.2001
Die Inschriften des Maništūsu		
pp. 75ff.:	Maništūsu 1	1.3.1
	Maništūsu 2	1.3.1 Dedicatory inscription
	Maništūsu 3	1.3.4
	Maništūsu 4	1.3.3
	Maništūsu 5	1.3.5
	Maništūsu B 1	1.3.2002
pp. 76 ff.:	Maništūsu B 2	1.3.2001

	No.	E2.
Die Inschiften des Narāmsîn		
pp. 81ff.:	Narāmsîn 1	1.4.10
	Narāmsîn 2	1.4.28
	Narāmsîn 3	1.4.13
	Narāmsîn 4	1.4.31
	Narāmsîn 5	1.4.24
	Narāmsîn 6	1.4.8.1
	Narāmsîn 7	1.4.8.2
	Narāmsîn 8	1.4.37
	Narāmsîn 9	1.4.35
	Narāmsîn 10	1.4.36
	Narāmsîn 11	1.4.27
	Narāmsîn 12	1.4.43
	Narāmsîn 13	1.4.4.4
	Narāmsîn 14	1.4.41
	Narāmsîn 15	1.4.40
	Narāmsîn 16	1.4.39
	Narāmsîn 17	1.4.15
	Narāmsîn 18	1.4.17
	Narāmsîn 19	1.4.16
	Narāmsîn 20	1.4.22
	Narāmsîn A 1	1.4.9
	Narāmsîn A 2	1.4.34
	Narāmsîn A 3	1.4.54
	Narāmsîn A 4	1.4.2025
	Narāmsîn A 5	1.4.52
	Narāmsîn A 6	1.4.20
	Narāmsîn A 7	1.4.19
	Narāmsîn B 1	1.4.2018
	Narāmsîn B 2	1.4.2002
	Narāmsîn B 3	1.4.14
	Narāmsîn B 4	1.4.2001
	Narāmsîn B 5	6.1.2001
	Narāmsîn B 6	1.4.2006
	Narāmsîn B 7	1.4.2005
	Narāmsîn B 8	1.4.2007
	Narāmsîn B 9	1.4.2010
	Narāmsîn B 10	1.4.48
Die Inschriften des Šarkališarrī		
pp. 113ff.:	Šarkališarrī 1	1.5.1
	Šarkališarrī 2	1.5.2
	Šarkališarrī 3	1.5.9
	Šarkališarrī 4	1.5.3
	Šarkališarrī 5	1.5.10
	Šarkališarrī 6 Text A	1.5.7
	Šarkališarrī 6 Text B	1.5.8
	Šarkališarrī 6 Text C	1.5.3.1
	Šarkališarrī B 1	1.5.2006
	Šarkališarrī B 2	1.5.2014
	Šarkališarrī B 3	1.5.2013
	Šarkališarrī B 4	1.5.2012
Die Inschriften des Eluldān		
p. 120:	Eluldān 1	1.12.1
Die Inschriften des Dudu		
p. 121:	Dudu 1	1.10.1
	Dudu 2	1.10.3
Die Inschriften des Šū-DUR.ÙL		
p. 122:	Šū-DUR.ÙL 1	1.11.1
	Šū-DUR.ÙL B 1	1.11.2003
Fragmente Altakkadischer Königinschriften		
pp. 123ff.:	Fragment 1	0.0.1005
	Fragment 2	0.0.1010
	Fragment 3	0.0.1003
	Fragment 4	1.4.32
	Fragment 5	0.0.1008

Gelb and Kienast, Königsinschriften (continued)

No.		E2.
Fragmente Altakkadischer Königinschriften (continued)		
	Fragment 6	0.0.1002
	Fragment 7	0.0.1006
	Fragment 8	0.0.1004
	Fragment 9	—
	Fragment 10	0.0.1007
	Fragment 11	0.0.1013
IV. Die Kopien von Inschriften der Könige von Akkade		
Die Kopien von Inschriften des Sargon		
pp. 157ff.:	Sargon C 1	1.1.1
	Sargon C 2	1.1.11; 1 1.12
	Sargon C 3	1.1.3
	Sargon C 4	1.1.2
	Sargon C 5	1.1.6
	Sargon C 6	1.1.7
	Sargon C 7	1.1.8
	Sargon C 8	1.1.13
	Sargon C 9	1.1.12
	Sargon C 10	1.1.14
	Sargon C 11	1.1.15 (first part)
	Sargon C 12	1.1.15 (second part)
	Sargon C 13	1.1.9
	Sargon C 14	1.1.5
	Sargon C 15	1.1.16.1
Die Kopien von Inschriften des Rīmuš		
pp. 191ff.:	Rīmuš C 1	1.2.4
	Rīmuš C 2	1.2.3
	Rīmuš C 3	1.2.5
	Rīmuš C 4	1.2.1
	Rīmuš C 5	1.2.2
	Rīmuš C 6	1.2.6
	Rīmuš C 7	1.2.9
	Rīmuš C 8	1.2.7
	Rīmuš C 9	1.2.18
	Rīmuš C 10	1.2.8
Die Kopien von Inschriften des Maništūšu		
pp. 220ff.:	Maništūšu C 1	1.3.1
	Maništūšu C 2	1.3.1 Dedicatory label
	Maništūšu C 3	1.3.2
Die Kopien von Inschriften des Narāmsîn		
pp. 226ff.:	Narāmsîn C 1	1.4.6 (first part); 1.4.3 (second part)
	Narāmsîn C 2	1.4.2
	Narāmsîn C 3	1.4.25
	Narāmsîn C 4	1.4.1
	Narāmsîn C 5 Text A	1.4.26
	Narāmsîn C 5 Texts B–C	1.4.5
	Narāmsîn C 6	1.4.23
	Narāmsîn C 7	1.4.1001

No.		E2.
Die Kopien von Inschriften des Narāmsîn (continued)		
	Narāmsîn C 8	1.4.49
	Narāmsîn C 9	1.4.12
	Narāmsîn C 10	1.4.50
	Narāmsîn C 11	1.4.1002
	Narāmsîn C 12	1.4.1003
	Narāmsîn C 13	1.4.46
	Narāmsîn C 14	1.4.45
	Narāmsîn C 15	1.4.7
	Narāmsîn C 16	1.4.33
	Narāmsîn C 17	1.4.47
	Narāmsîn C 18	1.4.20
	Narāmsîn C 19	1.4.48
Die Kopien von Inschriften des Šarkališarrī		
pp. 276ff.:	Šarkališarrī C 1	1.5.5
	Šarkališarrī C 2	1.5.6
	Šarkališarrī C 3	1.5.2
	Šarkališarrī C 4	
Fragmente von Kopien Altakkadischer Königinschriften		
pp. 283ff.:	Fragment C 1	0.0.1009
	Fragment C 2 (first part)	0.0.1009
	Fragment C 2 (second part)	1.10.2
	Fragment C 3	0.0.1011
	Fragment C 4	0.0.1012
	Fragment C 5	1.4.30.1
	Fragment C 6	1.4.30.2
	Fragment C 7	(is Ur III)
V. Die Inschriften der Könige von Gutium		
pp. 294ff.:	Gutium 1	2.14.1
	Gutium 2	11.12.1
	Gutium 3	11.13.1
	Gutium 4	8.1.2001
	Gutium C 1	2.1.1
	Gutium C 2	2.1.2
	Gutium C 3	2.1.3
VI. Die Inschriften Elamischer Herrscher		
p. 319:	Epir-mupi a	16.2.2002
	Epir-mupi b	16.2.2001
	Epir-mupi c	16.2.1
p. 320:	Elam 1 (Ilīšmānī)	16.3.1
pp. 361ff.:	MŠ 5 (Ištupilum 1)	3.5.3
	MŠ 6 (Ištupilum 2)	3.5.2
	MŠ 7 ((Ištupilum 3)	3.5.1
	MŠ 8 (Niwār-mēr)	3.4.1
IX. Varia		
p. 369:	Varia 2 (Aššur)	4.1.1
p. 377:	Varia 8 (Luristan 11)	0.0.1015
p. 384:	Varia 18 (Tell Mumbāqa)	14.1.2001

Grayson, RIMA 1

No.		E2.	No.		E2.
p. 7:	Ititi	4.1.1	p. 8	Azuzu	1.3.2002

Hirsch, AfO 20 (1963) pp. 1–82

No.		E2.
Sargon, Originalinschriften		
p. 2:	Sargon a 1	1.1.10
	Sargon a 2	1.1.4
Abschriften (with page reference to the edition of Hirsch):		
p. 2:	Sargon b 1 (34–37)	1.1.1
p. 3:	Sargon b 2 (37–39)	1.1.11,1.1.12
	Sargon b 3 (39)	1.1.11 Curse formula and colophon
	Sargon b 4 (39–40)	1.1.3
	Sargon b 5 (40)	1.1.3 Caption
	Sargon b 6 (40–44)	1.1.2
	Sargon b 7 (44–45)	1.1.6
p. 4:	Sargon b 8 (45–46)	1.1.7
	Sargon b 9 (46–47)	1.1.8
	Sargon b 10 (47–48)	1.1.13
	Sargon b 11 (48)	1.1.14
	Sargon b 12 (48–49)	1.1.12
	Sargon b 13 (49–50)	1.1.12
	Sargon b 14 (50–51)	1.1.15
	Sargon b 15 (51)	1.1.9
	Sargon b 16 (51–52)	1.1.9
Familie:		
p. 9:	No. 1 (Tašlultum)	1.1.2001
	No. 2 (Enḫedu'anna)	1.1.16
	2a (Siegel)	1.1.2004
	2b (Siegel)	1.1.2003
	2c (Siegel)	1.1.2005
	No. 3a (Obelisk des Maništūsu)	see commentary to E2.1.3
Rīmuš, Originalinschriten:		
p. 10:	Rīmuš a 1	1.2.11
	Rīmuš a 2	1.2.13
	Rīmuš a 3	1.2.17
	Rīmuš a 4	1.2.12
	Rīmuš a 5	1.2.10
	Rīmuš a 6	1.2.20
p. 11:	Rīmuš a 7	1.2.19
Abschriften (with page reference to the edition of Hirsch):		
p. 11:	Rīmuš b 1 (52–56)	1.2.4
	Rīmuš b 2 (56–57)	1.2.3
	Rīmuš b 3 (57–58)	1.2.5
	Rīmuš b 4 (58–59)	1.2.1
p. 12:	Rīmuš b 5 (59–61)	1.2.2
	Rīmuš b 6 (61)	1.2.2 Caption 9
	Rīmuš b 7 (61–65)	1.2.6
	Rīmuš b 8 (65)	1.2.6
	Rīmuš b 9 (65–65)	1.2.9
	Rīmuš b 10 (66)	1.2.9 Caption
	Rīmuš b 11 (66–68)	1.2.7
	Rīmuš b 12 (68–69)	1.2.18
Maništušu, Originalinschriften:		
p. 14:	Maništušu a 1	E3.1.1
	Maništušu a 3 (Obelisk des Maništušu) see commentary to E2.1.3	
	p. 15: Maništušu a 4	1.3.3
	Maništušu a 5	1.3.4
	Maništušu a 6	1.3.1 Dedicatory label

No.		E2.
Abschriften (with page reference to the edition of Hirsch)		
p. 15:	Maništušu b 1 (69–70)	1.3.1
	Maništušu b 2 (71)	1.3.1 Dedicatory label
	Maništušu b 3 (71–72)	1.3.2
Zeitgenössische Inschriften:		
p. 15:	Maništušu d 2 α	1.3.2001
	d 2 β	1.3.2002
	d 2 γ	0.0.1005
	Maništušu d 3	1.3.2003
Narâm-Sin, Originalinschriften:		
p. 17:	Narâm-Sin a 1	1.4.31
	Narâm-Sin a 2	1.4.13
	Narâm-Sin a 3	1.4.9
p. 18:	Narâm-Sin a 4	1.3.1
	Narâm-Sin a 5	1.4.41–3
	Narâm-Sin a 5	1.4.42
p. 18:	Naramsln a 6	1.4.27
	Narâm-Sin a 7	1.4.24
	Narâm-Sin a 8	1.4.41
	Narâm-Sin a 9	1.4.35
	Narâm-Sin a 10 α	1.4.15
p. 19:	Narâm-Sin a 10 β	1.4.17
	Narâm-Sin a 10 γ	1.4.16
	Narâm-Sin a 11	1.4.22
	Narâm-Sin a 12	1.4.43
Abschriften (with page reference to the edition of Hirsch):		
p. 19:	Narâm-Sin b 1	1.4.6.2
	Narâm-Sin b 2	1.4.2
p. 20:	Narâm-Sin b 3	to 1.4.2
	Narâm-Sin b 4 (72–73)	1.4.25
	Narâm-Sin b 5 (73–77)	1.4.26
p. 21:	Narâm-Sin b 6 (77–78)	1.4.5
	Narâm-Sin b 7	1.4.23
	Narâm-Sin b 8	1.4.1; 1.4.1001
Zeitgenössische Inschriften:		
p. 22:	Narâm-Sin d 1 α	1.4.2010
	d 1 β	1.4.2001
	d 1 γ	1.4.14
	d 1 δ	1.4.20
p. 23:	Narâm-Sin d 1 ε	1.4.2018
	Narâm-Sin d 2 α	1.4.50
	d 2 β	1.4.2004
	d 2 γ	1.4.2003
	d 2 δ	1.4.2008
	d 2 ε	1.4.2009
	d 2 ζ	1.4.2013
	d 2 η	1.4.2012
	d 2 θ	1.4.2016
	d 2 ι	1.4.2014
	d 2 κ	1.4.2020
	d 2 l	1.4.2023
p. 23 note 253:		1.4.2015
p. 24:	Narâm-Sin d 3	see commentary to E2.16
Familie:		
	p. 27: No. 1 (Enmenanna)	1.4.34
	No. 2 (Nabi'ulmaš)	1.4.54

Hirsch, AfO 20 (1963) pp. 1–82 (continued)

No.		E2.
Familie:		
	No. 3 (Ukīnulmaš)	1.4.50
	No. 4 (Lipitilī)	1.4.9
	No. 5 (Binkališarrī)	1.4.2023
Šarkališarrī, Originalinschriten:		
p. 28:	Šarkališarrī a 1	1.5.9
	Šarkališarrī a 2	1.5.1
	Šarkališarrī a 3	1.5.2
	Šarkališarrī a 4	1.5.3
	Šarkališarrī a 5	1.5.7
Abschriften:		
p. 28:	Šarkališarrī b	1.5.2
Zeitgenössische Inschrifen:		
p. 29:	Šarkališarrī d 1 α	1.5.2006
	d 1 β	1.5.2014
	d 1 γ	1.5.2013
	Šarkališarrī d 2 α	1.5.2003
	d 2 β	1.5.1.5.2004
p. 30:	Šarkališarrī d 2 γ	1.5.2007
Šarkališarrī, Zeitgenössische Inschrifen (continued):		
p. 30	d 2 δ	1.5.2008
	d 2 ε	1.5.2010
p. 31:	Šarkališarrī Bb	1.5.10
Binkališarrī:		
p. 31:	No. 1	1.4.2022
p. 31:	Elulu	1.12.1
Dudu:		
p. 31:	Dudu 1	1.10.1.1–2
Šu-DUR.ÙL:		
p. 32:	Šu-DUR.ÙL 1	1.11.2003
	Šu-DUR.ÙL 2	1.10.2001
	Šu-DUR.ÙL 3	1.11.2001
Verschiedene Inschriften:		
p. 32:	No. 1 (Ubil-Ištar)	0.0.1001
	No. 4 (Epir-mupi) (seal)	16.2.2002
p. 33	No. 4 (Epir-mupi) (seal)	16.2.2001
	No.4 (Epir-mupi) (seal)	16.2.1
	No. 5 Surruš-kīn	11.5.1
Inschriften unsicherer Zuordnung:		
p. 33:	No. 1	See commentary on p. 41
	No. 2	0.0.1010
	No. 4a	0.0.1002
	No. 4b	0.0.1006
	No. 5 (BM 98917)	1.4.28.1 (frgm. 3)
	No. 5 (BM 98918)	1.4.28.1 (frgm. 4)
	No. 6	0.0.1006
	No. 7	0.0.1008

Sollberger and Kupper, IRSA

No.		E2.
IIAla	(Bilingue)	1.1.1.1
IIAlb	(Bilingue)	1.1.11.1
IIAlc	(Ašlultum)	1.1.2001
IIAld	(En-ḫedu-ana)	1.1.16
IIA2a	(Rīmuš)	1.2.11
IIA2b		1.2.4.1
IIA2c		1.2.3.1
IIA2d		1.2.6.1
IIA2e		1.2.9.1
IIA3a	(Man-ištūšu)	1.3.4
IIA3b		1.3.1.6
IIA3c		1.3.2.1
IIA3d		1.3.2001
IIA4a	(Narām-Suen)	1.4.15
IIA4b		1.4.27
IIA4c		1.4.9
IIA4d		1.4.25
IIA4e		1.4.26
IIA4f		1.4.23
IIA4g		1.4.33
IIA4h		1.4.2018
IIA4i		1.4.2020
IIA4j		1.4.49
IIA4k		1.4.54
IIA4l		1.4.2002
IIA4m		1.4.2003
IIA4n		1.4.2001
IIA4o		1.6.1.2001
IIA4p		1.4.2004
IIA4q		1.4.2005
IIA4r		1.4.2006
IIA5a	(Šar-kali-šarrī)	1.5.2
IIA5b		1.5.9
IIA5c		1.5.1.5.10
IIA5d		1.5.2004
IIA5e		1.5.2012
IIA5f		1.5.2010
IIA6a	(Ēlul-dan)	1.12.1
IIA7a	(Dudu)	1.10.1
IIA8a	(Šū-turul)	1.11.1
IIA8b		1.11.2003
IIDla	(Šurus-kīn)	11.5.1
IID3a	(Nam-maḫani)	11.12.1
IID4a	(Lugal-ana-tuma)	11.13.1
IIE1a	(Ḫala-adda)	10.1.1
IIF1a	(Šar-addī-qubbišin)	8.1.2001
IIGla	(Epir-mupi)	16.2.1
IIJ1	(mentioned as missing)	2.1.1–3
IIJ2a	(Lā-ʾarāb)	2.14.1
IIJ3a	(Puzur-Suen)	2.18.1
IIJ4	see IID3a (Yarlagan)	11.12.1
IIJ5	see IID4a (Sium)	11.13.1
IIJ6	see IIK3a (Tirigan)	13.6.4
IIK3a	(Utu-ḫegal)	13.6.4
IIK3b		13.6.3
IIK3c		13.6.2001
IIIE4a	(Ištup-Ilum)	3.5.1
IIIE4b		3.5.2
IIIE6a	(Niwar-Mer)	3.4.1

Thureau-Dangin, SAK

No.		E2.
pp. 158f.	No. 9	6.1.2001
pp. 160ff.	No. 1 (Vase A)	1.2.20.1, 5–6, 35
	No. 6b (Vase B)	1.2.10
pp. 162f.	No. 6c (Vase C)	1.2.11.3
	No. 6d (Bruchstein)	1.2.19
	No. 7a (Streitkolben)	1.3.4
	No. 7b (Vase)	1.3.3
pp. 162f.	No. la (Backsteinstempel)	1.5.3.4a
	No. lb (Streitkolben)	1.5.9
	No. lc (Türangelstein A)	1.5.1
pp. 164f.	No. ld (Turangelstein B)	1.5.2
	No. le (Siegel A)	1.5.2003
	No. lf (Siegel B)	1.5.2004
	No. 19 (Siegel C)	1.5.2007
pp. 164f.:	No. lh (Siegel D)	1.5.2010
	No. 2a (Backsteinstempel)	1.4.15.3
	No. 2b (Vase A)	1.4.41.1
	No. 2c (Vase B)	1.4.4.1

No.		E2.
pp. 166f.:	No. 2d (Durchlochte Platte A)	1.4.27.2
	No. 2e (Durchlochte Platte B)	1.4.54
	No. 2f (Stele A)	1.4.24
pp. 166f.:	No. 29 (Stele B)	1.4.31
	No. 2h (Statue A)	1.4.13
pp. 168f.:	No. 2i (Statue B)	1.4.2002
	No. 2k (Siegel A)	1.4.2004
	No. 21 (Siegel B)	1.4.2023
	No. 2m (Siegel C)	1.4.2003
	No. 2n (Siegel D)	1.4.2014
	No. 2o (Siegel E)	1.4.2008
	No. 2p (Siegel F)	1.4.2016
	No. 2q (Siegel G)	1.4.2012
pp. 168f.:	No. 3a (Siegel A)	1.4.2022
	No. 3b (Siegel B)	1.4.2023
pp. 168f.:	No. 4 (Siegel)	0.0.1001
	p. 170f. No. 5a (Vase)	0.0.1010
pp. 170f.:	No. 5b (Stele)	See commentary to E2.1.2.II
	No. XI (Streitkolben)	2.14.1

Scores of Inscriptions

1 0 [*śar-um*-GI]
1 1 [...]
1 2 [...]

2 0 [lugal]-
2 1 [...]
2 2 [...]

3 0 [ag-ge-dè.KI]
3 1 [...]
3 2 [...]

4 0 [maškim]-
4 1 [...]
4 2 [...]-

5 0 [^{d}inanna]
5 1 [...]
5 2 [...]

6 0 [lu]gal-K[IŠ]
6 1 [lu]gal-K[IŠ]
6 2 [...]

7 0 [gúd]a-an-na
7 1 [gúd]a-an-na
7 2 [...]

8 0 ⸢lugal⸣-
8 1 ⸢lugal⸣-
8 2 [...]

9 0 ⸢kalam-ma⸣
9 1 ⸢kalam-ma⸣
9 2 [...]

10 0 énsi-gal-
10 1 énsi-gal-
10 2 [...]

11 0 ^{d}en-líl
11 1 ^{d}en-líl
11 2 [...]

12 0 uru unu.KI
12 1 uru unu.KI
12 2 [...]

13 0 e-ḫul
13 1 e-ḫul
13 2 [...]

14 0 ⸢bàd⸣-bi
14 1 ⸢bàd⸣-bi
14 2 [...]

15 0 e-ga-⸢sì⸣
15 1 e-ga-⸢sì⸣
15 2 [...]

16 0 lú-unu.KI-⸢ga-da⸣
16 1 lú-unu.KI-⸢ga-da⸣
16 2 [...]

17 0 GIŠ.tukul
17 1 GIŠ.tukul
17 2 [...]

18 0 ⸢e⸣-da-sìg
18 1 ⸢e⸣-da-sìg
18 2 [...]

19 0 TÙN.KÁR[A]
19 1 TÙN.KÁR[A]
19 2 [...]

20 0 e-NI-[sì]
20 1 e-NI-[sì]
20 2 [...]

21 0 lug[al-zà-ge-si]
21 1 lug[al-...]
21 2 [...]

22 0 [lugal]-
22 1 [...]
22 2 [...]

23 0 [unu.KI-ga-da]
23 1 [...]
23 2 [...]

24 0 [GI]Š.tuku[l]
24 1 [...]
24 2 [GI]Š.tuku[l]

25 0 [e]-d[a-sìg]
25 1 [...]
25 2 [e]-d[a-sìg]

26 0 ⸢e⸣-ga-dab_5
26 1 ⸢e-ga⸣-dab_5
26 2 ⸢e⸣-ga-dab_5

27 0 GIŠ.si-gar-ta
27 1 GIŠ.si-gar-ta
27 2 GIŠ.⸢si⸣-gar-ta

28 0 ká-^{d}en-líl-lá-šè
28 1 ká-^{d}en-líl-⸢lá⸣-šè
28 2 ká-^{d}en-líl-lá-šè

29 0 ⸢e⸣-túm
29 1 ⸢e⸣-túm
29 2 ⸢e⸣-túm

30 0 *śar-um*-GI
30 1 [...]
30 2 *śar-um*-GI

31 0 lugal-
31 1 [l]ugal-
31 2 lugal-

32 0 [a]g-ge-dè.KI
32 1 [a]g-ge-dè.KI
32 2 [ag]-ge-dè.KI

33 0 lú-úri.KI-ma-da
33 1 lú-úri.KI-ma-da
33 2 lú-úri.KI-ma-da

34 0 GIŠ.tukul
34 1 GIŠ.tukul
34 2 GIŠ.tukul

35 0 e-da-sìg
35 1 e-da-sìg
35 2 e-da-sìg

36 0 TÙN.KÁRA
36 1 TÙN.KÁRA
36 2 ⸢TÙN.KÁRA⸣

37 0 e-NI-sì
37 1 ⸢e⸣-NI-sì
37 2 e-NI-s[ì]

38 0 uru-ni
38 1 uru-ni
38 2 [...]

39 0 e-ḫul
39 1 e-ḫul (after erased ga-ga)
39 2 [...]

40 0 ⸢bàd⸣-bi
40 1 ⸢bàd⸣-bi
40 2 [...]

41 0 e-ga-⸢sì⸣
41 1 e-ga-⸢sì⸣
41 2 [...]

42 0 é-^{d}nin-⸢mar⸣.KI
42 1 é-^{d}nin-⸢mar⸣.KI
42 2 [...]

43 0 e-ḫul
43 1 e-ḫul
43 2 [...]

44 0 bàd-bi
44 1 bàd-bi
44 2 [...]

45 0 e-ga-⸢sì⸣
45 1 e-ga-⸢sì⸣
45 2 [...]

46 0 gú-kalam-bi
46 1 gú-kalam-bi
46 2 [...]

47 0 lagaš.KI-ta
47 1 lagaš.KI-ta
47 2 [...]

48 0 ⸢a⸣-ab-ba-šè na-x-ne
48 1 ⸢a⸣-ab-ba-šè na-x-ne
48 2 [...]

49 0 e-ḫul
49 1 e-ḫul
49 2 [...]

50 0 GIŠ.tukul-ni
50 1 GIŠ.tukul-ni
50 2 [...]

51 0 a-ab-ba-ka
51 1 a-ab-ba-ka
51 2 [...]

52 0 ì-luḫ
52 1 ì-luḫ
52 2 [...]

53 0 ⸢lú⸣-umma.KI-⸢da⸣
53 1 ⸢lú⸣-umma.KI-⸢da⸣
53 2 [...]

54 0 [GIŠ.tukul]
54 1 [...]
54 2 [...]

55 0 [e-da-sìg]
55 1 [...]
55 2 [...]

56 0 [TÙN.KÁRA]
56 1 [...]
56 2 [...]

57 0 [e-NI-sì]
57 1 [...]
57 2 [e-NI-sì]

58 0 [uru-ni]
58 1 [...]
58 2 [...]

59 0 [e-ḫul]
59 1 [...]
59 2 [...]

60 0 [bàd-bi]
60 1 [...]
60 2 [...]

61 0 [e-ga-sì]
61 1 [...]
61 2 [...]

62 0 [*śar-um*-GI]
62 1 [...]
62 2 [...]

63 0 ⸢lugal⸣-
63 1 ⸢lugal⸣-
63 2 [...]

64 0 kalam-ma-⸢ra⸣
64 1 kalam-ma-⸢ra⸣
64 2 [...]

65 0 ⸢^{d}en⸣-líl-le
65 1 ⸢^{d}⸢en⸣-líl-le
65 2 [...]

66 0 lú-[érim]
66 1 lú-[érim]
66 2 [...]

67 0 nu-na-⸢sum⸣
67 1 nu-na-⸢sum⸣
67 2 [...]

68 0 a-⸢ab⸣-[ba]-
68 1 a-⸢ab⸣-[ba]-
68 2 [...]

69 0 ⸢IGI.NIM⸣-ma-ta
69 1 ⸢IGI.NIM⸣-ma-ta
69 2 [...]

70 0 a-ab-ba-
70 1 a-ab-ba-
70 2 [...]

71 0 sig-⸢sig⸣-šè
71 1 sig-⸢sig⸣-šè
71 2 [...]

72 0 ^{d}⸢en-líl⸣-l[e]
72 1 ^{d}⸢en-líl⸣-l[e]
72 2 [...]

73 0 [mu-na-sum]
73 1 [...]
73 2 [...]

74 0 [ù]
74 1 [...]
74 2 [...]

75 0 [a-ab]-ba-
75 1 [a-ab]-ba-
75 2 [...]

76 0 [sig-sig]-ta
76 1 [...]-ta
76 2 [...]

77 0 [dumu-dum]u
77 1 [dumu-dum]u
77 2 [...]

78 0 [ag-ge-dè.KI]
78 1 [...]
78 2 [...]

79 0 n[am-énsi]
79 1 n[am-énsi]
79 2 [...]

80 0 mu-⸢kin(?)⸣-[x]
80 1 mu-⸢kin(?)⸣-[x]
80 2 [...]

81 0 lú-ma-[rí.KI]
81 1 lú-ma-[rí.KI]
81 2 [...]

82 0 lú-NIM.[KI]
82 1 lú-NIM.[KÎ]
82 2 [lú]-NI[M.KI]

83 0 (erasure)
83 1 (erasure)
83 2 [...]

84 0 igi-*śar-u*[*m*]-⸢GI⸣
84 1 igi-*śar-u*[*m*]-⸢GI⸣
84 2 igi-[*śa*]*r-u*[*m*]-GI]

85 0 lugal-
85 1 lugal-
85 2 ⸢lugal⸣-

86 0 kalam-ma-ka-šè
86 1 kalam-ma-ka-šè
86 2 ⸢kalam-ma-ka-šè⸣

87 0 ì-su$_{8}$-ge-éš
87 1 ì-su$_{8}$-ge-éš
87 2 ì-[...]

88 0 *śar-um*-GI
88 1 *śar-um*-GI
88 2 [...]

89 0 lugal-
89 1 lugal-
89 2 [...]-

90 0 kalam-ma-ke$_{4}$
90 1 kalam-ma-ke$_{4}$
90 2 [...]

91 0 kiš.KI
91 1 kiš.KI
91 2 [...]

92 0 ki-bé
92 1 ki-bé
92 2 [...]

93 0 bí-gi$_{4}$
93 1 bí-gi$_{4}$
93 2 [...]

94 0 uru-bé
94 1 uru-bé
94 2 [...]

95 0 ki-gub e-na-ba
95 1 ki-gub e-na-ba
95 2 [...]

96 0 ⸢lú mu-sar-ra-e⸣
96 1 ⸢ú mu-sar-ra-e⸣
96 2 [...]

97 0 ab-ḫa-lam-e-a
97 1 ab-ḫa-lam-e-a
97 2 [...]

98 0 ^{d}utu
98 1 ^{d}utu
98 2 [...]

99 0 suḫuš-a-ni
99 1 suḫuš-a-ni
99 2 [...]

100 0 ḫé-bù-re$_{6}$
100 1 ḫé-bù-re$_{6}$
100 2 [...]

101 0 numun-na-ni
101 1 numun-na-ni
101 2 [...]

102 0 ḫé-ga-ri-ri-ge
102 1 ḫé-ga-ri-ri-ge
102 2 [...]

Colophon

1 0 mu-sar-ra
1 1 mu-sar-ra
1 2 [...]

2 0 ki-gal-ba
2 1 ki-gal-ba
2 2 [...]

1 0 [*śar-ru*-GI]
1 1 [...]
1 2 [...]

2 0 [LUGAL]
2 1 [...]
2 2 [...]

3 0 [*a-kà-dè*.KI]
3 1 [...]
3 2 [...]

4 0 [MAŠKIM.GI$_4$]
4 1 [...]
4 2 [...]

5 0 [^{d}INANNA]
5 1 [...]
5 2 [...]

6 0 [LUGAL KIŠ]
6 1 [...]
6 2 [...]

7 0 [PA$_4$.ŠEŠ AN]
7 1 [...]
7 2 [...]

8 0 ⌈LUGAL⌉
8 1 ⌈LUGAL⌉
8 2 [...]

9 0 KALAM.MA.⌈KI⌉
9 1 KALAM.MA.⌈KI⌉
9 2 [...]

10 0 ÉNSI
10 1 ÉNSI
10 2 [...]

11 0 ^{d}*en-líl*
11 1 ^{d}*en-líl*
11 2 [...]

12 0 URU.KI
12 1 URU.KI
12 2 [...]

13 0 UNU.KI
13 1 UNU.KI
13 1 [...]

14 0 SAG.GIŠ.RA
14 1 SAG.GIŠ.RA
14 2 [...]

15 0 *ù*
15 1 *ù*
15 2 [...]

16 0 BÀD-*śu*
16 1 BÀD-*śu*
16 2 [...]

17 0 Ì.GUL.GUL
17 1 Ì.GUL.GUL
17 2 [...]

18 0 in REC 169
18 1 in REC 169
18 2 [...]

19 0 UNU.[KI]
19 1 UNU.[KI]
19 2 [...]

20 0 [*iš*$_{11}$-*ar*]
20 1 [...]
20 2 [...]

21 0 [URU.KI]
21 1 [...]
21 2 [...]

22 0 [SAG.GIŠ.RA]
22 1 [...]
22 2 [...]

23 0 [lugal-z]à-ge-si
23 1 [lugal-z]à-ge-si
23 2 [...]

24 0 ⸢LUGAL⸣
24 1 ⸢LUGAL⸣
24 2 [...]

25 0 [UN]U.KI
25 1 [UN]U.KI
25 2 [...]

26 0 *in* REC 169
26 1 *in* REC 169
26 2 [...]

27 0 ŠU.DU$_{8}$.A
27 1 ŠU.DU$_{8}$.A
27 2 Š[U.DU$_{8}$.A]

28 0 *in* SI.GAR-*rìm*
28 1 *in* SI.GAR-*rìm*
28 2 *i*[*n* SI.GAR]-⸢*rìm*⸣

29 0 *a-na* KÁ
29 1 *a-na* KÁ
29 2 *a-na* KÁ

30 0 ^{d}*en-líl*
30 1 ^{d}*en-líl*
30 2 ^{d}*en-líl*

31 0 *u-ru-úś*
31 1 *u-ru*-⸢*úś*⸣
31 2 *u-ru-úś*

32 0 *śar-ru*-GI
32 1 ⸢*śar-ru*-GI⸣
32 2 *śar-ru*-GI

33 0 LUGAL
33 1 LUGAL
33 2 LUGAL

34 0 *a-kà-dè*.KI
34 1 *a-kà-dè*.KI
34 2 *a-kà-dè*.KI

35 0 *in* REC 169
35 1 *in* REC 169
35 2 *in* REC 169

36 0 ÚRI.KI
36 1 ÚRI.KI
36 2 ⸢ÚRI⸣.[KI]

37 0 *iš*$_{11}$-*ar*
37 1 *iš*$_{11}$-*ar*
37 2 [...]

38 0 *ù*
38 1 *ù*
38 2 [...]

39 0 URU.KI
39 1 URU.KI
39 2 [...]

40 0 SAG.GIŠ.RA
40 1 SAG.GIŠ.RA
40 2 [...]

41 0 *ù*
41 1 *ù*
41 2 [...]

42 0 BÀD-*śu*
42 1 BÀD-*śu*
42 2 [...]

43 0 Ì.GUL.GUL
43 1 Ì.GUL.GUL
43 2 [...]

44 0 *é-nin-mar*.KI
44 1 *é-nin-mar*.KI
44 2 [...]

45 0 SAG.GIŠ.RA
45 1 SAG.GIŠ.RA
45 2 [...]

46 0 *ù*
46 1 *ù*
46 2 [...]

47 0 BÀD-*śu*
47 1 BÀD-*śu*
47 2 [...]

48 0 ⸢Ì.GUL.GUL⸣
48 1 ⸢Ì.GUL.GUL⸣
48 2 [...]

49 0 ⸢*ù*⸣
49 1 ⸢*ù*⸣
49 2 [...]

50 0 KALAM.MA.KI-*śu*
50 1 KALAM.MA.KI-*śu*
50 2 [...]

51 0 *ù*
51 1 (erasure) *ù*
51 2 [...]

52 0 *lagaš*(LA.BUR.ŠIR.RI).KI
52 1 *lagaš*(LA.BUR.ŠIR.RI).KI
52 2 [...]

53 0 *a-dì-ma*
53 1 *a-dì-ma*
53 2 [...]

54 0 *ti-a-am-tim*
54 1 *ti-a-am-tim*
54 2 [...]

55 0 SAG.GIŠ.RA
55 1 SAG.GIŠ.RA
55 2 [...]

56 0 GIŠ.TUKUL-*kí-śu*
56 1 GIŠ.TUKUL-*kí-śu*
56 2 [...]

57 0 *in ti-a-*⸢*am*⸣*-tim*
57 1 *in ti-a-*⸢*am*⸣*-tim*
57 2 [...]

58 0 Ì.LUḪ
58 1 Ì.LUḪ
58 2 [...]

59 0 UB.ME.KI
59 1 UB.ME.KI
59 2 [...]

60 0 ⸢*in* REC 169⸣
60 1 ⸢*in* REC 169⸣
60 2 [...]

61 0 [*iš*$_{11}$*-ar*]
61 1 [...]
61 2 [...]

62 0 [*ù*]
62 1 [...]
62 2 [...]

63 0 [URU.KI]
63 1 [...]
63 2 [...]

64 0 [SAG.GIŠ.RA]
64 1 [...]
64 2 [...]

65 0 [*ù* BÀD-śu]
65 1 [...]
65 2 [...]

66 0 [Ì.GUL.GUL]
66 1 [...]
66 2 [...]

67 0 [*śar-ru*-GI]
67 1 [...]
67 2 [...]

68 0 LUG[AL]
68 1 LUG[AL]
68 2 [...]

69 0 ⸢KALAM⸣.MA.[KI]
69 1 ⸢KALAM⸣.MA.[KI]
69 2 [...]

70 0 ^{d}*en-*⸢*líl*⸣
70 1 ^{d}*en-*⸢*líl*⸣
70 2 [...]

71 0 *ma-*[*ḫi-ra*]
71 1 *ma-*[*ḫi-ra*]
71 2 [...]

72 0 [*la i-dì-nu-śum*$_{6}$]
72 1 [...]
72 2 [...]

73 0 [*ti-a-am-ṭám*]
73 1 [...]
73 2 [...]

74 0 [*a-lí-tám*]
74 1 [...]
74 2 [...]

75 0 [*ù*]
75 1 [...]
75 2 [...]

76 0 [*śa-pil*]*-tám*
76 1 [*śa-pil*]*-tám*
76 2 [...]

77 0 ⸢^{d}⸣*en-líl*
77 1 ⸢^{d}⸣*en-líl*
77 2 [...]

78 0 *i-dì-nu-śum*$_{6}$
78 1 *i-dì-nu-śum*$_{6}$
78 2 [...]

79 0 *íś-tum-ma*
79 1 *íś-tum-ma*
79 2 [...]

80 0 *ti-a-am-tim*
80 1 *ti-a-am-tim*
80 2 [...]

81 0 *śa-*⸢*pil*⸣*-tim*
81 1 *śa-*⸢*pil*⸣*-tim*
81 2 [...]

82 0 DUMU.DUMU
82 1 DUMU.DUMU
82 2 [...]

83 0 *a-*⸢*kà-dè*⸣.KI
83 1 *a-*⸢*kà-dè*⸣.KI
83 2 [...]

84 0 ÉNSI-*ku*$_8$*-a-tim*
84 1 ÉNSI-*ku*$_8$*-a-tim*
84 2 [...]

85 0 [*u*]*-kà-lú*
85 1 [*u*]*-kà-lú*
85 2 [...]

86 0 *ma-rí*.KI
86 1 *ma-rí*.KI
86 2 [...]

87 0 *ù*
87 1 *ù*
87 2 [...]

88 0 NIM.KI
88 1 NIM.KI
88 2 [...]

89 0 *maḫ-rí-íś*
89 1 *maḫ-rí-íś*
89 2 [...]

90 0 *śar-*⸢*ru*-GI⸣
90 1 *śar-*⸢*ru*-GI⸣
90 2 [...]

91 0 LUGAL
91 1 LUGAL
91 2 [...]

92 0 KALAM.MA.KI
92 1 KALAM.MA.KI
92 2 [...]

93 0 *i-za-zu-ni*
93 1 *i-za-zu-ni*
93 2 [...]

94 0 ⸢*śar-ru*-GI⸣
94 1 ⸢*śar-ru*-GI⸣
94 2 [...]

95 0 LUGAL
95 1 LUGAL
95 2 [...]

96 0 KALAM.MA.KI
96 1 KALAM.MA.KI
96 2 [...]

97 0 *kiš*.KI
97 1 *kiš*.KI
97 2 [...]

98 0 *a-ša-rí-śu*
98 1 *a-ša-rí-śu*
98 2 [...]

99 0 *i-ni*
99 1 *i-ni*
99 2 [...]

100 0 URU.KI-*lam*
100 1 URU.KI-*lam*
100 2 [...]

101 0 *u-śá-ḫi-śu-ni*
101 1 *u-śá-ḫi-śu-ni*
101 2 [...]

102 0 *ša* DUB
102 1 *ša* DUB
102 2 [...]

103 0 ⸢*śu*$_4$⸣-*a*
103 1 ⸢*śu*$_4$⸣-*a*
103 2 [...]

104 0 *u-śa-sà-ku-ni*
104 1 *u-śa-sà-ku-ni*
104 2 [...]

105 0 dUTU
105 1 dUTU
105 2 [...]

106 0 SUḪUŠ-*śu*
106 1 SUḪUŠ-*śu*
106 2 [...]

107 0 *li-sú-uḫ*
107 1 *li-sú-uḫ*
107 2 [...]

108 0 *ù* ŠE.NUMUN-*śu*
108 1 *ù* ŠE.NUMUN-*śu*
108 2 [...]

109 0 *li-il-qù-ut*
109 1 *li-il-qù-ut*
109 2 [...]

Colophon

1 0 mu-sar-⸢ra⸣
1 1 mu-sar-⸢ra⸣
1 2 [...]

2 0 ⸢ki-gal-ba⸣
2 1 ⸢ki-gal-ba⸣
2 2 [...]

Caption 1

1 0 *śar-ru*-GI
1 1 *śar-ru*-GI
1 2 [...]

2 0 LUGAL
2 1 LUGAL
2 2 [...]

3 0 KALAM.MA.KI
3 1 KALAM.MA.KI
3 2 [...]

4 0 ⸢*ma*⸣-[...]
4 1 ⸢*ma*⸣-[...]
4 2 [...]

Lacuna

Caption 1

1 0 lugal-zà-⸢ge⸣-si
1 1 lugal-zà-⸢ge⸣-si
1 2 [...]

2 0 LUGAL
2 1 LUGAL
2 2 [...]

Caption 1′ (continued)

3 0 UNU.KI
3 1 UNU.KI
3 2 [...]

Caption 2′

1 0 mes-é
1 1 mes-é
1 2 x x

2 0 ÉNSI
2 1 ÉNSI
2 2 ÉNSI

3 0 ⌈UB⌉.ME.KI
3 1 [UB].⌈ME⌉.KI
3 2 ⌈UB.ME.KI⌉

Caption 3′

1 0 [...]
1 1 [...]
1 2 [...]

2 0 ⌈LUGAL⌉
2 1 [...]
2 2 ⌈LUGAL⌉

3 0 [...]
3 1 [...]
3 2 [...]

1 0 *šar-ru*-GI
1 1 [...-G]I
1 2 *šar-ru*-GI

2 0 LUGAL
2 1 LUGAL
2 2 LUGAL

3 0 *a-kà-dè*.KI
3 1 *a-kà-dè*.KI
3 2 *a-kà-dè*.KI

4 0 MAŠKIM.GI_4
4 1 MAŠKIM.GI_4
4 2 MAŠKIM.GI_4

5 0 ^{d}INANNA
5 1 ^{d}INANNA
5 2 ⸢^{d}INANNA⸣

6 0 LUGAL KIŠ
6 1 LUGAL KIŠ
6 2 LUGAL ⸢KIŠ⸣

7 0 PA_4.ŠEŠ AN
7 1 PA_4.ŠEŠ AN
7 2 PA_4.ŠEŠ AN

8 0 LUGAL
8 1 LUGAL
8 2 LUGAL

9 0 KALAM.MA.KI
9 1 KALAM.MA.KI
9 2 KALAM.MA.KI

10 0 ÉNSI
10 1 ÉNSI
10 2 ÉNS[I]

11 0 ^{d}*en-líl*
11 1 ^{d}*en-líl*
11 2 ^{d}*en*-⸢*líl*⸣

12 0 *in* ⸢REC 169⸣(KASKAL+[x])
12 1 *in* ⸢REC 169⸣(KASKAL+[x])
12 2 *in* ⸢REC 169⸣(KASKAL+[x])

13 0 UNU.KI
13 1 UNU.[KI]
13 2 UNU.KI

14 0 *$iš_{11}$-ar*
14 1 *$iš_{11}$-a*[*r*]
14 2 *$iš_{11}$-ar*

15 0 *ù*
15 1 *ù*
15 2 *ù*

16 0 50 ÉNSI
16 1 50 ÉNSI
16 2 50 ÉNSI

17 0 *in* ŠÍTA
17 1 *in* ŠÍTA
17 2 *in* ŠÍTA

18 0 *ìl-a-ba_4*
18 1 *ìl-a-ba_4*
18 2 *ìl-a-ba_4*

19 0 *ù*
19 1 *ù*
19 2 ⸢*ù*⸣

20 0 URU.KI
20 1 URU.KI
20 2 [...]

21 0 [S]AG.GIŠ.[RA]
21 1 [S]AG.GIŠ.[RA]
21 2 [...]

22 0 [*ù*]
22 1 [...]
22 2 [...]

23 0 B[ÀD-*šu*]
23 1 B[ÀD-*šu*]
23 2 [...]

24 0 ⸢Ì.GUL.GUL⸣
24 1 ⸢Ì.GUL.GUL⸣
24 2 [...]

25 0 *ù*
25 1 *ù*
25 2 [...]

26 0 lugal-zà-ge-si
26 1 lugal-zà-ge-si
26 2 [...]

27 0 LUGAL
27 1 LUGAL
27 2 [...]

28 0 UNU.KI
28 1 UNU.KI
28 2 [...]

29 0 in REC 169
29 1 in REC 169
29 2 [...]

30 0 ŠU.DU$_{8}$.A
30 1 ŠU.DU$_{8}$.A
30 2 [...]

31 0 *in ši-ga-rìm*
31 1 *in ši-ga-rìm*
31 2 [...]

32 0 *a-na* KÁ
32 1 *a-na* KÁ
32 2 [...]

33 0 ^{d}*en-lil*
33 1 ^{d}*en-lil*
33 2 [...]

34 0 *u-ru-úš*
34 1 *u-ru-úš*
34 2 [...]

35 0 *šar-ru*-GI
35 1 *šar-ru*-GI
35 2 [...]

36 0 LUGAL
36 1 LUGAL
36 2 [...]

37 0 *a-kà-dè*.KI
37 1 *a-kà-dè*.KI
37 2 [...]

38 0 ⸢*in*⸣ REC 169
38 1 ⸢*in*⸣ REC 169
38 2 [...]

39 0 ÚRI.KI
39 1 ÚRI.KI
39 2 [...]

40 0 *iš*$_{11}$*-ar*
40 1 *iš*$_{11}$*-ar*
40 2 [...]

41 0 *ù*
41 1 *ù*
41 2 [...]

42 0 URU.KI
42 1 URU.KI
42 2 [...]

43 0 SAG.GIŠ.⸢RA⸣
43 1 SAG.GIŠ.⸢RA⸣
43 2 [...]

44 0 ⸢*ù*⸣
44 1 ⸢*ù*⸣
44 2 [...]

45 0 B[ÀD-*śu*]
45 1 B[ÀD-*śu*]
45 2 [...]

46 0 Ì.G[UL.GUL]
46 1 Ì.G[UL.GUL]
46 2 [...]

47 0 [*é-nin-mar*.KI]
47 1 [...]
47 2 [...]

48 0 [SAG.GIŠ.RA]
48 1 [...]
48 2 [...]

49 0 [*ù*]
49 1 [...]
49 2 [...]

50 0 BÀD-*śu*
50 1 BÀD-*ś*[*u*]
50 2 ⸢BÀD⸣-*śu*

51 0 Ì.GUL.GUL
51 1 [Ì].GUL.GUL
51 2 ⸢Ì⸣.GUL.GUL

52 0 *ù*
52 1 *ù*
52 2 *ù*

53 0 KALAM.KI-*śu*
53 1 [KALA]M.KI-*śu*
53 2 KALAM.KI-*śu*

54 0 *ù*
54 1 *ù*
54 2 *ù*

55 0 *lagaš*(LA.BUR.ŠIR).KI
55 1 ⸢*lagaš*([LA.BU]R.ŠIR).⸢KI⸣
55 2 *lagaš*(LA.BUR.ŠIR).KI

56 0 *a-dì-ma*
56 1 [*a-d*]*ì-ma*
56 2 *a-dì-*⸢*ma*⸣

57 0 *ti-a-am-tim*
57 1 [*ti*]-⸢*a*⸣-*am-tim*
57 2 *ti-a-am-t*[*im*]

58 0 SAG.GIŠ.RA
58 1 [SAG].GIŠ.RA
58 2 SAG.GIŠ.RA

59 0 ⸢GIŠ⸣.TUKUL-*kí-śu*
59 1 [GIŠ.TUKU]L-*kí-śu*
59 2 ⸢GIŠ⸣.TUKUL-⸢*kí*⸣-*ś*[*u*]

60 0 *in ti-a-am-tim*
60 1 [*in t*]*i-a-am-*⸢*tim*⸣
60 2 *in ti-a-am-t*[*im*]

61 0 Ì.LUḪ
61 1 Ì.[LUḪ]
61 2 Ì.LUḪ

62 0 UB.ME.KI
62 1 UB.ME.[KI]
62 2 ⸢UB.ME⸣.KI

63 0 *in* REC 169
63 1 *in* ⸢REC 169⸣
63 2 *in* REC 169

64 0 *iš*$_{11}$*-ar*
64 1 *iš*$_{11}$*-ar*
64 2 *iš*$_{11}$*-ar*

65 0 *ù*
65 1 *ù*
65 2 *ù*

66 0 URU.KI
66 1 URU.KI
66 2 URU.KI

67 0 SAG.GIŠ.RA
67 1 SAG.GIŠ.RA
67 2 SAG.GIŠ.RA

68 0 ù
68 1 ù
68 2 ù

69 0 BÀD-*śu*
69 1 BÀD-*ś*[*u*]
69 2 BÀD-⸢*śu*⸣

70 0 Ì.GU[L.GUL]
70 1 Ì.GU[L.GUL]
70 2 Ì.G[UL.GUL]

71 0 *ś*[*ar-ru*-G]I
71 1 *ś*[*ar-ru*-G]I
71 2 *ś*[*ar-ru*-GI]

72 0 [LUGA]L
72 1 [LUGA]L
72 2 [...]

73 0 [KALAM.MA].KI
73 1 [...].KI
73 2 [...]

74 0 [*šu* ^{d}*en-l*]*íl*
74 1 [...-*l*]*íl*
74 2 [...]

75 0 *m*[*a-ḫi-r*]*a*
75 1 *m*[*a-ḫi-r*]*a*
75 2 [...]

76 0 *la* ⸢*i-dì-nu*⸣*-śum*$_{6}$
76 1 *la* ⸢*i-dì-nu*⸣*-śum*$_{6}$
76 2 [...]

77 0 *ti-a-*⸢*am-tám*⸣
77 1 *ti-a-*⸢*am-tám*⸣
77 2 [...]

78 0 *a-lí-*⸢*tám*⸣
78 1 *a-lí-*⸢*tám*⸣
78 2 [...]

79 0 ⸢*ù*⸣
79 1 ⸢*ù*⸣
79 2 [...]

80 0 *śa-pi*[*l-tám*]
80 1 *śa-pi*[*l-tám*]
80 2 [...]

81 0 [*i-dì-śum*$_{6}$]
81 1 [...]
81 2 [...]

82 0 [*íś-tum-ma*]
82 1 [...]
82 2 [...]

83 0 [t*i-a-am-tim*]
83 1 [...]
83 2 [...]

84 0 [*śa-pil-tim*]
84 1 [...]
84 2 [...]

85 0 [*a-dì-ma*]
85 1 [...]
85 2 [...]

86 0 [*ti-a-am-t*]*im*
86 1 [*ti-a-am-t*]*im*
86 2 [...]

87 0 [*a-lí*]-*tim*
87 1 [*a-lí*]-*tim*
87 2 [...]

88 0 [DUMU.DUM]U
88 1 [DUMU.DUM]U
88 2 [...]

89 0 *a-kà-*⌈*dè*⌉.KI
89 1 *a-kà-*⌈*dè*⌉.KI
89 2 [...]

90 0 ÉNSI-*ku*$_{8}$-*a-a-tim*
90 1 ÉNSI-*ku*$_{8}$-*a-a-tim*
90 2 [...]

91 0 *u-kà-lú*
91 1 *u-kà-lú*
91 2 [...]

92 0 *ma-rí*.KI
92 1 *ma-rí*.KI
92 2 [...]

93 0 *ù*
93 1 *ù*
93 2 [...]

94 0 NIM.KI
94 1 NIM.KI
94 2 [...]

95 0 *maḫ-rí-íś*
95 1 *maḫ-rí-íś*
95 2 [...]

96 0 *śar-ru*-GI
96 1 *śar-ru*-GI
96 2 [...]

97 0 LUGAL
97 1 LUGAL
97 2 [...]

98 0 KALAM.MA.KI
98 1 KALAM.MA.KI
98 2 [...]

99 0 *i-za-zu-ni*
99 1 *i-za-zu-ni*
99 2 [...]

100 0 *śar-ru*-GI
100 1 *śar-ru*-GI
100 2 [...]

101 0 LUGAL
101 1 LUGAL
101 2 [...]

102 0 KALAM.MA.KI
102 1 KALAM.MA.KI
102 2 [...]

103 0 [*k*]*iš*.KI
103 1 [*ki*]*š*.KI
103 2 [...]

104 0 ⸢*a*⸣-*ša-rí-šu*
104 1 ⸢*a*⸣-*ša-rí-šu*
104 2 [...]

105 0 ⸢*i*⸣-*ni*
105 1 ⸢*i*⸣-*ni*
105 2 [...]

106 0 *ù*
106 1 *ù*
106 2 [...]

107 0 URU.KI-*lam*
107 1 URU.KI-*lam*
107 2 URU.K[I-*lam*

108 0 *u-šá-ḫi-šu-ni*
108 1 [*u*]-*šá-ḫi-šu-ni*
108 2 *u-šá-ḫi-šu-n*[*i*]

109 0 *ša* DUB
109 1 [*ša*] ⸢DUB⸣
109 2 *ša* DUB

110 0 *šu*$_4$-*a*
110 1 [*šu*$_4$]-⸢*a*⸣
110 2 *šu*$_4$-*a*

111 0 *u-ša-sà-ku-ni*
111 1 *u-ša-sà-ku-ni*
111 2 *u*-⸢*ša*⸣-[...]

112 0 ^{d}*en-líl*
112 1 ^{d}*en-líl*
112 2 [...]

113 0 *ù*
113 1 *ù*
113 2 [...]

114 0 ^{d}UTU
114 1 ^{d}UTU
114 2 [...]

115 0 SUḪUŠ-*šu*
115 1 SUḪUŠ-*šu*
115 2 [...]

116 0 *li-sú-ḫa*
116 1 *li-sú-ḫa*
116 2 [...]

117 0 *ù*
117 1 *ù*
117 2 [...]

118 0 ŠE.NUMUN-*šu*
118 1 ŠE.NUMUN-*šu*
118 2 [...]

119 0 *li-il-qù-tá*
119 1 *li-il-qù-tá*
119 2 *l*[*i*-...]

120 0 *ma-ma-na*
120 1 *ma-ma-na*
120 2 *m*[*a*-...]

121 0 DÙL
121 1 DÙL
121 2 DÙ[L]

122 0 *śu*$_4$-⸢*a*⸣
122 1 *śu*$_4$-⸢*a*⸣
122 2 [...]

123 0 *u-a-*⸢*ḫa-ru*⸣
123 1 *u-a-*⸢*ḫa-ru*⸣
123 2 *u-*⸢*a*⸣-[...]

124 0 ᵈ⸢*en*⸣*-lí*l
124 1 ᵈ⸢*en*⸣*-líl*
124 2 ᵈ*e*[*n-líl*]

125 0 MU-*śu*
125 1 MU-*śu*
125 2 ⸢MU⸣-[*śu*]

126 0 *li-a-ḫir*$_X$(ḪA+ŠÚ)
126 1 *li-a-ḫir*$_X$(ḪA+ŠÚ)
126 2 *l*[*i-*...]

127 0 GIŠ.TUKUL-*śu*
127 1 GIŠ.TUKUL-*śu*
127 2 [...]

128 0 *li-iš-bir*$_5$
128 1 *li-iš-bir*$_5$
128 2 [...]

129 0 *maḫ-rí-íś*
129 1 *maḫ-rí-íś*
129 2 [...]

130 0 ᵈ⸢*en-líl*⸣
130 1 ᵈ⸢*en-líl*⸣
130 2 [...]

131 0 *e* DU
131 1 *e* DU
131 2 [...]

Colophon

1 0 mu-sar-ra ki-gal-ba
1 1 mu-sar-ra ki-gal-ba
1 2 [...]

2 0 igi-lugal-zà-ge-si-šè
2 1 igi-lugal-zà-ge-si-šè
2 2 [...]

3 0 a-ab-sar
3 1 a-ab-sar
3 2 [...]

1 0 *ìl-a-*ba_4
1 1 *ìl-a-*ba_4
1 2 *ìl-a-*ba_4

2 0 *il-śu*
2 1 [*:*]*l-śu*
2 2 *il-śu*

3 0 *śar-ru-*GI
3 1 *śar-ru-*GI
3 2 *śar-ru-*⸢GI⸣

4 0 LUGAL
4 1 LUGAL
4 2 LUGAL

5 0 KIŠ
5 1 KIŠ
5 2 K[IŠ]

6 0 *in* 9
6 1 ⸢*in* 9⸣
6 2 *in* 9

7 0 *ki-ṣé-rí*
7 1 *ki-ṣé-rí*
7 2 ⸢*ki*⸣*-ṣé-rí*

8 0 *a-kà-dè*.KI
8 1 *a-kà-dè*.KI
8 2 *a-kà-dè*.KI

9 0 URU.KI
9 1 URU.KI
9 2 URU.KI

10 0 UNU.KI
10 1 [UN]U.⸢KI⸣
10 2 UNU.⸢KI⸣

11 0 SAG.GIŠ.RA
11 1 [...]
11 2 SAG.GIŠ.RA

12 0 *ù*
12 1 [...]
12 2 *ù*

13 0 *in* REC 169
13 1 [...]
13 2 *in* REC 169

14 0 $iš_{11}$*-ar*
14 1 [...]
14 2 $iš_{11}$*-ar*

15 0 *ù*
15 1 *ù*
15 2 *ù*

16 0 ⸢50⸣ ÉNSI
16 1 ⸢50⸣ ÉNSI
16 2 Traces

17 0 *ù*
17 1 *ù*
17 2 (Traces)

18 0 LUGAL
18 1 LUGAL
18 2 (Traces)

19 0 $šu_4$*-ma*
19 1 $šu_4$*-ma*
19 2 (Traces)

20 0 ŠU.DU_8.A
20 1 ŠU.DU_8.A
20 2 [...]

21 0 *ù*
21 1 *ù*
21 2 [...]

22 0 *in na*-GUR$_8$-*za-am*.KI
22 1 *in na*-GUR$_8$-*za-am*.KI
22 2 [...]

23 0 REC 169
23 1 REC 169
23 2 [...]

24 0 *iš-ni-a-ma*
24 1 *iš-ni-a-ma*
24 2 [...]

25 0 *íś-ku$_8$-na-ma*
25 1 *íś-ku$_8$-na-ma*
25 2 [...]

26 0 *iš$_{11}$-ar*
26 1 *iš$_{11}$-ar*
26 2 [...]

27 0 *ù*
27 1 *ù*
27 2 [...]

28 0 ⌜*in*⌝ ÚRI.KI
28 1 ⌜*in*⌝ ÚRI.KI
28 2 [...]

29 0 *úś*-x-*tá-lí-śa-ma*
29 1 *úś*-x-*tá-lí-śa-ma*
29 2 [...]

30 0 *im$_4$-tá-aḫ-ṣa-ma*
30 1 *im$_4$-tá-aḫ-ṣa-ma*
30 2 [...]

31 0 *iš$_{11}$-ar*
31 1 *iš$_{11}$-ar*
31 2 [...]

32 0 *ù*
32 1 (erasure) *ù*
32 2 [...]

33 0 UB.ME.KI
33 1 UB.ME.KI
33 2 [...]

34 0 *in* REC 169
34 1 *in* REC 169
34 2 [...]

35 0 *iš$_{11}$-ar*
35 1 *iš$_{11}$-ar*
35 2 [...]

36 0 *ù*
36 1 *ù*
36 2 [...]

37 0 URU.KI
37 1 URU.KI
37 2 [...]

38 0 SAG.⌜GIŠ⌝.RA
38 1 SAG.⌜GIŠ⌝.RA
38 2 [...]

39 0 *ù*
39 1 *ù*
39 2 [...]

40 0 *lagaš*(LA.BUR.ŠIR).KI
40 1 *lagaš*(LA.BUR.ŠIR).KI
40 2 [...]

41 0 *in* REC 169
41 1 *in* REC 169
41 2 [...]

42 0 [*iš*$_{11}$*-ar*]
42 1 [...]
42 2 [...]

43 0 ⸢*ù*⸣
43 1 ⸢*ù*⸣
43 2 [...]

44 0 GIŠ.⸢TUKUL⸣-[*kí-śu*]
44 1 GIŠ.⸢TUKUL⸣-[...]
44 2 [...]

45 0 ⸢*in*⸣ [*ti-a-am-tim*]
45 1 ⸢*in*⸣ [...]
45 2 [...]

46 0 Ì.[LUḪ]
46 1 Ì.[...]
46 2 [...]

Colophon

1 0 ⸢mu⸣-sa[r-ra alan-na]
1 1 ⸢mu⸣-sa[rra ...]
1 2 [...]

2 0 ⸢ki-gal⸣-[bi nu-sar]
2 1 ⸢ki-gal⸣-[bi ...]
2 2 [...]

Caption

1′ 0 *ìl-a-ba*$_{4}$
1′ 1 [...]
1′ 2 *ìl-a-ba*$_{4}$

2′ 0 KALA.G[A]
2′ 1 KA[LA.GA]
2′ 2 KALA.G[A]

3′ 0 *ì-li*
3′ 1 [...]
3′ 2 *ì-li*

4′ 0 ^{d}*en-líl*
4′ 1 [...]
4′ 2 ^{d}*en-líl*

5′ 0 GIŠ.TUKUL
5′ 1 [...]
5′ 2 GIŠ.TUKUL

6′ 0 IN.NA.⸢SUM⸣
6′ 1 [...]
6′ 2 IN.NA.⸢SUM⸣

1 0 ⸢*a*⸣-*na* ^{d}*en-líl*
1 1 [...]
1 2 ⸢*a*⸣-*na* ^{d}*cn-líl*

2 0 *śar-ru*-GI
2 1 [...]
2 2 *śar-ru*-GI

3 0 LUGAL ⸢KIŠ⸣
3 1 [...]
3 2 LUGAL ⸢KIŠ⸣

4 0 SAG.GIŠ.RA
4 1 [...]
4 2 SAG.GIŠ.RA

5 0 NIM.KI
5 1 [...]
5 2 NIM.KI

6 0 *ù*
6 1 [...]
6 2 *ù*

7 0 *pá-ra*-⸢*aḫ*⸣-*śum*.KI
7 1 [...]
7 2 *pá-ra*-⸢*aḫ*⸣-*śum*.KI

8 0 *a-na* ^{d}*en-líl*
8 1 [...]
8 2 *a-na* ^{d}*en-líl*

9 0 A.MU.RU
9 1 [...]
9 2 A.MU.RU

10 0 *ša* DUB *śu*$_{4}$-*a*
10 1 [...]
10 2 *ša* DUB *śu*$_{4}$-*a*

11 0 *u-śa-sà-ku-ni*
11 1 [...]
11 2 *u-śa-sà-ku-ni*

12 0 ^{d}*en-líl*
12 1 [...]
12 2 ^{d}*en-líl*

13 0 *ù*
13 1 [...]
13 2 *ù*

14 0 ^{d}UTU
14 1 [...]
14 2 ^{d}UTU

15 0 ⸢SUḪUŠ-*śu*⸣
15 1 S[UḪUŠ-*śu*]
15 2 ⸢SUḪUŠ-*śu*⸣

16 0 *li-sú-ḫa*
16 1 *l*[*i*-...]
16 2 *li-sú-ḫa*

17 0 *ù*
17 1 [...]
17 2 *ù*

18 0 ŠE.N[UMUN-*śu*]
18 1 Š[E.NUMUN-*śu*]
18 2 ŠE.N[UMUN-*śu*]

19 0 *l*[*i-il-qù-tá*]
19 1 *l*[*i*-...]
19 2 [...]

Colophon 1

1 0 [m]u-⌈sar⌉-[ra]
1 1 [...]
1 2 [m]u-⌈sar⌉-[ra]

2 0 [ki-gal-ba]
2 1 [...]
2 2 [...]

Caption 1′

1 0 ⌈x-*su-uḫ-ru*⌉
1 1 ⌈x-*su-uḫ-ru*⌉
1 2 [...]

2 0 ÉNS[I]
2 1 ÉNS[I]
2 2 [...]

3 0 *ši-rí-ḫi-im*.[KI]
3 1 *ši-rí-ḫi-im*.[KI]
3 2 [...]

Caption 2′

1 0 *si-id-ga-*⌈*ù*⌉
1 1 *si-id-ga-*⌈*ù*⌉
1 2 [...]

2 0 GÌR.NÍTA
2 1 GÌR.NÍTA
2 2 [...]

3 0 *pá-ra-aḫ-*⌈*śum*⌉.[KI]
3 1 *pá-ra-aḫ-*⌈*śum*⌉.[KI]
3 2 [...]

Caption 3′

1 0 *sa*-NAM-*śi-m*[*u-ut*]
1 1 *sa*-NAM-*śi-m*[*u-ut*]
1 2 [...]

2 0 GÌR.NÍ[TA]
2 1 GÌR.NÍ[TA]
2 2 [...]

3 0 NIM.KI
3 1 NIM.KI
3 2 [...]

Caption 4

1 0 *lu-uḫ-iš-an*
1 1 *lu-uḫ-iš-an*
1 2 [...]

2 0 DUMU *ḫi-śi-*⌈*ib*⌉-[*ra-si-n*]*i*
2 1 DUMU *ḫi-śi-*⌈*ib*⌉-[*ra-si-n*]*i*
2 2 [...]

3 0 LUGAL
3 1 LUGAL
3 2 [...]

4 0 NIM.KI
4 1 NIM.KI
4 2 [...]

Caption 5′

1 0 *kum-du-pum*
1 1 *kum-du-pum*
1 2 [...]

Caption 5′ (continued)

2 0 ⸢DI⸣.[KU$_5$]
2 1 ⸢DI⸣.[KU$_5$]
2 2 [...]

3 0 [*pá-ra-aḫ-śum*.KI]
3 1 [...]
3 2 [...]

Caption 6′

1 0 [...]
1 1 [...]
1 2 [...]

2 0 8 L[Ú ...]
2 1 8 L[Ú ...]
2 2 [...]

3 0 x x x [...]
3 1 x x x [...]
3 2 [...]

4 0 x ⸢GIŠ⸣.TUKUL ⸢GIŠ.ERIN⸣
4 1 x ⸢GIŠ⸣.TUKUL ⸢GIŠ.ERIN⸣
4 2 [...]

Caption 7′

1 0 *ḫi-śi-ib-ra-si-ni*
1 1 *ḫi-śi-ib-ra-si-ni*
1 2 [...]

2 0 LUGAL
2 1 LUGAL
2 2 [...]

3 0 NIM.KI
3 1 NIM.KI
3 2 [...]

Caption 8′

1 0 x-RA.NE.NE A.AL.DAB$_5$
1 1 x-RA.NE.NE A.AL.DAB$_5$
1 2 [x].⸢E⸣ [...]

2 0 ŠU DU$_{10}$.BA A.AB.RI
2 1 ŠU DU$_{10}$.BA A.AB.RI
2 2 [...]

3 0 *ib-ba-li*
3 1 *ib-ba-li*
3 2 *ib-ba-l*[*i*]

Colophon 2

1 0 šà-bi an-na
1 1 šà-bi-an-x
1 2 šà-bi an-na

2 0 ki-gal-ba ^{d}en-líl ^{d}inanna
2 1 ki-gal-ba ^{d}en-líl ⸢^{d}inanna⸣
2 2 ki-gal-ba ^{d}en-líl ^{d}inanna

1 0 [*śar-um*-GI]
1 1 [...]
1 2 [...]

2 0 [lugal]-
2 1 [...]
2 2 [...]

3 0 [KIS]
3 1 [...]
3 2 [...]

4 0 [34 (x)] SAḪAR-ra
4 1 [...] SAḪAR-ra
4 2 [...]

5 0 [TÙN.KÁ]RA bí-sì
5 1 [TÙN.KÁ]RA bí-sì
5 2 [...]

6 0 bàd-bi
6 1 bàd-bi
6 2 [...]

7 0 ì-gul-gul
7 1 ì-gul-gul
7 2 [...]

8 0 zà-a-ab-ba-ka-šè
8 1 zà-a-ab-ba-ka-šè
8 2 [...]

9 0 má-me-luḫ-ḫa.KI
9 1 má-me-luḫ-ḫa.KI
9 2 [...]

10 0 má-má-gan.KI
10 1 má-má-gan.KI
10 2 [...]

11 0 má-tilmun.KI
11 1 má-tilmun.KI
11 2 [...]

12 0 kar-ag-ge-dè.KI-ka
12 1 kar-ag-ge-dè.KI-ka
12 2 [...]

13 0 bí-kéš
13 1 bí-kéš
13 2 [...]

14 0 ⌈*śar*⌉-*um*-GI
14 1 ⌈*śar*⌉-*um*-GI
14 2 [...]

15 0 ⌈lugal⌉
15 1 ⌈lugal⌉
15 2 [...]

16 0 du$_8$-du$_8$-⌈li⌉.KI-a
16 1 du$_8$-du$_8$-⌈li⌉.KI-(erasure)-a
16 2 [... .K]I-a

17 0 ^{d}da-gan-ra
17 1 ^{d}da-gan-ra
17 2 [^{d}da]-gan-ra

18 0 ki-a mu-na-za
18 1 ki-a mu-na-za
18 2 [... m]u-⌈na⌉-za

19 0 šùd mu-⌈na-de$_6$⌉
19 1 šùd mu-⌈na-de$_6$⌉
19 2 [...]

20 0 kalam-IGI.NIM
20 1 kalam-IGI.NIM
20 2 [...]

21 0 mu-na-sum
21 1 mu-na-sum
21 2 [...]

22 0 ma-rí.KI
22 1 ma-rí.KI
22 2 [...]

23 0 ià-ar-mu-ti.KI
23 1 ià-ar-mu-ti.KI
23 2 [...]

24 0 eb-la.KI
24 1 eb-la.KI
24 2 [...]

25 0 tir-
25 1 tir-
25 2 [...]

26 0 GIŠ.erin
26 1 GIŠ.erin
26 2 [...]

27 0 ḫur-sag-
27 1 ḫur-sag-
27 2 [...]

28 0 kù-ga-šè
28 1 kù-ga-šè
28 2 [...]

29 0 *śar-um*-GI
29 1 *śar-um*-GI
29 2 [...]

30 0 lugal
30 1 lugal
30 2 [...]

31 0 ⸢d⸣en-líl-le
31 1 ⸢d⸣en-líl-le
31 2 [...]

32 0 lú-gaba-ru
32 1 lú-gaba-ru
32 2 [...]

33 0 nu-mu-NI-tuk
33 1 nu-mu-NI-tuk
33 2 [...]

34 0 5,400 érin
34 1 5,400 érin
34 2 [...]

35 0 u$_{4}$-šú-šè
35 1 u$_{4}$-šú-šè
35 2 [...]

36 0 igi-ni-šè
36 1 igi-ni-šè
36 2 [...]

37 0 ninda ì-kú-e
37 1 ninda ì-kú-e
37 2 [...]

38 0 lú mu-⸢sar-ra-e⸣
38 1 lú mu-⸢sar-ra-e⸣
38 2 [...]

39 0 a[b]-ḫa-lam-e-a
39 1 a[b]-ḫa-lam-e-a
39 2 ⸢ab-ḫa-lam-e-a⸣

40 0 an-né
40 1 an-né
40 2 an-né

41 0 mu-ni
41 1 mu-ni
41 2 mu-ni

42 0 ḫé-ḫa-lam-e
42 1 ḫé-ḫa-lam-e
42 2 ⸢ḫé-ḫa-lam-e⸣

43 0 ^{d}en-líl-le
43 1 ^{d}en-líl-le
43 2 ^{d}en-líl-l[e]

44 0 numun-na-ni
44 1 numun-na-ni
44 2 numun-na-[ni]

45 0 ḫé-til-le
45 1 ḫé-til-le
45 2 ḫé-til-le

46 0 ^{d}inanna-ke_4
46 1 ^{d}inanna-ke_4
46 2 ^{d}inanna-⸢ke_4⸣

47 0 e x dumu-na-ni
47 1 [...]-⸢na⸣-ni
47 2 e x dumu-na-⸢ni⸣

48 0 ḫé-ku_5-⸢e⸣
48 1 [...]
48 2 ḫé-ku_5-⸢e⸣

Lacuna

Colophon 2

1 0 mu-sar-ra
1 1 [...]
1 2 mu-sar-ra

2 0 ki-gal-ba
2 1 [...]
2 2 ki-gal-ba

1 0 *ś*[*ar*]-⸢*ru*-GI⸣
1 1 *ś*[*ar*]-⸢*ru*-GI⸣
1 2 [...]

2 0 LUGAL
2 1 LUGAL
2 2 [...]

3 0 KIŠ
3 1 KIŠ
3 2 [...]

4 0 34 REC 169
4 1 34 REC 169
4 2 [...]

5 0 *iš*$_{11}$-*ar*
5 1 *iš*$_{11}$-*ar*
5 2 [...]

6 0 BÀD.BÀD
6 1 BÀD.BÀD
6 2 [...]

7 0 Ì.GUL.GUL
7 1 Ì.GUL.GUL
7 2 [...]

8 0 *a-dì-ma*
8 1 *a-dì-ma*
8 2 [*a-d*]*ì-ma*

9 0 *pu-ti*
9 1 *pu-ti*
9 2 ⸢*pu*⸣-*ti*

10 0 *ti-a-am-tim*
10 1 *ti-a-am-tim*
10 2 *ti-a-am-tim*

11 0 MÁ *me-luḫ-ḫa*
11 1 MÁ *me-luḫ-ḫa*
11 2 MÁ *me-luḫ-ḫa*

12 0 MÁ *má-gan*.KI
12 1 MÁ *má-gan*.KI
12 2 MÁ *má-gan*.KI

13 0 MÁ *tilmun*.KI
13 1 MÁ *tilmun*.KI
13 2 MÁ *tilmun*.KI

14 0 *in kà-rí-im*
14 1 *in kà-rí-im*
14 2 *i*[*n*] *kà-rí-im*

15 0 *ši a-kà-dè*.KI
15 1 *ši a-kà-dè*.KI
15 2 [...]-*dè*.KI

16 0 *ìr-ku-us*
16 1 *ìr-ku-u*[*s*]
16 2 [...]-*u*[*s*]

17 0 ⸢*śar*⸣-*r*[*u*-G]I
17 1 ⸢*śar*⸣-*r*[*u*-G]I
17 2 [...-G]I

18 0 [LUGAL]
18 1 [...]
18 2 [...]

19 0 *in tu-tu-li*.KI
19 1 ⸢*in*⸣ *tu-tu-li*.KI
19 2 *in tu-*[*tu*]-*l*[*i*.KI]

20 0 *a-na*
20 1 *a-na*
20 2 *a-na*

21 0 ^{d}*da-gan*
21 1 ^{d}*da-gan*
21 2 ⸢^{d}⸣[...]

22 0 *úś-kà-en*
22 1 *úś-kà-en*
22 2 *ú*[*ś*-...]

23 0 *ik-ru-ub*
23 1 ⸢*ik-ru-ub*⸣
23 2 *i*[*k*-...]

24 0 *ma-tá*[*m*]
24 1 *ma-tá*[*m*]
24 2 [...]

25 0 *a-lí-tám*
25 1 *a-lí-tám*
25 2 [...]

26 0 *i*-⸢*dì*⸣-*śum*$_6$
26 1 *i*-⸢*dì*⸣-*śum*$_6$
26 2 [...]

27 0 *ma-rí-am*.KI
27 1 *ma-rí-am*.KI
27 2 [...]

28 0 *ià-ar-mu-ti-a-am*.KI
28 1 *ià-ar-mu-ti-a-am*.KI
28 2 [...]

29 0 *eb-la*.KI
29 1 *eb-la*.KI
29 2 [...]

30 0 *a-dì-ma*
30 1 *a-dì-ma*
30 2 [...]

31 0 GIŠ.TIR
31 1 GIŠ.TIR
31 2 [...]

32 0 GIŠ.ERIN
32 1 GIŠ.ERIN
32 2 [...]

33 0 *ù*
33 1 *ù*
33 2 [...]

34 0 KUR.KUR
34 1 KUR.KUR
34 2 [...]

35 0 KÙ
35 1 KÙ
35 2 [...]

36 0 *śar-ru*-GI
36 1 *śar-ru*-GI
36 2 [...]

37 0 LUGA[L]
37 1 LUGA[L]
37 2 [...]

38 0 *šu* ^{d}⸢*en-líl*⸣
38 1 *šu* ^{d}⸢*en-líl*⸣
38 2 [...]

39 0 *ma-ḫi-ra*
39 1 *ma-ḫi-ra*
39 2 [...]

40 0 *la i-dì-śum*$_6$
40 1 *la i-dì-śum*$_6$
40 2 [...]

41 0 5,400 GURUŠ.GURUŠ
41 1 5,400 GURUŠ.GURUŠ
41 2 [...]

42 0 *u-um-śum*$_6$
42 1 *u-um-śum*$_6$
42 2 [...]

43 0 *ma-ḫar-śu*
43 1 *ma-ḫar-śu*
43 2 [...]

44 0 NINDA KÚ
44 1 NINDA KÚ
44 2 [...]

1 0 [*śar-ru*-GI]
1 1 [...]
1 2 [...]

2 0 [LUGAL]
2 1 [...]
2 2 [...]

3 0 [KIŠ]
3 1 [...]
3 2 [...]

4 0 30+[4 REC 169]
4 1 30+[4 REC 169]
4 2 [...]

5 0 *iš*$_{11}$-*a*[*r*]
5 1 *iš*$_{11}$-*a*[*r*]
5 2 [...]

6 0 URU.⌈KI⌉.UR[U KI]
6 1 URU.⌈KI⌉.UR[U.KI]
6 2 [...]

7 0 *sà-ar-ru-t*[*im*]
7 1 *sà-ar-ru-t*[*im*]
7 2 [...]

8 0 *u id* ⌈x⌉-[...]
8 1 *u id* ⌈x⌉-[...]
8 2 [...]

9 0 [...]
9 1 [...]
9 2 [...]

10 0 *u* [...]
10 1 *u* [...]
10 2 [...]

Lacuna

1′ 0 M[Á *má-gan*.KI]
1′ 1 M[Á ...]
1′ 2 [...]

2′ 0 M[Á *tilmun*.KI]
2′ 1 M[Á ...]
2′ 2 [...]

3′ 0 *i*[*n kà-rí-im*]
3′ 1 *i*[*n* ...]
3′ 2 [...]

4′ 0 *ši* ⌈*a*⌉-[*kà-dè*.KI]
4′ 1 *ši* ⌈*a*⌉-[...]
4′ 2 [...]

5′ 0 *ìr*-[*ku-us*]
5′ 1 *ìr*-[...]
5′ 2 [...]

6′ 0 *śar*-[*ru*-GI]
6′ 1 *śar*-[...]
6′ 2 [...]

7′ 0 LU[GAL]
7′ 1 LU[GAL]
7′ 2 [...]

8′ 0 [*in tu-tu-li*.KI]
8′ 1 [...]
8′ 2 [...]

9′ 0 [*a-na*]
9′ 1 [...]
9′ 2 [...]

10′ 0 ⸢^{d}⸣[*da-gan*]
10′ 1 [...]
10′ 2 ⸢^{d}⸣[...]

11′ 0 *ú*[*ś-kà-en*]
11′ 1 [...]
11′ 2 *ú*[*ś-...*]

12′ 0 *ik-ru-u*[*b*]
12′ 1 [...]
12′ 2 *ik-ru-u*[*b*]

13′ 0 *ma-tám*
13′ 1 [*ma*]-*tá*[*m*]
13′ 2 *ma-tám*

14′ 0 *a-lí-tám*
14′ 1 *a-*⸢*lí*⸣*-tám*
14′ 2 *a-l*[*í-tám*]

15′ 0 *i-dì-śum*$_{6}$
15′ 1 *i-dì-śum*$_{6}$
15′ 2 ⸢*i*⸣-[*dì*]-⸢*śum*$_{6}$⸣

16′ 0 *ma-rí-am*.[KI]
16′ 1 *ma-rí-*⸢*am*⸣.[KI]
16′ 2 *ma-rí-a*[*m*.KI]

17′ 0 *ià-ar-mu-ti-a-am*.<KI>
17′ 1 *ià-a*[*r-...*]
17′ 2 *ià-ar-mu-ti-a-am*.<KI>

18′ 0 *eb-la*.KI
18′ 1 [...]
18′ 2 *eb-la*.KI

19′ 0 [*a-dì*]-*ma*
19′ 1 [...]
19′ 2 [...]-*ma*

20′ 0 ⸢GIŠ⸣.T[IR] ⸢GIŠ.ERIN⸣
20′ 1 [...]
20′ 2 ⸢GIŠ⸣.T[IR] ⸢GIŠ.ERIN⸣

21′ 0 *ù* ⸢KUR.KUR⸣ K[Ù]
21′ 1 [...]
21′ 2 *ù* ⸢KUR.KUR⸣ K[Ù]

22′ 0 *śar-ru*-GI
22′ 1 [...]
22′ 2 *śar-ru*-GI

23′ 0 LUGAL KIŠ
23′ 1 [...]
23′ 2 LUGAL KIŠ

24′ 0 *šu* ^{d}*en-líl*
24′ 1 [...]
24′ 2 *šu* ^{d}*en-líl*

25′ 0 *ma-ḫi-ra*
25′ 1 [...]
25′ 2 *ma-ḫi-ra*

26′ 0 *la ì-dì-śum*$_{6}$
26′ 1 [...]
26′ 2 *la ì-dì-śum*$_{6}$

27′ 0 5,400 GURUŠ
27′ 1 [...]
27′ 2 5,400 GURUŠ

28′ 0 *u-um-śum*$_{6}$
28′ 1 [...]
28′ 2 *u-um-śum*$_{6}$

29′ 0 *ma-ḫar-śu*
29′ 1 [...]
29′ 2 *ma-ḫar-śu*

30′ 0 NINDA KÙ
30′ 1 [...]
30′ 2 NINDA KÙ

Colophon

1 0 ⸢mu-sar-ra alan-na⸣
1 1 [...]
1 2 ⸢mu-sar-ra alan-na⸣

Caption 1

1 0..NÌ.LA+IB UNU.KI
1 1 [...]
1 2 NÌ.LA+IB UNU.KI

Caption 2

1 0 lugal-zà-ge-si
1 1 [...]
1 2 lugal-zà-ge-si

2 0 LUGAL UNU.KI
2 1 [...]
2 2 LUGAL UNU.KI

Caption 3

1 0 lú-^{d}nanna
1 1 [...]
1 2 lú-^{d}nanna

2 0 LUGAL ŠEŠ.[UNU.K]I
2 1 [...]
2 2 LUGAL ŠEŠ.[UNU.K]I

Caption 4

1 0 NÌ.LA+IB Š[EŠ.UNU.KI]
1 1 [...]
1 2 NÌ.LA+IB Š[EŠ.UNU.KI]

Caption 5

1 0 NÌ.LA+IB UB.[ME.KI]
1 1 [...]
1 2 NÌ.LA+IB UB.[ME.KI]

Caption 6

1 0 mes-zi É[NSI]
1 1 [...]
1 2 mes-zi É[NSI]

2 0 *lag*[*aš*](LA.BUR.[ŠIR]).[KI]
2 1 [...]
2 2 *lag*[*aš*](LA.BUR.[ŠIR]).[KI]

Caption 7

1 0 mes-[é]
1 1 [...]
1 2 mes-[é]

2 0 É[NSI]
2 1 [...]
2 2 É[NSI]

3 0 ⸢UB⸣.M[E.KI]
3 1 [...]
3 2 ⸢UB⸣.M[E.KI]

Lacuna

1 0 *ś*[*ar-ru*-GI]
1 1 *ś*[*ar-ru*-GI]
1 2 [...]

2 0 [...]
2 1 [...]
2 2 [...]

3 0 [...]
3 1 [...]
3 2 [...]

4 0 [...]
4 1 [...]
4 2 [...]

5 0 [...]
5 1 [...]
5 2 [...]

6 0 [...]
6 1 [...]
6 2 [...]

7 0 [...]
7 1 [...]
7 2 [...]

8 0 [...]
8 1 [...]
8 2 [...]

9 0 [...]
9 1 [...]
9 2 [...]

10 0 x [...] x [...]
10 1 x [...] x [...]
10 2 [...]

11 0 *da-an*
11 1 *da-an*
11 2 [...]

12 0 ^{d}*en-líl*
12 1 ^{d}*en-líl*
12 2 [...]

13 0 *u-kál-lim*
13 1 *u-kál-lim*
13 2 [...]

14 0 *ma-ma-na*
14 1 *ma-ma-na*
14 2 *m*[*a-*...]

15 0 *pá-ni-śu*
15 1 *pá-ni-śu*
15 2 ⸢*pá*⸣-*n*[*i-śu*]

16 0 *ù-la*
16 1 *ù-la*
16 2 *ù-l*[*a*]

17 0 *u-ba-al*
17 1 *u-ba-al*
17 2 *u-ba-a*[*l*]

18 0 *ti-a-am-tám*
18 1 *ti-a-am-tám*
18 2 *ti-a-a*[*m-tám*]

19 0 *a-lí-tám*
19 1 *a-lí-tám*
19 2 *a-l*[*í-tám*]

20 0 *ù*
20 1 *ù*
20 2 ⸢*ù*⸣

21 0 *śa-pil-*[*tám*]
21 1 *śa-pil-*[*tám*]
21 2 x [...]

22 0 *i-dì-śum*$_6$
22 1 *i-dì-śum*$_6$
22 2 x [...]

23 0 *śar-ru*-GI
23 1 *śar-ru*-GI
23 2 *ś*[*ar-*...]

24 0 LUGAL
24 1 LUGAL
24 2 L[UGAL]

25 0 KIŠ
25 1 KIŠ
25 2 [...]

26 0 ⸢ra⸣-x [x x]
26 1 ⸢ra⸣-x [x x]
26 2 x-x [...]

27 0 GÌ[R.N[ÍTA]-*ś*[*u*]
27 1 [...]
27 2 GÌR.N[ÍTA]-*ś*[*u*]

Colophon

1 0 mu-⸢sar⸣-ra ki-gal-b[a]
1 1 [...]
1 2 mu-⸢sar⸣-ra ki-gal-b[a]

1 0 *śar-r*[*u*-GI]
1 1 *śar-r*[*u*-GI]
1 2 [...]

2 0 LU[GAL]
2 1 LU[GAL]
2 2 [...]

3 0 [KIŠ]
3 1 [...]
3 2 [...]

Lacuna of 6 lines

10 0 [*maḫ*]-*rí*-[*íś*]
10 1 [...]
10 2 [*maḫ*]-*rí*-[*íś*]

11 0 ^{d}*en-líl*
11 1 [...]
11 2 ^{d}*en-líl*

12 0 *śar-ru*-GI
12 1 [...]
12 2 *śar-ru*-GI

13 0 LUGAL KIŠ
13 1 [...]
13 2 LUGAL KIŠ

14 0 *ì-nu*
14 1 [...]
14 2 *ì-nu*

15 0 ^{d}*en-líl*
15 1 [...]
15 2 ^{d}*en-líl*

16 0 GIŠ.GIDRU
16 1 [...]
16 2 GIŠ.GIDRU

17 0 *i-dì-śum*$_{6}$-⸢*ma*⸣
17 1 *i-d*[*ì*-...]
17 2 *i-dì-śum*$_{6}$-⸢*ma*⸣

18 0 GÉŠTU
18 1 GÉŠ[TU]
18 2 GÉŠTU

19 0 *u-wa-ti-ir-śum*$_{6}$
19 1 [...]
19 2 *u-wa-ti-ir-śum*$_{6}$

20 0 [...] x x
20 1 [...]
20 2 [...] x x

21 0 *ú*-⸢*śa*⸣-*z*[*i-iz*]
21 1 [...]
21 2 *ú*-⸢*śa*⸣-*z*[*i-iz*]

22 0 DA-⸢x⸣
22 1 [...]
22 2 DA-⸢x⸣

23 0 *śar-ru*-GI
23 1 [...]
23 2 *śar-ru*-GI

24 0 ^{d}*en-líl*
24 1 [...]
24 2 ^{d}*en-líl*

25 0 *u-kál-lim*
25 1 *u-k*[*á-lim*]
25 2 *u*-⸢*kál*⸣-*lim*

26 0 *ma-ma-na*
26 1 *ma-ma-na*
26 2 *ma-ma-na*

27 0 *pá-ni-śu*
27 1 *pá-ni-śu*
27 2 [*pá-ni*]-*śu*

28 0 *ù-la*
28 1 *ù-la*
28 2 [*ù*]-*la*

29 0 *u-ba-al*
29 1 *u-ba-*⸢*al*⸣
29 2 *u-ba-al*

30 0 SUḪUŠ x x x
30 1 SUḪUŠ x [...]
30 2 SUHUŠ x x x

31 0 ŚA.DÚ *ì-li*
31 1 [...]
31 2 ŚA.DÚ *ì-li*

32 0 *ra-bí-um*
32 1 [...]
32 2 *ra-bí-um*

Colophon

1 0 mu-sar-ra ⸢alan⸣-na
1 1 [...]
1 2 mu-sar-ra ⸢alan⸣-na

1 0 en-ḫ[é]-du_7-an-na
1 1 en-ḫ[é]-du_7-an-na
1 2 [...-d]u_7-an-na

2 0 MUNUS.NUNUZ.ZI.^{d}NANNA
2 1 MUNUS.NUNUZ.ZI.^{d}NANNA
2 2 [...].^{d}NANNA

3 0 dam-^{d}nanna
3 1 dam-^{d}nanna
3 2 [dam]-⸢d⸣nanna

4 0 dumu-
4 1 dumu-
4 2 [dumu]-

5 0 ⸢*śar-ru*⸣-GI
5 1 ⸢*śar-ru*⸣-[GI]
5 2 [*śar-r*]*u*-GI

6 0 [lugal]-
6 1 [lugal]-
6 2 [lugal]-

7 0 ⸢KIŠ⸣
7 1 ⸢KIŠ⸣
7 2 [K]IŠ

8 0 [é-^{d}INAN]NA.ZA.ZA
8 1 [é-^{d}INAN]NA.ZA.ZA
8 2 [é-^{d}INAN]NA.ZA.ZA

9 0 [ur]i_5.KI-ma-ka
9 1 [...]
9 2 [ur]i_5.KI-ma-ka

10 0 [bára]-si-ga
10 1 [...]
10 2 [bára]-si-ga

11 0 [b]í-e-dù
11 1 [...]
11 2 [b]í-e-dù

12 0 bára banšur-an-na
12 1 [...-n]a
12 2 bára banšur-an-na

13 0 mu-šè bi-sa_4
13 1 mu-šè bi-[sa_4]
13 2 mu-šè bi-sa_4

1 0 *rí-mu-úś*
1 1 *rí-mu-úś*
1 2 *rí-mu-úś*

2 0 LUGAL
2 1 [...]
2 2 LUGAL

3 0 KIŠ
3 1 [...]
3 2 KIŠ

4 0 ⸢*in*⸣ REC 169
4 1 [...]
4 2 ⸢*in*⸣ REC 169

5 0 *adab*.KI
5 1 [...]
5 2 *adab*.KI

6 0 *ù*
6 1 [...]
6 2 *ù*

7 0 ⸢*zàbala*.KI⸣
7 1 [...]
7 2 ⸢*zàbala*.KI⸣

8 0 *iš*$_{11}$-⸢*ar*⸣
8 1 ⸢*iš*$_{11}$⸣-[*ar*]
8 2 ⸢*iš*$_{11}$-*ar*⸣

9 1 ⸢*ù*⸣
9 2 [*ù*]
9 3 ⸢*ù*⸣

10 0 15,720 LAL 2 GURUŠ.GURUŠ
10 1 ⸢15,720 LAL 2⸣ GURUŠ.GURUŠ
10 2 15,720 LAL 2 GURUŠ.GURUŠ

11 0 *u-śa-am-qí-it*
11 1 *u-śa-am-qí-it*
11 2 *u-śa-am-qí-it*

12 0 14,580 LAL 4 LÚ×ÉŠ
12 1 14,580 ⸢LAL 4⸣ LÚ×ÉŠ
12 2 14,580 LAL 4 LÚ×[x]

13 0 ŠU.DU$_{8}$.⸢A⸣
13 1 ŠU.DU$_{8}$.A
13 2 ŠU.DU$_{8}$.⸢A⸣

14 0 *ù*
14 1 *ù*
14 2 *ù*

15 0 mes-ki-gal-la
15 1 mes-ki-gal-la
15 2 mes-ki-ga[l-la]

16 0 ÉNSI
16 1 ÉNSI
16 2 ÉNSI

17 0 *adab*.KI
17 1 *adab*.KI
17 2 *ad*[*ab*.KI]

18 0 ŠU.DU$_{8}$.A
18 1 ŠU.DU$_{8}$.A
18 2 [...]

19 0 *ù*
19 1 *ù*
19 2 [...]

20 0 lugal-gal-zu
20 1 lugal-gal-zu
20 2 [...]

21 0 ÉNSI
21 1 ÉNSI
21 2 [...]

22 0 *zàbala*.KI
22 1 *zàbala*.KI
22 2 [...]

23 0 ŠU.DU$_8$.A
23 1 ŠU.DU$_8$.A
23 2 [...]

24 0 URU.KI-⸢*šu-ni*⸣
24 1 URU.KI-⸢*šu-ni*⸣
24 2 [...]

25 0 ⸢SAG.GIŠ⸣.[RA]
25 1 ⸢SAG.GIŠ⸣.[RA]
25 2 [...]

26 0 [*ù*]
26 1 [...]
26 2 [...]

27 0 [BÀD-*šu-ni*]
27 1 [...]
27 2 [...]

28 0 [Ì.GUL.GUL]
28 1 [...]
28 2 [...]

29 0 [*ù*]
29 1 [...]
29 2 [...]

30 0 [*in* URU.KI-*šu-ni*]
30 1 [...]
30 2 [...]

31 0 [N GURUŠ.GURUŠ]
31 1 [...]
31 2 [...]

32 0 *u*-⸢*šu-ṣí-am*⸣-*ma*
32 1 *u*-⸢*šu-ṣí-am*⸣-*ma*
32 2 [...]

33 0 *a-na*
33 1 *a-na*
33 2 [...]

34 0 *kà-ra-sí*-[*m*]
34 1 *kà-ra-sí-i*[*m*]
34 2 [...]

35 0 *iš*-⸢*kùn*⸣
35 1 *iš*-⸢*kùn*⸣
35 2 [...]

36 0 *ša* DU[B]
36 1 *ša* DU[B]
36 2 [...]

37 0 *šu*$_4$-*a*
37 1 *šu*$_4$-*a*
37 2 [...]

38 0 ⸢*u*⸣-*ša-sà*-⸢*ku-ni*⸣
38 1 ⸢*u*⸣-*ša-sà*-⸢*ku-ni*⸣
38 2 [...]

39 0 [^{d}]*en-líl*
39 1 [^{d}]*en-líl*
39 2 [...]

40 0 *ù*
40 1 *ù*
40 2 [...]
41 0 [^{d}]UTU

41 1 [^{d}]UTU
41 2 [...]

42 0 [SUḪUŠ-*šu*]
42 1 [...]
42 2 [...]

43 0 [*li-sú-ḫa*]
43 1 [...]
43 2 [...]

44 0 *ù*
44 1 *ù*
44 2 [...]

45 0 Š[E.NU]MUN-*šu*
45 1 Š[E.NU]MUN-*šu*
45 2 [...]

46 0 *l*[*i*]-*il*-⌈*qù*⌉-*tá*
46 1 *l*[*i*]-*il*-⌈*qù*⌉-*tá*
46 2 [...]

Colophon

1 0 ⌈mùš⌉ ki-gal ki-[ta]
1 1 ⌈mùš⌉ ki-gal ki-[ta]
1 2 [...]

2 0 egir-ra-⌈ni-šè⌉
2 1 egir-ra-⌈ni-šè⌉
2 2 [...]

1 0 *rí-mu-úś*
1 1 *rí-mu-úś*
1 2 [...]

2 0 [L]UG[AL]
2 1 [L]UG[AL]
2 2 [...]

3 0 KI[Š]
3 1 KI[Š]
3 2 [...]

4 0 *in* ⌈REC 169⌉
4 1 *in* ⌈REC 169⌉
4 2 [...]

5 0 ⌈UB.ME⌉.KI
5 1 ⌈UB.ME⌉.KI
5 2 [...]

6 0 ⌈*ù*⌉
6 1 ⌈*ù*⌉
6 2 [...]

7 0 KI.AN.KI
7 1 KI.AN.KI
7 2 [...]

8 0 *iš*$_{11}$-[*a*]*r*
8 1 *iš*$_{11}$-[*a*]*r*
8 2 [...]

9 0 *ù*
9 1 *ù*
9 2 [...]

10 0 ⌈8,900⌉ GURUŠ.GURUŠ
10 1 ⌈8,900⌉ GURUŠ.GURUŠ
10 2 [...]

11 0 [*u*]-*śa*-⌈*am*⌉-*qí*-⌈*it*⌉
11 1 [*u*]-*śa*-⌈*am*⌉-*qí*-⌈*it*⌉
11 2 [...]

12 0 ⌈3,540⌉ LÚ×KÁR
12 1 ⌈3,540⌉ LÚ×KÁR
12 2 [...]

13 0 [ŠU.DU$_8$.A]
13 1 [...]'
13 2 [...]

14 0 *ù*
14 1 [...]
14 2 *ù*

15 0 ⌈*en*⌉-x
15 1 [...]
15 2 ⌈*en*⌉-x

16 0 ÉNSI ⌈UB.ME⌉.KI
16 1 [...]
16 2 ÉNSI ⌈UB.ME⌉.KI

17 0 ŠU.DU$_8$.A
17 1 [...]
17 2 ŠU.DU$_8$.A

18 0 *ù*
18 1 *ù*
18 2 *ù*

19 0 lugal-KA
19 1 lugal-KA
19 2 lugal-KA

20 0 ÉNSI
20 1 ÉNSI
20 2 ÉNSI

21 0 KI.AN.KI
21 1 KI.AN.KI
21 2 KI.AN.KI

22 0 ŠU.DU$_8$.A
22 1 ŠU.DU$_8$.A
22 2 ŠU.DU$_8$.A

23 0 *ù*
23 1 *ù*
23 2 *ù*

24 0 URU.KI-*śu-ni*
24 1 ⌈URU⌉.K[I-...]
24 2 URU.KI-*śu-ni*

25 0 SAG.GIŠ.RA
25 1 SAG.GIŠ.[RA]
25 2 SAG.GIŠ.RA

26 0 *ù*
26 1 *ù*
26 2 *ù*

27 0 BÀD-*śu-ni*
27 1 BÀD-*śu-ni*
27 2 BÀD-*śu-ni*

28 0 Ì.GUL.GUL
28 1 Ì.GUL.GUL
28 2 Ì.GUL.GUL

29 0 *ù*
29 1 *ù*
29 2 *ù*

30 0 *in* URU.KI-*śu-ni*
30 1 *in* URU.KI-*śu-ni*
30 2 *in* URU.KI-*śu-ni*

31 0 3,600 GURUŠ.GURUŠ
31 1 3,600 GURUŠ.GURUŠ
31 2 3,600 GURUŠ.GURUŠ

32 0 *u-śu-ṣí-am-ma*
32 1 *u-śu-ṣí-am-ma*
32 2 *u-śu-ṣí-am-ma*

33 0 *a-na*
33 1 *a-na*
33 2 *a-na*

34 0 *kà-ra-śi-im*
34 1 *kà-ra-śi-im*
34 2 *kà-ra-śi-im*

35 0 *iś-kùn*
35 1 *iś-kùn*
35 2 *iś-kùn*

36 0 *ša* DUB
36 1 *ša* DUB
36 2 *ša* DUB

37 0 *śu*$_4$*-a*
37 1 *śu*$_4$*-a*
37 2 *śu*$_4$*-a*

38 0 *u-śa-sà-ku-ni*
38 1 *u-śa-sà-ku-ni*
38 2 <...>

39 0 ^{d}*en-líl*
39 1 ^{d}*en-líl*
39 2 <...>

40 0 ⌈*ù*⌉
40 1 ⌈*ù*⌉
40 2 <...>

41 0 ^{d}[UTU]
41 1 ⸢^{d}⸣[UTU]
41 2 <...>

42 0 [SUḪUŠ-*sú*]
42 1 [...]
42 2 <...>

43 0 [*li-sú-ḫa*]
43 1 [...]
43 2 <...>

44 0 [*ù*]
44 1 [...]
44 2 <...>

45 0 [ŠE.NUMUN-*šu*]
45 1 [...]
45 2 <...>

46 0 [*li-il-qù-tá*]
46 1 [...]
46 2 <...>

Colophon 1

1 0 múš ki-gal ki-ta
1 1 [...]
1 2 múš ki-gal ki-ta

2 0 gùb-bu-na
2 1 [...]
2 2 gùb-bu-na

Caption 1

1 0 *zi-nu-ba*
1 1 *zi-nu-ba*
1 2 *zi-nu-ba*

Caption 1 (continued)

2 0 ŠEŠ
2 1 ŠEŠ
2 2 ŠEŠ

3 0 ÉNSI
3 1 ÉNSI
3 2 É[NSI]

Caption 2

1 0 *a-ša-ar-mu-pi*$_5$
1 1 ⸢*a*⸣-*š*[*a*]-[*a*]*r-mu-pi*$_5$
1 2 *a-ša-ar-mu-p*[*i*$_5$]

2 0 SUKKAL-*šu*
2 1 SUKKAL-*šu*
2 2 [...]

Caption 3

1 0 lugal-gal-z[u](*Text:K[U])
1 2 lugal-g[al-x]
1 2 lugal-gal-z[u](*Text:K[U]

2 0 ÉNS[I]
2 1 ÉNS[I]
2 2 [...]

3 0 *zàbala*.KI
3 1 *zàbala*.KI
3 2 [...]

Caption 4

1 0 ur-^{d}EN.ZU
1 1 ur-^{d}EN.ZU
1 2 ur-^{d}EN.Z[U]

Caption 4 (continued)

2 0 SUKKAL-*śu*
2 1 SUKKAL-*śu*
2 2 [...]

Caption 5

1 0 lugal-KA
1 1 ⌈lugal⌉-KA
1 2 lugal-K[A]

2 0 É[N]SI
2 1 É[N]SI
2 2 [...]

3 0 KI.AN.KI
3 1 KI.AN.KI
3 2 [...]

Caption 6

1 0 giš-šà
1 1 giš-šà
1 2 giš-šà

2 0 GAL.SUKKAL-*śu*
2 1 GAL.SUKKAL-*śu*
2 2 G[AL.SUKKAL-*śu*]

Caption 7

1 0 ki-tuš-íd
1 1 ki-tuš-íd
1 2 ki-tuš-íd

2 0 ÉNSI
2 1 ÉNSI
2 2 [...]

Caption 7 (continued)

3 0 lagaš(LA.ŠIR.BUR).KI
3 1 lagaš(LA.ŠIR.BUR).KI
3 2 [...]

Caption 8

1 0 ad-da
1 1 ad-da
1 2 ad-da

2 0 GÌR.NITA
2 1 GÌR.NITA
2 2 [GÌR.NI]TA

Colophon 2

1 0 ki-gal ki-ta
1 1 ki-gal ki-ta
1 2 ki-gal ki(?)-ta(?)

2 0 šub-ba-meš
2 1 šub-ba-meš
2 2 [x-b]a-meš

Caption 9

1 0 *rí-mu-úś*
1 1 *rí-mu-úś*
1 2 *rí-mu-⌈úś⌉*

2 0 LUGAL
2 1 L[UGAL]
2 2 LUGAL

3 0 KIŠ
3 1 K[IŠ]
3 2 KIŠ

Caption 9 (continued)

4 0 *šu* ᵈ*en-líl*
4 1 *šu* [...]
4 2 *šu* ᵈ*en-líl*

5 0 *ma-ḫi-ra*
5 1 *ma-*[...]
5 2 *ma-ḫi-ra*

6 0 *la i-dì-śum*$_6$
6 1 ⌈*la*⌉ [...]
6 2 *la i-dì-śum*$_6$

Colophon 3

1 0 mu-sar-ra
1 1 [...]
1 2 mu-sar-ra

2 0 zà-ga-na
2 1 [...]
2 2 zà-ga-na

1 0 *rí-mu-úš*
1 1 *rí-mu-úš*
1 2 [...]

2 0 LUGAL
2 1 LUGAL
2 2 [...]

3 0 KIŠ
3 1 KIŠ
3 2 [...]

4 0 *in* REC 169
4 1 *in* REC 169
4 2 [...]

5 0 ⌈ŠEŠ⌉.UNU.KI
5 1 ⌈ŠEŠ⌉.UNU.KI
5 2 [...]

6 0 *ù*
6 1 *ù*
6 2 [...]

7 0 [*lagaš*(LA.ŠIR.BUR)].KI
7 1 [*lagaš*(LA.ŠIR.BUR)].KI
7 2 [...]

8 0 *iš*$_{11}$-⌈*ar*⌉
8 1 ⌈*iš*$_{11}$-*ar*⌉
8 2 ⌈*iš*$_{11}$⌉-[*ar*]

9 0 *ù*
9 1 *ù*
9 2 ⌈*ù*⌉

10 0 8,040 ⌈GURUŠ⌉
10 1 8,040 ⌈GURUŠ⌉
10 2 8,040 ⌈GURUŠ⌉

11 0 *u-śa-am-qí-it*
11 1 *u-*[*śa*]*-am-*[*qí-i*]*t*
11 2 *u-śa-*[*a*]*m-qí-it*

12 0 ⌈5,460⌉ LÚ×ÉŠ
12 1 ⌈5,460⌉ LÚ×ÉŠ
12 2 ⌈5,460⌉ LU×KÁR

13 0 ŠU.DU$_{8}$.A
13 1 ŠU.DU$_{8}$.A
13 2 ŠU.DU$_{8}$.A

14 0 *ù*
14 1 *ù*
14 2 *ù*

15 0 KA-kù
15 1 ⌈KA⌉-kù
15 2 [K]A-kù

16 0 LUGAL
16 1 LUGAL
16 2 LUGAL

17 0 ÚRI.KI
17 1 ÚRI.KI
17 2 ÚRI.KI

18 0 ŠU.DU$_{8}$.A
18 1 ŠU.DU$_{8}$.A
18 2 ŠU.DU$_{8}$.A

19 0 *ù*
19 1 *ù*
19 2 *ù*

20 0 ki-tuš-íd
20 1 [ki-t]uš(?)-íd
20 2 ki-tuš-íd

21 0 ÉNSI
21 1 [ÉNS]I
21 2 ÉNSI

22 0 *lagaš*(LA.ŠIR.BUR).KI
22 1 [...].KI
22 2 *lagaš*(LA.ŠIR.BUR).KI

23 0 ŠU.⸢DU$_8$⸣.A
23 1 [...].A
23 2 ŠU.DU$_8$.⸢A⸣

24 0 *ù*
24 1 ⸢*ù*⸣
24 2 ⸢*ù*⸣

25 0 [UR]U.KI-*šu-ni*
25 1 [URU.KI-*š*]*u-ni*
25 2 [UR]U.KI-*šu-ni*

26 0 SAG.GIŠ.RA
26 1 [SAG.GIŠ].RA
26 2 SAG.GIŠ.RA

27 0 *ù*
27 1 ⸢*ù*⸣
27 2 *ù*

28 0 BÀD-*šu-ni*
28 1 [...]-*ni*
28 2 BÀD-*šu-ni*

29 0 Ì.GUL.GUL
29 1 [Ì.GUL.GU]L
29 2 Ì.GUL.GUL

30 0 *ù*
30 1 ⸢*ù*⸣
30 2 *ù*

31 0 in URU.KI-*šu-ni*
31 1 [...]-*ni*
31 2 *in* URU.KI-*šu-ni*

32 0 5,985 GURUŠ
32 1 [... GURU]Š
32 2 5,985 GURUŠ

33 0 *u-šu-ṣí-am-ma*
33 1 *u-šu-ṣ*[*í-am*]-*m*[*a*]
33 2 *u-šu-ṣí-am-ma*

34 0 *a-na*
34 1 *a-n*[*a*]
34 2 ⸢*a*⸣-*na*

35 0 *kà-ra-ší-i*[*m*]
35 1 *kà-ra-ší-i*[*m*]
35 2 *kà-ra-ší-i*[*m*]

36 0 *iš-kùn*
36 1 *iš-kùn*
36 2 [*i*]*š-kùn*

37 0 *ša* DUB
37 1 *ša* DUB
37 2 [*ša*] DUB

38 0 *šu$_4$-a*
38 1 *šu$_4$-a*
38 2 *šu$_4$-a*

39 0 *u-ša-sà-ku-ni*
39 1 *u-*⸢*ša*⸣*-sà-ku-ni*
39 2 ⸢*u-ša*⸣-*sà*-⸢*ku-ni*⸣

40 0 ^{d}*en-líl*
40 1 ^{d}*en-líl*
40 2 ^{d}*en-líl*

41 0 *ù*
41 1 *ù*
41 2 *ù*

42 0 ^{d}UTU
42 1 ^{d}UTU
42 2 ⸢^{d}⸣UTU

43 0 SUḪUŠ-*śu*
43 1 SUḪUŠ-*śu*
43 2 SUḪUŠ-*śu*

44 0 *li-sú-ḫa*
44 1 *li-sú-ḫa*
44 2 *li-sú-ḫa*

45 0 *ù*
45 1 ⸢*ù*⸣
45 2 *ù*

46 0 ŠE.NUMUN-*śu*
46 1 [...]
46 2 ŠE.NUMUN-*śu*

47 0 *li-il-qù-tá*
47 1 [...]
47 2 *li-il-qù-tá*

Colophon

1 0 mu-sar gùb-ni-šè a-ab-sar
1 1 [...]
1 2 mu-sar gùb-ni-šè a-ab-sar

1 0 *rí-mu-úś*
1 1 *rí-mu-úś*
1 2 *rí-mu-úś*

2 0 LUGAL
2 1 LU[GAL]
2 2 LUGAL

3 0 KIŠ
3 1 [...]
3 2 KIŠ

4 0 *sú-ra-ma*
4 1 [...]
4 2 *sú-ra-ma*

5 0 *śar-ru-tám*
5 1 *śar-*[...]
5 2 *śar-ru-tám*

6 0 ^{d}*en-líl*
6 1 ^{d}*e*[*n-líl*]
6 2 ^{d}*en-líl*

7 0 *i-dì-nu-*⌈*śum*$_{6}$⌉
7 1 *i-dì-n*[*u-śum*$_{6}$]
7 2 *i-dì-nu-*⌈*śum*$_{6}$⌉

8 0 REC 169
8 1 R[EC 169]
8 2 REC 169

9 0 *šu-me-rí-im*
9 1 [...]
9 2 *šu-me-rí-im*

10 0 *ad ma-dì-íś*
10 1 [...]
10 2 *ad ma-dì-íś*

11 0 3 *iš*$_{11}$*-ar*
11 1 3 [...]
11 2 3 *iš*$_{11}$*-ar*

12 0 11,322 ⌈GURUŠ.GURUŠ⌉
12 1 [...]
12 2 11,322 ⌈GURUŠ.GURUŠ⌉

13 0 ⌈*u-śa*⌉*-am-q*[*í-it*]
13 1 [...]
13 2 ⌈*u-śa*⌉*-am-q*[*í-it*]

14 0 [N LÚ×KÁR]
14 1 [...]
14 2 [...] x [...]

15 0 ⌈ŠU.DU$_{8}$.A⌉
15 1 [...]
15 2 ⌈ŠU.DU$_{8}$.A⌉

16 0 ⌈*ù*⌉
16 1 [...]
16 2 ⌈*ù*⌉

17 0 KA-k[ù]
17 1 [...]
17 2 KA-k[ù]

18 0 LUGAL
18 1 ⌈LUGAL⌉
18 2 LUGAL

19 0 ÚRI.KI
19 1 ÚRI.KI
19 2 ÚRI.KI

20 0 ŠU.DU$_{8}$.A
20 1 ŠU.DU$_{8}$.A
20 2 ŠU.DU$_{8}$.A

21 0 *ù*
21 1 *ù*
21 2 *ù*

22 0 ÉNSI.ÉNSI-*śu*
22 1 ÉNSI.ÉNSI-*śu*
22 2 ÉNSI.ÉNSI-*śu*

23 0 ŠU.DU$_8$.A
23 1 ŠU.DU$_8$.⸢A⸣
23 2 ŠU.DU$_8$.A

24 0 *ù*
24 1 ⸢*ù*⸣
24 2 *ù*

25 0 *á-ra-ab-śu-nu*
25 1 *á-r*[*a-ab*]-*śu*-[*nu*]
25 2 *á-ra-ab-śu-nu*

26 0 *a-dì-ma*
26 1 ⸢*a*⸣-*d*[*ì-ma*]
26 2 [*a*]-*dì-ma*

27 0 *ti-a-am-tim*
27 1 *ti-a*-⸢*am*⸣-[*tim*]
27 2 [*t*]*i-a-am-tim*

28 0 *śa-pil*$_5$*-tim*
28 1 *śa-pil*$_5$*-tim*
28 2 *śa-pil*$_5$*-tim*

29 0 *il-qù-ut*
29 1 *i*[*l-q*]*ù*-⸢*ut*⸣
29 2 *il-qù-ut*

30 0 *ù*
30 1 *ù*
30 2 *ù*

31A 0 14,100
31A 1 (2×6,000)+(3×600)+(5×60)
31A 2 (2×6,000)+(3×600)+(5×60)

31B 0 GURUŠ.GURUŠ
31B 1 GURUŠ.GURUŠ
31B 2 GURUŠ.GURUŠ

32 0 *in* URU.KI.URU.KI
32 1 *in* URU.KI.URU.[KI]
32 2 *in* URU.KI.URU.KI

33 0 *šu-me-rí-im*
33 1 *šu-me-rí-i*[*m*]
33 2 [*š*]*u-me-rí-im*

34 0 *u-śu-ṣí-am-ma*
34 1 *u-śu*-⸢*ṣí-am*⸣-*ma*
34 2 [*u*]-⸢*śu-ṣí*⸣-*am-ma*

35 0 *a-na*
35 1 *a-na*
35 2 [...]

36 0 *kà-ra-śi-im*
36 1 *kà-ra-śi-im*
36 2 ⸢*kà-ra-śi-im*⸣

37 0 *íś-kùn*
37 1 *íś-kùn*
37 2 [...]

38 0 *ù*
38 1 *ù*
38 2 [...]

39 0 URU.KI.URU.KI-*śu-nu*
39 1 URU.KI.URU.KI-*śu-nu*
39 2 [...]

40 0 SAG.GIŠ.RA
40 1 SAG.GIŠ.RA
40 2 [...]

41 0 *ù*
41 1 *ù*
41 2 [...]

42 0 BÀD.BÀD-*šu-nu*
42 1 BÀD.BÀD-*šu-nu*
42 2 [...]

43 0 Ì.GUL.GUL
43 1 Ì.GUL.GUL
43 2 [...]

44 0 *u-lum*
44 1 *u-lum*
44 2 [...]

45 0 *in tù-a-rí-šu*
45 1 *in tù-a-rí-šu*
45 2 [...]

46 0 *ka-za-lu*.KI
46 1 *ka-za-lu*.KI
46 2 [...]

47 0 *na-ki-ir-ma*
47 1 ⸢*na-ki*⸣-*ir-ma*
47 2 *na*-⸢*ki*⸣-*ir-ma*

48 0 SAG.GIŠ.RA
48 1 SAG.GIŠ.RA
48 2 [...]

49 0 ⸢*in qar-bí*⸣
49 1 ⸢*in qar-bí*⸣
49 2 [...]

50 0 *ka-za-lu*.KI
50 1 *ka-za-lu*.KI
50 2 [...]

51 0 12,052 GURUŠ.GURUŠ
51 1 (2×6,000)+52 GURUŠ.GURUŠ
51 2 [...]

52 0 *u-ša-am-*qi_4*-it*
52 1 *u-ša-am-*qi_4*-it*
52 2 [...]

53 0 5,862
53 1 (1×6,000 LAL 2×60) + ⸢18⸣
53 2 [...]

54 0 LÚ×ÉŠ
54 1 LÚ×ÉŠ
54 2 [...]

55 0 ŠU.⸢DU_8⸣.A
55 1 ŠU.⸢DU_8⸣.A
55 2 [...]

56 0 ⸢*ù*⸣
56 1 ⸢*ù*⸣
56 2 [...]

57 0 *a-ša-ré-ed*
57 1 *a-ša-ré-ed*
57 2 *a-ša-r*[*é-ed*]

58 0 ÉNSI
58 1 ÉNS[I]
58 2 ÉNSI

59 0 *ka-za-lu*.KI
59 1 *ka-za-lu*.KI
59 2 [...]

60 0 ŠU.DU$_8$.A
60 1 ŠU.DU$_8$.A
60 2 ŠU.DU$_8$.[A]

61 0 *ù*
61 1 *ù*
61 2 ⸢*ù*⸣

62 0 BÀD-*śu*
62 1 BÀD-*śu*
62 2 BÀD.BÀD-*śu*

63 0 Ì.GUL.GUL
63 1 Ì.GUL.GUL
63 2 Ì.GUL.GUL

64A 0 ŠU+NÍGIN
64A 1 ŠU+NÍGIN
64A 2 ŠU+NÍGIN

64B 0 54,016
64B 1 (1×36,000)+(5×3,600)+16
64B 2 traces

64C 0 GURUŠ.GURUŠ
64C 1 GURUŠ.GURUŠ
64C 2 GURUŠ.GURUŠ

65 0 *a-dì mi-qi*$_4$*-tim*
65 1 [*a-dì m*]*i-qi*$_4$*-tim*
65 2 *a-dì mi-qi*$_4$*-tim*

66 0 *a-dì* ⸢LÚ×ÉŠ⸣
66 1 [...] ⸢LÚ×ÉŠ⸣
66 2 *a-dì* LÚ×KÁR

67 0 *a-dì* GURUŠ.GURUŠ
67 1 [...]
67 2 *a-dì* GURUŠ.GURUŠ

68 0 *šu-ut a-na*
68 1 [...]
68 2 *šu-ut a-na*

69 0 *kà-ra-sí-im*
69 1 [...]
69 2 *kà-ra-sí-im*

70 0 *íś-k*[*ùn-ni*]
70 1 [...]
70 2 *íś-k*[*ùn-ni*]

71 0 KASKAL.KI
71 1 [...]
71 2 KASKAL.KI

72 0 *šu-zu*-x
72 1 [...]
72 2 *šu-zu*-x

73 0 ^{d}UTU
73 1 [...]
73 2 ^{d}UTU

74 0 *ù*
74 1 [...]
74 2 *ù*

75 0 *il-a-ba*$_4$
75 1 [...]
75 2 *il-a-ba*$_4$

76 0 *ú-ma*
76 1 [...]
76 2 *ú-ma*

77 0 *la sú-ra-tim*
77 1 [...]
77 2 *la sú-ra-tim*

78 0 *lu kí-ni-íś-ma*
78 1 [...]
78 2 *lu kí-ni-íś-ma*

79 0 *ì-nu*
79 1 *ì-*[*nu*]
79 2 *ì-nu*

80 0 REC 169 *śu*$_4$*-a*
80 1 REC 169 *ś*[*u*$_4$*-a*]
80 2 REC 169 *śu*$_4$*-a*

81 0 DÙL-*śu*
81 1 DÙL-⸢śu⸣
81 2 DÙL-*śu*

82 0 *ib-ni-ma*
82 1 *ib-ni-ma*
82 2 *ib-ni-ma*

83 0 *a-na*
83 1 *a-na*
83 2 *a-na*

84 0 ^{d}*en-líl*
84 1 ^{d}*en-líl*
84 2 ^{d}*en-líl*

85 0 *śa-lí-mi-śu*
85 1 *śa-lí-mi-śu*
85 2 *śa-lí-mi-śu*

86 0 A.MU.RU
86 1 A.MU.RU
86 2 A.MU.RU

87 0 *ša* DUB
87 1 ⸢*ša* DUB⸣
87 2 *ša* DUB

88 0 *śu*$_4$*-a*
88 1 *ś*[*u*$_4$*-a*]
88 2 *śu*$_4$*-a*

89 0 *u-śa-sà-ku-ni*
89 1 *u-śa-sà-ku-ni*
89 2 *u-śa-sà-ku-ni*

90 0 ^{d}*en-líl*
90 1 ^{d}*en-líl*
90 2 ^{d}*en-l*[*íl*]

91 0 *ù*
91 1 *ù*
91 2 *ù*

92 0 ^{d}UTU
92 1 ^{d}UTU
92 2 ^{d}[UTU]

93 0 SUḪUŠ-*śu*
93 1 SUḪUŠ-*śu*
93 2 SUḪUŠ-*śu*

94 0 *li-sú-ḫa*
94 1 *li-sú-ḫa*
94 2 *li-su-ḫa*

95 0 *ù*
95 1 *ù*
95 2 *ù*

96 0 ŠE.NUMUN-*śu*
96 1 ŠE.NUMUN-*śu*
96 2 ŠE.NUMUN-*śu*

97 0 *li-il-qù-tá*
97 1 *li-il-qù-tá*
97 2 *li-il-qù-tá*

Colophon 1

1 0 ki-gal an-ta igi-ni-šè
1 1 ki-gal an-ta igi-ni-šè
1 2 <...>

2 0 ⸢a-ab-sar⸣
2 1 ⸢a-ab-sar⸣
2 2 <...>

Curse Formula

98 0 *ma-na-ma*
98 1 *mu$_4$-na-ma*
98 2 *ma-na-ma*

99 0 MU
99 1 MU
99 2 MU

100 0 *rí-mu-úś*
100 1 *rí-mu-úś*
100 2 *rí-mu-úś*

101 0 LUGAL
101 1 LUGAL
101 2 LUGAL

102 0 KIŠ
102 1 KIŠ
102 2 KIŠ

103 0 *u-śa-sà-ku-ni*
103 1 *u-śa-sà-ku-ni*
103 2 *u-śa-sà-ku-ni*

104 0 *al* DÙL
104 1 *al* DÙL
104 2 *al* DÙL

105 0 *rí-mu-úś*
105 1 *rí-mu-úś*
105 2 *rí-mu-úś*

106 0 MU-*śu*
106 1 MU-*śu*
106 2 MU-*śu*

107 0 *i-śa-kà-nu-ma*
107 1 *i-śa-kà-nu-ma*
107 2 *i-śa-kà-nu-ma*

108 0 DÙL-*mi-me*
108 1 DÙL-*mi-me*
108 2 DÙL-*mi-me*

109 0 *i*-[*qá-bi*]-⸢*ù*⸣
109 1 x x x ⸢*ù*⸣
109 2 *i*-[x x]-⸢*ù*⸣

110 0 ᵈ*en-líl*
110 1 ⸢ᵈ*en*⸣-[*lí*]*l*
110 2 ᵈ*en-líl*

111 0 *be-al*
111 1 *be-al*
111 2 *be-a*[*l*]

112 0 DÙL *śu$_4$-a*
112 1 DÙL *śu$_4$-a*
112 2 DÙL *śu$_4$*-⸢*a*⸣

113 0 *ù*
113 1 *ù*
113 2 *ù*

114 0 ᵈUTU
114 1 ᵈUTU
114 2 ᵈUTU

115 0 SUḪUŠ-*śu*
115 1 SUḪUŠ-*śu*
115 2 SUḪUŠ-*śu*

116 0 *li-sú-ḫa*
116 1 *li-sú-ḫa*
116 2 *li-su-ḫa*

117 0 *ù*
117 1 *ù*
117 2 *ù*

118 0 ŠE.NUMUN-*śu*
118 1 ŠE.NUMUN-⸢*śu*⸣
118 2 ŠE.NUMUN-*śu*

119 0 *li-il-qù-tá*
119 1 *li-il-qù-tá*
119 2 [*l*]*i-il-qù-tá*

120 0 ⸢NITA⸣
120 1 ⸢NITA⸣
120 2 [...]

121 0 *a i-dì-na-śum*$_6$
121 1 ⸢*a*⸣ *i-dì-*[*n*]*a-śum*$_6$
121 2 ⸢*a i-dì-na-śum*$_6$⸣

122 0 [*m*]*aḫ-rí-íś*
122 1 [*m*]*aḫ-rí-íś*
122 2 [...]

123 0 [*ì*]-*lí-śu*
123 1 [*ì*]-*lí-śu*
123 2 [...]

124 0 [*e*] DU
124 1 [*e*] DU
124 2 [...]

Colophon 2

1 0 lu[gal(?)...] x-ni-šè
1 1 lu[gal(?)...] x-ni-šè
1 2 [...]

Caption 1

2 0 ^{d}[...]
2 1 ^{d}[...]
2 2 [...]

3 0 *á-l*[*í-ik*]
3 1 *á-*[*lí-ik*]
3 2 [...]

4 0 *maḫ-*[*rí-śu*]
4 1 *maḫ-*[...]
4 2 [...]

Caption 2

1 0 *a-ša-*[*ré-ed*]
1 1 *a-ša-*[*ré-ed*]
1 2 [...]

2 0 É[NSI]
2 1 É[NSI]
2 2 [...]

3 0 ⸢*ka*⸣-[*zal-lu*.KI]
3 1 ⸢*ka*⸣-[*zal-lu*.KI]
3 2 [...]

Lacuna

Caption 1′

1 0 *e*[*n*-...]
1 1 *e*[*n*-...]
1 2 [...]

2 0 É[NSI]
2 1 É[NSI]
2 2 [...]

3 0 UB.ME.⸢KI⸣
3 1 UB.ME.⸢KI⸣
3 2 [...]

Caption 2′

1 0 ^{d}*u-um*
1 1 ^{d}*u-um*
1 2 [...]

2 0 *á-lí-ik*
2 1 *á-lí-ik*
2 2 [...]

3 0 ⸢*maḫ*⸣-*rí-śu*
3 1 ⸢*maḫ*⸣-*rí-śu*
3 2 [...]

Caption 3′

1 0 KA-kù
1 1 KA-kù
1 2 [...]

2 0 LUGAL
2 1 LUGAL
2 2 [...]

Caption 3′ (continued)

3 0 ÚRI.KI
3 1 ÚRI.KI
3 2 [...]

Colophon 3

1 0 ki-gal-ba egir
1 1 ki-gal-ba egir
1 2 [...]

2 0 lú-^{d}da-mu
2 1 lú-^{d}da-mu
2 2 [...]

1 0 *rí-mu-úś*
1 1 [...]
1 2 *rí-mu-úś*

2 0 LUGAL
2 1 [...]
2 2 LUGAL

3 0 KIŠ
3 1 [...]
3 2 KIŠ

4 0 *ì-nu*
4 1 [...]
4 2 *ì-nu*

5 0 *kà-za-lu*.KI
5 1 [...]
5 2 *kà-za-lu*.KI

6 0 SAG.⸢GIŠ⸣.RA-*ni*
6 1 [...]
6 2 SAG.⸢GIŠ⸣.RA-*ni*

7 0 [*in*] ⸢REC 169⸣
7 1 [*in*] ⸢REC 169⸣
7 2 [*in*] ⸢REC 169⸣

8 0 *kà-za-lu*.KI
8 1 ⸢*ka*⸣-*za-lu*.KI
8 2 *kà-za-lu*.KI

9 0 12,052 GURUŠ.GURUŠ
9 1 12,052 [...]
9 2 12,052 GURUŠ.GURUŠ

10 0 *u-śa-am-qí-it*
10 1 [*u*]-⸢*śa*⸣-[*am*]-⸢*qí*⸣-*i*[*t*]
10 2 *u-śa-am-qí-it*

11 0 5,864 LÚ×ÉŠ
11 1 5,864 LÚ×ÉŠ
11 2 5,864 LÚ×KÁR

12 0 ŠU.DU$_8$.A
12 1 ⸢ŠU.DU$_8$.A⸣
12 2 ŠU.DU$_8$.A

13 0 *ù*
13 1 ⸢*ù*⸣
13 2 *ù*

14 0 *a-ša-ré-ed*
14 1 ⸢*a*⸣-*ša*-[*ré-ed*]
14 2 *a-ša-ré-ed*

15 0 ÉNSI
15 1 ÉN[SI]
15 2 ⸢ÉNSI⸣

16 0 *kà-za-lu*.KI
16 1 [...-*l*]*u*.KI
16 2 *kà-za-lu*.KI

17 0 ŠU.DU$_8$.A
17 1 [ŠU.D]U$_8$.A
17 2 ŠU.D[U$_8$].A

18 0 *ù*
18 1 ⸢*ù*⸣
18 2 *ù*

19 0 BÀD-*śu*
19 1 [B]ÀD-⸢*śu*⸣
19 2 BÀD-*śu*

20 0 Ì.GUL.GUL
20 1 Ì.GUL.GUL
20 2 [...]

21 0 *ša* DUB
21 1 *ša* DUB
21 2 *ša* DUB

22 0 *śu*$_4$-*a*
22 1 *śu*$_4$-*a*
22 2 *śu*$_4$-*a*

23 0 *u-śa-sà-*⸢*ku*⸣*-ni*
23 1 *u-śa-sà-*⸢*ku*⸣*-ni*
23 2 <...>

24 0 ^{d}*en-líl*
24 1 ^{d}*en-líl*
24 2 <...>

25 0 ⸢*ù*⸣
25 1 ⸢*ù*⸣
25 2 <...>

26 0 ^{d}⸢UTU⸣
26 1 ^{d}⸢UTU⸣
26 2 <...>

27 0 SUḪUŠ-*śu*
27 1 SUḪUŠ-*śu*
27 2 <...>

28 0 ⸢*li-sú*⸣*-ḫa*
28 1 ⸢*li-sú*⸣*-ḫa*
28 2 <...>

29 0 ⸢*ù*⸣
29 1 ⸢*ù*⸣
29 2 <...>

30 0 ŠE.NUMUN-⸢*śu*⸣
30 1 ŠE.NUMUN-⸢*śu*⸣
30 2 <...>

31 0 *li-i*[*l*]*-qù-tá*⸣
31 1 *li-i*[*l*]*-qù-tá*⸣
31 2 <...>

Ex. 2 puts after line 23: áš-bal-bi šu-bi na-nam

Colophon

1 0 mùš ki-gal ki-ta
1 1 x ki-gal ki-ta
1 2 mùš ki-gal ki-ta

2 0 á-zi-da-na
2 1 ⸢á-zi⸣-da-na
2 2 á-zi-da-na

1 0 *rí-mu-úś*
1 1 *rí-mu-úś*
1 2 ⸢*rí*⸣-*mu-úś*

2 0 LUGAL
2 1 LUGAL
2 2 LUGAL

3 0 KIŠ
3 1 KIŠ
3 2 KIŠ

4 0 *in* REC 169
4 1 *in* REC 169
4 2 *i*[*n*] ⸢REC 169⸣

5 0 *a-ba-al-ga-maš*
5 1 [...*a*]*l-ga-maš*
5 2 *a-ba-al-ga-maš*

6 0 ⸢LUGAL⸣
6 1 ⸢LUGAL⸣
6 2 L[UGAL]

7 0 *pá-ra-aḫ-śum*.KI
7 1 *pá-ra-aḫ-śum*.KI
7 2 [...-*ś*]*um*.KI

8 0 *iš*$_{11}$-*ar*
8 1 *iš*$_{11}$-*ar*
8 2 *iš*$_{11}$-*ar*

9 0 *ù*
9 1 *ù*
9 2 *ù*

10 0 *za-ḫa-ra*.KI
10 1 *za-ḫa-ra*.KI
10 2 [*za*]-⸢*ḫa*⸣-*ra*.KI

11 0 *ù*
11 1 *ù*
11 2 *ù*

12 0 NIM.KI
12 1 NIM.KI
12 2 ⸢NIM⸣.KI

13 0 *in qab*$_x$(DA)-*lí*
13 1 *in qab*$_x$(DA)-*lí*
13 2 *in qab*$_x$(DA)-*lí*

14 0 *pá-ra-aḫ-śum*.KI
14 1 *pá-ra-aḫ-śum*.KI
14 2 ⸢*pá-ra*⸣-*aḫ-śum*.KI

15 0 *a-na*
15 1 *a-na*
15 2 *a-na*

16 0 REC 169
16 1 REC 169
16 2 REC 169

17 0 *ip-ḫu-ru-ni-im-ma*
17 1 *ip-ḫu-ru-ni-im-ma*
17 2 ⸢*ip-ḫu*⸣-[*ru-ni-i*]*m-ma*

18 0 *iš*$_{11}$-*ar*
18 1 *iš*$_{11}$-*ar*
18 2 *iš*$_{11}$-⸢*ar*⸣

19 0 *ù*
19 1 *ù*
19 2 *ù*

20 0 16,212 GURUŠ.GURUŠ
20 1 16,212 GURUŠ.GURUŠ
20 2 16,212 ⸢GURUŠ⸣.GURUŠ

21 0 *u-śa-am-*qi_4*-it*
21 1 *u-śa-am-*qi_4*-it*
21 2 *u-śa-am-qí-it*

22 0 4,216 LÚ×ÉŠ×
22 1 4,216 LÚ×ÉŠ
22 2 4,216 ⌈LÚ×X⌉

23 0 ŠU.DU_8.⌈A⌉
23 1 [...]
23 2 ŠU.DU_8.⌈A⌉

24 0 ⌈*ù*⌉ *e-maḫ*(?)*-si-n*[*i*]
24 1 [...]
24 2 ⌈*ù*⌉ *e-maḫ*(?)*-si-n*[*i*]

25 0 LUGAL NIM.KI Š[U.DU_8.A]
25 1 [...]
25 2 LUGAL NIM.KI Š[U.DU_8.A]

26 0 *ù kà-la-ma*
26 1 [...]
26 2 *ù kà-la-ma*

27 0 x x x NIM.KI ŠU.DU_8.A
27 1 [...]
27 2 x x x NIM.KI ŠU.DU_8.A

28 0 *ù si-id-ga-ù*
28 1 [...] s[*i-id-ga*]-⌈*ù*⌉
28 2 *ù si-id-ga-ù*

29 0 GÌR.NÍTA
29 1 ⌈GÌR⌉.NÍTA
29 2 GÌR.NÍTA

30 0 *pá-ra-aḫ-śum*.KI
30 1 *pá-ra-aḫ-śum*.KI
30 2 *pá-ra-aḫ-śum*.KI

31 0 ŠU.D⌈U⌉$_8$.A
31 1 ŠU.DU_8.A
31 2 ŠU.DU_8.A

32 0 *ù*
32 1 *ù*
32 2 *ù*

33 0 *śar*-GA-PI
33 1 ⌈*śar*⌉-GA-PI
33 2 *śar*-GA-PI

34 0 GÌR.NÍTA
34 1 [GÌ]R.NÍTA
34 2 GÌR.NÍTA

35 0 *za-ḫa-ra*.KI
35 1 ⌈*za*⌉-[*ḫa-r*]*a*.KI
35 2 *za-ḫa-ra*.KI

36 0 ŠU.DU_8.A
36 1 ŠU.D[U_8.A]
36 2 ⌈ŠU⌉.DU_8.A

37 0 *in ba-rí-ti*
37 1 *in ba-rí-ti*
37 2 [*i*]*n* ⌈*ba-rí-ti*⌉

38 0 *a-wa-an*.KI
38 1 *a-wa-an*.KI
38 2 [...]

39 0 *ù*
39 1 *ù*
39 2 [...]

40 0 *śu-śi-im*.KI
40 1 *śu-śi-im*.KI
40 2 [...]

41 0 *in* ÍD
41 1 *in* ÍD
41 2 [...]

42 0 *qáb-lí-tim*
42 1 *qáb-lí-tim*
42 2 [...]

43 0 *ù*
43 1 *ù*
43 2 [...]

44 0 *bí-ru-tám*
44 1 *bí-ru-tám*
44 2 [...]

45 0 *in a-ša-ar* URU
45 1 *in a-ša-ar* URU
45 2 [...]

46 0 *al-⸢śu⸣-nu*
46 1 *al-⸢śu⸣-nu*
46 2 [...]

47 0 *íś-⸢pu⸣-uk*
47 1 *íś-⸢pu⸣-uk*
47 2 [...]

48 0 *ù*
48 1 *ù*
48 2 [...]

49 0 URU.KI.URU.KI
49 1 URU.KI.URU.KI
49 2 [...]

50 0 NIM.KI
50 1 NIM.KI
50 2 [...]

51 0 SAG.⸢GIŠ⸣.RA
51 1 SAG.⸢GIŠ⸣.RA
51 2 [...]

52 0 *ù*
52 1 *ù*
52 2 [...]

53 0 BÀD.BÀD-*śu-nu*
53 1 BÀD.BÀD-*śu-nu*
53 2 [...]

54 0 Ì.GUL.GUL
54 1 Ì.GUL.GUL
54 2 [...]

55 0 *ù*
55 1 *ù*
55 2 [...]

56 0 SUḪUŠ
56 1 SUḪUŠ
56 2 [...]

57 0 ⸢*pá-ra-aḫ-śum*.KI⸣
57 1 ⸢*pá-ra-aḫ-śum*.KI⸣
57 2 [...]

58 0 [*in* KALAM]
58 1 [...]
58 2 [...]

59 0 [NIM.KI]
59 1 [...]
59 2 [...]

60 0 [*i-sú-uḫ-ma*]
60 1 [...]
60 2 [...]

61 0 [*rí-mu-úš*]
61 1 [...]
61 2 [...]

62 0 [LUGAL]
62 1 [...]
62 2 [...]

63 0 [KIŠ]
63 1 [...]
63 2 [...]

64 0 NIM.[KI]
64 1 NIM.[KI]
64 2 [...]

65 0 *i-be-al*
65 1 *i-be-al*
65 2 [...]

66 0 ^{d}*en-líl*
66 1 ^{d}*en-líl*
66 2 [...]

67 0 *u-kál-lim*
67 1 *u-kál-lim*
67 2 [...]

68 0 *in śa-an-tim*
68 1 *in śa-an-tim*
68 2 [...]

69 0 *śa-lí-íś-tim*
69 1 *śa-lí-íś-tim*
69 2 [...]

70 0 *ša-ti*
70 1 *ša-ti*
70 2 [...]

71 0 ^{d}*en-líl*
71 1 ^{d}*en-líl*
71 2 [...]

72 0 *śar-ru*$_{x}$(URU×A)*-tám*
72 1 *śar-ru*$_{x}$(URU×A)*-tám*
72 2 [...]

73 0 *i-dì-nu-śum*$_{6}$
73 1 *i-dì-nu-śum*$_{6}$
73 2 [...]

74 0 ŠU+NIGÍN 9,624
74 1 ŠU+NIGÍN 9,624
74 2 [...]

75 0 GURUŠ.GURUŠ
75 1 GURUŠ.GURUŠ
75 2 [...]

76 0 *a-dì mi-qi*$_{4}$*-tim*
76 1 *a-dì mi-qi*$_{4}$*-tim*
76 2 [...] x [...]

77 0 *a-dì* LÚ×ÉŠ
77 1 *a-dì* LÚ×ÉŠ
77 2 [...] x [...]

78 0 ^{d}UTU
78 1 ^{d}UTU
78 2 ⌈^{d}⌉UTU

79 0 *ù*
79 1 *ù*
79 2 *ù*

80 0 *il-a-ba*$_{4}$
80 1 *il-a-ba*$_{4}$
80 2 ⌈*il*⌉*-a-ba*$_{4}$

81 0 *ú-má*
81 1 *ú-má*
81 2 *ú-má*

82 0 *la sú-ra-tum*$_8$
82 1 *la sú-ra-tum*$_8$
82 2 *la sú-ra-tum*$_8$-

83 0 *lu kí-ni-íś-ma*
83 1 *lu kí-ni-íś-*[*ma*]
83 2 *lu kí-ni-íś-ma*

84 0 *ì-nu*
84 1 [...]
84 2 *ì-nu*

85 0 REC 169
85 1 [...]
85 2 REC 169

86 0 *śu*$_4$*-a*
86 1 [...]
86 2 *śu*$_4$*-a*

87 0 DÙL-*śu*
87 1 [...]
87 2 DÙL-*śu*

88 0 *i*[*b-ni*]*-ma*
88 1 [...]
88 2 *i*[*b-ni*]*-ma*

89 0 *a-na*
89 1 [...]
89 2 *a-na*

90 0 ^{d}*en-líl*
90 1 [...]
90 2 ^{d}⸢*en*⸣-*líl*

91 0 *śa-lí-mi-śu*
91 1 [...]
91 2 *śa-lí-mi-śu*

92 0 A.MU.RU
92 1 [...]
92 2 A.MU.RU

93 0 *ša* DUB
93 1 [...]
93 2 *ša* DUB

94 0 *śu*$_4$*-a*
94 1 [...]
94 2 *śu*$_4$*-a*

95 0 *u-śa-sà-ku-ni*
95 1 [...]
95 2 *u-śa-sà-ku-ni*

96 0 ^{d}*en-líl*
96 1 [...]
96 2 ^{d}*en-líl*

97 0 *ù*
97 1 [...]
97 2 *ù*

98 0 ^{d}UTU
98 1 ⸢d⸣UTU
98 2 ^{d}UTU

99 0 SUḪUŠ-*śu*
99 1 SUḪUŠ-*śu*
99 2 SUḪUŠ-*śu*

100 0 *li-sú-ḫa*
100 1 *li-sú-ḫa*
100 2 *li-sú-ḫa*

101 0 *ù*
101 1 ⸢*ù*⸣
101 2 *ù*

102 0 ŠE.NUMUN-*śu*
102 1 ŠE.N[UMUN-*śu*]
102 2 ŠE.NUMUN-*śu*

103 0 *li-il-qù-tá*
103 1 *li-i*[*l*]*-qù-*⸢*tá*⸣
103 2 *li-il-qù-tá*

Colophon 1

1 0 ki-gal ⸢á-gùb-ni⸣-šè
1 1 ki-gal ⸢á-gùb-ni⸣-šè
1 2 <...>

2 0 ⸢a-ab⸣-sar
2 1 ⸢a-ab⸣-sar
2 2 <...>

Curse formula

104 0 *ma-na-ma*
104 1 *ma-na-ma*
104 2 *ma-na-ma*

105 0 MU
105 1 ⸢MU⸣
105 2 MU

106 0 *rí-mu-úś*
106 1 ⸢*rí-mu*⸣*-úś*
106 2 *rí-mu-úś*

107 0 LUGAL
107 1 LUGAL
107 2 LUGAL

108 0 KIŠ
108 1 KIŠ
108 2 KIŠ

109 0 *u-śa-sà-ku-ma*
109 1 *u-śa-sà-ku ma*
109 2 ⸢*u*⸣*-śa-sà-*⸢*ku*⸣*-ma*

110 0 *al* DÙL
110 1 *al* DÙL
110 2 *al* DÙL

111 0 *rí-mu-úś*
111 1 *rí-*⸢*mu*⸣*-úś*
111 2 *rí-mu-úś*

112 0 MU-*śu*
112 1 MU-*śu*
112 2 MU-*śu*

113 0 *i-śa-kà-nu-ma*
113 1 *i-śa-kà-*⸢*nu*⸣*-ma*
113 2 *i-śa-kà-nu-ma*

114 0 DÙL-*mi-me*
114 1 DÙL-*mi-me*
114 2 DÙL-*mi-me*

115 0 *i-qá-bi-ù*
115 1 *i-q*[*á*]*-*⸢*bi*⸣*-ù*
115 2 *i-qá-bi-ù*

116 0 ^{d}*en-líl*
116 1 ^{d}*en-líl*
116 2 ^{d}*en-líl*

117 0 *be-al*
117 1 *be-al*
117 2 *be-al*

118 0 DÙL *šu*$_4$-*a*
118 1 DÙL *šu*$_4$-*a*
118 2 DÙL *šu*$_4$-*a*

119 0 *ù*
119 1 *ù*
119 2 *ù*

120 0 ^{d}UTU
120 1 ^{d}UTU
120 2 ^{d}UTU

121 0 SUḪUŠ-*šu*
121 1 SUḪUŠ-*šu*
121 2 SUḪUŠ-*šu*

122 0 *li-sú-ḫa*
122 1 *li-sú-ḫa*
122 2 *li-sú-ḫa*

123 0 *ù*
123 1 ⸢*ù*⸣
123 2 *ù*

124 0 ŠE.NUMUN-*šu*
124 1 [...]
124 2 ŠE.NUMUN-*šu*

125 0 *li-il-qù-tá*
125 1 [...]
125 2 *li-il-qù-tá*

126 0 NITA
126 1 [...]
126 2 NITA

127 0 *a i-dì-na-šum*$_6$
127 1 [...]-*na-šum*$_6$
127 2 *a i-dì-na-šum*$_6$

128 0 *maḫ-rí-iś*
128 1 *maḫ-rí-iś*
128 2 *maḫ-rí-iś*

129 0 *ì-lí-šu*
129 1 *ì-lí-šu*
129 2 ⸢*ì*⸣-*lí-šu*

130 0 *e* DU
130 1 ⸢*e*⸣ DU
130 2 *e* DU

131 0 30 MA.NA
131 1 30 MA.NA
131 2 30 MA.NA

132 0 KÙ.GI
132 1 KÙ.GI
132 2 KÙ.GI

133 0 3,600 MA.NA
133 1 3,600 MA.NA
133 2 3,600 MA.NA

134 0 URUDU
134 1 URUDU
134 2 URUDU

135 0 300 IR$_{11}$ GÉME
135 1 300 IR$_{11}$ GÉME
135 2 [x]+100 IR$_{11}$ GÉME

136 0 *ì-nu*
136 1 *ì-nu*
136 2 [*ì*]-*nu*

137 0 NIM.KI
137 1 NIM.KI
137 2 NIM.KI

138 0 *ù*
138 1 *ù*
138 2 ⸢*ù*⸣

139 0 *pá-ra-*⸢*aḫ*⸣*-śum*.KI
139 1 *pá-ra-*⸢*aḫ*⸣*-śum*.KI
139 2 *pá-ra-*[*aḫ-ś*]*um*.KI

140 0 SAG.GIŠ.RA-*ni*
140 1 SAG.GIŠ.RA-*ni*
140 2 SAG.GIŠ.RA-*n*[*i*]

141 0 *u-ru-a-am-ma*
141 1 *u-ru-a-am-ma*
141 2 *u-ru-a-am-*⸢*ma*⸣

142 0 *a-na*
142 1 ⸢*a*⸣*-na*
142 2 ⸢*a-na*⸣

143 0 ᵈ*en-líl*
143 1 ⸢ᵈ⸣*en-líl*
143 2 ᵈ*en-líl*

144 0 A.MU.RU
144 1 [A].MU.RU
144 2 A.MU.RU

Colophon 2

1 1 [...-b]i-šè [...s]ar
1 2 mu-sar-ra ki-gal-ba

Caption 1

1 0 *rí-mu-úś*
1 1 [...]
1 2 *rí-mu-úś*

2 0 LUGAL
2 1 [...]
2 2 LUGAL

3 0 KIŠ
3 1 [...]
3 2 KIŠ

4 0 *šu* ᵈ*en-líl*
4 1 [...]
4 2 *šu* ᵈ*en-líl*

5 0 *ma-ḫi-ra*
5 1 [...]
5 2 *ma-ḫi-ra*

6 0 ⸢*la*⸣ *i-dì-śum*$_6$
6 1 [...]
6 2 ⸢*la*⸣ *i-dì-śum*$_6$

Colophon 3

1 0 mu-sar-ra
1 1 [...]
1 2 mu-sar-ra

2 0 zà-ga-na
2 1 [...]
2 2 zà-ga-na

1 0 *rí-m[u-ú]ś*
1 1 *rí-m[u-úś]*
1 2 [...]
1 3 [...-*ú*]*ś*
1 4 [...-*ú*]*ś*

2 0 LUGAL
2 1 LU[GAL]
2 2 [...]
2 3 [LU]GAL
2 4 [LU]GAL

3 0 K[I]Š
3 1 K[I]Š
3 2 [...]
3 3 [KI]Š
3 4 [KI]Š

4 0 *in* REC 169
4 1 *in* [REC 169]
4 2 *in* REC 169
4 3 [*in*] ⸢REC 169⸣
4 4 *in* REC 169

5 0 *a-ba-al-ga-maš*
5 1 *a-ba-a*[*l*-...]
5 2 *a-ba-al*-⸢*ga-maš*⸣
5 3 [...]-⸢*maš*⸣
5 4 *a-ba-al-ga-maš*

6 0 LUGAL
6 1 [LU]GAL
6 2 LUGAL
6 3 [...]
6 4 LUGAL

7 0 *pá-ra-aḫ-śum*.KI
7 1 [*pá*]-⸢*ra-aḫ-śum*⸣.KI
7 2 *pá-ra-aḫ-śum*.KI
7 3 [...-*śu*]*m*.KI
7 4 *pá-ra-aḫ-śum*.KI

8 0 *iš*$_{11}$*-ar*
8 1 ⸢*iš*$_{11}$*-ar*⸣
8 2 *iš*$_{11}$*-ar*
8 3 [*iš*$_{11}$]-*ar*
8 4 *iš*$_{11}$*-ar*

9 0 *ù*
9 1 *ù*
9 2 *ù*
9 3 *ù*
9 4 *ù*

10 0 *si-id-ga-ù*
10 1 *si-id-ga-ù*
10 2 *si-id-ga-ù*
10 3 [*s*]*i-id-ga-ù*
10 4 *si-id-ga-ù*

11 0 GÌR.NITA-*śu*
11 1 ⸢GÌR⸣.NITA-*śu*
11 2 GÌR.NITA-*śu*
11 3 [GÌ]R.NITA-*śu*
11 4 GÌR.NITA-*śu*

12 0 ŠU.DU$_{8}$.A
12 1 ŠU.⸢DU$_{8}$⸣.A
12 2 ŠU.DU$_{8}$.A
12 3 [ŠU].DU$_{8}$.A
12 4 ŠU.DU$_{8}$.A

13 0 *in ba-rí-ti*
13 1 *in ba*-⸢*rí-ti*⸣
13 2 *in ba-rí-ti*
13 3 [*in b*]*a*-⸢*rí-ti*⸣
13 4 *in ba-rí-ti*

14 0 *a-wa-an*.KI
14 1 [*a-w*]*a-an*.KI
14 2 *a-w*[*a-a*]*n*.KI
14 3 [...]
14 4 *a-wa-an*.KI

15 0 *ù*
15 1 *ù*
15 2 *ù*
15 3 [...]
15 4 *ù*

16 0 *śu-śi-im*.KI
16 1 ⸢*śu-śi-im*⸣.KI
16 2 *śu-śi-i*[*m*.KI]
16 3 [...]
16 4 ⸢*śu*⸣-*śi-im*.<KI>

17 0 *in* ÍD
17 1 *in* Í[D]
17 2 *in* ÍD
17 3 [...]
17 4 *in* ÍD

18 0 *qab*$_{x}$(DA)-*lí-tim*
18 1 *qa*[*b*$_{x}$((DA)-[...]
18 2 *qab*$_{x}$((DA)-[...]
18 3 [...-*t*]*im*
18 4 *qab*$_{x}$((DA)-*lí-tim*

19 0 *ù*
19 1 ⸢*ù*⸣
19 2 *ù*
19 3 ⸢*ù*⸣
19 4 *ù*

20 0 *bí-ru-tám*
20 1 *bí-r*[*u-tám*]
20 2 *bí-r*[*u-tám*]
20 3 [...-*tá*]*m*
20 4 *bí-ru-tám*

21 0 *in a-ša-ar* URU
21 1 *in a-ša-*[*ar*]
21 2 *in a-ša-a*[*r*] ⸢URU⸣
21 3 [...]
21 4 *in a-ša-ar* URU

22 0 *al-śu*
22 1 [...]
22 2 *al-śu*
22 3 [...]
22 4 *al-śu*

23 0 *íś-pu-uk*
23 1 [...]
23 2 *íś-*⸢*pu-uk*⸣
23 3 [...]
23 4 *íś-pu-uk*

24 0 *ù*
24 1 [...]
24 2 *ù*
24 3 [...]
24 4 *ù*

25 0 SUḪUŠ
25 1 [...]
25 2 SUḪUŠ
25 3 S[UḪUŠ]
25 4 SUḪUŠ

26 0 *pá-ra-aḫ-śum*.KI
26 1 [...]
26 2 *pá-ra-aḫ-śum*.KI
26 3 *pá-r*[*a-* ...]
26 4 *pá-ra-aḫ-śum*.KI

27 0 *in* KALAM
27 1 [...]
27 2 *in* KALAM
27 3 *i*[*n* KALAM]
27 4 *in* KALAM

28 0 NIM.KI
28 1 [...]
28 2 NIM.KI
28 3 NIM.[KI]
28 4 NIM.KI

29 0 *i-sú-uḫ-ma*
29 1 [...]
29 2 *i-sú-uḫ-ma*
29 3 *i-sú-⸢uḫ⸣-ma*
29 4 *i-sú-uḫ-ma*

30 0 *rí-mu-úš*
30 1 [...]
30 2 *rí-mu-úš*
30 3 [...]
30 4 *rí-mu-úš*

31 0 LUGAL
31 1 [...]
31 2 LUGAL
31 3 [...]
31 4 LUGAL

32 0 KIŠ
32 1 [...]
32 2 KIŠ
32 3 [...]
32 4 KIŠ

33 0 NIM.KI
33 1 [...]
33 2 NIM.KI
33 3 [...]
33 4 NIM.KI

34 0 *i-be-al*
34 1 [...]
34 2 *i-be-al*
34 3 [...]
34 4 *i-be-al*

35 0 ^{d}*en-líl*
35 1 [...]
35 2 ^{d}*en-líl*
35 3 [...]
35 4 ^{d}*en-líl*

36 0 *u-kál-lim*
36 1 [...]
36 2 *u-kál-lim*
36 3 [...]
36 4 *u-kál-lim*

37 0 ^{d}UTU
37 1 ⸢^{d}⸣UTU
37 2 ^{d}UTU
37 3 [...]
37 4 ^{d}UTU

38 0 *ù*
38 1 *ù*
38 2 *ù*
38 3 [...]
38 4 *ù*

39 0 *ìl-a-ba*$_4$
39 1 *ìl-a-ba*$_4$
39 2 *ìl-a-ba*$_4$
39 3 [...]
39 4 *ìl-a-ba*$_4$

40 0 *ú-má*
40 1 *ú-má*
40 2 *ú-má*
40 3 [...]
40 4 *ú-má*

41 0 *la sú-ra-tum*$_8$
41 1 *la sú-ra-tum*$_8$
41 2 *la sú-ra-tum*$_8$
41 3 [...]
41 4 *la sú-ra-tum*$_8$

42 0 *lu kí-ni-íš-ma*
42 1 *lu kí-ni-íš-ma*
42 2 *lu kí-ni-íš-ma*
42 3 [...]
42 4 *lu kí-ni-íš-ma*

43 0 *ša* DUB
43 1 *ša* DUB
43 2 *ša* DUB
43 3 [...]
43 4 ⌈*ša*⌉ DUB

44 0 *śu*$_4$*-a*
44 1 *śu*$_4$*-a*
44 2 *śu*$_4$*-a*
44 3 [...]
44 4 ⌈*śu*$_4$⌉*-a*

45 0 *u-śa-sà-ku-ni*
45 1 *u-śa-sà-ku-ni*
45 2 *u-śa-sà-ku-ni*
45 3 [...]
45 4 [*u-ś*]*a-sà-ku-ni*

46 0 ^{d}*en-líl*
46 1 ^{d}*en-líl*
46 2 ^{d}*en-líl*
46 3 [...]
46 4 ^{d}*en-líl*

47 0 *ù*
47 1 *ù*
47 2 *ù*
47 3 [...]
47 4 *ù*

48 0 ^{d}UTU
48 1 ^{d}UTU
48 2 ^{d}UTU
48 3 [...]
48 4 ^{d}UTU

49 0 SUḪUŠ-*śu*
49 1 SUḪUŠ-*śu*
49 2 SUḪUŠ-*śu*
49 3 [...]
49 4 SUḪUŠ-*śu*

50 0 *li-sú-ḫa*
50 1 *li-sú-ḫa*
50 2 *li-sú-ḫa*
50 3 [...]
50 4 *li-sú-ḫa*

51 0 *ù*
51 1 *ù*
51 2 *ù*
51 3 [...]
51 4 *ù*

52 0 ŠE.NUMUN-*śu*
52 1 ŠE.NUMUN-*śu*
52 2 ŠE.NUMUN-*śu*
52 3 [...]
52 4 ŠE.NUMUN-*śu*

53 0 *li-il-qù-tá*
53 1 *li-il-qù-tá*
53 2 *li-il-qù-tá*
53 3 [...]
53 4 *li-il-qù-tá*

Colophon

1 0 mu-sar-ra
1 1 mu-sar-ra
1 2 mu-⌈sar⌉-ra
1 3 [...]
1 4 <...>

2 0 ŠEN.*za-ḫum*
2 1 ŠEN.*za-ḫum*
2 2 ŠEN.*za-ḫum*
2 3 [...]
2 4 <...>

1 0 [*rí*]-⸢*mu-úš*⸣
1 1 [...]
1 2 [*rí*]-⸢*mu-úš*⸣

2 0 ⸢LUGAL⸣
2 1 [...]
2 2 ⸢LUGAL⸣

3 0 KIŠ
3 1 [...]
3 2 KIŠ

4 0 [^{d}*en-líl*]
4 1 [...]
4 2 [...]

5 0 [KALAM.MA.KI]
5 1 [...]
5 2 [...]

6 0 ⸢*ka-la-ma*⸣
6 1 ⸢*ka-la-ma*⸣
6 2 [...]

7 0 *i-dì-šum*$_6$
7 1 *i-dì-šum*$_6$
7 2 [...]

8 0 *ti-a-am-tám*
8 1 *ti-a-am-tám*
8 2 [...]

9 0 *a-lí-tám*
9 1 *a-lí-tám*
9 2 [...]

10 0 *ù*
10 1 *ù*
10 2 [...]

11 0 ⸢*ša*⸣-*pil*$_5$-*tám*
11 1 ⸢*ša*⸣-*pil*$_5$-*tám*
11 2 [...]

12 0 *ù*
12 1 *ù*
12 2 [...]

13 0 ŠA.DÚ-*e*
13 1 ŠA.DÚ-*e*
13 2 [...]

14 0 *kà-la-šu-nu-ma*
14 1 *kà-la-šu-nu-ma*
14 2 [...]

15 0 *a-na*
15 1 *a-na*
15 2 [...]

16 0 ^{d}*en-líl*
16 1 ^{d}*en-líl*
16 2 [...]

17 0 *u-kà-al*
17 1 *u-kà-al*
17 2 [...]

18 0 *ša* DUB
18 1 *ša* DUB
18 2 [...]

19 0 *šu*$_4$-*a*
19 1 *šu*$_4$-*a*
19 2 [...]

20 0 *u-ša-sà-ku-ni*
20 1 *u-ša-sà-ku-ni*
20 2 [...]

21 0 ^{d}*en-líl*
21 1 ^{d}*en-líl*
21 2 [...]

22 0 *ù*
22 1 *ù*
22 2 [...]

23 0 ^{d}UTU
23 1 ^{d}UTU
23 2 [...]

24 0 SUḪUŠ-*šu*
24 1 SUḪUŠ-*šu*
24 2 [...]

25 0 *li-sú-*⸢*ḫa*⸣
25 1 *li-sú-*⸢*ḫa*⸣
25 2 [...]

26 0 *ù*
26 1 *ù*
26 2 [...]

27 0 ŠE.⸢NUMUN⸣-*šu*
27 1 ŠE.⸢NUMUN⸣-*šu*
27 2 [...]

28 0 *li-il-qù-tá*
28 1 *li-il-qù-tá*
28 2 [...]

Colophon 1

1 0 mu-sar-ra [k]i-gal-ba
1 1 mu-sar-ra [k]i-gal-ba
1 2 [...]

Caption

1 0 *rí-mu-*⸢*úš*⸣
1 1 *rí-mu-*⸢*úš*⸣
1 2 [...]

2 0 LUGAL
2 1 LUGAL
2 2 [...]

3 0 KIŠ
3 1 KIŠ
3 2 [...]

4 0 SAG.GIŠ.R[A]
4 1 SAG.GIŠ.R[A]
4 2 [...]

5 0 N[IM.KI]
5 1 N[IM.KI]
5 2 [...]

6 0 [*ù*]
6 1 [...]
6 2 [...]

7 0 ⸢*pá*⸣-*r*[*a-aḫ-šum*.KI]
7 1 ⸢*pá*⸣-*r*[*a-aḫ-šum*.KI]
7 2 [...]

Colophon 2

1 0 ⸢zà⸣-g[a-na a-ab-sar]
1 1 ⸢zà⸣-g[a-na a-ab-sar]
1 2 [...]

1 0 *a-na*
1 1 *a-na*
1 2 ...
1 3 [...]
1 4 [...]

2 0 ^{d}EN.ZU
2 1 ^{d}EN.ZU
2 2 ...
2 3 [...]
2 4 [...]

3 0 *rí-mu-úś*
3 1 *rí-mu-úś*
3 2 ...
3 3 [...]
3 4 [...]

4 0 LUGAL
4 1 LUGAL
4 2 ...
4 3 [..]
4 4 [...]

5 0 KIŠ
5 1 KIŠ
5 2 ...
5 3 [...]
5 4 [...]

6 0 *ì-nu*
6 1 *ì-nu*
6 2 ...
6 3 [...]
6 4 *ì-nu*

7 0 NIM.KI
7 1 NIM.KI
7 2 ...
7 3 [...]
7 4 [NI]M.[KI]

8 0 *ù*
8 1 *ù*
8 2 ...
8 3 [...]
8 4 ⸢*ù*⸣

9 0 *pá-ra-aḫ-śum*.KI
9 1 *pá-ra-aḫ-śum*.KI
9 2 ...
9 3 [*pá-ra-a*]*ḫ-śum*.K[I]
9 4 *pá-ra-aḫ-śu*[*m*.KI]

10 0 SAG.GIŠ.RA-*ni*
10 1 SAG.GIŠ.RA-*ni*
10 2 ...
10 3 [SAG.GIŠ].⸢RA⸣-[*ni*]
10 4 SAG.GI[Š.RA-*ni*]

11 0 *in* NAM.RA.AK
11 1 *in* NAM.RA.AK
11 2 ...
11 3 *in* NAM.RA.AK
11 4 [...]

12 0 NIM.KI
12 1 NIM.KI
12 2 ...
12 3 NIM.KI
12 4 [...]

13 0 A.MU.RU
13 1 A.MU.RU
13 2 ...
13 3 A.MU.RU
13 4 [...]

1 0 [*a-na*]
1 1 [...]
1 2 [...]

2 0 [^{d}UTU]
2 1 [...]
2 2 [...]

3 0 *r*[*í-mu-úš*]
3 1 [...]
3 2 *r*[*í-mu-úš*]

4 0 LUG[AL]
4 1 [...]
4 2 LUG[AL]

5 0 KI[Š]
5 1 [...]
5 2 KI[Š]

6 0 *i*-[*nu*]
6 1 [...]
6 2 *i*-[*nu*]

7 0 N[IM.KI]
7 1 [...]
7 2 N[IM.KI]

8 0 [*ù*]
8 1 [...]
8 2 [...]

9 0 ⸢*pá-ra-aḫ-šum*.KI⸣
9 1 ⸢*pá-ra-aḫ-šum*.KI⸣
9 2 [...]

10 0 SAG.GIŠ.RA-*ni*
10 1 SAG.GIŠ.RA-*ni*
10 2 [...]

11 0 *in* ⸢NAM.RA⸣.[AK]
11 1 *in* ⸢NAM.RA⸣.[AK]
11 2 [...]

12 0 [NIM.KI]
12 1 [...]
12 2 [...]

13 0 [A.MU.RU]
13 1 [...]
13 2 [...]

1 0 *a-n*[*a*]
1 1 *a*-[*na*]
1 2 *a-n*[*a*]

2 0 [d]E[N.ZU]
2 1 [d]E[N.ZU]
2 2 [...]

3 0 *r*[*í-mu-úš*]
3 1 *r*[*í-mu-úš*]
3 2 [...]

4 0 LU[GAL]
4 1 LU[GAL]
4 2 [...]

5 0 K[IŠ]
5 1 K[IŠ]
5 2 [...]

6 0 *ì*-[*nu*]
6 1 *ì*-[*nu*]
6 2 [...]

7 0 [NIM.KI]
7 1 [...]
7 2 [...]

8 0 [*ù*]
8 1 [...]
8 2 [...]

9 0 [*pá-ra-aḫ-šum*.KI]
9 1 [...]
9 2 [...]

10 0 [SAG.GIŠ.RA-*ni*]
10 1 [...]
10 2 [...]

11 0 [*in* NAM.RA.AK]
11 1 [...]
11 2 [...]

12 0 [NIM.KI]
12 1 [...]
12 2 [...]

13 0 [A.MU.RU]
13 1 [...]
13 2 [...]

1 0 *rí-mu-úś*
1 1 [...]
1 2 ...
1 3 [*r*]*í-mu-úś*
1 4 *rí-mu-úś*

2 0 LUGAL
2 1 L[UGAL]
2 2 ...
2 3 [L]UGAL
2 4 LUGAL

3 0 KIŠ
3 1 KI[Š]
3 2 ...
3 3 [K]IŠ
3 4 KIŠ

4 0 SAG.GIŠ.RA
4 1 SAG.GIŠ.R[A]
4 2
4 3 [SAG].GIŠ.RA
4 4 SAG.GIŠ.RA

5 0 NIM.KI
5 1 NIM.KI
5 2 ...
5 3 [NIM].KI
5 4 NIM.KI

6 0 *ù*
6 1 *ù*
6 2 ...
6 3 ⌈*ù*⌉
6 4 *ù*

7 0 *pá-ra-aḫ-śum*.KI
7 1 *pá-ra-aḫ-śum*.KI
7 2 ...
7 3 [...]
7 4 [*pá-r*]*a-aḫ-śum*.KI

1 0 [*rí-mu-úš*]
1 1 [...]
1 2 [...]
1 3 [*rí-mu-úš*]

2 0 [lugal]-
2 1 [...]
2 2 [...]
2 3 [...]

3 0 [KIŠ]
3 1 [...]
3 2 [...]
3 3 [...]

4 0 [u_4-ul-lí-a-ta]
4 1 [...]
4 2 [...]
4 3 [...]

5 0 [^{d}en-líl-ra]
5 1 [...]
5 2 [...]
5 3 [...]

6 0 [lú na-me]
6 1 [...]
6 2 [...]
6 3 [...]

7 0 [al]an-a[n-na]
7 1 [...]
7 2 [...]
7 3 [al]an-a[n-na]

8 0 nu-ta-dím
8 1 ⸢nu⸣-ta-⸢dím⸣
8 2 [...]
8 3 nu-ta-dím

9 0 *rí-mu-úš*
9 1 [*r*]*í-mu-úš*
9 2 [...]
9 3 *rí-mu-úš*

10 0 lugal-
10 1 lugal-
10 2 [...]
10 3 lugal-

11 0 KIŠ
11 1 KIŠ
11 2 [...]
11 3 [K]IŠ

12 0 alan-na-ni an-na-kam
12 1 alan-na-ni (erasure) ⸢an⸣-na-kam
12 2 [...]
12 3 alan-na-ni an-na-kam

13 0 ì-dím
13 1 [ì]-dím
13 2 [...]
13 3 ì-dím

14 0 igi-^{d}en-líl-lá-šè
14 1 igi-⸢^{d}⸣en-líl-lá-šè
14 2 [...]
14 3 igi-^{d}en-líl-lá-šè

15 0 ì-gub
15 1 ì-gub
15 2 [...]
15 3 ì-gub

16 0 NI.UL-
16 1 NI.UL-
16 2 [...]
16 3 NI.UL-

17 0 dingir-re-ne-ka
17 1 dingir-re-ne-ka
17 2 [...]
17 3 dingir-re-ne-ka

18 0 me-te-ni
18 1 me-te-ni
18 2 [...]
18 3 me-te-ni

19 0 ì-ŠID
19 1 ì-ŠID
19 2 [...]
19 3 ì-ŠID

20 0 lú
20 1 lú
20 2 [...]
20 3 lú

21 0 im-sar-ra-e
21 1 im-sar-ra-e
21 2 [...]
21 3 im-sar-ra-e

22 0 ab-ḫa-lam-me-a
22 1 ab-ḫa-lam-me-a
22 2 [...]
22 3 [a]b-ḫa-lam-me-a

23 0 ^{d}en-líl ^{d}utu-bi
23 1 ^{d}en-líl ^{d}utu-bi
23 2 [...]
23 3 [^{d}en]-líl ^{d}[...]

24 0 suḫuš-sa-ni
24 1 suḫuš-sa-ni
24 2 [...]
24 3 suḫuš-sa-⸢ni⸣

25 0 ḫé-bu$_x$(PAD)-re$_6$-ne
25 1 ḫé-bu$_x$(PAD)-re$_6$-⸢ne⸣
25 2 [...]
25 3 ḫé-bu$_x$(PAD)-r[e$_6$]-n[e]

26 0 [numun-na-n]i
26 1 [...]
26 2 [numun-na-n]i
26 3 [...]

27 0 ḫé-ri-ri-ge-ne
27 1 [...-n]e
27 2 ḫé-ri-ri-ge-ne
27 3 [...]

Colophon 1

1 0 ⸢mu-sar-ra URUDU⸣.ŠEN.*za*-⸢*ḫum*⸣
1 1 ⸢mu-sar-ra URUDU⸣.ŠEN.*za*-⸢*ḫum*⸣
1 2 [...]
1 3 [...]

Colophon 2

1 0 mu-sar-ra
1 1 [...]
1 2 [...]
1 3 mu-sar-ra

2 0 ti-x-bi-ni
2 1 [...]
2 2 [...]
2 3 ti-x-bi-ni

3 0 *rí-mu-úš*-kam
3 1 [...]
3 2 [...]
3 3 *rí-mu-úš*-kam

1 0 [*rí-mu-úš*]
1 1 [...]
1 2 [...]
1 3 [...]

2 0 [LUGAL]
2 1 [...]
2 2 [...]
2 3 [...]

3 0 [KIŠ]
3 1 [...]
3 2 [...]
3 3 [...]

4 0 [*íš-tum da-ar*]
4 1 [...]
4 2 [...]
4 3 [...]

5 0 [*a-na* ^{d}*en-líl*]-*l*[*e*](?)
5 1 [...]
5 2 [...]
5 3 [*a-na* ^{d}*en-líl*]-*l*[*e*](?)

6 0 [*m*]*a-na-ma*
6 1 [...]
6 2 [...]
6 3 [*m*]*a-na-ma*

7 0 DÙL KÙ.AN
7 1 [...]
7 2 [...]
7 3 DÙL KÙ.AN

8 0 *la ib-ni*
8 1 *la* ⸢*ib*⸣-*ni*
8 2 [...]
8 3 *la ib-ni*

9 0 *rí-mu-úš*
9 1 *rí-mu-úš*
9 2 [...]
9 3 *rí-mu-úš*

10 0 LUGAL
10 1 LUGAL
10 2 [...]
10 3 LUGAL

11 0 KIŠ
11 1 KIŠ
11 2 [...]
11 3 KIŠ

12 0 DÙL-*šu*
12 1 DÙL-*šu*
12 2 [...]
12 3 DÙL-*šu*

13 0 *ša* KÙ.AN
13 1 *ša* KÙ.AN
13 2 [...]
13 3 *ša* KÙ.AN

14 0 *ib-ni-ma*
14 1 *ib-ni-ma*
14 2 [...]
14 3 *ib-ni-ma*

15 0 IGI-*me* ^{d}*en-líl*
15 1 IGI-*me* ^{d}*en-líl*
15 2 [...]
15 3 IGI-*me* ^{d}*en-líl*

16 0 *i-za-az*
16 1 *i-za-az*
16 2 [...]
16 3 *i-za-*[*az*]

17 0 DA-*íś ì-li*
17 1 DA*íś ì-li*
17 2 [...]
17 3 DA-*í*[*ś* ...]

18 0 MU-*śu*
18 1 MU-*śu*
18 2 [...]
18 3 MU-[*śu*]

19 0 *u-śa-mi-id*
19 1 *u-śa-mi-id*
19 2 [...]
19 3 *u-śa-m*[*i-id*]

20 0 *ša* DUB
20 1 *ša* DUB
20 2 [...]
20 3 *ša* D[UB]

21 0 *śu*$_{4}$*-a*
21 1 *śu*$_{4}$*-a*
21 2 [...]
21 3 *śu*$_{4}$*-a*

22 0 *u-śa-sà-ku-ni*
22 1 *u-śa-sà-ku-ni*
22 2 [...]
22 3 *u-śa-sà-ku-ni*

23 0 ^{d}*en-líl*
23 1 ^{d}*en-líl*
23 2 [...]
23 3 ^{d}*en-l*[*íl*]

24 0 *ù*
24 1 *ù*
24 2 [...
24 3 (erasure) ⸢*ù*⸣

25 0 ^{d}UTU
25 1 ^{d}UTU
25 2 [...]
25 3 [^{d}]UTU

26 0 SUḪUŠ-*śu*
26 1 SUḪUŠ-*śu*
26 2 [...]
26 3 ⸢SUḪUŠ⸣-*śu*

27 0 *li-sú-ḫa*
27 1 *li-sú-ḫa*
27 2 [...]
27 3 [*l*]*i-sú-ḫa*

28 0 *ù*
28 1 *ù*
28 2 [*ù*]
28 3 *ù*

29 0 ŠE.NUMUN-*śu*
29 1 ŠE.NUMUN-*śu*
29 2 [...]
29 3 [ŠE.NU]MUN-*śu*

30 0 *li-il-qù-tá*
30 1 *li-il-qù-tá*
30 2 [*li-il-q*]*ù*-[*tá*]
30 3 [*li*]-*il*-[*qù-t*]*á*

Colophon 2

1 0 mu-sar-ra
1 1 [...]
1 2 [...]
1 3 mu-sar-ra

Colophon 2 (continued)

2 0 ti-x-bi-ni
2 1 [...]
2 2 [...]
2 3 ti-x-bi-ni

3 0 *rí-mu-úś*-KAM
3 1 [...]
3 2 [...]
3 3 *rí-mu-úś*-KAM

1 0 *ma-an-íś-tu-śu*
1 1 [...]
1 2 [...]
1 3 [...]
1 4 [...]
1 5 [...]
1 6 *ma-an-íś-tu-śu*
1 7 *ma-an-íś-tu-*[*śu*]
1 8 [...]*-tu-*[*ś*]*u*

2 0 LUGAL
2 1 [...]
2 2 [...]
2 3 [...]
2 4 [...]
2 5 [...]
2 6 LUGAL
2 7 LUGAL
2 8 [...]

3 0 KIŠ
3 1 [...]
3 2 [...]
3 3 [...]
3 4 [...]
3 5 [...]
3 6 KIŠ
3 7 K[IŠ]
3 8 [...]

4 0 *ì-nu*
4 1 [...]
4 2 [...]
4 3 [...]
4 4 [...]
4 5 [...]
4 6 *ì-nu*
4 7 ⌈*ì*⌉*-nu*
4 8 [...]

5 0 *an-ša-an*.KI
5 1 [...]
5 2 [...]
5 3 [...]
5 4 [...]
5 5 [...]
5 6 *an-ša-an*.KI
5 7 *an-ša-a*[*n*.KI]
5 8 [...]

6 0 *ù*
6 1 [...]
6 2 [...]
6 3 [...]
6 4 [...]
6 5 [...]
6 6 *ù*
6 7 [...]
6 8 [...]

7 0 *ši*$_4$*-rí-ḫu-um*.KI
7 1 [...]
7 2 [...]
7 3 [...]
7 4 [...]
7 5 [...]
7 6 *ši*$_4$*-rí-ḫu-um*.KI
7 7 [...]
7 8 [...]-⌈*um*.KI⌉

8 0 SAG.GIŠ.RA-*ni*
8 1 [...]
8 2 [...]
8 3 [...]
8 4 [...]
8 5 [...]
8 6 SAG.GIŠ.RA-*ni*
8 7 [...]
8 8 SAG.GIŠ.RA-*ni*

9 0 *ti-a-am-tàm*
9 1 [...]
9 2 [...]
9 3 [...]
9 4 [...]
9 5 [...]
9 6 *ti-a-am-tàm*
9 7 [...]
9 8 *ti-a-am-tàm*

10 0 *śa-pil-tàm*
10 1 [...]
10 2 [...]
10 3 [...]
10 4 [...]
10 5 [...]
10 6 *śa-pil-tàm*
10 7 [...]
10 8 *śa-pil-tàm*

11 0 MÁ.MÁ GIŠ.LA-*e*
11 1 [...]
11 2 [...]
11 3 [...]
11 4 [...]
11 5 [...]
11 6 MÁ.MÁ GIŠ.LA-*e*
11 7 [...]
11 8 MÁ.MÁ GIŠ.LA-*e*

12 0 *u-śa-bì-ir*
12 1 [...]
12 2 [...]
12 3 [...]
12 4 [...]
12 5 [...]-[*i*]*r*
12 6 [*u-śa*]-[*b*]*ì-ir*
12 7 [...]
12 8 *u-śa-bì-ir*

13 0 URU.KI.URU.KI
13 1 [...]
13 2 [...]
13 3 [...]
13 4 UR[U...]
13 5 [... U]RU.KI
13 6 [...]
13 7 [...]
13 8 URU.KI.URU.KI

14 0 *a-bar-ti*
14 1 [...]
14 2 [...]
14 3 [...]
14 4 *a-b*[*ar-ti*]
14 5 [...-*t*]*i*
14 6 *a-*⸢*bar-ti*⸣
14 7 [...]
14 8 *a-bar-ti*

15 0 *ti-a-am-tim*
15 1 *ti-a-*⸢*am-tim*⸣
15 2 [...]
15 3 *ti-*⸢*a*⸣-[...]
15 4 *t*[*i-*...]
15 5 [*ti*]-⸢*a*⸣-*am-tim*
15 6 *ti-a-am-tim*
15 7 [...]
15 8 *ti-a-am-tim*

16 0 32 *a-na*
16 1 32 *a-na*
16 2 [x]+10+2 *a-*⸢*na*⸣
16 3 32 *a-*[*na*]
16 4 30+1+[1] [...]
16 5 [30]+2 *a-na*
16 6 33 *a-na*
16 7 [...]
16 8 33 *a-na*

17 0 REC 169
17 1 REC 169
17 2 ⸢REC 169⸣(KASKAL+⸢x⸣)
17 3 ⸢REC 169⸣(KASKAL+⸢x⸣)
17 4 ⸢REC 169⸣(KASKAL+[x])
17 5 ⸢REC 169⸣([K]ASKAL+x)
17 6 REC 169
17 7 [...]
17 8 REC 169

18 0 *ip-ḫu-ru-nim-ma*
18 1 *ip-ḫu-ru-nim-ma*
18 2 *ip-ḫu-r*[*u*]*-nim-ma*
18 3 *ip-ḫu-r*[*u*]*-nim-m*[*a*]
18 4 *i*[*p-ḫu-ru*]*-nim-*[*ma*]
18 5 *ip-ḫu-ru-nim-ma*
18 6 *ip-ḫu-ru-nim-ma*
18 7 [...]
18 8 [...]

19 0 *iš*$_{11}$*-ar*
19 1 *iš*$_{11}$*-ar*
19 2 *iš*$_{11}$*-a*[*r*]
19 3 [*i*]*š*$_{11}$*-a*[*r*]
19 4 ⸢*iš*$_{11}$⸣-[*ar*]
19 5 *iš*$_{11}$*-ar*
19 6 *iš*$_{11}$*-ar*
19 7 [...]
19 8 [...]

20 0 *ù*
20 1 *ù*
20 2 [...]
20 3 [...]
20 4 [...]
20 5 *ù*
20 6 *ù*
20 7 [...]
20 8 [...]

21 0 URU.KI.URU.KI-*śu-nu*
21 1 URU.KI.URU.KI-*śu-nu*
21 2 [...]
21 3 [...]
21 4 [...]
21 5 URU.KI.URU.KI-⸢*śu*⸣-[*nu*]
21 6 URU.KI.URU.KI-*śu-nu*
21 7 [...]
21 8 [...]

22 0 SAG.GIŠ.RA
22 1 SAG.GIŠ.RA
22 2 [...]
22 3 [...]
22 4 [...]
22 5 [...]
22 6 SAG.GIŠ.R[A]
22 7 [...]
22 8 [...]

23 0 EN.EN-*śu-nu*
23 1 EN.EN-*śu-nu*
23 2 [...]
23 3 [...]
23 4 [...]
23 5 [...]
23 6 EN.E[N-...]
23 7 [...]
23 8 [...]

24 0 [*u-ś*]*a-am-*[*q*]*í-it*
24 1 [*u-ś*]*a-am-*[*q*]*í-it*
24 2 [...]
24 3 [...]
24 4 [...]
24 5 [...]
24 6 [...]
24 7 [...]
24 8 [...*-q*]*í-*[*i*]*t*

25 0 *ù*
25 1 ⌈*ù*⌉
25 2 [...]
25 3 [...]
25 4 [...]
25 5 [...]
25 6 [...]
25 7 [...]
25 8 ⌈*ù*⌉

26 0 *íš-tu*[*m-ma*]
26 1 [...]
26 2 [...]
26 3 [...]
26 4 [...]
26 5 [...]
26 6 *í*[*š-tum-ma*]
26 7 [...]
26 8 [*í*]*š-tu*[*m-ma*]

27 0 *i*[*d-ké-ás-su-nu-ma*]
27 1 [...]
27 2 [...]
27 3 [...]
27 4 [...]
27 5 [...]
27 6 *i*[*d-*...]
27 7 [...]
27 8 x x [...]

28 0 *a-dì-*⌈*ma*⌉
28 1 [...]
28 2 [...]
28 3 [...]
28 4 [...]
28 5 [...]
28 6 *a-dì-*⌈*ma*⌉
28 7 [...]
28 8 [*a*]*-d*[*ì-ma*]

29 0 *ḫu-rí* KÙ
29 1 [...]
29 2 [...]
29 3 [...]
29 4 [...]
29 5 [...]
29 6 *ḫu-rí* KÙ
29 7 [...]
29 8 [...]

30 0 *íl-qù-ut*
30 1 [...]
30 2 [...]
30 3 [...]
30 4 [...]
30 5 [...]
30 6 *íl-qù-ut*
30 7 [...]
30 8 *í*[*l-qù-ut*]

31 0 ŚA.DÚ-*e*
31 1 [...]
31 2 [...]
31 3 [...]
31 4 [...]
31 5 [...]
31 6 ⌈ŚA⌉.DÚ-*e*
31 7 [...]
31 8 Ś[A ...]

32 0 *a-bar-ti*
32 1 [...]
32 2 [...]
32 3 [...]
32 4 [...]
32 5 [...]
32 6 *a-bar-ti*
32 7 [...]
32 8 *a-*[...]

33 0 *ti-a-am-tim*
33 1 [...]
33 2 [...]
33 3 [...]
33 4 [...]
33 5 [...]
33 6 *ti-a-am-tim*
33 7 [...]
33 8 *t*[*i*-...]

34 0 *śa-pil-tim*
34 1 [...]
34 2 [...]
34 3 [...]
34 4 [...]
34 5 [...]
34 6 *śa-pil-tim*
34 7 [...]
34 8 *śa-pi*[*l-tim*]

35 0 NA$_4$.NA$_4$-⸢*sú*⸣-*nu* GI$_6$
35 1 [...]
35 2 [...]
35 3 [...]
35 4 [...]
35 5 [...]
35 6 NA$_4$.NA$_4$-⸢*śu*⸣-*nu* GI$_6$
35 7 [...]
35 8 NA$_4$.NA$_4$-[*śu*]-*nu* G[I$_6$]

36 0 *i-pu-*⸢*lam-ma*⸣
36 1 [...]
36 2 [...]
36 3 [...]
36 4 [...]
36 5 [...]
36 6 [...]-⸢*lam-ma*⸣
36 7 [...]
36 8 *i-pu-l*[*am-ma*]

37 0 *in* MÁ.MÁ
37 1 [...]
37 2 [...]
37 3 [...]
37 4 [...]
37 5 [...]
37 6 [...]
37 7 [...]
37 8 *in* MÁ.MÁ

38 0 *i-ṣa-*[*na-ma*]
38 1 [...]
38 2 [...]
38 3 [...]
38 4 [...]
38 5 [...]
38 6 [...]
38 7 [...]
38 8 *i-ṣa-*[...]

39 0 *in kar-rí-*<*im*>
39 1 [...]
39 2 [...]
39 3 [...]
39 4 [...]
39 5 [...]
39 6 [...]
39 7 [...]
39 8 *in kar-rí-*<*im*>

40 0 *ši a-kà-dè*.KI
40 1 [...]
40 2 [...]
40 3 [...]
40 4 [...]
40 5 [...]
40 6 [...]
40 7 [...]
40 8 *ši a-kà-dè*.KI

41 0 *ìr-ku*$_{8}$*-us*
41 1 [...]
41 2 [...]
41 3 [...]
41 4 [...]
41 5 [...]
41 6 [...]
41 7 [...]
41 8 *ìr-ku*$_{8}$*-us*

42 0 DÙL-*śu*
42 1 [...]
42 2 [...]
42 3 [...]
42 4 [...]
42 5 [...]
42 6 [...]
42 7 [...]
42 8 DÙL-*śu*

43 0 *ib-ni*
43 1 [...]
43 2 [...]
43 3 [...]
43 4 [...]
43 5 [...]
43 6 [...]
43 7 [...]
43 8 *ib-ni*

44 0 *a-na*
44 1 [...]
44 2 [...]
44 3 [...]
44 4 [...]
44 5 [...]
44 6 [...]
44 7 [...]
44 8 *a-na*

45 0 [^{d}*en-líl!*]
45 1 [...]
45 2 [...]
45 3 [^{d}*en-líl*]
45 4 [^{d}UTU]
45 5 [^{d}UTU]
45 6 [^{d}*en-líl*]
45 7 [^{d}*en-líl*]
45 8 ^{d}EN.ZU

46 0 A.MU.RU
46 1 [...]
46 2 [...]
46 3 [...]
46 4 [...]
46 5 [...]
46 6 [...]
46 7 [...]
46 8 A.MU.RU

47 0 ^{d}UTU
47 1 ⸢^{d}⸣[...]
47 2 [...]
47 3 [...]
47 4 [...]
47 5 [...]
47 6 [...]
47 7 [...]
47 8 ^{d}UTU

48 0 *ù*
48 1 *ù*
48 2 [...]
48 3 [...]
48 4 [...]
48 5 [...]
48 6 [...]
48 7 [...]
48 8 *ù*

49 0 *il-a-ba*$_4$
49 1 *il-a-ba*$_4$
49 2 [...]
49 3 [...]
49 4 [...]
49 5 [...]
49 6 [...]
49 7 [...]
49 8 [...]

50 0 *ú-má*
50 1 *ú-má*
50 2 [...]
50 3 [...]
50 4 [...]
50 5 [...]
50 6 [...]
50 7 [...]
50 8 [...]

51 0 *la sú-ra-tum*
51 1 *la sú-ra-tum*
51 2 [...]
51 3 [...]
51 4 [...]
51 5 [...]
51 6 [...]
51 7 [...]
51 8 [...]

52 0 *lu kí-ni-íś-ma*
52 1 *lu kí-ni-íś-ma*
52 2 [...]
52 3 [...]
52 4 [...]
52 5 [...]
52 6 [...]
52 7 [...]
52 8 [...]

53 0 *ša* DUB
53 1 *ša* DUB
53 2 [...]
53 3 [...]
53 4 [...]
53 5 [...]
53 6 [...]
53 7 [*ša*] ⸢DUB⸣
53 8 [...]

54 0 *śu*$_4$*-a*
54 1 *śu*$_4$*-a*
54 2 [...]
54 3 [...]
54 4 [...]
54 5 [...]
54 6 [...]
54 7 ⸢*śu*$_4$*-a*⸣
54 8 [...]

55 0 *u-sá-sà-ku-ni*
55 1 *u-sá-sà-ku-ni*
55 2 [...]
55 3 [...]
55 4 [...]
55 5 [...]
55 6 [...]
55 7 [*u-sá*]*-sà-*⸢*ku*⸣-[*ni*]
55 8 [...]

56 0 ⸢^{d}⸣*en-líl*
56 1 ^{d}UTU
56 2 [...]
56 3 [...]
56 4 [...]
56 5 [...]
56 6 [...]
56 7 ⸢^{d}⸣*en-líl*
56 8 [...]

57 0 *ù*
57 1 *ù*
57 2 [...]
57 3 [...]
57 4 [...]
57 5 [...]
57 6 [...]
57 7 *ù*
57 8 [...]

58 0 ^{d}UTU
58 1 [^{d}]INANNA
58 2 [...]
58 3 [...]
58 4 [...]
58 5 [...]
58 6 [...]
58 7 ^{d}UTU
58 8 ^{d}[...]

59 0 SUḪUŠ-*śu*
59 1 [SUḪUŠ]-*śu*
59 2 [...]
59 3 [...]
59 4 [...]
59 5 [...]
59 6 [...]
59 7 SUḪUŠ-*śu*
59 8 SUḪUŠ-*śu*

60 0 *li-sú-ḫa*
60 1 [...]
60 2 [...]
60 3 [...]
60 4 [...]
60 5 [...]
60 6 [...]
60 7 *li-sú-ḫa*
60 8 *li-sú-ḫa*

61 0 *ù*
61 1 [...]
61 2 [...]
61 3 [...]
61 4 [...]
61 5 [...]
61 6 [...]
61 7 ⸢*ù*⸣
61 8 (erasure) *ù*

62 0 ŠE.NUMUN-*śu*
62 1 [...]
62 2 [...]
62 3 [...]
62 4 [...]
62 5 [...]
62 6 [...]
62 7 ŠE.NUMUN-*śu*
62 8 ŠE.NUMUN-*śu*

63 0 *li-il-qù-tá*
63 1 [...]
63 2 [...]
63 3 [...]
63 4 [...]
63 5 [...]
63 6 [...]
63 7 [*l*]*i*-⸢*il*⸣-*qù-tá*
63 8 *li-il-qù-tá*

Colophon

1 0 mu-s[ar-ra]
1 1 [...]
1 2 [...]
1 3 [...]
1 4 [...]
1 5 [...]
1 6 [...]
1 7 mu-s[ar-ra]
1 8 [...]

2 0 [ki-gal-b]a
2 1 [...]
2 2 [...]
2 3 [...]
2 4 [...]
2 5 [...]
2 6 [...]
2 7 [ki-gal-b]a
2 8 [...]

Dedicatory label

1 0 *ma-an-iś-tu-śu*
1 1 [...]
1 2 [...]
1 3 [...]
1 4 [...]
1 5 [...]-*ś*[*u*]
1 6 ⌜*ma-an*⌝-*iś*-[*tu*]-*śu*
1 7 *ma-an-iś-tu-śu*
1 8 [...]

2 0 LUGAL
2 1 [...]
2 2 [...]
2 3 [...]
2 4 [...]
2 5 [LU]GAL
2 6 [LUG]AL
2 7 LUGAL
2 8 [...]

3 0 KIŠ
3 1 [...]
3 2 [...]
3 3 [...]
3 4 [...]
3 5 [K]IŠ
3 6 [KI]Š
3 7 KIŠ
3 8 [...]

4 0 *a-na*
4 1 [...]
4 2 [...]
4 3 [...]
4 4 [...]
4 5 [*a*]-*na*
4 6 *a-n*[*a*]
4 7 *a-na*
4 8 [...]

5 0 ᵈ*en-líl*
5 1 [...]
5 2 [...]
5 3 [ᵈ*en-líl*]
5 4 [ᵈUTU]
5 5 [ᵈU]TU
5 6 ᵈ*en-l*[*íl*]
5 7 ᵈ*en-líl*
5 8 [ᵈEN.ZU]

6 0 A.MU.RU
6 1 [...]
6 2 [...]
6 3 [...]
6 4 [...]
6 5 [A.MU].RU
6 6 A.MU.RU
6 7 A.MU.RU
6 8 [...]

Colophon 2

0 1 mu-sar-ra ki-gal-ba
1 1 [...]
2 1 [...]
3 1 [...]
4 1 [...]
5 1 [...]
6 1 mu-sar-ra ki-gal-ba
7 1 mu-sar-ra ki-gal-ba
8 1 [...]

1 0 ^d^*en-líl*
1 1 ^d^*en-líl*
1 2 ^d^*en-líl*
1 3 [...]

2 0 *ma-an-iś-tu-śu*
2 1 *ma-an-iś-tu-śu*
2 2 *ma-an-iś-tu-śu*
2 3 [...]

3 0 LUGAL
3 1 LUGAL
3 2 LUGAL
3 3 [...]

4 0 KIŠ
4 1 KIŠ
4 2 KIŠ
4 3 [...]

5 0 ^d^*en-líl*
5 1 ^d^*en-líl*
5 2 ^d^*en-líl*
5 3 [...]

6 0 *u-śa-ar-bí-śu*
6 1 *u-ś[a-a]r-bí-śu*
6 2 *u-śa-ar-bí-śu*
6 3 *u-śa-a[r-bí-śu]*

7 0 MU-*śu*
7 1 MU-*śu*
7 2 ⌜MU⌝-*śu*
7 3 *śum*$_6$-[*śu*]

8 0 *i-bí*
8 1 *i-bí*
8 2 *i-bí*
8 3 *i-b*[*í*]

9 0 *ù*
9 1 *ù*
9 2 *ù*
9 3 ⌜*ù*⌝

10 0 [GI]Š.GIDRU
10 1 [GIŠ].⌜GIDRU⌝
10 2 [GI]Š.⌜GIDRU⌝
10 3 [GIŠ].GI[DRU]

11 0 *śar-ru-tim*
11 1 [...]
11 2 *śar-ru-tim*
11 3 x [...] x

12 0 ⌜*i-dì*⌝-*śum*$_6$
12 1 ⌜*i-dì-śum*$_6$⌝
12 2 [*i-d*]*ì-śum*$_6$
12 3 [...]

13 0 *ša* DUB
13 1 *ša* DUB
13 2 [*ša*] ⌜DUB⌝
13 3 [...]

14 0 *śu*$_4$-*a*
14 1 *śu*$_4$-*a*
14 2 *śu*$_4$-*a*
14 3 [...]

15 0 *u-śa-sà-ku-ni*
15 1 ⌜*u*⌝-[*ś*]*a-sà-ku-ni*
15 2 [*u-śa-s*]*à-ku-ni*
15 3 [...]

16 0 ^d^*en-líl*
16 1 ^d^*en-líl*
16 2 [...]
16 3 [...]

17 0 *ù*
17 1 *ù*
17 2 *ù*
17 3 [...]

18 0 ^{d}UTU
18 1 ⌈^{d}UTU⌉
18 2 ^{d}UTU
18 3 [...]

19 0 ⌈SUḪUŠ-*śu*⌉
19 1 ⌈SUḪUŠ-*śu*⌉
19 2 [...]
19 3 [...]

20 0 [*l*]*i-sú-ḫa*
20 1 [...]
20 2 [*l*]*i-sú-ḫa*
20 3 [...]

21 0 [*ù*]
21 1 [...]
21 2 [...]
21 3 [...]

22 0 [ŠE.NUMUN]-⌈*śu*⌉
22 1 [...]
22 2 [...]-⌈*śu*⌉
22 3 [...]

23 0 [*li-il-qù-tá*]
23 1 [...]
23 2 [...]
23 3 [...]

24 0 [...]
24 1 [...]
24 2 [...]
24 3 [...]

25 0 [...]
25 1 [...]
25 2 [...]
25 3 [...]

26 0 [...] x x
26 1 [...] x x
26 2 [...]
26 3 [...]

27 0 [...] x
27 1 [...] x
27 2 [...]
27 3 [...]

28 0 [...] x
28 1 [...] x
28 2 [...]
28 3 [...]

Lacuna

Rev. col. ii

16 0 *na-<ra-am>*-^{d}<EN.ZU>
16 1 *na-<ra-am>*-^{d}<EN.ZU>
16 2 *na*-[...]-^{d}[...]

17 0 *da-núm*
17 1 *da-núm*
17 2 *d*[*a-núm*]

18 0 *in ši-ip-rí*
18 1 *in ši-ip-rí*
18 2 *i*[*n* ...]

19 0 ^{d}INANNA
19 1 ^{d}INANNA
19 2 ⸢d⸣[...]

20 0 *il-šu*$_4$
20 1 *il-šu*$_4$
20 2 [...]

21 0 LUGAL
21 1 LUGAL
21 2 [...]

22 0 *a-kà-dè*.KI
22 1 *a-kà-dè*.KI
22 2 [...]

23 0 *ù*
23 1 *ù*
23 2 [...]

24 0 LUGAL
24 1 LUGAL
24 2 [...]

(Blank)

25 0 [...] x
25 1 [...] x
25 2 [...]

26 0 [...] x
26 1 [...] x
26 2 [...]

27 0 [...-*l*]*im*
27 1 [...-*l*]*im*
27 2 [...]

28 0 [...] x
28 1 [...] x
28 2 [...]

29 0 É[N]SI
29 1 É[N]SI
29 2 [...]

30 0 ^{d}*en-líl*
30 1 ^{d}*en-líl*
30 2 [...]

31 0 GÌR.NITA
31 1 GÌR.NITA
31 2 [...]

32 0 *il-a-ba*$_4$
32 1 *il-a-ba*$_4$
32 2 [...]

33 0 MAŠKIM.GI$_4$
33 1 MAŠKIM.GI$_4$
33 2 [...]

34 0 x x
34 1 x x
34 2 [...]

35 0 *ir-ni-*[*na*.I_7]
35 1 *ir-ni-*[*na*.I_7]
35 2 [...]

Rev. col. iii

1 0 *mu-kí-in*
1 1 *mu-kí-in*
1 2 [...]

2 0 SUḪUŠ.SUḪUŠ
2 1 SUḪUŠ.SUḪUŠ
2 2 [...]

3 0 *a-kà-dè*.KI
3 1 *a-kà-dè*.KI
3 2 [...]

4 0 *mu-tar-rí*
4 1 *mu-tar-rí*
4 2 [...]

5 0 *dú-un-nim*
5 1 *dú-un-nim*
5 2 [...]

6 0 *a-na*
6 1 *a-na*
6 2 [...]

7 0 *kà-lí*
7 1 *kà-lí*
7 2 [...]

8 0 *in* É
8 1 *in* É
8 2 [...]

9 0 ^{d}*en-*⌈*líl*⌉
9 1 ^{d}*en-*⌈*líl*⌉
9 2 [...]

10 0 [...]
10 1 [...]
10 2 [...]

11 0 [...]
11 1 [...]
11 2 [...]

12 0 [...].KI
12 1 [...].KI
12 2 [...]

13 0 [...]-*na*
13 1 [...]-*na*
13 2 [...]

14 0 šu-bi igi(?) 2(?)-àm
14 1 šu-bi igi(?) 2(?)-àm
14 2 [...]

15 0 *ì-nu*
15 1 *ì-nu*
15 2 [...]

16 0 *ki-ib-<ra-tum*$_8$>
16 1 *ki-ib-<ra-tum*$_8$>
16 2 [...]

17 0 *ar-<ba-um*>
17 1 *ar-<ba-um*>
17 2 [...]

18 0 *íš-ti-ni-íš* <*i*-KIR-*ni-šu*$_4$>
18 1 *íš-ti-ni-íš*
18 2 *i*[*š-ti*]-*n*[*i-íš*]

19 0 *śar in śar-rí*
19 1 *śar in śar-rí*
19 2 *śar i*[*n* ...]

20 0 *ma-na-ma*
20 1 *ma-na-ma*
20 2 *ma-na-ma*

21 0 *la i-mu-ru*
21 1 *la i-mu-ru*
21 2 *la i-mu-ru*

22 0 *ì-nu*
22 1 *ì-nu*
22 2 *ì-nu*

23 0 *na-ra-am*-^{d}EN.ZU
23 1 *na*-<*ra-am*>-^{d}<EN.ZU>
23 2 *na-ra-am*-^{d}EN.ZU

24 0 *da-núm*
24 1 *da-núm*
24 2 *da-núm*

25 0 *in śi-ip-rí*
25 1 *in śi-ip-rí*
25 2 *in śi-ip-rí*

26 0 ^{d}INANNA
26 1 ^{d}INANNA
26 2 ^{d}INANNA

27 0 *kà-lu*$_5$*-ma*
27 1 *kà-lu*$_5$*-ma*
27 2 *kà-lu*$_5$*-ma*

28 0 *ki-ib-ra-*⸢*tum*$_8$⸣
28 1 *ki-*⸢*ib-ra-tum*$_8$⸣
28 2 *ki-ib-ra-t*[*um*$_8$]

29 0 *ar-ba-um*
29 1 ⸢*ar*⸣-*ba*-[*um*]
29 2 *ar-ba-u*[*m*]

30 0 *íś-ti-ni-íś*
30 1 *íś*-[*ti*]-*ni-íś*
30 2 *íś-ti-ni-íś*

31 0 *i*-KIR-*ni-śu*$_4$*-ma*
31 1 *i*-KIR$_X$(ḪA)-*ni-śu*$_4$*-ma*
31 2 *i*-KIR-*ni-śu*$_4$*-ma*

32 0 *im-ḫu-ru-nim*
32 1 [*i*]*m-ḫu-ru-nim*
32 2 *im-ḫu-ru-ni*[*m*]

33 0 ⸢LUGAL(?)⸣-*am*(?)
33 1 ⸢LUGAL(?)⸣-*am*(?)
33 2 LU[GAL(?) ...]

34 0 [...]
34 1 [...]
34 2 [...]

35 0 [...]-⸢*ù*⸣
35 1 [...]-⸢*ù*⸣
35 2 [...]

36 0 [...-DA]M(?)
36 1 [...-DA]M(?)
36 2 [...]

Rev. col. iv

1 0 [x]-IŠ-*ti*
1 1 [x]-IŠ-*ti*
1 2 [...]

2 0 [...]-*tim*
2 1 [...]-*tim*
2 2 [...]

3 0 [*in*] DI.KU$_5$
3 1 [*in*] DI.KU$_5$
3 2 [...]

4 0 [^{d}*en*]-*líl*
4 1 [^{d}*en*]-*líl*
4 2 [...]

5 0 [...] NE
5 1 [...] NE
5 2 [...]

6 0 [...] x
6 1 [...] x
6 2 [...]

7 0 *iḫ*(?)-*ma*(?)-ZI(?)
7 1 *iḫ*(?)-*ma*(?)-ZI(?)
7 2 [...]

8 0 ^{d}[*e*]*n*-*l*[*íl*]
8 1 ^{d}[*e*]*n*-*l*[*íl*]
8 2 [...]

9 0 *be-lí-śu*
9 1 *be-lí-śu*
9 2 [...]

10 0 *in* [...]
10 1 *in* [...]
10 2 [...]

11 0 MU [...]
11 1 MU [...]
11 2 [...]

12 0 [...]
12 1 [...]
12 2 [...]

13 0 [...]
13 1 [...]
13 2 [...]

14 0 [...] *ši* x [...]
14 1 [...] *ši* x [...]
14 2 [...]

15 0 [x] *ši-la*
15 1 [x] *ši-la*
15 2 [...]

16 0 [...]-*ù*
16 1 [...]-*ù*
16 2 [...]

17 0 [...] x
17 1 [...] x
17 2 [...]

18 0 [...] UD(?)
18 1 [...] UD(?)
18 2 [...]

19 0 *ù*
19 1 *ù*
19 2 [...]

20 0 *ti*-[*a-am-ti*]*m*
20 1 *ti*-[*a-am-ti*]*m*
20 2 [...]

21 0 *i-in*(?) [x (x)]
21 1 *i-in*(?) [x (x)]
21 2 [...]

22 0 IŠ-[...]
22 1 IŠ-[...]
22 2 [...]

23 0 *i-*⌈*bi*⌉-[*ir-m*]*a*
23 1 *i-*⌈*bi*⌉-[*ir-m*]*a*
23 2 [...]

24 0 *m*[*á-gan*.K]I
24 1 *m*[*á-gan*.K]I
24 2 [...]

25 0 ⌈*qáb*⌉*-li*
25 1 ⌈*qáb*⌉*-li*
25 2 [...]

26 0 *ti-*[*a*]*-am-tim*
26 1 *ti-*[*a*]*-am-tim*
26 2 [...]

27 0 SAG.GIŠ.RA
27 1 SAG.GIŠ.RA
27 2 [...]

28 0 *ù*
28 1 *ù*
28 2 [...]

29 0 GIŠ.TUKUL-*kí-šu*$_{4}$
29 1 GIŠ.TUKUL-*kí-šu*$_{4}$
29 2 [...]

30 0 *i*[*n*] *ti-a-am-tim*
30 1 [*in*] *ti-a-am-tim*
30 2 *i*[*n ti*]*-a-am-t*[*im*]

31 0 *ša-píl-tim*
31 1 [*ša*]-⌈*píl*⌉*-tim*
31 2 *ša-píl-*⌈*tim*⌉

32 0 Ì.LUḪ
32 1 Ì.[LU]Ḫ
32 2 Ì.LUḪ

33 0 *na-ra-am-*^{d}EN.ZU
33 1 *na-<ra-am>-*^{d}<EN.ZU>
33 2 *na-ra-am-*^{d}EN.ZU

34 0 *da-núm*
34 1 *d*[*a-núm*]
34 2 *da-núm*

35 0 *in ši-ip-rí*
35 1 *in š*[*i-ip-rí*]
35 2 *in ši-ip-rí*

36 0 ^{d}INANNA
36 1 ^{d}[INANNA]
36 2 ^{d}INANNA

37 0 *ì-nu*
37 1 [...]
37 2 *ì-nu*

38 0 ^{d}*en-líl*
38 1 [...]
38 2 ^{d}⌈*en*⌉*-líl*

39 0 DI.KU$_{5}$-*šu*
39 1 D[I.KU$_{5}$-*šu*]
39 2 ⌈DI.KU$_{5}$⌉-*šu*

40 0 *i-dì-nu-ma*
40 1 [...]
40 2 *i-dì-nu-ma*

41 0 *ù*
41 1 [...]
41 2 *ù*

Rev. col. v

0 0 *ṣé-ra-at*
1 1 *ṣé-ra-*⌈*at*⌉
2 2 *ṣé-ra-at*

2 0 NI.SI$_{11}$
2 1 NI.SI$_{11}$
2 2 NI.SI$_{11}$

3 0 *qá-ti-ís-su*
3 1 *qá-ti-ís-su*
3 2 *qá-ti-ís-su*

4 0 *i-dì-nu*
4 1 *i-dì-nu*
4 2 *i-dì-nu*

5 0 *ù*
5 1 *ù*
5 2 *ù*

6 0 *na-e*
6 1 *na-e*
6 2 *na-e*

7 0 *e-er-tim*
7 1 *e-er-tim*
7 2 *e-er-tim*

8 0 *la i-dì-nu-šum*$_{6}$
8 1 *la i-dì-nu-šum*$_{6}$
8 2 *la i-dì-nu-šum*$_{6}$

9 0 DUG(?).KUR.KU.DÙ [Ì]
9 1 DUG(?).KUR.KU.DÙ [Ì]
9 2 DUG(?).KUR.KU.DÙ

10 0 [IGI-*me*] ⌈^{d}*en-líl*⌉
10 1 [...]
10 2 [IGI-*me*] ⌈^{d}*en-líl*⌉

11 0 [...]
11 1 [...]
11 2 [...]

12 0 [...]
12 1 [...]
12 2 [...]

13 0 [...]
13 1 [...]
13 2 [...]

14 0 [...]
14 1 [...]
14 2 [...]

15 0 [A].MU.RU
15 1 [A].MU.RU
15 2 [...]

16 0 *ma-na-ma*
16 1 *ma-na-ma*
16 2 [...]

17 0 MU
17 1 MU
17 2 [...]

18 0 *na-<ra-am>-*^{d}<EN.ZU>
18 1 *na-<ra-am>-*^{d}<EN.ZU>
18 2 [...]

19 0 LUGAL
19 1 LUGAL
19 2 [...]

20 0 *a-kà-dè*.KI
20 1 *a-kà-dè*.KI
20 2 [...]

21 0 GÌR.NITA «DÙ»
21 1 GÌR.NITA «DÙ»
21 2 [...]

22 0 *ìl-a-ba*$_4$
22 1 *ìl-a-ba*$_4$
22 2 [...]

23 0 *u-śa-sà-ku-ni*(!)
23 1 *u-śa-sà-ku-ni*(!)
23 2 [...]

24 0 *al* DUG(?).KUR.KU.DÙ Ì
24 1 *al* DUG(?).KUR.KU.DU Ì
24 2 [...]

25 0 *na-*<*ra-am*>-^{d}<EN.ZU>
25 1 *na-*<*ra-am*>-^{d}<EN.ZU>
25 2 [...]

26 0 MU-*śu*
26 1 MU-*śu*
26 2 [...]

27 0 *i-śa-kà-nu-ma*
27 1 *i-śa-kà-nu-ma*
27 2 [...]

28 0 DUG(?).KUR.KU.DÙ Ì-*me*
28 1 DUG(?).KUR.KU.DÙ Ì-*me*
28 2 [...]

29 0 *i-qá-bì-ù*
29 1 *i-qá-bì-ù*
29 2 [...]

30 0 *ù*
30 1 *ù*
30 2 [...]

31 0 LÚ.KAS$_4$
31 1 LÚ.KAS$_4$
31 2 [...]

32 0 LÚ-*lam*
32 1 LÚ-*lam*
32 2 [...]

33 0 *ša-ni-am*
33 1 *ša-ni-am*
33 2 [...]

34 0 *u-kál-la-mu-ma*
34 1 *u-kál-la-mu-ma*
34 2 [...]

Rev. col. vi

1 0 MU-*śu*$_4$-*me*
1 1 MU-*śu*$_4$-*me*
1 2 [...]

2 0 *pi-ší-iṭ-ma*
2 1 *pi-ší-iṭ-ma*
2 2 [...]

3 0 MU-*mi-me*
3 1 MU-*mi-me*
3 2 ⌜MU-*mi*⌝-*me*

4 0 *śu-ku*$_8$-*un*
4 1 *śu-ku*$_8$-*un*
4 2 *śu-ku*$_8$-*un*

5 0 *i-qá-bì-ù*
5 1 *i-qá-bì-ù*
5 2 *i-qá-bì-ù*

6 0 ^{d}INANNA-
6 1 ^{d}INANNA-
6 2 ^{d}INANNA-

7 0 *an-nu-ni-tum*
7 1 *an-nu-ni-tum*
7 2 *an-nu-ni-tum*

8 0 AN
8 1 AN
8 2 AN

9 0 ^{d}*en-líl*
9 1 ^{d}*en-líl*
9 2 ^{d}⸢*en-líl*⸣

10 0 *ìl-a-ba*$_4$
10 1 *ìl-a-ba*$_4$
10 2 *ìl-a-*[*ba*$_4$]

11 0 ^{d}EN.ZU
11 1 ^{d}EN.ZU
11 2 ^{d}EN.ZU

12 0 ^{d}UTU
12 1 ^{d}UTU
12 2 ^{d}UTU

13 0 ^{d}[*nergal*]
13 1 ^{d}[...]
13 2 [...]

14 0 ⸢^{d}⸣*u-um*
14 1 [...]
14 2 ⸢^{d}⸣*u-um*

15 0 ⸢^{d}⸣*nin-kar*
15 1 [...]
15 2 ⸢^{d}⸣*nin-kar*

16 0 ⸢*ì*⸣*-lu*
16 1 [...]
16 2 ⸢*ì*⸣*-lu*

17 0 *ra-bí-ù-tum*
17 1 [...]
17 2 *ra-bí-ù-tum*

18 0 *in* ŠU.NÍGIN-*šu-nu*
18 1 [...]
18 2 *in* ŠU.NÍGIN-*šu-nu*

19 0 *ar-ra-tám*
19 1 [*ar-ra-t*]*ám*
19 2 *ar-ra-tám*

20 0 [*l*]*a-mu-tám*
20 1 [*la-m*]*u-tám*
20 2 [*l*]*a-mu-ut-tám*

21 0 *li-ru-ru-úš*
21 1 *li-ru-ru-úš*
21 2 [*l*]*i-ru-ru-úš*

22 0 GIDRU *a-na*
22 1 GIDRU *a-na*
22 2 [...] ⸢*a*⸣*-na*

23 0 ^{d}*en-líl*
23 1 ^{d}*en-líl*
23 2 [^{d}*e*]*n-líl*

24 0 *e u-kí-il*
24 1 *e u-kí-il*
24 2 [...] x x

25 0 *śar-ru*$_9$(URU)*-tám*
25 1 *śar-ru*$_9$(URU)*-tám*
25 2 [...]

26 0 *a-na*
26 1 *a-na*
26 2 [...]

27 0 dINANNA
27 1 dINANNA
27 2 [...]

28 0 *e iṣ-ba-at*
28 1 *e iṣ-ba-at*
28 2 [...]

29 0 d*nin-ḫur-sag*
29 1 d*nin-ḫur-sag*
29 2 [...]

30 0 *ù*
30 1 *ù*
30 2 [...]

31 0 d*nin-tu*
31 1 d*nin-tu*
31 2 [...]

32 0 NITA
32 1 NITA
32 2 [...]

33 0 *ù*
33 1 *ù*
33 2 [...]

34 0 MU
34 1 MU
34 2 [...]

35 0 *a i-dì-na-śum*$_6$
35 1 *a i-dì-na-śum*$_6$
35 2 [...]

36 0 *ra*-x
36 1 *ra*-x
36 2 [...]

37 0 *śar-ru*$_9$(URU)*-śu*
37 1 *śar-ru*$_9$(URU)*-śu*
37 2 [...]

Rev. col. vii

1 0 [d]IŠKUR
1 1 [d]IŠKUR
1 2 [...]

2 0 *ù*
2 1 *ù*
2 2 [...]

3 0 d*nisaba*
3 1 d*nisaba*
3 2 [...]

4 0 ⸢*śi*$_4$⸣*-rí-iḫ-śu*$_4$
4 1 ⸢*śi*$_4$⸣*-rí-iḫ-śu*$_4$
4 2 [...]

5 0 *e u-śu-śi-ra*
5 1 *e u-śu-śi-ra*
5 2 [...]

6 0 dEN.KI
6 1 dEN.KI
6 2 [...]

7 0 I_7-*śu*$_4$
7 1 I_7-*śu*$_4$
7 2 [...]

8 0 *sà-ki-kà-am*
8 1 *sà-ki-kà-am*
8 2 [...]

9 0 *li-im-dú-ud*
9 1 *li-im-dú-ud*
9 2 [...]

1 0 *na-ra-am-*^{d}EN.ZU
1 1 *na-ra-am-*^{d}EN.ZU
1 2 *na-ra-am-*^{d}EN.ZU
1 3 *na-ra-am-*^{d}EN.ZU
1 4 [*n*]*a-ra-am-*[^{d}]EN.[ZU]

2 0 LUGAL
2 1 LUGAL
2 2 LUGAL
2 3 LUGAL
2 4 LU[GAL]

3 0 *ki-ib-ra-tim*
3 1 *ki-ib-ra-tim*
3 2 *ki-ib-ra-tim*
3 3 *ki-ib-ra-tim*
3 4 *ki-ib-*[*ra-tim*]

4 0 *ar-ba-im*
4 1 *ar-ba-im*
4 2 *ar-ba-im*
4 3 *ar-ba-im*
4 4 *ar-*[*ba-im*]

5 0 BUR
5 1 BUR
5 2 BUR
5 3 BUR
5 4 B[UR]

6 0 NAM.RA.AK
6 1 NA[M.]RA.AK
6 2 NAM.RA.AK
6 3 NAM.RA.AK
6 4 N[AM.RA.AK]

7 0 *má-gan*.KI
7 1 *má-gan*.KI
7 2 *má-gan*.KI
7 3 *má-gan*.KI
7 4 [...]

Col. i′

Lacuna

1′ 0 [*a-n*]*a*
1′ 1 [...]
1′ 2 [*a-n*]*a*

2′ 0 [^{d}EN].⸢ZU⸣
2′ 1 [...]
2′ 2 [^{d}EN].⸢ZU⸣

3′ 0 [*áś-ru*]-*uk*(Text: AZ)
3′ 1 [...]
3′ 2 [*áś-ru*]-*uk*(Text: AZ)

4′ 0 [*ma-n*]*a-ma*
4′ 1 [...]
4′ 2 [*ma-n*]*a-ma*

5′ 0 [MU]-*mi*
5′ 1 [...]
5′ 2 [MU]-*mi*

6′ 0 ⸢*a*⸣ *u-śa-sí-ik*
6′ 1 [...]
6′ 2 ⸢*a*⸣ *u-śa-sí-ik*

7′ 0 [DÙ]L-*mi*
7′ 1 [...]
7′ 2 [DÙ]L-*mi*

8′ 0 [*ma-ḫa-ar*]
8′ 1 [...]
8′ 2 [...]

9′ 0 [^{d}EN.ZU]
9′ 1 [...]
9′ 2 [...]

10′ 0 [*li-zi-iz*]
10′ 1 [...]
10′ 2 [...]

Lacuna

Col. ii′

1 0 *ma-na-ma*
1 1 *ma-na-ma*
1 2 [...]

2 0 MU-*mi*
2 1 MU-*mi*
2 2 [...]

3 0 *na-ra-am*-^{d}EN.ZU
3 1 *na-ra-am*-^{d}EN.ZU
3 2 [...]

4 0 *da-nim*(!)
4 1 *da-nim*(!)
4 2 [...]

5 0 LUGAL
5 1 LUGAL
5 2 [...]

6 0 *ki-ib-ra-tim*
6 1 [...]
6 2 *ki-ib-ra-tim*

7 0 *ar-ba-im*
7 1 *ar-ba-im*
7 2 [...]

8 0 *u-śa-sà-ku-ma*
8 1 *u-śa-sà-ku-ma*
8 2 [...-*m*]*a*

9 0 *al* DÙL
9 1 *al* DÙL
9 2 [...]

10 0 *na-ra-am-*^{d}EN.ZU
10 1 *na-ra-am-*^{d}EN.ZU
10 2 [...^{d}E]N.ZU

11 0 *da-nim*
11 1 *da-nim*
11 2 [...]

12 0 MU-*šu*
12 1 MU-*šu*
12 2 [...]

13 0 *i-ša-kà-nu-ma*
13 1 *i-ša-kà-nu-ma*
13 2 ⸢*i-sá-kà*⸣-[*nu*]-*ma*

14 0 DÙL-*mi-me*
14 1 DÙL-*mi-me*
14 2 DÙL-*mi-me*

15 0 *i-qá-bi-ù*
15 1 *i-qá-bi-ù*
15 2 *i-qá-bi-ù*

16 0 *ù* LÚ-*lam*
16 1 *ù* LÚ-*lam*
16 2 *ù* LÚ-*lam*

17 0 *na-kà-ra-am*
17 1 *na-kà-ra-am*
17 2 *na-kà-ra-am*

18 0 *u-kál-la-mu-ma*
18 1 *u-kál-la-mu-ma*
18 2 *u-kál-la-mu-ma*

19 0 MU-*šu-me*
19 1 MU-*šu-me*
19 2 MU-*šu-me*

20 0 *pi*$_5$-*ši*$_x$(SU$_4$)-*iṭ-ma*
20 1 *pi*$_5$-*ši*$_x$(SU$_4$)-*iṭ-ma*
20 2 *pi*$_5$-⸢*ši*$_x$(SU$_4$)-*iṭ-ma*⸣

21 0 MU-*mi*
21 1 MU-*mi*
21 2 MU-*mi*

22 0 *šu-ku*$_8$-*un*
22 1 *šu-ku*$_8$-*u*[*n*]
22 2 *šu-ku*$_8$-*un*

23 0 *i-qá-bi-ù*
23 1 *i-qá-bi-ù*
23 2 *i-qá-bi-ù*

24 0 ^{d}EN.ZU
24 1 ^{d}EN.ZU
24 2 ^{d}EN.⸢ZU⸣

25 0 *be-al*
25 1 *be-al*
25 2 *be-al*

26 0 DÙL ⸢*šu*$_4$⸣-*a*
26 1 DÙL ⸢*šu*$_4$⸣-*a*
26 2 DÙL *šu-a*

27 0 *ù* ^{d}INANNA-
27 1 *ù* ^{d}INANNA-
27 2 *ù* ^{d}INANNA-

28 0 *an-nu-ni-tum*
28 1 *an-nu-ni-*⸢*tum*⸣
28 2 *an-nu-ni-tum*

29 0 AN
29 1 A[N]
29 2 AN

30 0 ^{d}*en-líl*
30 1 ^{d}*en-líl*
30 2 ⸢^{d}⸣*en-líl*

31 0 *ìl-a-ba*$_4$
31 1 *ìl-a-ba*$_4$
31 2 [*il*]-⸢*a*⸣-*ba*$_4$

32 0 [^{d}][EN].ZU
32 1 ⸢^{d}⸣[EN].ZU
32 2 [^{d}EN].⸢ZU⸣

33 0 [^{d}]UTU
33 1 [^{d}]UTU
33 2 [^{d}UT]U

Col. iii′

1 0 ^{d}*nergal*
1 1 ^{d}*nergal*
1 2 [...]

2 0 ^{d}*u-um*
2 1 ^{d}*u-um*
2 2 [...]

3 0 ^{d}*nin-kar-ak*
3 1 ^{d}*nin-kar-ak*
3 2 [...]

4 0 DINGIR *ra-bí-ù-tum*
4 1 DINGIR *ra-bí-ù-tum*
4 2 [...]

5 0 *in* ŠU.NÍGIN-*śu*$_4$-*nu*
5 1 *in* ŠU.NÍGIN-*śu*$_4$-*nu*
5 2 [...]

6 0 *ar*(Text: Ù)-*ra-tám*
6 1 *ar*(Text: Ù)-*ra-tám*
6 2 [...]

7 0 *la-mu-tám*
7 1 *la-mu-tám*
7 2 [...]

8 0 *li-ru-ru-úś*
8 1 *li-ru-ru-úś*
8 2 [...]

9 0 GIDRU
9 1 GIDRU
9 2 [...]

10 0 *a-na* ^{d}*en-*⸢*líl*⸣
10 1 *a-na* ^{d}*en-*⸢*líl*⸣
10 2 [...]

11 0 *śar-ru-tám*
11 1 *śar-ru-tám*
11 2 [...]

12 0 *a-na* ^{d}INANNA
12 1 *a-na* ^{d}INANNA
12 2 [...]

13 0 *a u-kí-il*
13 1 *a u-kí-il*
13 2 [...]

14 0 *maḫ-rí-íś*
14 1 *maḫ-rí-íś*
14 2 [...]

15 0 *ì-lí-śu*
15 1 *ì-lí-śu*
15 2 [...]

16 0 *a* DU
16 1 *a* DU
16 2 [...]

17 0 ^{d}*nin-ḫur-sag-gá*
17 1 ^{d}*nin-ḫur-sag-gá*
17 2 [^{d}*nin-ḫur-sag*]-⸢*gá*(?)⸣

18 0 *ù*
18 1 *ù*
18 2 *ù*

19 0 ^{d}*nin-tu*
19 1 ^{d}*nin-tu*
19 2 [^{d}*ni*]*n-tu*

20 0 NITA *ù*
20 1 NITA *ù*
20 2 NITA ⸢*ù*⸣

21 0 MU
21 1 MU
21 2 [M]U

22 0 [*a*] *i-dì-na-śum*$_6$
22 1 [*a*] *i-dì-na-śum*$_6$
22 2 [...-*śu*]*m*$_6$

23 0 ⸢^{d}⸣IŠKUR
23 1 ⸢^{d}⸣IŠKUR
23 2 [...]

24 0 *ù* ^{d}*nisaba*
24 1 *ù* ^{d}*nisaba*
24 2 [...]

25 0 [*ś*]*i-rí-iḫ-śu*
25 1 [*ś*]*i-rí-iḫ-śu*
25 2 [...]

26 0 *a* ⸢*ù*⸣-*śe-śi*-⸢*ra*⸣
26 1 *a* ⸢*ù*⸣-*śe-śi*-⸢*ra*⸣
26 2 [...]

27 0 ⸢^{d}⸣EN.⸢KI⸣
27 1 ⸢^{d}⸣EN.⸢KI⸣
27 2 [...]

28 0 ÍD-*sú*
28 1 ÍD-*sú*
28 2 [...]

29 0 A *li-im-dú-ud*
29 1 A *li-im-dú-ud*
29 2 [...]

30 0 *ù* GIŠ.TÚG.PI(Text: KAM)
30 1 *ù* GIŠ.TÚG.PI(Text: KAM)
30 2 [...]

31 0 *a u+ra*(Text: SIKIL)-*pí*-IŠ(Text: MA)
31 1 *a u+ra*(Text: SIKIL)-*pí*-IŠ(Text: MA)
31 2 [...]

32 0 *u-rí*-⸢IŠ⸣
32 1 *u-rí*-⸢IŠ⸣
32 2 [...]

Col. iv′

Caption 1′

1 0 [AN.TA (x)] NE
1 1 [AN.TA (x)] NE
1 2 [...]

2 0 ⸢*im-li*⸣*-ik*
2 1 ⸢*im-li*⸣*-ik*
2 2 [...]

Caption 2′

3 0 KI.[TA] GÌR.NITA
3 1 KI.[TA] GÌR.NITA
3 2 [...]

Caption 2 (continued)

4 0 KI.EN.GI KI.URI
4 1 KI.EN.GI KI.URI
4 2 [...]

5 0 lugal-uru-si
5 1 lugal-uru-si
5 2 [...]

Col. v′

(traces)

Narām-Sîn E2.1.4.6 page 113

Col. i

1 0 ^{d}*en-líl*
1 1 [...]
1 2 ^{d}*en-líl*

2 0 *il-śu*
2 1 [...]
2 2 *il-śu*

3 0 *ìl-a-ba*$_4$
3 1 [...]
3 2 *ìl-a-ba*$_4$

4 0 KALA *ì-li*
4 1 [...]
4 2 KALA *ì-li*

5 0 [*i*]*l*-⸢*la*⸣-*at-śú*
5 1 [...]
5 2 [*i*]*l*-⸢*la*⸣-*at-śú*

6 0 [*na*]-*ra-am*-[^{d}]EN.ZU
6 1 [...]
6 2 [*na*]-*ra-am*-[^{d}]EN.ZU

7 0 [*d*]*a-núm*
7 1 [...]
7 2 [*d*]*a-núm*

8 0 [LU]GAL
8 1 [...]
8 2 [LU]GAL

9 0 [*ki-ib-r*]*a-tim*
9 1 [...]
9 2 [*ki-ib-r*]*a-tim*

10 0 [*ar-ba-im*]
10 1 [...]
10 2 [...]

Lacuna

1′ 0 [*in kiš*.KI]
1′ 1 [...]
1′ 2 [...]

2′ 0 ⸢*ip-ḫur*⸣-*kiš*
2′ 1 ⸢*ip-ḫur*⸣-*kiš*
2′ 2 [...]

3′ 0 *śar-ru*$_x$(URU×A)-*śúm*(ZUM)
3′ 1 *śar-ru*$_x$(URU×A)-*śúm*(ZUM)
3′ 2 [...]

4′ 0 *i-śi*$_{11}$-⸢*ù*⸣
4′ 1 *i-śi*$_{11}$-⸢*ù*⸣
4′ 2 [...]

5′ 0 *ù*
5′ 1 *ù*
5′ 2 [...]

6′ 0 *in* UNU.KI
6′ 1 *in* UNU.KI
6′ 2 [...]

7′ 0 amar-gírid
7′ 1 amar-gírid
7′ 2 [...]

8′ 0 *śar-ru*$_x$(URU×A)-*śúm*(ZUM)-*ma*
8′ 1 *śar-ru*$_x$(URU×A)-*śúm*(ZUM)-*ma*
8′ 2 [...]

9′ 0 *i-śi$_{11}$-ù*
9′ 1 *i-śi$_{11}$-ù*
9′ 2 [...]

10′ 0 *ip-ḫur-kiš*
10′ 1 *ip-ḫur-kiš*
10′ 2 [...]

11′ 0 LUGAL
11′ 1 LUGAL
11′ 2 [...]

12′ 0 *kiš*.KI
12′ 1 *kiš*.KI
12′ 2 [...]

13′ 0 *u-ṣa-bi-àm-ma*
13′ 1 *u-ṣa-bi-àm-ma*
13′ 2 [...]

14′ 0 1 *kiš*.KI
14′ 1 1 *kiš*.KI
14′ 2 [...]

15′ 0 1 *gú-du$_8$-a*
15′ 1 1 *gú-du$_8$-a*
15′ 2 [...]

16′ 0 1 A.ḪA.KI
16′ 1 1 A.ḪA.KI
16′ 2 [...]

17′ 0 1 ZIMBIR (AN.UD.KIB.NUN).KI
17′ 1 1 ZIMBIR (AN.UD.KIB.NUN).KI
17′ 2 [...]

18′ 0 1 *ka-zal-lu*.KI
18′ 1 1 *ka-zal-lu*.KI
18′ 2 1 [...]

19′ 0 1 *gir$_{13}$-tab*.KI
19′ 1 1 *gir$_{13}$-tab*.KI
19′ 2 1 [...]

20′ 0 [1 *a-p*]*i$_5$-ak*.KI
20′ 1 [1 *a-p*]*i$_5$-ak*.KI
20′ 2 [...]

21′ 0 [1 ... .K]I
21′ 1 [1 ... .K]I
21′ 2 [...]

Lacuna

1″ 0 [ŚA].DÚ-*ì*
1″ 1 [ŚA].DÚ-*ì*
1″ 2 [...]

2″ 0 MAR.DÚ.KI
2″ 1 MAR.DÚ.KI
2″ 2 [...]

3″ 0 *in ba-rí-ti*
3″ 1 *in ba-rí-ti*
3″ 2 [...]

4″ 0 A.ḪA.KI
4″ 1 A.ḪA.KI
4″ 2 [...]

5″ 0 *ù*
5″ 1 *ù*
5″ 2 [...]

6″ 0 ÚR×Ú.KI
6″ 1 ÚR×Ú.KI
6″ 2 [...]

7″ 0 *in* SIG_7-*rí*
7″ 1 *in* SIG_7-*rí*
7″ 2 [...]

8″ 0 dEN.ZU
8″ 1 dEN.ZU
8″ 2 [...]

9″ 0 *íš-dú-ud-ma*
9″ 1 *íš-dú-ud-ma*
9″ 2 [...]

10″ 0 REC 169
10″ 1 REC 169
10″ 2 [...]

11″ 0 *u-qá-e*
11″ 1 *u-qá-e*
11″ 2 [...]

12″ 0 *na-ra-am*-dEN.ZU
12″ 1 *na-ra-am*-dEN.ZU
12″ 2 [...]

13″ 0 *da-núm*
13″ 1 *da-núm*
13″ 2 *da-núm*

14″ 0 GURUŠ.GURUŠ-*šu*
14″ 1 GURUŠ.GURUŠ-*šu*
14″ 2 GURUŠ.GURUŠ-*šu*

15″ 0 É-*ba*-AT
15″ 1 É-*ba*-AT
15″ 2 É-*ba*-AT

16″ 0 -*ma*
16″ 1 -*ma*
16″ 2 -*ma*

17″ 0 *a-kà-dè*.KI
17″ 1 *a-kà-dè*.KI
17″ 2 *a-kà-dè*.KI

18″ 0 ŠU.DU_8.A-*ma*
18″ 1 ŠU.DU_8.A-*ma*
18″ 2 ŠU.DU_8.A-*ma*

19″ 0 *a-na* dUTU
19″ 1 *a-na* dUTU
19″ 2 *a-na* dUTU

20″ 0 *è-dì-il*
20″ 1 *è-dì-il*
20″ 2 ⌈*è-dì*]-[x]

21″ 0 dUD-*šu*
21″ 1 dUD-*šu*
21″ 2 [...]

22″ 0 *kiš*.KI-*ši-um*
22″ 1 *kiš*.KI-*ši-um*
22″ 2 [...]

Col. ii

Lacuna

1′ 0 [...*š*]*u*-⌈*nu*⌉
1′ 1 [...*š*]*u*-⌈*nu*⌉
1′ 2 [...]

2′ 0 *u-šá-zé*
2′ 1 *u-šá-zé*
2′ 2 [...]

3′ 0 *ù*
3′ 1 *ù*
3′ 2 [...]

4′ 0 *bí-bí-in-na-at-śu-nu*
4′ 1 *bí-bí-in-na-at-śu-nu*
4′ 2 [...]

5′ 0 *u-gal-li-ib*
5′ 1 *u-gal-li-ib*
5′ 2 [...]

6′ 0 *e*-NI
6′ 1 *e*-NI
6′ 2 [...]

7′ 0 *i-tá-kir*$_9$
7′ 1 *i-tá-kir*$_9$
7′ 2 [...]

8′ 0 *sá-bi-a*
8′ 1 *sá-bi-a*
8′ 2 [...]

9′ 0 *in* SIG$_7$-*rí*
9′ 1 *in* SIG$_7$-*rí*
9′ 2 [...]

10′ 0 ^{d}EN.ZU
10′ 1 ^{d}EN.ZU
10′ 2 [...]

11′ 0 REC 169
11′ 1 REC 169
11′ 2 [...]

12′ 0 *íś-ku*$_8$-*na-ma*
12′ 1 *íś-ku*$_8$-*na-ma*
12′ 2 [...]

13′ 0 *i-tá-aḫ-za-ma*
13′ 1 *i-tá-aḫ-za-ma*
13′ 2 [...]

14′ 0 *in* DI.KU$_5$
14′ 1 *in* DI.KU$_5$
14′ 2 [...]

15′ 0 ^{d}INANNA-
15′ 1 ^{d}INANNA-
15′ 2 [...]

16′ 0 *an-nu-ni-tum*
16′ 1 *an-nu-ni-tum*
16′ 2 [...]

17′ 0 *na-ra-am*-^{d}EN.ZU
17′ 1 *na-ra-am*-^{d}EN.ZU
17′ 2 [...]

18′ 0 *da-núm*
18′ 1 *da-núm*
18′ 2 [...]

19′ 0 *in* REC 169
19′ 1 *in* REC 169
19′ 2 [...]

20′ 0 *in* A.ḪA.KI
20′ 1 *in* A.ḪA.KI
20′ 2 [...]

21′ 0 [*k*]*iš*.KI-[*š*]*i-am*
21′ 1 [*k*]*iš*.KI-[*š*]*i-am*
21′ 2 [...]

22′ 0 [*iš*$_{11}$-*a*]*r*
22′ 1 [*iš*$_{11}$-*a*]*r*
22′ 2 [...]

23′ 0 [*ù*]
23′ 1 [...]
23′ 2 [...]

24′ 0 ^{m}*ì*-⸢*lí*⸣-*ré-ṣí*
24′ 1 ^{m}*ì*-⸢*lí*⸣-*ré-ṣí*
24′ 2 [...]

25′ 0 GÌR.NÍTA
25′ 1 GÌR.NÍTA
25′ 2 [...]

26′ 0 ^{m}DINGIR-*mu-da*
26′ 1 ^{m}DINGIR-*mu-da*
26′ 2 [...]

27′ 0 ^{m}*i-bí*-^{d}*za-ba*$_4$-*ba*$_4$
27′ 1 ^{m}*i-bí*-^{d}*za-ba*$_4$-*ba*$_4$
27′ 2 [...]

28′ 0 ^{m}*im*$_4$-*tá-lik*
28′ 1 ^{m}*im*$_4$-*tá-lik*
28′ 2 [...]

29′ 0 ^{m}*puzur*$_4$-^{d}ASAR
29′ 1 ^{m}⸢*puzur*$_4$⸣-^{d}ASAR
29′ 2 ^{m}*puzur*$_4$-^{d}ASAR

30′ 0 NU.BÀNDA-*ù*
30′ 1 NU.BÀNDA-*ù*
30′ 1 NU.BÀNDA-⸢*ù*⸣

31′ 0 *kiš*.KI
31′ 1 *kiš*.KI
31′ 2 *kiš*.KI

32′ 0 *ù*
32′ 1 *ù*
32′ 2 ⸢*ù*⸣

33′ 0 ^{m}*puzur*$_4$-^{d}*nin-gal*
33′ 1 ^{m}*puzur*$_4$-^{d}*nin-gal*
33′ 2 ^{m}*puzur*$_4$-^{d}*ni*[*n-gal*]

34′ 0 ÉNSI
34′ 1 ÉNSI
34′ 2 É[NSI]

35′ 0 A.ḪA.KI
35′ 1 A.ḪA.KI
35′ 2 [...]

36′ 0 ^{m}DINGIR-SIPA
36′ 1 ^{m}DINGIR-SIPA
36′ 2 [...]

37′ 0 NU.BÀNDA-*śu*
37′ 1 NU.BÀNDA-*śu*
37′ 2 [...]

38′ 0 ^{m}*ku*$_8$-*lí-zum*
38′ 1 ^{m}*ku*$_8$-*lí-zum*
38′ 2 [...]

39′ 0 NU.BÀNDA
39′ 1 NU.BÀNDA
39′ 2 [...]

40′ 0 *éreš*.KI
40′ 1 *éreš*.KI
40′ 2 [...]

41′ 0 ^{m}*e-dam*(Text: SAL.DA)-*u*
41′ 1 ^{m}*e-dam*(Text: SAL.DA)-*u*
41′ 2 [...]

42′ 0 NU.BÀNDA
42′ 1 NU.BÀNDA
42′ 2 [...]

43′ 0 *gú-du*$_8$*-a*.KI
43′ 1 *gú-du*$_8$*-a*.KI
43′ 2 [...]

Col. iii

Lacuna

1′ 0 ᵐDINGIR-x
1′ 1 ᵐDINGIR-x
1′ 2 [...]

2′ 0 ÉNSI
2′ 1 ÉNSI
2′ 2 [...]

3′ 0 BAR.KI
3′ 1 BAR.KI
3′ 2 [...]

4′ 0 ᵐ*da-da*
4′ 1 ᵐ*da-da*
4′ 2 [...]

5′ 0 ÉNSI
5′ 1 ÉNSI
5′ 2 [...]

6′ 0 *a-pi*$_5$*-ak*.KI
6′ 1 *a-pi*$_5$*-ak*.KI
6′ 2 [...]

7′ 0 ŠU.NÍGIN 300 GURUŠ
7′ 1 ŠU.NÍGIN 300 GURUŠ
7′ 2 [...]

8′ 0 *ra-bí-a-ni*
8′ 1 *ra-bí-a-ni*
8′ 2 [...]

9′ 0 *ù*
9′ 1 *ù*
9′ 2 [...]

10′ 0 4,932 LÚ×ÉŠ
10′ 1 (600×8)+(60×2) +10+2 LÚ×ÉŠ
10′ 2 [...]

11′ 0 *in* REC169
11′ 1 *in* REC169
11′ 2 [...]

12′ 0 *i-ik-mi*
12′ 1 *i-ik-mi*
12′ 2 [...]

13′ 0 *ù*
13′ 1 *ù*
13′ 2 [...]

14′ 0 *a-dì-ma*
14′ 1 *a-dì-ma*
14′ 2 [...]

15′ 0 *kiš*.KI
15′ 1 *kiš*.KI
15′ 2 [...]

16′ 0 *ìr-da-śu*$_4$*-ma*
16′ 1 *ìr-da-śu*$_4$*-ma*
16′ 2 [...]

17′ 0 *ù*
17′ 1 *ù*
17′ 2 [...]

18′ 0 *al le-ti*
18′ 1 *al le-ti*
18′ 2 [...]

19′ 0 *kiš*.KI
19′ 1 *kiš*.KI
19′ 2 [...]

20′ 0 KÁ
20′ 1 KÁ
20′ 2 [...]

21′ 0 ^{d}*nin-kár*
21′ 1 ^{d}*nin-kár*
21′ 2 [...]

22′ 0 REC 169
22′ 1 REC 169
22′ 2 [...]

23′ 0 *iš*$_{11}$*-ni-a-ma*
23′ 1 *iš*$_{11}$*-ni-a-ma*
23′ 2 [...]

24′ 0 *íš-ku*$_{8}$*-na-ma*
24′ 1 *íš-ku*$_{8}$*-na-ma*
24′ 2 [...]

25′ 0 [*i-tá*]*-aḫ-*⸢*za-ma*⸣
25′ 1 [*i-tá*]*-aḫ-*⸢*za-ma*⸣
25′ 2 [...]

26′ 0 *in* DI.[KU$_{5}$]
26′ 1 *in* DI.[KU$_{5}$]
26′ 2 [...]

27′ 0 *an-nu-ni-tum*
27′ 1 *an-nu-ni-tum*
27′ 2 ⸢*an-nu*⸣-[*ni-tum*]

28′ 0 *ù*
28′ 1 *ù*
28′ 2 ⸢*ù*⸣

29′ 0 AN-*nim*
29′ 1 AN-*nim*
29′ 2 AN-*nim*

30′ 0 ⸢*na-ra-am*⸣-^{d}EN.ZU
30′ 1 ⸢*na-ra-am*⸣-^{d}EN.ZU
30′ 2 *na-ra-am*-^{d}EN.ZU

31′ 0 *da-núm*
31′ 1 *da-núm*
31′ 2 *da-núm*

32′ 0 *in* REC 169
32′ 1 *in* REC 169
32′ 2 *in* REC 169

33′ 0 *in kiš*.KI
33′ 1 *in kiš*.KI
33′ 2 [...]

34′ 0 *kiš*.KI*-ši-am*
34′ 1 *kiš*.KI*-ši-am*
34′ 2 [...]

35′ 0 *iš*$_{11}$*-ar*
35′ 1 *iš*$_{11}$*-ar*
35′ 2 [...]

36′ 0 *ù*
36′ 1 *ù*
36′ 2 [...]

37′ 0 ^{m}*puzur*$_{4}$-^{d}*nu-muš-da*
37′ 1 ^{m}*puzur*$_{4}$-^{d}*nu-muš-da*
37′ 2 [...]

38′ 0 ÉNSI
38′ 1 ÉNSI
38′ 2 [...]

39′ 0 *ka-zal-lu*.KI
39′ 1 *ka-zal-lu*.KI
39′ 2 [...]

40′ 0 ^{m}*da-núm*
40′ 1 ^{m}*da-núm*
40′ 2 [...]

41′ 0 NU.BÀNDA
41′ 1 NU.BÀNDA
41′ 2 [...]

42′ 0 BAR.KI
42′ 1 BAR.KI
42′ 2 [...]

43′ 0 ^{m}*pu*-BALA
43′ 1 ^{m}*pu*-BALA
43′ 2 [...]

44′ 0 NU.BÀNDA
44′ 1 NU.BÀNDA
44′ 2 [...]

45′ 0 *a-pi*$_5$*-ak*.KI
45′ 1 *a-pi*$_5$*-ak*.KI
45′ 2 [...]

Lacuna

Col. iv

Lacuna

1′ 0 ^{m}*i*-⸢*dì*⸣-[DINGIR]
1′ 1 ^{m}*i*-⸢*dì*⸣-[DINGIR]
1′ 2 [...]

2′ 0 ÉNSI
2′ 1 ÉNSI
2′ 2 [...]

3′ 0 *gú-du*$_8$*-a*.KI
3′ 1 *gú-du*$_8$*-a*.KI
3′ 2 [...]

4′ 0 ^{m}⸢*ì-lí-íś*⸣*-tá-*⸢*kál*⸣
4′ 1 ^{m}⸢*ì-lí-íś*⸣*-tá-*⸢*kál*⸣
4′ 2 [...]

5′ 0 ÉNSI
5′ 1 ÉNSI
5′ 2 [...]

6′ 0 ZIMBIR(AN.UB.KIB.NUN).KI
6′ 1 ZIMBIR(AN.UD.KIB.NUN).KI
6′ 2 [...]

7′ 0 ^{m}*sá-lim-be-lí*
7′ 1 ^{m}*sá-lim-be-lí*
7′ 2 [...]

8′ 0 ÉNSI
8′ 1 ÉNSI
8′ 2 [...]

9′ 0 *gir*$_{13}$*-tab*.KI
9′ 1 *gir*$_{13}$*-tab*.KI
9′ 2 [...]

10′ 0 ^{m}*qì-śum*$_6$
10′ 1 ^{m}*qì-śum*$_6$
10′ 2 [...]

11′ 0 ÉNSI
11′ 1 ÉNSI
11′ 2 [...]

12′ 0 *éreš*.KI
12′ 1 *éreš*.KI
12′ 2 [...]

13′ 0 ^{m}*i-tá*-DINGIR
13′ 1 ^{m}*i-tá*-DINGIR
13′ 2 [...]

14′ 0 ÉNSI
14′ 1 ÉNSI
14′ 2 [...]

15′ 0 *dal-ba-at*.KI
15′ 1 *dal-ba-at*.KI
15′ 2 [...]

16′ 0 ^{m}*im*$_4$*-tá-lik*
16′ 1 ^{m}*im*$_4$*-tá-lik*
16′ 2 [...]

17′ 0 NU.BÀNDA
17′ 1 NU.BÀNDA
17′ 2 [...]

18′ 0 A.ḪA.KI
18′ 1 A.ḪA.KI
18′ 2 [...]

19′ 0 ŠU.NÍGIN 10 ME GURUŠ
19′ 1 ŠU.NÍGIN 10 ME GURUŠ
19′ 2 [...]

20′ 0 *ra-bí-a-ni*
20′ 1 *ra-bí-a-ni*
20′ 2 [*ra*]-*b*[*í-a-ni*]

21′ 0 *ù*
21′ 1 *ù*
21′ 2 ⸢*ù*⸣

22′ 0 2,025 LÚ×ÉŠ
22′ 1 (600×3)+(60×3) +(10×4)+5 LÚ×ÉŠ
22′ 2 (600×?)+(60×3) +(10×?)+5 LÚ×KÁR

23′ 0 *in* REC 169
23′ 1 *in* ⸢REC 169⸣
23′ 2 *in* REC 169

24′ 0 *i-ik-mi*
24′ 1 *i-ik-mi*
24′ 2 *i-ik-mi*

25′ 0 *ù*
25′ 1 *ù*
25′ 2 *ù*

26′ 0 *a-na*
26′ 1 *a-na*
26′ 2 ⸢*a*⸣*-na*

27′ 0 [U]D.KIB.NUN.⸢I₇⸣-*tim*
27′ 1 [U]D.KIB.NUN.⸢I₇⸣-*tim*
27′ 2 [U]D.KIB.NUN.⸢I₇⸣-*tim*

28′ 0 *u-ma-li-šu-*⸢*nu*⸣
28′ 1 *u-ma-*⸢*li*⸣*-šu-*⸢*nu*⸣
28′ 2 [*u-m*]*a-li-*[...]

29′ 0 *ù*
29′ 1 *ù*
29′ 2 ⸢*ù*⸣

30′ 0 URU.KI-*lam*
30′ 1 URU.KI-*lam*
30′ 2 [...]-⸢*lam*⸣

31′ 0 *kiš*.KI
31′ 1 *kiš*.KI
31′ 2 [...].KI

32′ 0 SAG.GIŠ.RA
32′ 1 SAG.GIŠ.RA
32′ 2 [SAG.GIŠ].RA

33′ 0 *ù*
33′ 1 *ù*
33′ 2 ⸢*ù*⸣

34′ 0 BÀD-*śu*
34′ 1 BÀD-*śu*
34′ 2 [...]-*śu*

35′ 0 Ì.GUL.GUL
35′ 1 Ì.GUL.GUL
35′ 2 [Ì.G]UL.GUL

36′ 0 *ù*
36′ 1 *ù*
36′ 2 *ù*

37′ 0 ÍD
37′ 1 ÍD
37′ 2 [Í]D

38′ 0 *in qer-bí-śu*
38′ 1 *in qer-bí-śu*
38′ 2 [...] *qer-bí-śu*

39′ 0 *u-śu-ṣí*
39′ 1 *u-śu-ṣí*
39′ 2 *u-śu-ṣí*

40′ 0 *ù*
40′ 1 *ù*
40′ 2 [...]

41′ 0 *qè-ré-eb*
41′ 1 *qè-ré-eb*
41′ 2 [...]

42′ 0 URU.KI-*lim*
42′ 1 URU.KI-*lim*
42′ 2 [...]

43′ 0 2,525 GURUŠ.GURUŠ
43′ 1 (600×4)+(60×2)
+5 GURUŠ.GURUŠ
43′ 2 [...]

44′ 0 *u-śa-am-qì-it*
44′ 1 *u-śa-am-qì-it*
44′ 2 [...]

45′ 0 *ù*
45′ 1 *ù*
45′ 2 [...]

Lacuna

Col. v

Lacuna

1′ 0 [...]
1′ 1 [...]
1′ 2 [...]

2′ 0 *da*-[...]
2′ 1 *da*-[...]
2′ 2 [...]

3′ 0 ⸢*ù*⸣
3′ 1 ⸢*ù*⸣
3′ 2 [...]

4′ 0 *kiš*.[KI]-*š*[*i*-x]
4′ 1 *kiš*.[KI]-*š*[*i*-x]
4′ 2 [...]

5′ 0 DU [...]
5′ 1 DU [...]
5′ 2 [...]

6′ 0 ᵐ[amar-girid]
6′ 1 ᵐ[amar-girid]
6′ 2 [...]

7′ 0 L[UGAL]
7′ 1 L[UGAL]
7′ 2 [...]

8′ 0 UNU.⌈KI⌉
8′ 1 UNU.⌈KI⌉
8′ 2 [...]

9′ 0 *u-ṣa-b*[*i*]-*àm-ma*
9′ 1 *u-ṣa-b*[*i*]-*àm-ma*
9′ 2 [...]

10′ 0 1 UNU.KI
10′ 1 1 UNU.KI
10′ 2 [...]

11′ 0 1 ÚRI.[KI]
11′ 1 1 ÚRI.[KI]
11′ 2 [...]

12′ 0 1 *lagaš*.KI
12′ 1 1 *lagaš*.KI
12′ 2 [...]

13′ 0 1 *umma*.KI
13′ 1 1 *umma*.KI
13′ 2 [...]

14′ 0 1 *adab*.KI
14′ 1 1 *adab*.KI
14′ 2 [...]

15′ 0 1 *šuruppak*.KI
15′ 1 1 *šuruppak*.KI
15′ 2 1 [...]

16′ 0 1 IN.KI
16′ 1 1 IN.KI
16′ 2 1 x [...]

17′ 0 1 NIBRU.K[I]
17′ 1 1 NIBRU.K[I]
17′ 2 1 N[IBRU.KI]

18′ 0 *íš-tum-ma*
18′ 1 *íš-tum-ma*
18′ 2 ⌈*íš-tum*⌉-[*ma*]

19′ 0 *ti-a-am-tim*
19′ 1 *ti-a-am-tim*
19′ 2 *ti-a-a*[*m-tim*]

20′ 0 *śa-píl-tim*
20′ 1 *śa-píl-tim*
20′ 2 *śa-píl-t*[*im*]

21′ 0 *id-ké-áś-su-nu-ma*
21′ 1 *id-ké-áś-su-nu-ma*
21′ 2 *id-ké*-⌊*áś*⌋-*su-nu-ma*

22′ 0 *ba-rí-ti*
22′ 1 *ba-rí-ti*
22′ 2 *ba-rí-ti*

23′ 0 URU×UD.KI
23′ 1 URU×UD.KI
23′ 2 URU×UD.KI

24′ 0 *ù*
24′ 1 *ù*
24′ 2 *ù*

25′ 0 *áš-na-ak*.KI
25′ 1 *áš-na-ak*.K[I]
25′ 2 *áš-na-ak*.KI

26′ 0 *íś-dú-ud-ma*
26′ 1 [...]
26′ 2 *íś-dú-ud-ma*

27′ 0 REC 169
27′ 1 ⌈REC 169⌉
27′ 2 REC 169

28′ 0 *u-qá-e*
28′ 1 *u-qá-*⌈*e*⌉
28′ 2 *u-qá-e*

29′ 0 *na-ra-am-*ᵈEN.ZU
29′ 1 *na-ra-am-*ᵈEN.ZU
29′ 2 *na-ra-am-*ᵈEN.ZU

30′ 0 *da-núm*
30′ 1 *da-n*[*úm*]
30′ 2 *da-núm*

31′ 0 *íś-má-śu₄-*⌈*ma*⌉
31′ 1 *íś-m*[*á-śu₄-ma*]
31′ 2 *íś-*⌈*má*⌉*-śu₄-*⌈*ma*⌉

32′ 0 *íś-t*[*um*]
32′ 1 *íś-t*[*um*]
32′ 2 [...]

33′ 0 *kiš*.[KI]
33′ 1 *kiš*.[KI]
33′ 2 [...]

34′ 0 DA-*í*[*ś-śu*]
34′ 1 DA-*í*[*ś-śu*]
34′ 2 [...]

35′ 0 *ig-r*[*u-úś*]*-m*[*a*]
35′ 1 *ig-r*[*u-úś*]*-m*[*a*]
35′ 2 [...]

36′ 0 ⌈REC 169⌉
36′ 1 ⌈REC 169⌉
36′ 2 [...]

37′ 0 *íś-k*[*u₈*]*-na-*[*ma*]
37′ 1 *íś-k*[*u₈*]*-na-*[*ma*]
37′ 2 [...]

38′ 0 *i-tá-*[*aḫ*]*-za-*[*ma*]
38′ 1 *i-tá-*[*aḫ*]*-za-*[*ma*]
38′ 2 [...]

39′ 0 *in* DI.[KU₅]
39′ 1 *in* D[I.KU₅]
39′ 2 [...]

Col. vi

Lacuna

1′ 0 *u-*[...]
1′ 1 [...]
1′ 2 *u-*[...]

2′ 0 x [...]
2′ 1 [...]
2′ 2 x [...]

3′ 0 *ša a*[*l* ...] x x
3′ 1 [...]
3′ 2 *ša a*[*l* ...] x x

4′ 0 *ša* [...] Lacuna
4′ 1 [...]
4′ 2 *ša* [...]

5′ 0 I_7 x [...]
5′ 1 [...]
5′ 2 I_7 x [...]

6′ 0 *u-śu-*[*ṣí*]
6′ 1 [...]
6′ 2 *u-śu-*[*ṣí*]

7′ 0 *ù*
7′ 1 [...]
7′ 2 *ù*

8′ 0 *ma* x [x]
8′ 1 [...]
8′ 2 *ma* x [x]

9′ 0 ⸢*ù*⸣
9′ 1 [...]
9′ 2 ⸢*ù*⸣

10′ 0 ᵐluga[l-nì-zu]
10′ 1 [...]
10′ 2 ᵐluga[l-nì-zu]

11′ 0 ÉNS[I]
11′ 1 [...]
11′ 2 ÉNS[I]

12′ 0 [NI]BRU.[KI]
12′ 1 [...]
12′ 2 [NI]BRU.[KI]

13′ 0 [x] x x [x]
13′ 1 [...]
13′ 2 [x] x x [x]

Col. i

(Not preserved)

Col. ii

Lacuna

1′ 0 [ì-nu]
1′ 1 [...]
1′ 2 [...]

2′ 0 [ki-ib-ra-tum]
2′ 1 [...]
2′ 2 [...]

3′ 0 [ar-ba-um]
3′ 1 [...]
3′ 2 [...]

4′ 0 [íś-ti-ni-í]ś
4′ 1 [...]
4′ 2 [...-í]ś

5′ 0 [i-KIR-ni]-śu$_4$
5′ 1 [...]
5′ 2 [...]-śu$_4$

6′ 0 [in rí-m]a-[t]i
6′ 1 [...]
6′ 2 [...-m]a-[t]i

7′ 0 [x-n]im$_4$
7′ 1 [...]
7′ 2 [x-n]im$_4$

Col. iii

Lacuna

1′ 0 [ki-ib-ra-tum]
1′ 1 [...]
1′ 2 [...]

2′ 0 [ar-ba-um]
2′ 1 [...]
2′ 2 [...]

3′ 0 í[ś-t]i-ni-íś
3′ 1 [íś-t]i-[ni]-[í]ś
3′ 2 í[ś-ti]-ni-í[ś]

4′ 0 im$_4$-ḫu-ru-ni-śu$_4$-ma
4′ 1 [im$_4$-ḫ]u-ru-ni-[śu$_4$]-ma
4′ 2 im$_4$-ḫu-r[u]-ni-śu$_4$-m[a]

5′ 0 [íś-t]e$_4$
5′ 1 [íś-t]e$_4$
5′ 2 [...]

6′ 0 [^{d}en-l]íl
6′ 1 [^{d}en-l]íl
6′ 2 [...]

Col. iv

Lacuna

1′ 0 [kà-la-śu]-nu-m[a]
1′ 1 [...]-nu-m[a]
1′ 2 [...]

2′ 0 iš$_{11}$-ar
2′ 1 iš$_{11}$-ar
2′ 2 [...]

Col. iv (continued)

3′ 0 *ù*
3′ 1 *ù*
3′ 2 [...]

4′ 0 *śar-rí-śi-in*
4′ 1 *śar-rí-śi-in*
4′ 2 [...]

5′ 0 *šu-ut in ra-m*[*a*-x]-*at*
5′ 1 *šu-ut in ra-m*[*a*-x]-*at*
5′ 2 [...]

6′ 0 *i*-[*śi*$_{11}$-*ù-nim*]
6′ 1 *i*-[...]
6′ 2 [...]

Col. v

1 0 *ik-mi*-[(x)]
1 1 *ik-mi*-[(x)]
1 2 [...]

2 0 *in* GIŠ.SI.GAR-*im*
2 1 *in* GIŠ.SI.GAR-*im*
2 2 [...]

3 0 *maḫ-rí-íś*
3 1 *maḫ-rí-íś*
3 2 [...]

4 0 ^{d}*en-líl*
4 1 ^{d}*en-líl*
4 2 [...]

5 0 *a-bí-śu*
5 1 *a-bí-śu*
5 2 [...]

6 0 [*u-śá-rí-ib*]
6 1 [...]
6 2 [...]

Lacuna

Col. vi

1 0 [MÁ.GUR$_8$].MÁ.GUR$_8$
1 1 [...].MÁ.GUR$_8$
1 2 [...]

2 0 [*a-kà-d*]*è*.KI
2 1 [*a-kà-d*]*è*.KI
2 2 [...]

3 0 [URU.KI-*l*]*í-śu*
3 1 [URU.KI-*l*]*í-śu*
3 2 [...]

4 0 *u-kí-in-nu*
4 1 [...-*i*]*n-nu*
4 2 *u-kí-i*[*n-nu*]

5 0 *ù*
5 1 ⌈*ù*⌉
5 2 ⌈*ù*⌉

6 0 *ki-i*[*b-ra-t*]*im*
6 1 [...-*t*]*im*
6 2 *ki-i*[*b-*...]

7 0 *a*[*r-ba-im*]
7 1 [...]
7 2 *a*[*r-ba-im*]

8 0 x [...]
8 1 [...]
8 2 x [...]

Lacuna

Col. vii

1 0 [...]
1 1 [...]
1 2 [*a-k*]*à-dè*.KI

2 0 [U]RU.KI-*lí-šu*
2 1 [...]
2 2 [U]RU.KI-*lí-šu*

3 0 ⸢*ù*⸣
3 1 [...]
3 2 ⸢*ù*⸣

4 0 [*ki-i*]*b-ra-tum*
4 1 [...]
4 2 [*ki-i*]*b-ra-tum*

5 0 [*ar-b*]*a*-⸢*um*⸣
5 1 [...]
5 2 [*ar-b*]*a*-⸢*um*⸣

Lacuna

Col. viii

(Not preserved)

1 0 *na-ra-am-*^{d}EN.ZU
1 1 *na-ra-am-*^{d}EN.ZU
1 2 *na-ra-am-*^{d}EN.ZU
1 3 *na-ra-am-*^{d}EN.ZU

2 0 *da-núm*
2 1 *da-núm*
2 2 *da-núm*
2 3 *da-núm*

3 0 LUGAL
3 1 LUGAL
3 2 LUGAL
3 3 LUGAL

4 0 *ki-ib-ra-tim*
4 1 *ki-ib-ra-tim*
4 2 *ki-ib-ra-*⸢*tim*⸣
4 3 *ki-ib-ra-tim*

5 0 *ar-ba-im*
5 1 *ar-ba-im*
5 2 *ar-ba-im*
5 3 *ar-ba-im*

6 0 *ša-ir*
6 1 *ša-ir*
6 2 *ša-ir*
6 3 *ša-ir*

7 0 10 LAL 1 REC 169
7 1 10 ⸢LAL⸣ 1 REC 169
7 2 10 LAL 1 REC 169
7 3 10 LAL 1 REC 169

8 0 *in* MU 1
8 1 *in* MU 1
8 2 *in* MU 1
8 3 *in* MU 1

9 0 *íś-tum*
9 1 *íś-tum*
9 2 *íś-tum*
9 3 *íś-tum*

10 0 REC 169.REC 169
10 1 REC 169.REC 169
10 2 REC 169.REC 169
10 3 REC 169.REC 169

11 0 *śu*$_{4}$*-nu-ti*
11 1 *śu*$_{4}$*-nu-ti*
11 2 *śu*$_{4}$*-nu-ti*
11 3 *śu*$_{4}$*-nu-ti*

12 0 *iš*$_{11}$*-ar-ru*
12 1 *iš*$_{11}$*-ar-ru*
12 2 *iš*$_{11}$*-ar-ru*
12 3 *iš*$_{11}$*-*⸢*ar*⸣*-ru*

13 0 *ù*
13 1 *ù*
13 2 *ù*
13 3 *ù*

14 0 *śar-rí-śu-nu* 3
14 1 *śar-rí-śu-nu* 3
14 2 *śar-rí-śu-nu* 3
14 3 *śar-rí-śu-nu* 3

15 0 *i-ik-mi-ma*
15 1 *i-ik-mi-ma*
15 2 *i-ik-mi-ma*
15 3 *i-ik-mi-ma*

16 0 *maḫ-rí-íś*
16 1 *maḫ-rí-íś*
16 2 *maḫ-rí-íś*
16 3 *maḫ-rí-íś*

17 0 ^{d}*en-líl*
17 1 ^{d}*en-líl*
17 2 ^{d}*en-líl*
17 3 ^{d}*en-líl*

18 0 *u-śa-rí-ib*
18 1 *u-śa-rí-ib*
18 2 *u-śa-rí-ib*
18 3 *u-śa-rí-ib*

19 0 *in u-mi-śu*
19 1 *in u-mi-śu*
19 2 *in u-m[i]-śu*
19 3 *in u-mi-śu*

20 0 *li-pi*$_5$*-it-ì-li*
20 1 *li-pi*$_5$*-it-ì-li*
20 2 *li-pi*$_5$*-it-ì-li*
20 3 *li-pi*$_5$*-⸢it⸣-ì-li*

21 0 DUMU-*śu*
21 1 DUMU-*śu*
21 2 DUMU-*śu*
21 3 DUMU-*śu*

22 0 ÉNSI
22 1 ÉNSI
22 2 ÉNSI
22 3 ÉNSI

23 0 *mára-da*.KI
23 1 *[m]ára-da*.KI
23 2 *mára-da*.KI
23 3 *mára-da*.KI

24 0 É
24 1 É
24 2 É
24 3 É

25 0 ^{d}*lugal-mára-da*
25 1 ^{d}*lugal-mára-da*
25 2 ^{d}*lugal-mára-da*
25 3 ^{d}*lugal-mára-da*

26 0 *in mára-da*.KI
26 1 *in mára-da*.KI
26 2 *in mára-da*.KI
26 3 *in mára-da*.KI

27 0 *ib-ni*
27 1 *ib-ni*
27 2 *ib-ni*
27 3 *ib-ni*

28 0 *ša* DUB
28 1 *ša* DUB
28 2 *ša* DUB
28 3 *ša* DUB

29 0 *śu*$_4$*-a*
29 1 *śu*$_4$*-a*
29 2 *śu*$_4$*-a*
29 3 *śu*$_4$*-a*

30 0 *u-śa-sà-ku-ni*
30 1 *u-śa-sà-ku-ni*
30 2 *u-śa-sà-k[u-n]i*
30 3 *u-śa-sà-ku-ni*

31 0 ^{d}UTU
31 1 ^{d}UTU
31 2 ^{d}UTU
31 3 ^{d}UTU

32 0 *ù*
32 1 *ù*
32 2 *ù*
32 3 *ù*

33 0 ^{d}*lugal-mára-da*
33 1 ^{d}*lugal-mára-da*
33 2 ^{d}*lugal-mára-da*
33 3 ^{d}*lugal-mára-da*

34 0 SUḪUŠ-*śu*
34 1 SUḪUŠ-*śu*
34 2 SUḪU[Š]-⸢*śu*⸣
34 3 SUḪUŠ-*śu*

35 0 *li-sú-ḫa*
35 1 *li-sú-ḫa*
35 2 *l*[*i*]-[*s*]*ú-ḫa*
35 3 *li-sú-ḫa*

36 0 *ù*
36 1 *ù*
36 2 *ù*
36 3 *ù*

37 0 ŠE.NUMUN-*śu*
37 1 ŠE.NUMUN-*śu*
37 2 ŠE.NUMUN-*śu*
37 3 ŠE.NUMUN-*śu*

38 0 *li-il-qù-tá*
38 1 *li-il-qù-tá*
38 2 *li-il-qù-t*[*á*]
38 3 *li-il-qù-tá*

1 0 [^{d}*na-ra*]-*am*-[^{d}EN].ZU
1 1 [^{d}*na-ra*]-*am*-[^{d}EN].ZU
1 2 [...]

2 0 [BA.D]ÍM
2 1 [BA.D]ÍM
2 2 [BA.DÍ]M

3 0 [É] ⸢^{d}⸣EN.ZU
3 1 [É] ⸢^{d}⸣EN.ZU
3 2 [É ^{d}E]N.ZU

1 0 [(^{d})*na-ra-am*-^{d}]EN.ZU
1 1 [(^{d})*na-ra-am*-^{d}]EN.ZU
1 2 [...]

2 0 [LUGA]L
2 1 [LUGA]L
2 2 [...]

3 0 [*ki-ib-ra-ti*]*m*
3 1 [*ki-ib-ra-ti*]*m*
3 2 [...]

4 0 ⸢*ar-ba-im*⸣
4 1 ⸢*ar-ba-im*⸣
4 2 [...]

5 0 *ì-nu*
5 1 *ì-nu*
5 2 [...]

6 0 ḪAR-*ša-ma-at*.KI
6 1 ḪAR-*ša-ma-at*.KI
6 2 [...]

7 0 *en*-⸢*a*⸣-[*r*]*a-am*
7 1 *en*-⸢*a*⸣-[*r*]*a-am*
7 2 [...]

8 0 *ù*
8 1 *ù*
8 2 *ù*

9 0 AM
9 1 AM
9 2 AM

10 0 *in qab*$_x$(DA)-*lá-ì*
10 1 *in qab*$_x$(DA)-*lá-ì*
10 2 *in qab*$_x$(DA)-⸢*lá-ì*⸣

11 0 *ti-ba-a*[*r*]
11 1 *ti-ba-a*[*r*]
11 2 *ti-ba-a*[*r*]

12 0 ŚÁ.DÚ-*im*
12 1 ŚÁ.DÚ-*im*
12 2 ŚÁ.DÚ-*im*

13 0 *śu*$_4$-*ma*
13 1 *śu*$_4$-*ma*
13 2 *śu*$_4$-*ma*

14 0 *u-śa-am-qí-it-śu*
14 1 *u-śa-am-qí-it-śu*
14 2 *u-śa-am-qí-it-śu*

15 0 *tám-ši-il-śu*
15 1 *tám-ši-il-śu*
15 2 *tám-ši*$_x$(SU$_4$)-*il-śu*

16 0 *ib-ni-ma*
16 1 *ib-ni-ma*
16 2 [*i*]*b-ni-ma*

17 0 *a-na*
17 1 *a-na*
17 2 ⸢*a*⸣-*na*

18 0 ^{d}*en-líl*
18 1 ^{d}*en-líl*
18 2 ⸢^{d}⸣*en-líl*

19 0 *a-b*[*í*]-*śu*
19 1 <...>
19 2 *a-b*[*í*]-*śu*

20 0 A.MU.RU
20 1 A.MU.RU
20 2 A.MU.RU

21 0 *ša* DUB
21 1 *ša* DUB
21 2 *ša* D[UB]

22 0 *śu*$_4$-*a*
22 1 *śu*$_4$-*a*
22 2 *śu*$_4$-⸢*a*⸣

23 0 *u-śa-sà-ku-ni*
23 1 *u-śa-sà-ku-ni*
23 2 *u-śa-sà-k*[*u-ni*]

24 0 ^{d}*en-líl*
24 1 ^{d}*en-líl*
24 2 ^{d}*en-líl*

25 0 *ù*
25 1 *ù*
25 2 *ù*

26 0 ^{d}UTU
26 1 ^{d}UTU
26 2 ^{d}UTU

27 0 SUḪUŠ-*śu*
27 1 SUḪUŠ-*śu*
27 2 SUḪUŠ-*śu*

28 0 *li-sú-ḫa*
28 1 *li-sú-ḫa*
28 2 *li-sú-ḫa*

29 0 *ù*
29 1 *ù*
29 2 *ù*

30 0 ŠE.NUMUN-*śu*
30 1 ŠE.NUMUN-*śu*
30 2 [...]

31 0 *li-il-qù-tám*
31 1 *li-il-qù-tám*
31 2 [...]

1 0 *na-ra-am-*^{d}EN.ZU
1 1 *na-ra-am-*^{d}EN.ZU
1 2 *na-ra-am-*^{d}EN.ZU

2 0 LUGAL
2 1 LUGAL
2 2 LUGAL

3 0 *a-kà-dè*.KI
3 1 *a-kà-dè*.KI
3 2 *a-kà-dè*.KI

4 0 *śa-pí-ir*
4 1 *śa-pí-ir*
4 2 *śa-pí-ir*

5 0 KIŠ MI KAM
5 1 KIŠ MI KAM
5 2 KIŠ MI KAM

6 0 KALAM
6 1 KALAM
6 2 KALAM

7 0 NIM.KI
7 1 NIM.KI
7 2 NIM.KI

8 0 *kà-lí-śa-ma*
8 1 *kà-lí-śa-ma*
8 2 *k*[*à*]*-lí-śa-ma*

9 0 *a-dì-ma*
9 1 *a-dì-ma*
9 2 [...]

10 0 *pá-ra-aḫ-śum*.KI
10 1 *pá-ra-aḫ-śum*.KI
10 2 [...]

11 0 *ù*
11 1 *ù*
11 2 [...]

12 0 KALAM
12 1 KALAM
12 2 [...]

13 0 [Š]UBUR$^{\textit{śu-bar-tim}}$.KI
13 1 [Š]UBUR$^{\textit{śu-bar-tim}}$.KI
13 2 [...]

14 0 *a-dì-ma*
14 1 *a-dì-ma*
14 2 [...]

15 0 GIŠ.TIR
15 1 GIŠ.TIR
15 2 [...]

16 0 [GI]Š.ERIN
16 1 [GI]Š.ERIN
16 2 [...]

17 0 *ù*
17 1 *ù*
17 2 [...]

18 0 [*ì*]*-nu*
18 1 [*ì*]*-nu*
18 2 [...]

19 0 [*a*]*-na*
19 1 [*a*]*-na*
19 2 [...]

20 0 *tal-ḫa-dim*.[K]I
20 1 *tal-ḫa-dim*.[K]I
20 2 [...]

21 0 *i-lí-ku*
21 1 *i-lí-ku*
21 2 [...]

22 0 KASKAL.KI *śu*$_4$-a
22 1 KASKAL.KI *śu*$_4$-a
22 2 [...]

23 0 *śar in śar-rí*
23 1 *śar in śar-rí*
23 2 [...]

24 0 *ma-na-ma*
24 1 *ma-na-ma*
24 2 [...]

25 0 *la i-lí-ik*
25 1 *la i-lí-ik*
25 2 [...]

26 0 *na-ra-am-*^{d}EN.ZU
26 1 *na-ra-am-*^{d}EN.ZU
26 2 [...]

27 0 LUGAL
27 1 LUGAL
27 2 [...]

28 0 *a-kà-dè*.KI
28 1 *a-kà-dè*.KI
28 2 [...]

29 0 *i-lí-ik-ma*
29 1 *i-lí-ik-ma*
29 2 [...]

30 0 ^{d}INANNA
30 1 ^{d}INANNA
30 2 [...]

31 0 *ma-ḫi-ra*
31 1 *ma-ḫi-ra*
31 2 [...]

32 0 *la id-dì-śum*$_6$
32 1 *la id-dì-śum*$_6$
32 2 [...]

33 0 ÉNSI.ÉNSI
33 1 ÉNSI.ÉNSI
33 2 [...]

34 0 ŠUBUR.KI
34 1 ŠUBUR.KI
34 2 [...]

35 0 (Erasure) *ù*
35 1 (Erasure) *ù*
35 2 [...]

36 0 EN.EN
36 1 EN.EN
36 2 [...]

37 0 *a-lí-a-tim*
37 1 *a-lí-a-tim*
37 2 [...]

38 0 NIDBA-*ś*[*u-nu*]
38 1 NIDBA-*ś*[*u-nu*]
38 2 [...]

39 0 [*m*]*aḫ-rí-*[*śu*]
39 1 [*m*]*aḫ-rí-*[*śu*]
39 2 [...]

40 0 *u-śa-r*[*í-bu*]
40 1 *u-śa-r*[*í-bu*]
40 2 [...]

41 0 [...]
41 1 [...]
41 2 [...]

42 0 [...]
42 1 [...]
42 2 [...]

43 0 [...]
43 1 [...]
43 2 [...]

44 0 N[AM(?)-...]
44 1 N[A.M(?)-..]
44 2 [...]

45 0 *a-l*[*a*]
45 1 *a-nla*]
45 2 [...]

46 0 *i*-R[I-x-*a*]*m*
46 1 *i*-R[I-x-*a*]*m*
46 2 [...]

47 0 *na-ra-am-*[d]EN.ZU
47 1 *na-ra-am-*[d]EN.ZU
47 2 [...]

48 0 LUGAL
48 1 LUGAL
48 2 [...]

49 0 *a-kà-dè*.KI
49 1 *a-kà-dè*.KI
49 2 [...]

50 0 *a-na*
50 1 *a-na*
50 2 [...]

51 0 [d]*nin-gublaga*
51 1 [d]*nin-gublaga*
51 2 [...]

52 0 A.MU.RU
52 1 A.MU.RU
52 2 [...]

53 0 *ša* DUB
53 1 *ša* DUB
53 2 [...]

54 0 *u-śa-sà-ku-ni*
54 1 *u-śa-sà-ku-ni*
54 2 [...]

55 0 [d]*nin-gubalag*
55 1 [d]*nin-gubalag*
55 2 [...]

56 0 *be-al*
56 1 *be-al*
56 2 [...]

57 0 DÙL *śu*$_4$*-a*
57 1 DÙL *śu*$_4$*-a*
57 2 [...]

58 0 *ù*
58 1 *ù*
58 2 [...]

59 0 [d]UTU
59 1 [d]UTU
59 2 [...]

60 0 SUḪUŠ-*śu*
60 1 SUḪUŠ-*śu*
60 2 [...]

61 0 *li-sú-ḫa*
61 1 *li-sú-ḫa*
61 2 [...]

62 0 ŠE.NUMUN-*šu*
62 1 ŠE.NUMUN-*šu*
62 2 [...]

63 0 *li-il-qù-tá*
63 1 *li-il-qù-tá*
63 2 [...]

64 0 NI[TA-*sú*]
64 1 NI[TA-*sú*]
64 2 [...]

65 0 ⌜*ù*⌝
65 1 ⌜*ù*⌝
65 2 [...]

66 0 [MU]-*šu*
66 1 [MU]-*šu*
66 2 [...]

67 0 [*a*] ⌜*i*⌝-*dì-na-šum*$_6$
67 1 [*a*] ⌜*i*⌝-*dì-na-šum*$_6$
67 2 [...]

68 0 *maḫ-rí-íš*
68 1 *maḫ-rí-íš*
68 2 [...]

69 0 [*i*]-*lí-šu*
69 1 [*i*]-*lí-šu*
69 2 [...]

70 0 [*a*] DU
70 1 [*a*] DU
70 2 [...]

1 0 ^{d}*na-ra-am*-^{d}EN.ZU
1 1 ^{d}*na-ra-am*-^{d}EN.ZU
1 2 ^{d}*na-ra-am*-^{d}EN.ZU
1 3 ^{d}*na-ra-am*-^{d}EN.ZU

2 0 *da-núm*
2 1 *da-núm*
2 2 *da-núm*
2 3 *da-núm*

3 0 LUGAL
3 1 LUGAL
3 2 LUGAL
3 3 LUGAL

4 0 *ki-ib-ra-tim*
4 1 *ki-ib-ra-tim*
4 2 *ki-ib-ra-tim*
4 3 *ki-ib-ra-tim.*

5 0 *ar-ba-im*
5 1 *ar-ba-im*
5 2 *ar-ba-im*
5 3 *ar-ba-im*

6 0 SAG.GIŠ.RA
6 1 SAG.GIŠ.RA
6 2 SAG.GIŠ.RA
6 3 SAG.GIŠ.RA

7 0 *ar-ma-nim*.KI
7 1 *ar-ma-nim*.KI
7 2 *ar-ma-nim*.KI
7 3 *ar-ma-nim*.KI

8 0 *ù*
8 1 *ù*
8 2 [...]
8 3 *ù*

9 0 *eb-la*.KI
9 1 *eb-la*.KI
9 2 [...]
9 3 *eb-la*.KI

Obverse

Ex. 1 Obv. Col. i

Lacuna

1′ [^{d}*na-ra-am-*^{d}EN.ZU]
2′ [*da-núm*]
3′ [LUGAL]
4′ ⸢*ki*⸣-*i*[*b-ra-tim*]
5′ *ar-ba-i*[*m*]
6′ SAG.GIŠ.RA
7′ UŠ.GI
8′ *ša-bir*$_{5}$
9′ GIŠ.TUKUL
10′ ŠUBUR.KI
11′ *kà-lí-ì-śu*
12′ *mu-kí-in*
13′ SUḪUŠ.SUḪUŠ
14′ *um-ma-nim*.KI

Ex. 2 Col. i′

Traces of the last signs of five lines.

Ex. 1 Obv. Col. ii

Lacuna

1′ x [...]
2′ *a-b*[*u-*...]
3′ *úś-ba-al-k*[*i-it-ma*]
4′ *u-ṣa-ab-bi-à*[*m*]
5′ *íś-tum-*[*ma*]
6′ *tu-tu-*[*uš-šè*.KI]
7′ *ù*
8′ KALAM.K[I-*śu*]
9′ *ur-k*[*i-*...]

Ex. 2 Col. ii′

1 x x.KI
2 *ù*
3 ⸢KALAM⸣.KI-śu
4 *ḫa-ḫu-un*.KI
5 *ù* <KALAM.KI-*śu*>
6 *a-dì-ma*
7 ⸢KALAM(?)⸣.KI
8 [...] x x

Lacuna

1′ [...].KI
2′ *ù*
3′ [KALAM.K]I-*śu*
4′ [...].KI
5′ [...].KI
6′ [*ù* KALA]M.KI-śu
7′ [x] *im*(?)-*ul*(?).KI
8′ x *ùḫ*(?)-*ḫu*.KI
9′ ⸢ḪAR(?)⸣-*a-núm*.KI
10′ ⸢*ù*⸣ KALAM.KI-*śu*
11′ *gal*(?)-*áš*.KI
12′ ḪAR-*ba-ak*(?).KI
13′ ⸢*a*⸣-*li-we*.KI
14′ [*ḫ*]*a-śu-an-šè*.KI
15′ [x]-*in-šè*.KI
16′ [*ù* K]ALAM.KI-*śu*

Ex. 2 Col. iii′ and ex. 1 Rev.

10 *ù a-*⸢*dì*⸣*-m*[*a*]
11 [...]
12 *ù a-*⸢*dì*⸣*-m*[*a*]

20 KALAM.K[I]
21 [...]
22 KALAM.K[I]

Ex. 2 Col. iii′ and ex.1 Rev.

3 0 *ki*-x-*e-na-á*[*š*].⌈KI⌉
3 1 [...]
3 2 *ki*-x-*e-na-á*[*š*].⌈KI⌉

4 0 LAGABxTIL-*šè*.KI
4 1 [...]
4 2 LAGABxTIL-*šè*.KI

5 0 *ù* KALAM.KI-*śu*
5 1 [...] KALAM.KI-[*śu*]
5 2 *ù* KALAM.KI-*śu*

6 0 *tu-tu-uš-šè*.K[I]
6 1 *tu-tu-u*[*š-šè*.KI]
6 2 *tu-tu-uš-šè*.K[I]

7 0 *ù* KALAM.K[I-*śu*]
7 1 ⌈*ù*⌉ KALAM.KI-[*śu*]
7 2 *ù* KALAM.K[I-*śu*]

8 0 *ne-ri*-x-[....KI]
8 1 *ne-ri*-x-[....KI]
8 2 ⌈*ne-ri*⌉-[....KI]

9 0 *ù*
9 1 ⌈*ù*⌉
9 2 *ù*

10 0 KALAM.K[I-*śu*]
10 1 KALAM.K[I-*śu*]
10 2 KALAM.K[I-*śu*]

11 0 [x] ⌈x⌉ [...]
11 1 [x] ⌈x⌉ [...]
11 2 [...]

Lacuna

Ex. 2 Col. iii′

1′ *ù* [...]
2′ *ga*-[...]
3′ SIPA(?) [...]
4′ *šu*-x [...] x [...]
5′ *ši*-x-NI-[....KI]
6′ *śa-ak-nu* [...]
7′ x-*tir-šè*.KI
8′ *zum-ḫi-in-núm*.KI
9′ *ù* KALAM.KI-*śu*
10′ *nin*$_9$(SAL+KU)-*li-in-su-è*.K[I]
11′ *mu-luḫ*.⌈KI⌉
12′ ABxU-*sig*-⌈*ge*⌉.K[I]
13′ *su-ùḫ*-[...]

Reverse

Ex. 2 Col. iv′

1 *kum-ti*-x [...]
2 *ù* KALA[M.KI-*śu*]
3 *šè-wi-i*[*n* ....KI]
4 *šu-un*-x[....KI]
5 *ù* KALAM.K[I-*śu*]
6 *śu-a-we*.K[I]
7 *ù* KALAM.KI-*śu*
8 *a-zu-ḫi-núm*.K[I]
9 ⌈*ù*⌉ KALAM.KI-*śu*
10 *íś-tum-ma*
11 SAG.GIŠ.RA-*ù-ś*[*u*]
12 *ba-al-ṭì-śu*
13 14 ⌈BÀD⌉
14 ⌈*a-na*⌉ [...]

Lacuna

1′ ḪAR(?) NE [....KI]
2′ *ku-um-ra-at*.KI
3′ *ir-in-da*.KI

Ex. 2 Col. iv′ (continued)

4 *ù* KALAM.MA-*śu*
5′ *àm-mi-lu*.KI
6′ *ù* KALAM.KI-*śu*

Ex. 2 Col. v′

1 [x] x x x.KI
2 [*ù* KALA]M.⸢KI-*śu*⸣
3 [...] *šè*.KI
4 [...]-*in-núm*.KI
5 [*ù* K]ALAM.KI-*śu*
6 [...] x KI
7 [*ù* KAL]AM.KI-*śu*
8 [...]-⸢*we*⸣.KI
9 [ù KA]LAM.KI-śu
10 [...].KI
11 [*ù* KAL]AM.KI-*śu*
12 [...-*š*]*è*.KI
13 [...].KI
14 [...].KI
15 [...] x

Lacuna

1′ [*ù* KALAM.K]I-*śu*
2′ [*a-d*]*ì-ma*
3′ [...].KI
4′ [*ù*] URU.KI.URU.KI
5′ [*a*]-*bar-ti*
6′ [I]DIGNA.I₇

1 0 *a-na*
1 1 *a-na*
1 2 [...]
1 3 [...]
1 4 [...]

2 0 *il-a-ba*$_4$
2 1 *il-a-ba*$_4$
2 2 [...]
2 3 [...]
2 4 [...]

3 0 ^{d}*na-ra-am-*^{d}EN.ZU
3 1 ^{d}*na-ra-am-*^{d}EN.ZU
3 2 [...]
3 3 [...]
3 4 [...]

4 0 *da-núm*
4 1 *da-núm*
4 2 [...]
4 3 [...]
4 4 [*d*]*a-*[*núm*]

5 0 LUGAL
5 1 LUGAL
5 2 [...]
5 3 [...]
5 4 LUGAL

6 0 *ki-ib-ra-tim*
6 1 *ki-ib-ra-tim*
6 2 [...]
6 3 [...]
6 4 *ki-ib-ra-tim*

7 0 *ar-ba-im*
7 1 *ar-ba-im*
7 2 [...]
7 3 [...]
7 4 *ar-ba-im*

8 0 SAG.GIŠ.RA
8 1 SAG.GIŠ.RA
8 2 [...]
8 3 [...]
8 4 SAG.GIŠ.RA

9 0 *ar-ma-nim*.KI
9 1 *ar-ma-nim*.KI
9 2 [...]
9 3 [...]
9 4 *ar-ma-nim*.KI

10 0 *ù*
10 1 *ù*
10 2 [...]
10 3 [...]
10 4 *ù*

11 0 *eb-la*.KI
11 1 *eb-la*.KI
11 2 [...]
11 3 [...]
11 4 *e*[*b*]*-l*[*a*.KI]

12 0 *ù*
12 1 *ù*
12 2 [...]
12 3 [...]
12 4 [...]

13 0 NIM.KI
13 1 NIM.KI
13 2 [...]
13 3 [...]
13 4 [...]

14 0 A.MU.RU
14 1 A.MU.RU
14 2 A.M[U.RU]
14 3 [...]
14 4 [...]

15 0 *kàr-šum*
15 1 *kàr-šum*
15 2 *kàr-*[*šum*]
15 3 [...]
15 4 [...]

16 0 *šu* SUKKAL-*li*
16 0 *šu* SUKKAL-*li*
16 1 ⌜*šu*⌝ SUKKAL-*li*]
16 3 *šu* SUK[KAL-*li*]
16 4 [...]

17 0 ÉNSI
17 1 ÉNSI
17 2 ÉN[SI]
17 3 [É]NSI
17 4 [...]

18 0 *ni-qum*.KI
18 1 *ni-qum*.KI
18 2 [*ni*]*-q*[*um*]
18 3 *ni-qum*.KI
18 4 [...]

19 0 IR$_{11}$-*sú*
19 1 IR$_{11}$-*sú*
19 2 [...]
19 3 IR$_{11}$-*sú*
19 4 [...]

1 0 ^{d}*en-líl*
1 1 ^{d}*en-líl*
1 2 ^{d}*en-líl*

2 0 *u-kál-lim*
2 1 *u-kál-lim*
2 2 *u-kál-lim*

3 0 *śar-kà-lí*-LUGAL-*rí*
3 1 *śar-kà-lí*-LUGAL-*rí*
3 2 *śar-kà-lí*-LUGAL-*rí*

4 0 *da-núm*
4 1 *da-núm*
4 2 *da-núm*

5 0 LUGAL
5 1 LUGAL
5 2 LUGAL

6 0 *a-kà-dè*.KI
6 1 *a-kà-dè*.KI
6 2 *a-kà-dè*.KI

7 0 ^{ba}DÍM
7 1 ^{ba}DÍM
7 2 ^{ba}DÍM

8 0 *é-kur*
8 1 *é-kur*
8 2 *é-kur*

9 0 É
9 1 É
9 2 É

10 0 ^{d}*en-líl*
10 1 ^{d}*en-líl*
10 2 ^{d}*en-líl*

11 0 *in* NIBRU.KI
11 1 *in* NIBRU.KI
11 2 *in* NIBRU.KI

12 0 *ša* DUB
12 1 *ša* DUB
12 2 *ša* DUB

13 0 *śu*$_4$*-a*
13 1 *śu*$_4$*-a*
13 2 *śu*$_4$*-a*

14 0 *u-śa-sà-ku-ni*
14 1 *u-śa-sà-ku-ni*
14 2 *u-śa-sà-ku-ni*

15 0 ^{d}*en-líl*
15 1 ^{d}*en-líl*
15 2 ^{d}*en-líl*

16 0 *ù*
16 1 *ù*
16 2 *ù*

17 0 ^{d}UTU
17 1 ^{d}UTU
17 2 ^{d}UTU

18 0 *ù*
18 1 *ù*
18 2 *ù*

19 0 ^{d}INANNA
19 1 ^{d}INANNA
19 2 ^{d}INANNA

20 0 SUḪUŠ-*śu*
20 1 SUḪUŠ-*śu*
20 2 SUḪUŠ-*śu*

21 0 *li-sú-ḫu*
21 1 *li-sú-ḫu*
21 2 *li-sú-ḫu*

22 0 *ù*
22 1 *ù*
22 2 *ù*

23 0 ŠE.NUMUN-*śu*
23 1 ŠE.NUMUN-*śu*
23 2 ŠE.NUMUN-*śu*

24 0 *li-il-qù-tu*
24 1 *li-il-qù-tu*
24 2 *li-il-qù-tu*

1 0 ^{d}*śar-kà-lí*-LUGAL-*rí*
1 1 ^{d}*śar-kà-lí*-LUGAL-*rí*
1 2 ^{d}*śar-kà-lí*-LUGAL-*rí*
1 3 ^{d}*śar-kà-lí*-LUGAL-*rí*
1 4 ^{d}*śar-kà-lí*-LUGAL-*rí*

2 0 DUMU *da-dì* ^{d}*en-líl*
2 1 DUMU *da-dì* ^{d}*en-líl*
2 2 DUMU *da-dì* ^{d}*en-líl*
2 3 DUMU *da-dì* ^{d}*en-líl*
2 4 DUMU *da-dì* ^{d}*en-líl*

3 0 *da-núm*
3 1 *da-núm*
3 2 *da-núm*
3 3 *da-núm*
3 4 *da-núm*

4 0 LUGAL
4 1 LUGAL
4 2 LUGAL
4 3 LUGAL
4 4 [L]UGAL

5 0 *a-kà-dè*.KI
5 1 *a-kà-dè*.KI
5 2 *a-kà-dè*.KI
5 3 *a-kà-dè*.KI
5 4 *a-kà-dè*.K[I]

6 0 *ù*
6 1 *ù*
6 2 *ù*
6 3 *ù*
6 4 *ù*

7 0 *bù-ú-la-ti*
7 1 *bù-ú-la-ti*
7 2 *bù-ú-la-ti*
7 3 *bù-ú-la-ti*
7 4 *bù-*⸢*ú-la*⸣*-ti*

8 0 ^{d}*en-líl*
8 1 ^{d}*en-líl*
8 2 ^{d}*en-líl*
8 3 ^{d}*en-líl*
8 4 [^{d}*e*]*n-líl*

9 0 ^{ba}DÍM
9 1 ^{ba}DÍM
9 2 ^{ba}DÍM
9 3 ^{ba}DÍM
9 4 [^{ba}]DÍM

10 0 *é-kur*
10 1 *é-kur*
10 2 *é-kur*
10 3 *é-kur*
10 4 ⸢*é*⸣*-kur*

11 0 É ^{d}*en-líl*
11 1 É ^{d}*en-líl*
11 2 É ^{d}*en-líl*
11 3 É ^{d}*en-líl*
11 4 [É] ⸢^{d}⸣*en-líl*

12 0 *in* NIBRU.KI
12 1 *in* NIBRU.KI
12 2 *in* NIBRU.KI
12 3 *in* NIBRU.KI
12 4 [*i*]*n* NIBRU.KI

13 0 *ša* DUB
13 1 *ša* DUB
13 2 *ša* DUB
13 3 *ša* DUB
13 4 [*š*]*a* DUB

14 0 *śu*$_4$*-a*
14 1 *śu*$_4$*-a*
14 2 *śu*$_4$*-a*
14 3 *śu*$_4$*-a*
14 4 [*śu*$_4$]*-a*

15 0 u-śa-sà-ku-ni
15 1 <u>-śa-sà-ku-ni
15 2 u-śa-sà-ku-ni
15 3 u-śa-sà-ku-ni
15 4 [u]-śa-sà-ku-ni

16 0 ^{d}en-líl
16 1 ^{d}en-líl
16 2 ^{d}en-líl
16 3 ^{d}en-líl
16 4 ^{d}en-líl

17 0 ù
17 1 ù
17 2 ù
17 3 ù
17 4 ù

18 0 ^{d}UTU
18 1 ^{d}UTU
18 2 ^{d}UTU
18 3 ^{d}UTU
18 4 ^{d}UT[U]

19 0 SUḪUŠ-śu
19 1 SUḪUŠ-śu
19 2 SUḪUŠ-śu
19 3 SUḪUŠ-śu
19 4 [SUḪ]UŠ-ś[u]

20 0 li-sú-ḫa
20 1 li-sú-ḫa
20 2 li-sú-ḫa
20 3 li-sú-ḫa
20 4 [l]i-sú-ḫa

21 0 ù
21 1 ù
21 2 ù
21 3 ù
21 4 ù

22 0 ŠE.NUMUN-śu
22 1 ŠE.NUMUN-śu
22 2 ŠE.NUMUN-śu
22 3 ŠE.NUMUN-śu
22 4 ŠE.NUMUN-śú

23 0 li-il-qù-tá
23 1 li-il-qù-tá
23 2 li-il-qù-tá
23 3 li-il-qù-tá
23 4 li-i[l-qù]-tá

1 0 *śar-kà-lí*-LUGAL-*rí*
1 1 *śar-kà-lí*-LUGAL-*rí*
1 2 *śar-kà-lí*-LUGAL-*rí*

2 0 LUGAL
2 1 LUGAL
2 2 LUGAL

3 0 *a-kà-dè*.KI
3 1 *a-kà-dè*.KI
3 2 *a-kà-dè*.KI

1 0 *du-du*
1 1 [*du-d*]*u*
1 2 *du-du*

2 0 *da-núm*
2 1 [*da-n*]*úm*
2 2 *da-núm*

3 0 LUGAL
3 1 [LU]GAL
3 2 LUGAL

4 0 *a-kà-dè*.KI
4 1 [*a-kà-d*]*è*.KI
4 2 *a-kà-dè*.KI

1 0 ^{d}nin-ḫur-sag
1 1 ^{d}nin-ḫur-sag
1 2 ^{d}nin-ḫur-sag
1 3 ^{d}nin-ḫur-sag
1 4 ^{d}nin-ḫur-sag

2 0 ama-dingir-re-ne-ra
2 1 ama-dingir-re-ne-ra
2 2 ama-dingir-re-ne-ra
2 3 ama-dingir-re-ne-ra
2 4 ama-dingir-re-ne-ra

3 0 lú-^{d}utu
3 1 lú-^{d}utu
3 2 lú-^{d}utu
3 3 lú-^{d}utu
3 4 lú-^{d}utu

4 0 énsi-
4 1 énsi-
4 2 énsi-
4 3 énsi-
4 4 énsi-

5 0 umma.KI-ke$_4$
5 1 umma.KI-ke$_4$
5 2 umma.KI-ke$_4$
5 3 umma.KI-ke$_4$
5 4 umma.KI-ke$_4$

6 0 nam-ti-la-ni-šè
6 1 nam-ti-la-ni-šè
6 2 nam-ti-la-ni-šè
6 3 nam-ti-la-ni-šè
6 4 nam-ti-la-ni-šè

7 0 tillà-ki-ág-na
7 1 tillà-ki-ág-na
7 2 tillà-ki-ág-na
7 3 tillà-ki-ág-na
7 4 tillà-ki-ág-na

8 0 é mu-na-dù
8 1 é mu-na-dù
8 2 é mu-na-dù
8 3 é mu-na-dù
8 4 é mu-na-dù

9 0 uš-bi mu-du$_{10}$
9 1 uš-bi mu-du$_{10}$
9 2 <...>
9 3 uš-bi mu-du$_{10}$
9 4 <...>

10 0 temen-bi mu-si
10 1 temen-bi mu-si
10 2 <...>
10 3 temen-bi mu-si
10 4 <...>

11 0 me-bi šà-bi-a
11 1 me-bi šà-bi-a
11 2 <...>
11 3 me-bi šà-bi-a
11 4 <...>

12 0 si im-ma-ni-sá
12 1 si im-ma-ni-sá
12 2 <...>
12 3 si im-ma-ni-sá
12 4 <...>

1 0 ^{d}ereš-ki-gal
1 1 ^{d}ereš-ki-gal
1 2 ^{d}ereš-ki-gal
1 3 ^{d}ereš-ki-gal

2 0 nin-ki-u$_{4}$-šu$_{4}$-ra
2 1 nin-ki-u$_{4}$-šu$_{4}$-ra
2 2 nin-ki-u$_{4}$-šu$_{4}$-ra
2 3 nin-ki-u$_{4}$-šu$_{4}$-ra

3 0 lú-^{d}utu
3 1 lú-^{d}utu
3 2 lú-^{d}utu
3 3 lú-^{d}utu

4 0 énsi-umma.KI
4 1 énsi-umma.KI
4 2 énsi-umma.KI
4 3 énsi-umma.KI-ke$_{4}$

5 0 dumu-^{d}nin-isin$_{x}$(IN)-nam-ka-ke$_{4}$
5 1 dumu-^{d}nin-isin$_{x}$(IN)-nam-ka-ke$_{4}$
5 2 dumu-^{d}nin-isin$_{x}$(IN)-nam-ka-ke$_{4}$
5 3 <...>

6 0 nam-ti-la-ni-šè
6 1 nam-ti-la-ni-šè
6 2 nam-ti-la-ni-šè
6 3 nam-ti-la-ni-šè

7 0 ki-^{d}utu-è
7 1 ki-^{d}utu-è
7 2 ki-^{d}utu-è
7 3 ki-^{d}utu-è

8 0 ki-nam-tar-re-da
8 1 ki-nam-tar-re-da
8 2 ki-nam-tar-re-da
8 3 ki-nam-tar-re-da

9 0 é mu-na-dù
9 1 é mu-na-dù
9 2 é mu-na-dù
9 3 é mu-na-dù

10 0 gaba-ba a bí-in-gi
10 1 gaba-ba a bí-in-gi
10 2 gaba-ba a bí-in-gi
10 3 gaba-ba/ a bí-in-gi-in

11 0 mu-bi pa bí-in-è
11 1 mu-bi pa bí-in-è
11 2 mu-bi pa bí-in-è
11 3 mu-bi/ pa bí-in-è

1	0	^{d}nanše
1	1	^{d}nanše
1	2	^{d}nanše
1	3	^{d}nanše
1	4	...
1	5	...
1	6	...
1	7	^{d}nanše
1	8	^{d}nanše
1	9	^{d}nanše
1	10	^{d}nanše
1	11	...
2	0	nin-uru$_{16}$
2	1	nin-uru$_{16}$
2	2	nin-uru$_{16}$
2	3	nin-uru$_{16}$
2	4	...
2	5	...
2	6	...
2	7	nin-uru$_{5}$.
2	8	nin-uru$_{16}$
2	9	nin-uru$_{5}$
2	10	nin-uru$_{6}$
2	11	...
3	0	nin-in-dub-ba-ra
3	1	nin-in-dub-ba-<ra>
3	2	nin-⸢in⸣-[d]ub-⸢ba⸣-ra
3	3	nin-in-dub-ba-ra
3	4	...
3	5	...
3	6	...
3	7	nin-in-dub-ba-ra
3	8	nin-in-dub-ba-ra
3	9	nin-in-dub-ba-ra
3	10	nin-in-dub-ba-ra
3	11	nin-in-dub-ba-<ra>
4	0	^{d}utu-ḫé-gál
4	1	^{d}utu-ḫé-gál
4	2	^{d}⸢utu⸣-ḫé-gál
4	3	^{d}utu-ḫé-gál
4	4	...
4	5	...
4	6	...
4	7	^{d}utu-ḫé-gál
4	8	^{d}utu-ḫé-gál
4	9	^{d}utu-ḫé-gál
4	10	^{d}utu-ḫé-gál
4	11	...
5	0	lugal-an-ub-da-limmu$_{5}$-ba-ke$_{4}$
5	1	lugal-an-ub-da-limmu$_{5}$-ba-ke$_{4}$
5	2	lugal-an-ub-[d]a-limmu$_{5}$-ba-ke$_{4}$
5	3	lugal-an-ub-da-limmu$_{5}$-ba-ke$_{4}$
5	4	...
5	5	...
5	6	...
5	7	lugal-an-ub-da-limmu$_{5}$-ba-[ke$_{4}$]
5	8	lugal-an-ub-da-limmu$_{5}$-ba-ke$_{4}$
5	9	lugal-an-ub-da-limmui-ba-ke$_{4}$
5	10	lugal-an-ub-da-limmu$_{5}$-ba-ke$_{4}$
5	11	...
6	0	ki-sur-ra-lagaš.KI
6	1	ki-sur-ra-lagaš.KI-⸢x⸣
6	2	ki-sur-ra-lagaš.KI-ka
6	3	ki-sur-ra-lagaš.KI
6	4	ki-sur-ra-lagaš.KI.
6	5	...
6	6	...
6	7	ki-sur-ra-lagaš.KI
6	8	ki-sur-ra-lagaš.KI-ka
9	9	ki-sur-ra-lagaš.KI!
6	10	ki-sur-ra-lagaš.KI-[k]a(?)
6	11	ki-sur-<ra>-lagaš.KI

7	0	lú-uri$_5$.KI-ke$_4$
7	1	<..>
7	2	lú-uri$_5$.KI-ke$_4$
7	3	ú-ŠEŠ.<AB>.KI-ke$_4$
7	4	lú-uri$_5$.KI
7	5	...
7	6	..
7	7	lú-uri$_5$.KI-ke$_4$
7	8	lú-uri$_5$.KI-ke$_4$
7	9	lú-uri$_5$.KI-ke$_4$
7	10	ú-uri$_5$.KI-ke$_4$
7	11	lú-uri$_5$-ma
8	0	inim bí-gar
8	1	inim bí-gar
8	2	inim bí-[g]ar
8	3	inim bí-gar
8	4	...
8	5	...
8	6	...
8	7	inim bí-gar
8	8	inim bí-gar
8	9	inim bí-gar
8	10	inim bí-gar
8	11	...
9	0	šu-na mu-ni-gi$_4$
9	1	šu-na mu-ni-gi$_4$
9	2	šu-na mu-⌜ni⌝-gi$_4$
9	3	šu-na mu-ni-gi$_4$
9	4	...
9	5	...
9	6	...
9	7	šu-na mu-ni-gi$_4$
9	8	šu-na mu-ni-gi$_4$
9	9	šu-na mu-ni-gi$_4$
9	10	šu-na mu-ni-gi$_4$.
9	11	...

1 0 ^{d}nanna
1 1 ^{d}nanna
1 2 ^{d}nanna
1 3 ...
1 4 ...
1 5 ^{d}[nanna]
1 6 ^{d}[nanna]

2 0 lugal-a-ni
2 1 lugal(Text: LÚ)-a-ni
2 2 [lug]al-a-ni
2 3 ...
2 4 ...
2 5 luga[l-a-ni]
2 6 luga[l-a-ni]

3 0 lú-sa$_6$-ga
3 1 lú-sa$_6$-ga
3 2 lú-s[a$_6$-ga]
3 3 ...
3 4 ...
3 5 lú-[sa$_6$-ga]
3 6 l[ú-sa$_6$-ga]

4 0 énsi-
4 1 énsi-
4 2 [éns]i
4 3 ...
4 4 ...
4 5 én[si]-
4 6 én[si]-

5 0 uri$_5$.KI-ma-ke$_4$
5 1 uri$_5$.KI-ma-ke$_4$
5 2 [u]ri$_5$.KI-m[a-ke$_4$]
5 3 ...
5 4 ...
5 5 [u]ri$_5$.KI-m[a-ke$_4$]
5 6 [u]ri$_5$.KI-m[a-ke$_4$]

6 0 ki-sur-ra-né
6 1 ⌜ki⌝-sur-ra-né
6 2 [k]i-sur-ra-né
6 3 ...
6 4 ...
6 5 ki-[...]
6 6 ki-sur-r[a-né]

7 0 KA-ta mu-na-ta-è
7 1 KA-ta mu-na-ta-è
7 2 KA-ta [mu-na]-ta-[è]
7 3 ...
7 4 ...
7 5 KA-[...]-ta-è
7 6 KA-ta m[u-na]-ta-U[D.DU]

8 0 bára mu-na-si
8 1 bára mu-si
8 2 bára mu-na-s[i]
8 3 ...
8 4 ...
8 5 bára mu-[na-si]
8 6 [b]ára mu-n[a-si]

www.ingramcontent.com/pod-product-compliance
Lightning Source LLC
Chambersburg PA
CBHW080743250525
26957CB00044B/183